THE
SECRET ROOTS
OF
CHRISTIANITY

THE SECRET ROOTS OF CHRISTIANITY

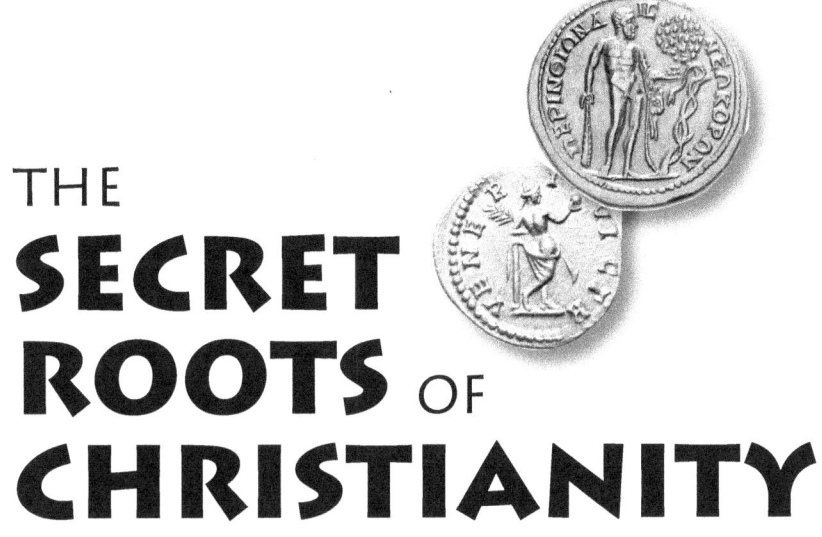

Decoding Religious History with Symbols on Ancient Coins

DAVID WRAY

NUMISMATICS AND HISTORY

Copyright © 2012 by David Wray

All rights reserved. No part of this book may be reproduced in any form or by any electronic or mechanical means, including information storage and retrieval systems, without written permission from the publisher except in the case of brief quotations embodied in critical articles and reviews. For information, address Numismatics and History, 139 Damon Road, Needham, MA 02494

Published by Numismatics and History, Needham, Massachusetts

Library of Congress Control Number: 2012920973

ISBN: 978-0-9885567-0-6

Cover and interior design by Glenna Collett
Editing by Sylvia Dovner
Proofreading by Joanna Eng
Index by Joan Croce
Coin photos for cover and book parts supplied by the Classical Numismatic Group, Inc.
Map photograph on cover by javarman3

Printed in the United States of America

CONTENTS

Preface		IX
Introduction	Regarding the Existence of Secret Roots of Christianity	XIII

	PART ONE	**ANCIENT SICILY: A MICROCOSM OF ANCIENT MEDITERRANEAN CULTS**	1
1		Sicily's Land and People	3
2		Creation Mythology, Gods, and Monsters of Ancient Greek Sicily	17
3		Native Sicilian Mythology	37
4		Other Mythologies on Sicily	57

	PART TWO	**A MYTHOLOGICAL MYSTERY TOUR OF ANCIENT CULTS**	79
5		The Impact of Ancient Greek Mystery Cults	81
6		The Salvation of Herakles	107
7		Ancient Greek Religious Themes That Helped Shape History	127
8		Ideas about Evolution: The Importance of Persistence through Change	149

PART THREE — HELLENIZATION: TRANSFORMING MEDITERRANEAN POLITICS, RELIGIOUS BELIEFS, AND PHILOSOPHIES — 165

9 The Dawn of the Hellenistic Age — 167
10 The Hellenization of Eastern Cults — 189
11 Dangerous Ideas: Hellenistic Philosophies and the Emergence of Rome on the World Stage — 217

PART FOUR — IMPERIALISTIC, RELIGIOUS, AND CIVIL WAR — 235

12 Adversarial Vision: Shaping Rome's Early Interactions with Hellenistic Cults — 237
13 The Hellenistic Cult of Mithras: Shaping Western Understanding of God and the Universe — 265
14 The Life and Times of Gaius Marius: Retooling the Roman War Machine and Sharpening the Game of Politics — 301
15 Lucius Cornelius Sulla: Hero, Dictator, and Creative Master of War — 331

PART FIVE — BECOMING A STAR: HOW JULIUS CAESAR OBTAINED POPULAR RECOGNITION AS A GOD — 351

16 Julius Caesar and the First Triumvirate — 353
17 Amassing Power: Julius Caesar's Conquest of Gaul and Defeat of Pompey the Great — 387
18 Julius Caesar's Journey toward Apotheosis — 421

PART SIX — THE CULT OF THE EMPEROR: RULE OF THE WEST SUPPORTED BY SYMBOLS AND LANGUAGE OF DIVINITY   451

19   The Alliance of Marc Antony and Cleopatra: How the New Dionysos and the Living Incarnation of Isis Came to Oppose the Son of God   453

20   A Civil War Portrayed as a Clash of Gods for Control of the Universe   479

21   The Inauguration of a New Spiritual Age   501

PART SEVEN — INFLUENCES ON THE BIRTH, LIFE, AND CRUCIFIXION OF JESUS CHRIST   525

22   Herodian Judea: The Nativity of Jesus   527

23   The Reign of Tiberius: The Life and Ministry of Jesus   569

24   Pontius Pilate's Administration: The Crucifixion of Jesus   609

25   The Birth of a Thousand Cults   641

Index   679

PREFACE

This book is dedicated to great collectors, lovers of history who preserve important artifacts that otherwise would be lost.

I am a collector of ancient coins, a frequent visitor of museum coin galleries, numismatic conventions, and auctions in search of rare coins with strange symbols. When I find an interesting coin, I search through reference literature—numismatic, historical, and archaeological—attempting to understand the coin's symbols and how they relate to history. Many coins in my collection contain symbols that remain mysterious despite my best efforts to decode them; however, some coins seem to come alive with meaning when I finally discover the right piece of information.

For example, the coin that began my journey toward writing this book portrayed a naked man chasing a woman as though to ravish her. Manufactured (*minted*) 2500 years ago on a Greek island, the coin puzzled me because it expressed regional pride using an image that I regarded as obscene and violent, so I investigated further. Eventually, I found an archaeological report about excavations on a neighboring island called Samothrace. The report presented information about the oldest historical Greek mystery cult. Excavation of an initiation hall revealed pictures that told a story about one of the first men in the world. He came to Samothrace, encountered one of the first women, and kidnapped her. Her brothers chased the kidnapper, caught him, and intended to execute him. However, the woman had fallen in love with her kidnapper. Instead of an execution, her family celebrated a marriage. Gods attended the marriage and gave gifts that brought blessings to all humanity. The greatest gift was the secret for obtaining a happy life after death. Greeks from all over the Mediterranean region sought to learn the secret through initiation in the Samothracian mysteries. Connecting numismatics, history, and archaeology allowed me to recognize the coin as a statement of piety and devotion—not obscenity and violence. The coin advertised a cult that brought substantial revenue to the island by selling an early type of salvation.

Numismatics offers insight into public and personal histories through the use of symbols that speak of ambitions of ancient rulers, everyday concerns of common Greeks and Romans, and economic forces that powered ancient Mediterranean markets. Examining an ancient coin, one sees a combination of substance and symbol that transcends limitations of space and time, offering a glimpse of the living past. Through collecting and researching ancient coins, I discovered a complex untold story about developments in religious history that prepared the West for the emergence of Christianity.

The Secret Roots of Christianity took ten years to write and was tested in a classroom for six of those years: The author taught a course by the same name in the RISE Program at Rivier University in Nashua, New Hampshire. Presenting readers with ancient symbols and a judicious mix of historical and archaeological information, *The Secret Roots of Christianity* surveys a broad range of religious history. Readers will discover important stories that they never knew existed, knowledge of which will help them chart new paths in their own investigations of religious history. However, many unfamiliar names in the stories may seem difficult to pronounce and remember. Readers should not worry about being able to pronounce or remember unusual names. Most of the names distinguish characters and places that are important in brief stories but never reappear in the book again. Relatively few difficult names will recur throughout the book, and familiar contexts will make those names easy to remember. If necessary, one always can use the Index to learn more about a strange name.

In the making of this this book, I owe debts to many people. In particular, an exquisitely talented production team helped transform my original manuscript into a finished product. Sylvia Dovner edited the book, helping me organize information as well as address issues related to content and presentation. Glenna Collett designed the book and its cover, and Joanna Eng proofread the book. Joan Croce took on the particularly daunting challenge of indexing the book. The beauty and ease of use of the finished book comes directly from the talents of this fine team.

The Classical Numismatic Group, Inc. (CNG), contributed most of the pictures of ancient coins that appear in this book. I investigated the possibility of using coin images from museums and other scholarly sources, but CNG was the only source willing to provide the many images that the book needed. Victor England, the president of CNG, allowed me unrestricted access to his company's database of coin images. Further, Travis Markel of CNG checked my selections and sent me a collection of the highest quality coin images that CNG could provide.

I am indebted to fellows of the Society Historia Numorum (SHN) for sharing many years of original research in numismatics and ancient history, information that opened my eyes to the unique window that coins open to the past. Jamie Knapp believed in my project from the beginning, reading early drafts of the book and offering constructive criticism. Ken Mayo made it possible for me to teach courses in the RISE Program at Rivier University, providing a live audience for testing each new draft of the book. Sherry Briggs gave me editing suggestions, and Prue Fitts, John Bittner, Linda Fenton, Don Squires, and Emilio Favorito all contributed ideas and information related to their areas of expertise. Pankaj Tandon introduced me to Eastern iconography and numismatics related to Indian numismatics, which points to largely unexplored connections among Zoroastrian, Hindu, Buddhist, and Christian religious history. Asher Keshet contributed information and assistance until his untimely death, and Sarah Keshet contributed important photographs in his memory.

Members of other numismatic organizations also provided assistance, reviewing early manuscripts for both style and substance.

Paul Levine, Phil Mattera, Paul Murphy, Dennis McAvoy, and Alan Yarbrough in the Massachusetts Ancient Numismatics Association (MANA) provided generous assistance. Members of the Boston Numismatic Society (BNS) offered advice and encouragement.

Michael Molnar contributed key information connecting astrology, Roman numismatics, and early Christian history in his wonderful book *The Star of Bethlehem: Legacy of the Magi*. He read an early draft of my book and offered strong encouragement. In addition, he graciously listened to my ideas, gave me helpful criticism, and sent me important reference literature.

Last, but far from least, I am grateful to my family for giving me support and encouragement for so many years. I'm deeply grateful to Ella Wray (my wife) for her devotion. I also owe much to John Wray (my father), to Lewis Wray (my son), and to Mary Burger (my cousin). Without my family's support, I never could have completed this ambitious project.

INTRODUCTION

REGARDING THE EXISTENCE OF SECRET ROOTS OF CHRISTIANITY

Understanding the roots and earliest development of Christianity requires knowledge about cultic beliefs, politics, and historical events long before the birth of Jesus.

Few historians have attempted to write a history of Christian roots because the subject is vast and complicated. Most prefer instead to tell a traditional story that begins already well-rooted in Judeo-Christian tradition. Traditional histories of Christianity generally begin no earlier than two thousand years ago. Accustomed to these types of histories, many people in the West assume that all important religious history before Jesus consisted of biblical history related to Judea, a tiny spot on the coast of the eastern Mediterranean Sea.

To a well-educated Greek or Roman living sometime between the death of Jesus and the legalization of Christianity by Constantine the Great in 313 A.D., our modern Western understanding of religious history would have seemed absurd. Jews came from a small country with traditions that most Greeks and Romans in ancient times regarded

FIGURE I-1. Cross-Shaped *Idol of Pomos* on Modern 2 Euro Coin. European Union, Cyprus, 2008 A.D.

as uncharacteristic of the wider Mediterranean region. While no one could deny a certain popular appreciation among some Romans for Jewish literature, Jewish history (first translated into Greek in the third century B.C.), beliefs, and practices applied mostly to Jews.

Many Romans found it difficult to take Christianity seriously because they saw Christian beliefs and practices as a haphazard conglomeration of pre-Christian material. For example, even the cross, formally adopted as a Christian symbol in the fourth century A.D., had broad pre-Christian religious associations: Crosses symbolized goddesses giving birth, simultaneously representing fertility and the transition between life and death. From Cyprus, the modern coin in Figure I-1 portrays a five-thousand-year-old cross, illustrating that the earliest religious use of crosses had nothing to do with Christianity. While Jesus preached to Jews in Judea, Roman coins portrayed busts of Venus wearing cross-shaped earrings. When pagans converted to Christian cults, pre-Christian traditions and symbols accompanied the new converts. The pagan origins of new Christian symbols became less visible over time, particularly after Christians made paganism illegal at the end of the fourth century A.D. For all practical purposes, the pre-Christian origins of many Christian beliefs, practices, and iconography became secret.

Different from any other history of the origins of Christianity, this book surveys pre-Christian cults and history to uncover secret roots of Christianity. Beginning hundreds of years before the birth of Jesus and ending approximately a century after his death, a complex story emerges, describing how religious symbols, philosophy, historical events, and politics conspired to prepare the Western world to become Christian: The first pagan converts shaped Christianity by adopting it; and then more pagans embraced Christianity because much of it already was familiar. After only a few hundred years, Christianity became the dominant religion in the West.

DIFFICULTIES IN PERCEIVING SECRET HISTORY

Advances in religion, history, and science have transformed human society so much that, in modern times, we have difficulty relating to life in ancient times. Then, people lived in a universe that seemed vastly different from ours. Even modern uses of the words *religion*, *history*, and *science* get in the way of accurately perceiving the past.

For example, the word religion is a relatively new creation that fails to describe the nature of religious worship two thousand years ago. Referring to Judaism, Christianity, and paganism during the first century A.D. as religions helps obscure the fact that large, centrally organized religions didn't exist in the West until the beginning of the third century A.D.[1] Christians began speaking broadly of Christianity, Judaism, and paganism only as religious authorities confronted the problem of identifying acceptable and unacceptable forms of worship. Before the third century A.D., only relatively small cults existed: People worshipped gods that often were recognized generally throughout a large region; however, individual communities adjusted cult beliefs and practices to make them consistent with local culture and the

---

[1]Steve Mason, Professor of History at York University, Toronto, Canada, wrote a brief history of terms like *Jew*, *pagan*, and *Christian* in "Judaism—Back to Basics," in *Biblical Archaeology Review*, Vol. 35, No. 6. Professor Mason concluded that, "Paradoxically, Christians appear to have invented both Judaism and paganism."

personalities of local priests. Today, we commonly speak about Jews, Christians, and pagans in the first century A.D. but neglect to acknowledge that a Christian cult in Galilee differed from a Christian cult in Ephesos, a Jewish cult in Alexandria differed from a Jewish cult in Jerusalem, and a pagan Cult of Zeus in Tarsos differed from a pagan Cult of Zeus in Syracuse. Before the third century A.D., the earliest Christian cults differed greatly from place to place, often incorporating numerous elements from local pagan cults.

The word history describes a discipline that also has changed substantially from ancient to modern times. Ancient Greeks and Jews wrote histories of the world that commonly portrayed interactions between gods and human beings. In ancient times, miracles in a story assured readers of the story's importance. Modern readers sometimes interpret such a story as a trustworthy account describing a moment when different physical laws prevailed in the universe. However, a sophisticated reader of history understands that historians in ancient times wrote to meet the expectations of readers of their day, not the expectations of modern readers. For example, trustworthy ancient historians wrote about Constantine the Great during the fourth century A.D. stating that, at different times, he experienced signs and communications from the Greek god Apollo and from God as worshipped by Roman Christians. Do Constantine's experiences prove that both gods exist?

The word science also means something different today than in ancient times. Two thousand years ago, the practice of science included meditation, sacrifice, religious inquiry, astrology, metaphorical mathematics, and investigations into natural laws by thought experiments. What we call science in modern times didn't exist until the scientific method was developed in the seventeenth century A.D. It would seem ungracious not to acknowledge people like Archimedes, Aristotle, and Hipparchus as great scientists; however, it's a mistake to understand any ancient scientific achievement as something separate from ancient religious beliefs.

Any attempt to investigate the roots of Christianity automatically brings ancient and modern assumptions about religion, history, and science into conflict. Attempting to speak more accurately about the localized nature of ancient religious beliefs, this work generally uses the word *cult* instead of *religion*. In addition, pre-Christian historical accounts involving religious beliefs and miracles are placed on an equal footing with Christian accounts involving religious beliefs and miracles. As much as possible, information about ancient religious beliefs is presented with respect.

USING COINS TO DISCOVER SECRET ROOTS

Just as modern paleontologists investigate the evolution of plants and animals by arranging fossils in a progression from oldest to newest, this book uses coins to investigate religious history. Arranging coins and other datable artifacts in a progression from older to younger offers an evolutionary view of religious iconography, which connects symbols, politics, and history into a graphic record. Comparing this graphic record with a historical account of events, ideas, and religious beliefs provides insights simply not available any other way.

The topics discussed in the book were identified by surveying images on ancient coins, arranging them by date and theme, and connecting them with historical events. Numismatic iconography connected rulers, citizens, allies, and enemies and portrayed all aspects of ancient religious life. As Christianity benefits Christians today, ancient cults benefited pagan worshippers by offering:

- Relationship with divinity
- Ways to pray
- Inspiration through relics and exemplary lives
- Atonement and forgiveness
- Healing and miracles
- Understanding of life mysteries
- Salvation after death
- Comforting of grief

Minted for the first time in the West approximately 2650 years ago in Asia Minor, coins survive from almost every place in the ancient civilized world. Just as fossils document increasing biological sophistication from lower layers of rock to higher ones, images on coins arranged from earlier times to later times offer a remarkable view of religious evolution. Further, coins connect well with documented layers of human history from the seventh century B.C. to the first century A.D.

Information Available from Coins

What can coins reveal? Coins are like photographs. By looking at a family photo album, one can compare clothing that grandparents wore when they were young with clothing that the grandchildren currently wear. One can compare old and new fashions that sometimes point to big differences between old and new ways of life. For important events that happened to the family, photos help document the influences and effects related to those events.

Just like photos in a family album, images on coins portray important moments in the histories of people. Arranging coins in chronological order reveals changes over decades, centuries, and millennia, just as arranging fossils in chronological order makes biological evolution visible over geological ages. By collecting coins, one can assemble photo albums that represent gods, miracles, and historical events that symbolically parallel the development of the Western world.[2]

Ancient coins and other small artifacts bear witness to events and symbols that influenced religious history. For example, holding an ancient coin minted under Pontius Pilate during the year of the crucifixion of Jesus brings one in direct contact with physical and symbolic material perceived by people involved with the birth of Christianity. Whether you are a Christian, a Jew, an agnostic, or an atheist, the material in this book will help you understand the historical background surrounding the birth of Christianity.

When describing coins, this book uses simple numismatic conventions. Numismatists speak of the front of a coin as its *obverse* and the back of a coin as its *reverse*. When a picture presents both sides of a coin, the obverse generally appears on the left and the reverse appears

---

[2]For beginning collectors, the chapters of this book offer ideas about collecting coins related to religious themes. Almost all the coins in the illustrations can be purchased at coin shows and auctions.

FIGURE I-2. Coin of a Modern Christian King Displaying Symbols that Refer to His Astrological Birth Chart. Kingdom of Naples and Sicily, Ferdinand IV, AR Piastre, 1791 A.D.

on the right. The customary description of a coin usually describes what it portrays, where it came from, its metal composition (AU for gold, AR for silver, and AE for copper or bronze), the ruler who authorized it, its denomination, and the date of its *minting*, or manufacture by a *celator*. For AE coins of uncertain denomination, a number, like "AE 26," indicates the diameter of the coin in millimeters.

Images on coins can prove surprising, often revealing much more information than one realizes at first glance. For example, consider the relatively modern silver piastre in Figure I-2. Minted in Naples under Ferdinand IV, King of Naples and Sicily during the period 1751 to 1799, the obverse of the coin (about the size of an American silver dollar) bears portraits of Ferdinand IV and his Austrian wife, Queen Maria Carolina. The reverse portrays astronomical symbols: the earth, the sun, and zodiacal constellations. Knowing a little about the history of science, one might guess that an enlightened ruler at the end of the eighteenth century A.D. intended the coin to honor famous scientists, men like Nicolaus Copernicus, Johannes Kepler, and Isaac Newton, whose work from the sixteenth to the eighteenth centuries A.D. uncovered the laws of planetary motion.

However, look more closely at the coin's reverse. Naturally (to Ferdinand), Sicily and Naples occupy the center of the world. Just beyond the *legend* ("Soli Reduci," which means, "To the return of the sun"), the sun shines beneath an astrological symbol (a goat) that represents the constellation *Capricorn* (sun sign for December 23–January 20). When one learns that Ferdinand IV celebrated his birthday on January 12, one suddenly realizes that this Christian king portrayed a symbolic representation of his astrological birth chart on his coinage. Instead of showing the earth going around the sun, the coin actually portrays zodiacal constellations and a small sun circling the earth.

From the examination of images on a single eighteenth century coin, questions emerge concerning the relationship between astrology and Christianity:

- When did Christians first encounter astrology?
- Why did Christianity tolerate the pagan practice of astrology?
- How did astrology grow so important that a Christian ruler placed his astrological birth chart on official state coinage?

By examining astrological symbols on ancient coins, one discovers fascinating information about the religious importance of astrology in the West over many centuries. Questions then arise regarding how astrology and other pre-Christian religious beliefs related to the birth and early development of Christianity.

A Glimpse of the Secret Roots of Christianity

Traditional religious history preserves a rarely acknowledged secret that Christianity developed from at least three ancient roots: a Western structural root derived from Mediterranean Greek culture, an Eastern spiritual root from Anatolia and Persia, and a literary Jewish historical root, which masked the other roots and supported the idea that Christians had taken the place of Jews in relationship with God by entering a new covenant with Jesus. Each root contributed something special to the development of Christianity as follows:

- Supported by pagan iconography and rhetoric, the Western root imprinted Christianity with Greek spirit in a Hellenistic universe.

- The Eastern root filled the Greek construct with magic, focused humanity on a divine mission, and infused popular reverence for goddesses into Christian beliefs about the Virgin Mary.
- The literary Jewish root played two contradictory roles: Jewish scripture served as the reliable witness that proved Jesus to be both God and savior; and double-edged moral lessons in the *Old Testament* explained catastrophic events in the first century A.D. as divine judgment against Jews, supporting beliefs by early pagan converts to Christianity that Romans were good, Jews were bad, and God abandoned Jews for treacherously murdering Jesus.

Drawing from both visible and secret roots, Christians freed themselves from paying for salvation from mystery cults while preserving the ability to worship a virgin-born hero with all the trappings of a solar deity; also, they adopted Jewish history while congratulating themselves for possessing different beliefs and practices than Jews. However, the benefits of keeping some roots secret came at a cost: Separation from mysteries associated with goddess cults meant that Christianity never maintained an easy relationship with women and sex; in addition, science and history became dangerous.

This book contains seven parts. The first three parts provide an overview of the diversity, depth, and richness of religious beliefs, practices, and iconography in the ancient Greek world that influenced modern Western culture and religion. The fourth, fifth, and sixth parts describe how the West developed under Roman influence. Then the seventh part focuses on the life of Jesus and the emergence of Christian cults in the first century A.D.

Ancient Sicily: A Microcosm of Ancient Mediterranean Cults.

During the seventh century B.C., Greeks founded new colonies along the Mediterranean coast, which spread Greek culture and helped prepare an important foundation for Christianity in the West. Part One introduces representative examples of Western mythology and cults as expressed by Greek and other Mediterranean ethnicities[3]

---

[3] In ancient times, people often regarded inhabitants of different cities as representatives of different ethnicities.

that interacted on Sicily. By surveying Sicilian cults, one glimpses disconnected elements of Christianity among popular cult influences during Greek colonization. One also can recognize important Greek structural contributions to Christianity, which differ from Semitic contributions and continue to survive in the West, for example:

- Christianity acquired a Greek spirit of optimism, which expresses itself in a popular belief that pagan times were terrible but Christianity improved everything. However, history never characterized Jews as possessing a spirit of optimism: For example, some Jews believed in their souls' survival after death and some did not.
- Christians, pagan Greeks, and Jews all shared beliefs that the creation of the universe occurred approximately five thousand years ago and that, afterward, events occurred like the creation of the first man and woman and occasional global floods that cleansed the earth of impious humans. In the universes of Christians and pagan Greeks, guilt from sin could be inherited; but Jews, while believing that sinful nature and even punishment could be inherited, generally believed that all humans were born innocent.
- Both pagan Greeks and Christians believed that one great male deity dominated spiritual life in the universe and that he often delegated lower-level responsibilities to lesser spiritual beings; but Jewish history commonly portrays Jews as denying the validity of worshipping more than one spiritual being, even though archaeology often provides more complicated views of Jewish spiritual life.

Greeks also pioneered standard methods for improving religious beliefs, practices, and iconography. Greek gods originated in different lands around the Mediterranean Sea, however, their cults traveled, rose, and fell among Mediterranean populations depending on the perceived benefits that their worship brought their followers. Greeks integrated foreign gods into their cults in ways similar to the Christian acquisition of saints. Immigrant Greeks on Sicily encountered at least one Sicilian cult that featured a deity who, like Jesus, was born on December 25, was treacherously murdered, and then resurrected specifically to offer hope to mankind. Also, like Christianity, the most advanced Sicilian cults offered salvation to true believers.

A Mythological Mystery Tour of Ancient Cults. Pagans who lived virtuous lives and who paid for initiation into spiritual mysteries achieved salvation, obtaining access after death to the Elysian Fields, a pleasant underground realm analogous to heaven where souls would live forever. Part Two explores how Western cults that offered salvation often exhibited features characteristic of modern Christianity. For example, Greeks pioneered the use of theater, iconography, athletic competition, relics, and philosophy to achieving salvation, developing religious practices that continue to exist in Western culture but did not exist in ancient Jewish culture.

Many elements of modern Christianity originated as pagan elements thousands of years ago that were reinterpreted as originally Christian. For example, conceived by a supreme deity and a virgin, the Greek hero Herakles metaphorically represented the idea that no man lies beyond redemption. Elements of pagan stories about Herakles entered Jewish stories of the strong-man Samson, and iconography related to Herakles' search for the apples of the Hesperides influenced Christian iconography about the Garden of Eden. From the East, ancient Zoroastrians believed that a hero born of a virgin would precipitate the End of Days, which included the destruction of a spiritual entity that was the source of all evil. Strangely, Jewish literature condemned Greek religious influences but remained silent about Zoroastrian religious influences, many of which found their way into Christianity.

Hellenization: Transforming Mediterranean Politics, Religious Beliefs, and Philosophies. Part Three explores the importance to Christianity of religious ideas flowing freely east and west. Alexander the Great conducted a series of extraordinary conquests that briefly unified important European and Asian civilizations, thus establishing a record of military successes that excited the imagination of every general who came after him. During the resulting *Hellenistic Age*, Alexander's successors ruled vast empires and oversaw the merging of religious beliefs and practices from the West with those of the East. Greeks equated Eastern spiritual entities with gods in the Greek pantheon, and Eastern spiritual innovations like ecstatic worship, astrology, and magic began to enter the West. Hellenistic rulers, often portraying themselves as gods to their subjects, modified Eastern cults and used them as tools for promoting social harmony. Many Eastern peoples, Judean Jews in particular, began to see Hellenistic domination as an unacceptable threat to their beliefs and culture.

No subject lay beyond the consideration of Hellenistic philosophical inquiry. Perhaps a man could become a god, perhaps gods didn't exist, and perhaps viewing religious beliefs and practices as flexible elements of a technology for changing society justified making improvements to any barbarian cult. Modern religious beliefs differ greatly from Hellenistic religious beliefs. Nevertheless, Christianity owes more to Alexander the Great than to Jewish Kings like King Solomon and Judah Maccabee: Hellenistic scholars ensured the enduring importance of Jewish religious history in the *Old Testament* by translating it into Greek. In a world where every educated person read Greek, Jewish history exhibited important advantages over many local mythologies and histories: Jewish history concisely presented a fairly consistent history of the world, which combined common Mediterranean mythological and historical elements while generally avoiding the demonization of specific ethnicities. Further, Jewish literature made an unprecedented case for one set of laws applying equally to everyone, regardless of a person's wealth or status. Hellenistic readers appreciated the virtues of Jewish ethics while discounting the descriptions of undesirable Jewish laws and cultural practices.

Imperialistic, Religious, and Civil War. Throughout the third and second centuries B.C., the Roman Republic expanded rapidly and increasingly dominated the Mediterranean world. However, even as Roman power stretched beyond the Italian peninsula, unexpected existential threats confronted Rome with confounding regularity. During this period, spectacular military losses from encounters with brilliant foreign generals introduced Rome to the utility of sophisticated Hellenistic ideas. Only the emergence of talented Roman generals at the right times preserved the Roman Republic, however, over time, talented Roman generals posed their own grave threats to the Roman Republic. Paradoxically, by expanding and opening itself to Hellenistic ideas Rome opened itself to being conquered: Rome used the island of Sicily as a staging ground for its invasion of the Mediterranean world; and Hellenistic cults used slave centers like Sicily and Delos and intellectual centers like Tarsos, Pergamon, and Alexandria as staging grounds for the religious invasion of Rome.

Beginning with Part Four, religious preparations for the West to accept Christianity can be tracked with the transmission of Eastern cults westward into Rome. Lacking Greek sophistication, Roman worship originally comprised mostly solemn rituals and sacrifices without combining salvation, fertility, and sex into sophisticated mysteries. However, the worship of Eastern goddesses by great generals broke the artificial barriers between Roman culture and Eastern cults: The Anatolian Cult of *Cybele* established a formal presence in Rome, the Cult of *Isis* (an analogue of Christianity's Cult of Mary) increased the power of Rome's poor and working classes, and cults of the *Syrian Aphrodite* established a strong presence among commoners and slaves in Rome. Some of the most important models for interactions between Christianity and other religions first developed during this period in Rome: the first religious persecutions (including Rome's first expulsion of Jews in 139 B.C.), the first true believers who suffered death rather than abandon their faith, and the use of religious beliefs by slaves and poor people to confront their wealthy masters. Particularly suited for Rome, a new Hellenistic cult developed specifically for warriors: The Cult of *Mithras* entered Rome surreptitiously and began shifting Western culture toward the worship of a *solar deity* (a dying and resurrecting god of the sky born on December 25) as well as toward believing that, after death, virtuous souls found eternal life in the sky instead of in plutonic caverns beneath the surface of the earth.

Becoming a Star. As described in Part Five, Julius Caesar and Pompey the Great, the last great generals of the Roman Republic, contended against each other for dominion over the Mediterranean world. During events brimming with historical and metaphorical significance, Julius Caesar, Pompey, and a third Roman general established the First Triumvirate, a new way of governing the Roman Republic. The three generals exhibited public personas that turned politics into a real-time morality play. Their struggles inadvertently resulted in the creation of the Roman Empire as well as establishing the political and religious conditions encountered by Jesus and his family in Judea.

Julius Caesar minted coins that connected his family's mythological origins to his successes. Representing himself as a descendant of the goddess Venus, Julius Caesar lived a life in which myth and reality seemed inextricably combined. A talented engineer and general, he used engineering and science to improve the lives of common Romans as well as to obtain decisive tactical advantages in battles with powerful enemies. A powerful orator, he masterfully swayed public opinion, easily taking charge in every situation. In international relations, he outshone every other leader such that every historical conflict and interaction contributed to his reputation as the most powerful man in the world. While preparing an assault on the Parthian Empire (attempting to equal the achievements of Alexander the Great) Julius Caesar was treacherously murdered by jealous members of Rome's privileged class. Rome then entered a strange period when the common people of Rome asserted power over government officials. Popular respect for Julius Caesar gave young Octavian, the nephew and heir of Julius Caesar, the opportunity to become one of the most powerful men of Rome. When a bright comet appeared in the sky during Julius Caesar's funeral games, Romans began believing that, for the first time in recorded history, a man who had lived and died among them had ascended into the sky and become a god.

The Cult of the Emperor. In Part Six, Octavian Caesar used his talent for self-promotion to connect popular ideas about the divinity of his uncle Julius Caesar to propaganda asserting Octavian's own divinity. A master of symbolism and spin, Octavian used his status as Son of God to obtain enough credit and flexibility to successfully consolidate power over Rome. He then strove to extend his power over the Mediterranean region, contending against Marc Antony and Cleopatra, ambitious rulers who also claimed divinity. By achieving victory in a conflict popularly portrayed as a war among gods, Octavian obtained sufficient power to complete the momentous transition of Rome from a Republic to an Empire. Taking the name Augustus, which means revered, he developed new political symbols and language portraying his reign as the dawn of a new spiritual age.

By the beginning of the new millennium in 1 A.D., during the early childhood of Jesus, Augustus ruled the Roman Empire as the divine son of the god Julius Caesar. Many events in the lives of Julius and Augustus Caesar metaphorically prefigured events in the life of Jesus, as portrayed in the canonical gospels in the *New Testament*. In addition, important novelties in Roman culture, for example, the mature iconography and language of Augustan propaganda, Eastern goddess worship, and the worship of solar deities like Mithras, lay ready and waiting to be applied appropriately to Christianity. By popularizing himself and Julius Caesar as saviors of Rome, Augustus did more to prepare Roman acceptance of Jesus and Christian dominance of the West than any of the twelve apostles who survived Jesus.

Influences on the Birth, Life, and Crucifixion of Jesus. Two thousand years ago, Jewish saviors rose, inspired attacks against Rome, and then fell, establishing a tradition of *catastrophic messianism* that many Jews believed would bring the Kingdom of God to earth. Part Seven portrays the political and religious atmosphere during the life of Jesus. Born during the reign of Augustus, Jesus lived as a traditional Nazarene, worshipping God and following Jewish laws. He avoided using iconography and followed a teacher noted for condemning Jews who incorporated Hellenistic ideas into Jewish faith. However, rapidly changing circumstances in Judea's relationship with Rome provoked social turmoil in Judea. Jews took offense at Roman worship of Julius Caesar and Augustus as gods, and met attempts to import Rome's Cult of the Emperor to Judea with anger.

Looking only in the *New Testament*, it's difficult to see Jesus. Although the canonical gospels portray him as a practitioner of catastrophic messianism, his words were recorded in Greek language, his biblical quotes referred to a Greek version of the *Bible* instead of a non-Hellenistic Hebrew version, and even his metaphors related to Greek gods and Eastern cults. The history of the first century A.D. after the crucifixion of Jesus shows that Christians adjusted their portrayals of

Jesus to suit political circumstances after his death. In the canonical gospels, one can find evidence that Jesus existed, but heavily modified speech and stories form an anachronistic haze around the real man.

EVERYONE LIVES DURING *MODERN* TIMES

Frequently misunderstood and ignored by people today, pagan life and Christian life were similar in many respects. During pagan times, people prayed, families worshipped together, worshippers sought blessings and guidance, great teachers imparted religious insights, gods miraculously healed the sick, governments accredited religious teachers, and cities funded socially beneficial religious institutions. Like modern Christians, pre-Christian pilgrims traveled to distant sacred locations to see relics, to worship with famous mystics, and to achieve deeper levels of religious understanding. Some pilgrims were healed from serious ailments and some obtained profound experiences of personal salvation. The most important insights about pagan and Christian religious beliefs come from their similarities, not their differences.

Pre-Christian Mediterranean societies continually updated and improved their religious beliefs with the latest innovations available in an active and diverse theological marketplace. Facing all the prospects for disasters and material uncertainties that characterized living in ancient times, pagan populations always utilized the most powerful ideas of divinity and salvation available. Over time, small changes in religious beliefs and practices added up to an evolutionary period of religious transformation. Everything changed; however, somehow, everything also stayed the same. As we live our lives in times that we consider modern, ancient rules and habits continue to govern how we think and act.

Without studying the past, we simply have no way of seeing the antiquity of many aspects of our lives. This book attempts to provide enough history and mythology to let images from the past speak for themselves. For this, we first need to understand a few ancient ideas about the nature of the universe, certain aspects about the worship of ancient gods, and important characteristics about ancient cultures around the Mediterranean Sea. Our investigation begins by looking at the early history of a diverse microcosm of the ancient Greek world at the center of the Mediterranean Sea—the multicultural island of Sicily.

PART ONE

Marriage of Underworld Deities in a Sicilian Mystery Cult

ANCIENT SICILY
A MICROCOSM OF ANCIENT MEDITERRANEAN CULTS

Beginning in the seventh century B.C., *Greek mythology shaped history's first Mediterranean mystery cults, the spiritual grandparents of modern Christianity.*

CHAPTER
1

SICILY'S LAND AND PEOPLE

> Offering life after death like Christianity, mystery cults came to Sicily attached to mythologies that helped early settlers explain and cope with the island's diverse cultures and geography.

During an adventurous age in the eighth and seventh centuries B.C., waves of immigrants from Europe and Africa came to Sicily, a place inhabited by native tribes since prehistoric times. Competing European powers first colonized the eastern shore. In the northeast, some colonists came to build new lives after fleeing persecution at home. Some colonists made friends with the natives, but others conquered and enslaved native populations. Over time, an overwhelming tide of Europeans pushed the indigenous tribes westward.

Despite periodic native rebellions, the European settlers expanded their territory, established more settlements, and improved their standard of living. Attracted by the possibilities of living a good life, even more new immigrants came from a variety of different lands. Sicily became a melting pot of different races, cultures, and ideas.

One could describe the history of the United States of America in similar terms. In a broad sense, the early history of Sicily parallels U.S. history—with a few important differences:

- Ancient Sicily never unified into a single country. However, great wars over Sicilian territory determined the rise or fall of empires.
- Rather than affirming democracy, Sicily ultimately helped to defeat the city-state of Athens, one of the world's earliest and greatest democracies.
- Sicily helped shape the development of the ancient world by enabling the growth of the Roman Empire and by influencing the development of Christianity.
- Rome used policies it developed for enslaving Sicily and siphoning its wealth as a model for subjugating captured territories throughout the Mediterranean region.

SICILY'S CULTURAL DIVERSITY

This book begins with Sicily because people came to Sicily from every Mediterranean shore. Greeks, Phoenicians, and Romans competed directly on Sicily; and Rome expanded into an empire only after conquering Sicily first. Much of what we know about Greek cults reached us through the Romans, and much of Rome's knowledge of Greek cults came to Rome from Sicilian Greek colonies. Many Greek myths reached us already strongly attached to Sicilian geography and natural history. Sicily shows how the forces of nature, culture, and competition shaped cults in ancient times.

The largest island in the Mediterranean Sea, Sicily has played many important roles in history. On this island, Phoenicians taught Romans the practice of crucifying enemies. Slave-grown Sicilian grain nourished Republican Rome, and policies invented for administering a subjugated Sicily scaled easily into policies for governing the expanding Roman Empire. In later periods of history, Christian saints performed miracles on Sicilian soil, the Holy Roman Empire used the island to stage armies bound for the Crusades, and a tolerant, multicultural medieval society on Sicily contributed to the birth of the Renaissance in Florence. Even when the Black Death came to Europe, the disease came first to Sicily.

At its best, the history of Sicily proves that a dynamic mix of cults and cultures can lead to greatness. Settlers from Italy, Spain, Turkey, the Middle East, and Africa competed with native peoples to secure Sicilian resources and to sell Sicilian products. It took only two centuries of intensive competition and growth for successful Greek colonies on the island to rival the economic and cultural influence of Greece.

The history of Sicily also hints at the operation of long-term justice, or at least irony, as inhabitants that traded in slaves fell into service as slaves of others. In the earliest literary mention of Sicily, the *Odyssey* refers to Sicily's indigenous tribes as traders of slaves. When European colonists arrived, they obtained slaves in wars against Sicily's indigenous tribes. Then, periodically over hundreds of years, wars among natives, Europeans, and Africans brought extreme reversals in fortune, including slaughter and enslavement, to population centers all over the island. Eventually, Romans harnessed almost everyone on Sicily as slaves to produce food for Rome. Rome then used the agricultural wealth and strategic location of Sicily to help build and dominate a Mediterranean empire.

SICILY'S GEOGRAPHICAL DIVERSITY

Sicily's triangular shape inspired its ancient name, Trinacria (triangle). A little larger than the state of Vermont, the island touches three seas, a different sea with each of its three sides: the Tyrrhenian Sea on the north coast, the Ionian Sea on the east coast, and the Mediterranean Sea on the southwest coast. A two-mile-wide strait (the Strait of Messina) separates the northeast corner of the island from the "toe" of the Italian peninsula. (See Figure 1-1.)

A chain of mountains, extending Italy's Calabrian Apennines, runs east-to-west along the north coast of the island. Two mountains in this chain exceed six thousand feet in height. In Figure 1-1, a white spot in the northeast marks snow-covered Mount Etna—well over ten thousand feet tall. Europe's highest active volcano, the mountain has a circumference of 87 miles at its base. Currently the second most active volcano in the world, Mount Etna has the longest documented history of eruptions of any volcano—more than 190 eruptions in 2500 years. Ancient texts[1] say that Mount Etna erupted in 479, 425, and 396 B.C.

Sicily's largest coastal plain extends south and west of Mount Etna. The whole island slopes south, away from northern mountains, in a hilly incline toward the Ionian and Mediterranean Seas. The north and east coasts possess steep banks and deep water, while the topography of the southwestern coast features many lagoons, marshes, shallow seas, and sandbanks.

ABSORPTION OF RELIGIOUS INFLUENCES

Since Greek culture first developed, Greek sailors traded with indigenous populations on every coast of the Mediterranean Sea. Egypt and the Middle East have absorbed elements of Greek culture since Minoan times in the second millennium B.C. During the eighth and seventh centuries B.C., Greek colonists established new communities on many foreign shores. Wealthy Greek cities like Corinth, Megara, and Naxos sent shiploads of colonists to found Greek towns on the coasts of France, Italy, Sicily, and all around the Black Sea. In some places, Greek influence percolated farther inland.

From their original home on the Lebanese coast, Phoenicians also colonized the Mediterranean, especially North Africa and Spain. Phoenicians traveled farther than Greeks, well beyond the Pillars of Herakles (the ancient name of the Strait of Gibraltar between Spain and Morocco), but they focused more on trade than on colonization. Still, the independent city-state of Carthage achieved greatness, and its navy battled Rome's for domination of the Mediterranean Sea.

All around the Mediterranean Sea, Greeks and Phoenicians spread new religious ideas along with their trade goods. Philosophies and cults from ancient centers of civilization like Egypt and Babylon (and

---

[1] A description of Mount Etna's eruptions of 479 B.C. appears in *The Odes of Pindar* Ode 1, Decade 5. The eruption of 425 B.C. was mentioned in the *History of the Peloponnesian Wars* (3.116) by Thucydides, and the eruption of 396 B.C. was mentioned in the *Historical Library* book xiv by Diodorus Siculus.

FIGURE 1-1. Landforms of Sicily and Three Surrounding Seas

some even farther east) greatly influenced the development of Western religion. In the center of the Mediterranean, Sicily absorbed religious influences from all the cultures around it, particularly the Greek.

Of great importance, sophisticated Greek *mystery cults* emerged around the same time that Greeks colonized Sicily. Colonists from Naxos brought early ideas about salvation to Sicily along with a mystery cult. Their priests guarded secrets (the mysteries) that enabled initiates to negotiate favorable treatment after death from King Hades and Queen Persephone. Supplicants obtained access to these mysteries only after dreams and signs came to them from the gods. Prospective initiates purified themselves and paid priests for the privilege of initiation. Then, after suffering long ceremonies involving hunger, darkness, ritual death, and rebirth, successful initiates received the jealously guarded secrets.

Born in the East,[2] mystery cults came west only gradually. While ancient Greeks embraced these cults, Romans viewed them with

---

[2]While the true origin of mystery cults remains unknown, evidence for the earliest example in European history was found on the island of Samothrace in the northeastern Aegean Sea.

suspicion. Sicily fulfilled its most pivotal role in world history as Greek power declined in the Mediterranean and Roman power increased. Just as Rome used Sicily to help invade the East, Eastern cults used Sicily to invade Rome and the West.

AN EXAMPLE FROM GREEK MYTHOLOGY

Shown in Figure 1-2, a replica of the Aphrodite Panel of the *Ludovisi Throne*[3] provides an interesting visual metaphor of the emergence of Greek Sicily. A decorative element on a throne used during Greek initiation rituals, the Aphrodite panel portrays three women. The sleeve of the leftmost woman indicates that she wears a Doric *peplos*. One makes a peplos by folding a long rectangular piece of cloth end-to-end, cutting a hole for the head, stitching the sides leaving arm-holes, and then shaping the garment into a dress with pins and a belt. The woman on the right wears an Ionic *chiton*, a completely different style of dress. One makes a chiton by first making a cloth tube, sewing one end to accommodate a head, cutting holes in the side, attaching sleeves, and then shaping the garment with a belt.

Between them, the two women support a third woman, a central figure dressed only in a revealing, diaphanous gown. Barely visible, the gown forms delicate ripples below her neck. A modest royal diadem on her head signifies that this woman rules as a queen. Why does this panel show women in Dorian and Ionian costumes attending a queen?

Dressed in different ethnic styles, the two supporting women represent the participation of both Dorian and Ionian Greek women in some important event. Just as the *Bible* says that all Arabs and Jews descend from sons of Abraham, Greek mythology says that Dorian and Ionian Greeks descend from two different sons of Kreousa, a daughter

---

[3]Controversial in recent years, the original Ludovisi Throne in the Museo Nazionale Romano of Palazzo Altemps in Rome has attracted accusations of forgery on stylistic grounds. A majority of scholars currently accept it as authentic. In 1982, Professor Margherita Guarducci identified its provenance: a temple located in Marasà (on the toe of Italy) that was rebuilt approximately in 480 B.C.

FIGURE 1-2. Replica of Aphrodite Panel of the Ludovisi Throne

of King Erichthonius of Athens. Dorians descend from Kreousa's son, Dorus, and Ionians descend from her other son, Ion.

Evolving over hundreds of years and blending traditions from many different places, Greek mythology includes a wide variety of stories that frequently contradict each other in substance and time frame. Different myths, expressing different regional religious traditions, present contradictory genealogies of Dorian and Ionian Greeks. For example, Dorian myths emphasize the importance of Dorian culture by saying that Kreousa bore both sons by her husband Xouthos, but Dorus was the older and wiser brother. Conversely, Ionian myths say that Kreousa bore her mortal son, Dorus, by Xouthos, but she bore Ion, her semi-divine son, after having relations with the god Apollo.

Just as the Aphrodite Panel displays two ethnic varieties of dress, modern authorities associate the panel with two completely different mythological stories. In one story, Cronos (God of Time) castrated his father, Uranus (God of the Sky), and threw the severed genitals into the sea. Generated from the resulting mixture of sea-foam, blood, and semen, Aphrodite, the Goddess of Love, emerged on the shores of Cyprus, nude and fully grown. Some authorities believe the Aphrodite Panel shows the birth of Aphrodite with two Fates helping to lift her from the sea.

However, a more likely possibility associates this scene with the annual emergence of Persephone from the underworld. The myth of Persephone explained the changing seasons, and mystery rituals related to Persephone (for example, the Eleusinian Mysteries) frequently used decorated thrones. According to this interpretation, the scene shows two mortal women, a Dorian Greek and an Ionian Greek, lifting Persephone from the earth as part of a Springtime mystery ritual.

Greek mythology from Sicily identifies Enna, a town near the center of the island, as the place where Hades, God of the Underworld, abducted Persephone (Goddess of both the Spring and the Underworld). Hades then carried her to his underground Kingdom of the Dead and made her his queen. After Persephone disappeared, the unquenchable grief of Persephone's mother, Demeter (Goddess of Nature), brought unending Winter to the Earth.

Life on Earth survived only because Zeus (King of the Gods) negotiated a deal between Demeter and Hades. They agreed that Persephone could spend one part of every year in the underworld and another part on the surface of the Earth. Closely related to the mysteries at Eleusis (near Athens), a cult related to Demeter and Persephone at Enna included sacred rituals for mortals to participate annually in the Springtime reemergence of Persephone[4] from the underworld and the return of fertility to the earth.

Because both Dorian and Ionian Greeks colonized Italy and Sicily in the eighth century B.C., it makes sense that the Aphrodite panel illustrates the participation of both Dorians and Ionians in the Springtime return of Persephone to Sicily. Greek history even suggests why the goddess looks with particular favor on the woman wearing the Doric

---

[4]As another example of different regional religious traditions, Syracusans (Dorians) believed that Persephone divided her time equally (six months at a time) in the realms of life and death; however, the Eleusinian (Ionian) tradition said that Persephone spent only four months of every year with Hades. Chapter 2 discusses the Cult of Demeter and Persephone on Sicily at greater length.

peplos. Around the time that an unknown artist carved the throne, Dorians fled Spartan persecution on the Peloponnese Peninsula. New Dorian immigrants flooded northeastern Sicily and related communities on the toe of Italy (the original location of the Ludovisi Throne). While expressing an inclusive sentiment by carving women from both Dorian and Ionian cultures, the artist (perhaps a new immigrant) nevertheless portrayed divine favor toward the Dorian.

REGIONAL GODS

Like politics, all cults are local. Yet, historically, all cults seem to come from someplace else. In ancient times even the twelve Olympian Gods[5] originally came from different lands. Cults of three Olympian goddesses emerged from different continents during a time when most of the world worshipped a divine mother of many names: the Cult of Aphrodite, the Goddess of Love, came from Cyprus (Europe); the Cult of Athena, Goddess of Wisdom, came from Libya (Africa); and the Cult of Artemis, Goddess of the Hunt, came from Turkey (Asia).

Nations did not exist in the West during the early years of Greek and Phoenician colonization. Instead, large cities throughout the Mediterranean region dominated their surrounding territories and operated as independent city-states. Almost every city-state worshipped its own special gods. Still, Greeks and Phoenicians everywhere recognized similar male-centric hierarchies of gods.

The sky god Baal ruled the Phoenician gods of Carthage and Tyre, while Zeus ruled Greek gods from the top of Mount Olympus on the border between Macedonia and Thessaly. Athenians chose Athena as the symbol of their city-state, but they still recognized Zeus as King of the Gods. Sparta, a city-state devoted to the development of an elite class of warriors, acquired distinction as the only Greek people to build a temple to Ares, God of War. Much later, Rome, too, built temples to the God of War, but Rome used Ares' Roman name, Mars.

---

[5]The different regional religious traditions expressed in Greek mythology make it impossible to identify any single definitive set of twelve Olympian Gods. See Chapter 2 for further discussion of this point.

THE COLONIZATION OF SICILY

On the small island of Sicily native cults first emerged organically from the native population, tribes of *Sicans* and *Sicels* that had occupied Sicily since the Stone Age. Sometime after the Trojan War[6], refugees from Asia Minor called *Elymians* brought Eastern cults to northwestern Sicily. By the eighth century B.C., Phoenician sailors from Carthage, the most important North African city-state, brought Phoenician and Egyptian cults to west-Sicilian trading posts that eventually turned into Carthaginian colonies. Carthage built a culture that combined influences from Spain, ancient Egypt, and barbarian western portions of Africa with the original Phoenician culture that founders of Carthage had carried from the Middle East.

Beginning in the eighth century B.C., wealthy Greek city-states launched shiploads of colonists that landed on the eastern and southern coasts of Sicily. Some Greek colonists sought to escape conflicts at home, but most saw their adventure as an investment toward continuing their aristocratic way of life. Either way, new Greek colonists seized prime Sicilian real estate and staffed their plantations with native slaves.

All the new colonists brought cults from home. Like early settlers that came to America, Greek settlers conducted religious rituals to help found their colonies. Greek rituals usually included preliminary consultation with an oracle, often at Delphi. Colonists then traveled as the oracle directed, seeking to recognize the divinely approved location of the colony by means of a special sign. Colonists dedicated a new colony by bringing sacred fire to it from their mother city and by ceremonially blessing the community. Founders also created a mythological or religious justification for colonization.

For hundreds of years, conflicts among numerous ethnicities and city-states made life precarious for the inhabitants of Sicily. Even during the best of times, Greeks and Phoenicians engaged in piracy and small-scale warfare. Greeks effectively closed the Strait of Messina to Phoenicians, while Phoenicians made routes south and west of Sicily extremely dangerous for Greeks.

---

[6]Modern scholars generally date the Trojan War to the thirteenth century B.C.

Chapter 1 | Sicily's Land and People   13

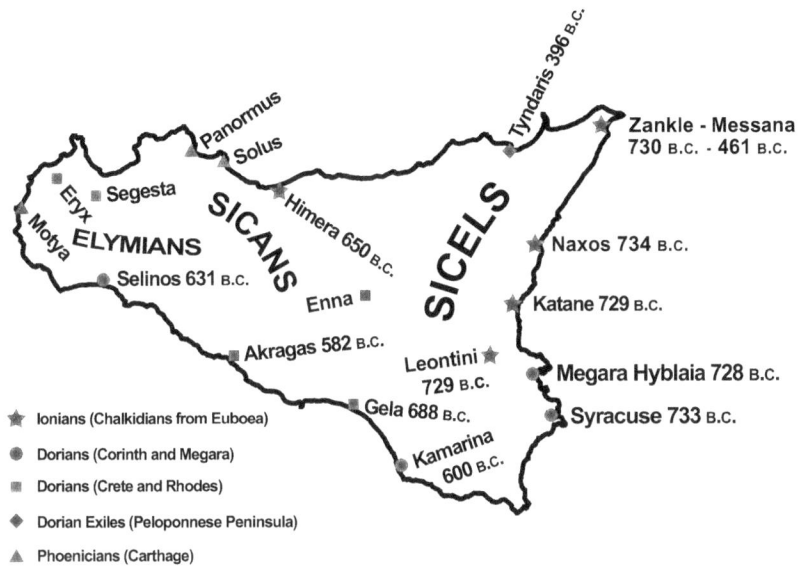

FIGURE 1-3. Greek and Phoenician Colonies on Sicily and General Territories of Indigenous Populations

No other part of the Mediterranean contained so many different cults in such a small area. By the end of the seventh century B.C., a number of distinct groups of people lived on Sicily. (See Figure 1-3.)

- Similar to the tribal cultures that bounded the west and north of the ancient Greek world, two separate indigenous tribes occupied most of central Sicily: Sicels and Sicans.
- Traditionally identified as descendants of refugees from the Trojan War, Elymians already occupied communities in northwest Sicily—for example, Eryx, Segesta, and Entella—when Greeks arrived in the seventh century B.C.
- History's first colonists of Sicily, Ionian Greeks, arrived on the east coast of the island in the mid-eighth century B.C. An Ionian leader named Theocles led a group of settlers from the Greek islands of Euboea and Naxos, and they named their settlement Naxos (734 B.C.). Five years later, Theocles and his settlers captured land from native Sicels and founded Leontini and Katane (729 B.C.). Euboeans

also settled in Zankle-Messana (730 B.C.), and then expanded to Himera (650 B.C.).
- Almost immediately after Ionian Greeks colonized Naxos, Dorian Greeks from Corinth established the colonies of Syracuse (733 B.C.) and Megara Hyblaia (728 B.C.).
- From Carthage, only a hundred miles south of Sicily, Phoenicians tried to halt the western expansion of Greeks on Sicily by colonizing earlier trading centers, like Motya, Panormus, and Solus.

In later centuries, mostly Dorian Greeks came to Sicily:

- Dorian settlers from Crete and Rhodes established a settlement at Gela (688 B.C.) and expanded a century later to Akragas (582 B.C.). These settlers also established some control over inland settlements: Eryx and Segesta in the northwest, as well as the sacred town of Enna located in the heart of Sicily.
- Dorian Greeks colonized Selinos (651 B.C.) and Kamarina (600 B.C.).
- Messenians fleeing persecution from Spartans on the Peloponnese Peninsula settled in northeastern Sicily and changed the name of Zankle to Messana in 461 B.C.
- In 396 B.C., after the Peloponnesian War with Athens, Syracuse helped Dorian exiles found a colony named Tyndaris west of Messana.

THE SIGNIFICANCE OF COLONIZATION

Over time, Sicily prospered and acquired ever-increasing importance for both Greeks and Phoenicians. Greek colonies and Carthaginian colonies differed in an important way: Greek colonies quickly became independent from their founding cities, while the Phoenician colonies on Sicily always remained loyal to Carthage. A hundred years after its founding on the southeast corner of Sicily, Syracuse surpassed even Athens among the great cities in the ancient world. Many Sicel and Sican communities successfully allied themselves with their more-successful neighbors in Greek or Phoenician city-states. However, the native communities that had retreated inland to inaccessible parts of the island did not participate directly in the rising prosperity of Sicily.

Even though Greeks came to Sicily well after the creation of most Greek myths, the island still contributed much to Greek mythology. Indigenous Sicilian culture and natural history shaped the personalities of Greek gods and inspired stories about famous monsters. Sicily also figured prominently in myths concerning the creation of the world.

CHAPTER

2

CREATION MYTHOLOGY, GODS, AND MONSTERS OF ANCIENT GREEK SICILY

Greek mythology comprises stories about creation, a history of one god dominating a host of lesser spiritual beings, and teachings about humanity's need for faith in struggles against evil.

Between the arrival of the first Greek colonies on Sicily in the seventh century B.C. and the Roman invasions of Sicily in the third century B.C., Greek mythology evolved into a jumble of ancient stories, of which relatively few survived to reach modern times. As described in Chapter 1, Greeks in different locations around the Mediterranean Sea adjusted their myths over time to reflect local cultural traditions.[1] For example, Dorians told stories related to Dorian lands (the Peloponnese Peninsula and mainland Greece) and Ionians told stories related to Ionian lands (Athens, the Greek islands, or Ionia on the west coast

---

[1]This chapter introduces Greek gods and creation mythology by selectively extracting story elements from a number of divergent ancient sources in an attempt to produce a largely consistent story. See Chapter 25 for a discussion of similar approaches commonly taken in discussions about the life of Jesus.

of Asia Minor). Though Greeks built their stories from broadly shared cultural elements, the stories also incorporated elements related to local prejudices, geography, and contacts with other cultures. Having evolved separately, the multitude of seemingly related Greek myths often expressed incompatible time frames and divergent points of view.

CREATION OF THE UNIVERSE

In the beginning, Gaea (the Earth) created herself out of chaos and ruled the universe alone. As the first virgin goddess, she gave birth to undifferentiated sky—the god Uranus—who then ruled everything, even Gaea. Uranus had children by his mother: huge, monstrous, and powerful children. To ensure that he stayed in control, Uranus imprisoned his children in Tartarus, the deepest part of the underworld.

But one son, Cronos, escaped imprisonment, rebelled, and defeated his father. Cronos castrated Uranus, mortally wounding him and reshaping the universe. Cronos separated Earth and sky (Gaea and Uranus) and started time. On the surface of the Earth, gods, giants, and nymphs emerged from the semen and blood of Uranus.

Cronos then freed some of his imprisoned siblings from Tartarus. Of the most powerful giants—the first three Cyclopes (each with a single eye), the three Hecatonchires (each with fifty heads and a hundred arms and hands), and the Titans (half human and half snake)—Cronos freed only his own kind: his eleven Titan brothers and sisters. Figure 2-1 graphically summarizes these early stages of the creation of the universe according to Greek mythology.

As metaphors go, any early story about the creation of the universe that begins with the creation of matter (Gaea), space (Uranus), and time (Cronos) seems worthy of respect. Modern scientists began thinking in similar terms about the origins of the universe only after Albert Einstein[2] linked matter, space, and time with his *general theory*

---

[2] Albert Einstein won the Nobel Prize in Physics in 1921. For developing theories of relativity and for contributing to the creation of quantum theory, he often is described as the father of modern physics.

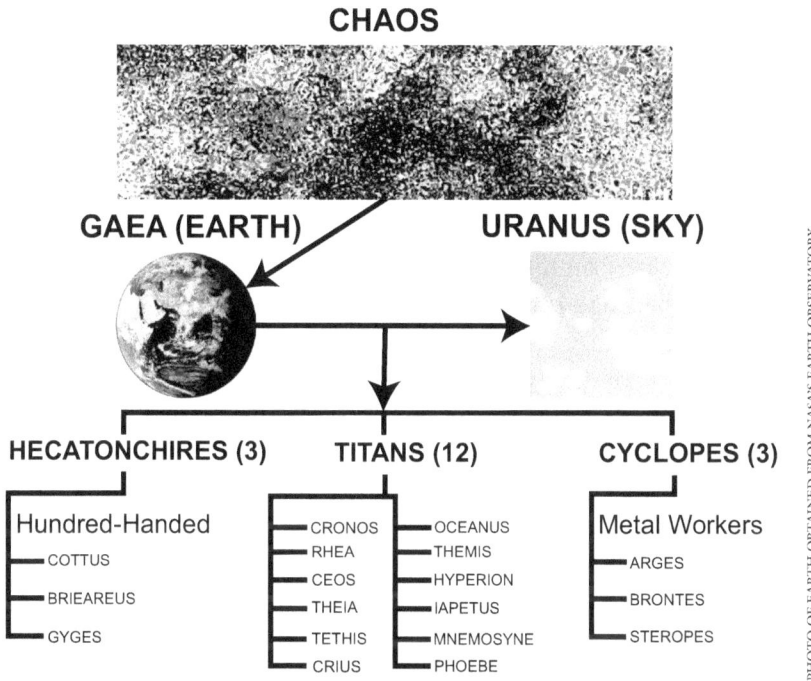

FIGURE 2-1. Greek Mythological Genealogy of the Universe

of relativity. Mythological creation stories even possess metaphorical similarities with modern cosmological theory: Myths speak about the creation of Cyclopes, Titans, and Hecatonchires, and modern cosmology speaks about a generation of giant stars that existed in the early universe. Just as Greek myths of Gaea's first children explain the origins of all substance and life, modern cosmology says that the explosive deaths of ancient giant stars generated the heavy elements that compose the earth and make life possible.

ZEUS, THE NEW RULER OF THE UNIVERSE

Cronos married his Titan sister, Rhea (Goddess of Mountains, Forests, and Commerce), and ruled the universe from his throne on Sicily.

Like his father, Cronos feared that his children would kill him. However, instead of locking his children away, Cronos swallowed each child immediately after Rhea gave birth to it. Cronos swallowed Hades (God of the Underworld), Poseidon (God of the Sea), Demeter (Goddess of Agriculture), Hera (Goddess of Childbirth and Marriage), and Hestia (virgin Goddess of the Hearth)—but Zeus escaped because Rhea fooled Cronos and gave him a rock to swallow instead.

Raised in secret on the island of Crete, Zeus eventually grew strong enough to challenge his father's rule. First, he freed his father's siblings, the one-eyed Cyclopes and the fifty-headed, hundred-handed Hecatonchires. In gratitude, the Cyclopes gave Zeus the weapons of thunder and lightning.

His grandmother, Gaea, encouraged Zeus to rebel. Armed with his new weapons, he led an army of giants against Cronos' opposing force of Titans. Recognizing the inevitable, most of the Titans surrendered to Zeus. At the moment of victory, Zeus seized his father and made him vomit all the gods that he had swallowed.

Having won the first war, Zeus dominated his grandmother (Gaea) and enjoyed mastery over all heaven and Earth. To prevent future threats, he imprisoned Cronos and his few remaining loyal Titans. Zeus threw them all into Tartarus and assigned the Hecatonchires to guard them. Zeus then established his throne and palace above Mount Olympus.

Establishing the reign of the Olympian Gods, Zeus divided responsibilities for controlling earthly affairs among his brothers, sisters, and children. He appeased the stronger gods (his immediate brothers and sisters) by giving each of them responsibility for a major portion of the universe. While retaining dominion over heaven and Earth, Zeus allocated responsibility for the underworld to Hades, the oceans to Poseidon, all of vegetative nature to Demeter, the homes of all mortals to Hestia, and the concerns of women to Hera.

Greek mythology speaks of "Twelve Olympian Gods," but few lists of these gods agree on the same twelve.[3] Most lists of twelve gods

---

[3] Often associated with the twelve cycles of the moon in a year, twelve is an important recurring number in mythology and religion; for example, the twelve constellations of the zodiac, the twelve tribes of Israel, and the twelve apostles.

FIGURE 2-2. Ancient Numismatic Representations of Olympian Gods

begin with the thirteen (fifteeen counting Eros and Persephone) Olympian Gods in Figure 2-2 and exclude one of the gods that didn't live on Mount Olympus (for example, Hades, Hestia, or Demeter). Hades lived in the underworld; Hestia lived in the homes of mortals; and Demeter lived in nature. After leaving Mount Olympus, Demeter gave her place among the gods to Dionysos, the God of Wine that she or her daughter bore with Zeus. Some lists include Hebe (Goddess of Youth), Persephone (Queen of the Underworld, daughter of Demeter and Zeus), and/or Helios (God of the Sun).

Aphrodite (Zeus' aunt) ruled love and sexual attraction. Ares and Hephaistos (Zeus' sons by Hera) governed war and metalworking, respectively. Athena (Zeus' daughter by Metis) served as a warlike Goddess of Crafts and Wisdom. The fraternal twins, Apollo and Artemis (Zeus' two children by Leto), ruled a number of concerns. Apollo's domain included prophecy, music, and healing, and he sometimes ruled the sun. Artemis ruled wild animals, hunting, and the healing of children. Hermes (Zeus' son by Maia, a daughter of the Titan,

Atlas) ruled thought and business, and he also served as Zeus' personal messenger.

Just as modern religions dedicate enormous cathedrals to a supreme deity, ancient Greeks dedicated enormous temples to Zeus, the ruler of the Olympian Gods. Theron, the Sicilian dictator of Akragas (modern Agrigento on the southern coast of Sicily), celebrated his victory over the Carthaginians in the Battle of Himera (modern Imera on the northern coast of Sicily) in 480 B.C. by building a temple of Zeus. Measuring 56 meters wide, 113 meters long, and 40 meters high, the temple stood as high as a twelve-story building and extended wider and longer than a modern football field. Theron built this temple slightly higher, slightly wider, and slightly longer than the temple of Zeus in the nearby city of Selinos. Even with modern building techniques, heavy construction equipment, and lightweight building materials, few modern religious structures can compare with these ancient temples of Zeus.

From Mount Olympus, Zeus ruled the universe aided by a divine hierarchy of lesser spiritual beings. While modern Christians emphasize the differences between monotheism and polytheism, the God of Christianity also rules over a hierarchy of cherubim, seraphim, angels, and saints. Historical investigation of the Christian divine hierarchy even suggests that some Christian entities originated as pagan deities.[4]

TYPHON'S ATTACK

After Zeus defeated Cronos, Gaea thought Zeus had betrayed her. She wanted revenge, and she wanted to regain sovereignty over herself and the universe. Coincidentally, she also had another child, Typhon. (See Figure 2-3.) Even today, Typhon remains the monster most intimately

---

[4] Examples of saints with suspicious origins include: Saint Cornely of horned beasts who connects with Cernunnos, the horned Celtic God of Animals; Saint Bridgit who connects with Brighid, a Celtic goddess analogous to the Greek goddess Athena; and Saint George, a Christian soldier in Diocletian's army who was a dragon-slayer like the North African deity Anat. (See Figure 4-3.)

FIGURE 2-3. Typhon (Side B) from a Chalkidian Black-Figured Hydria with Zeus and Typhon, ca. 550 B.C.

identified with Sicily. Gaea bore this son by Tartarus, the deepest and darkest hidden part of herself.

All the Olympian Gods feared Typhon. His legs, two massive vipers, supported a head and body that appeared mostly human; but he stood so tall that his head brushed against the stars. Some said that fifty serpents grew in place of fingers on each of his two hands. Others said that he had two hundred hands, each with fifty serpents. Typhon also had wings, pointy ears, and as many as ninety-nine animal heads (lions, leopards, boars, and bulls) emerging from various parts of his body. Fire shot from his eyes, and molten rock erupted in firestorms from his mouth.

When Typhon attacked Mount Olympus, all the Olympian Gods except Zeus ran away to Egypt and hid in the form of animals. Only Zeus stayed to fight for control of the universe, and he lost. Fulfilling his mother's desire for vengeance, Typhon defeated Zeus and rendered him helpless by slicing the muscles and tendons from Zeus' hands and feet. Typhon wrapped the muscles and tendons in a bearskin and stored the bundle in a cave. There, he ordered the dragon-woman, Delphyne, to guard them.

Zeus never lost hope. One tradition says that Cadmus, one of the earliest humans, helped Zeus. Another tradition says that Hermes and Aegipan (a monstrous son of Zeus symbolized by Capricorn, part goat and part fish) helped Zeus. One way or another, Zeus recovered his muscles and tendons and restored the use of his hands and feet. With help from the Fates, he defeated Typhon and imprisoned the monster beneath Sicily. However, even in defeat, Typhon continued to cause trouble. When he raged, firestorms from his mouth produced eruptions of lava, smoke, and ash on Mount Etna.

Typhon had children. His family included monsters like the hundred-headed Echidna, the multi-headed Hydra, Orthos (the two-headed dog of three-bodied Geryon), the Chimera (fire-breathing female monster, part lion, part goat, and part serpent), the Graiai (three old crones that shared one eye and one tooth), and Kerberos (the multi-headed guard-dog of the underworld). Typhon's grand-children included the Sphinx and the Nemean lion. As a wild land associated with Typhon and his relatives, Sicily grew famous for its monsters.

While seemingly unrelated to specific ancient cults, the story of Typhon helped Greeks relate to cultures with other, vastly different beliefs. For example, Greeks thought it scandalous that Egyptians worshipped gods shaped like animals. Still, the story of Typhon allowed Greeks to believe that they worshipped the same gods as the Egyptians. Egyptians simply had come to know the gods when they disguised themselves as animals and hid from Typhon.

THE MARRIAGE OF HERA AND ZEUS

At first, Hera wanted nothing to do with her younger brother, even though he ruled over her as King of the Gods. However, Zeus demanded everything his way. One day, Zeus disguised himself as a grubby and disheveled cuckoo bird and flew to Hera. She took pity on the small creature, picked it up, and held it to her breast—whereupon, Zeus returned to his natural form and raped her. Hera married Zeus as a way of avoiding the public shame of rape. She probably never loved Zeus, but she bore him many divine children and she hated his infidelities. Almost all their children reflected some element of pain in their relationship, especially Eris (Goddess of Discord and Strife), Eileithyia (Goddess of Childbirth), Ares (quarrelsome God of War), and Hephaistos (ugly and lame God of Volcanoes and Metalworking)

Zeus honored friendships and always kept his word, but he never promised fidelity in marriage. He earned his reputation as a philanderer. He not only married many times, but he also conducted numerous affairs with goddesses, creatures, and mortal women.

Zeus and Hera fought often. When Hephaistos, the ugliest god, tried to defend his mother, Zeus grabbed Hephaistos' legs and threw the god all the way to the island of Lemnos. Two nymphs, Thetis and Eurynome, hid badly injured Hephaistos in a cave and nursed him back to health. However, Hephaistos never regained full use of his legs.

When Hephaistos' strength returned, Zeus refused to allow the lame god to come back to Mount Olympus. Even Hera rejected him because of his disability, but, encouraged by Thetis and Eurynome, Hephaistos mastered the art of magical craftsmanship. When he presented Zeus with an assortment of miraculous objects, Zeus gave permission for Hephaistos to return to Mount Olympus, but Hephaistos eventually abandoned Mount Olympus for a workshop on Sicily.

In the family of Zeus, one sees the metaphorical power of Greek myths to represent human experience. Though times have changed greatly over the past couple thousand years, one still can analyze modern family conflicts in terms of qualities governed by Zeus' wife and children. Mythology also helps us understand how differently we live from our ancestors and how much Western culture has changed.

THE WAR WITH THE GIANTS

The island of Sicily played a prominent role in the last major threat to the Olympian Gods, a war against one hundred giants. Because of this war, many myths connect Sicily with Hephaistos, Gaea, and Athena (the warrior Goddess of Wisdom). The story of Athena begins with Zeus' very first marriage, long before the birth of Hephaistos. Although most people think of Hera as Zeus's only wife, he married Hera only after marrying four or five other female divinities, not counting mistresses. His first wife, Metis (the original Goddess of Wisdom), suffered a tragic but unsurprising fate soon after she became pregnant. Gaea warned Zeus that, if Metis gave birth to a son, the son would become greater than his father. Zeus' father, Cronos, solved this sort of problem by swallowing babies. Recognizing the danger of being tricked by the Goddess of Wisdom, Zeus solved the problem differently; he changed Metis into a fly and swallowed her before she gave birth.

Some time later, after many years and several more wives, Zeus suddenly experienced an unendurable headache that would not go away. Hephaistos, the lame God of Metalworking, helped his father by splitting Zeus' forehead with an axe. Fully grown, armed, and ready for battle, Athena leaped from Zeus' exposed brain, and Zeus recovered from his surgery.

Meanwhile, after Zeus defeated Typhon, Gaea's desire for vengeance increased even more. Using a reserve supply of blood from Uranus, Gaea conceived and gave birth to the most powerful giant ever, hundred-armed Enkeladus. Carefully preparing a new rebellion, Gaea sent this giant and ninety-nine others to Mount Olympus to attack the gods.

Emerging from the three westernmost prongs of the Chalkidian Peninsula in southern Macedonia, the giants waged war against the Olympian Gods all over the Earth. A stone carving[5] from a temple of Hera in Selinos, an ancient Sicilian city west of modern Agrigento, commemorates a key moment in the victory of the gods over the giants. The carving shows Athena lifting the island of Sicily and crushing Enkeladus beneath it. (See Figure 2-4.) Perhaps the mountains on the northern part of Sicily outline the giant's body beneath them, or perhaps a fiery cave beneath Mount Etna imprisons both Typhon and

---

[5]Though damaged, the carving in Figure 2-4 (currently in the Regional Archaeological Museum in Palermo) shows Athena lifting something (triangular Sicily) and crushing Enkeladus beneath it.

Chapter 2 | Creation Mythology, Gods, and Monsters   27

FIGURE 2-4. Athena Crushing Enkeladus Beneath Sicily, Carving from "Temple E" at Selinunte (Selinos), Sicily

Enkeladus. Regardless, Greek mythology says that Enkeladus still lives, and the whole island shakes whenever he moves.

After the defeat of the hundred giants, nothing ever again challenged Zeus for dominion over the universe. In such a position, a god like Zeus might feel some loss, as if no opportunity remained for achieving anything meaningful. Many Greeks believed that Zeus began to consider issues related to human salvation at this moment of divine history.[6]

THE FIRST CYCLOPES

Other than its association with creation mythology, Sicily mostly links with Greek myths about monsters. Stories of monsters connect to

---

[6]See Chapter 4.

geographical features of the island (for example, Mount Etna, Europe's most active volcano) as well as to Sicily's long role as meeting place for different cultures. Because Romans transmitted Greek mythology to the modern world, and because Sicily sometimes offered refuge to enemies of Rome, perhaps stories of monsters related to Sicily survived better than stories of monsters farther away.

After the war with the giants ended, Hephaistos chose Sicily as the best location for his workshop; Typhon's mouth served as the perfect forge, and earthquakes by Enkeladus helped mix and shape magic alloys. Also, even though the Cyclopes had given Zeus thunder and lightning, someone still needed to manufacture these weapons. Hephaistos forged lightning bolts and thunder for Zeus, as well as weapons, armor, and magical devices for the other Olympian Gods. For example, Hephaistos forged Poseidon's trident and Hades' Helmet of Invisibility.

The first generation of Cyclopes—Brontes (Thunderer), Steropes (Flasher), and Arges (Brightener)—helped Hephaistos in his labors under Mount Etna. Skilled and loyal workers, the Cyclopes served Zeus and Hephaistos well. Ironically, the Cyclopes' skill and loyalty eventually doomed them. Their few good qualities made them perfect targets for revenge after Zeus killed Apollo's son, Asclepius, the world's greatest healer.

Not only could Asclepius heal the sick, but he also could raise the dead. Hades complained that Asclepius would empty the underworld by bringing people back to life. Zeus solved the problem by killing Asclepius, and Apollo, seeking revenge, killed the Cyclopes. Sicilians say the ghosts of Brontes, Steropes, and Arges haunt the slopes of Mount Etna to this day.

The myths about Asclepius and the Cyclopes show that even divine power had limits in Greek mythology. The death of Asclepius affirmed that mortals must always die, and the death of the Cyclopes indicated that even Zeus couldn't have an infinite number of thunderbolts. In fact, early Christianity incorporated Greek concepts that placed limits on divinity.[7]

---

[7]See Chapter 13.

MONSTROUS HAPPENINGS

Some myths say that Poseidon had children by Thoosa (a sister of the monsters, Skylla and Medusa) and created a second generation of Cyclopes who could not work metal. Mythology remembers these Cyclopes, especially Polyphemus, as savage, man-eating Sicilian shepherds. In the *Odyssey*, Odysseus blinded Polyphemus to prevent the monster from eating members of Odysseus' ship's crew. Sometime later, Poseidon healed Polyphemus, who continued to participate in mythological stories of Sicily—especially those concerning Polyphemus' unrequited love for the sea nymph Galatea.

The sea-going Greeks considered Poseidon,[8] ruler of the oceans, very nearly as powerful as Zeus, but Poseidon could not win a fight against his brother. When Poseidon's giant daughter, Charybdis, tried to increase the size of her father's realm by flooding dry lands, Zeus chained her to the seabed. Even though confined to an underwater cave between Italy and Sicily in the Strait of Messina, Charybdis sucked down water three times a day, forming enormous whirlpools.

Although he could not rebel against all-powerful Zeus, Poseidon developed a strong rivalry with Zeus' favorite daughter, Athena. For example, when Poseidon and Athena competed to become the patron god of Athens, Poseidon gave the city a well that never emptied. Unfortunately, the well always contained seawater. The Athenians chose Athena as victor in this competition because she gave Athens the olive tree, the first source of Athens' wealth.

But Poseidon didn't always lose against Athena. Well before the Trojan War, Athena came to Hephaistos' workshop to order a new set of armor and weapons. She offered payment, but Hephaistos refused, insisting that his only payment would be love. The virgin goddess agreed. Continually seeking opportunities for revenge against Athena, Poseidon somehow learned about this agreement.

When Hephaistos finished Athena's armor, Poseidon saw an opportunity to embarrass the virgin goddess. He told Hephaistos that

---

[8] Homer's *Odyssey* describes Poseidon as walking on water and controlling wind and waves, similar to the depiction of Jesus in *John* 6:16–21 and *Mark* 4:35–40.

Athena was on her way to his workshop intending to make passionate love with him. When Athena arrived, wanting only to pick up her armor and weapons, Hephaistos attempted to rape her. Athena fought and escaped, but not before Hephaistos "spilled his seed" on her thigh. Athena wiped her leg clean with a piece of wool that she then dropped on the earth (perhaps on Sicilian soil). This impregnated Gaea who gave birth to a child, Erichthonius (earth-born). Gaea rejected Erichthonius, so Athena raised him. The ancestor of Dorian and Ionian Greeks, Erichthonius became the first King of Athens.

Elements of Greek creation myths resonate powerfully with the historical roots of Western culture. Some myths seem to describe a prehistoric transfer of religious power from worship of a divine mother to worship of a divine father. Perhaps the Cyclopes represent an ancient Greek view of the native inhabitants of Sicily before Greek colonization. Strangely, the story of Hephaistos' rape of Athena seems to have foretold the future. Metaphorically, it prefigured the fatal weakening of Athens when Syracuse (a powerful city on the southeast corner of Sicily) defeated Athens' navy in 413 B.C. Also, just as Athena nurtured Erichthonius, the future King of Athens, Greek culture and Sicilian grain metaphorically nurtured a young Rome that grew and achieved dominion over all Greece, including Athens.

ATHENA'S REVENGE

The great wealth of Syracuse contributed to Athens' defeat in the fifth century B.C. and attracted fatal attention from Rome in the third century B.C. A Greek named Archias founded Syracuse on the southeast corner of Sicily in 734 B.C. When Archias consulted the oracle at Delphi before traveling to Sicily,[9] the oracle told him to choose between health and wealth. Archias chose wealth. To ancient Greeks, this explained why the excellent harbor, fresh springs, and fertile soil of Syracuse brought wealth to the colony.

---

[9]See *The Geography* 6.2.4 by Strabo. Born in Pontus in the middle of the first century B.C., Strabo traveled extensively in the ancient world and wrote about philosophy, history, and geography as a proponent of Roman imperialism.

Chapter 2 | Creation Mythology, Gods, and Monsters

FIGURE 2-5. Athena and Medusa, Sicily, Syracuse, Second Democracy, AU Didrachm, ca. 410–406 B.C.

The obverse of a gold coin from Syracuse shows Athena wearing her helmet. (See Figure 2-5.) The reverse of this coin displays the head of Medusa, the lone mortal sister of two other Gorgons, Stheno and Euryale. Medusa's head hangs from Athena's Aegis, a flexible shield made from the impenetrable hide of the goat that nursed baby Zeus on Crete.

Greek myths describe the Gorgons as three monster sisters that had snakes instead of hair. Gorgons also had tusks, brass hands, and gold wings. Any man who looked at a Gorgon turned to stone. Originally, however, Medusa looked very different from her two ugly sisters. She was beautiful.

Medusa's parents, Phorcys (the old man of the sea) and Ketos (Phorcys' sister, sometimes a beautiful nymph and sometimes a sea dragon), produced beautiful children as well as monstrous children. Famous for her exquisite hair, Medusa was even more beautiful than her lovely sister, Skylla. Medusa originally lived happily in North Africa, perhaps roaming beautiful beaches on the Libyan coast. Just as Phoenicians from North Africa came to trade on Sicily, the beautiful young Medusa must have visited Sicily where she bore two children by Hephaistos. These children, Caca (the Goddess of Excrement) and Cacus (a three-headed, fire-breathing giant) moved from Sicily to the Palatine hill of Rome in the centuries before Rome existed. Cacus and Caca lived together in a cave on the Palatine hill around the time when Herakles boxed King Eryx of Sicily in the myth of the red cattle of Geryon.[10]

Eventually, things went badly for Medusa after she made love to Poseidon in a temple of Athena—or perhaps Poseidon raped her there. Regardless, sex in the temple angered Athena so much that she took horrible revenge against Medusa. Athena transformed Medusa's beautiful black hair into writhing snakes. The goddess also gave Medusa brass hands, tusks, and gold wings so that Medusa looked exactly like her ugly Gorgon sisters.

This horrible revenge did not satisfy Athena, who continued to nurse a grudge. When the hero, Perseus (the ancestor of the Persians), needed help acquiring the head of Medusa, Athena helped him obtain magic objects so he could succeed in this task. Athena even helped guide the blade of the harpé (the sickle-shaped weapon that Cronos had used to castrate his father, Uranus) when Perseus got close enough to cut off Medusa's head.

After Perseus cut off the Gorgon's head, two children by Poseidon emerged fully grown from her neck: Pegasus (the winged horse) and Chrysaor (the battle giant). Pegasus became a messenger between Hephaistos and Zeus, carrying deliveries of fresh thunderbolts from Mount Etna to Mount Olympus. Chrysaor fathered Geryon, from whom Herakles stole the famous red cattle in stories that connect Sicily and Rome.

Athena took two vials of blood from Medusa's body, one from her left side and one from her right side. Blood from Medusa's left side could heal any disease, even raise the dead; Athena gave this vial to Asclepius. Blood from Medusa's right side could instantly destroy any living thing; Athena kept this vial. The remainder of Medusa's blood magically transformed into the snakes of the Libyan Desert.

Athena also kept Medusa's head[11] and attached it to the center of her Aegis. Inspired by this story, Greek soldiers often portrayed a head of Medusa on their shields or armor. Possessing the power to transform any man who looked at her into stone, Medusa personified male

---

[10]See Chapter 4.
[11]However, in ancient times, numerous tourists visited an ancient barrow grave near the temple of Artemis in the Greek city of Argos, the supposed repository of the authentic head of Medusa. See the *Description of Greece* 2.21.5 by Pausanias.

fears of female sexuality. Placed on a shield, an image of her ghastly face and writhing snakes offered the possibility of magically petrifying an enemy long enough to land a mortal blow.

Medusa's relationship with Hephaistos connects myths of Medusa directly with Sicily. More importantly, however, Medusa came to represent a double-edged power to affirm life and to destroy it. By the second century B.C., Hellenistic Greeks associated the stories of Medusa with a new cult[12] that emphasized the need for humans to choose between a path of light and a path of darkness.

THE TRANSFORMATION OF SKYLLA

Like her sister, Medusa, Skylla transformed from a beautiful young woman into a hideous monster. When she was young, Skylla played nude on the sands of beautiful Sicilian beaches. She avoided men and socialized only with sea nymphs, especially with her close friend, Galatea. From time to time, Galatea must have complained to Skylla about the Cyclops, Polyphemus, who chased her and annoyed her. Skylla might have answered by bragging about her success in avoiding men. One day, however, while Skylla walked alone and nude along a beautiful beach, Glaucus, a son of Poseidon, emerged from the sea and fell in love with her. Glaucus approached Skylla, but she ran away, completely horrified.

Glaucus made the mistake of going to Circe, sorceress daughter of the Sun (Sol), to complain about being treated badly by Skylla. Circe loved Glaucus and grew angry with Skylla, an unwelcome competitor for Glaucus' affections. The sorceress poisoned the water in Skylla's favorite cove with magic herbs. The next time Skylla went swimming, she transformed into a ferocious monster. Her legs changed into a dragon's body, and the foreparts of six vicious dogs grew from her sides, serving as monstrous legs and feet. (See Figure 2-6.)

Skylla lived in a cave overlooking the Strait of Messina. Some days, she rested, enjoyed the view, and took care of domestic chores. Other days, she patrolled the sea, snatching sailors and destroying ships.

---

[12]See Chapter 13.

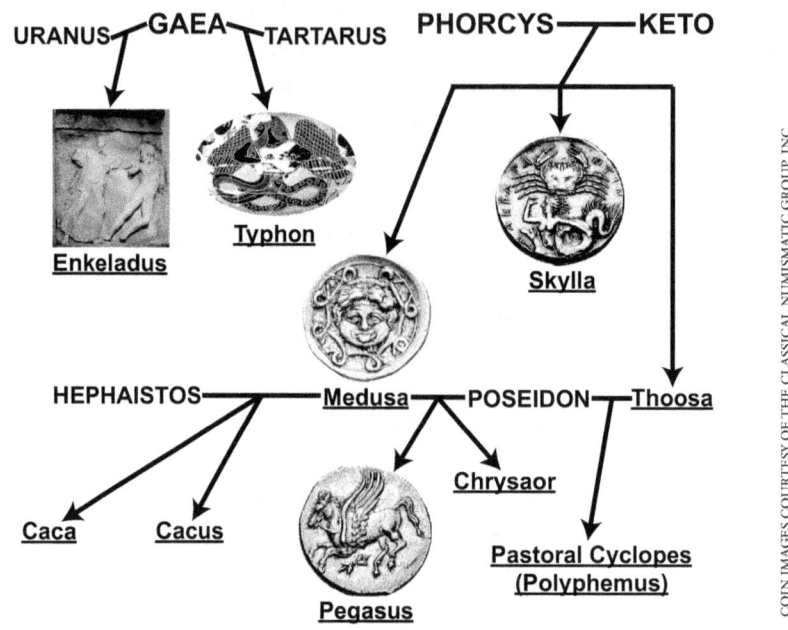

FIGURE 2-6. Genealogy of Monsters Related to Sicily

When the Argonauts, a crew of ancient Greece's greatest heroes, sailed to Sicily searching for the Golden Fleece, they confronted the dangers of Skylla, Charybdis, and Sirens (woman-headed birds) in the Strait of Messina. With help from Glaucus, the heroes passed safely. Later, Herakles killed Skylla during one of his many labors when she snatched cattle from him. However, Skylla's father, Phorcys, prodded her back to life by stabbing her flesh with burning sticks.

Through numerous adventures and changes, Glaucus continued to love Skylla and to reject Circe, which infuriated Circe. Eventually, Circe gave up on Glaucus and turned him into a monster as well.

With Glaucus out of the way, Poseidon made love with Skylla. Afterwards, perhaps to prevent the birth of strange children, Poseidon transformed Skylla into a coastal cliff. Near Messina, you still can find Skylla's cave and Skylla herself in the form of a cliff. Since the very beginnings of history, worshippers have used places and artifacts to prove that religious events really happened.

SICILIAN *GENESIS*

Just as the Christian *Bible* associates stories in *Genesis* with the Middle East, Greek myths associate stories of events soon after the creation of the universe with Sicily. Ancient Greeks filled the gap between creation and history with divine genealogies. In Sicily's case, most of the genealogies concerned monsters. Figure 2-6 displays images and relationships among several generations of monsters related to the island.

In the center of the Mediterranean, Sicily holds the immortal remains of Gaea's two great children, Typhon and Enkeladus, monsters who competed with Zeus for control of the universe. Cadmus and the Fates helped Zeus defeat Typhon, and Herakles helped Zeus defeat Enkeladus. (Part Two of this book provides details about the life of Herakles.) Gaea's grandchildren, Phorcys and Ketos, also gave rise to a complex genealogy of monsters (for example, Skylla and Polyphemus) connected to Sicily.

In their myths, ancient Greeks expressed faith in a relationship between humanity and gods in a universe where terrifying monsters always lay waiting just out of sight. Only with faith, courage, and help from the gods could ancient Greeks hope to prosper.

However, religious beliefs existed on Sicily long before the Greeks ever got there. Because Sicily occupies such a central location in Western geography and history, and because Sicilian Greek colonies grew wealthy so quickly, Greek settlers preserved some information about native cults that never fit well with immigrant Greek beliefs. In the surviving traces of native Sicilian mythology, one glimpses pieces of ancient cults that were lost in processes of transformation and evolution.

CHAPTER
3

NATIVE SICILIAN MYTHOLOGY

> Mythology and history connect in unexpected ways: Sometimes history shapes mythology; sometimes mythology shapes history; and sometimes one can't tell where mythology ends and history begins.

The first mythology and cults on Sicily came with its first immigrants, probably many thousands of years ago during the Stone Age. Successive waves of immigration then brought new peoples and new ideas to Sicily, to influence and mix with older populations and traditions. In the eighth century B.C., Greek historians documented three separate ethnic groups living as natives on Sicily: Sicans, Sicels, and Elymians. However, well before the first historical Greek settlers, Mycenaean Greeks and Phoenicians also influenced Sicily.

Sicilian, Phoenician, and Greek mythologies mixed and merged over centuries as immigrant and native populations competed for the best Sicilian lands. Sometimes native populations equated native gods with Greek and Phoenician gods, and sometimes Greek and Phoenician immigrants incorporated native gods into flexible pantheons of nature deities—particularly as river gods and nymphs. Over time, the merging of gods and myths encapsulated information about inter-ethnic relations in a form that looked like history. City-states then used the "facts" of this history to imbue enmities, alliances, and trade relationships with a measure of sanctity.

SICANS

Representing the earliest inhabitants of Sicily, Sicans migrated from Italy during the Neolithic Period. Neolithic artifacts made by Sicani ancestors have turned up all over the island. The artifacts include stone tools, pottery, and burial niches—especially on the northwestern and southeastern parts of Sicily. However, by the time that Greeks colonized Sicily, Sicans occupied only a thin band across the west-central portion of Sicily from Hyccara (near Panormus) in the north to Omphal (near Akragas) in the south. (See Figure 1-3.) The name, Omphal, suggests that this town may have served as an ancient divinatory center. Like the omphalos at Delphi, the name may identify the town as the navel of the island. Alternatively, the name might come from the Sicani language and have nothing to do with the Greek word, omphalos.

Members of a pre-literate, prehistoric society, Sicans failed to preserve thousands of years of their history, ideas, and culture for future Sicilians. Still, one can find clues about the texture of their lives by viewing their artifacts, especially in the archaeological museums in Palermo and Agrigento. Except for Sicilian place names and myths involving Mycenaean Greeks, little information about Sicans has survived.

MYCENAEAN GREEKS

Elements of Greek mythology must have arrived on Sicily earlier than the historical immigration of Greeks in the eighth century B.C. In modern times, archaeologists have found imported wares on Sicily that document trade between indigenous Sicilians and Mycenaean Greeks beginning at least as early as the fourteenth century B.C., and trade continued until Mycenaean culture declined in the twelfth and eleventh centuries B.C. While archaeologists have not identified

Mycenaean colonies on Sicily, material remains—ceramics, fibulae, and a Mycenaean type of tomb—strongly suggest that permanent Mycenaean settlements existed at widely separated locations on Sicily.[1]

Members of an influential culture with traditions recorded in the *Iliad* and the *Odyssey*, Mycenaean Greeks voyaged all around the Mediterranean Sea. Historical information about Mycenaean culture can be found in Egyptian records of the "Sea Peoples"[2] in Biblical stories about the Philistines. On Sicily, myths related to Daidalos, the greatest of all Greek craftsmen, preserve the memory of a Mycenaean presence.

SICELS

In the eighth century B.C. Sicels occupied most of Sicily. Greek settlers believed that Sicels came to Sicily from the Italian peninsula sometime after the Trojan War. Sicel material culture resembles Sicani material culture. Even the names of these two ethnic groups resemble each other etymologically. Sicels established their principal city, Zankle, on the Strait of Messina. Sicel communities then spread steadily west and south. Zankle became ancient Messana, which eventually became modern Messina.

More history survives about Sicels than about any other native Sicilian ethnic group. Sicel communities survived well into historical times when Sicel warriors served as mercenaries for wealthy Greek communities. In the fifth century B.C., a famous leader named Ducetius led an unsuccessful Sicel rebellion against the dominant Greek rulers of Sicily. Most of the surviving information about Sicel mythology comes from Greek history about Ducetius, from Greek place names, and from Sicel coins minted during Ducetius' rebellion.

---

[1] See *Use and Appreciation of Mycenaean Pottery in the Levant, Cyprus, and Italy (ca. 1600–1200 B.C.)* p. 203 by Gert Jan van Wijngaarden.
[2] The "Great Harris Papyrus" (*Papyrus British Museum 9999*) records that Ramesses III of Egypt (1220–1155 B.C.) battled "Sea Peoples" that included "Peleshet" (Philistines), "Shardana" (Sardinians?), and "Denyen" (Mycenaean Greeks?). Scholars speculate that the attack by a coalition of these tribes against Egypt reflected catastrophic pressures throughout the Mediterranean region responsible for the collapse of Mycenaean civilization around that time.

ELYMIANS

The *Odyssey* refers to two groups on Sicily, Sicans and Sicels, but only vaguely in the context of the procurement of slaves. By the eighth century B.C., a third ethnic population, Elymians, lived in a few hill forts in northwestern Sicily. The Elymians believed their ancestors fled the destruction of ancient Troy—just as Romans believed that the Trojan prince, Aeneas, fled Troy and gave rise to a line that produced Romulus and Remus, the founders of Rome. Artifacts from Elymian settlements reflect Near Eastern influences, particularly Phoenician and Egyptian. Elymians named their major towns (for example, Eryx, Segesta, and Elima) after great Elymian mythological heroes.

The Elymian goddess cult at Eryx survived through times when Greeks dominated Sicily because Elymians allied with Phoenicians. After Romans came to Sicily and defeated both Greeks and Phoenicians, the cult thrived because of the mythological connection with ancient Troy that Elymians shared with the Romans. However, because Romans perceived the Elymian cult solely through their shared connection with ancient Troy, they recorded little information otherwise about Elymian culture and beliefs. Still, isolated fragments of distinctly Elymian mythology have survived.

PHOENICIANS

Some religious influences also came to Sicily from African cultures. Phoenicians from Carthage (near modern Tunis) built trading posts on Sicily as early as the ninth century B.C. They established permanent settlements on Sicily only in response to Greek colonization. Phoenicians then needed permanent, fortified settlements to protect their trade interests with Sicily.

Because Phoenicians competed aggressively with Romans in ancient history and lost, the Romans destroyed Phoenician writings and failed to record much about Phoenician religious beliefs on Sicily. However, Phoenicians originally immigrated to Carthage from Tyre, a city on the coast of Lebanon that still uses its ancient name. In Carthage, Phoenician cults and mythology fused elements from North Africa and the Middle East.

A MERGING OF GREEK AND SICANI MYTHOLOGY

Echoing the ancient Mycenaean connection with Sicily, Sicilian myths associate the northern Sicani town of Hyccara with the Greek hero, Daidalos, and his son, Ikaros. A famous Greek inventor during the Greek Heroic Age,[3] Daidalos originally lived and worked on Crete. King Minos, a son of Zeus and Europa and the father of Ariadne, ruled Crete as its first king. When King Minos refused to sacrifice a perfect bull to Poseidon, the god took revenge by making King Minos' wife, Pasiphae, fall in love with the bull. Pasiphae then asked Daidalos to build a device that would make it possible for her to make love with the bull.

Daidalos made a device shaped like a cow that would contain and protect Pasiphae as she enjoyed the amorous activities of the perfect bull. Apparently, the device worked. King Minos never suspected that his wife cheated on him in any way until she gave birth to the Minotaur.

To punish his wife's infidelity, King Minos imprisoned the Minotaur in a maze that Daidalos had designed. King Minos then threw Daidalos and his son, Ikaros, in jail. Daidalos and Ikaros escaped from jail using wings invented by Daidalos. During the escape, however, Ikaros flew too close to the sun, which melted the wax that attached the feathers to Ikaros' wings. Leaving a trail of feathers, Ikaros plunged to earth and died. Daidalos traveled alone to Sicily and took refuge with the King Cocalus of Camicus, a Sicani city near ancient Akragas (modern Agrigento).

---

[3]Greek historians generally thought the Heroic Age began around 1400–1300 B.C., several generations before the Trojan War, and that it ended a generation or so after the Trojan War. Mythological roots related to Daidalos may well extend deeper, perhaps originating in the Middle East by the beginning of the second millennium B.C.

Still seeking revenge, King Minos sent warriors to search for Daidalos. When they reported his location, King Minos led a raiding party to Sicily intending to capture Daidalos and return him to prison. While King Minos and King Cocalus established a friendly diplomatic relationship, Daidalos prepared a trap for King Minos. Daidalos rigged a bathtub so he could fill it instantly with boiling water. That night, when the daughters of King Cocalus enticed King Minos to bathe, boiling water engulfed him, killing him before he could bring any harm to Daidalos.

When the kingdom of Crete learned of Minos' death, its navy set sail intending to destroy the city of Camicus. However, Poseidon favored Daidalos. The powerful God of the Sea prevented the Cretan navy from reaching Sicily by devastating the fleet with storms. Eventually, Daidalos left Camicus and founded his own city on the northeast coast of Sicily. He named the city Hyccara in honor of his dead son, Ikaros.

Hundreds of years after the decline of Mycenaean Greek civilization, early in the fifth century B.C., King Theron of Akragas used the myth about Daidalos and the death of King Minos to improve his diplomatic relationship with Crete. King Theron "discovered" the Bronze Age grave of King Minos near Akragas. He sent the contents of this grave with gifts and ambassadors to Crete,[4] ostensibly returning the bones and possessions of King Minos to his homeland.

This historical act of King Theron shows that ancient Greeks actively investigated the remains of earlier cultures. When possible, ancient Greeks even associated the remains with mythological stories. Whether he believed that he had discovered the remains of King Minos or not, King Theron used bones from an ancient grave as a means for improving foreign relations and furthering his political ambitions.

FORCES FOR CHANGE IN THE EIGHTH CENTURY B.C.

Colonization by Greeks meant conflict, displacement, and enslavement for native populations on Sicily. Because Sicani, Sicel, and Elymian

---

[4] See the *Library of History* 4.79.4 by Diodorus Siculus.

communities generally saw themselves as separate and independent from their neighbors, they never formed a unified front against Greek invaders. During the first hundred years of Greek colonization, invading Greek settlers (Siceliots) captured and occupied all of the east coast, most of the south coast, and somewhat less of the north coast of Sicily. Siceliots enslaved many Sicels and pushed others from their coastal homes to defensible hill forts toward the middle of the island.

While the earliest inhabitants of Sicily possessed their own religious beliefs, distinctly different from those of Greeks and Phoenicians, Sicans, Sicels, and Elymians slowly adopted Greek and Phoenician beliefs over time. Native Sicilian communities preserved some aspects of their original religious traditions and slowly allowed others to fade away. However, religious influences went both ways between Sicels and Greeks. Both peoples honored the Sicel town Enna, near the center of Sicily, as a sacred location for worshipping Demeter and her daughter Persephone. At ancient cultic sites like Enna, native Sicilians reinterpreted their ancient cults, adding imported practices and mythology like new clothing for ancient gods.

As Greek cities came to dominate Sicily, native Sicilians acquired Greek language and culture. By the time that Romans came to Sicily in the third century B.C., not much remained of Sicani, Sicel, and Elymian culture and cults. Still, coins show that Greeks preserved many native Sicilian myths and traditions, particularly when they affirmed qualities that the Greeks admired.

TOKENS OF ANCIENT SICILIAN CULTURE

Over time, Greek Siceliots came to honor ancient Sicilian heroes. Just as the United States honored the courage of a Native American woman, Sacagawea, by placing her portrait on the Sacagawea Dollar, Syracuse honored the courage of Leukaspis, a Sicani hero, by placing his image on a silver drachm. (See Figure 3-1.) By honoring Leukaspis, one of six Sicani heroes who fought Herakles,[5] this coin honors patriotic defense

---

[5]The greatest of all Dorian Greek heroes, Herakles performed twelve labors that took him all over the known Greek world. Chapter 6 discusses the place of Herakles in Greek mythology.

FIGURE 3-1. Athena and Dolphins, and Semi-Divine (Naked) Leukaspis Defending an Altar. Sicily, Syracuse, AR Drachm, ca. 405 B.C.

of country. Of course, invincible Herakles killed all six Sicani heroes, but, at a critical moment in Syracusan history, this coin told everyone that Syracusan soldiers would resist unto death any foreign invasion.

Greeks also preserved remnants of native culture by retaining original place names. For example, Dorian Greeks from Crete and Rhodes established a colony named Gela just west of the Gela River in 688 B.C. Both Sicans and Greeks believed in river gods. In the Sicani language, Gela means extreme cold, which aptly describes the temperature of the Gela River. Figure 3-2 shows a tetradrachm that personifies the river god Gelas as a swimming, man-headed bull. Greek colonists often preserved the names of Sicani and Sicel gods as the names of their local river god and nymph. On their coins, Siceliots portrayed river gods and nymphs with symbols derived from Greek mythology.

THE FIRST GREEK RIVER GOD

The oldest brother of all rivers, Achelous flows between the ancient mainland Greek states of Aitolia and Akarnania. This river played important roles in Greek mythology. For example, Achelous started the Great Flood at Zeus' command. Also, for the royal house of

FIGURE 3-2. Nike (Victory) Crowning Horses after a Race, and Personification of Gelas, a Greek/Sicani River God. Sicily, Gela, AR Tetradrachm, ca. 450–440 B.C.

Thebes, Achelous' deep waters had the power to wash away guilt and moral stain.

Early in the Greek Heroic Age, Herakles competed with Achelous for the love of the Aitolian princess, Deinara. Herakles defeated Achelous even though the river god had the ability to change his shape. While wrestling with Herakles, Achelous first changed into a snake, but Herakles almost strangled Achelous. When he changed into a bull, Herakles tore off one of the bull's horns.

Nymphs retrieved the horn and gave it to Amaltheia, Goddess of Plenty. In modern times, we still remember this horn. As a place to store Amaltheia's possessions, it became known as the *Cornucopia*, the "Horn of Plenty."

Consistent with the myth of Achelous and Herakles, Greeks portrayed Achelous as a man-headed bull, or sometimes as a man-headed snake. Ancient Greeks believed that the Titans, Oceanus and Tethys, parented three thousand rivers, three thousand nymphs, and numerous other divine personages—including Phorcys, the father of Medusa and Skylla. Mythology mostly identified river gods as male (an important exception is the Styx River, which circled nine times around Hades'

FIGURE 3-3. Nike Awarding Victory to Racer, and Himera, Sacrificing with Pan Bathing in a Lion Fountain. Sicily, Himera, AR Tetradrachm, ca. 420–409 B.C.

underworld and possessed a female spirit), but Greeks generally associated both a male river god and a female nymph with every important river. On Sicily, the first Greek coins portray river gods as man-headed bulls. Later images portray river gods shaped like humans, but with short horns on their foreheads to indicate their divinity. Sicel communities, especially, represented old Sicel gods as human-shaped river gods with "devil's horns."

Possibly because Achelous once flooded the entire world, he sometimes traveled far from home. On Sicily, stories of his visits affirmed both the antiquity and the importance of local cults, rivers, and land forms. With one important exception in Syracuse, no other river god left his river to visit other parts of the world.

EXAMPLES OF SICILIAN RIVER GODS AND NYMPHS

Sicilian Greeks portrayed nymphs as beautiful young women. The tetradrachm in Figure 3-3 shows Himera, the fountain nymph, pouring a sacrificial offering onto a flaming altar. In the background, Pan bathes in warm spring water from the famous lion fountains of Himera (the

FIGURE 3-4. Surviving Lion Fountains in the Regional Archaeological Museum in Palermo, Sicily

town). Some of the original lion-headed fountains of Himera still can be seen in Sicily at the Regional Archaeological Museum in Palermo. (See Figure 3-4.)

Of the three virgin goddesses (Athena, Persephone, and Artemis) that Greeks associated with Sicily, Athena favored the region around Himera's springs. There, Himera made hot water flow from the earth so Athena's favorite mortal, Herakles, could bathe and rest. Perhaps because of the fountain nymph's fame, history has forgotten the name of the god associated with Himera's river.

An ancient didrachm from the Dorian Greek town, Kamarina, portrays the river god Hipparis and his nymph Kamarina. (See Figure 3-5.) On the obverse of this coin, Hipparis gazes to his right. A small horn on his head makes him look very much like a modern image of the Devil. On the reverse, a swan carries Kamarina on its back in the middle of her sacred lake. The reverse image appears reminiscent of the myth about the seduction of Leda by Zeus in the form of a swan. However, this swan strains to carry Kamarina across the lake at top speed, and Kamarina's robe billows in the wind.

Because of Sicily's variety of ethnic roots and mythologies, river gods and nymphs played important roles in Sicilian mythology. They provided a means of access for native Sicilian mythology into Greek

FIGURE 3-5. Sicilian River God, Hipparis, and His Nymph, Kamarina. Sicily, Kamarina, AR Didrachm, before 405 B.C.

mythology. Centuries later, images of river gods on ancient Sicilian coins may have inspired medieval Christian images of Satan.

OTHER TIES BETWEEN SICILY AND GREEK MYTHOLOGY

The two coins in Figure 3-6 illustrate more ways that native Sicilian traditions contributed richness and variety to existing Greek mythology. The top coin comes from Lipara, one of the Aeolian Islands north of Sicily. The obverse of the top coin displays a portrait of Aeolus. While one tradition identifies Aeolus as an early King of Thessaly—a grandson of Prometheus (the Titan who gave fire to mortals), and a brother of Dorus (progenitor of Dorian Greeks)—a different tradition identifies him as the King of Winds, the son of Poseidon and Melanippe (daughter of the centaur, Chiron). As King of Winds, Aeolus lived on the Aeolian Islands just north of Sicily. In the *Odyssey*, this king gave Odysseus a bag of winds to help him sail home.

The bottom coin in Figure 3-6 comes from Messana, the ancient Sicel capital just across the Strait of Messina from the toe of Italy. The

FIGURE 3-6. Top: Aeolus and Stylized Stern of Galley. Aeolian Islands, Lipara, Hemilitron, 425–400 B.C. Bottom: Pelorias and Possibly King Pheraimon or Orion. Sicily, Messana, AE Litra, 310–288 B.C.

obverse of the lower coin portrays Pelorias, the nymph of three sacred lakes on the sickle-shaped arc of land that encloses Messina Bay. Possessing neither a label (the letters next to the figure identify the city, Messana) nor characteristic devices, the warrior on the reverse of the lower coin cannot be identified for certain. However, mythology offers interesting possibilities. The warrior might represent battle-ready King Pheraimon, a semi-divine son of Aeolus. Alternatively, this coin may provide one of the few ancient images of Orion. The inhabitants of ancient Messana may have identified the semi-divine warrior on the reverse of the lower coin in Figure 3-6 as Pheraimon, Orion, Zanclus, Gegenus, or even someone else.

Aeolus married Gyane, the daughter of King Liparus. (From Gyane came *cyan*, the English word for the color, sky-blue.) They lived together on a cloud above the island of Lipara and raised twelve children—six sons and six daughters. Each son married one of his sisters. At least two of the couples moved to Sicily where the sons became Sicel kings. Pheraimon, the first King of Zankle-Messana, ruled northeast Sicily. His brother, Androkles, ruled northwest Sicily.

Nobody knows the original name of the city that Pheraimon ruled. Its first known name, Zankle (Sickle), came from an early king, Zanclus, the son of Gegenus. The name of the city changed to Messana early in the fifth century B.C. after settlers came to Sicily from Messenia on the Peloponnese Peninsula.

Myths like these offer hints about authentic ancient connections between Greeks and native Sicilians. The names of heroes and gods may reflect the names of real people. Sometimes myths seem so close to history that one can glimpse the authentic lives underneath the stories.

ORION ON SICILY

Myths about Orion suggest him as another possible identification of the warrior on the bottom coin in Figure 3-6. A number of contradictory stories cluster around the life of Orion, but the tradition most relevant to Sicily identifies his birthplace as Oreios at the foot of Mount Telethrios on the island of Euboea. This tradition connects stories of Orion with the capture of the early Sicel city of Zankle by Chalkidian colonists from Euboea.

The son of Euryale (a daughter of King Minos) and Poseidon, Orion surpassed all other mortals in size, strength, and beauty. Poseidon gave his son not only the ability to walk on water, but also a fine ocean-going steed, part horse and part sea-serpent, the hippocamp. (See Figure 3-7.) Greek mythology identifies Orion as the greatest hunter of all time, but he possessed serious character flaws; for example, he had a bad habit of stalking and raping women.

He lived in Zankle during the time of King Zanclus and performed amazing feats of strength. Orion narrowed the Strait of Messina by building the sickle-shaped arc of land where the nymph Pelorias lived. Orion also built a promontory for the city with a temple of Poseidon on top. These achievements represent the most positive aspects of myths about Orion.

Chapter 3 | Native Sicilian Mythology   51

FIGURE 3-7. Athena, and Orion's Ocean-Going Steed, the Hippocamp. Sicily, Syracuse, AE Litra, ca. 390 B.C.

After completing his work in Zankle, Orion traveled to Syracuse on the southeast corner of Sicily. There, he stayed on Ortygia Island, the home of his good friend, Artemis, to live with her and hunt. One myth says that Orion met his death there, either stung by a scorpion sent by Gaea or killed by Artemis. Artemis may have killed him by accident, tricked into doing so by Apollo (Apollo disapproved of his sister's boyfriend), or Artemis may have killed him on purpose for sexually violating one of her virgin companions.

Regardless, mythology credits Artemis' grief and prayers to Zeus for placing Orion in the sky in remembrance of his manliness. Granted immortality as a constellation among the stars, Orion still pursues women, perpetually following the Pleiades, an open star cluster called the "Seven Sisters" by ancient Greeks. Just as Orion chased these women in life, his constellation continues to chase the Seven Sisters across the Winter sky.

In ancient times, stories about Orion helped Sicilians feel like they understood the history of their land and sky. For modern readers, the stories combine fabulous tales with information about how it felt to live in ancient society.

FIGURE 3-8. Chthonic Nymph or Goddess Offering Her Breast to a Snake, and River God. Sicily, Selinos, AR Litra, ca. 400 B.C.

ACHELOUS' VISIT TO SICILY

The elder brother of all rivers and an uncle of Medusa and Skylla, Achelous visited both Sicily and Lipara at least once. On Lipara, Achelous met and seduced Perimele, the daughter of Aeolus. From this union, Perimele gave birth to two children, Hippodamas and Orestes (different from the son of Agamemnon, also named Orestes, who killed his mother). To punish his daughter for her affair with Achelous, Aeolus threw her into the sea. Rather than let Perimele die, Poseidon transformed Perimele into an island next to Lipara.

The inhabitants of Selinos, Sicily, believed that Achelous fathered their local nymph, Eurymedusa. The obverse of the coin in Figure 3-8 may represent Eurymedusa breastfeeding a snake. The reverse carries the image of her uncle Selinos in the form of a man-headed bull, looking just like his older brother, Achelous.

Eurymedusa's story has not survived, but archaeology suggests that the coin in Figure 3-8 may portray Demeter or Persephone. Numerous artifacts recovered at Selinos show the presence of an ancient *chthonic* (underworld) cult that worshipped Zeus Melichios,[6] Demeter, and

---

[6]The Cult of Zeus Melichios worshipped Zeus in the form of a snake.

Persephone. In the form of a snake, Zeus mated with Demeter who gave birth to their child, Persephone. Later, Zeus again took the form of snake to mate with his daughter, Persephone, and thus fulfilled a prophecy by Fate that the child, Dionysos, would become the savior of all mankind.

At the time that Selinos minted the coin in Figure 3-8, inhabitants of the city may have identified the seated woman as Demeter, Persephone, or Eurymedusa. Likewise, the snake might have represented Zeus Melichios or an unknown consort or child of Eurymedusa. Regardless, the ancient cultic center of Selinos probably rivaled the Greek Cult of Demeter and Persephone at Enna. Comparing the inconsistent multitude of surviving myths helps show that a variety of ancient cults slowly merged into a smaller number of cults. The Enna cult survived longer than the Selinos cult. Still, iconography from the chthonic cult at Selinos possesses its own distinctive charm.

A GREEK RIVER GOD AND NYMPH IN SYRACUSE

Of all Sicily's river gods and nymphs, the most famous pair, Arethusa and Alpheios, did not originate on Sicily. Both immigrated to Sicily's greatest city, Syracuse, from a foreign land. Arethusa and Alpheios both originally came from a region called Olympia on the Peloponnese Peninsula of Greece.

A close friend of the goddess Artemis, Arethusa shared many of her friend's passions and characteristics—she loved nature, she liked to hunt, and she disliked the company of men. One hot day, while hunting near Olympia with Artemis, Arethusa decided to cool off by swimming in a river. She jumped in the water, but immediately felt something terribly wrong.

Arethusa ran out of the river, and close behind came Alpheios, the God of Olympia's Alpheios River. Arethusa ran, but Alpheios ran faster. Arethusa called out to Artemis for help, so Artemis wrapped Arethusa in a thick cloud to hide her. Knowing that Arethusa was in the cloud, Alpheios saw that he had trapped her, and he called to her expressing

FIGURE 3-9. Illustration of the Story of Arethusa and Alpheios from Ovid's *Metamorphoses*, Book 5, Plate 53, by Baur, 1703

his love. (See Figure 3-9.) Artemis transformed Arethusa into a stream so she could escape—but Alpheios recognized Arethusa in the water and also transformed himself, intending to mingle his water with hers. Instantly, Artemis cracked opened the earth so Arethusa could escape into the crack—but Alpheios flowed after her. Arethusa raced through the earth to Ortygia Island, Artemis' sacred home just off the coast of Syracuse, but Alpheios flowed faster. The two streams blended and erupted as a single freshwater spring on the island, their waters forever merged. Affirming this divine connection between Syracuse and Olympia, Syracuse built an extravagant treasury in Olympia around 480 B.C.

The myth of Arethusa and Alpheios directly affirmed the sacred connection between mainland Greece and Sicily. It justified the Greek colonization of Sicily while suggesting that Sicily would produce something important and new by combining different cultures. By honoring this myth, Syracusans remained Greek no matter how much they mixed with other ethnic groups.

FIGURE 3-10. Sicel River God, Adranos. Sicily, Adranon, AE Hemidrachm, 344–336 B.C.

LOST SICEL GODS

Sicel cities displayed their ancient gods on coins after Ducetius' rebellion, particularly during a flowering of Sicel pride in the fourth century B.C. The coin in Figure 3-10 shows a portrait of the Sicel god Adranos. Much more than a river god, the horned god Adranos possessed attributes similar to those of both Ares and Hephaistos. Modern scholars suggest that the Phoenicians introduced worship of Adranos to Sicels as a composite of the Phoenician gods, Adar and Moloch. The Sicilian cult of Adranos considered dogs sacred, as did the Phoenician cults of Adar (God of Lightning and Thunder) and Moloch (Sun God). Possessing the ability to identify thieves and unbelievers,[7] more than a thousand dogs lived at the temple of Adranos on Mount Etna.

Knowledge of some Sicel gods reached modern times only because of labeled images on Sicel coins. However, some stories of Sicel gods survived without associated images. On Mount Etna, for example, Sicels worshipped the Palikoi, twin demon children of Zeus and the nymph Thaleia (one of the Graces—"Rejoicing"). After making love with Zeus, Thaleia feared vengeance from Hera so Thaleia asked the Earth to swallow her. Eventually, Thaleia gave birth to twin boys who

---

[7]See *On the Characteristics of Animals* 11.20 by Claudius Aelianus. Bred for hunting on harsh volcanic terrain, dogs from the breed, Cirneco dell'Etna, still exist on Sicily.

emerged from Mount Etna in the form of twin sulfur springs. Sicels originally offered human sacrifices to the Palikoi. Both Greeks and Sicels honored the temple of the two brothers as a sanctuary for runaway slaves.

The pieces of native Sicilian mythology that survived without combining with Greek mythology seem to provide authentic glimpses into the lives of ancient native Sicilians. Often, they seem to connect with the hard lives of slaves or of refugees in mountainous regions away from coastal lands dominated by Greeks. Still, the pieces help round out the picture of life on ancient Sicily.

The most persistent of ancient Sicilian mythology and cultic traditions survived in combination with Greek influences. Perhaps the most important combination happened quickly: The ancient native Sicilian cults at Selinos and Enna combined easily with mystery stories of Demeter, Persephone, and Dionysos brought by the first Greek settlers at Naxos.

CHAPTER
4

OTHER MYTHOLOGIES ON SICILY

Ancient Sicilian cults from diverse ethnic groups began connecting with Greek iconography and mythological histories about the origins of salvation.

From the seventh to the third centuries B.C., the mixing of cultures on Sicily provided for the development of important multi-ethnic religious understandings that Romans in later centuries would build into the foundation of the Roman Empire. New beliefs arrived on Sicily with each wave of new immigrants. Native Sicilian and Greek beliefs slowly merged and other ethnic cults and mythologies also entered the mix. Significant non-Greek influences came from Phoenician and Elymian gods. However, important as a force for unification, a sophisticated Greek mystery cult, the Cult of Dionysos, arrived with the first Ionian settlers. Offering salvation[1] to all who sought it, Greek mysteries proved so attractive on Sicily that every ethnic group began using Greek iconography to represent their gods. In the spread of Greek salvation iconography one sees the beginnings of a multi-ethnic interconnecting of gods and mythologies into a single broad fabric.

---

[1] In this book, salvation generally refers to the ability of a virtuous soul to obtain an afterlife in circumstances characterized as eternal and pleasant.

In the seventh century B.C., mystery cults like the Cult of Dionysos began spreading to new locations throughout the Mediterranean region. Mystery cults mixed powerful ideas about survival after death with mythology, religious beliefs, and understandings about the nature of the world. As the cults spread and evolved in new lands, they preserved salvation themes from the original cults but they acquired new cultic myths that incorporated the natural history and cultural elements of their new locations. Both public and private story elements supporting the cults changed by traveling, but the new cults retained symbolic connections to the myths and deities of the earlier cults, often portraying their relatedness in terms of an expanding family of deities: The new cults honored brothers, sisters, children, and associates of earlier salvation-oriented deities.

CROSS-CULTURAL ACCESS TO MYSTERIES AND SALVATION

Salvation meant something different in ancient times than it does today. Originally, ancient Greeks generally believed that nothing awaited a person after death other than mixing with darkness and dirt beneath the surface of the earth. Beginning around the time that Greeks colonized Sicily, mystery cults began to spread the news across the Mediterranean Sea that secret knowledge allowed human souls to obtain access to a better realm after death. Knowing secrets communicated only during initiation into a mystery cult, a newly deceased soul could obtain eternal life in the *Elysian Fields*, a pleasant underworld realm of eternal Spring and Summer.

Ancient mysteries comprised stories with well-known public parts as well as secretly communicated parts. The public parts consisted of popular myths involving, for example, weddings attended by gods, visits to the underworld by semi-divine heroes, and sex between underworld deities and nature goddesses. Over time, mysteries spread into every Mediterranean culture, and they preserved symbolic connections with each other. Diverse cultures often used identical religious iconography as well as similarly themed mystery myths. In addition, mysteries frequently preserved a metaphorical history of their spread in the genealogies of their deities, newer cults honoring relatives or associates of deities from older cults.

As a melting pot, Sicily served as a key location where diverse traditions (Ionian, Dorian, Phoenician, Elymian, Sicel, and Sican) reinterpreted at least the public parts of mysteries and incorporated them into their cultures. Coins of all the ethnic groups on Sicily show that they used similar iconography of gods associated with mysteries, connecting images of Greek gods like Zeus, Hades, Persephone, Demeter, Herakles, and Dionysos with differently named gods from other ethnic traditions. However, the secret parts of ancient mysteries connected more intimately with specific cults, cultures, and ethnicities at specific locations, combining guided experiences, religious teachings, and passion plays in culturally appropriate ways. The secret parts of ancient mysteries mostly have been lost—priests and initiates guarded these secrets well—but brilliant efforts by modern scholars[2] have begun to reveal a few long-forgotten secrets of mysteries.

PHOENICIAN CULTS AND MYTHOLOGY

Most of the Phoenician cults that Carthaginians brought to Sicily first traveled to Africa from the ancient Canaanite city of Tyre. In the ninth century B.C., Princess Elissa of Tyre (who became Queen Dido of Carthage) led an expedition of Phoenician colonists that founded the North African city of Carthage. Later, as the Carthaginians built an empire based on trade, their culture absorbed African influences (particularly from Egypt) as well as Greek influences. Meanwhile, Phoenician cults in Tyre also changed, absorbing influences from farther east. Over time, Phoenician cults in Carthage came to differ significantly from Phoenician cults in Tyre.

Phoenician settlers on Sicily mostly came from Carthage and worshipped Carthaginian gods. By the sixth century B.C., Phoenicians on Sicily used many of the same images of gods that Sicilian Greeks used.

---

[2]For examples of modern scholars uncovering lost secrets of ancient mystery cults, see *Greek Mysteries: The Archaeology and Ritual of Ancient Greek Secret Cults* edited by Michael B. Cosmopoulos or *The Origins of the Mithraic Mysteries: Cosmology and Salvation in the Ancient World* by David Ulansey.

FIGURE 4-1. Carthaginian Goddess, Tanit, Portrayed as the Greek Goddess, Persephone, and Horse and Palm Tree. Siculo-Punic, AR Tetradrachm, ca. 330 B.C.

Despite looking like Greek gods, Carthaginian gods possessed attributes more characteristic of the gods of Egypt and the Near East than the gods of Mount Olympus. Carthaginians believed in many gods, but primarily worshipped a trinity comprising Tanit, Baal-Hammon, and Eshmoun.

Tanit, the most popular of the Carthaginian gods, resembled the Greek goddesses Demeter, Persephone, Artemis, and Aphrodite. Tanit ruled the harvest and granted good fortune in human affairs. A Goddess of Motherhood and the Moon, she also ruled the affairs of women. Coins of Carthage and Phoenician Sicily often portrayed Tanit with her sacred symbols: horse, crescent moon, and palm tree. Carthaginians also associated Tanit with symbols related to mystery and salvation; for example, an opium poppy[3] head and dolphins surround Tanit in Figure 4.1, symbols of salvation frequently associated with Persephone. The husband of Tanit, Baal-Hammon resembled both Baal of the Near East and Amon of Egypt. Almighty lord of the universe, he ruled from the sky and governed human affairs, storms, growth, and fertility. Carthaginians celebrated his birthday on December 25, identifying

---

[3]Ancient cultures associated opium with salvation because of its power to ease pain and save lives. Some mysteries incorporated the use of opium in their initiation ceremonies.

FIGURE 4-2. Carthaginian God, Melqart, Portrayed as Greek Hero-God, Herakles, and Horse, Wheat, and Palm Tree. Siculo-Punic AR Tetradrachm, ca. 300 B.C.

Baal-Hammon as a *solar deity*. Solar deities generally underwent death and rebirth during the winter solstice[4] (annual lowest declination of the sun in the northern hemisphere).

In Phoenician mythology, Baal-Hammon once quarreled with Mot, God of the Underworld. Mot killed Baal-Hammon and ate him. Baal-Hammon's sister, Anat,[5] forced Mot to regurgitate her brother, and then resurrected him by placing his body in the hollowed-out trunk of an evergreen tree. In modern times, people in the West still associate evergreen trees with religious celebrations on December 25.

Carthaginians worshipped Eshmoun as the God of Health and Healing. Images of Eshmoun resemble those of the Greek God of Healing, Asclepius. Carthaginians and Phoenicians on Sicily also worshipped Melqart, a lesser god who possessed the attributes of Poseidon, Apollo, Ares, and Hephaistos. Carthaginians portrayed Melqart with features of the Greek god Herakles. (See Figure 4-2.)

---

[4]Even though the winter solstice usually occurs on December 21, ancient astronomers couldn't confirm the sun's movement toward higher declinations until several days after the solstice.
[5]Known as "dragon-slayer" and "defender of cities," the goddess Anat may be the root source of Christian legends about Saint George and the dragon.

FIGURE 4-3. Siculo-Punic Images of Anat and Reshef Portrayed as Athena, and a Divine Archer. Sicily, Solus, AE Tetras, Fourth Century B.C.

Even though Phoenicians used the same religious symbols for their gods that Greeks used for the Olympian Gods, certain attributes, myths, and practices of worship of Phoenician gods differed considerably from those of the Olympian Gods. For example, knowing only the mythology and history of Greek Sicily, one might look at symbols on a coin of the Phoenician town of Solus (see Figure 4-3) and identify the obverse image as a bust of Athena. The reverse shows an unknown warrior advancing right with a bow and arrow. Since Pheraimon, the legendary first King of Zankle-Messana might have appeared as a warrior on a coin of Messana in eastern Sicily (that is, on the reverse of the lower coin in Figure 3-6), one might be tempted to identify the warrior on this west Sicilian coin as Androkles, Pheraimon's brother and the legendary first ruler of western Sicily. However, the inhabitants of Phoenician Solus might have looked at the obverse of this coin and seen their goddess Anat, the sister of Baal-Hammon who saved him from Mot. Phoenicians worshipped Anat as a war goddess and called her "Dragon-Slayer" and "Defender of Cities." The warrior on the reverse might represent Reshef, Anat's husband, a Phoenician God of Thunder and War.

Nobody knows for certain the details relating iconography, mythology, and worship of Phoenician deities in ancient Sicily. Even in North

Africa at well-preserved cultic centers, archaeologists struggle to determine basic and important aspects of Carthaginian worship. For example, ancient historians said that worshippers sacrificed living children[6] to the gods of Carthaginian cults, but modern archaeologists argue about whether or not this was true.[7]

ELYMIAN CULTS AND MYTHOLOGY

Historians and archaeologists know even less about Elymian cults and mythology. Excavations of Elymian cultic sites reveal piles of ashes and bones from religious offerings, but archaeologists don't even know the names of the gods that Elymians worshipped. Only a few details concerning Elymian cults have survived: Sicilian coins and Roman history preserved a few intriguing tidbits of Elymian mythology along with the names of local heroes.

Like the Phoenicians and Greeks on Sicily, Elymians came from someplace else. An ancient Elymian temple on a mountaintop at Eryx in northwestern Sicily continued operating into the time of Imperial Rome. During pre-Roman Hellenistic times, Siceliots generally called the goddess of this temple Aphrodite. Coin images show her seated on a throne holding a dove, her sacred animal. (See Figure 4-4.) Roman historians called her Venus Erice. In Eryx, Sicilians and visiting Romans worshipped Venus in a style reminiscent of the worship of Astarte, an ancient fertility goddess in the Middle East; they worshipped her with ecstatic dances and sacred prostitution.

Elymians believed that, after the Trojan War, a Trojan maiden named Segesta came to western Sicily. Near a place where a hot river merged with a cold river, she mated with the local river god Krimissos

---

[6]In the first century B.C., a Sicilian Greek historian wrote that Carthaginians originally had sacrificed the "noblest of their sons" but that they then turned to buying and raising children specifically for sacrifice. See the *Library of History* 20:14 by Diodorus Siculus.

[7]For a sample of the debate, see articles in the Nov/Dec 2000 issue of *Archaeology Odyssey* magazine: "An Odyssey Debate: Were living Children Sacrificed to the Gods? No." by M'hamed Hassine Fantar, and "An Odyssey Debate: Were living Children Sacrificed to the Gods? Yes." by Joseph A. Greene and Lawrence E. Stager.

FIGURE 4-4. Nike Crowning Racer, and Aphrodite of Eryx and Eros Pondering a Dove. Sicily, Eryx, AR Tetradrachm, ca. 410–400 B.C.

while he was in the form of a dog. Her child Aegestes grew up and founded the main Elymian cities: Segesta (named after Aegestes' mother), Entella, and Eryx. Probably to avoid the embarrassment of canine ancestry, Elymians claimed to descend from Aegestes' best friend, Elimo, a Trojan prince. With images of Aegestes, Krimissos, and Segesta, the Segestan tetradrachm in Figure 4-5 displays an unusual and noteworthy family portrait.

In later centuries, Romans tolerated the strange religious practices of the Elymians because Roman mythology supported the connection between the Elymians and ancient Troy. Romans believed that the founder of Rome descended from a Trojan prince named Aeneas, the son of Venus and a noble Trojan named Anchises. Father and son had wandered the Mediterranean after the defeat of Troy. Soon after they reached Sicily, Anchises died near Eryx. Aeneas buried his father at the future location of the temple of Venus Erice and then continued to wander. Eventually Aeneas settled among the hills that would become Rome. Romans believed that the Temple of Venus Erice honored the divine mother and the mortal father of the Roman race.

According to Virgil, a heroic Elymian king named Eryx forced a violent encounter with Herakles. When Herakles drove the red cattle

FIGURE 4-5. Aegestes and Dogs (Krimissos as a Dog?), and Segesta. Sicily, Segesta, AR Tetradrachm, ca. 400 B.C.

of Geryon through Italy, Eryx stole the herd's prize bull and took it to Sicily. Herakles pursued Eryx and demanded that he return the bull, but Eryx challenged Herakles to decide the matter with a boxing match. A son of Aphrodite and the Elymian King Butes, Eryx boxed skillfully and heroically, but he died under the powerful fists of Herakles. (A contradictory tradition maintains that Herakles didn't kill Eryx. Instead, Eryx died in a different adventure when Perseus showed him the head of Medusa.)

The Elymians also must have felt kinship with Ganymede, the Trojan cupbearer of Zeus. Originally, Hebe, the Goddess of Youth, served as Zeus' cupbearer, but she lost her job after she accidentally indecently exposed herself. Apparently, Zeus had wanted to replace her anyway because he already had his eye on Ganymede, a beautiful young man whose brother, Ilos, founded Ilium (Troy). No sooner had Zeus relieved Hebe of her duties, than he transformed into an eagle and, swooping to earth, snatched Ganymede away from his family. Ganymede served as Zeus' catamite (passive male lover) in exchange for immortality and eternal youth. Of course Hebe was then free to marry Herakles when he eventually joined the Olympian Gods.[8]

---

[8]See Chapter 6.

TWO SETS OF DIVINE TWINS ON SICILY

The Greek Sicilian cities of Tyndaris and Katane exemplify ways that similar mythic traditions sometimes came to Sicily reflecting different origins and traditions. The Tyndareans came as exiles from the Peloponnese Peninsula, and the Kataneans came as immigrants from the island of Euboea. Both cities celebrated twin brothers with divine honors: Tyndaris celebrated Castor and Polydeukes, known as the *Dioscuri*;[9] and Katane celebrated Amphinomus and Anapias, known as the Katanean brothers. In Tyndaris, Greek exiles transplanted and modified a Dorian tradition of honoring divine twins from their lost homeland. In Katane, Ionian colonists generated a similar, new tradition based on the natural history of their new homeland.

After Sparta defeated Athens in the Peloponnesian War, Spartans cleansed their homeland of turncoats and rebellious *helots*[10] by sending them into exile. In 396 B.C., Dionysos, the tyrant of Syracuse, founded a city on the north coast of Sicily as a place to accept the exiled Greeks. Even though expelled by Spartans, the exiles continued to celebrate Peloponnesian traditions. They named their city Tyndaris in memory of the Dorian myth about Tyndareos, the first Spartan king, a man who competed for his wife's (Leda's) affections with Zeus.

In the form of a swan, Zeus mated with Leda. She bore four children from two eggs: Helen (who became Helen of Troy) and Polydeukes from one, and Clytemnestra and Castor from the other. Heroes of myths like the Caledonian Boar hunt, Castor and Polydeukes descended in the end to cattle thievery and inter-tribal feuding. When Castor died in a petty skirmish, Zeus consoled Polydeukes by offering him immortality, but Polydeukes refused to abandon his brother to the underworld. Polydeukes negotiated with Zeus for both brothers to share immortality, each brother alternately spending a day in the underworld followed by a day on Mount Olympus.

The Peloponnesian exiles at Tyndaris created myths that Tyndareos, Castor, and Polydeukes originally lived in Zankle on Sicily. By

---

[9]The Dioscuri appear in our modern skies as the constellation, Gemini.
[10]The helots were Peloponnesians forced to work as slaves for the Spartans.

Chapter 4 | Other Mythologies on Sicily   67

FIGURE 4-6. Helen of Troy (?) and the Gemini Twins (Dioscuri). Sicily, Tyndaris, AE 20, ca. 254–214 B.C.

honoring Castor and Polydeukes—the embodiment of transcendent brotherly love—as Sicilians, the inhabitants of Tyndaris honored themselves as spiritually superior to Spartans. In Figure 4-6 the obverse of a coin from Tyndaris portrays either Helen of Troy or Tyndaris, the sister of Tyndareos. The reverse of the coin portrays the Dioscuri.

In Katane, two brothers similarly received divine honors, though fewer details of their story have survived. Known as the Katanean brothers, Amphinomus and Anapias rescued their parents from a catastrophic eruption of Mount Etna. Miraculously overcoming dangers from lava, falling rocks, poison gas, and rampaging animals, the brothers lifted their parents and carried them to safety. Honored as demigods in Katane, the Katanean brothers symbolized transcendent filial piety. (See Figure 4-7.)

MYTHS ABOUT DEMETER AND PERSEPHONE

Long before the arrival of Greeks on Sicily, an unknown goddess and her daughter established their home at Enna. This cult competed with similar cults around the Greek world, especially with a cult at Eleusis near Athens. All these cults worshipped a nature/fertility goddess (for

FIGURE 4-7. Dionysos, and Katanean Brothers: Amphinomus Carrying his Father and Anapias Carrying his Mother. Sicily, Katane, AE 20, sometime after 212 B.C.

example, Demeter) and/or her daughter (for example, Persephone), and they usually included mysteries related to a child by a powerful underworld deity (for example, Zeus Melichios or Hades). Greeks associated the child with wheat (for example, Brimos) and/or with grapes (for example, Dionysos). By the time that Greek culture dominated the island, all Sicilians associated the area around Enna with Demeter and Persephone. All ethnic groups of Sicily—Dorians, Ionians, Sicels, Sicans, Phoenicians, and Elymians—recognized the importance of mysteries associated with this Cult of Demeter and Persephone.

In the surviving mythology about Demeter and Persephone, one can see that ancient Greeks shaped the story to fit the needs of a specific culture or region.[11] If more versions of the myth had survived, we would know more about cultural variation in the ancient world. In connection with this cult on Sicily, much of the Western world came to recognize Sicily as the birthplace of wheat. Given to humanity by Persephone, Queen of the Underworld, wheat represented more than merely a nutritious staple; it also symbolized the possibility of salvation.

The same day that Athena buried the hundred-armed giant, Enkeladus, under Sicily, Hades drove his chariot from the underworld to

---

[11]See Chapter 5.

Chapter 4 | Other Mythologies on Sicily   69

FIGURE 4-8. Nike Crowning Eros for Extending the Empire of Love, Skylla Below, and Demeter and Dolphins on Reverse. Sicily, Syracuse, AR Tetradrachm, ca. 405 B.C.

see what caused the earth to shake so much. The land had just settled. While Demeter busied herself growing new vegetation to cover the earth's scars from the recent war, young Persephone picked opium poppies in a field. Hades slowed his chariot to get a better look at Persephone, but he didn't notice Aphrodite and Eros (winged God of Erotic Love) watching nearby.

Suddenly perceiving a way to expand her empire of love, Aphrodite whispered to Eros to shoot an arrow into Hades' heart. Perhaps transformed by love's arrow, perhaps operating under a secret agreement with Zeus, or perhaps influenced by the power of his own sudden lust, Hades seized Persephone and dragged her to the underworld. On the obverse of the coin in Figure 4-8, Nike (winged Goddess of Victory) crowns Eros with a victory wreath for extending the rule of love to the underworld. Beneath Eros and his chariot, Skylla provides local color. On the reverse, dolphins surround Demeter (or Persephone?), who appears grim, but reconciled.

Frantic at the disappearance of her daughter, Demeter neither ate nor drank. Carrying a torch by night, she searched the entire world without resting, but she couldn't find Persephone anywhere. One day near Athens, she met Celeus, the King of Eleusis.

Even though Demeter's suffering and self-neglect hid that she was a goddess, Celeus and his family treated Demeter with respect, consideration, and generosity. Observing loving interactions among Celeus, his wife, and their infant son (Triptolemus), the goddess decided to reward them. When King Celeus invited Demeter to stay in their household as an honored guest, she accepted and looked for an opportunity to make Triptolemus immortal.

First, Demeter prepared Triptolemus by feeding him milk mixed with the juice of opium poppies. Then, late at night, she began a ritual to burn the mortality from his body. Discovering Demeter passing the young boy through flames, the boy's mother shrieked in horror and ruined the process. Demeter revealed who she was and scolded the mother. In no mood to waste more time with mortals, Demeter abandoned the house of Celeus and renewed the search for her daughter.

Suffering deeply from the loss of her daughter, Demeter continued to wander all over the world. Some Greeks believed that Poseidon raped Demeter on the Peloponnese Peninsula, resulting in the birth of another daughter named Despoena.[12] Eventually Arethusa, the Syracusan water nymph of the freshwater spring on Ortygia Island, told Demeter that Hades had taken Persephone to the underworld.

At first Demeter blamed Sicily for the abduction by Hades. However, Arethusa testified that Hades alone had abducted Persephone near the Syracusan spring, Kyane, and that the land of Sicily was innocent. Arethusa claimed impartiality because she loved her original home on the Peloponnese Peninsula and lived like a stranger on Sicily. Hecate (a magical moon goddess) and Helios (the sun) also confirmed to Demeter that Hades had abducted Persephone completely on his own.

After that, Demeter stopped doing much of anything. As she mourned the loss of Persephone, plants stopped growing. Realizing that Demeter's grief would bring death to all the plants and animals on Earth, Zeus, the father of Persephone, decided to intervene. He ordered Hermes to go to the underworld and negotiate with Hades for Persephone's release.

---

[12]See Chapter 5.

Hades loved Persephone and didn't want to lose her. He agreed that she could leave only if she had suffered as much in the underworld as her mother had suffered on the surface of the Earth. That is, Persephone could leave only if she had refused to consume food and water like her mother. When asked, Persephone admitted she once consumed the juice from several pomegranate seeds. That wasn't much, so Hades agreed to a compromise: She could spend eight months of every year with her mother on the surface of the Earth, but must spend four months of every year with Hades in the underworld.[13]

This myth explains the annual cycle of Spring, Summer, Fall, and Winter. The Earth's seasons track Demeter's mood. Plants begin to die in Fall as Persephone enters the underworld to live with Hades, and new plants emerge in Spring then she returns to the surface of the Earth. A symbol of renewed life among the living and the dead, Persephone offered hope for salvation.

After concluding the agreement with Hades, Demeter occasionally returned to Eleusis to spend time with Triptolemus. Eventually she sent a chariot pulled by dragons to bring him to Mount Olympus. There, she taught him the secrets of agriculture: how to plow the earth, how to grow useful plants, how to harvest crops, and how to store them. Because of her affection for Triptolemus, and because her daughter ruled as Queen of the Underworld, Demeter also taught Triptolemus mysteries: Demeter taught Triptolemus how to navigate the underworld and what to say to obtain access to the Elysian Fields.

When he returned to Eleusis, Triptolemus taught the secrets of agriculture to all mankind. He also founded a temple at Eleusis where priests guarded Demeter's mysteries and initiated worthy mortals with secret rituals. The Eleusinian Mysteries offered humanity divine knowledge of how to live a good life and how to find a pleasant eternity after death.

Rivaling Syracusan elements in the myth described above, another Sicilian tradition identified a field near Enna at Lake Pergusa as the location where Hades leaped from the underworld, seized Persephone,

---

[13]Some traditions said that Persephone divided her time equally, six months above ground and six months in the underworld.

FIGURE 4-9. Demeter or Persephone, and Triptolemus. Sicily, Enna, AE 23, ca. 42–36 B.C.

and dragged her underground to make her queen of his Kingdom of the Dead. All Sicily honored Enna as a place of mystery and magic. As at Eleusis near Athens, priests performed ceremonies at Enna to help ensure the return of fertility to the earth through the Springtime emergence of Persephone from the underworld. Priests also conducted initiation ceremonies that offered salvation through the knowledge of mysteries. The coin from Enna in Figure 4-9 portrays either Demeter or Persephone on the obverse and Triptolemus (sowing wheat?) on the reverse.

THE RELATIONSHIP BETWEEN DIONYSOS AND SICILY

The great god that helped unify the many threads of Sicilian mythologies into a single fabric with themes of nature, madness, salvation, and sex came to Sicily from the Greek island of Naxos. In 734 B.C., Greek colonists from Naxos founded a new Naxos, the first Greek colony on Sicily, and they brought the Cult of Dionysos with them. Naxos settlers claimed that both lands, their ancient homeland and their new colony, had helped nurture Dionysos, God of Wine, Ecstasy, and Fertility. Like

Athena, Dionysos emerged from a body part of Zeus—his thigh. Also like Athena, Dionysos got there in a very strange way.

After observing humans for a while, Zeus wanted more for them than a short, brutish life followed by an endless night of mud and corruption. Acting at the direction of Fate, Zeus decided to father a new god Dionysos who would become the savior of all mankind. Zeus impregnated Dionysos' mother, either Demeter or Persephone, possibly on the island of Sicily at Selinos.

The first birth of Dionysos also probably occurred on Sicily. Perpetually jealous of her husband's infidelities, Hera enlisted Titans to watch for an opportunity to kidnap and murder the divine child. Slowly, the baby grew from an infant into a toddler. Eventually, a day came when the toddler wandered too far away from his parents. The Titans captured baby Dionysos, cooked him, and ate him.[14] Arriving too late to save the whole child from being eaten, Athena succeeded in recovering only the child's still-beating heart. Dutifully, she carried it to Zeus.

At this time, Zeus loved a mortal woman named Semele.[15] Zeus liquefied the baby's heart and gave it to Semele to drink. Of course this made Semele pregnant, and it gave Hera a new target for jealousy and vengeance. This time, Hera pretended friendship with Semele. Eventually, Hera easily tricked Semele into making Zeus give her a gift that would kill her.

One day, when Zeus promised to give Semele anything she asked, Semele requested (at Hera's suggestion) that Zeus come to her just like he came to Hera on Mount Olympus. Zeus begged Semele to reconsider, and to choose anything else instead. Coached by Hera, Semele demanded that Zeus grant her the full glory of his presence.

Regretfully, Zeus honored his promise, but Semele's mortal flesh could not endure Zeus' unshielded divinity. Semele burned to ashes, but Zeus preserved Semele's developing fetus from destruction. Having no womb, Zeus ripped open his thigh and sewed it closed around the fetus.

---

[14]See Chapter 5.

[15]Semele was the daughter of Cadmus and Harmonia, important mythical figures in the earliest historical mystery cult at Samothrace. See Chapter 5.

IGURE 4-10. Dionysos and His Stepfather, Silenos. Sicily, Naxos, AR Tetradrachm, ca. 430–420 B.C.

Zeus gave birth to Dionysos, the twice born, on the island of Naxos. There, Zeus entrusted the child to Semele's sister Ino and her husband Athamas to raise. Ino and Athamas took great pains to protect the child from Hera. They hid him by raising him as a girl, but the deception didn't work for long. When Hera discovered the truth about Dionysos, she drove Ino and Athamas mad. Because of Hera, these loving parents killed their own children, and again Zeus had to save little Dionysos.

After this, Dionysos moved a lot. Many cities claimed to have played a part in raising him. Once, Zeus even transformed the child into a goat and hid him with nymphs. It appears, however, that Dionysos lived longest and best on the island of Sicily with his foster father, Silenos (Pan's son who ruled as King of Satyrs).

The coin in Figure 4-10 displays a bust of Dionysos wreathed with ivy on the obverse and Dionysos' drunken foster father, Silenos, on the reverse. Silenos holds a *kantharos* (cup) full of wine in his right hand, and his left hand grasps a *thyrsos*, a type of wand associated only with Dionysos that represented fertility and transformation. In *The Cyclops*, the only Greek satyr play that has survived to modern times, the playwright Euripides portrays a comic interaction between Silenos and the Cyclops, Polyphemus. Drunk with the wine of Odysseus, Polyphemus mistakes ugly old Silenos for Zeus' cupbearer, Ganymede, and carries the protesting King of Satyrs to a cave to make love with him.

As a grown man, Dionysos traveled the world performing miracles[16] and bringing divine ecstasy to his followers. Once, somewhere on the Mediterranean Sea, pirates captured Dionysos intending to ransom or kill him. Dionysos transformed the pirates into dolphins. Often associated with Demeter, Persephone, and Arethusa on Sicily, dolphins served humanity by saving shipwrecked sailors from drowning at sea.

When the Ionian hero, Theseus, abandoned Ariadne, the daughter of King Minos, on the island of Naxos, Dionysos found her and married her. Dionysos might have honeymooned with Ariadne on Sicily, a place where she could meet his family as well as visit the grave of her father. Association with Ariadne connected Dionysos with the earliest Greek mythology on Sicily.

The stories of Demeter, Persephone, and Dionysos provide entertainment to modern readers, but ancient Greeks took mystery stories seriously. As the public face of a mystery cult, these stories connected metaphorically with information communicated only during secret initiation. Experiencing the hidden part of mysteries gave initiates more than the promise of future salvation: Initiations transformed people's lives and even healed the sick. No initiates ever disclosed mysteries associated with Demeter, Persephone, and Dionysos; revealing them would have brought suffering in life as well as after death. Not a single description of these mysteries survives, only tantalizing clues.

BRINGING SALVATION TO ALL MEDITERRANEAN CULTURES

Archaeologists have found many ancient Greek graves, on Sicily and elsewhere, that contain gold foil inscribed with notes. The notes tell the newly dead spirit where to go, what to do, and—most importantly—what to say to Persephone, Queen of the Underworld. Initiates of

---

[16]Greeks credited Dionysos with the original miraculous transformation of water into wine through growth and processing of grapes.

mystery cults associated a mysterious child of Persephone (Brimos or Dionysos) simultaneously with important agricultural products and with knowledge that made salvation possible. At festivals and initiations, Greeks performed "Passion Plays" showing critical moments in the lives of Demeter, Persephone, and Dionysos. Pious pilgrims also traveled to holy sites on Sicily to sacrifice, to pray, and to attempt to assure a pleasant afterlife for their souls.

Over time, as the ethnic groups on Sicily mixed and interrelated, they all used coins with symbols that referred to mysteries of Demeter, Persephone, and Dionysos. The coins also carried symbols that referred to values and histories associated with specific ethnicities. Still, all the ethnicities, mythologies, and cults on ancient Sicily serve only to introduce a few important types among many variations in lands around the Mediterranean Sea.

Greeks influenced all Mediterranean cults and cultures through trade and colonization. North coastal regions in particular worshipped the Olympian Gods and believed in Greek myths about the creation of the universe. Ancient Greek influence persisted over centuries and millennia so that, in the West, we still tell stories about Greek gods to our children, and we still occasionally use pagan Greek iconography.

Away from the coastal regions, north and south of the Mediterranean Sea, local tribal cults possessed mythologies and practices more similar to Sicel and Sicani cults than to Greek cults. Information about these cults and myths largely has been lost. The sparse history of indigenous cults on Sicily reflects how rarely Greeks recorded information about these cults. Ancient Greeks didn't consider "barbarian" cults worth investigating. Regardless, many foreign gods found their way into the Greek pantheon as titans, nymphs, river gods, and monsters.

In the eastern Mediterranean region, non-Greek cultic traditions prevailed in Syria and Egypt. Syrian-style cults survived on Sicily among the Elymians. Near the Elymians, Carthaginian colonies practiced cults that combined Syrian, Egyptian, and North African influences. Regardless, during the early stages of Greek colonization, Eastern and African influences trickled slowly into Greek culture.

To understand the sources of western religion, one must examine not just varieties of peoples, mythologies, and cults, but also important themes and characteristic stories that often transcended ethnicity and place of origin. All the mythologies and cults around the Mediterranean Sea possessed common themes and story elements, and images on ancient coins serve as a useful means of introducing them. Examining common numismatic themes in ancient cults and relating them to modern religion can help modern people appreciate the realities of ancient life.

PART TWO

Numismatic Advertisement for a Profitable Mystery Cult

A MYTHOLOGICAL MYSTERY TOUR OF ANCIENT CULTS

Many pieces of ancient cults survive unrecognized in the modern world.

CHAPTER
5

THE IMPACT OF ANCIENT GREEK MYSTERY CULTS

Mysteries combined passion plays, mystical teachings, and salvation long before the birth of Christianity.

The earliest well-documented mystery cult appeared in Samothrace in the seventh century B.C. However, earlier evidence of chthonic worship at many sites in the Mediterranean region suggests that cults similar to historic mystery cults were widespread and varied and that they originated in a time deep in human prehistory. Concerned with healing, fertility, life after death, and personal transformation, some cults focused on supporting customs that helped local culture work. Other cults acquired international reputations as centers for teaching advanced knowledge.

To describe what they sought from initiation into mysteries, ancient Greeks sometimes used the word *salvation*, generically seeking help with a variety of personal issues. Some worshippers of mystery cults sought initiation to deal with problems involving health or family. Others wanted to acquire power, enhance their status, improve their personal effectiveness, purify themselves, express their devotion, preserve their lives from danger, or ensure their survival after death.

Priests of mystery cults, the best practical psychologists of their day, skillfully designed rituals of mystery cults by combining many types of sophisticated ancient knowledge—the best art, rhetoric, technology, and craftsmanship of every sort. The earliest Greek plays portrayed mystery stories, high priests of mystery cults practiced the most advanced Greek science, and initiates of mystery cults occupied the highest positions in ancient Greek society. While mystery cults coexisted with Jewish and Christian cults, Jewish and Christian leaders struggled to deter their followers from seeking initiation. In later centuries, after Western Christianity finally won the war against pagan cults, Christian leaders had discredited mystery cults so successfully that Christians abandoned many of the highest expressions of ancient culture. From music to advanced mathematics, much of the best of ancient knowledge was lost.

THE MECHANISM OF MYSTERY CULTS

The desire for salvation always connects with fears associated with the central problems of existence: the possibilities of losing one's being to nothingness (death) or to uncontrollable, overwhelming sensation (madness). As a central problem of life, the certainty of death in everyone's life serves as a background consideration that helps emphasize the importance of every other human problem: A pang of hunger or thirst feels sharper because of the existence of death by starvation; loneliness and shame enhance fears of disappearing into nothingness; and, even in grief, losing a loved one underscores the possibility of losing oneself.

Few people can bear to focus for long on the central problems of existence. Instead, feeling powerless and victimized by their own generic level of anxiety, people sometimes lose their sense of well-being by focusing their attention on uncontrollable aspects of their lives. By permanently reducing anxiety associated with a central issue of existence (like the fear of death), initiation into a mystery cult could help people feel their power instead of their weakness and refocus their attention on controllable circumstances. By helping people confront the central problems of existence, mystery cults acquired a reputation for helping people resolve or diminish a variety of personal problems.

Using religious rituals and theater as tools, priests of mystery cults guided initiates through metaphorical analogues of great personal transformations; forcing initiates to confront their fears about death, nothingness, and madness, the priests then led initiates to experience rebirth or even the presence of God. Initiations carefully orchestrated feelings of hunger, thirst, loneliness, shame, and grief and transformed them slowly into joy accompanied by feasting and enlightened celebration. Priests sometimes enhanced initiation experiences using tools like technology (for example, seemingly "miraculous" acoustic and pneumatic effects), drugs, sex, and alcohol. However, unreliable tools could put the whole initiation at risk. Abstinence, confession, and hardship were tools that reliably adjusted the consciousnesses of initiates while giving priests as much control as possible.

If ancient worshippers sought miracles from initiation, both history and archaeology confirm that many people obtained what they sought. Successful initiates recorded the importance of mystery cults in their lives in frescoes, in sculpture, in plays, and in grateful testimonials at temples and other centers of worship. Initiations sometimes produced miraculous healings of body and mind; the lame walked, the blind saw, and the tormented found peace.

THE ORIGINS OF RELIGIOUS THEATER

Archaeological evidence for the existence of mystery cults extends into prehistory, particularly in Turkey, Greece, and Crete. The most well-known forms of ancient mystery cults comprise chthonic mysteries connected with Demeter, Persephone, and Hades. Large concentrations of artifacts at Eleusis and Delphi on mainland Greece, on the island of Samothrace, and even on Sicily at Enna and Selinos identify these places among others as major centers for ancient mysteries. At places like these, the combining of mythology and ritual as a tool of initiation gave birth to theater.

Greek myths connected sacred places and mystical teachings with stories about the origins of salvation. The reenactment of mythological events gave worshippers a vicarious experience of the origins of salvation that broadened their understanding and enriched their lives. After their emergence in the sacred spaces of mystery cults, the first plays gave rise to an enduring and deeply influential art form.

Initiations into mysteries—usually described as chthonic, Dionysiac, Bacchic, or Orphic—continued until Christianity outlawed and expunged this form of worship. Christians replaced the *orgia* (solemn religious rituals and salvation-oriented plays) of ancient Greek mysteries with a new brand of the same thing. Yet, early Christians vilified ancient mystery cults so successfully that the meaning of the word *orgy* changed from a religious ritual to a party featuring sex and strong drink. Modern Christians have forgotten that straight-laced Roman pagans accused early Christians of licentiousness and immorality when they first came to Rome.

In fact, almost all religious traditions always have supported family values. While it's true that human mores and circumstances have varied greatly from place to place and from time to time, traditions that failed to help people in their everyday lives simply did not last. Extreme, immoral, and unhealthful mystery cults[1] certainly existed; however, worshippers generally experienced mystery stories, no matter how peculiar by modern standards, as life-affirming passion plays.

THE MYSTERIES OF SAMOTHRACE

The Mysteries of Samothrace, currently the oldest historical mystery cult, told the story of Cadmus (one of the earliest men) and Harmonia (the daughter of Ares and Aphrodite). Cadmus taught humanity about agriculture, bronze working, and the alphabet. Harmonia served humanity as the personification of harmony and agreement.

A son of King Agenor of Tyre as well as a grandson of Poseidon, Cadmus lived during the Heroic Age when men as large and strong as giants lived in easy relationship with gods. Cadmus helped Zeus (King of the Olympian Gods) defeat the monster, Typhon. Cadmus also founded the Greek city of Thebes. As instructed by Athena, he populated the city by sowing the soil with serpent's teeth. Warriors grew from the teeth and fought each other until only five remained. These five warriors established the five noble families of Thebes.

---

[1]For example, modern sensibilities would not have approved of the rites of Crete's opium goddess Gazi.

Zeus treacherously repaid Cadmus' help escaping the monster Typhon by abducting Cadmus' sister, Europa, the woman who gave her name to Europe. Hermes, the God of Messengers, led his father Zeus, hidden in the form of a white bull, to a beach near Tyre where Europa played with her friends. Looking like a beautiful and gentle white bull, Zeus enticed Europa to mount him. Then, still in the form of a bull, Zeus plunged into the sea and carried her to Crete.

Hoping to recover his daughter, King Agenor ordered his sons, Cilix, Phoenix, Cadmus, and Thasos to search for their sister and not to return until they found her. Eventually, Phoenix established the land of the Phoenicians, Cilix settled the country of Cilicia, and Thasos ended up on the island of Thasos. All of them founded great city-states, but none succeeded in finding Europa.

While searching for Europa on the island of Samothrace, Cadmus saw beautiful Harmonia. Instantly aroused, he seized the young woman, carried her to his ship, and sailed away. Harmonia's outraged brothers, Jason and Dardanus, sailed after Cadmus and caught him. They brought him back to Samothrace intending to execute him, but Harmonia had fallen in love with Cadmus, and Samothrace celebrated a wedding instead of an execution, the only wedding ever attended by both gods and mortals.

The public part of the Samothracian Mysteries celebrated the story of Cadmus and Harmonia that culminated in a wedding where gods gave gifts to humanity. Regarding the secret part of the Samothracian Mysteries, the wedding symbolically affirmed the kinship between humans and gods because both descended from Earth and sky (Gaea and Uranus). When Cadmus died, the gods allowed him to live in the Elysian Fields, a pleasant part of the underworld. The Mysteries of Samothrace probably instructed initiates how to follow Cadmus to a better place after death based on a covenant between gods and men at his wedding. For hundreds of years, Samothrace regularly conducted initiations into these mysteries. Even Philip II of Macedon, the father of Alexander the Great, sought and obtained initiation in the Mysteries of Samothrace.[2]

---

[2] Philip met Olympias, Alexander's mother, during initiation and they married soon after. See *Life of Alexander* 2:2 by Plutarch.

FIGURE 5-1. Cadmus Chasing Harmonia, and Punchmark. Macedon, Siris, AR Stater, ca. 500 B.C.

Of course, Macedon may have enjoyed a special connection with the Mysteries of Samothrace. From Siris, Macedon, the coin in Figure 5-1 displays symbolism closely related to the Samothracian myth of Cadmus and Harmonia. The coin's obverse shows an aroused, semi-divine (naked) male seizing a woman, exactly as Samothracian mythology said that Cadmus seized Harmonia. On the reverse of the coin, a large, square punch mark indicates that the coin came from the beginning of the fifth century B.C., a time when Macedonian tribal groups struggled to dominate each other. The coin provides evidence for longstanding regional respect for these mysteries.

Those already familiar with Greek mythology will find parallels between the story of Cadmus and Harmonia and stories of the abductions of Helen of Troy. Helen's abduction by Paris started the Trojan War; however, Theseus abducted Helen before Paris did. Helen's brothers, Castor and Polydeukes (the Gemini twins), chased Theseus by ship, recaptured Helen, and safely returned her to Sparta. Ancient Peloponnesians honored Helen's brothers as protectors of sailors, just as Samothracians honored Harmonia's brothers. One also can see parallels in the relationship between Cadmus and Harmonia with other mythological relationships, sometimes between Hermes and Persephone and sometimes between Hades and Persephone. Some myths seem to identify Cadmus with Hermes, a god frequently represented as *ithyphallic* (with an erect phallus).

Cadmus and Harmonia had four daughters and one son. They named one of their daughters Semele. The name of this daughter connects the cult of Samothrace with the Cult of Dionysos. The stories of different Greek mystery cults often connect with each other, revealing an underlying genealogy of influence, colonization, and cult evolution.

EVIDENCE OF LOST MYSTERIES

Zeus carried Europa all the way to Gortyna on the island of Crete. Then he changed into an eagle and ravished her. The obverse of the coin in Figure 5-2 displays images of Europa and an eagle in a plane tree, and the reverse portrays Zeus in the form of a bull. On the obverse, Europa lifts her veil with her right hand and embraces Zeus (in the form of an eagle) with her left. Resting his head beneath Europa's breasts, the eagle mates with her and flaps his wings. All around the ancient Mediterranean Sea, women commonly wore veils. In those days, a woman symbolically opened herself to marriage and intimacy by lifting her veil. Because numismatic depictions of sexual process often refer to local mysteries, this coin suggests that the inhabitants of Gortyna celebrated Mysteries of Europa. Perhaps ancient Cretans believed that Europa bargained with Zeus concerning the fate of her descendants' souls.

Later, Europa married Asterion, King of Crete. As Queen of Crete, she raised three sons by Zeus: Minos, Rhadamanthus, and Sarpedon. After death, two of her sons served as judges in the underworld. Three judges[3] determined the fate of humans in the underworld: Aecus,[4] Rhadamanthus, and Minos. Aecus represented Greeks from Europe, Rhadamanthus represented Greeks from Asia, and Minos cast the deciding vote whenever the other judges disagreed. Rhadamanthus' son, Gortys, founded Gortyna. Europa's third son, Sarpedon (possibly

---

[3] See *Gorgias* 523a by Plato.
[4] Aecus, King of Aegina, was the son of Zeus (in the form of an eagle or of fire) by the daughter of a river god. Zeus made subjects for his son by transforming ants on the island into human beings.

88   Part Two | A Mythological Mystery Tour

FIGURE 5-2. Zeus as an Eagle Ravishing Europa in a Plane Tree, and Bull. Crete, Gortyna, AR Stater, ca. 280 B.C.

conflated with a great hero with the same name who died in the Trojan War) established the Kingdom of Lycia on a peninsula in southeastern Asia Minor.

The ancestors and descendents of Europa symbolized social and spiritual relationships between the inhabitants of ancient Gortyna and the world around them. Similarly, today's Christians use genealogies in the *Bible* to explain the inheritance of original sin, the relationship between Arabs and Jews, the divine heritage of Jesus, and so forth. Modern historians and archaeologists look to biblical and Greek mythological genealogies for clues about ancient migrations and relationships among prehistoric tribal groups.

PYTHAGOREAN MYSTERIES

More than merely psychological roller coaster rides, some mysteries also served as a mechanism for communicating knowledge in specialized disciplines like mathematics, astronomy, and technology. In ancient times, teachers sometimes communicated sophisticated knowledge only to initiates who proved worthy of receiving the information.

Chapter 5 | Impact of Ancient Greek Mystery Cults   89

FIGURE 5-3. Sacrificial Tripod and Heron, and Incuse Design—Possibly Designed to Encode Pythagorean Teachings. Bruttium, Croton, AR Nomos, ca. 530–500 B.C.

Early in the sixth century B.C., for example, Pythagoras conducted initiations into mysteries related to the Cult of Demeter and Persephone, but he included elements of mathematics, harmonics, and other types of divine knowledge. We remember Pythagoras as a teacher of the *Pythagorean Theorem* relating lengths of the sides of a right triangle in the famous formula: $A^2 + B^2 = C^2$. However, Greeks of his day knew Pythagoras as a semi-divine miracle-worker, the most famous inhabitant of Croton, a coastal city at the foot of Italy.

The city of Croton minted the coin in Figure 5-3 during the lifetime of Pythagoras. Some numismatists speculate that the peculiar design of these coins, comprising similar positive (protuberant) and negative (depressed) images, relates to his philosophical teachings. At its most basic level of symbolism, the coin serves as a metaphorical expression of the relationship between the spiritual and material worlds: The obverse and reverse images look the same at first, but on close examination they don't look the same at all. The relationship between one side and the other—between fullness and emptiness applied to an instrument of devotion (the tripod)—may have symbolized teachings by Pythagoras about the body and soul.

Like Jesus, Pythagoras wrote nothing that has survived, but many ancient historians wrote about Pythagoras. Some described him as a child of Apollo and a mortal woman named Parthenis (a name derived from the Greek word for virgin). Pythagoras left his birthplace, Samos, perhaps to avoid persecution.[5] He traveled and studied in Egypt, Babylon, and even India before finally settling in Croton. Like other mystery teachers, Pythagoras divided his students into beginners (those who heard basic teachings like mythological stories) and advanced groups. He taught a variation of Dionysian Mysteries that encouraged initiates to live an "Orphic Life," that is, a life dedicated to nonviolence against all living things. In communities that he founded, men and women possessed equal status; they shared possessions and ate only vegetarian food. Neophytes took a five-year vow of silence. Pythagoreans rose at dawn to worship the sun, and then spent the rest of the day in study and thoughtful activity. In the evening, followers ate a communal meal, perhaps followed by readings and discussion of Pythagorean ideas.

According to Pythagoras, numbers caused everything in the universe, physical and spiritual. In such a universe, one could acquire wisdom only through numerical studies like mathematics, geometry, music, and astronomy. Ancient teachings about numbers, like "five" causes color, "six" causes cold, "seven" causes health, "eight" causes love, etc., may derive from original teachings of Pythagoras. Also, hints of strange Pythagorean rituals have survived, for example, in descriptions of initiates reading words written in blood on a mirror illuminated by light reflected from the full moon.[6] Pythagoras taught that souls lived forever. Endowed by Hermes[7] with the power to remember everything, including his past lives, Pythagoras taught that, at death, souls migrated to new incarnations under the guidance of Demeter.

The first philosopher to declare that the Earth (as a round ball) circled the sun, Pythagoras healed the sick, calmed rough winds, raised

---

[5]Some sources say that Pythagoras fled Samos to escape the tyranny of Polycrates who seized control of the island around 538 B.C. Others say that Pythagoras entered Egypt with a letter of introduction from Polycrates.
[6]See *History of Mathematics* p. 74 by David Eugene Smith.
[7]Pythagoras taught that Hermes was the wisest of gods and that he guided human souls after death from their bodies to an appropriate spiritual region.

the dead, and walked on water. However, the city-state of Croton eventually perceived his teachings, his communities, and his growing influence as a threat. Eventually, Croton expelled Pythagoras, who moved to nearby Taras (future Tarentum). Taras expelled Pythagoras at the age of ninety-five, and he died four years later in Metapontum on the Anatolian Peninsula. His death underscores an unfortunate consequence of passing knowledge in secrecy; sometimes profound knowledge, hard-won by the greatest of ancient minds, failed to survive the extinction of small, highly intellectual mystery cults.

Regardless, Greeks would judge all future religious teachers (for example, Jesus) against Pythagoras' resume:

- Birth foretold by the Oracle of Delphi
- Born of a virgin
- Lived previously (born again)
- Known to his followers as the Son of God
- Taught about the immortality of human souls
- Descended to the realm of Hades and returned
- Suffered a violent death
- Followers performed miracles in the name of Pythagoras

Many scholars have gone to great lengths proving that the followers of Jesus did not copy a list of Pythagoras' miracles into the gospels. However, one cannot help but see a connection between Christian writings and Pythagorean ideas.

OTHER TEACHERS AND TEACHINGS OF MYSTERIES

After the death of Pythagoras, a Pythagorean mystic[8] named Empedocles performed miracles and wrote philosophical verses in Akragas, Sicily. Empedocles not only healed individuals, but he even stopped a plague in the nearby city of Selinos by recommending the drainage of

---

[8]Teachers or initiates of mysteries often are called mystics.

FIGURE 5-4. Coin Minted to Celebrate Halting of a Plague by the Pythagorean Mystic, Empedocles. Sicily, Selinos, AR Tetradrachm, ca. 450 B.C.

a local swamp. Similar to other miracle workers, Empedocles did not die, but rose bodily into the realm of the gods. The tetradrachm in Figure 5-4 celebrates the elimination of plague in Selinos after the city followed the advice of Empedocles. On the obverse, Artemis holds the reins of a chariot while Apollo, her brother, shoots arrows of plague. On the reverse, the river god Selinos places offerings on an altar to appease Apollo's wrath.

Pythagoras' ideas strongly influenced Plato (the greatest of ancient Greek philosophers) as well as numerous other mystics, philosophers, and scientists through the ages. Pythagoras knew of the existence of irrational numbers. He used a value of π (pi) equal to $22/7$, an approximation derived by comparing the diameter of a circle with its circumference, mathmatically determined by averaging the perimeters of polygons inscribed and circumscribed around the circle. (See Figure 5-5.) Pythagoreans approximated the square root of three as $265/153$, a number known to mystics as "the Number of the Fish." Hundreds of years after Pythagoras died, Pythagorean mystics continued to teach combinations of spirituality, mathematics, and science in Alexandria, Athens, Tarsos, and the Near East.

Obscure hints of mysticism based on numbers and geometry survive in modern Christianity. If one uses a protractor first to draw a

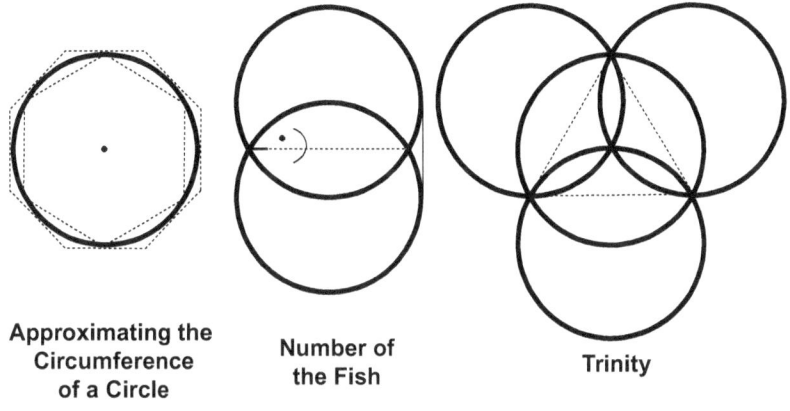

FIGURE 5-5. Geometric Diagrams Depicting the Approximation of Pi, the Origins of the Number of the Fish, and a Geometric Metaphor of Trinity—an Equilateral Triangle with Sides Equal to the Number of the Fish

circle with a unit radius, then to draw an identical circle with its center on the edge of the first circle, one obtains an image like the middle drawing in Figure 5-5. As long as both circles have the same unit radius, the distance between the two points of intersection of the two circles measures approximately 265/153 units. If you sketch a tail, a little mouth, an eye, and a gill, you can appreciate why people called this length the Number of the Fish. The rightmost diagram in Figure 5-5 shows that an inscribed equilateral triangle inside a unit circle will have three sides that each measure 265/153 units. In the last chapter of the most mystical gospel in the *New Testament*,[9] Jesus appeared to his disciples for the third time since his death after the disciples caught 153 fish. Supporting a cult that represented itself with the image of a fish, early Christian gospels incorporated Pythagorean-style miracles, symbolism, and mysteries.

The followers of both mystery cults and Christianity often have described the benefits of their faiths in similar terms. For example, in *The Bacchae*, a play written by Euripides around 410 B.C., the chorus enters after the opening speech by Dionysos and speaks of the joy of being initiated into heavenly mysteries and leading a holy life on a

---

[9] See *John* 21.

mountain, purified from every sin. Similar mystical sentiments might have been uttered by the companions of Jesus who accompanied him during his "Transfiguration" on Mount Tabor.[10]

A DORIAN VARIATION OF ELEUSINIAN MYSTERIES

An interesting variation of the Eleusinian Mysteries developed in ancient Greek herding societies. Myths from these societies illustrate how mystery cults played an important role in making some cultures work. Men from herding tribes of ancient Arcadia (central Peloponnese Peninsula) often obtained wives by raiding neighbor villages and kidnapping young women. The kidnapped women then had to overcome feelings of rage about their treatment as they adjusted to their new lives. To keep a society functioning with this kind of institutionalized abuse, Arcadians used mystery cults to deliver powerful emotional support to the kidnapped women. Special Arcadian Mysteries guided these women toward acceptance of their new roles as wives of their kidnappers and as mothers of their kidnappers' children.

In Arcadia, mysteries included stories about Persephone's abduction and Demeter's search for her daughter with an added twist; as Demeter searched all over the world, Poseidon (ancient Greek God of the Sea) lustfully stalked the goddess. For a long time, Demeter eluded Poseidon. Once, however, she hid from him by changing into a horse. Having observed her transformation, Poseidon changed into a horse as well. Disguised as just another member of the herd, Poseidon surprised Demeter and raped her.

Demeter hated Poseidon for what he'd done, but Zeus would not tolerate strong grievances between Olympian Gods. When Demeter's hate passed, she bathed in the Ladon River. Subsequently, she bore two children, a daughter named Despoena and an immortal horse named Areion. The obverse of the coin in Figure 5-6 depicts "Furious Demeter" (Demeter Erinys). On the coin's reverse, Demeter's young

---

[10]See the gospel of *Matthew* 17:1–9.

Chapter 5 | Impact of Ancient Greek Mystery Cults   95

FIGURE 5-6. Furious Demeter and Her Son, Areion. Arcadia, Thelpusa, AR Obol, ca. 370-350 B.C.

son, Areion, prances across a field. A horse of heroes, Areion carried men like Herakles and Adrastus[11] in famous battles.

The coin displays images of Demeter and Areion as public images related to Arcadian mysteries, but no images survive of Despoena. Because only initiates could speak the name *Despoena* out loud in Arcadia, the nature of this goddess appears to relate to secret parts of the local mysteries. Surviving mythology indicates that Despoena (like Artemis, Goddess of the Hunt) grew into a young tomboy goddess. The hound, her sacred animal, accompanied her everywhere. Even though Demeter and Poseidon must have reconciled, neither god cared for Despoena. Instead, a male Titan named Anytos raised her.

EVIDENCE OF MACEDON'S DORIAN ANCESTRY

In northern Greece, Macedonians claimed to descend from Dorians like the Arcadians on the Peloponnese Peninsula. Macedon's royal house even claimed direct descent from Herakles. Located on the

---

[11] Herakles gave Areion as a gift to Adrastus, King of Argos, who later led an army with six heroic allies in the war known as the "Seven against Thebes."

FIGURE 5-7. Image of Poseidon in the Form of an Ithyphallic Ass, and Punchmark. Macedon, Mende, AR Tetrobol, 510–480 B.C.

Chalkidian peninsula, near the birthplace of Orion (legendary hunter and stalker of women), the Macedonian town of Mende must have possessed traditions similar to those of ancient Arcadia. In this context, the ithyphallic ass on the obverse of a coin from Mende (see Figure 5-7) corresponds to the story of Poseidon stalking Demeter. Consistent with minting practices in the early fifth century B.C., this coin's reverse displays only punch marks. Perhaps unrecorded Mysteries of Mende included rites of reconciliation for women to forgive kidnapping and sexual assault by their husbands.

In general, Greeks thought it amusing, if not obscene, to represent the primary aspect of a divinity as partly or wholly animal. Ancient Greek literature has preserved numerous derogatory comments about Egyptian religious beliefs expressing this prejudice. Greeks used the myth of Typhon to explain that Egyptian beliefs about their gods' appearances originated during the time when Olympian Gods lived in Egypt, disguising themselves as animals to hide from Typhon. However, Greeks understood completely when a male god found it necessary to disguise himself as an animal in order to have sex with an unwilling female.

Christian iconography sometimes shows surprising connections to primitive Greek religious conceptions. The *New Testament* does not go into detail as to precisely how Jesus miraculously appeared as a developing fetus inside the body of his mother. However, paintings of this event (Annunciation) in many churches often show the Holy Spirit flying in the form of a dove toward Mary, an unsuspecting virgin.

HINTS OF RELIGIOUS EVOLUTION IN MYTHOLOGICAL GENEALOGY

The participation of the Titan, Anytos, in the myth about Despoena again illustrates the interconnection of ancient mysteries in different places. Anytos the Titan connects Dionysos to ancient mysteries at Delphi, the place where Apollo killed an ancient monster snake named Python. In general, shared elements connected diverse mystery stories at many of the great centers of chthonic rites, places like Delphi, Eleusis, Selinos, and Enna. For nine months of every year, Delphi celebrated rites of Apollo, including one day a month for his famous oracle. Using the same temple, Delphi dedicated the other three months of every year to the worship of Dionysos.

As mentioned in Chapter 4, Hera enlisted a band of Titans to exact vengeance on Zeus and Persephone after the birth of Dionysos. Anytos led the band. The Titans dressed in silly clothes and clown-face makeup, and they brought gifts of tricky toys to baby Dionysos. Engaging him with amusing antics, they lured the young god away from the protection of his parents.

The Titans carried Dionysos to Delphi where they slaughtered the young god, cut him to pieces, and cooked him in a pot. Though they consumed the flesh of young Dionysos, Athena found his still-beating heart and carried it back to Zeus. The temple at Delphi might have preserved sacred relics of the first incarnation of Dionysos, perhaps even remnants of the original cannibalistic feast.

The Eleusinian initiation ceremony included killing a small sheep or goat (a kid) and cooking it in its mother's milk, which may have represented the cooking of baby Dionysos by the Titans. In a ceremony of symbolic cannibalism, initiates identified with the murderers of Dionysos as they ate the kid stew, incorporating the sacrificed god into the core of their being. Modern Christians perform a similar symbolic act, eating the body and drinking the blood of Jesus, in the ceremony of the Eucharist.

THE CULT OF ASCLEPIUS

To settle claims of Asclepius' origins by rival city-states, the Oracle at Delphi declared that Asclepius came from Epidauros in Argolis on the Peloponnese Peninsula where he founded his healing cult. Eumolpus, the first priest of the Eleusinian Mysteries, initiated Asclepius to give him access to the region where miraculous healing occurs—the underground path between life and death. The same priests that guided initiations at Eleusis also served as healers and teachers in the Cult of Asclepius at Epidauros. The priests (called Eumolpids) dedicated the first day of every Eleusinian initiation to mysteries of Asclepius, the God of Healing. The mysteries even accepted seekers of salvation who arrived late as long as they arrived sometime during that first day.

The obverse of the top coin in Figure 5-8 portrays Asclepius' father, Apollo Maleatus (Apollo as healer). The reverse shows Asclepius, enthroned, holding a snake. Snakes and dogs assisted Asclepius with healing. The obverse of the lower coin in Figure 5-8 shows Asclepius gazing right, while the reverse portrays his wife, Epione (the Goddess of Easing Pain), carrying medicine. Epione bore many children, including Panakaia (the Goddess of Medicine), Hygeia (a Goddess of Health and Bathing), Iaso (Goddess of Recuperation from Illness), Aceso (Goddess of Healing Processes), Aglaea (Brilliance, the youngest of the three charities), and Telesphoros (the God of Convalescence).

Healing cults provided the best option in ancient times for dealing with serious health issues. The Asclepion of Epidauros trained healers and priests in the use of drugs and medical procedures. Ancient healers used natural remedies like spices, herbs, opium, and silphium. While many ancient medicines contained the same drugs that doctors use

FIGURE 5-8. Coins Related to Healing Cult at Epidauros. Top: Argolis, Epidauros, AR Drachm, ca. 260 B.C., Bottom: Argolis, Epidauros, AE 18, ca. 225–200 B.C.

today, natural sources delivered uncertain amounts of healing drugs mixed with a variety of other, unnecessary ingredients.

The fame of Cyrenean silphium (a plant similar to fennel or celery) caused that plant's extinction sometime during the first century A.D. Ancients used silphium as a food, a spice, and a medicine. Apollo gave the first silphium plant to the nymph Cyrene, and the best silphium grew around the North African city named after her. Ancient healers knew of silphium's effectiveness as a diuretic, as a purgative, as a means of cleansing afterbirth from the womb, and as a contraceptive for women.[12] The obverse of the top coin in Figure 5-9 shows the nymph Cyrene seated between a silphium plant and its fruit. The reverse portrays the North African god Amon.

Almost every large city possessed an Asclepion,[13] but the famous temple complex at Epidauros attracted supplicants and students

---

[12]See *Natural History* 22:49 by Pliny the Elder.
[13]Worshippers in ancient times also sought healing from other gods, for example, Mên, Eshmoun, Isis, and Apollo (sometimes from the Oracle at Delphi).

throughout the ancient world. This healing sanctuary contained hot baths, dormitories, shrines, and a theater for performing rituals and religious plays. In addition, a central building, called an enkoimitiria, served as a place where supplicants practiced *incubation*, curing disease through dreams.

Sometimes dreams told a sick person to go to a particular Asclepion. There, priests might treat his illness with drugs, salves, rituals, and sacrifices. When signs revealed that a patient needed incubation,[14] priests prepared the patient with counseling, rituals, and drugs, and then led the person to a specific place in the enkoimitiria to sleep. (Men and women slept apart from each other.) Instructing the patient not to fear anything the god might reveal, the priest then left the person to sleep…and to dream.

Found at every Asclepion in the ancient world, miracle texts recorded healings of a wide variety of ailments—blindness, lameness, skin diseases—serious illnesses of all sorts. The texts report that patients sometimes awoke in the enkoimitiria completely healed. Other times, Asclepius sent patients a dream that taught them how to treat their disease.

At Epidauros, miracle texts document particular success in treating barrenness in women. In one miracle text, a woman cured of infertility described her experience: While she slept, the god came to her in the form of a giant snake; he rested on her stomach, and she conceived. Modern physicians suggest that ancient techniques for curing infertility proved effective because priests combined sleeping potions with special "hands-on" servicing of female clients.

Honoring the Asclepion at Pergamon, the lower coin in Figure 5-9 portrays Asclepius on the obverse and his symbol, the staff of Asclepius, on the reverse. Wrapped by a single snake, the staff served as an ancient symbol of healing. During the American Civil War, military doctors adopted a different symbol to represent them: the caduceus (a symbol of Hermes), a winged staff entwined with two snakes. In

---

[14]The practice of incubation did not end with paganism. For example, the Martyrium of Saint Philip (a building marking the site of the execution of the apostle Philip) in Hierapolis (Pamukkale, Turkey) was designed to serve as an enkoimitiria. Christians practiced incubation there until the building was destroyed by earthquake and fire in the seventh century A.D.

Chapter 5 | Impact of Ancient Greek Mystery Cults

FIGURE 5-9. Coins Related to Healing Cults at Cyrene and Pergamon. Top: Cyrenaica, Cyrene, AR Tetradrachm, ca. 485–475 B.C., Bottom: Mysia, Pergamon, AE 15, 133–27 B.C.

ancient times, messengers carried a caduceus to obtain safety traveling through war zones, but that symbol (like Hermes) also could represent legal and illegal enterprises focused on making profits. During the 1970s the American Medical Association changed their symbol from the caduceus to the staff of Asclepius. At the present time, some medical organizations use the caduceus and some use the rod of Asclepius. Noticing which symbol organizations choose to represent themselves can provide interesting insights about their focus: whether they see themselves as healers, messengers, businessmen, or thieves.

A CONNECTION BETWEEN DIONYSOS AND EROTIC LOVE

The obverse of the coin in Figure 5-10 portrays a bust of Dionysos, the savior that Zeus fathered to bring salvation to the human race. He wears both a royal diadem and a wreath of ivy. The reverse shows Herakles holding a lion skin and club—divine power radiates from

FIGURE 5-10. Dionysos, and Herakles as Symbols of Spiritual Salvation. Thracian Islands, Thasos, AR Tetradrachm, 168–148 B.C.

his naked body. The legend on the reverse says "Herakles" on the right, "Soter" (the Greek word for savior) on the left, and "Thasion" beneath, indicating that the city-state of Thasos minted the coin.

A common symbol of Dionysos, the so-called "heart-shaped" ivy leaves that crown Dionysos illustrate how elements of ancient cults, disconnected from their source, still exist in modern times. During the three days around the full moon (the 11th, 12th, and 13th days) of the lunar month, Anthesterion[15]—approximately equivalent to February—ancient Greeks celebrated a festival of Dionysos called Anthesteria. This festival of flowers and new wine marked the time of year when Dionysos yielded the shrine at Delphi to Apollo. For hundreds of years, ancient Greeks honored erotic love during this mid-February festival, often describing it as "the Marriage of God." It simultaneously commemorated the anniversaries of Zeus' relationships with Persephone and Semele, the two conceptions of Dionysos, and the day that Dionysos took Ariadne to be his wife. Eros, the God of Erotic Love, ruled the last day of the festival when mature women participated in

---

[15]Like Jews and Muslims today, ancient Greeks determined the end and beginning of months based on the phase of the moon.

symbolic marriages with Dionysos. Young virgins also celebrated lesser unions with the god.

Our modern celebration of Valentine's Day on February 14 preserves echoes of the ancient festival of Anthesteria. It serves as just one example among many of the ancient practices and images that persist in our modern world as unconscious memories of the past. Consistent with the longstanding connections between Herakles and Dionysos, the Church of Santa Maria in Cosmedin, Rome—the church that preserves the relics of Saint Valentine—also contains the ruins of a temple of Herakles in its basement.

INFLUENCES ON JUDEO-CHRISTIAN SCRIPTURE

Long after the death of ancient mystery cults, their traditions still echo inside Judeo-Christian practices and literature. Before entering service as novitiates, Catholic nuns march down church aisles clothed as "brides of Christ." Personal testimonials of female Christian mystics[16] provide evidence for a longstanding connection between eroticism and Christian mysticism. Further, *New Testament* scripture[17] explicitly describes salvation in terms of marriage to Jesus.

Ancient Greek religious beliefs influenced Judeo-Christian scripture in other ways as well. The coin in Figure 5-11 comes from Eleusis, the cultic center of the Eleusinian Mysteries. The obverse side of the coin shows Triptolemus sitting in a winged chariot magically pulled into the sky by snakes. The reverse displays a pig. Part of the preparation for initiation at Eleusis consisted of carrying a small pig into the sea. Sins and impurities would pass into the pig, which the prospective initiate then would sacrifice to Demeter and Persephone. An echo of this tradition survives in the gospel of *Mark*. Jesus drove a legion of demons from an

---

[16]The sixteenth century Spanish nun, Saint Teresa de Ávila, wrote accounts of erotic encounters with Jesus.
[17]For examples, see *Ephesians* 5:22–33, and see also *Revelations* 19:7–9, 21:1–2, and 21:9–10.

FIGURE 5-11. Triptolemus in His Winged Serpent Chariot, and Pig Used by Prospective Initiates in Purification Ceremonies. Attica, Eleusis, AE 15, 340–335 B.C.

outcast and tormented man into a herd of swine, which then charged into a lake and drowned to the last pig.[18] The story doesn't make much sense in modern terms; however, in the days when Christianity competed with the Eleusinian Mysteries, the story directly affirmed the saving power of Jesus as greater than that of Dionysos.

Similarly, the context of competition between Judaism and Greek mystery cults provides insight about the Jewish prohibition against eating a kid seethed in its mother's milk.[19] This prohibition did not arise as a commandment to treat animals ethically. Instead, it resembles other Jewish restrictions against participating in foreign religions—like not eating meat from creatures sacrificed to strange gods and not inquiring into the nature of other religions.[20]

This overview of mystery and healing cults provides a glimpse of institutions that offered salvation during ancient times. Though ancient

---

[18]See *Mark* 5:1–20. Controversial evidence that Jesus taught mysteries that competed directly with Eleusinian Mysteries can be found in *The Secret Gospel: The Discovery and Interpretation of the Secret Gospel According to Mark*, by Professor Morton Smith of Columbia University.
[19]See *Exodus* 34:26.
[20]See *Exodus* 34:15–16 and *Deuteronomy* 12:30.

experiences of seeking salvation remain irretrievably lost, one avenue for insight lies open. As passion plays offered insight to ancient mystics, mythology offers vicarious experiences of ancient lives to modern scholars. In particular, the life of Herakles helps show how ancient Greeks understood important dichotomies in their religious lives, for example: piety and sacrilege, purity and impurity, free will and fate.

CHAPTER
6

THE SALVATION OF HERAKLES

Both ancient Greeks and early Christians saw Herakles as proof that no man was beyond salvation's reach.

No single mythological character provides broader insight into ancient Greek ideas about salvation than Herakles. Like other saviors, he was conceived when the ruler of the universe (Zeus) impregnated a virtuous young virgin with divine ancestry. Herakles possessed towering strength and grave weaknesses. Sometimes, he behaved piously and heroically, and sometimes he behaved despicably and sacrilegiously.

Born into complicated family circumstances, Herakles lacked self-control and easily got into trouble. Hera hated him and sought to destroy him, but Athena helped him when she could. Regardless, he met every situation that came his way with characteristic strength, courage, and stubbornness—sinning, redeeming himself, accomplishing heroic feats, and laying the geopolitical foundation for the classical Greek world.

Herakles matured into a hero capable of helping gods, but he never lost the ability to make mistakes. At the instant of his death, expecting nothing, he ascended bodily to heaven and became a god. As the only member of the Greek pantheon who lived and died as a mortal, he offered hope to every human who wanted a good afterlife.

HERAKLES' ANCESTRY

Like every other mortal, Herakles was born into a situation, a collection of politics and rivalries that had been accumulating for centuries. His mother, Alcmene (a young virgin impregnated by Zeus), descended from Zeus through Perseus, a semi-divine hero that Eastern Greeks associated with salvation. Members of Alcmene's family were key players in complicated world events. Through no fault of his own, Herakles inherited friends, enemies, possibilities, and problems—just by being born.

Years earlier, Zeus had miraculously impregnated Perseus' mother, Danae, by showering her with golden rain. Ancient representations of this event portray a stream of drops floating toward Danae, just as beams of light point toward Mary in Christian Annunciation[1] paintings. Danae gave birth to Perseus, the hero who slew Medusa and saved Princess Andromeda from a monster (Ketos[2]). Perseus married Andromeda, who bore him four children. The first son, Perses, founded the Persian race. Three other sons created the circumstances that shaped Herakles' life: Two sons of Perseus, Alcaeus and Sthenelus, shared rule over Thasos, Tiryns, and Mycenae; and the third son gave rise to the Taphians, a race of pirates and slave traders from the Greek island, Taphos, off the coast of Akarnania. (See Figure 6-1.)

Although Alcaeus and Sthenelus shared rule over Thasos, Tiryns, and Mycenae, Alcaeus took primary responsibility for the Peloponnese city-states, Tiryns and Mycenae, and Sthenelus mostly ruled the distant island of Thasos. After Alcaeus died, his sons, Electryon and Amphitryon, inherited their father's responsibilities. The city-state of

---

[1] Annunciation paintings usually portray beams of light directed toward Mary. In the light, one sometimes finds a dove or even a tiny fetus floating toward the Virgin. See Chapter 13.
[2] Ancient Greeks frequently portrayed Ketos as a dragon. The monster still appears in our night sky in two forms: around the North Star as the constellation Draco (dragon) and below the zodiac as the constellation Ketos (whale).

Chapter 6 | The Salvation of Herakles   109

FIGURE 6-1. Map of Southern Greece and Peloponnese Peninsula

Tiryns crowned Electryon king; however, Electryon and Amphitryon still shared control over all three city-states with their uncle, Sthenelus.

As King of Tiryns, Electryon fathered nine heroic sons and a daughter named Alcmene (Herakles' mother). The daughter grew into such a beautiful and virtuous young woman that Electryon's brother, Amphitryon, fell in love with her. Since Alcmene reciprocated Amphitryon's love, Electryon gave her to his brother in marriage. Unfortunately, just before the wedding ceremony, Taphian pirates raided the king's herds, stealing his cattle and killing all nine of his sons. Electryon made Amphitryon promise not to consummate his marriage with Alcmene until after he had avenged the dead sons and regained the stolen cattle of Tiryns.

Electryon, Amphitryon, and Sthenelus fought a long, complicated war against the Taphians but could not defeat them. Poseidon had helped found the Taphian race through his love of a granddaughter of Perseus. Because of this love, Poseidon granted Pteralaos, King of the Taphians, a magical invincibility symbolized by a single golden hair on his head. As long as the hair grew on Pteralaos' head, Taphian pirates could resist the mightiest efforts of any army, including the combined forces of Tiryns, Mycenae, and Thasos. Because Electryon, Amphitryon, and Sthenelus could not defeat the Taphians, they could not avenge the deaths of Electryon's sons and Amphitryon could not consummate his marriage with Alcmene.

However, Electryon and Amphitryon recaptured the cattle of Tiryns, and then they argued between themselves. Agitated by the loud voices, a bull charged the two brothers. Amphitryon swung his club. Bouncing off the bull, the club accidentally struck and killed Electryon. Without intending to harm anyone, Amphitryon stained his soul with one of the worst of all sins—the murder of his own brother!

In the eyes of gods and men, Amphitryon's guilt demanded his expulsion from Tiryns. He renounced all claims to kingship, and the people of Tiryns crowned Sthenelus their king. The king then sent Amphitryon and his family into exile, including Alcmene and her younger half-brother, Licymnius.

King Creon of Thebes (the city founded by Cadmus) accepted the exiled family. Creon sympathized with Amphitryon because Thebes also had suffered a series of scandals that rocked the Theban royal family. For example, Creon's brother-in-law, King Oedipus, recently had blinded himself because he couldn't stand the guilt of accidentally killing his father and marrying his mother. Also, King Creon had to order the execution of Antigone, the daughter by Oedipus' incestuous union, for publicly flouting Creon's order not to bury the dead body of her traitor brother. For the comparatively minor infraction of accidentally killing a brother, King Creon conducted purification ceremonies to free Amphitryon from the spiritual pollution of his brother's death. Further, Creon allowed the exiles to live near Thebes' Electra gate, and he gave Amphitryon an army so he could continue prosecuting war against the Taphians to avenge Electryon's dead sons.

Through all these changes, Alcmene remained true to her father's wishes and the memory of her dead brothers; she continued to refuse sex with her husband. Amphitryon fought the Taphians for a long time. Eventually, Comaetho, a Taphian princess, fell in love with Amphitryon and betrayed her father by cutting the single golden hair from his head. Deprived of their invincibility, the Taphians lost the war against Amphitryon and his Theban army. Amphitryon killed as many Taphians as honor and vengeance required, and then he marched his army quickly homeward toward Thebes. At last, having fulfilled his promise, he eagerly looked forward to consummating his marriage with Alcmene.

But during Amphitryon's absence, Zeus had coveted Alcmene. Zeus changed form to look exactly like Amphitryon, and then entered Thebes in advance of the victorious army. To prove to Alcmene that the army had avenged Alcmene's brothers, Zeus gave her a golden cup from the Taphian royal house. Together, Zeus and Alcmene drank from the cup, went to bed, and conceived Herakles.

When Amphitryon returned, he also slept with Alcmene, but consummation quickly turned to dismay and confusion. Amphitryon expressed outrage that someone else already had taken Alcmene's virginity. Alcmene, on the other hand—shocked at her husband's accusations—pointed to the golden cup and defended her virtue with quiet dignity. Only Tiresias, the blind seer of the House of Thebes, could explain that a god had visited Alcmene in the form of her husband. Tiresias finally convinced Amphitryon not to blame his wife because no mortal woman could have prevented a god from taking her virginity.

But Hera blamed Alcmene. Always jealous of Zeus' affairs with other women, Hera could not punish Zeus. However, with careful planning, she could punish Alcmene.

The circumstances of Herakles' conception connect him with important ancient literature[3] about morality and justice. Ancient Greeks understood sin in terms of spiritual pollution. Though Amphitryon never intended to harm his brother, causing the accidental death brought as much spiritual pollution as intentional murder. Because an impure soul could not find peace after death, Amphitryon immediately sought purification from any king or priest who would accommodate the request.

Just as myths about Herakles weave like a connecting thread throughout Greek mythology, his myths also connect Greek mythology to the *Bible*. For example, the story about the Taphian pirates

---

[3]For example, the playwrights Aeschylus, Euripides, and Sophocles wrote moral tragedies about the royal house of Thebes that sheltered Herakles' mortal parents, Amphitryon and Alcmene.

connects to the biblical story about Samson and Delilah. Like the King of the Taphians, Samson possessed divine strength symbolized by his hair. As the Taphian princess, Comaetho, weakened her father by cutting his hair, Delilah similarly weakened Samson. Connections like this between Greek mythology and biblical stories predisposed ancient Greeks favorably toward the first Greek translations of the *Bible*.

HERAKLES' BIRTH AND INFANCY

Nine months after conceiving Herakles, Alcmene went into labor. Zeus bragged to Hera that his next descendent would rule all the lands around him. Hera made Zeus swear to the truth of this statement. Then she sent her daughter, Eileithyia, Goddess of Childbirth, to sit outside the door of Alcmene's birthing room. There, Eileithyia prevented Herakles' birth by sitting with her legs crossed and interlacing her fingers.

Meanwhile, Hera advanced the pregnancy of the wife of Sthenelus, a grandson of Zeus by Danae. Hera ensured a quick and easy birth for Sthenelus' child, Eurystheus, while Alcmene suffered seven days in labor. Eileithyia intended not just to delay Alcmene's labor, but to kill both mother and child.

Eileithyia would have succeeded in killing Alcmene if one of her midwives hadn't saved her. While Alcmene suffered in grim silence, the midwife emerged from Alcmene's room and thanked Eileithyia for finally allowing delivery. Surprised at the news, Eileithyia uncrossed her legs and fingers and ran to see what had happened. This action let Alcmene deliver twins: Herakles (the semi-divine son of Zeus) and Iphicles (the mortal son of Amphitryon). Hera punished the tricky midwife by changing her into a weasel.

Alcmene gave her grandfather's name, Alcaeus, to baby Herakles. Young Alcaeus wouldn't acquire the name *Herakles* until he went to Delphi years later. Until then, both Alcmene and young Alcaeus had to beware of Hera.

Once, Hera sent two enormous snakes to kill baby Alcaeus. As Iphicles gurgled and played like a normal child, Alcaeus fought the snakes and killed them both. On the coin in Figure 6-2, the obverse depicts a

Chapter 6 | The Salvation of Herakles   113

FIGURE 6-2. Alcaeus (Baby Herakles) Strangling Snakes Sent by Hera. Boeotitia, Thebes, AR Stater, ca. 425–395 B.C.

Boeotian shield, while the reverse portrays Herakles as an infant fighting Hera's snakes. Observing the encounter, Amphitryon understood that he had fathered Iphicles, but a god had fathered Alcaeus.

Fearing Hera's anger, Alcmene once abandoned baby Alcaeus in the woods, but a goddess protected him. A friend of Herakles throughout his life, the goddess Athena rescued the baby and obtained a small measure of revenge against Hera. Athena tricked Hera into nursing Alcaeus by taking advantage of her well-developed maternal instincts. But baby Alcaeus bit much too hard and Hera recognized him. Angrily, she cast the baby away, milk spurting from her breast. The little milk that Alcaeus drank helped make him stronger and more divine. The spilled milk flowed across the heavens and remains visible today as the Milky Way.

In the pre-Christian Western world, the symbol of a goddess nursing a young god or a mortal became an important symbol of salvation. For example, worshippers of the goddess Isis sometimes portrayed salvation with the image of the goddess nursing the young savior Harpokrates. Other times, worshippers portrayed her nursing an old man, mercifully bestowing eternal life with her milk.[4]

---

[4]Nursing images entered Christian iconography when early Christians preserved symbols associated with the worship of Isis and incorporated them into the Cult of Mary. See Chapter 25.

HERAKLES AS A YOUNG MAN

As young Alcaeus matured, he grew skillful and strong. The greatest teachers of the age flocked to Thebes to teach him: Autolycus, son of Hermes and father of Odysseus, taught wrestling; Castor, one of the Gemini twins, taught armored warfare; King Eurytus of Oechalia taught archery; Cheiron, the centaur, taught hunting; and Amphitryon, Alcaeus' father, taught chariot racing. Alcaeus excelled in all his studies except music.

Alcaeus didn't like music and especially didn't like learning to play the lyre. Music accentuated Alcaeus' greatest weaknesses: impulsiveness and a certain lack of sensitivity. When Linus, a muse's son, struck Alcaeus for not paying attention in music class, Alcaeus struck Linus on the head with a lyre. Shocked that Linus died from the blow, Alcaeus grieved deeply. As would happen repeatedly in his life, Alcaeus suffered so much remorse that others forgave him. People saw that Alcaeus was a good young man. Technically, he had acted only in self-defense—the problem was that he was so strong!

So Amphitryon sent young Alcaeus to herd sheep in Thespiae until passions cooled down in Thebes. Amphitryon reasoned that Alcaeus would find it more difficult to get into trouble in the country surrounded by sheep than in the city where people accidentally might make him angry. In Thespiae, he guarded the flocks of King Thespius at the foot of Mount Cithaeron. There, Alcaeus encountered a lion that came to feast on the king's sheep.

With his bare hands, Alcaeus fought and killed the Cithaerian lion. Perhaps representing this event, the reverse of the coin in Figure 6-3 shows semi-divine (naked) Herakles as a young man battling a lion. The obverse of the coin portrays a bust of Apollo. King Thespius was so impressed with the young man's strength, skill, and beauty that the king ordered entertainment for Alcaeus for fifty nights. Coincidently, the king had fifty daughters. Each night the king introduced Alcaeus to a new daughter. One daughter refused Alcaeus, but all the other daughters became pregnant. Two daughters bore twins. In less than a year, Alcaeus fathered fifty-one children.

FIGURE 6-3. Alcaeus (Young Herakles) Strangling a Lion. Paeonia, AR Tetradrachm, 359–335 B.C.

Alcaeus returned to Thebes to discover that King Erginus of Minyan Orchomenus had conquered and disarmed the Theban army. Further, the king had demanded that Thebes pay a tribute of one hundred head of cattle. Learning that emissaries from Minyan Orchomenus soon would come to collect the cattle, Alcaeus quickly organized young Theban males and armed them with old weapons stored in the city's temples. When the emissaries of King Erginus arrived, Alcaeus led his youthful army in battle against them. After defeating the emissaries, Alcaeus cut off their noses, ears, and hands. He hung the severed body parts around the emissaries' necks, and sent them home with a different tribute for King Erginus.

This portion of Herakles' life shows that, for ancient Greeks, spiritual pollution did not always result from causing a person's death. Though he had killed Linus, Alcaeus did not acquire spiritual pollution because Linus had struck Alcaeus first. However, Amphitryon had to send Alcaeus away because friends of Linus might seek revenge. A man's friends could kill for revenge without incurring moral pollution. Of course, when Alcaeus returned, everyone thought highly of him after he fought the emissaries from Minyan Orchomenus, killing some and mutilating others, saving Thebes from having to pay tribute.

HERA'S REVENGE: PAIN AND POLLUTION

King Erginus launched another war against Thebes, but Alcaeus defeated the invaders. This time, Creon of Thebes demanded and received a tribute of 200 head of cattle from King Erginus. King Creon awarded highest honors to Alcaeus, including marriage to Princess Megara. Alcaeus and Megara enjoyed a wonderful period of wealth, happiness, and honor and soon produced three beautiful sons. Hera chose this moment for terrible revenge, bringing ruin to Alcaeus' life.

Alcaeus always had shown a tendency to fly into uncontrolled rage with little provocation. Catching Alcaeus at a weak moment (while he was drunk), Hera drove Alcaeus into a mad rage. He killed his three sons and his wife before anyone could stop him. He also attacked his father, and would have killed him, except Athena knocked Alcaeus unconscious with a rock. For centuries thereafter, the citizens of Thebes venerated the rock as a sacred relic. They called it the Sober Stone.

When Alcaeus returned to his senses, no human being could have suffered greater remorse. Neither King Creon, nor any of the Thebans, could stand to punish Alcaeus because no punishment could hurt him more than he already had hurt himself. Tormented by guilt, Alcaeus exiled himself from Thebes.

His friend, Theseus, convinced Alcaeus not to kill himself, arguing that only cowards committed suicide. Theseus took Alcaeus to Athens to seek guidance from the priests of Athena, but they could not help. Abandoning Athens, he then traveled to Delphi to ask the Oracle how a wretch such as he could wash away the stain of murdering his family. If any man ever needed salvation, Alcaeus did.

Contrary to her reputation for providing confusing answers, the Oracle at Delphi spoke clearly to Alcaeus; she told him to change his name to Herakles (Glory to Hera), to deliver himself to King Eurystheus (Sthenelus' son who had inherited kingship over Thasos, Tiryns, and Mycenae), and to perform ten labors of the king's choosing. Without delay, Alcaeus adopted the name Herakles and presented himself to King Eurystheus. Herakles took the only option available to him to cleanse his soul from an unbearable burden of spiritual pollution.

THE LABORS OF HERAKLES

No man ever performed mightier deeds than Herakles. King Eurystheus tasked his cousin with a series of labors that took him to the edges of the world—even to Hades and back. Yet Herakles successfully performed every labor no matter how impossible it seemed. He even performed two extra labors because Eurystheus found reasons not to count two. Figure 6-4 displays images from ancient coins related to Herakles' twelve labors.

In brief, the twelve labors are as follows:

1. *Strangling the Nemean Lion*: Impenetrable skin rendered the giant lion invulnerable to weapons, but Herakles used one of the lion's own claws to skin it and afterward used the skin as armor.
2. *Killing the Echidna/Lernian Hydra*: Every time Herakles struck off one of the hydra's heads, two new ones grew back. Iolaus, the son of Herakles' twin half-brother (Iphicles) helped by scorching the bloody stump each time Herakles knocked off a head. Because Iolaus helped, Eurystheus chose not to count this labor. Herakles saved blood from the hydra to poison his arrows. Eventually, the poison would bring about Herakles' own death.
3. *Capturing the Keryneian Doe*: Herakles captured this impossibly elusive doe by wounding it on the hoof. Then he had to explain to the goddess Artemis what he was doing with her sacred animal.
4. *Capturing the Erymanthian Boar*: Herakles carried this enormous animal alive back to Eurystheus. Terrified, Eurystheus hid in a pot. After this labor, Herakles briefly joined Jason and the Argonauts.[5]
5. *Cleaning the Augean Stables*: Herakles asked King Augeas of Elis to pay for this labor if the hero could complete it in a single day. Augeas agreed because he thought the task impossible to finish so quickly. Herakles diverted a nearby river that cleaned the stables

---

[5] In a series of adventures reminiscent of the *Odyssey*, Jason, a grandson of Aeolus, recruited the greatest heroes of Greece's Heroic age in a quest to obtain the Golden Fleece. Because they sailed on a ship named Argo, mythology refers to the heroes collectively as Argonauts. The Argonauts included the Gemini twins, Asclepius, Orpheus, and many other demigods and heroes.

FIGURE 6-4. Representations of the Labors of Herakles on Ancient Coins

in less than a day, but the king refused to pay. Further, Eurystheus refused to count this labor because he required that Herakles neither request nor receive payment for any labor. Because of this labor, Herakles eventually founded the Olympic Games in honor of his father, Zeus.

6. *Chasing Away the Stymphalian Birds*: The dung from these birds poisoned the land, and they could kill men with their brass claws and iron feathers. Athena helped Herakles evict the birds from Stymphalos by giving him a magic noisemaker crafted by Hephaistos, the lame God of Metalworking.

7. *Capturing the Cretan Bull*: King Minos no longer wanted this bull after his wife gave birth to the Minotaur. Herakles captured the bull, took it to King Eurystheus, and later released it. After that, the bull ravaged the land of Marathon until Theseus killed it.

8. *Capturing the Man-Eating Mares of Diomedes*: King Diomedes of Thrace fed these dangerous mares with human flesh. During this labor, Herakles wrestled Death and won, ensuring that a friend's wife remained alive.

9. Obtaining the Girdle of Hippolyte, the Amazon Queen: Events in this complex adventure motivated Herakles to conduct a personal

war against Troy. Afterward, King Priam rebuilt Troy and fortified the city with great walls, which set the stage for the Trojan War.

10. *Capturing the Red Cattle of Geryon*: This adventure competes favorably with the most surreal stories of modern fiction. Herakles built the Pillars of Herakles at the entrance of the Mediterranean Sea. He sailed in the giant Cup of Helios and founded the Celtic race in an affair with Celtine, daughter of Bretannus. Herakles also killed the remaining two Gorgons, completing the job begun by his great-grandfather, Perseus.

11. *Fetching Golden Apples from the Tree of Life in the Garden of the Hesperides*:[6] In this adventure, Herakles killed a giant serpent named Ladon who guarded the tree. He also killed the Caucasian Eagle that fed on Prometheus' liver, and he briefly took Atlas' place carrying the whole universe (not the world!) on his shoulders. Passing the universe back and forth inadvertently sloshed the oceans of the Earth, which saved the Argonauts from death by dehydration. After Herakles showed the apples to Eurystheus, Athena restored them to the Garden of the Hesperides.

12. *Fetching Kerberos, Hades' Three-Headed Dog Who Guarded the Entrance to the Underworld*: Eumolpus, the first priest of Demeter at Eleusis, initiated Herakles in the Eleusinian Mysteries so he could enter the realm of Hades and return safely. Herakles spoke with gods and dead souls, saved Theseus from the Chair of Forgetfulness, and (with Hades' permission) carried three-headed, snake-tailed Kerberos back to Eurystheus. Upon the completion of the twelfth labor, Eurystheus issued his last request to Herakles: return of the dreadful beast to Hades!

By completing the world's first and most extreme twelve-step program, Herakles cleansed his soul of spiritual pollution from the murder of his family. For thousands of years, pagans and Christians have found

---

[6]Early Christians associated the Garden of the Hesperides with the Garden of Eden. The *Bible* does not identify the "forbidden fruit" in the Garden of Eden. However, during the first few centuries after the death of Jesus, Western Christians connected classical images of Venus (nude) holding a golden apple and Herakles (nude) taking apples after killing the serpent, Ladon, with the story of Adam and Eve, which influenced popular identification of the fruit as an apple.

comfort and inspiration in these stories about Herakles. Submitting to divine will (as expressed by the Oracle of Delphi) and energetically applying himself to tasks that seemed impossible, Herakles proved that miracles come when needed and no human being lies beyond salvation.

Throughout history, students of mythology have searched the stories of Herakles for hidden wisdom. Students of astrology, magic, and alchemy have found correspondences between Herakles' twelve labors and occult teachings. For example, a work called *Hieroglyphica* (portions dating to the fifth century A.D.) in the Biblioteca Medicia, Laurenziana, in Florence, Italy, refers to Herakles in magical symbolic terms. Also, astrologers always have speculated on the correspondences between the twelve labors and the twelve signs of the zodiac.[7]

MORE POLLUTION, AND EVEN SACRILEGE

Unfortunately, after working so hard to purify his soul, Herakles also proved that even the strongest man has weaknesses that repeatedly can lead him astray. After completing the labors, he couldn't stop having adventures and taking new wives. From time to time, he also continued to lose control of himself and commit violent acts in blind rage.

Once, when the great archer, King Eurytus of Oechalia, offered his daughter, Iole, as first prize in an archery contest, Herakles entered the contest and won easily. Fearing that Herakles might accidentally kill his daughter, Eurytus refused Herakles his prize and even accused him of stealing some cattle. Seething with anger, Herakles left the kingdom of Oechalia with nothing to show for his efforts but dishonor.

Eurytus' son, Iphitus, disagreed with his father's actions. Iphitus believed that Herakles deserved Iole's hand in marriage because he had acted honorably and won the contest fairly. Eurytus banished his son for expressing this opinion too strongly. Iphitus then approached Herakles to discuss the possibility of raising an army and conquering the kingdom of Oechalia. Before discussing anything, Herakles flew

---

[7]For a relatively modern example of astrological commentary derived from the mythology of Herakles, see *The Labours of Hercules: An Astrological Interpretation* by Alice A. Bailey.

into a rage at the sight of Iphitus and murdered him. Again, Herakles acquired a burden of guilt by murdering an innocent man.

After the murder, the Kings of Pylus and Sparta refused to purify Herakles, earning his bitter enmity forever. Then a terrible disease struck Herakles. He traveled to Delphi, to learn of a cure, but this time the Oracle of Delphi refused to answer his questions. Because the Oracle had failed him, Herakles seized the Tripod of Apollo and marched away to set up his own oracle.

Apollo rushed to earth to preserve the sanctity of his temple. The god would have fought Herakles, but Zeus separated the two with the blast of a thunderbolt. Herakles explained that he just wanted to learn how he could recover from his illness and purify himself again. Obtaining permission from Apollo to speak, the Oracle instructed Herakles to sell himself into slavery for three years and to give the money he obtained to King Eurytus as payment for Iphitus' life.

Herakles sold himself to the highest bidder, Omphale, Queen of Lydia, who subjected him to three years of shameful service. Omphale dressed in Herakles' lion skin and carried his club, and she made Herakles dress like a woman. For three years, Herakles worked in women's clothes doing women's work like spinning, weaving, and needlepoint. At the end of three years, Omphale freed Herakles and married him. She even bore Herakles a son.

In ancient times, temporarily assuming attributes associated with the opposite gender was a symbolic path toward finding wisdom. When the Theban seer, Tiresias,[8] encountered two copulating snakes, he changed into a woman when he killed the female snake with his staff. He remained a woman for seven years until he killed the male snake with the same staff. With the staff and snakes, he made the caduceus, a magical device with transformative power, and gave it to Hermes. Changing genders gave Tiresias powers of prophecy, clairvoyance, and wisdom. Though Herakles only adopted women's clothing for a few years, his marriage to Omphale indicates that he at least obtained a measure of tolerance from the experience.

---

[8]Tiresias was one of the most famous seers of the ancient Greek world. He appears in surviving tragic plays about the royal house of Thebes, for example, *Oedipus the King* and *Antigone* by Sophocles and *The Bacchae* by Euripides.

THE MATURE HERO

Herakles fought a war against Troy, inadvertently initiating events that led to the future Trojan War. Then Hera shipwrecked him on Cos. Because the inhabitants of Cos attacked Herakles, he killed their king. However, a hero of Cos succeeded in severely wounding Herakles. Because of this, Zeus punished Hera for harassing Herakles. (Perhaps Zeus also cast Hephaistos out of heaven at this time for attempting to defend Hera.)

Zeus knew that he needed Herakles. The Oracle at Delphi had prophesied that the Olympian Gods would not win the war against the hundred giants without help from the most powerful of all mortals. Herakles recuperated from his wounds just in time to join the Olympian Gods in battle. He even helped Zeus kill a giant that attempted to rape Hera.

After helping Zeus win the war against the giants, Herakles spent his later years fighting more wars, settling old grudges, making new friends and enemies, and establishing the ruling houses of city-states that would participate in the Trojan War. He generally avoided acquiring further spiritual pollution (at least in ancient Greek terms), and Hera stopped harassing him. After defeating King Augeas of Elis (settling an old score with the king who had refused to pay for cleaning his stables), Herakles founded the Olympic Games in honor of his father, Zeus. Perhaps referring to the Olympic Games, the obverse of the coin in Figure 6-5 portrays two wrestlers competing. The reverse of the coin shows Herakles ready for battle: naked, brandishing a club, and shielding himself with his impenetrable lion skin.

The mature Herakles continued having problems with impulse control. Once, he promised to protect a new ally, King Cepheus of Tegea. The very next day, Herakles ravished the king's daughter instead of protecting the king in battle.

In one of his later adventures, Herakles won the hand of Deinara (daughter of King Oeneas of Calydon) by defeating Achelous, the river god.[9] Deinara loved Herakles and bore him three children. Herakles

---

[9]See Chapter 3 for a description of Herakles' fight with Achelous.

FIGURE 6-5. Numismatic Reference to the Founding of the Olympic Games by Herakles. Pisidia, Selge, AR Stater, ca. 300 B.C.

loved Deinara, but he still ravished other women from time to time, especially while helping Deinara's father conquer and despoil other cities. Once, when King Oeneas threw a banquet to honor Herakles, the hero accidentally killed the king's nephew who served as cupbearer. Both the king and his brother (the father of the cupbearer) forgave Herakles, but he couldn't forgive himself. He exiled himself and Deinara from Calydon.

After leaving Calydon, Herakles and Deinara eventually came to the Evenus River in Aitolia. A centaur ferryman named Nessus offered to carry Deinara to the other side. Herakles and Deinara accepted the centaur's offer with gratitude. By the time Nessus reached the far riverbank with Deinara, Herakles had swum only halfway across. Nessus then proceeded to ravish Deinara.

Herakles wounded Nessus with an arrow dipped in the most deadly of all poisons, Hydra blood. This poison proved fatal to Nessus, but not before he had ensured the death of Herakles. As the centaur lay dying, he told Deinara that she should collect and keep a vial of his blood. Then, if she ever worried about keeping the love of Herakles, she should sprinkle the blood on a garment and give it to him to wear. Nessus knew that Hydra's poison on Herakles' clothing, even diluted by blood, would kill as certainly as on the tip of an arrow.

THE DEATH OF HERAKLES

Despite the passage of time, Herakles still fumed that King Eurytus long ago had refused to award Princess Iole as first prize in the archery contest, so Herakles attacked the kingdom of Oechalia. He quickly defeated the king and seized Iole as a concubine. He then readied sacrifices to thank Zeus for victory. Wishing to cleanse himself before the sacrifices, Herakles prepared to bathe and sent a runner home to fetch fresh clothes.

Fearing that Herakles would fall in love with Iole, Deinara sprinkled Nessus' blood on the garments that she sent. Herakles emerged from his bath, dried himself, and put on the clothes. Instantly, searing pain racked his body. He tore off the clothes, but Hydra poison inevitably proved fatal. Dying an agonizing, slow death, Herakles returned home. Poor Deinara attempted to commit suicide when she learned what she'd done, but Artemis transformed the tormented woman into a guinea fowl.

Accepting his fate, Herakles built his own funeral pyre. As he stood on the pyre, he asked people around him, including many of his sons, to light the fire. Only one son responded, so Herakles gave his bow to this son. The fire grew, and then lightning struck the pyre, consuming it in an instant. Though witnesses to these events searched the ashes, nobody ever found any of Herakles' remains.

Athena took Herakles, now a god, bodily up to heaven on Mount Olympus. There, Hera and Herakles reconciled. Hera gave Herakles permission to marry Hebe, the Goddess of Youth—Hera's daughter and Herakles' half-sister. As a god who had lived the life of a severely flawed mortal, Herakles transcended mortality through faith and vigorous action. He acquired a cult following that not only survived as the world transformed from Greek to Roman, but even grew stronger.

THE GRAND UNIFIER OF GREEK MYTHOLOGY

Even though no editor ever redacted a consistent compilation of ancient Greek mythology, all Greek myths cast themselves relative to events in Herakles' life. King Oedipus ruled Thebes before the birth of Herakles, and the Trojan War happened after his death. While alive, Herakles traveled the known world, killed monsters, and met every other hero of his age. He begat hundreds of children who became heroes and founded city-states, and he influenced how Greek tribes related to each other long after his death.

From a religious point of view, Herakles exemplified the moral issues of a simpler, more brutal age. Even so, Eumolpus, the first priest of Eleusis, initiated Herakles in one of the world's first and most sophisticated mystery cults. Powerful enough to speak directly with gods, Herakles asked for divine help when he needed it and even bargained with divine decrees. Yet, the ancient Greek everyman could see himself in Herakles and aspire to the hero's wisdom and virtues. By becoming a god, Herakles became the divine advocate of humanity, a god who could explain the mortal point of view even to Zeus.

By the time that Greek versions of Jewish scripture first appeared in Egypt in the third century B.C., nobody remembered the sources of mythological stories. Many Greek myths and biblical stories seemed to correspond with each other, and Greek scholars could debate with Jewish scholars about which stories came first. Regardless, the similarities between Greek myths and biblical stories encouraged Greek respect for Jewish scriptures.

Even after Christianity established itself as the dominant religion of the West, Christians continued to view Herakles as an important symbol of salvation. Further, Herakles established a tradition of religious devotion that continues in the world today: Herakles founded the Olympic Games as a means of worshipping his father, Zeus. Though we celebrate the games differently than Greeks did thousands of years ago, one can still view modern athletes participating in the games as acts of devotion.

CHAPTER
7

ANCIENT GREEK RELIGIOUS THEMES THAT HELPED SHAPE HISTORY

Christianity inherited a pre-Christian reverence for athletics, historical traditions, fossils, meteorites, omens, and Eastern ideas.

As we study the past, we recognize the purposes of even unfamiliar religious practices because the uses of spiritual practices and belief always have remained the same: Religion gives us confidence as we faithfully prepare for challenges in our lives; it imbues our ethics with meaning; it connects us to our ancestors; and it helps us accept the mortality of ourselves and our loved ones. Although Western religion has evolved considerably since the life of Jesus, our unchanging human needs always have determined the uses of religious beliefs.

Just as the uses of religion have stayed the same, certain structural elements of religious belief—themes—survived the transition from ancient to modern times. We often focus on the differences between old and new themes rather than their similarities. For example, we no longer believe in Asclepius, mythological heroes, and magic; instead we believe in spiritual healing, saints, and miracles. Similarly, modern Christians might easily discount the salvation-related mysteries of ancient times as pagan superstition, yet still believe in heaven, hell, and the imminence of the Rapture.[1]

Exploring ancient religious themes can help us recognize the persistence of ancient practices in modern times almost like echoes of our ancestors' lives. However, because themes have changed their appearance, we don't always recognize them easily: Because we no longer explicitly recognize athletics as an element of religious practice, we no longer notice the connection between athletics and religion that persists in modern times; because we no longer believe in Greek mythology, we fail to notice religious meaning in our continuing use of mythological references; because we don't remember pagan religious practices, we fail to connect our modern veneration of Christian relics with ancient veneration of artifacts associated with Greek myths; and because Western technology now gives us easy access to ideas, histories, and cultures in the modern world, we fail to notice how the roots of Western religion developed and matured in the East and then migrated slowly to the West, producing an evolving Western religious tradition that didn't resemble its current form until long after the life of Jesus.

ATHLETIC GAMES

In ancient times, Greek city-states honored Olympian Gods, especially Zeus, Apollo, and Poseidon, with athletic games. Because athletic competitions had not yet separated from religious festivals, Greeks participated in athletic games as acts of religious devotion. Collectively known as the Panhellenic Games, a sequence of the six most important ancient athletic games occurred every four years in a cycle known as an *Olympiad*: one near Olympia (the Olympic Games) honoring Zeus, one at Pythia honoring Apollo, two at Nemea honoring Zeus, and two at Isthmia honoring Poseidon. Ancient Greeks considered all Panhellenic Games sacred, comparable to the Eleusinian Mysteries.

---

[1]Many modern Christians use the word Rapture to describe events related to the End of Days. During Rapture, Christians who believe appropriately will levitate physically toward heaven, leaving everyone else on Earth to suffer judgment.

The games provided opportunities for top athletes to compete and for the best athletes to achieve fame throughout the Greek world. Only free, male Greeks unstained by certain crimes participated in the games. However, qualifying Greeks from anywhere in the ancient Greek world could come to the games and participate. Reflecting the Greeks' association of nudity with divinity, athletes competed nude in all events of the Panhellenic Games except in chariot races and the special footrace for contestants wearing armor. As a practical matter, the rules of competition allowed athletes to wear a *kynodesme*, a strap that restrained the penis.

The Olympic Games

The history of the Olympic Games, the first and most sacred of all the Panhellenic Games, goes back at least to the eighth century B.C. According to the ancient system of dates (counting Olympiads), Herakles founded the Olympic Games in 776 B.C. The Olympic Games continued until a Christian emperor (Theodosius I) outlawed them in 393 A.D.

The first Olympic Games included only religious rituals and a single race, the *stadion*. In this race athletes ran a distance that measured 600 times the length of Herakles' feet. By the third century B.C., however, the games expanded to include up to twenty events—for example, footraces for longer distances, a footrace wearing armor, wrestling, boxing, the *pankration*, and the *pentathlon*. The pankration event mixed wrestling, boxing, and other fighting techniques with rules prohibiting only biting and gouging. The pentathlon competition comprised five separate events: stadion, wrestling, javelin throw, long jump, and discus throw.

The coins in Figure 7-1 show nude athletes participating in the three events related only to the pentathlon: The obverse of the top left coin (from Akragas, Sicily) carries a bust of Apollo, while the reverse displays a javelin-thrower; the obverse of the top right coin carries a bust of the Roman emperor, Phillip II, while the reverse displays a long-jumper marking his distance; and the obverse of the lower coin portrays a discus-thrower and a tripod, while the reverse displays a

FIGURE 7-1. Coins Portraying Nude Pentathletes: Javelin-Thrower (Top Left), Long-Jumper (Top Right), and Discus-Thrower (Bottom). Sicily, Akragas, AE 23, ca. 279–200 B.C.; Thrace, Bizya, Philip II, AE Assarion, ca. 244–247 A.D.; and Cos, AR Triple Siglos, ca. 480–475 B.C.

crab. On the lower coin, the tripod emphasizes the religious nature of the games: Greeks lit fires on top of tripods and sprinkled religious offerings in the flames. The crab represents the city-state of Cos.

Except for a priestess of Demeter, and possibly young girls, sacred law forbade women from watching Olympic events. If a woman dared to watch, the community condemned her for sacrilege and threw her from the top of the Typaion Cliff. Despite the prohibition against viewing men's games, young women competed in their own ritual games in honor of Hera. Also, despite the ancient emphasis on games for men, one mythological tradition says that men's and women's games at Olympia originated together, primarily because of a woman.

The Mythological Basis of The Olympic Games

The story of Briseis, the woman who inspired the first games[2] at Olympia in honor of Hera and Zeus, comes from the Trojan War, one of the greatest events in Greek religious history. Olympian gods and their

---
[2] This section describes a popular mythological tradition inconsistent with myths about Herakles founding the Olympic Games.

FIGURE 7-2. Achilles, and His Mother, Thetis. Thessaly, Larisa Kremaste, AE 19, ca. 300–270 B.C.

heroic children fought on both sides of this conflict. Achilles, the greatest of all Greek heroes, sacked Lyrnessus (a Cilician town near Troy) and killed Briseis' husband and brothers. Seizing Briseis as a prize of war, Achilles made her his concubine.

Even though Achilles murdered her family, Briseis regarded him as a gentle and honorable protector. Later, when Agamemnon (the commander of the Greek forces fighting Troy) seized Briseis as his own concubine, Achilles stopped fighting for the Greeks. The bitter disagreement between Agamemnon and Achilles over Briseis provides much of the dramatic tension in the *Iliad*. Troy's fate is sealed only after Agamemnon returned Briseis to Achilles. Achilles' mother, a sea-nymph named Thetis, brought new armor (divinely crafted by Hephaistos) to her son, who then reentered the war. The obverse of the coin in Figure 7-2 displays the face of Achilles, and the reverse portrays Thetis carrying the new armor as she rides on a sea-going hippocamp.

Achilles died helping ensure the defeat of Troy, but Briseis (under her real name of Hippodameia) survived the war and then married King Pelops.[3] According to this mythological tradition, King Pelops

---

[3] As an example of the contradictory genealogies that run throughout Greek mythology, Herakles, a great-grandson of King Pelops, must have lived after the Trojan War, yet Herakles' children founded the royal houses of the Greek city-states that fought against Troy.

organized the first Olympic Games as funeral games for Hippodameia's father. Hippodameia established the Heraean Games at the same time as a way of thanking Hera for marriage to Pelops.

For the first Heraean Games, Hippodameia selected a committee of sixteen women to organize rituals and footraces for young girls in honor of Hera. By the sixth century B.C., Elis[4] and the nearby city of Pisa regularly established committees of sixteen noble women to organize Heraean Games in the Olympic Stadium at the ritual center known as Olympia. At the Games, young female competitors dressed in small tunics that hung from a strap on their left shoulder. The tunic exposed an athlete's right breast and formed a short skirt that ended just above the athlete's knees. Custom and law prevented adult men from viewing the Heraean Games, but young boys watched the competition keenly.

The tradition of athletic games begun by ancient Greeks has contributed much to Western culture. Some of the earliest standard measures of time and distance came from athletic games. Greeks measured the passing of years by Olympiads and long distances by stadii.[5] We still remember the names of some of the greatest ancient athletes.[6] In addition, many important historical events, both ancient and modern, have occurred in the context of athletic games. For example, ancient Rome recognized Julius Caesar as a god when a comet appeared at his funeral games,[7] and, in modern times, the world remembers Jesse Owens' victories in the Berlin Summer Olympics of 1936 as a symbolic victory of American racial diversity over Nazi Aryanism.[8]

AN INFLUENTIAL RELIC FROM THE TROJAN WAR

Myths often connected widely separated locations in the ancient world and influenced history in peculiar, far-reaching ways. The reverse of

---

[4]Elis was the capital of the Peloponnesian city-state also known as Elis.
[5]In ancient times, one stadion measured a distance between 177 and 200 meters.
[6]A cook named Coroebus of Elis won the first stadion race in the first Olympics.
[7]See Chapter 20.
[8]Adolf Hitler used pseudo-science to assert the existence and inherent superiority of a tall, white-skinned, blond-haired, blue-eyed race of Aryan ancestors of Germans.

Chapter 7 | Ancient Greek Religious Themes   133

FIGURE 7-3. Coin Showing Three Generations of Trojan Royalty on Its Reverse: Anchises, Aeneas, and Askanios. Mysia, Parium. Emperor Gallienus, AE 27, ca. 253–268. A.D.

the Roman coin in Figure 7-3 portrays an event that connects the founding of ancient Rome with myths about the Trojan War: Prince Aeneas flees Troy carrying his aged father, Anchises, and holding the hand of his young son, Askanios. In his lap, Anchises clutches a special shrine that contains the Palladium, a statue of Pallas Athena that Vestal Virgins preserved in their temple in the Roman Forum as a sacred relic of the Trojan War.

Aeneas and his family boarded ships with other fleeing Trojans; abandoned their defeated homeland; and encountered numerous adventures all across the ancient Mediterranean. In his book, the *Aeneid*, Virgil[9] describes how Aeneas almost married Queen Dido (formerly Princess Elissa of Tyre), the first Phoenician ruler of Carthage. Later, when Anchises died on Sicily, Aeneas founded the important Temple of Aphrodite near his father's grave in the Elymian[10] city, Eryx. Aeneas then led the Trojan refugees to Italy, where they founded communities and noble families that eventually gave rise to Rome.

---

[9]Virgil is generally recognized as the greatest Roman poet. Toward the end of the first century B.C., his poetry about Roman origins generated public pride at the beginning of the Roman Empire, just as Henry Wadsworth Longfellow's poetry in the nineteen century A.D. generated public pride in the origins of the United States.
[10]See Chapter 4 for information about the Elymians.

As Rome evolved from a Republic to an Empire (from the third century B.C. to the first century B.C.), Romans always granted special privileges to the places connected to Rome's mythological ancestry. They honored the Temple of Aphrodite in Eryx, referring to it as the Temple of Venus Erice. The people of Eryx remained free, even after the Romans reduced most of the rest of Sicily to slavery. In Asia Minor, the citizens of Troas (ancient Troy) enjoyed privileges and tax-free status that neighboring cities could only envy. Rome's mythological connection with ancient Troy also eased the adoption of the first foreign cult by Rome, the cult of the Eastern mother-goddess Cybele.[11]

A LIVING TRADITION FROM THE TROJAN WAR

The coin in Figure 7-4 provides an opportunity to explore an example of the importance and persistence of living traditions related to ancient mythology. On the coin's obverse, a bust of Persephone, Queen of the Underworld, affirms the salvation available to all initiated Greeks after death. The coin's reverse displays Ajax of Locris, nude and semi-divine. The city-state of Locris[12] minted this coin in the fourth century B.C., not just to remember Ajax, a famous Locrian hero who fought in the Trojan War, but also to honor a religious obligation that Locrians fulfilled on Ajax's behalf for centuries.

Ajax, Prince of Locris, fought on the Greek side of the Trojan War as one of Greece's greatest warriors. Nevertheless, when Troy fell, he committed an act of sacrilege. Rampaging with other Greek soldiers through the dying city, Ajax chased Kassandra, the prophetess who had foretold the defeat of Troy. When Kassandra ran into the Temple of Athena for refuge, Ajax violated the sanctity of the temple; he seized Kassandra and raped her. For this sacrilege, Ajax and his ship never reached home. Athena wrecked his ship and killed Ajax with lightning.

Locrian religious tradition honored this story as sacred truth. Every year, the citizens of Locris sent two young virgins to serve in the

---

[11]See Chapter 12.
[12]Locris was a city-state of central Greece, just west of the island of Euboea.

FIGURE 7-4. Persephone, and Locrian Ajax. Locris, Opuntia, AR Stater, 356–338 B.C.

Temple of Athena at Troy to atone for the sin of Ajax. Locris paid this religious debt every year for centuries—perhaps for a thousand years.[13]

FOSSILS AS RELIGIOUS RELICS

In the ancient world, relics and traditions proved the truth of mythological stories and affirmed the validity of Greek religious beliefs. Greek pilgrims traveled great distances to view relics in temples and sanctuaries, and even to visit topography associated with the mythological past. In certain mountains, fossil seashells proved the truth of myths about great floods. On the island of Samos, a red patch of flat ground full of giant mammal bones[14] was identified as the "Field of Blood," the place where the god Dionysos led an army mounted on war elephants in a bloody battle against giant Amazons.[15] In modern times, the deposits of Miocene[16] fossils on Samos are famous. Numerous examples of

---

[13]See *Ancient Greek Cults: A Guide* p. 51 by Jennifer Lynn Larson.
[14]Regarding the Field of Blood, see Greek Question 56 in *Roman and Greek Questions* by Plutarch. For a thorough review of ancient uses of fossils, see *The First Fossil Hunters* by Adrienne Mayor.
[15]The Amazons were a warlike tribe of giant warrior women during Greek mythology's Heroic Age.
[16]The Miocene geological epoch extended from 5 million to 23 million years ago.

giant mammal fossils from fossil beds on Samos appear in natural history galleries in museums across Europe and the United States.

Throughout ancient Greek society, artifacts in numerous temples proved the validity of mythological history and religious traditions. In the Iliad, Homer repeatedly compares heroes who fought in the Trojan War to the men of his time. Ancient heroes stood much taller than ordinary men and threw rocks that even the strongest men of Homer's time couldn't lift. Because certain prehistoric mammal bones often look a lot like human bones, only much larger, ancient Greeks identified fossils as the remains of both monsters and heroes. Homer believed in the existence of giant heroes because he had examined giant bones preserved in temples and venerated as sacred relics.

In 560 B.C., the Oracle of Delphi told Spartan clients that they would not defeat the city-state of Tegea (a regional rival) unless Sparta recovered the bones of Orestes. Herodotus[17] describes how Spartans found the bones of Orestes, a hero over ten feet tall, and returned them to Sparta. Based on Herodotus' account, a modern classical scholar[18] has speculated that Orestes' bones consisted of large mammal bones from Pleistocene[19] deposits near Olympia. After obtaining the fossil bones, Sparta defeated Tegea and set events in motion that ultimately led to the Peloponnesian War.[20]

The portrayal of the monster, Ketos, on the obverse of the coin from Caria[21] in Figure 7-5 provides numismatic evidence that ancient Greeks used fossil bones to model images of mythological monsters. The reverse of the coin displays a star surrounded by a lattice frame. Below the coin, two images of fossil ichthyosaur skulls in the British Museum are provided for comparison. Herakles killed Ketos to

---

[17]See the *Histories* 1.67–68 by Herodotus. A Greek historian who lived during the fifth century B.C., Herodotus is commonly regarded in the West as the "Father of History."
[18]See *The First Fossil Hunters* p. 111 by Adrienne Mayor.
[19]The Pleistocene geological epoch extended from 12,000 to 2.5 million years ago.
[20]Between 431–404 B.C., Sparta victoriously led the Peloponnesian League in war against the Athenian Empire. History remembers this event as the Peloponnesian War.
[21]Situated on the western shores of the Anatolian Peninsula, the city-state of Caria contained a large population of Greeks. Persia incorporated Caria as a satrapy in the sixth century B.C. Caria also gave its name to a geological epoch slightly over 200 million years ago famous for rock deposits in which the largest known ichthyosaur fossils have been discovered.

Chapter 7 | Ancient Greek Religious Themes   137

FIGURE 7-5. Comparison of Numismatic Portrait of the Monster, Ketos, with Fossil Ichthyosaur Skulls. Caria, Kindya, AR Tetrobol, ca. 510–490 B.C.

save Hesione, daughter of Laomedon, King of Troy. Modern paleontologists see considerable similarity between this image of Ketos and ichthyosaur fossils that sometimes erode from the cliffs around Caria. Looking at the fossil skull of a fully grown ichthyosaur, a giant marine reptile with a body up to 60 feet long, who could doubt that only a giant hero like Herakles or Perseus could slay such a monster?

Until recently, archaeologists often discarded fossil remains that they discovered in excavations of ancient temples. An archaeologist would not record the discovery of a fossil bone, assuming it didn't show anything more than natural weathering of rocks and the burial of ancient sites by water-borne materials. Archaeologists have begun to recognize only recently that some paleontological artifacts found at ancient sites once served as sacred relics of the mythological past.

A Sacred Fossil Associated with King Pelops

In a myth that connects King Pelops with Demeter, Pelops' father, King Tantalus, offered Pelops as a child sacrifice to the Olympian Gods. King Tantalus cooked the sacrificed child and served him to the gods in a stew. Distracted because her daughter had recently gone to the underworld, Demeter absent-mindedly ate a shoulder. All the other Olympian Gods perceived something wrong with the stew and refused to eat. After the gods discovered what Tantalus had done, Zeus arranged for eternal punishment of Tantalus in the underworld.[22] Hephaistos crafted a new shoulder for Pelops out of ivory; then the gods reassembled him and brought him back to life. When Pelops grew older, Poseidon fell in love with Pelops and carried him to heaven. Poseidon and Pelops lived together among the gods on Mount Olympus until Zeus required that Pelops leave.

After King Pelops died, Greeks from Elis displayed his giant ivory shoulder blade as a sacred relic. Warriors from Elis carried Pelops' shoulder bone with them to Troy to ensure their victory.[23] After the Greeks won the Trojan War, Elis lost King Pelops' shoulder when the ship carrying the relic sank on its way home. Later, however, a fisherman miraculously caught the giant shoulder and returned it to the city-state of Elis, where the relic's arrival coincided with the end of a terrible plague. Priests stored the giant fossil at Olympia in a bronze chest in a sanctuary called the Pelopion.[24]

The original giant scapula revered as Pelops' shoulder probably was a semi-mineralized mammoth bone from a deposit of Pleistocene fossils near Olympia. The fossil would have measured 3–4 feet long, 2–3 feet wide, and would have weighed 66–110 pounds. After being cleaned and polished, it might easily have resembled ivory. After the original relic was lost at sea, the fisherman probably netted a different,

---

[22]In the underworld, King Tantalus was *tantalized* in a pool beneath the branches of a fruit tree: Whenever he reached for a piece of fruit to eat, the branch holding it would move away, and whenever he knelt to drink, the pool would empty.
[23]This is another temporal contradiction of Greek Mythology; how could King Pelops marry Briseis after the Trojan War if his shoulder already was a sacred relic?
[24]See the *Description of Greece* 5.13.1–4 by Pausanias.

Miocene-era fossil scapula from the sunken land-bridge in the shallow seas around Euboea. The Oracle of Delphi identified the new fossil as the lost shoulder of Pelops, which was then returned to Olympia. In this way, the original artifact no more than 2.5 million years old may have been replaced by an artifact many millions of years older—not that it made any difference to the reverent and faithful.[25]

A Modern Sacred Fossil

In modern times we wonder how anyone could have believed the disjointed and silly Greek myths that we sometimes read to children. But in the ancient world, these stories provided context for understanding everything that people saw and experienced: They explained the greatest mysteries of the universe. Besides, the Greek practice of supporting ancient morality tales with questionable artifacts did not end with paganism. Unique and mysterious artifacts have always proven useful to Christianity.

For example, a fourth century church, the Cathedral of the Assumption of Saint Mary, in Rab, Croatia, preserves an important Christian relic—the skull of Saint Christopher, patron saint of travelers. The early church in Constantinople certified its significance and authenticity. The skull confirmed both the strength and unsightly features of the saint affectionately known as "Dog Face."

Inheritors of Greek religious traditions, early Christians sometimes presented artifacts as religious relics because of their appearance and availability, not because of any factual relationship they held to the events they supposedly proved. Saint Christopher's skull bears an elongated profile—from his heavy brow ridges to the protuberance at the rear of his skull (called an occipital bun)—characteristic of Neanderthal man, an extinct near-human species whose last members died out between 25,000 and 30,000 years ago. To early Christians, the "dog-like" appearance of a rare fossil Neanderthal skull proved that it belonged to Saint Christopher.

---

[25]See *The First Fossil Hunters* pp. 109–110 by Adrienne Mayor.

METEORITES

Ancient Greeks read sacred history from landforms and constellations, and saw proof of the power of gods in the sun, wind, and seas. On those rare instances when a meteorite fell from the sky, people believed that the stone was sacred and that the gods had communicated something important. The obverse of the ancient coin in Figure 7-6 displays a winged deity (perhaps Nike), while the reverse carries an image of a conical object. Even though the precise meanings of many numismatic symbols have been lost, archaeology and literature often can provide insight. The cone on the reverse of this coin appears to reflect ancient religious traditions related to meteorites.

In many cities around the Mediterranean Sea, people carved meteorites into conical shapes and used them to represent deities. Ancient Greeks enshrined meteorites at Pessinus (Galatia) representing the goddess Cybele, at Paphos (Crete) representing the goddess Aphrodite, at Emesa (Syria) representing the local sun god Heliogabalus, and at many other places. In excavations at Paphos, Cyprus, archaeologists found the famous conical meteorite called the Xoanon that represented Aphrodite.

Various literary sources associate meteors and meteorites with deities. The *Iliad* describes the goddess Athena appearing like a brilliant meteor as she rushed to carry out Zeus' orders during the Trojan War.[26] Even the *New Testament*[27] refers to an image of Artemis of Ephesos that fell from the sky that the city guarded as the goddess herself. Early Byzantine Christians called these meteorites *baetyls* (from ancient Semitic for "House of God") and referred to meteorites as the homes of pagan deities.

Images of meteorites appear on Arabian coins extending into late Imperial Roman times. Connected with this pagan tradition, a black meteorite from pre-Islamic times still rests in the eastern corner of the Ka'ba in Mecca. Even today this stone serves as a mysterious axis of worship in the Islamic faith.

---

[26] See the *Iliad* 4:75–77 by Homer.
[27] See *Acts* 19:23–36.

FIGURE 7-6. Winged Deity, and Sacred Meteorite (Baetyl) Carved into Conical Shape. Caria, Caunus, AR Stater, ca. 410–390 B.C.

OMENS

In ancient times, when people believed that every detail of life revealed the intimate connection between humans and gods, something as insignificant as a sneeze could assume great importance as an omen. Ancient Greeks thought that sneezes brought messages from the gods. In the *Odyssey*, Penelope wished aloud that her husband, Odysseus, would return and get rid of the suitors that harassed her so terribly; and her son sneezed.[28] To Penelope, this foretold that her husband would return soon to slaughter the suitors.

In the beginning of the fourth century B.C., Xenophon[29] recorded the story of a Greek mercenary army in Persia. The Royal Persian Army had just executed the Greek army's employer, a rebel Persian leader who had paid the Greeks well. Xenophon lectured the Greek

---
[28] See the *Odyssey* 17:505–550 by Homer.
[29] Xenophon was a soldier, mercenary, and historian who wrote eyewitness descriptions of events during the transition between the fifth and fourth centuries B.C.

mercenaries, outlining a plan for them to escape from Persia by way of a dangerous path north. At a key moment during his speech, a soldier sneezed.[30] Every man in the army bowed to Xenophon and accepted him as their divinely ordained leader.

EASTERN IDEAS: ZOROASTRIAN TRADITIONS

Born in a sacred land called Aryana Vaejah (probably somewhere within the modern boundaries of Kazakhstan) between 1400 and 1100 B.C., the prophet Zoroaster built a fascinating monotheism out of ancient traditions of nature worship. Modern historians credit Zoroaster with the invention of important religious concepts, such as physical resurrection at the End of Days and a Last Judgment by a trinity comprising three aspects of a single god.[31] These concepts later became important parts of Christianity.

Zoroastrian Creation of the Universe

According to Zoroaster, two spiritual deities came into being at the beginning of time as twins, Ahura Mazda and Angra Mainyu. Ahura Mazda chose to express his being with order, wisdom, goodness, and light. Angra Mainyu chose to express his being with evil and darkness. After deliberation, Ahura Mazda willed the destruction of his evil twin. To help accomplish this, Ahura Mazda created the physical universe.

First, Ahura Mazda divided himself into three parts: Mazda (the spirit of wisdom), Varuna (the spirit of the spoken word), and Mithra (the spirit of covenant). These spirits divided into other spirits, often dividing by threes and often associating with other spirits in threes. In this fashion, Ahura Mazda created angelic spirits called *ahuras* and a physical universe characterized by seven creations: a sky of stone like a spherical shell, water filling the lower part of the shell, earth floating in the water, plants growing on the earth, animals living among the

---
[30]See the *Anabasis* 3.2 by Xenophon.
[31]For a discussion of Zoroastrian history and beliefs that appear in this section, see *Zoroastrianism: Its Antiquity and Constant Vigour* by Mary Boyce.

plants, man living among all these creations, and light from Ahura Mazda illuminating everything.

For the most part, Ahura Mazda confined Angra Mainyu to a realm of darkness in a deep pit at the center of the world next to a mountain named Hara. From this pit of darkness, Angra Mainyu generated sin, sickness, and pain. To oppose Ahura Mazda's ahuras, Angra Mainyu created evil spirits called *daevas*.

The Foundation of Zoroastrian Ethics

Ancient Zoroastrians generally addressed Ahura Mazda by any of his three main aspects. While each aspect operated independently from the others, no aspect existed separately from the one wise god. Similarly, the essence of Ahura Mazda filled all that he created. Spiritual beings, operating separately from physical reality, could participate in the essence, substance, and processes of physical reality.

Zoroastrians worshipped Ahura Mazda as a wise lord of goodness and light. Commonly represented as a winged solar disk (sometimes with a male torso), Ahura Mazda ruled heaven and emanated spiritual light from the sun, moon, and every fire in every hearth. All light contained the essence of Ahura Mazda. Because the creations of Angra Mainyu tried to pollute those of Ahura Mazda, the physical universe served as a battleground where the twin gods struggled, good against evil. In the material world, every person must choose whether to serve Ahura Mazda by following a path of righteousness or to serve Angra Mainyu by doing evil. Symbolically, Angra Mainyu achieved his greatest victory by committing his greatest sin, polluting fire with the darkness of smoke.

Comparing Zoroastrianism and Hinduism

Hinduism and Zoroastrianism apparently developed side by side around the time of the introduction of chariots in regions north of India. Comparisons of Hindu and Zoroastrian scriptures suggest that Zoroaster served as a priest in an ancient herding society that a Hindu warrior society occasionally raided. In complementary fashion,

Zoroastrian scriptures speak about riders of chariots as invading forces that serve evil, while the earliest Hindu texts speak of Hindu gods as powerful riders of chariots.

Just as Zoroastrian and Hindu scriptures seem to describe the same history from opposite points of view, Zoroastrians and Hindus perceive the universe differently from each other. Hindus developed religious beliefs involving a multitude of deities: Souls evolve by migrating from life to life, yet the fundamental nature of the universe never changes; it always contains a necessary balance of both good and evil. Zoroaster taught instead that the universe had a beginning, that each human lives a single life in which he must choose between good and evil, and that good will triumph over evil at the End of Days.

Zoroastrian Afterlife and Prophesied Savior

At death, a person's spiritual soul separates from the physical body. At sunrise on the fourth day after death, the soul goes to the top of Mount Hara at the center of the world. Appearing as a fiery trinity comprising Mithra (spirit of covenants), Rasnu (spirit of judgment), and Sraosa (spirit of hearkening to god), Ahura Mazda judges each soul. In the presence of Sraosa, Rasnu holds the scales that weigh the sum of a soul's good deeds against the sum of the soul's evil deeds, and Mithra pronounces judgment. The virtuous soul crosses a wide bridge from the top of Mount Hara to the sky, a realm of multiple heavens ruled by Ahura Mazda. For the evil person, the bridge contracts to the width of a spear-blade. The evil soul then slips and falls into the mouth of Hell on the north side of Mount Hara. In Hell, the evil soul suffers torment at the hands of daevas generated by Angra Mainyu.

Zoroaster said that good will battle evil for one cosmic year comprising twelve cosmic months. Zoroaster probably taught that each cosmic month lasted a thousand normal years, but later teachers expanded this time frame. The struggle between good and evil will reach a climax when a savior (Saosyant) appears on Earth. Just as Zoroaster introduced revolutionary seed ideas among his people on the banks of Lake Urmia, Zoroaster left his physical seed in the lake itself. Someday a virgin, pure in spirit, will bathe in the lake and conceive Zoroaster's child. This child will give final instruction to humanity and precipitate the End of Days.

Zoroastrian Eschatology

At the End of Days, Ahura Mazda will defeat Angra Mainyu, as good must necessarily triumph over evil. At a critical moment, Ahura Mazda will unite heaven and Earth. Then he will level the earth and make all the earth's metals flow into a giant molten river. Every person who ever lived (all the good souls in heaven and all the evil souls in Hell) will resurrect physically and fall into the molten river.

Spirits in the metal will protect virtuous people, but the molten river will burn and consume everything evil. After cleansing humanity, the molten river will pour into the mouth of Hell, consuming the evil essence of Angra Mainyu and sealing Hell forever. Blessed humanity then will consume a sacred meal with Ahura Mazda who will restore every person's perfect physical body, unblemished and immortal. Humanity then will live in the purified realm of Ahura Mazda forever.

The Persian Empire: A Zoroastrian Crucible

Zoroaster's religious concepts easily connected with other spiritual beliefs. To Zoroastrians, the gods and monsters of pagan mythology corresponded to ahuras and daevas. Spiritual beliefs and philosophies from the earliest civilizations of western Asia helped shape the Zoroastrianism that was adopted by Persia. Then, the Persian Empire took its Zoroastrian beliefs north to the Russian steppes, south to Egypt, east to India, and west to lands washed by the Mediterranean Sea.

In eastern Mediterranean lands, symbols of Ahura Mazda appear on ancient coins in a variety of mythological contexts. In Figure 7-7, the obverse of the top coin from Samaria portrays a mythical horned bird. The reverse portrays the Egyptian god Bes wearing a winged mustache and a feathered headdress. A winged solar disk of Ahura Mazda appears above the crown of Bes. The obverse of the lower left

FIGURE 7-7. Three Coins Showing Zoroastrian Influence. Top: Samaria, AR Obol, ca. 375–333 B.C. Bottom left: Cilicia, Tarsos, Tarkumuwa (Datames), Satrap of Cilicia and Cappadocia, AR Stater 384–360 B.C. Bottom right: Cilicia, Mallos. AR Tetrobol, ca. 425–385 B.C.

coin from Tarsos, Cilicia, shows Baal of Tarsos enthroned among religious symbols like grapes, wheat, and an eagle-tipped scepter. On the reverse, a winged solar disk of Ahura Mazda hovers to the right of a seated Persian satrap examining an arrow. The obverse of the bottom right coin from Mallos, Cilicia, portrays Ahura Mazda as a god with four wings holding the sun.

Zoroastrian Influences on the West

Believing in a single ruling god that consisted only of goodness, Plato had difficulty explaining the existence of evil. Zoroastrian priests, however, easily identified the source of evil and emphasized the necessity for each person to choose an ethical path. Strongly influenced by both Zoroastrian ideas as well as ancient astronomical traditions, Eastern religious traditions generally looked upon the sky as a region of purity and the ultimate home for successful human souls.

After the conquests of Alexander the Great, Western Greek civilization quickly embraced philosophical and religious ideas from the East. Greeks even wrote that Pythagoras studied with Zoroaster in

Babylon. From the opposite point of view, Persians saw Greek invaders as agents of Angra Mainyu. From the beginning of the Hellenistic Age at the end of the fourth century B.C., Zoroastrians developed apocalyptic literature maintaining that the evil empires of Macedonian rulers would precipitate the coming of the Zoroastrian savior. Throughout the Middle East, worshippers of Ahura Mazda generated expectations that the collapse of the last Hellenistic empires (the Seleukids and the Ptolemies) would mark the beginning of the End of Days.[32] Living for centuries under Persian rule, Jews (among others) in Egypt, Judea, and Anatolia gradually adopted this belief.

By the first century A.D., Zoroastrian ideas had percolated through the Middle East and mixed seamlessly with other traditions. In constant ferment, the East expected the imminent arrival of a savior who would bring the End of Days. In his letter to Ephesos, Saint Paul described Christianity in terms of a spiritual war[33] between God's realm of light and the devil's realm of darkness. In fact, Christianity incorporated many distinctive aspects of Zoroastrianism, such as the importance of trinity, the joys of heaven and the torments of Hell, a soul's ascension on the fourth day after death into a realm of multiple heavens, and physical resurrection of good people at the End of Days to inhabit a purified unification of heaven and Earth.

Up to the early fourth century B.C., however, few Eastern ideas had found their way into Greek mythology. Greeks believed that Persian Zoroastrians descended from Perseus, the Greek father of Perses, but Greeks feared and mistrusted Persians. With completely different religious points of view, Persians and Greeks understood the universe differently: They entertained completely different ideas about the origin of the Earth, the purpose of mankind, and the evolution of different races throughout the world.

---

[32]See *Zoroastrianism: Its Antiquity and Constant Vigour* pp. 149–150 by Mary Boyce.
[33]See *Ephesians* 6:10–13.

CHAPTER
8

IDEAS ABOUT EVOLUTION

THE IMPORTANCE OF PERSISTENCE THROUGH CHANGE

> Religious ideas from ancient times passed from pagan cults into Christianity, but Christianity welcomed some ideas more than others.

Before the twentieth century, mankind simply did not possess the tools necessary to understand DNA differences between species and the interrelation of all life. Without advanced chemistry, comparative physiology, worldwide communications technology, and physical data confirming the age of the Earth, it was anybody's guess how humans came to exist. Yet, sooner or later, everyone needs some way of understanding their place in humanity and humanity's place in the world and the universe.

Sooner or later, some event happens that threatens our existence—a personal health threat, a threat to our family, a threat to our nation, or a threat to our world. Based on our understanding of what we are, where we came from, and how we relate to the world, we attempt to respond appropriately to threats. Yet, as we grow older, our understanding of ourselves and our world changes from day to day. One of humanity's most important survival skills has been an ability to enshrine key ideas that let us determine appropriate courses of action during times of existential stress. For key ideas to be valuable, they must be flexible but they must not change easily. We feel the power of religion because it guards key ideas that we use to define ourselves as humans living in an uncertain world. We feel a personal connection with religion because of its longstanding role in defining humanity and helping it survive: It helps us as we mature, playing different roles in our evolving lives; it helps us cooperate in groups to accomplish large projects; and it helps our species survive stress in a constantly changing environment.

History allows us to see changes to humanity over thousands of years, and it also lets us see what has persisted. We can see differences in human understandings of where we came from; we can see important ways that societies have changed over time; and we can see humanity's reactions to long-term changes in the Earth's environment. We also can see similarities between modern ideas and ancient ideas; we can see the persistence of ancient symbols over time; and we even can see examples of the persistence of ancient behaviors that survive the abandonment of ancient beliefs and that reconnect with new beliefs and new justifications.

COMPARING ANCIENT AND MODERN IDEAS ABOUT EVOLUTION

Ancient Greeks possessed a much freer understanding of evolution than we have now. They believed that a human being consisted of a body made of earthy material and a soul made of spiritual material, and they believed that humanity changed over time. Because Greek mythology spoke of many heroes as *autochthonous* or earth born, it seemed perfectly reasonable that, with assistance from a god, some men (like Erichthonius[1]) might emerge directly from the earth. In such a world, human beings might evolve in various ways, but not

---

[1]Chapter 2 relates how Gaea gave birth to Erichthonius, the first king of Athens, as a consequence of Hephaistos' unsuccessful attempt to rape Athena.

necessarily in ways that we associate with evolution today. Open to a broad range of possibilities, some ancient Greeks believed that:

- Evolution occurred spiritually, intellectually, and/or physically, with these aspects evolving individually or in combination.
- Some humans evolved from animals, and some did not.
- Humans became smaller over time.
- Children inherited abilities based on their parents' education, choices, and achievements.
- Some souls evolved by learning lessons over many lives.
- Humanity might have gotten worse instead of better.
- Evolution might recur in cycles.
- Gods alternately destroyed and recreated humanity as they changed the world.

Since the nineteenth century A.D., research focused on the theory of evolution has helped biology become the latest scientific discipline (joining astronomy, physics, and geology) to demonstrate the incompatibility of scientific evidence and fundamentalist religion. In modern times, we think of evolution as something that began with the first appearance of life on Earth several billion years ago: Life changed through slow processes involving hereditary transmission of characteristics from parent to child and survival of the fittest offspring. With increasingly sophisticated tools, modern science has begun to unravel the complex story how all existing species on Earth emerged through incremental changes—information transmission errors—while copying DNA from parent to child sequentially over billions of years. In contrast, modern fundamentalists vigorously assert the literal truth of documents that have suffered their own information transmission errors.[2] Modern religious fundamentalists generally condemn scientific understandings that differ from histories of the world in religious works like the *Bible* or *Koran* as sacrilege.

Because Greeks freely explored ideas about evolution in their philosophy and mythology, they originated many ideas that people still use to speak of human and cultural evolution. In the sixth century B.C., the

---

[2] See Chapter 25 for a discussion of some of the ways that transmission errors have affected text in the *New Testament*.

great philosopher, Pythagoras (like a modern New Age mystic), taught that evolution happened spiritually as human souls experienced many lives by migrating from one body to another. Taking a contrary point of view, his contemporary, the Ionian philosopher Anaximander (like a modern evolutionary biologist), taught that evolution related only to bodies: Living creatures originally came from moisture influenced by warmth, and human beings evolved gradually from simpler animals, slowly changing over many generations. From a different perspective, Greek mythology said that different types of humans had lived during different periods of time, which were referred to as ages.

MYTHOLOGY ABOUT EVOLUTION

In the late eighth century B.C., Hesiod[3] wrote that humanity evolved by passing through a number of ages: a Golden Age, a Silver Age, a Bronze Age, a Heroic Age, and an Iron Age. Although modern archaeologists adopted this terminology and still speak about ages of humanity, ancient ideas about ages differed from the modern understanding of ages, which is tied to the dating of technological developments in cultures. Hesiod said that humans of one mythological age generally did not evolve physically into humans of the next mythological age. Instead, he identified five completely separate races of humans that existed on Earth during different ages since creation: a Golden Race, a Silver Race, a Bronze Race, a Heroic Race, and an Iron Race. The timelines in Figure 8-1 (events and time frames according to scientific, mythological, and biblical models for the history of the universe[4]) illustrate the use of mythical terminology by science and the use of mythical timescale by Judeo-Christian tradition.

The **Golden Age** began during the reign of Cronos, a Titan who ruled the universe from a throne somewhere on Sicily. In this ideal

---

[3]Hesiod, one of the earliest Greek poets, may have been a contemporary of Homer.
[4]Dates and events listed in the timelines are offered only as general points of comparison. For example, instead of defining a single "Stone Age," science tracks technological development by culture so that dates for many Stone Ages vary considerably. Also, biblical chronology experts are continually developing new timelines based on new interpretations of the *Bible*.

Chapter 8 | Ideas About Evolution   153

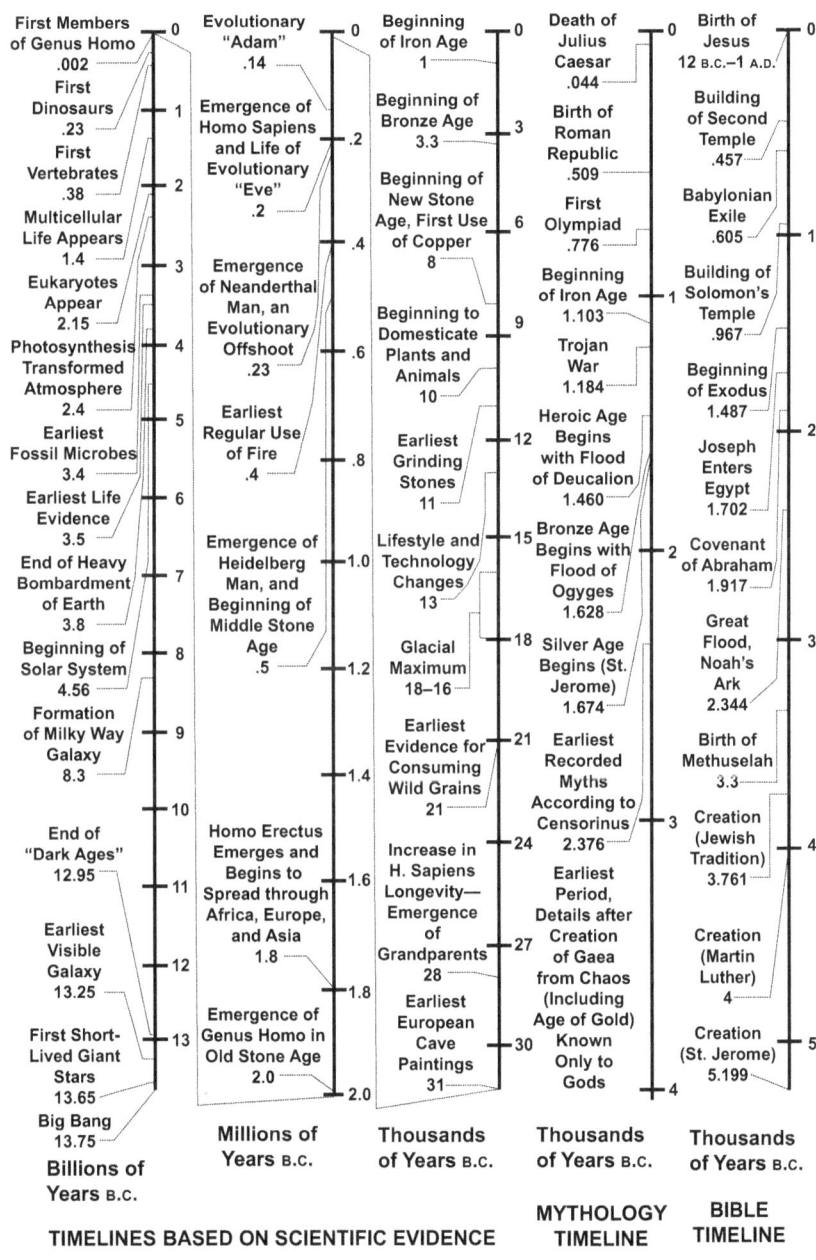

FIGURE 8-1. Timelines of the Universe and of Human Existence Comparing Scientific, Mythological, and Biblical Perspectives.

time, the Golden Race lived in peace. No wild creatures harmed them, and animals during this time didn't even harm each other. The Earth nurtured all creatures with an abundance of fruits, nuts, and honey during an endless Spring. The Golden Race knew nothing of laws, property, punishments, and war because individuals shared everything and acted only honorably. Nobody ever grew old or infirm. Instead, everyone lived long lives and eventually died peacefully. The Golden Race honored the gods, and the gods loved the Golden Race. This first race of humanity eventually disappeared, however, because they neither married nor bore children. As spirits, they continue to watch over the Earth.

The **Silver Age** began under the rule of Zeus after his lover, Leto (Goddess of Light), gave birth to the twin gods, Apollo and Artemis, on the island of Delos. (See map in Figure 8-2.) During the Silver Age, Zeus limited Spring and shaped the year with four seasons. The Silver Race lived as children for a hundred years. After childhood they suddenly aged, lived briefly as adults, and then died. The Silver Race procreated; they built homes in caves and bushes and planted seeds to grow food; but they generally lived foolishly and frequently insulted the gods. Zeus punished the Silver Race for impiety by sending a great flood during the reign of Ogyges (a son of either Cadmus or Poseidon), the first King of Boeotia (the area around Thebes). Greek mythology remembers this flood as the Ogygian Deluge. Some modern writers have attempted to connect the story of the Ogygian Deluge with the giant eruption of the Thera caldera on the Greek island, Santorini, around 1610 B.C. However, Plato dated this flood approximately to 10,000 B.C., a time that some modern geologists associate with catastrophic flows of water between the Aegean Sea and the Black Sea after the last Ice Age.[5]

During the **Bronze Age**, Zeus created the Bronze Race out of ash trees. Hesiod describes the Bronze Race as strong, stern, hard-hearted, violent, and war loving. The first humans to use bronze weapons and armor, they even built their homes out of bronze. The Bronze Race

---

[5]Although no consensus exists among geologists concerning the timing, amount, and direction of flooding, evidence of large flows of water between the Aegean Sea and the Black Sea has fueled speculation that sudden catastrophic events associated with flows between these seas may have inspired Western myths about great floods.

Chapter 8 | Ideas About Evolution   155

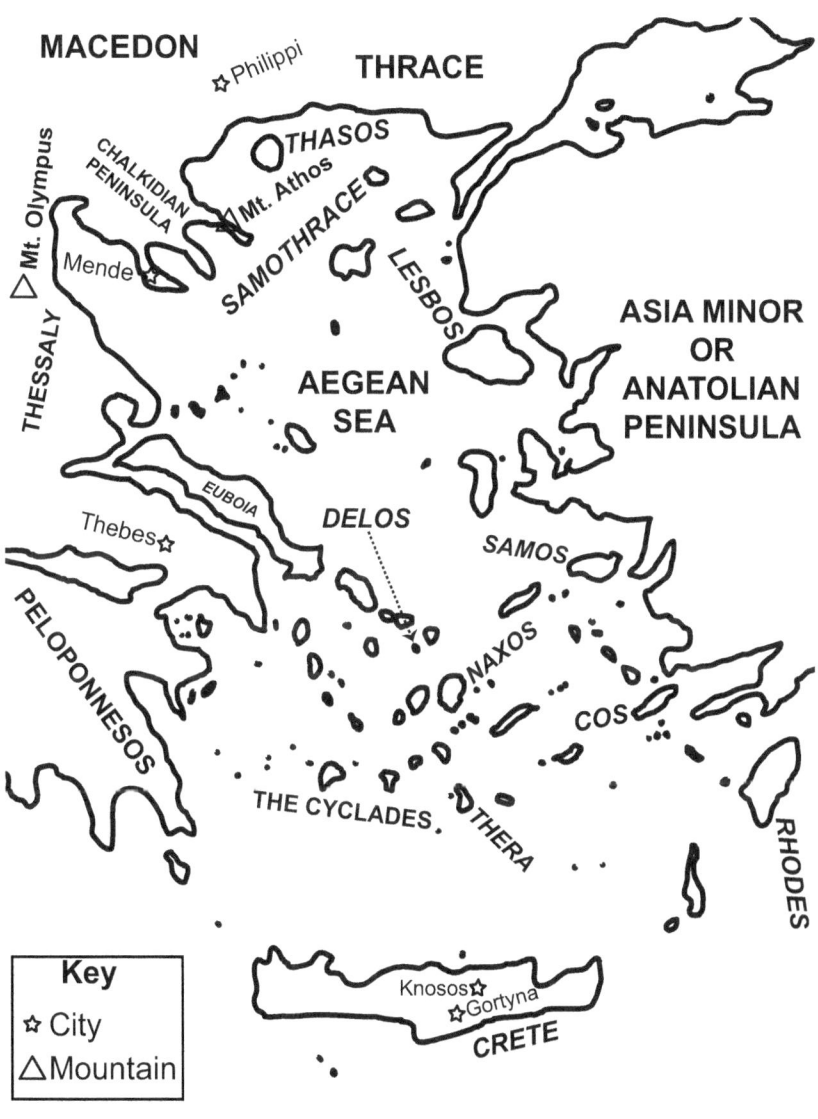

FIGURE 8-2. Map of the Aegean Sea.

may have destroyed themselves through their love of violent conflict, or Zeus may have sent another great flood to destroy them. Mythology associates Deucalion, a son of the Titan, Prometheus (remembered as the bringer of fire to mankind), with the great flood that ended the

Bronze Age. When Zeus decided to send a flood to destroy the Bronze Race, Prometheus told Deucalion, which allowed him to save himself and his family.

During the **Heroic Age**, after the Flood of Deucalion, Zeus made a noble race of giant, semi-divine heroes. This age is the only one in Greek mythology in which humanity improved from the previous age. Greek heroes associated with gods and battled other heroes. For example, the Doric hero, Herakles, and the Ionian hero, Theseus, pursued fantastic adventures. Also, many heroic sons of Herakles participated in the Trojan War. In a short time, most of the heroes died from wars and adventures. Zeus permitted the noblest heroes to live after death on the Isles of the Blessed somewhere near the western edge of the world.

The **Iron Age** began before the Heroic Age ended. While great heroes lived short, spectacular, mythological lives, Deucalion and his wife helped create the next race of humanity, the Iron Race. In the Iron Age—the current age—gods no longer associated with humans. People no longer shared the Earth, but marked it with boundaries, and they stole treasures that gods hid in the depths of the Earth. All humanity lived with misery and evil: They lusted for profit; they betrayed each other; and they struggled to live petty, dishonorable lives. Zeus planned to destroy the current race of humanity when the time came that babies are born already old, and humans live lives of unbridled villainy and impiety.

CREATION OF HUMANITY: VARIOUS MYTHS

Greek myths tell conflicting stories about the creation of the current race of mankind. In one myth, an Earth goddess named Cura made the first man out of water and clay, and then Cura asked Zeus to give the man a soul. In another myth, Prometheus (Forethought) made Deucalion, the first Iron Age human, out of clay, and Athena gave him a soul. Pausanias, a Greek traveler in the second century A.D., records that a small town named Panopeus near Delphi in central Greece preserved two rocks that smelled like human flesh. Local Greeks honored these rocks as relics of the clay that was used to make Deucalion.[6]

In another myth, Prometheus' Oceanid wife, Clymene, bore Deucalion, the first Iron Age man. Prometheus' brother, Epimetheus (Afterthought) and his wife, Pandora,[7] conceived Pyrrha, the first Iron Age woman. Or perhaps Clymene was Prometheus' mother and Pandora was the first Iron Age woman. Regardless, Deucalion and his wife (Pyrrha or Pandora) survived the great flood at the end of the Bronze Age by floating in a large wooden box to a mountain—Mount Parnassus, Mount Tomaros, Mount Etna, Mount Athos, or some other sacred mountain depending on local traditions. To repopulate the Earth, Deucalion and Pyrrha threw stones, "bones of their mother," behind them. The stones consisted of living rock, parts of an ancient Earth goddess. Each stone changed into a new human being; Deucalion's stones changed into men and Pyrrha's changed into women.

Greek myths credit the Titan, Prometheus, for making life bearable for Iron Age humanity. Prometheus tricked Zeus into accepting bones wrapped in fat as religious offerings. That way, humans could eat the good parts of sacrificed animals after burning the waste parts for the gods. In addition, Prometheus gave both fire and knowledge (for example, mathematics, medicine, and divination) to humanity. For giving these gifts to mankind, Zeus chained the Titan to a rock in the Caucasus Mountains and ordered an eagle to eat his liver. Every night Prometheus' liver would regenerate, and every day the eagle would eat the liver again. Condemned to suffer this torment until a descendent of Zeus ended it, Prometheus eventually regained his freedom when Herakles killed the eagle and tore the chains from the rock.

Zeus also punished humanity for receiving Prometheus' gifts. Zeus gave Pandora a box (actually a large storage pot called a *pithos*) and forbade her from opening it. Leaving Pandora with Deucalion, Zeus knew that Pandora would open the box despite his prohibition. In this way, qualities like pain, jealousy, and plague—all the miseries of Iron Age humanity—escaped from the box into the world.

The Mediterranean Sea provided easy access among Greek, Anatolian, Near Eastern, and Egyptian civilizations (see the map in Figure

---

[6]See the *Description of Greece* 1.4.3 by Pausanias.
[7]Just as Christians identify Eve as the source of original sin, pagan Greeks identified Pandora as the source of all the ills that plague mankind.

8-3), and religious ideas moved from culture to culture as easily as trade goods. Accordingly, the most sophisticated and enduring of Mediterranean cults evolved as mythological blends adapted to specific cultures. By the time that Jews produced a codified biblical history of the universe in *Genesis*, pagans throughout the Mediterranean would have recognized important elements of their own ancient traditions in the text. In Hebrew, Adam means earth and Eve means life. The Judeo-Christian God made Adam out of earth just as Cura or Prometheus made Deucalion out of clay. Noah resembles Deucalion; Eve resembles Pandora; and so on. Early Christian writers even used the similarities between pagan mythological history and biblical history as evidence for the validity of Christianity.

ANATOLIAN GODDESSES: GREAT MOTHERS OF HUMANITY

In Greek mythology, an ancient mother goddess helped Deucalion and Pyrrha/Pandora repopulate the Earth. Sometimes the goddess transformed clay or rocks into people, and sometimes the goddess merely assisted by installing souls in bodies. Regardless, Greeks mostly looked to the goddess cults of Anatolia to identify the mother goddess who helped give birth to the Iron Race.

Because the ancient land of Anatolia (Turkey) had been occupied, fought over, and fragmented for thousands of years, different Anatolian city-states knew the Great Mother by different names—Kubaba, Cybele, Artemis, Mâ, Mater, Meter, etc. In some traditions the Great Mother not only gave rise to the Iron Race, but she remained a virgin and later conceived a savior without intercourse. Sometimes, however, she conceived a savior through intercourse with a god and magically restored her virginity after the savior's birth. Yet the goddess always possessed a core set of characteristics: Always the mother, lover, and consort of another great god, the goddess presided over creation, mercy, prophecy, and death. Awesome ruler of life and death, the Great Mother granted fertility to land, people, and animals, yet she also granted blood-lust to warriors and received the dead from battle with loving, maternal care. Near Troy, an ancient temple at Pessinus

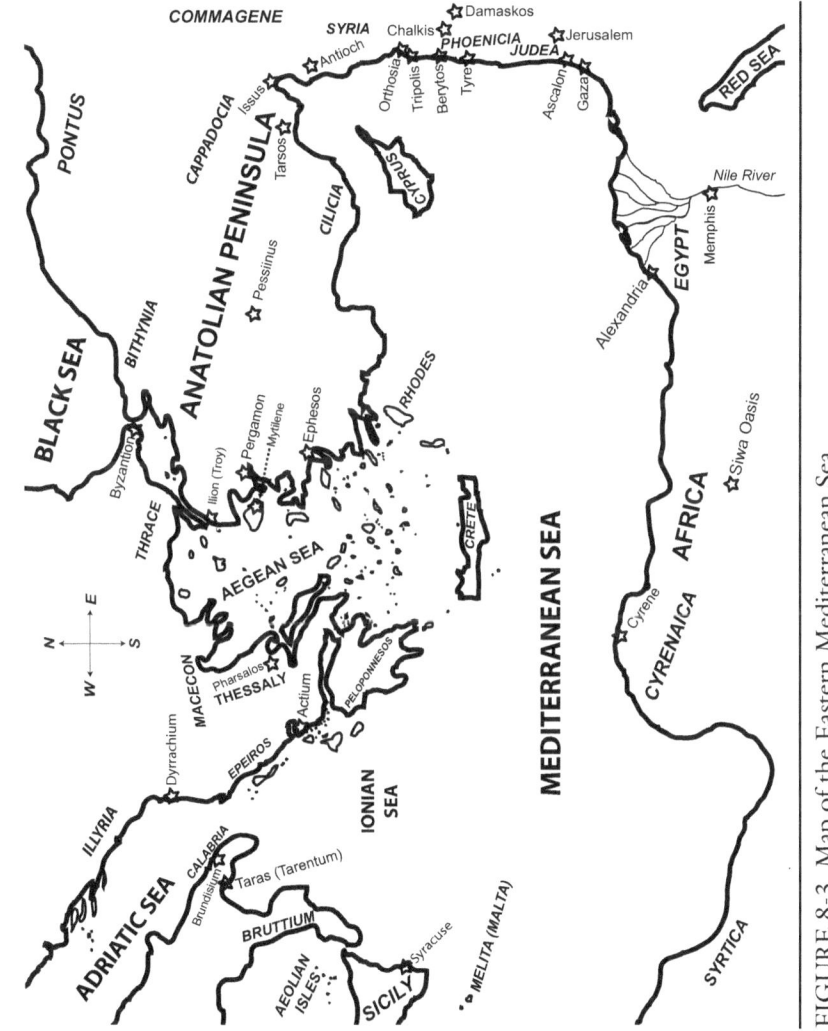

FIGURE 8-3. Map of the Eastern Mediterranean Sea.

housed a meteorite, the sacred home of the goddess Cybele, also known as the Great Mother of Mount Ida. Not far away, in Ephesos, people worshipped a similar goddess, also associated with a meteorite; and Ephesians called her Artemis.

Ancient statues of Artemis of Ephesos (for example, see Figure 8-4) portray her with protuberances that modern eyes associate with multiple breasts.[8] However, in ancient times, priests hung the scrota of sacrificed bulls around the goddess's neck, and neophytes committed themselves to her service by castrating themselves publicly during her annual festivals. Ancient eyes saw the protuberances on her statues as offerings of male scrota instead of female breasts.

THE PERSISTENCE OF SYMBOLS THROUGH HISTORY

Loosely coupled, common symbols and persistent religious practices often echo strangely across the centuries. Some religious symbols get dropped, some get preserved, but the underlying meanings of religious symbols and practices can get all mixed up. For example, symbols on the coin and the statue in Figure 8-4 came from the same place, but from two completely different worlds. Minted in the geometric period during the seventh century B.C., the coin represents an archaic Greek goddess cult. The statue was carved sometime around the beginning of the fourth century A.D. after the cult had been Hellenized, imported by Republican Rome, and then reinterpreted by Imperial Rome.

Just as the United States of America represents its economic and military might numismatically (for example, with an eagle and arrows on a Washington quarter), ancient Ephesians communicated their strength using the symbols on the coin in Figure 8-4. One of the world's oldest two-sided coins, it was minted in electrum (a gold and silver alloy) approximately in 625 B.C. The obverse displays a geometric

---

[8]Some scholars believe the statues are decorated with breasts because of ancient claims that Amazons, giant warrior women of the Heroic Age, were said to have founded the first temple at Ephesos. (See the *Hymn to Artemis* 3.233 by Callimachus.) Spiritual children of the Great Mother, Amazon women cut off their right breasts so they wouldn't interfere with shooting arrows.

FIGURE 8-4. Bee and Flower Symbols Associated with the Cult of Artemis of Ephesos, and Statue of Artemis of Ephesos, ca. third to fourth century A.D., in the Museo Archaeologico Nazionale in Naples, Italy.

representation of a honeybee, and the reverse displays a punch mark shaped like a flower. Ancient Ephesians kept bees, traded honey, and represented their ancient mother goddess as a bee. Ephesians called the High Priest of Artemis of Ephesos the king bee, and referred to virgin priestesses as honeybees. Simultaneously honoring the local cult, advertising honey, and warning neighbors that its army could sting any attacker, the bee and flower symbols affirmed the power of the city-state's faith, economy, and military.

In Figure 8-4, the statue of Artemis on the right came from a late Roman temple. Just below the coin, an enlarged view of the statue near the goddess's feet shows images of a bee and flower. A sculptor carved the bee and flower on the statue almost a thousand years after the same images first appeared on coins. Under the Romans, the Cult of Artemis of Ephesos proved successful, but not as successful as the Cult of Cybele, a similar goddess from the nearby city of Pessinus.

By the time Ephesian artists carved the statue of Artemis in Figure 8-4, Romans had transplanted the Cult of Cybele from Pessinus to Rome and had included the worship of Artemis of Ephesos in the same state cult. The statue of Artemis wears a crown shaped like a city tower, just like Cybele's crown, and the statue's black face recalls Cybele's sacred meteorite that priests carried from Pessinus to Rome in 204 B.C. The black face of this statue also resembles faces on ancient "Black Madonna" statues of the Virgin Mary in old European churches.

After Constantine I announced public support of Christianity in the Edict of Milan in 313 A.D., the Cult of Artemis of Ephesos continued its long-standing function as a Roman state cult. Christian Roman emperors continued to support the Temple of Artemis of Ephesos for 70 years until Theodosius I closed all pagan temples in 391 A.D. Forty years after that, the Christian Council of Ephesos established the Cult of the Virgin Mary and gave her titles previously held only by earlier virgin goddesses like Cybele and Artemis, for example, Magna Mater (the Great Mother) and the Queen of Heaven. The statue may have come from one of the 48 temples of the Great Mother that the Council of Ephesos converted into shrines of the Virgin Mary in 431 A.D. Many traditional images of the Virgin Mary portray her wearing a crown shaped like Cybele's. In addition, ancient statues of Mary as a black virgin persist in old European churches as symbolic echoes of black virgin goddesses of the pagan past.

THE PERSISTENCE OF ANCIENT RELIGIOUS PRACTICES

With bloody orgies of ecstatic self-mutilation, the worship of Artemis of Ephesos affirmed every prejudice that a modern Christian might have against paganism. Yet some of the earliest Christians struggled to incorporate ecstatic aspects into Christianity. Ancient Christian cults that incorporated ecstatic practices (similar to those used in classical goddess worship) competed directly with Eastern goddess cults and sometimes expanded into empire-wide Christian movements. In the second century A.D., a castrated priest of Cybele named Montanus[9] converted to Christianity and preached an ecstatic version of worship

---

[9] In the late second century A.D., Montanus taught a form of Christianity that included practices from the worship of Cybele like ecstatic prophesy and speaking in tongues.

called Montanism. Tertullian, the creator of the Church's doctrine of the Holy Trinity, adopted Montanism in the third century A.D. Also, many early Christians (for example, Origen, a Church Father who lived in Alexandria in the early third century A.D.) castrated themselves like priests of Cybele.

Over many centuries, the Christian Church has struggled in vain to expunge Montanist-style heresies. Despite official church dogma condemning self-mutilation, the current list of Christian saints contains at least 72 names of persons claimed to have been eunuchs.[10] In addition, isolated ecstatic Christian cults (for example, the Skoptsy[11] of Russia) exist even today. No clear causal path connects practices of the ancient ecstatic Cults with those of modern ecstatic Christians. However, conflicts between ecstatic and non-ecstatic religious practices echo across the centuries as a recurring theme in the struggle between centralized and decentralized control over Christian worship.

COMPARING ANCIENT AND MODERN CHRONOLOGIES

In the late fourth century A.D., the Christian writer, Jerome,[12] tried to create a chronology of world history by reconciling the writings of Hellenistic Greek writers like Apollodorus[13] and Diodorus Siculus[14] (the Sicilian) with the writings of Eusebius,[15] the Father of Church History. Jerome accepted Eusebius' date for the Great Flood of Noah as 2958 B.C. Jerome also accepted the Greek mythological ages as historical and assigned dates to them. Jerome thought the Golden Age lasted from 1710–1674 B.C., the Silver Age from 1674–1628 B.C., the Bronze Age from 1628–1472 B.C., and the Heroic Age from 1460–1103 B.C.

---

[10]The Byzantine Church reserved eight senior positions exclusively for eunuchs. See *Sex: A User's Guide* pp. 71–72 by Stephen Arnott.
[11]From the late eighteenth century to the mid-twentieth century, the Skoptsy of Russia practiced castration of men and mastectomy of women as a means of controlling lust.
[12]Jerome, an Illyrian Christian priest of the late fourth century A.D., formerly considered a saint, is best known for his translation of the *Bible* known as the *Vulgate*.
[13]Apollodorus was a Greek historian who lived in Athens in the second century B.C.
[14]Diodorus Siculus was a Sicilian Greek historian who lived during the first century B.C.
[15]Eusebius became Bishop of Caesarea in Palestine in 314 A.D.

In its earliest writings about the history of the universe, Christianity incorporated a chronology that blended pagan and Jewish traditions.

Some ancient beliefs about evolution even found their way into modern science. Hesiod's description of the sequential appearance of human races in ages inspired nineteenth century archaeologists to designate characteristic periods of human technological development as the Stone Age, the Bronze Age, and the Iron Age. Modern archaeologists agree with Hesiod—that he lived during the Iron Age and that Greeks and Trojans fought a war during the Bronze Age—but the archaeologists define these ages only in terms of the material remains of culture.

It's interesting to compare Jerome's chronology with findings from modern science. Evolutionary Biologists have proposed an "Eve Hypothesis" that claims that all modern humans descend from a single African female who lived approximately 200,000 years ago. To archaeologists, Jerome's date for the end of the Silver Age seems to coincide with the currently accepted date for the eruption of Thera (~1610 B.C.), and his date for the end of the Heroic Age corresponds well with the currently accepted date for the destruction layer associated with Homeric Troy (~1180 B.C.).

In the fourth century B.C., ancient Greek priests, playwrights, poets, and philosophers valued the ability of Greek mythology to explain humanity's role in the world. However, variations among myths about the origins, ages, and races of humanity underscored the fundamental weakness of Greek mythology: Even though all Greeks generally knew similar stories, no responsible authority existed who could integrate the numerous incompatible variations of Greek myths and ensure consistency among them. All around the Mediterranean Sea, city-states preserved clear and detailed stories that told how their founders related to the first humans, but those stories rarely joined well with stories from other places.

PART THREE

Deified Alexander the Great and Seated Athena Holding Nike

HELLENIZATION
TRANSFORMING MEDITERRANEAN POLITICS, RELIGIOUS BELIEFS, AND PHILOSOPHIES

In the Golden Age of Hellenism, successors of Alexander the Great declared themselves gods, homogenized Eastern cults, and oversaw the development of ideas and literature that helped shape Christianity.

CHAPTER

9

THE DAWN OF THE HELLENISTIC AGE

While conquering the East, Alexander the Great merged Eastern and Western cults in ways that shifted the spiritual foundations of the West.

From the late fourth century B.C. when Alexander the Great campaigned in Asia until 30 B.C. when Rome defeated Egypt (the last Hellenistic empire), *Hellenization* shaped much of the World's understanding of spirituality. Hellenization refers generally to the adoption of Greek ways by non-Greek cultures, but Alexander's military advance through the Persian Empire brought transfomation to both the West and the East. Before his conquests, differences between East and West restricted flows of information and products, but the creation of Alexander's short-lived empire opened enduring flows in both directions.

Bringing a higher standard of living to both the East and the West, Alexander the Great benefitted the world that came after him. To the East, he brought Greek medicine and numerous model Greek cities (usually named Alexandria[1]) with advanced architecture, theaters, and temples, and to the West, he brought the treasures of the East: exotic

---

[1] Alexander may have founded as many as 57 separate cities named Alexandria.

trade goods, sophisticated new crafts, and new philosophical and religious ideas. He unified most of the known civilized world, installing Greek rulers from Anatolia and Egypt to Afghanistan. After Alexander, Easterners and Westerners understood their world differently.

Alexander's personality influenced the world that came after him as much as any of his accomplishments. Possessing immense ambition and almost miraculous abilities, he sought and received recognition as a deity in the East. Many of his successors deified themselves and struggled to rebuild the vast empire that had been lost after Alexander's death. Even though his successors never rebuilt Alexander's empire, they quickly ensured that much of the world spoke the Greek language, adopted Greek artistic conventions, and studied Greek philosophy. Greek myths and philosophies influenced the East, and Zoroastrian, Hindu, and Buddhist ideas influenced the West. Eastern ideas profoundly transformed Western philosophy during the Hellenistic Age, fueling a cultural blossoming sometimes called the Golden Age of Hellenism.

Among the many accomplishments of Alexander, his conquest of the Persian Empire brought an awareness of Jewish culture to the West. While great cultures of the East—Egypt, Assyria, Babylon, and Persia—had long recorded interactions with Jews, Greeks had paid little attention to the kingdoms of Judah and Israel. Writing in the fifth century B.C., Herodotus, known as the Father of Western History, mentioned Palestine[2] but failed to mention Jews at all. Also, despite the numerous references to money in the *Old Testament*, no Jewish coins have been found that date earlier than the fourth century B.C., a time when Persia controlled Jewish territories and when coins bearing Jewish names and symbols first began to appear.

THE PERSIAN EMPIRE

In the middle of the sixth century B.C., Cyrus the Great (a Zoroastrian) began merging large states—Neo-Babylonia, Neo-Assyria, Medea,

---
[2]Greeks called the region Palestine because Greek settlers named Philistines established colonies in the region during the twelfth century B.C., almost a thousand years before the conquests of Alexander the Great.

Lydia, Egypt, and even parts of India[3]—into the largest empire the world had yet known. He ruled this empire with an administration that respected the customs and cults of all his subjects. In 530 B.C., he died in battle attempting to expand the empire further north into the steppes of Kazakhstan and Uzbekistan.

Cambyses II, a son of Cyrus, reigned briefly. Although he continued expanding the Persian Empire into central Asia as well as south and west into Egypt and Libya, internal attempts to usurp control of the empire caught him by surprise. Hopes for a dynasty of Cyrus ended with Cambyses II's death in 522 B.C., however Persia soon entered its finest period. Darius I eliminated all other contenders for the throne and expanded the empire in all directions. An enlightened ruler, he continued to promulgate the unifying policies of Cyrus.

Darius continued expanding the Persian Empire east to the Indus Valley, north to the Black Sea and the Danube River, south to Egypt, and west almost to Athens. In one of the key historical moments that helped preserve Western culture, General Miltiades of Athens defeated the forces of Darius I in 490 B.C. at the Battle of Marathon, which forced the Persian army to withdraw from Europe and return to Asia.

Under King Xerxes, Persia attempted one more time to expand its empire west in 480 B.C. However, an Athenian once again saved Western culture: Themistocles defeated the Persian navy in the straits near Salamis (an island in the Saronic Gulf near Athens). Persia never again invaded Greece. Instead, the empire focused on solidifying its control over rebellious Egyptians in Egypt and Greeks in Asia.

PERSIAN RELIGIOUS TOLERANCE

Profound cultural differences separated Eastern and Western consciousness in the fourth century B.C. Fundamentally optimistic and independent, Greeks combined a belief in multiple gods with a belief in personal freedom. A man's reach depended on his ability. With a little help from one god or another, a person could aspire to anything.

---

[3] From a modern perspective, the parts of "India" conquered by Persia and Alexander mostly occupy the modern nation of Pakistan.

However, monotheistic[4] Persians had a more hierarchical, mission-oriented view of the universe: All virtuous people owed allegiance to Ahura Mazda in the war against evil. The best to which a common Persian could aspire was to live a virtuous life while avoiding pain and disaster as much as possible. As the earthly representative of Ahura Mazda, the Persian King of Kings demanded submission and obeisance from his subjects. Forced to accommodate Eastern traditions, Greeks in Asia found it offensive to bow to Persian leaders.

Still, Persians treated the different cultures in their empire with respect, tolerating Greek and Eastern gods because Zoroastrians recognized Ahura Mazda as the source of everything good in the universe. To the extent that a foreign deity taught virtue and wisdom, that deity existed as an aspect of Ahura Mazda. By reinterpreting the nature of foreign deities, Zoroastrianism embraced and strongly influenced all non-Zoroastrian cults in the Persian Empire.

BAAL AND HIS CONSORTS

In the Levant from Asia Minor to just north of Egypt, Eastern Greek and Western Semitic city-states worshipped local versions of a male god frequently called Baal. Even if the local deity had a different name (for example, Hadad) worshippers might refer to the deity as Baal, Adon, or Adonai, which were Semitic appellations for lord or master. People generally understood gods called Baal as storm gods or solar deities. In some cults, only priests spoke the real name of the deity, and they did so only on special occasions. Greeks associated Baal sometimes with Cronos and sometimes with Zeus. Gods called Baal generally ruled with consorts and sometimes ruled a small number of lesser deities. Consorts of Baal in different regions included goddesses like Baalat, Asherah, Astarte, Tanit, and Cybele.

By combining both Zoroastrian and local religious images on local coinage, Persians affirmed tolerance of religious diversity while

---

[4]Zoroastrianism incorporates both monotheism and dualism: Everything good comes from Ahura Mazda who eventually will destroy Angra Mainyu, the source of all evil.

Figure 9-1. Coin Showing the Gods, Ahura Mazda and Baal of Issus. Cilicia, Issus, Persian Satrap Tiribazos, AR Stater, 386–380 B.C.

simultaneously encouraging the reinterpretation of non-Persian deities. For example, the Anatolian coin in Figure 9-1 combines both Zoroastrian and local religious iconography: The obverse displays an image of the great Zoroastrian God of Persia, Ahura Mazda; the reverse portrays Baal of Issus, standing and holding an eagle and a scepter. Ahura Mazda holds a lotus flower in his left hand (not visible on this coin), and a flower (either lily or lotus) crowns the scepter of Baal.

The obverse of the coin in Figure 9-2 portrays the Anatolian god Baal of Tarsos looking like Greek Zeus on his throne holding an eagle. The coin's reverse may symbolize an astrological event—the Springtime defeat of the Winter constellation, Taurus the bull, by the Summer constellation, Leo the lion—or, it may refer to a lost story about the origin of Baal of Tarsos or the founding of his city. History failed to record details about the cults and mythologies of most Baals. However, like Ahura Mazda, Eastern Baals generally lived in the sky and dominated the universe more completely than Greek Zeus. After the conquests of Alexander, Syrian traders and slaves began moving throughout the Hellenized Western world spreading the idea of an all-powerful deity that ruled the universe from his home in the sky.

Figure 9-2. Baal of Tarsos with Astrological Symbols. Cilicia, Tarsos, Satrap Mazaios, AR Stater, ca. 361–334 B.C.

ATARGATIS: THE SYRIAN APHRODITE

Numerous goddess cults thrived under the Persians in Syria, varying from town to town throughout the region. However, despite all the Baalats, Asherahs, Astartes, and other female deities, Atargatis acquired an international reputation as the Great Goddess of Syria. The obverse of the coin in Figure 9-3 portrays Atargatis, commonly referred to as the White Goddess or the Syrian Aphrodite. The coin's reverse portrays a priest of the goddess riding in a cart. Atargatis ruled as an Earth goddess and mistress of beasts, and her husband (usually Hadad or Baal) ruled the heavens and controlled storms and lightning. Descending from Middle Eastern goddesses like Ishtar, Asherah, and Astarte, Atargatis often ruled as a member of a triad that included her husband, Baal, and her lover, Adonis. Adonis descended from gods named Dumuzi, Tammuz, and Adonai. He governed mysteries of life and death as he divided his year, like Persephone, living six months above ground with Atargatis and six months in the underworld as the lover of the Queen of the Dead.

In the beginning of time, divine fish (remembered as the constellation, Pisces) left an egg on the banks of the Euphrates. Doves found the egg and hatched Atargatis. The doves fed the young goddess and

Figure 9-3. Great Goddess of Syria, Atargatis, and Priest Riding in Cart in the Sacred City, Bambyce (Hierapolis). Syria, Cyrrhestica, Bambyce, Priest-King Abdhad, AR Didrachm, ca. 340–332 B.C.

protected her. When she accidentally fell into a pool at Bambyce, fish saved her. Fish and doves[5] remained sacred to this goddess, particularly the fish in the sacred pool of Bambyce.

In Bambyce, a purple-robed, gold-crowned priest-king ruled over 300 white-robed priests in a lavishly decorated temple of Atargatis. To join the priesthood, men sometimes castrated themselves and made an offering of their own bloody flesh. At special ceremonies of ecstatic dance, worshippers flagellated themselves with many-tailed whips and sliced their arms with swords and axes. Twice daily, priests sacrificed to the goddess in an atmosphere sanctified by incense, chanting, and music from flutes, castanets, and drums. Also twice daily, priests sacrificed to Hadad in silence. Sometimes they sacrificed children.

JEWISH CULTS UNDER THE PERSIANS

Modern Jews and Christians share many popular misconceptions about ancient Jewish cults, for example, that all Jews were strict monotheists, that Solomon built their only temple in Jerusalem, that Jewish cultic practices differed radically from pagan cultic practices, that Jewish law

---

[5]Because of this regional religious bias, fish and doves also play special roles in Christian scripture.

was based on vengeance (an eye for an eye), and that Jews never made images of their god. Contrary to popular belief, several different Jewish cults[6] existed under the Persians—Babylonian, Samaritan, Egyptian, and perhaps others—each with its own temple or temples.[7] Most Jewish cults worshipped a single god, but Jewish cults in a world that worshipped numerous other gods differed considerably from modern monotheistic religions that assert that only one god exists. In its current form, the *Hebrew Bible* explicitly refers to at least 23 pagan deities, mostly asserting greater power of the Jewish god but never stating that pagan deities did not exist. Jewish cults ambiguously referred to their god as Lord, just as other cults did throughout the Middle East. In fact, Jewish cultic worship strongly resembled the cultic worship of supreme deities like Baal, Zeus, and Ahura Mazda, gods who dominated all other spiritual beings in the universe. Solomon's temple, built with the traditional styling of a Northern Syrian long-room temple,[8] provided a place for Jews to sacrifice animals, burn incense, and perform religious rituals just as pagan temples provided for non-Jewish populations. Jewish temples existed outside of Jerusalem, and some Jews made images of their god; some Jews even believed that their god ruled with a consort named Asherah.[9]

Sharing many religious practices with Eastern cults that ranged from Egypt to Anatolia, Jewish Cults distinguished themselves by their reverence for written teachings called *Torah* (in modern times, the first five books of the *Old Testament*), which specified Jewish purity laws, obligations, and proscriptions. The *Torah* also served as the foundation for a particularly egalitarian and fair legal system. Other ethnic groups in the Middle East had created different laws for nobles, commoners, and

---

[6]The *Hebrew Bible* reflects the diversity of Jewish cults that existed before the text was codified. One of the easiest ways to see this is by comparing the two different accounts of creation that appear in *Genesis*, the Elohist creation story (*Genesis* 1:1–2:3) and the Yahwist creation story (beginning in *Genesis* 2:4).
[7]By the dawn of the Christian era, dozens of Jewish cults existed, each characterized generally by the degree to which it connected to a specific personality or ethnic group adhering to a particular blend of Semitic, Greek, Babylonian, and Egyptian ideas.
[8]See "Temple Architecture: What Can Archaeology Tell Us About Solomon's Temple?" by Volkmar Fritz in *Biblical Archaeology Review*, July/August 1987, pp. 38–45, and pp. 48–49.
[9]See "Understanding Asherah—Exploring Semitic Iconography" by Ruth Hestrin in *Biblical Archaeology Review*, Sept./Oct. 1991, pp. 50–59.

Chapter 9 | The Dawn of the Hellenistic Age   175

Figure 9-4. Coin of Tarsos Displaying City Towers, Possibly Representing Jerusalem. Cilicia, Tarsos, Satrap Mazaios, AR Stater, ca. 361–334 B.C.

slaves, sometimes requiring the punishment of a perpetrator's entire family for a minor offense to a nobleman. In contrast, Jews possessed a single set of laws that applied equally from the lowest to the highest levels of Jewish society. Also, contrary to popular understanding, the Jewish principle of an "eye for an eye" (known as *Lex Talionis*) limited punishment more than prescribing it: Punishments had to be appropriate to wrongs, and even slaves were entitled to monetary compensation for bodily harm caused by masters.[10] Although modern readers see Jewish laws as prescribing a code of vengeance, Jewish laws expressed the innovative view that justice should be administered equally to all members of a society and that damage to a "tooth, an eye, a hand, or a foot" should be punished with no more than equivalent damage (usually a monetary equivalent) to the perpetrator of the crime.

Minted by the Persian *satrap* (governor), Mazaios,[11] the coin in Figure 9-4 emphasizes the importance of Tarsos as an administrative center, the size of the administered region, and the importance of Jews

---

[10] See the analysis of *Exodus* 21:24–27 in *JPS Torah Commentary: Exodus* p. 127 by Nahum Sarna.
[11] Persia controlled its vast empire by dividing it into large provinces and installing governors, each governor (satrap) responsible for the health and stability of a single province as well as for implementing the policies and directives of the Persian emperor. Mazaios, the Persian satrap who surrendered Babylon to Alexander the Great, continued working afterward in Alexander's Persian administration.

within it. Like the coin in Figure 9-2, the obverse of the coin in Figure 9-4 portrays Baal, and the reverse portrays a lion attacking a bull over towers of a city wall. Text on the reverse hints that the towers and wall refer to the towers and wall surrounding Jerusalem.

Scholars usually have translated the text on the reverse of this coin as "Mazaios governor of Transeuphrates and Cilicia." However, the Aramaic inscription uses phraseology similar to that found in the *Hebrew Bible*. As described in the book of *Nehemiah*, the Persian administration of Artaxerxes I allowed Jerusalem to rebuild its city walls in the middle of the fifth century B.C. Biblical numismatics authority, David Hendin, translates the inscription as, "Mazaios who is over beyond the river and Cilicia." The similarity of this text to a descriptive phrase used seven times in the books of *Ezra* and *Nehemiah* led Hendin to suggest that this coin portrays towers of the wall around Jerusalem. Thus, the language and symbols on the coin in Figure 9-4 connect it directly with the completion of Jerusalem's walls as well as the codification of the *Hebrew Bible*, events that occurred around the same time under Persian administration.[12]

Persian rulers rewarded cooperative states and punished rebellious ones. Perhaps because they respected Zoroastrian monotheism, Jerusalem Jews cooperated with Persian imperial administration and, in return, received funding for city projects and a large measure of self-rule. In contrast, many former Greek city-states chafed under Persian rule and continually looked for opportunities to liberate themselves from oriental despotism. When tested, Persian rulers ruthlessly put down regional rebellions involving Greeks, Egyptians, and ambitious members of the Persian royal family.[13]

Babylonian Jews

Before Cyrus created the Persian Empire, King Nebuchadnezzar of Babylon had repeatedly conquered Judea (in 597, 586, and 581 B.C.) and taken most of the Jewish population in and around Jerusalem to Babylon. In particular, Nebuchadnezzar destroyed Jerusalem,

---

[12]See the *Guide to Biblical Coins,* 4th edition, pp. 100–103, by David Hendin.
[13]Xenophon, a Greek mercenary, provided a vivid description of events surrounding the rebellion by Cyrus the Younger around 400 B.C. in *The Persian Expedition.*

Figure 9-5. Portrait of Persian Satrap; God of Judah on Throne with Wing and Wheel Viewed by Moses or Ezekiel. Judah, AR Drachm, 370–333 B.C.

including Solomon's Temple, as punishment for the Jewish uprising in 586 B.C.

Jerusalem Jews adapted to their new life in Babylon, an ancient cultural center with a royal library containing centuries of recorded history. After Cyrus incorporated Babylon into the Persian Empire, the status of Jews changed from a captive people to just another minority. Jews acquired Persian educations and rose to high positions in the service of the Persian King. The Jewish Holiday of Purim featuring the story of Queen Esther survives as an encapsulated memory of the experience of Babylonian Jews in the Persian Empire.

As Jews in Babylon struggled to preserve the Jerusalem cult without a temple, they began collecting and editing their most important religious texts. A relatively small captive nation, these Jews accomplished for Judaism what no Greek ever accomplished for ancient Greek mythology: They integrated a broad and diverse set of religious documents into a single, rich, fairly consistent patchwork of Jewish sacred texts. With stories indebted to both Mediterranean and Babylonian sources, these texts told the story of Jews from the beginning of the universe to the Jewish captivity in Babylon. When Babylonian Jews returned to Jerusalem, they brought their sacred scriptures with them.

During the fourth century B.C., Jerusalem Jews minted coins that bore images of the God of Moses. The obverse of the coin in Figure 9-5 probably shows the face of a Persian satrap, but the reverse portrays a deity. Consistent with images of Baal and Zeus, the deity sits on a throne and holds an eagle—yet the throne recalls Ezekiel's vision of God's chariot with a winged wheel (*Ezekiel* 1:4–28). The bearded face in the lower right corner might represent Ezekiel, or it might represent Moses. The script spells the word, Yehud (Judah), in ancient Hebrew. The iconography and inscription connects the coin directly to Jews and the city of Jerusalem in the Persian province of Judah.

Samaritan Jews

However, King Nebuchadnezzar never deported all Jews to Babylon. Remaining near Mount Gerizim, the site where Joshua built an altar and pronounced his blessings, Samaritans considered themselves the guardians of the original and authentic Jewish cult. When Jews began to return from Babylon to Jerusalem during the time of King Cyrus[14] around 536 B.C., Samaritan Jews and Jerusalem Jews represented similar but antagonistic cults.[15] By the fourth century B.C., Jerusalem Jews had restarted their cult in the Second Temple, had rebuilt the walled city of Jerusalem, and had largely completed the canonization of their official Jewish scriptures. Possibly in response to the canonization of scriptures in Jerusalem, Jews in Samaria canonized similar sacred scriptures[16] that contained key differences from the Jerusalem text.

Samaritans worshipped their god in Shechem. The Samaritan *Torah* directed the building of a temple on top of Mount Gerizim and the offering of sacrifices to occur only there. The ancient Samaritan sect survives today in the towns of Nablus and Holon in modern Israel and still preserves its version of the *Torah*. Other Jewish sects may well have used their own, slightly different versions of the *Torah* and *Hebrew Bible* that have not survived.[17]

---

[14]Cyrus the Great is the only non-Jew in the *Hebrew Bible* to be referred to as "God's Messiah" (see *Isaiah* 45:1), which means "God's anointed." This term otherwise refers to the Jewish priests and kings anointed with holy oil as part of their assumption of office. (See *Exodus* 30:22–25.)

[15]To Samaritans, Jews returning from Babylon even had offensive names. The name of Queen Esther's cousin, Mordecai, honored Marduk, the patron deity of Babylon.

[16]Texts of the *Old Testament* used by Christians reflect influences from Babylonian, Samaritan, Egyptian, and possibly other versions of Jewish scripture.

[17]Some Phrygian Jews conflated Yahweh with Attis and Jupiter Sabazius. See *Oriental Religions in Roman Paganism* pp. 62–64 by Franz Cumont.

Chapter 9 | The Dawn of the Hellenistic Age   179

Figure 9-6. Picture of Deity with Three Faces as Well as Five Silver Coins for the Jewish Pidyon Ha' Ben Ceremony. Samaria, AR Obol, ca. 375–333 B.C.

The Samaritan coin in Figure 9-6 bears ancient Jewish symbolism that reveals strong Eastern influence. On the reverse, a pile of five Athenian tetradrachms symbolizes the five shekels of silver paid during a Jewish Pidyon Ha' Ben ceremony. As prescribed in *Numbers* 18:15, a non-priestly Jewish family presented its first-born son to a temple priest on the thirty-first day after the child's birth. The priest and the family then conducted a Pidyon Ha' Ben ceremony, during which the parents paid the priest five silver coins to redeem their baby. Seemingly unrelated to known Jewish cults, the image on the obverse portrays a deity with three faces.

Consistent with Zoroastrian and Chaldaean ideas, supreme deities throughout Syria commonly possessed three aspects. A priest might address such a deity using three different names, yet the deity would remain one. Evidence that this idea influenced Jews comes from Roman descriptions of the god of the Jews as having multiple heads like snake-legged Typhon.[18] To Samaritan Jews, the faces on the coin in Figure 9-6 expressed the power and mystery of God while affirming the obligation for all Jews to live according to the laws of the *Torah*.

---

[18]For a Roman myth associating the Jewish god Yahweh with Typhon, see *Of Isis and Osiris* 31.363C–D by Plutarch. See *The Masks of God: Occidental Mythology* pp. 274–275 by Joseph Campbell for Hellenistic images of Yahweh as a snake-legged deity.

Egyptian Jews

Little information has survived concerning the special attributes of Egyptian Jewish cults;[19] however, the *Old Testament* documents a long-standing connection between Jews and Egypt. The Jewish Patriarch, Jacob, may have ruled Egypt as a Hyksos[20] King, and *Exodus* describes how Jewish tribes abandoned Egypt for their new home in the Promised Land during the reign of Ramses II.[21] In Egypt, Jews may well have been influenced by the heretic pharaoh Akhenaten[22] who changed the official Egyptian cult into a monotheistic reverence for the sun during the fourteenth century B.C. Jewish royal seals commonly used Egyptian solar symbols to connect Jewish royalty with divinity. For example, Hezekiah's seal, found on numerous jar handles from the beginning of the seventh century B.C., portrayed an Egyptian winged solar disk as a reference to divinity. While Persia controlled Egypt, the good relationship between Persians and Jews extended also to Jews in Egypt: Describing the results of the Persian invasion of Egypt, a papyrus[23] from Upper Egypt said that the Persians destroyed the temples of Egyptian gods, but they did not damage the Jewish temple on Elephantine Island.

The two Jewish kingdoms in Palestine (Judah and Israel) often combined iconography from Egypt and the Middle East. For example, the obverse of the Samaritan coin in Figure 9-7 comes from Middle Eastern iconography and represents a Cherub—not a chubby flying baby (Greek Eros) that decorates modern Valentine's Day cards, but the powerful winged creature referenced in the *Bible*.[24] Cherubim dwelled with God and served him in the Holy of Holies of the Jewish temple. Ancient art portrayed them in a variety of forms and always

---

[19]Excavations of the Jewish temple on Elephantine Island in Egypt have produced evidence that some Egyptian Jews associated their God with the Egyptian ram-headed god Khnum, part of a divine triad that included his consort Satis and her daughter Anuket.
[20]The Hyksos were Semites who ruled Egypt during the seventeenth and sixteenth centuries B.C.
[21]Rameses II, Pharaoh of Egypt from 1279–1213 B.C., is commonly identified as the pharaoh in Exodus.
[22]Akhenaten ruled as Pharaoh of Egypt from approximately 1350–1335 B.C.
[23]See the Elephantine papyrus, *Petition to Bagoas*, in the Sayce-Cowley collection.
[24]Some Theologians believe that *Ezekiel* 10:14 provides evidence that a Cherub had the face of a bull.

Chapter 9 | The Dawn of the Hellenistic Age   181

Figure 9-7. Composite Creature (Cherub?) and a Naked Deity Portrayed as Egyptian Creator God. Samaria, AR Hemiobol, ca. 375–333 B.C.

combined attributes of different animals: the wings of an eagle; the body of a bull or lion; the head of a bull, lion, or man; and, sometimes, the hands of a man.

The reverse of the coin in Figure 9-7 portrays a naked human form. In the fourth century B.C., nude images on Eastern coins represented deities. This deity masturbates, just as the sun god Ra—the first God of Egypt and the divine creator of all things—generated the universe in an act of masturbation. To Egyptians, the world's existence required a continuing act of creation.[25] Regarding the bird clutched in the deity's hand,[26] this Egyptian symbol sometimes identified a creator god and sometimes symbolized the power of a deity or a pharaoh over people.

Numismatists usually refer to the coin in Figure 9-7 as a temple boy[27] type, sometimes hinting that the coin's design referred to temple boys working as male prostitutes in fourth century B.C. Samaria.

---

[25] As a full participant in the divine mythology of Egypt, a pharaoh's wife often took the religious title, "Hand of God," to represent her erotic role in Egyptian creation rituals.
[26] In Greek iconography, a deity with an eagle universally represented Zeus.
[27] The Cypriot "temple boy" was portrayed as a chubby two-year-old sitting on his left leg with his right foot close to his body and his right knee pointing up. Referring to an Eastern tradition of temple care for orphaned or vulnerable young children, temple boys usually wore protective amulets and sometimes a shirt, but most exposed their genitals without touching them. Sometimes they held a small creature (chicken or rabbit) in one hand as they leaned on their other arm. In Figure 9-7, the vigorous naked youth portrayed with an eagle represents a deity, not a temple boy.

Even if such a tradition existed, the iconography of this coin remains obscure: Is the boy giving or receiving an eagle for performing an obscene act of personal gratification? Surviving ancient literature fails to document any tradition of temple boy prostitution in Samaria. If this coin had come from ancient Egypt, archaeologists would not hesitate to identify the deity as the sun god Ra creating the universe. From Samaria, a region with a long tradition of combining symbols from Egypt and the Middle East, this coin expresses respect and devotion to the all-powerful God of Jews.[28]

ALEXANDER'S INVASION OF PERSIA

The Persian Empire attempted to use its wealth and influence to manipulate and weaken its many Greek neighbors. By the middle of the fourth century B.C., an ambitious Macedonian king named Philip II wanted to punish the Persians for meddling in Greek politics. Toward this end, he sought opportunities to inflame the persistent dissatisfaction of Asian Greek communities. Philip dreamed of someday invading and conquering Asia, but challenges in Greece kept him too preoccupied to attempt such a venture.

Born in 356 B.C. to King Philip II, Alexander III of Macedon (Alexander the Great) seized all the opportunities that his privileged position offered. The most brilliant philosopher of the day, Aristotle, taught Alexander science, philosophy, rhetoric, medicine, and literature. Philip II, an excellent general, taught Alexander the skills of war and practical leadership. More importantly, Alexander's own character continually placed him in positions where he could exercise and develop these skills.

While Philip II led his army against Byzantion, sixteen-year-old Alexander ruled as Regent of Macedon, led his first victorious military campaign, and founded a city named Alexandropolis. When Philip II marched against the combined forces of Athens and Thebes

---

[28]For other examples of the religious use of phallic symbols by Jews on amulets, see *The Masks of God: Occidental Mythology* pp. 274–275 by Joseph Campbell.

at Chaeronea, eighteen-year-old Alexander led the cavalry wing that defeated the previously invincible Sacred Band of Thebes. Twenty-year-old Alexander assumed the title of King of Macedon after a royal bodyguard assassinated Philip II in Aegae. Within two years of his coronation, Alexander had consolidated control over Greece and mobilized an army against the Persians in Asia Minor. See Figure 9-8 for a timeline of Alexander's life.

Immediately after crossing the Hellespont from Europe to Asia Minor, Alexander the Great began defeating Persian forces and proclaiming the liberation of Greek cities. Beginning with his first victories over wealthy cities in Anatolia, Alexander minted thousands of new tetradrachms like the coin in Figure 9-9. The obverse of this coin portrays the young king wearing a lion skin hat like Herakles because Macedonians believed that their king descended directly from the famous Dorian hero. On the reverse, Zeus (Herakles' divine father) sits on his throne on Mount Olympus, his scepter surmounted by a flower,[29] mostly overlapping the beaded edge on this coin.

Retreating Persian forces initiated a scorched-earth policy: They destroyed cities, crops, and food-stores in advance of Alexander. Tarsos, the capital of Cilicia and an important Persian administrative center, barely escaped destruction. The Persians delayed destroying Tarsos too long, believing they could hold Alexander at the Cilician Gates, an easily defended mountain pass. (See the map in Figure 9-10.) Alexander surprised the Persians by capturing the Cilician Gates at night and then forcing his way quickly to Tarsos. The Greeks of Tarsos welcomed Alexander as their city's savior. The city's central location between East and West as well as its usefulness supporting Alexander's push south helped ensure Tarsos' future as a major Hellenistic cultural center.

At Tarsos, Alexander received the first reports concerning the Persian response to his overwhelming success in Anatolia and imminent invasion of Syria. Darius III ordered the finest soldiers from every administrative region of Persia to congregate in Syria under his

---

[29]Tetradrachms of Alexander the Great often portray the scepter of Zeus surmounted by a flower (lily or lotus blossom), a cross, or an eagle—symbols commonly associated with Eastern cults of Zeus.

Figure 9-8. Timeline of the Life of Alexander the Great.

Figure 9-9. Alexander the Great as Herakles, and Zeus, Enthroned. AR Tetradrachm, 333–327 B.C.

command. When Alexander finally marched east, an excellent army many times larger than his own waited to challenge him.

VICTORY AT ISSUS FOLLOWED BY A DECADE OF EMPIRE BUILDING

At the decisive Battle of Issus in 333 B.C., Alexander the Great confronted Darius III, Great King of Persia, Anatolia, Egypt, Bactria, and the Indus Valley. Outnumbered more than three to one,[30] the Macedonian army nonetheless decisively defeated Darius. The Persian king escaped, but Alexander captured Darius' mother and wives. To these Persian women, Alexander's conduct appeared so noble that Darius' mother disowned her son and adopted Alexander the Great. Alexander effectively conquered the Persian Empire in a single battle, but it still took years to assert control over the empire and to finish off Darius.

After defeating Darius III at Issus, Alexander marched his soldiers south through Syria and Phoenicia, offering peace but not tolerating insults. When he sent ambassadors to the fortified island city of Tyre,

---

[30]The modern historian, Will Durant, estimated Alexander's force at Issus as fewer than 30,000 men, and Darius' as more than 600,000.

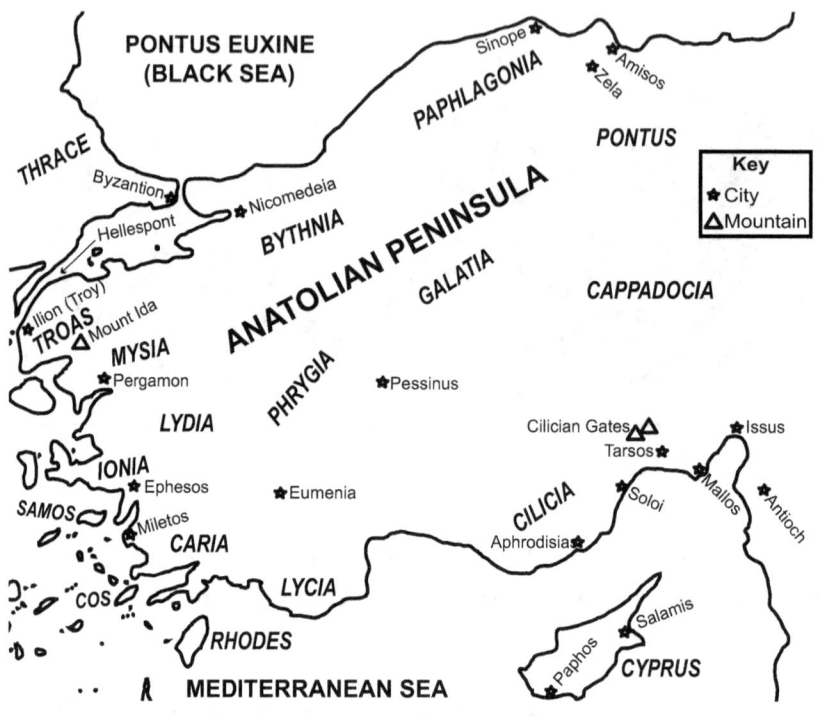

Figure 9-10. Map of Anatolian Peninsula.

the city treacherously murdered them and threw their bodies into the sea. Alexander resolved to make an example of the city. He built a land bridge to the island 200 yards wide and half a mile long. After a long and bitter struggle—at the cost of seven months and 400 Macedonian lives—Alexander slaughtered more than 7,000 Tyrians and sold more than 30,000 into slavery. The rough treatment of Tyre reduced further opposition as the relatively small Macedonian force asserted control over the western part of the Persian Empire. Even today, Alexander's land bridge still connects the city of Tyre to the mainland, a surviving reminder of the city's crushing defeat.

As Alexander advanced, he always honored local deities as if they were identically equivalent to Greek gods. For example, he identified the goddess Atargatis as Hera and the god Hadad as Zeus. When Alexander marched through Israel and Judah on his way to Egypt, he passed through the Samaritan town of Shechem, probably recognizing the god of Samaritan Jews as Zeus and sacrificing to him in the temple at Mount Gerizim.[31]

After ensuring that he controlled the port cities of West Asia (denying Darius any military use of the Persian navy), Alexander raced to secure Egypt, a strategic supplier of grain. Egypt welcomed the conqueror and crowned him pharaoh in Memphis. Afterward, when he visited a famous Egyptian Oracle at the Siwa Oasis, Egyptian priests confirmed the popular suspicion that Zeus,[32] not Philip, had fathered the young conqueror just as Zeus had fathered Herakles. Alexander's official connection with divinity established a precedent for his successors, called the *Diadochi*, to claim links with divinity as well.

By 331 B.C., Alexander had conquered all of western Asia and most of North Africa. It took him four more years to march across Asia, kill Darius III, establish a Greek presence in Afghanistan, and invade India. Spending his last few years dealing with various forms of mutiny and rebellion, Alexander returned to Persepolis in 324 B.C. On the tenth or eleventh of June in 323 B.C., he died in Babylon approximately a month before his thirty-third birthday.

AFTER THE DEATH OF ALEXANDER THE GREAT

A conqueror other than Alexander might have persisted in seeing every foreign cult as worshipping a different god, which would have preserved the boundaries between different cultures. Such a conqueror might have tolerated some cults and persecuted others, and after his death the world quickly would have returned to the way it was before. Instead, Alexander the Great helped foster a world view that only one hierarchy of gods existed in the universe, all of them ruled by Zeus. By establishing the equivalence between Eastern and Western deities, Alexander initiated a complex mixing of Eastern and Western cults and laid a spiritual foundation for the broad acceptance of one supreme

---

[31] Despite Josephus' description of Alexander's sacrifice in the Jerusalem Temple (see *Antiquities of the Jews* 11.317–345), most scholars believe that Alexander the Great passed through Shechem and never visited Jerusalem.

[32] In Egypt, a popular myth said that the last Egyptian pharaoh, Nektanebo, took the form of Amon-Ra and had intercourse with Alexander's mother in Macedon.

deity as the ruler of the universe.[33] Building on the tolerant and unifying policies initiated under Persian rule, Alexander the Great facilitated the creation of a spiritual and intellectual environment that helped big ideas and large enterprises take shape in the Western world.

After Alexander died, his generals roughly divided his empire—Cassander ruled Macedon, Lysimachus ruled Thrace, Ptolemy ruled from Egypt to Syria, and Seleukos ruled from Mesopotamia to Bactria—and they battled among themselves for a generation. Nevertheless, the rulers who had derived power from their association with Alexander oversaw processes of Hellenization that gave rise to a glorious age of clarification, transformation, and cultural homogenization. Throughout the known world, an educated class arose among the multitude of ethnicities; people who spoke, read, and wrote in Greek combined Eastern and Western influences to create fine works of art, literature, and science.

Like Alexander, the Diadochi generally respected different cultures in their empires. They preserved infrastructure, honored sophisticated knowledge, and connected similar concepts in the East and West. Believing that everyone worshipped the same gods by different names, they worshipped Baal of the Middle East as Zeus; they worshipped Isis of Egypt as Demeter and Aphrodite; and they built temples to combination deities that integrated Eastern and Western religious ideas in new cities throughout their empires.

---

[33]To appreciate the importance of this idea, consider what happens in a society when two men worship different, equally powerful deities. When one man asks the other how many head of cattle he has, no accurate reply can be given. A truthful answer might fuel jealous interactions between competing gods, and accurately counted livestock might die. A society that worships multiple, equally powerful deities avoids taking accurate inventories, distrusts communications, and even questions the existence of any single truth about the universe. The author first encountered this issue while designing a socioeconomic survey for a polytheistic tribe in Abyei, Sudan, in 1977.

CHAPTER
10

THE HELLENIZATION OF EASTERN CULTS

> Shaping Eastern cults according to Hellenistic tastes, Alexander's successors oversaw revisions of cult mythologies, the creation of Western astrology, and production of a Greek version of the *Old Testament*.

The adventures of Alexander the Great in Asia set the standard by which all future military leaders would measure themselves, yet military exploits alone fail to explain the degree to which he changed the world. Alexander founded Greek-style cities throughout the world that contained temples to hybrid deities like Zeus/Ahura Mazda and Hera/Cybele, which encouraged Hellenistic Greeks to think of exotic foreign deities as regional expressions of Greek ones. Subsequently, the creative merging of Eastern and Western ideas, known as Hellenization, helped transform civilization throughout Europe, Asia, and North Africa.

Greek mythology traveled East. For example, Herakles entered Buddhism and transformed into Vajrapani, one of the three aspects of Buddha that served as protective deities. Vajrapani represented Buddha's power, while two other deities represented Buddha's wisdom and compassion. Figure 10-1 illustrates the remarkable preservation

Figure 10-1. Left: Bust of Hadrian, and Sandan (Herakles) Standing on the Back of a Horned Lion. Tarsos, AR Tridrachm, 117–138 A.D. Right: Carved Doors Portraying Taa Raa Ban (Vajrapani) on the Back of a Stylized Lion. Palace of Rama I (Eighteenth Century A.D.), Bangkok, Thailand.

of Herakles' iconography across time and distance: On the left, a coin from Tarsos minted during the second century A.D. portrays Herakles as the local hero, Sandan, standing on the back of a horned lion; on the right, carved wooden doors in the eighteenth century palace of Rama I in Bangkok, Thailand, portray the god Taa Raa Ban (a local version of Vajrapani) standing on the back of a stylized lion as he guards the entrance to a Buddhist sanctuary.

Asian iconography and ideas traveled both East and West. Traveling East, Atargatis transformed into the Buddhist deity Hariti.[1] As far East as Japan, Boreas, the Greek God of the North Wind, influenced the development of Fujin, one of the eldest Shinto gods. Traveling West, abstract Buddhist and Hindu notions that associated life with illusion, evil, and suffering slowly shifted the temper of Hellenistic philosophy away from fundamental optimism toward a desire to avoid pain.

---

[1] Hariti was a child-devouring ogress that Buddha converted into a protector of women and children.

Even so, the first two centuries of the Hellenistic Age, from 300 B.C. to 100 B.C., produced the greatest scientific achievements of the ancient world. In the third century B.C., Eratosthenes of Cyrene (a city in Libya) and his Alexandrian students calculated the circumference of the Earth as 28,675 miles, approximately 15 percent larger than the measure we now accept. Aristarchus of Samos claimed that the Earth revolved around the sun, affirming a Copernican solar system almost two thousand years before Copernicus. Archimedes discovered the lever, specific gravity, and basic principles of integral calculus. Most significantly, by discovering the precession of the Earth's equinoxes in the second century B.C., Hipparchus of Rhodes profoundly influenced the West's concept of the universe, which created a quiet but deeply felt philosophical revolution.[2]

Perhaps the single most influential idea from the East to enter Greek consciousness was that a human being, particularly a ruler, could become a god. Egyptians honored their pharaoh as an incarnation of the god Horus. In Persia, the King of Kings possessed a measure of divinity as Ahura Mazda's representative on Earth. However, Alexander's own deification, strongly supported by Eastern customs, established a precedent for deifying his Greek successors.

A HELLENISTIC PERSPECTIVE ON DIVINITY

Greeks myths supported the belief that some mortals, particularly heroes conceived by gods with mortal virgins, might possess divine attributes. Zeus raised some mortal heroes into the sky as constellations: Examples include Herakles, the Dioscuri (the Gemini twins), and Perseus. Herakles possessed the power to accomplish great deeds, but he needed Athena to help him think things through; the Dioscuri (the only Greek example of purebred humans to become divine) had to share a single divinity between them, and Perseus acquired special divinity from association with the Hellenistic Cult of Mithras. Regardless, Greeks rarely considered it possible for mortals to obtain any

---

[2]See Chapter 13.

Figure 10-2. Alexander the Great as Zeus/Amon. Lysimachus, Thrace, Lysimacheia Mint, AR Tetradrachm, 305–281 B.C.

kind of divine favor greater than a pleasant afterlife among heroes and chthonic deities in a special part of the underworld.

However, a few Greek rulers inspired short-lived religious cults before the time of Alexander the Great, for example: Lysander[3] the Spartan, Empedocles[4] of Akragas, and Dion[5] of Syracuse. Alexander's teacher[6] wrote that a ruler of truly outstanding talent and ability belonged outside the jurisdiction of a state's laws. Such an exceptional man operated as a law unto himself, and his subjects might reasonably consider their ruler a god among men.

After the death of Alexander, people widely thought of him as a god. Lysimachus[7] minted the tetradrachm in Figure 10-2 portraying

---

[3]Killed during a skirmish with Thebans in 395 B.C., Lysander led Sparta to victory over Athens in the Peloponnesian War.
[4]An influential Pythagorean philosopher in the fifth century B.C., Empedocles originated cosmological teachings about the generation of the universe from four elements: earth, air, fire, and water. When he disappeared, many people said that he had transformed directly into a god.
[5]One of Plato's finest students, Dion of Syracuse counseled two successive tyrants of Syracuse. The first sold Plato into slavery, and the second exiled Dion when he became too popular. When Dion returned to Syracuse and brought an end to tyranny, the Syracusan Assembly prayed to him as to a god. He was assassinated before he could implement a new Syracusan government.
[6]See *Politics*, Book 3.13, 1284a, 10–13), by Aristotle.
[7]A Diadochus (successor of Alexander), Lysimachus eventually ruled Thrace, Asia Minor, and Macedonia.

Alexander on the obverse with a horn of Amon[8] growing out of his head. On the coin's reverse, Athena, the Goddess of Wisdom, sits on a throne holding Nike, the winged Goddess of Victory. Coins like this one represent Alexander as an incarnation of Zeus/Amon, a symbolic union of "God, the Father" and "God, the Son."

Modern historians debate whether or not Alexander ever proclaimed himself a god. However, the Oracle at the Siwa Oasis confirmed that Zeus/Amon fathered Alexander, and he eventually adopted the Persian ceremony of *proskynesis*,[9] requiring even free-born Greeks to prostrate themselves before him. While in India, Alexander minted gold coins with the first portraits of himself possessing attributes of Amon.[10]

HELLENIZATION OF SYRIAN AND ANATOLIAN CULTS

After the death of Alexander in 323 B.C., fifty years of war among his successors, the Diadochi, made life hard and unpredictable especially in Syria and Anatolia. History records more about battles and the personalities of competitors than about social and religious changes. However, during this period of instability, a Eumolpid[11] named Timotheus traveled through Anatolia searching for the key to unify Eastern cults of goddesses frequently associated with Aphrodite in the West.

As one of the earliest religious accommodations of Hellenism, Greeks had identified Atargatis as the goddess who helped Deucalion and Pyrrha repopulate the Earth after the Great Flood of Deucalion.[12] Seleukid rulers renamed Bambyce,[13] calling it Hierapolis (the holy

---

[8] Frequently identified with the sun as Amon-Ra, Amon ruled other Egyptian deities as a divine generative principle sometimes known as "lord of the phallus." Amon was identified by Greeks as Zeus and by Phoenicians as Baal (hence, the Phoenician solar deity Baal-Hammon).
[9] The practice of proskynesis involved kissing towards and prostrating oneself before a person with higher rank.
[10] See "Ptolemy's Alexandrian Postscript" by Frank Holt in *Saudi Aramco World* Nov/Dec 2006.
[11] Eumolpus, the first priest of the Eleusinian Mysteries, founded a clan of priests at Eleusis called Eumolpids.
[12] See Chapter 8.
[13] A center for the worship of Atargatis, Bambyce was located near Aleppo, Syria.

city), and said that Deucalion built the city's first temple where the goddess miraculously transformed rocks into human beings. Greeks didn't worry about cult details that contradicted Greek mythology such as the relationship between Atargatis and fish, portrayals of the goddess with webbed feet, and numerous inconsistent variations of Atargatis cults throughout Syria. Going beyond the simplistic Hellenization of Atargatis, Timotheus investigated Eastern cultic details and mythological histories, striving to connect the divine core that unified all Eastern goddesses with the Eleusinian Mysteries in the West.

Timotheus studied the mysteries of goddesses like Cybele and Mâ. The *Galli* of Pessinus (priests of Cybele) gave him access to secret documents, which allowed Timotheus to write a scholarly work that focused on the Cult of Cybele as the center of a broad system of *Phrygian* (Central Anatolian) mysteries. By Hellenizing the cultic practices and traditions of Cybele, Timotheus encouraged Greeks to accept Eastern goddess cults in general as special instances of the Cult of Cybele.

Identifying Atargatis and Cybele as different aspects of the same goddess, Timotheus clarified the story that connected Cybele with Deucalion and Pyrrha. After the creation of the Iron Race, Zeus admired the fertility of the goddess as well as her generosity. Suddenly attracted to the goddess, Zeus descended from Mount Olympus and attempted to seduce her. The goddess tried to resist, but she couldn't prevent the king of the gods from doing what he wanted. Zeus impregnated the naked rock, which then bore a *hermaphroditic*[14] child named Agdistis.

Agdistis expressed himself passionately through lustful, violent acts associated with both male and female inclinations. These unnatural acts disgusted the Olympian Gods so much that Dionysos resolved to fix the problem. While Agdistis slept in a drunken stupor, Dionysos tied one end of a rope around Agdistis' testicles, and the other end around Agdistis' feet. When the sleeping god wakened and stood up, he castrated himself. Blood flowed from his open wound and fertilized the earth. A bush grew from the bloody earth and magically filled with ripe pomegranates.

---

[14]In Greek mythology, the child of Hermes and Aphrodite had both male and female sex organs and was called Hermaphroditus. Even today, we call a person with both male and female sex organs a hermaphrodite.

A local princess, Nana, daughter of King Sangarios, picked one of the beautiful pomegranates, clutched it to her breast, and immediately became pregnant. When King Sangarios discovered that his daughter was pregnant, he locked her in a room intending to starve her to death; but Cybele secretly fed Nana and kept her alive. After Nana gave birth to a boy, the king ordered that the child be abandoned in the wilderness, but ibexes adopted and raised him. The wild boy grew up healthy and strong, and Phrygians called him Attis, after attagis, the Phrygian name for ibex. Cybele loved both Agdistis and Attis. Agdistis passionately loved Attis as well.

One day, while drinking with King Midas of Phrygia, Attis mentioned just how passionately Agdistis loved him. Disgusted by this news, King Midas told Attis that he should not submit to the shame of such an incestuous and unnatural relationship. King Midas suggested instead that Attis consider marrying a princess of Phrygia, namely, King Midas' daughter. After some discussion, Attis agreed.

When the fateful day of the royal marriage arrived, King Midas locked the gates of the capital city so nothing outside could disturb the wedding. Cybele knew, however, that she could ensure Attis' safety only by preventing the marriage. She broke through the city walls with her head, which explains why the goddess wears a crown of city towers.[15] Agdistis then ran into the town and infected the wedding guests with madness.

Out of control, King Midas castrated himself, and his daughter slashed her breasts. Horrified, Attis ran from the city. He continued to run until, exhausted, he stopped next to an evergreen tree. There, Attis castrated himself. Lifting his bloody testicles into the air, he screamed for Agdistis to take them and then died. Violets grew from the earth moistened by his blood.

Cybele picked up Attis' testicles, washed them, and gave them sacred burial. Agdistis and King Midas' daughter wept over the body of Attis, and then the daughter killed herself. After Cybele buried the young girl, a bitter almond tree grew from her grave.

---

[15] Different from the royal diadems of Hellenistic rulers, the crown of Cybele inspired designs for the earliest crowns of the Virgin Mary as well as for crowns of medieval European rulers.

Figure 10-3. Cybele and Hermes. Lesbos, Mytilene, Electrum Hecte, ca. 412–378 B.C.

Agdistis begged Zeus to restore life to Attis. Zeus wanted to help somehow, but Destiny allowed Zeus to restore only the barest minimum of life:[16] Attis' hair continued to grow; his body remained fresh; and he could move one finger. Agdistis founded a cult to protect and take care of Attis.

More complex than the Greek goddess of love, Eastern Aphrodites, like Atargatis and Cybele, governed issues related to life, death, fertility, and war for worshippers throughout Syria and Asia Minor. Traditional images of both goddesses portrayed them seated on thrones and crowned with city towers; however, Atargatis sometimes looked like a mermaid and Cybele usually appeared with lions. Worshippers of Atargatis honored Bambyce as their goddess's sacred home, and devotees of Cybele believed that their goddess lived in a large black meteorite in her temple at Pessinus in Galatia.

Numerous cults throughout the East told stories about local Aphrodites different from the story recorded by Timotheus. With Hellenistic flexibility, a coin like the one in Figure 10-3 could be viewed as honoring a variety of cults that featured goddesses and gods in complicated relationships: Aphrodite and Hermes, Cybele and Agdistis, Cybele and

---

[16]Later cults of Attis believed in full physical resurrection of the god.

Attis, and even Cybele and Hermes. The obverse of the coin portrays a goddess, like Cybele, wearing a crown of city towers, and the reverse portrays a god wearing a *petasus*—the characteristic hat of Hermes and an easily recognizable reference to a hermaphroditic deity.

Eastern Aphrodites were worshipped with music from timbrels, cymbals, flutes, horns, drums, and even banging swords against shields. Priests and priestesses participated in wild dances, slicing their arms with axes and swords. Special holidays often included passion plays that illustrated dramatic events from stories of the gods' lives. Worshippers of Attis decorated evergreen trees to celebrate his resurrection. More extreme than other cults, the Cult of Cybele accepted new priests only after they castrated themselves.

HELLENIZATION OF EGYPTIAN CULTS

Different from all other cults that developed around the Mediterranean Sea, Egyptian cults honored gods that looked like animals. Egyptian gods were complicated: A single god could take the form of many animals. Traditional Egyptians worshipped Isis in forms such as Sekhmet (a lioness), Hathor (a cow), Bastet (a cat), and even Thermoutis (a snake). Greek literature ridiculed Egyptian gods and expressed contempt for people that worshipped them. Alexander the Great didn't live long enough to address the peculiarities of Egyptian cults, but his boyhood friend and trusted general, Ptolemy (see Figure 10-4), faced the issue head-on after he seized an empire that comprised all of Egypt and much of the Levant.

To legitimize his rule as pharaoh, Ptolemy stole the body of Alexander the Great as it traveled from Babylon to Macedon. Carrying the body to Egypt, Ptolemy built a great tomb for Alexander in the most magnificent of the world's many Alexandrias and crowned the city with the Pharos, the most famous of all ancient lighthouses. Gathering experts in all fields, Ptolemy inaugurated enlightened policies that influenced the entire Hellenistic world. To house art and manuscripts that he had collected from distant parts of the world, he built a temple of the muses called the *Museion* (the first museum). He started

Figure 10-4. Ptolemy I, Soter. Egypt, AU Pentadrachm, 305–282 B.C.

numerous projects to Hellenize Egyptian cults and Eastern mysticism rendering Eastern religious ideas more accessible to Greeks. In some cases, projects that Ptolemy initiated continued for centuries. Alexandrians gave Ptolemy the nickname "Soter," or savior.

To manage the process of Hellenizing Egyptian cults, Ptolemy hired the Eumolpid, Timotheus, a scholar already famous for Hellenizing the Anatolian cult of Cybele. Timotheus worked with Manetho, a priest of Isis from Heliopolis. Together these men reshaped Egyptian mythology in ways intended to satisfy conservative Egyptian devotees along the Nile Valley as well as Greek Eleusinian initiates in Alexandria. Though modern scholars debate whether or not any Egyptian cult ever met the strict definition of a mystery cult, Timotheus and Manetho adjusted important Egyptian cults to make them consistent with the Eleusinian Mysteries.

Hellenized Egyptian mythology began with familiar stories about traditional gods in human form: At the beginning of time, only the sun god Ra existed. Impregnating himself (see Figure 9-7), he created the gods of air (Shu), moisture (Tefnut), earth (Geb), and sky (Nut). Earth and sky mated and gave birth to Seth, Nephthys, Isis, and Osiris. Seth, God of Thunder, married Nephthys, Goddess of the Dead. Osiris, the first King of the Nile, married Isis, Goddess of Fertility.

Seth's wife, Nephthys, coveted Osiris. Once, Nephthys got Osiris drunk and seduced him. From this union, Nephthys gave birth to Osiris' son, Anubis. Seth had never liked his brother, Osiris. Now, jealous and angry that Nephthys had borne a son by Osiris, Seth prepared to take revenge.

First, Seth tricked Osiris into climbing inside a magic casket. Then, Seth poured molten lead over Osiris, killing him, and threw the lead-filled casket into the Nile River. When Nephthys learned what Seth had done, she left him. When Isis learned, she grieved and searched for the remains of her lost husband.

In the traditional Egyptian myth, Isis soon recovered her husband's body. She charmed the procreative parts of Osiris with magic, and then she changed into a bird to mate with him. From this union, Isis conceived Horus, and then she worked with the god Thoth to bring all the parts of Osiris back to life. Timotheus changed this story by incorporating elements from Greek myths associated with Persephone, a goddess celebrated as a virgin and a mother who bore a divine child (Dionysos) that was murdered and then came to life again to become the god of salvation.

In Timotheus' new, expanded story, the casket (filled with lead!) floated down the Nile and out to sea. Eventually, the casket washed ashore next to a giant tree near Byblos, Phoenicia. There, over many years, the tree grew and slowly engulfed the casket until it rested completely inside the giant tree. At this point, the King of Phoenicia ordered the tree cut down and installed as a pillar in his palace.

Meanwhile, grief-stricken Isis wandered all over the world searching for her husband/brother. After many years, she arrived in Phoenicia where the king and his family comforted her out of their nobility and kindness. Not recognizing the divinity of Isis, the king and queen offered the goddess a job as nursemaid to the prince, and Isis accepted.

As a blessing for the royal house of Phoenicia, Isis decided to make the princely child immortal. Over the course of several nights, Isis passed the boy through fire to burn the mortality from his body. One night, the queen saw Isis place the child into a fire. The queen screamed and woke the palace in alarm. Isis stopped transforming the

Figure 10-5. Serapis with Cerberus, and Isis Nursing Harpokrates.

child and revealed herself as a goddess. She then walked to the pillar that contained Osiris and commanded it to open. Recovering the casket of Osiris, she left the palace and returned to Egypt.

In Egypt, Seth found the body of Osiris in its casket. Still angry, Seth tore the body into numerous parts and scattered them all over the world. With the help of Thoth and Anubis, Isis gathered the parts and put Osiris back together. In this new, Hellenized myth, Isis brought Osiris back to life as Serapis, Lord of the Underworld.

To Alexandrian Greeks, Serapis represented a combination of Zeus and Hades. On the left in Figure 10-5, Serapis sits on his throne. Cerberus, the two-headed guardian of the entrance to the underworld, sits at Serapis' side. The container[17] on Serapis' head was a device for

---

[17]Called a *modius* or a *calathus*, the container represented baskets used as standard units of dry measure. A modius was approximately equivalent to a peck, and a calathus was approximately equivalent to a bushel.

measuring harvested grain or fruit, which represents the god's role in generating fertility and life.

Next to the picture of Serapis, Isis (virgin goddess and divine mother) nurses her son Horus. Greeks called the nursing child Harpokrates. Mysteries of Isis might have identified the nursing child sometimes as the mortal son of the King of Phoenicia and sometimes as Isis' divine child by Serapis: Harpokrates. Worshippers of Isis sometimes portrayed the goddess nursing an old man. With iconography emphasizing both mystery and mercy, these Hellenized deities offered the possibility of eternal life to all mankind.

The Hellenistic Cult of Isis differed significantly from traditional Egyptian cults. Timotheus packaged the cult for export as worship of a universal divine female. Portrayed only in human form, the Hellenistic Isis encompassed all aspects of all goddesses. Sailors worshipped Isis Pharia (a lighthouse goddess) or Isis Pelagia (the goddess who sailed all the seas looking for the body of her dead husband). Other Hellenistic Greeks worshipped Isis as Aphrodite, Hera, Artemis, Cybele, Rhea, Hestia, Leto, Tyche, Nike, Nemesis, Astarte, and more. Further, Isis possessed a special power greater than the powers of most foreign deities: Simple faith and devotion to Isis brought worshippers eternal life in a favored place in the land of the dead.

The matching Cult of Serapis helped round out the offering of Hellenized Egyptian cults by pairing Isis with a supreme male deity. Dread God of the Underworld, Serapis combined salvation aspects of Osiris, the pre-Ptolemaic God of the Underworld, with aspects of fertility and domination. Outside of Egypt, however, the cult proved less popular than the Cult of Isis.

Temples of Isis spread quickly to Hellenistic cities in Ptolemaic times. Delos, Delphi, Corinth, Lesbos, Cos, Rhodes, Ephesos, Maroneia (Thrace), and Thessalonica (Macedonia) all built temples of Isis. Her symbols commonly included the rose, the crown of Isis, and the *ankh*[18] (Egyptian cross). Worshippers purified themselves with

---

[18]The earliest known crosses used for religious purposes appeared around 3000 B.C. in both Egypt and Cyprus. As the ankh in Egypt and the symbol of Venus (♀) in Cyprus, the cross represented a goddess in the standard ancient birthing position: squatting with extended arms supported by other women. See "Souskiou: Hidden Valley of the Idol Makers" by Andrew Selkirk in *Current World Archaeology*, #43, pp. 34–39.

Figure 10-6. Pre-Christian Examples of the Chi-Rho Symbol. Calabria, Tarentum, AR Nomos, ca. 281–272 B.C., and Ptolemy III, Egypt, AE 43, ca. 246–221 B.C.

baptism in Nile water, they lived chaste lives, and they sometimes crawled long distances on their knees to beg for blessings from the goddess. On Delos, Priests of Isis wore the same style of black robes that Christian monks adopted centuries later. At special celebrations of Isis, worshippers danced to music from timbrels and tambourines as well as to the sounds of a special rattle called a *sistrum*.

On behalf of Isis, Hellenistic Greeks popularized the use of some symbols that later acquired special Christian significance. For example, crosses, particularly the Egyptian cross, became common symbols of eternal life as the Hellenistic Cult of Isis spread throughout the Western world. In later centuries, Christian *Gnostics*[19] in Egypt popularized the use of this cross, calling it the crux ansate, or cross with a handle. Even early examples of what would become the Christian *Chi-Rho*[20] monogram began to appear in Hellenistic contexts during the third century B.C. For example, in Figure 10-6, a Chi-Rho monogram

---

[19] Originally, both Jewish and Christian forms of Gnosticism existed. Christian Gnosticism taught that salvation lay in finding Christ within oneself. See Chapter 25.
[20] In the third century A.D., Constantine the Great introduced a monogram combining the Greek letters Chi (X) and Rho (P), which became a symbol of Christianity.

appears on the reverse of the top coin next to semi-divine Taras riding a dolphin (salvation-related iconography); on the reverse of the lower coin between the eagle's legs, the Chi-Rho symbol appears as the personal monogram of Ptolemy III.

After the death of Ptolemy I, Ptolemy II built the Great Library of Alexandria to house his father's personal collection of manuscripts. Attracting the finest minds in the Hellenistic world, the library supported ongoing research and education, becoming the world's greatest existing repository of knowledge and the most prestigious center for education and scientific research. During a period when few people distinguished between religious beliefs, philosophy, and science, the Great Library of Alexandria facilitated progress in all three disciplines.

HELLENIZATION OF BABYLONIAN CULTS

Ptolemy I didn't confine his religious innovations solely to Egyptian cults. In Babylon, he already had encountered Persian Zoroastrianism in a form that employed practices of divination, astronomy, and magic. Many of these practices originally came from earlier cultures—Sumerians, Assyrians, and Chaldaeans—that had occupied Babylon hundreds, even thousands of years earlier.

Greeks had long used magic in the form of simple curses and charms. In Egypt, traditional magic included spells that bound great gods to the will of mortals. However, outside Egypt, animal-headed gods failed to find many adherents and few Hellenistic Greeks believed that prayers, incense, spells, or even sacrifices could force a mighty god like Zeus to change the course of destiny. In contrast to Greek and Egyptian magic, Babylonian magic promised deep understanding of the universe, profound abilities to foresee the future, and reliable influence over elemental spirits, which intrigued Hellenistic Greeks.

Babylonian priests, called *magi* (the source of the word *magic*), had a reputation for successfully combining science, cultic beliefs, and philosophy into a system that brought occult powers within mortal reach. Many Greeks wanted Babylonian knowledge, but someone needed to translate Babylonian beliefs in a way that made sense to Greeks. The perfect person to accomplish this task came to Ptolemy's court and produced works of enduring importance: a Babylonian religious consultant named Berosus.

A priest of the god Bel (Lord)-Marduk (the patron deity of Babylon associated with vegetation, water, magic, and judgment), Berosus gave Western philosophers the keys for understanding how Babylonians systematized knowledge. Just as Timotheus had introduced Greek mythological elements into traditional Egyptian cults, Berosus combined an Eastern, spiritual approach to material science with advanced Hellenistic philosophy. From a tradition that sometimes affirmed and sometimes opposed Zoroastrianism, Berosus revealed new understandings of astronomy, demonology, and philosophy for consideration by Western priests and philosophers. Ultimately, writings that he produced opened the door to magical religious practices, not just for Hellenistic scholars, but also for Christians and Jews in the first millennium A.D.[21]

Mixing Babylonian Material Science and Greek Philosophy

Though now lost, the works of Berosus provided a history of the universe that connected the merging and transformation of materials with stories about the interactions of hidden spirits. Greeks already believed in minor gods like nymphs, Pan, and Nike. For example, Sicilian Greeks honored Pan and Nike on the coin in Figure 10-7. On the obverse, Pan, a horned nature god (part goat and part man), personified the natural wisdom that herders acquired from working with land and animals. On the reverse, the winged goddess Nike delivered recognition for victories to those who struggled successfully in athletic competition or war. The images on this coin expressed a city's pride in the industry, cleverness, and success of its citizens. Belief in minor gods like these predisposed Greeks to believe that elemental spirits could influence health and material processes.

---

[21]Archaeological evidence of Jewish magic has been found in the form of incantation bowls, papyri, inscriptions, and amulets. In addition, the *Babylonian Talmud* includes a little information (mostly criticism) about magical practices of Jews. See Chapter 25 for a brief discussion of Christian magic.

Chapter 10 | The Hellenization of Eastern Cults 205

Figure 10-7. Pan, and Nike; Minor Deities Who Served as Models for Demons and Angels. Sicily, Himera, AE Hemilitron, ca. 420–407 B.C.

Before Alexander the Great, Greek travelers had visited the East and returned bringing wisdom to the West. Among them, Democritus, credited in modern times with discovering the concept of atoms, wrote a work called *Physical and Mystical Teachings* around 400 B.C. In this work, he claimed to have summoned the spirit of the Zoroastrian prophet, Ostanes, who revealed the secrets of material magic. Expecting even greater insights from the works of Berosus, Hellenistic philosophers carefully studied his writings hoping to find new ways to understand and influence the universe.

The works of Berosus provided a new language for speaking about material and psychological transformation. As Hellenistic philosophers investigated ways of bringing Babylonian elementals and semi-divine spirits under contol, Babylonian metaphysics laid the foundations for European alchemy and magic. Western scholars began using abstruse descriptions of interactions between spirits to encode knowledge that combined chemistry, metallurgy, and spirituality. Over the centuries, Greek nature gods like Pan evolved into demon helpers of occult scientists, and Nikes evolved into angels.[22]

---

[22] Angels originally did not resemble the winged goddess Nike. The earliest Christian art generally depicted angels as man-like messengers without wings.

Mixing Greek, Babylonian, and Egyptian Astronomy

Hellenistic astronomy connected Greek myths, mathematics, thousands of years of astronomical data, and important events recorded in historical archives. Influenced by Berosus, Alexandrian philosophers struggled to convert their unprecedented wealth of information into a unified system that exposed the underlying mechanism of fate in the universe. Combining observation and reason, they used geometry to measure the universe, and they made scientific discoveries that would stand unequalled for more than a thousand years. However, the Eastern belief that fate was written in the stars also gained strength. The sky seemed like a more appropriate place than a mountain top for gods to make their home, and some Western scholars began to consider the sky as the source and destination of all souls.

Egypt understood the critical importance of changes in the heavens, particularly in the early morning sky. As the sun travels approximately one degree per day along the ecliptic, stars and planets pass from invisibility in the sun's glare into visibility in the early morning sky. Each star and planet emerges for the first time every year just before sunrise on the date called its *heliacal* (solar) rising. Every year, around mid-July in the modern calendar, Egyptian priests searched the morning sky for the heliacal rising of *Sothis*,[23] the brightest star in Earth's night sky. The first appearance of Sothis marked the Egyptian New Year and the beginning of the Nile flood, which determined the prosperity of Egypt. The height of the Nile flood indicated the prospects for Egypt's agricultural success in the forthcoming year. A low flood brought starvation: Not enough land would produce food. A high flood also brought starvation: Saturated ground caused seeds to rot instead of grow. When the flood was just right, Egypt prospered. Egyptian priests studied astronomical cycles attempting to predict details about the Nile flood.

Having collected astronomical observations of stars and planets for thousands of years, Egyptian priests recognized the existence of long cycles. During the reign of Ptolemy I, Egypt used the 365-day Sothic

---

[23]The modern name for Sothis is Sirius. We call it the Dog Star because it resides in the constellation *Canis Major* (Greater Dog).

calendar, a calendar that comprised twelve 30-day months and five extra days of sacred festival. However, a *sidereal* year (a year based on the Earth's true period of revolution around the sun) lasts approximately 365¼ days. The ¼ day discrepancy caused the days of the Egyptian calendar to drift approximately ¼ day earlier every year. For example, as July 20 (the traditional date of the Egyptian New Year) drifted ¼ day earlier each year over many years, July 20 moved slowly into the Spring, then the Winter, then the Fall, and then finally returned to its official place in Summer at the heliacal rising of Sothis. Because the heliacal rising of Sothis connected directly to the true sidereal year, the actual heliacal rising appeared to drift later from year to year, moving completely through the calendar in 1461 years. Every 1461 years (one *Sothic cycle*), the heliacal rising of Sothis advanced through the Egyptian calendar and ultimately returned to July 20, the traditional date of the New Year.

Under the guidance of Berosus, the astronomical traditions of Egypt and Babylon combined well. Both traditions encouraged thinking about long cycles. The archives of Babylon contained records of historical events and astronomical observation collected over thousands of years by Sumerians, Assyrians, and Chaldaeans. Generations of magi had distilled the teachings that Berosus carried to Alexandria. Confidently writing from a Babylonian perspective that astronomical cycles influenced all human activities, Berosus inspired Alexandrian scholars to reinterpret mythology and history in terms of astronomical observations and to use what they learned to predict future events. With abundant data extending thousands of years into the past, Hellenistic scholars in Egypt combined Greek mythology, Egyptian historical records, and Berosus' teachings into an influential new understanding of the influence of astronomical cycles on human affairs.

Only part of the Hellenization of Eastern and Western astronomies survived to reach modern times: Hellenistic scientific theories failed to survive the Dark Ages, but the mythological and magical parts of ancient astronomy, *astrology*, persisted. Astrology served as a tool for kings, priests, and commoners in both pagan and Christian times. Relatively true to its Hellenistic form, the art of astrology continues to thrive in the age of science—with just a few extra planets.

HELLENISTIC INFLUENCE ON THE *BIBLE*

Although the Jewish cult in Jerusalem made a point of resisting foreign influences, the translation of Hebrew scripture into Greek facilitated the Hellenization of Jewish cults. Continuing the policies of his father, Ptolemy II commissioned the translation of the Hebrew *Torah*.[24] Legend says that seventy-two Jewish scholars worked independently translating the *Torah* into Greek. The scholars generated seventy-two separate translations, all word-for-word identical to each other and all faithful to the original Hebrew text. However, which original text did the translations match? At least two different Jewish cults existed during the time of Ptolemy II, each with its own version of the *Torah*: a Jerusalem version and a Samaritan version (*Samaritan Pentateuch*).

The full Ptolemaic version of the *Hebrew Bible*, called the *Septuagint* in honor of the original seventy-two translators of the *Torah*, survived to the present day only in Latin, that is, translated into Latin from the original Greek. The text grew over time, eventually incorporating most surviving Hebrew scripture, but the Latin text also includes scribal modifications, mistranslations, and details that betray origins in opposing Jewish sects. As a Latin translation of Hellenistic Greek Jewish scripture, the *Septuagint* differs significantly from the Masoretic text of the *Hebrew Bible* used by Jews today, just as the Masoretic text of the *Torah* differs from the *Samaritan Pentateuch*. Of the six thousand differences between the Masoretic text of the *Torah* and the *Samaritan Pentateuch*, the *Septuagint* follows the Samaritan version approximately two thousand times.

From its beginning sometime during the first half of the third century B.C., the process of translating sacred Jewish writings into Greek continued with varying degrees of quality for more than two centuries. By 200 B.C., discrepancies between the Ptolemaic Greek version of the *Bible* and Hebrew scriptures caused so much concern that several scholars[25] created completely new Greek versions. By the end of the

---

[24]After canonization, the *Torah* comprised the first five books of the *Old Testament*: *Genesis, Exodus, Leviticus, Numbers,* and *Deuteronomy*.
[25]We know the names of three scholars who generated revised translations of the *Hebrew Bible* in Greek in the second century B.C.: Aquila, Theodotion, and Symmachus. Aquila may even have generated a version of the *Hebrew Bible* in Aramaic.

first century B.C., dozens of different Jewish sects existed, perhaps with no two sects agreeing completely on any single set of canonical texts.

The *Septuagint* seems to reflect certain Greek predilections like the birth of salvation-oriented heroes (for example, Dionysos and Herakles) by virgins who experienced unusual congress with the most powerful god in the universe: In an important biblical passage,[26] a word that means "young woman" in the Masoretic text was translated as "virgin"[27] in the *Septuagint*, which indicated to Greeks that a virgin someday would conceive a new savior. Either Hellenistic translators adjusted the Hebrew text to meet Greek standards or they chose an unusual textual variation as their Hebrew source, a variation which no longer exists. Regardless, the translated Jewish scriptures impressed Hellenistic Greeks: The *Septuagint* integrated familiar stories (that is, stories similar to Greek myths) seamlessly into a whole religious history from the creation of the universe to times of recent memory.

AN EXAMPLE OF AN OPPORTUNISTIC HELLENISTIC CULT

Ruling large empires with many diverse cults, Hellenistic rulers freely modified cults to suit their own personal tastes, political circumstances, and social agendas. A reference to an opportunistic, politically motivated cult survives in the name of an asterism that still graces modern skies, *Coma Berenices*.[28] This is the traditional name of an open star cluster that looks like a large fuzzy spot in the sky near the constellation, Leo. The story of how this asterism got its name helps show how rulers flexibly used cults to solve regional problems during the third century B.C. The story also illustrates the complex relations within and between empires during the Hellenistic Age.

In the first half of the third century B.C., Ptolemy II (the father of both Ptolemy III and Berenike) fought a long, unproductive war

---
[26]See Isaiah 7:14.
[27]Over the centuries, this version of the *Bible* proved especially important for justifying the existence of Christianity separate from Judaism: Use of the word *virgin* turned mistranslated text into an important prophecy of the virgin birth of Jesus.
[28]Coma Berenices means the "Hair of Berenike."

against Antiochus II of the Seleukid Empire. Eventually deciding to pursue a diplomatic solution to the conflict, Ptolemy II offered his daughter, Berenike, in marriage to Antiochus II. Ptolemy II also offered an enormous dowry—the total revenues of Egypt's possessions in Syria—on condition that Antiochus II abandon his previous wife and children and name only the children of Berenike as his successors. Antiochus II agreed.

Around the same time, Ptolemy II secured peace on Egypt's western border by marrying his son (Ptolemy III) to a different Berenike, the daughter of King Magus of Cyrene. The half-brother[29] of Ptolemy II, King Magus of Cyrene shared many Greek ancestors with the Ptolemies of Egypt. Based on numismatic representations, the two Berenikes (Ptolemy III's sister as well as his new wife) looked almost like twins.

All went well for approximately seven years. Antiochus II honored his agreement with Ptolemy II, and the Ptolemies and the Seleukids lived in peace. One Berenike lived as Princess of Egypt, and the other lived as Empress of the Seleukid Empire. Both women bore children recognized as legitimate heirs to great Hellenistic empires.

Trouble developed in 246 B.C. Both Ptolemy II and Antiochus II died that year. Antiochus II died first under suspicious circumstances while visiting his ex-wife in Ephesos. Soon after that, Ptolemy II died of natural causes in Alexandria. Ptolemy II's son ascended the throne of Egypt as Ptolemy III, and Berenike from Cyrene became Queen Berenike II of Egypt. In the Seleukid Empire, however, Antiochus II's ex-wife said that Antiochus had changed his will at the last minute: Instead of leaving the empire to the children of Berenike, he left the empire to the oldest son (Seleucus II) of his ex-wife. Finding herself in a precarious political situation in Antioch, Empress Berenike of the Seleukid Empire wrote Ptolemy III, her brother, for help.

As quickly as he could, Ptolemy III installed Berenike II on the throne of Egypt, prepared an army for war, and marched to Antioch to help his sister. Upon reaching Antioch, he discovered that Seleukid partisans already had killed both his sister and her son, but Berenike's

---

[29]Ptolemy II and Magus of Cyrene both were sons of Berenike I, the wife of Ptolemy I.

friends had taken care to keep the deaths secret. Ptolemy continued to conceal his sister's death and wrote ghost letters from his sister to local rulers petitioning their support against Seleucus II. Ptolemy fought the Seleukids for five years. He won new territory for Egypt, but he failed to conquer the Seleukid Empire. Eventually, when he heard about political unrest in Alexandria, Ptolemy III posted defensive forces in his new possessions and quickly marched home to protect his throne.

The great poet, Callimachus (second Chief Librarian of the Great Library of Alexandria and teacher of Eratosthenes) wrote a poem that immortalized events surrounding Ptolemy III's return. Callimachus wrote that Berenike II offered her hair to Aphrodite in Zephyrium for the safe return of her husband. Overnight, the hair disappeared, and Berenike feared that someone had committed sacrilege by stealing the hair. However, the great astronomer of the time, Conon of Samos, comforted the unhappy queen. He said that Zeus had transported Queen Berenike's hair to heaven; Conon had discovered Berenike's hair glowing in the night sky. In this way, the gods had expressed divine favor toward Ptolemaic rule and the queen's hair glowing in the sky helped rally public support during a difficult time in Egypt.

Modern astronomy has revealed additional information about this episode in Egyptian history. In 239 B.C., around the time that Ptolemy III returned to Egypt, Halley's Comet passed through the constellation, Leo. For some time, Coma Berenices and Halley's Comet appeared together, like twin fuzzy patches in the clear Egyptian sky, until Halley's Comet finally moved on and disappeared. The association of the comet, the poem, and the political difficulties reveals the opportunistic nature of cultic veneration of Queen Berenike's hair. Further, the appearance of the open star cluster and the comet so close together must have reminded Egyptians of the other Berenike, Ptolemy III's sister.

Minted during the reign of Ptolemy III, the coins in Figure 10-8 display portraits of women on their obverses and twin symbols on either side of the cornucopia on their reverses: the gold quarter drachm displays two stars and the silver pentadrachm displays two caps. In the light of historical and astronomical events, the star and cap symbols on the two coins connect the appearance of Halley's comet near Coma

Figure 10-8. Numismatic Portraits of Berenike II, and Stars and Caps Symbolic of Dioscuri. AU Quarter Drachm and AR Pentadrachm of Berenike.

Berenices with the minor Hellenistic cult invented in 239 B.C. to divert attention and defuse public unrest. Not all numismatists agree on which Berenike graced the obverses of these coins with her portrait. Nevertheless, twin caps[30] or stars on Greek and Roman coins commonly represented the Dioscuri.[31] Just as the Dioscuri shared divinity, the two caps and the two stars on the coins in Figure 10-8 appear to refer to a divinity shared between the two Berenikes, the sister and wife of Ptolemy III, which makes these stars and caps the only reference to both a comet and an open star cluster ever to appear on coins.

One year after the appearance of Halley's Comet, a public proclamation referenced the divinity of Ptolemy III as well as the divinity of his sister and his wife. The "Canopic Decree" of 238 B.C. thanked

---

[30]The coin in Figure 4-6 shows the Dioscuri, or Gemini Twins, wearing the caps that became their symbols. Twin stars represent the constellation, Gemini.
[31]The story of the Dioscuri is discussed in Chapter 4. Because the Dioscuri regained their sister, Helen, from Theseus after he kidnapped her by ship, Alexandrians worshipped the twins as protectors of seafaring traders.

Ptolemy and "Berenike, his sister and his wife." Referring to Ptolemy III and the Berenikes as "Benefactor Gods," even though one Berenike was dead, the decree thanked them for supporting Egyptian cults, implementing a strong national defense, and importing grain to ameliorate a famine. The decree also said that Ptolemy III instituted a modern calendar, establishing that after three years of 365 days there should be a leap year of 366 days. The decree provided, "...for a one-day feast of the Benefactor Gods to be added every four years to the five additional days before the New Year."[32] In this way, Ptolemy III stabilized the year so that a date always corresponded closely to a specific part of every season.

After Ptolemy III died, the cult of Berenike's Hair became little more than a historical poem supporting astronomical folklore. Egypt also soon forgot Ptolemy III's innovative calendar. However, within two centuries, Julius Caesar brought the same calendar to Rome and the Western world. The Julian calendar[33] operated in the West unchanged until 1528 when a decree of Pope Gregory XIII refined the calendar further.

CONDITIONING THE WORLD FOR RELIGIOUS CHANGE

The Hellenization of Eastern cults played an enormous role in the historical development of Western religion. The Greek rulers that inherited Alexander's empire struggled to associate all known cults of their world with Greek deities they already understood. With the help of consultants, the rulers standardized mythological elements of Eleusinian mysteries—for example, the birth of a hero after divine impregnation of a beautiful virgin, the murder and subsequent resurrection of a salvation deity, and sincere attempts by the most powerful god in the universe to improve the afterlives of humans—adding them to

---

[32] A full translation of the Canopic Decree can be found in *Records of the Past*, Series 1, Volume VIII, by S. Birch.
[33] Like the story of the two Berenikes, the story of Julius Caesar includes the fortuitous appearance of a comet. See Chapter 19.

salvation-oriented religious cults in non-Greek cultures throughout their empires. Ptolemaic Alexandria became a center for interpreting and adjusting the Hellenistic World's philosophies and cultic beliefs to suit Greek tastes.

At the Library of Alexandria, the intellectual center of the Hellenistic world, Berosus opened rich new fields of practical inquiry. That a wise person might predict future events, control natural forces, and even use supernatural means to influence destiny seemed reasonable. The good reputation of modern science comes from the ability of scientists to produce predictable results. In Hellenistic Egypt, the intellectual ancestors of modern scientists hoped to obtain similar certainty by reading destiny in the movements of planets and stars and by formalizing techniques for marshaling unseen spiritual forces. A new intellectual climate and thousands of years of data from the East promised almost miraculous possibilities for the brilliant, the learned, and the inspired.

In the East, some people accepted reinterpretation of their local deities, and some didn't. Inhabitants of large cities like Alexandria fully embraced the modified cults of Isis and Serapis, but conservative farmers in the Egyptian countryside quietly clung to the worship of traditional animal deities. Regardless, the modified Egyptian cults began spreading to Greek cities around the Mediterranean Sea. Encouraged by a new ability to approach all goddesses through Isis, Hellenistic populations began looking past the trappings of specific cults in seeking relationships with divinity.

Under Alexander's successors, populations became mobile and less attached to local gods. Philosophies, technologies, and cultic beliefs easily passed East and West as it became safer for people to travel long distances. Taking advantage of an Eastern tendency to deify rulers, Hellenistic rulers adopted practices that blurred the distinction between divine and mortal beings: adjusting local cults, importing foreign cults, and even opportunistically creating new cults to suit personal, political, and social objectives. Many Hellenistic rulers created short-lived cults that identified the rulers and their families as gods.

Around the Mediterranean Sea, Hellenized populations approached religious beliefs and practices more generically. Uprooted by wars as well as by opportunities for profit and trade, Easterners tended to congregate in new communities, each one comprising a unique mix of relocated slaves, merchants, and migrant craftsmen. Attempting to recreate mystery doctrines similar to those from their past, communities developed new cults that contained elements of widely shared belief. Most new cults resembled Dionysian Mysteries carefully adjusted to reflect the origins, values, and aspirations of community members.

Everywhere, encouraged by the increased availability of foreign literature translated into Greek, people began to think more freely about religious beliefs and philosophy. Over time, specific local religious traditions declined in importance. Some Hellenistic philosophers suggested that the stories of gods merely recalled vague history and that deification originated from honors paid to great mortals. In fact, for the first time in history, respectable scholars freely considered the possibility that gods did not exist.

CHAPTER
11

DANGEROUS IDEAS

HELLENISTIC PHILOSOPHIES AND THE EMERGENCE OF ROME ON THE WORLD STAGE

> With the maturation of Hellenistic cults and philosophies, the East possessed important elements of Christianity, which needed only long-term antagonism from Rome to travel, strengthen, and organize around the life story of Jesus.

The most important components of Christianity existed before the birth of Jesus. For example, the translation of Jewish scriptures into Greek made accounts of Semitic morality and sacred history available for consideration by Hellenistic philosophers and priests. In addition, important elements of Christian iconography, belief, and practice appeared in cults that worshipped solar deities like Baal/Hammon, in salvation-oriented mystery cults like those of Dionysos, and in cults of mother goddesses like Isis. Many Hellenistic cults exhibited isolated features identical to those incorporated by Christianity in the first few centuries A.D. However, it took Romans to teach Western cultures to persecute followers of undesirable cults, which ultimately taught Christians to make war because of religious beliefs.

After the death of Alexander the Great in 323 B.C., Hellenism culturally affirmed beliefs that later characterized Christianity: For example, in the empires ruled by Diadochi, Eastern populations accepted that one male deity controlled the universe, perhaps employing a multitude of other spiritual beings to execute his will; the almighty ruler of the universe sometimes influenced the fate of humanity by impregnating a worthy virgin who then bore a heroic, divine son; and, after fulfilling his purpose among mortals (frequently oriented toward the salvation of humanity), the hero returned to the source of his divinity, his father. As shown by posthumous images of Alexander the Great, some Hellenists even perceived the heroic son of god as simultaneously separate from and combined with his divine father after death. (See Figure 10-2 for a portrayal of Alexander as Zeus/Amon.) However, Hellenistic religious beliefs consistent with Christianity don't look Christian to modern eyes, mostly because Hellenism did not oppose non-Christian religious beliefs.

Religious beliefs, practices, and iconography mingled flexibly in the great Hellenistic empires during the centuries before Jesus. Free to pursue spiritual and intellectual truth wherever it might lead, Hellenistic philosophers investigated atheistic, agnostic, and theistic ethical systems. Four philosophical movements competed for intellectual dominance during the Hellenistic Age: the minor movements of Cynicism and Skepticism, and the major movements of Epicureanism and Stoicism. *Cynicism* taught that gods did not exist and encouraged the turning away from desire. Casting doubt on the existence of gods, *Skepticism* taught the ultimate inadequacy of human reason as a tool for grappling with important questions. Asserting that, if gods existed, they would care little about humanity, *Epicureanism* encouraged its followers to live in a way that minimized pain. *Stoicism* usually maintained that God existed—sometimes that many gods existed—but Stoic belief varied according to intellectual fashion. Over the centuries, Stoicism grew more important at the expense of the other three movements, eventually providing a framework for the development of Christian philosophy.

With the development and spread of the theistic Hellenistic philosophy called Stoicism, every positive religious idea necessary for the emergence of Christianity expressed itself somewhere within the empires of Alexander's successors. However, other than the personality of Jesus, the most important element of Christianity that was absent during the Hellenistic Age was a profound intolerance of non-Christian beliefs. For Christianity to develop and separate itself from other Hellenistic systems, its seed ideas needed to spread from the civilized East to the relatively unsophisticated West, they needed to organize separately from pagan cults, and they needed to precipitate in a revolutionary movement against the authorities who affirmed other systems. A Hellenistic set of Judeo-Christian beliefs organized in opposition to other cults only because Rome—a brutal, self-serving, pagan empire—showed the way. Rome emerged as an example of both fundamental opposition to Hellenism as well as a model for expediently incorporating Hellenistic elements from time to time. Eventually, during the first century A.D., political strife in the Roman Empire precipitated a broad Judeo-Christian revolutionary movement that characterized tolerant, flexible Hellenism as evil.

During the third century B.C., not long after Alexander's death, Greek culture flowered intellectually, spiritually, artistically, and economically. However, intent on seizing the wealth of Hellenistic society, the lean and mean Roman culture began to emerge on the world stage by the end of the century. The Mediterranean World became acquainted with Rome over the course of three international wars: the Pyrrhic War, the First Punic War, and the Second Punic War. Focusing first on learning to stand up to Hellenistic navies and armies, Rome began to dominate Mediterranean territories, enthusiastically acting as a nemesis against Hellenistic tolerance and sophistication. Before long, Rome had conquered the Greek peninsula and began looking eastward toward the homeland of the Jews. Striving always to keep itself Roman while dominating the Hellenistic world, Rome embraced some Hellenistic cults and rejected others. Only after defeating Hellenistic empires did Rome consider that Hellenism offer anything of value other than wealth, slaves, and military tactics. Over time, Rome developed into exactly the sort of self-conflicted antagonist of Hellenism that the West needed to develop, grow, and ultimately receive Christianity.

THE PREEMINENT PRE-HELLENISTIC PHILOSOPHER: PLATO

Writing a generation before the Hellenistic Age in the early fourth century B.C., the Athenian philosopher, Plato, developed a broad range of ideas that formed the foundation of Western philosophy. Believing that reliance on evidence from one's senses led to ambiguities and contradictions, he dogmatically identified reason as the most important tool to investigate the nature of reality. Among his ideas, for example, he theorized that abstractions (for example, a color, a virtue, or even the idea of a tree) and objects were things that had different kinds of being. Plato thought that abstractions possessed a type of divine existence: incorporeal, incorruptible, and immortal, but still perceptible to mortal human beings. To interact with something physical, humans used their physical bodies. To interact with abstractions like numbers, goodness, and beauty, humans used something else—their souls. If human souls shared the same type of being as abstractions, human souls must live forever and learning really was a type of remembering. Likewise, a universal soul called *God* must also exist and live forever.

A generation before the influx of Zoroastrian ideas in the West, Plato believed that only one universal soul (one God) existed, but he had difficulty explaining the presence of evil in the world. A surviving dialogue of Plato, *Epinomis*, includes Eastern ideas (for example, the possible existence of an evil universal soul) that resemble Zoroastrian concepts. However, most scholars today don't believe that Plato wrote this dialogue. Instead, they suggest that an unknown philosopher wrote the dialogue to lend credence to a particular Hellenistic school's teachings about Eastern ideas.

After Plato's death, Alexander's teacher, Aristotle, emerged as the last great Greek philosopher to enjoy the pre-Hellenistic atmosphere of philosophical optimism. Before learning that he needn't bother, he built the foundations of many new fields of Western thought, for example: ethics, politics, physics, logic, zoology, geography, and so on. After Aristotle, Eastern ideas shifted the temper of Greek philosophical endeavor away from optimism toward a pessimistic desire to escape suffering and evil.

AN ATHEISTIC HELLENISTIC PHILOSOPHY: CYNICISM

Diogenes, the most famous of the Cynics, valued simple goodness, loved virtue, and rejected all conventions. He thought that only the extinction of desire made virtue possible. Only without desire—free from fear—could any human consider and choose a moral path. Because the world awards material success randomly, he considered worldly goods and riches worthless. Similarly, he branded popular qualities like honor, wisdom, and happiness as lies. Diogenes rejected all refined philosophy, just as he rejected religious beliefs, governments, delights of the senses, and notions like private property, marriage, and slavery.

To his followers, he affirmed the concept of brotherhood, not only with all men but also with all animals. He recommended that people find truth by living close to nature. The word, *cynic*, derives from the Greek word for dog-like (*kunikos*) because Diogenes reputedly lived like a dog; he slept in a large pottery casket, fed himself by begging, and offended common decency by performing private acts in public. When Alexander the Great visited the philosopher and asked if he wanted any favor, Diogenes asked only that Alexander stand aside and not block the sun. This encounter impressed Alexander so much that he said: If he weren't Alexander, he would want to be Diogenes.

Though Cynicism became fashionable for a while in Alexandria, the philosophy acquired a bad reputation. Popular Cynicism didn't require abstinence from good things, only a superficial indifference to them—as well as to family, to benefactors, to obligations, and so on. Practitioners used the philosophy to justify any behavior whatsoever, giving rise to the modern meaning of the word, *cynic*.

AN AGNOSTIC HELLENISTIC PHILOSOPHY: SKEPTICISM

From Alexander's army, a veteran named Pyrrho developed the formal system of doubt called Skepticism. Skeptical with regard to senses, logic, and morals, and aware of great differences in values among different cultures scattered across the world, Pyrrho believed that no rational grounds existed for preferring any course of action over another. In an uncertain world, he advocated a common sense approach: One should follow the customs of the country in which one lived; one should worship without belief; and one should enjoy life without asking too many questions. Pyrrho doubted all the self-evident premises from which logical arguments began because philosophers could argue both sides of any question, seemingly with equal validity.

Far from opening new lines of philosophical inquiry, Pyrrho's ideas developed into a dogma that affirmed that nobody knew anything and that nobody could know anything. To some degree, the movement freed its followers from worry. Also, consistent with modern ideas about the importance of self-esteem, it allowed ignorant people to consider themselves as wise as the learned.

A HUMANISTIC HELLENISTIC PHILOSOPHY: EPICUREANISM

A sufferer of painful illnesses throughout his life, the philosopher, Epicurus, created a dogma that valued tranquility as well as simple delights associated with taste, hearing, sight, love, friendship, and so on. To Epicurus, virtue consisted of prudence in pursuit of pleasure. Epicureans valued the absence of pain more than the presence of pleasure, and they tried to live in ways that minimized or avoided fear. Rejecting customary rules of dignity, Epicurus accepted slaves, children, and prostitutes among his students. He also treated all his students like friends.

Epicurus recommended that his followers live moderately, avoid public life, and avoid sex.[1] He loved pleasures of the body, but he

---

[1] Later Epicurean teachers said that sex without passion wouldn't harm a person.

rejected luxury because indulgence in luxury damaged health. Maintaining that properly educated people could experience happiness under any circumstances, even under torture, Epicurus enjoined his followers to live simple lives: Surviving on voluntary contributions, they ate mostly bread and drank mostly water.

Epicurus believed that gods probably existed because many people believed in them, but he thought that the activities and opinions of mortals would have mattered little to a god. Believing that immortality of the soul would make release from pain impossible, he rejected the idea that humans survived after death. Instead, he taught that small particles (called atoms) composed everything in the world, including breath, heat, and even souls. At death, soul particles detached themselves from the human body and scattered. Detached soul particles neither maintained personalities nor suffered from bodily sensations.

Epicurus rejected divination, astrology, and magic as useless superstition. He considered science useful for providing rationalistic explanations of natural phenomena—as long as the explanations avoided mentioning gods—but he saw no point in choosing between competing explanations. His dogma remained popular among educated Greeks and Romans until the end of the Roman Republic in the late first century B.C.[2]

A THEISTIC HELLENISTIC PHILOSOPHY: STOICISM

The philosopher, Zeno, founded Stoicism in the first part of the third century B.C. He believed that that nothing happened by chance and that material laws determined everything that happened. Adapting the materialistic theories of Heraclitus,[3] Zeno taught that everything

---

[2] During late Roman Republic times, Octavian Caesar campaigned against Epicureanism as part of his efforts to restore traditional Roman virtues and cults in contrast to Marc Antony's support for Hellenism. See Chapters 20 and 21.
[3] The pre-Socratic philosopher, Heraclitus of Ephesos, taught an obscure philosophy in the beginning of the fifth century B.C. Identifying change as the central principle of the universe, he said that opposites possessed a hidden unity, that everything came to pass in accordance with something called the *Logos*, and that basic elements—air, earth, and water—originally came from fire.

evolved from fire. Fire evolved sequentially into water, earth, and air. At the end of a long cycle, everything returned to its source, the original fire (sometimes called God and sometimes called Zeus).

Zeno taught that all things came from an underlying unity called nature, and that everything existed balanced by its opposite. God existed as the soul of the world. Every human soul was a part of God, and everything moved according to divine plan. Free from considerations of desire, a virtuous person directed his will in harmony with nature. Evil people embraced desire and lived virtuously only if forced to do so. Because virtue depended only on will, not on circumstances, a person's circumstances (including health, happiness, and possessions) simply didn't matter. Some Stoics believed that the soul died with the body. Others believed that, at death, a wise man's light, clear soul drifted toward heaven to live among the stars, while an evil man's heavy, dark soul fell like ash to mix with muddy earth. Some Stoics even believed that a moral universe might require evil souls to reincarnate.

Of the four important Hellenistic movements, Stoicism achieved the greatest popularity. Over time, Stoicism incorporated much of Plato's philosophy, justified systems of multiple gods, and sometimes embraced and sometimes ridiculed astrology, divination, and magic. Always maintaining the central importance of humanity and the Earth,[4] Stoic philosophy flexibly affirmed whatever most people wanted to believe. Stoics came to believe that ethics determined the laws that governed all material interactions. Through correct application of ethics and logic, Stoic philosophers expected to be able to derive all scientific laws. For 500 years after Alexander, most rulers of Mediterranean empires declared themselves as followers of Stoicism.

DECLINING FAITH IN REASON LEADING TO CHRISTIAN PHILOSOPHY

As the Hellenistic Age progressed, scholars lost faith in the potency of reason as illustrated by changes in curriculum in Plato's Academy in

---

[4]Prefiguring the heresy trial of Galileo in 1633, the Stoic, Cleanthes of Assos (third century B.C.), urged that Aristarchus of Samos be charged with impiety for maintaining that the sun, not the Earth, occupied the center of the universe. See Chapter 13.

Athens. Beginning in the late fourth century B.C., the academy affirmed pure reason and rejected astrology, divination, and magic. However, as Eastern ideas slowly transformed Western thought during the third century B.C., the academy moved away from Platonism and embraced Skepticism. Focusing on declarations in Platonic dialogues by Socrates that he didn't know anything, teachers at the academy came to value verbal cleverness more than truth. By the beginning of the second century B.C., the academy trained students to argue both sides of any proposition skillfully without regard to substance. In the middle of the first century B.C., Plato's Academy abandoned Skepticism for Stoicism and began teaching courses in astrology, divination, and magic.

Even after the death of Jesus, the shift in philosophical temper away from reason and toward mysticism and dogma continued for centuries, which supported the increasing popularity of Christianity. In the third century A.D., Plotinus[5] packaged a metaphysical strain of stoicism with Neo-Pythagorean[6] ideas into an influential philosophy called Neo-Platonism.[7] Neo-Platonists asserted the existence of one god in three parts (being, essence, and incarnation). They also claimed that Judeo-Christian metaphysics were earlier and more fundamental than Platonic and Hellenistic metaphysics.

THE RISE OF ROME

From its earliest beginnings in the eighth century B.C., Rome oriented its society around war. Roman mythology expressed this priority through the genealogy of Rome's founders: Mars (the Roman name for Ares), the God of War, sired Romulus and Remus (the twins who founded Rome) by raping the virgin, Rhea Sylvia, a direct descendant of Venus (the Roman name for Aphrodite) and Anchises through the Trojan prince, Aeneas. All of the oldest and noblest Roman families

---
[5]Plotinus' ideas can be found in his book, the *Enneads*.
[6]Espousing a combination of Pythagorean and Platonic ideas in the second century A.D., the Neo-Pythagorean philosopher, Numenius of Apamea, sometimes is described as the Father of Neo-Platonism.
[7]In the late fourth and early fifth centuries A.D., Neo-Platonism powerfully influenced Saint Augustine, one of the greatest Christian philosophers, who reported two mystical experiences consistent with Neo-Platonic ideas.

shared violent origins: The first Roman men obtained wives by seizing them from a neighboring tribe, the Sabines.[8]

Rome didn't accomplish much in its first centuries. In the seventh century B.C., Roman control reached the coast of the Tyrrhenian Sea, but Etruscan neighbors seized Rome and placed it under their monarchy until the end of the sixth century B.C. After liberating itself from its last Etruscan king in 509 B.C., Rome initiated a republican form of government. By the end of the fifth century B.C., Rome captured a powerful neighboring city-state, the Veii, and began to grow.

Despite setbacks, Rome grew stronger and tied its economic well-being to territorial expansion and domination of its neighbors. However, Celts sacked Rome in 396 B.C., creating a searing memory of what it meant to lose a war. Nevertheless, the fourth century B.C. saw a steady increase in Roman power. Every year, just before the harvest season, Roman citizens banded together into an army and invaded their neighbors. Sometimes the army merely weakened neighbors by depriving them of their harvest. Other times, Romans displaced the inhabitants of desirable land and colonized it. If opponents defended themselves too well, the Romans seized people as well as property and sold all the captives as slaves.

Rome dominated the Italian peninsula by the beginning of the Hellenistic age and soon competed directly with Greeks and Phoenicians for control of the Mediterranean Sea. By the end of the fourth century B.C., Rome began to threaten Greek colonies in Italy. Rome then won three important wars: the Pyrrhic War (281–275 B.C.); the First Punic War (264–242 B.C.); and the Second Punic War (218–202 B.C.). By the end of the third century B.C., Rome became the dominant power on the Mediterranean Sea.

The Pyrrhic War

Early in the third century B.C., Agathocles of Syracuse ruled a small empire of Greek colonies on Sicily and the southern Italian peninsula. Until his death in 289 B.C., he protected his empire from threats by

---

[8]This event is immortalized in myth as "The Rape of the Sabine Women."

Rome and Carthage with a combination of local forces and mercenaries. Afterward, Rome made incursions south, threatening Tarentum, the largest Greek colony in Southern Italy. For protection, Tarentum looked across the Adriatic Sea to King Pyrrhus of Molossia, the leader of a coalition of northwestern Greek states called the Epirote League.

A son-in-law of Agathocles of Syracuse, King Pyrrhus had earned a reputation as a powerful king and a successful general. Italian Greeks and Sicilian Greeks both sought his protection: Italian Greeks wanted protection from Rome and Sicilian Greeks wanted protection from opportunistic attacks by Carthage. Pyrrhus couldn't resist the opportunity to expand his empire. First, he secured his position at home by forming an alliance with the King of Macedon. Then, Pyrrhus launched his army west intending to rule willing Greek subjects as well as to conquer the upstart barbarians of Rome.

Pyrrhus won battles. Italian and Sicilian Greek cities even hailed Pyrrhus as their king. However, to this day, Pyrrhus' name survives as an adjective of dubious merit. We speak of a *Pyrrhic victory* as one not worth winning because of its enormous cost to the victor. After six years of Pyrrhic victories and increasing familiarity with Pyrrhus' despotic tendencies, Italian and Sicilian Greeks lost confidence in his leadership and slowly withdrew their support. In 275 B.C., Pyrrhus abandoned everything he had won and returned home to Epeiros. From the *Pyrrhic War*, Romans learned that they could stand up to a substantial Greek army.

The First Punic War

Just before he died, old King Agathocles of Syracuse hired Italian mercenaries to fight against Carthage.[9] After the king's death, the mercenaries remained on Sicily, unpaid and unhappy. They captured the Greek city of Messana, killed all the men, and kept the women as their wives. The mercenaries also harassed Greek neighbors who supposedly were protected by Syracuse.

---

[9] Founded by the Phoenician Princess Elissa of Tyre, Carthage became the dominant naval power on the Mediterranean Sea by the beginning of the third century B.C.

For decades, Messana successfully resisted raids from Syracusan forces, but attacks kept coming. Just when defeat seemed imminent, Carthaginians came powerfully to Messana's aid. Afterward, discomfort with the continuing presence of a Carthaginian garrison inside the city moved some of Messana's inhabitants to ask Rome for help. More concerned about limiting the influence of Carthage than helping a gang of mercenaries, Rome accepted the invitation and entered the first of its three wars against Carthage, the *First Punic War*.

The war lasted 23 years until 241 B.C. Despite complex political maneuvering by mercenaries and Sicilian Greeks, the conflict boiled down to a struggle between Rome and Carthage for control of Sicily. Rome fought Carthaginian forces on Sicily, in Africa, and even on the high seas. During this war, Carthaginians taught Romans how to make an impression when executing an enemy: The Carthaginians crucified Roman captives. To achieve victory, Rome learned how to build and operate a world-class navy, how to maintain armies in foreign lands, and how to defeat the ruthless military of Carthage.

In the decisive engagement of the war, a sea-battle (called the Battle of the Aegates Islands) just west of Sicily, Roman vessels devoid of masts, sails, and provisions—stripped of everything unnecessary for battle—nimbly out-maneuvered and rammed Carthaginian vessels that were burdened with provisions, equipment, and replacement land forces. The destruction of half the Carthaginian fleet left Carthaginian forces on Sicily at the mercy of Rome, which ultimately forced Carthage to surrender. As the new dominant naval power in the western Mediterranean, Rome subjected Carthage to harsh terms that virtually guaranteed another Punic war. Still, Rome's victory initiated decades of unhindered Roman expansion around the Mediterranean Sea.

Success gave Rome uncontested possession of Sicily, though Syracuse and a few other cities remained mostly free because they had allied themselves with Rome. The opportunity to administer Sicily as a foreign territory subject to the will of the Roman Senate[10] allowed

---

[10] Beginning with Sicily, Rome assigned the administration of a provincial territory to the higheset bidder, which reduced bureaucracy and gave provincial governors free license to squeeze subject territories with little concern for ethics or human suffering.

the creation and testing of foreign governance policies designed to siphon treasures and wealth from a captured land. Roman entrepreneurs quickly carved Sicily into huge plantations staffed with slaves and tasked them with growing grain to feed the people of Rome.

An Introduction to the Second Punic War

Fought from 218–202 B.C., the *Second Punic War* brought Rome into direct confrontation with the power of Hellenistic ideas. From the Carthaginian general, Hannibal,[11] Rome learned a memorable lesson that advanced military tactics could multiply the effectiveness of soldiers while simultaneously protecting them from injury. Further, when Syracuse allied with Carthage, Rome learned a different lesson from the great scientist, Archimedes: that advanced war machines could neutralize a powerful invading force.

By 218 B.C., Rome and Carthage both craved war. As the international interests of these two powers increasingly came into conflict, particularly over territory and resources in Spain, Hannibal seized the opportunity to make war on Rome. Roman military leaders soon learned that a truly brilliant military commander could achieve victories against armies vastly outnumbering his own and lose few soldiers doing so. Famously, Hannibal led his army, including elephants, over the Alps into northern Italy. There, he marched at will throughout Italy. Time and again, Rome attacked Hannibal with numerically superior forces, but Rome's army suffered grave losses in every battle while Hannibal's emerged relatively unscathed.

Nevertheless, Hannibal possessed too small an army to capture the city of Rome. He needed additional troops, but neither politically divided Carthage nor terrorized Italian communities would supply him with sufficient reinforcements. After great successes early in the war, Hannibal achieved only a prolonged stalemate in Italy as Romans learned to avoid facing him in battle. Instead, Romans punished Hannibal's allies, captured distant Carthaginian colonies, and slowly

---

[11]Widely regarded as one of the greatest generals of all time, Hannibal commmanded Carthaginian military forces in the late third century B.C.

prepared to attack Carthage itself. Decided mostly by Rome's strategy of attrition, wearing down the will of Carthage while refusing to engage its most capable commmander, the Second Punic War lasted sixteen long years.

The Roman Conquest of Syracuse

In 214 B.C., seeing opportunity in Hannibal's successes in Italy and encouraged by Carthaginian agents, Syracuse stopped sending tribute to Rome and reclaimed Sicilian territory that Rome had seized in the First Punic War. In spite of continuing problems with Hannibal, Rome scraped together an army to teach Syracuse a lesson. Once again, however, Rome learned about the power of sophisticated thought: Whenever a Roman force attacked Syracuse, the inventions of Archimedes[12] completely confounded the Romans' best efforts. As Roman warships approached the city from far away, giant Syracusan catapults threw five-hundred-pound stones that hit the ships and sank them. When Roman ships got closer to the city, strange machines focused the sun's light, not only igniting ships' sails but also roasting men alive. If ships got close enough to attack the city directly, mechanical claws reached over the city walls, lifted the ships, shook off the men, and then dropped the ships to sink in the bay. The Roman army could attack Syracuse, but they could not defeat a city defended by Archimedes.

Nobody knows how long Syracuse might have held out. A peace party in Syracuse made a small opening in Syracuse's wall so they could negotiate terms for peace with the Roman general, but no negotiations took place. Taking full advantage of the opportunity, Roman soldiers widened the hole and poured through it. Once inside, Roman soldiers indiscriminately slaughtered Syracusan citizens. A Roman soldier even killed Archimedes. Eventually Syracusan soldiers repelled the Romans, but the Romans had critically weakened the city. With Archimedes dead, the city soon fell.

---

[12]One of the greatest scientists in antiquity, Archimedes advanced mathematics, astronomy, physics, and engineering. His few writings that survived the Middle Ages served as a significant source of ideas at the beginning of the Renaissance.

CHARACTERISTICS OF ROMAN DOMINATION

After defeating Syracuse in 212 B.C., Rome squeezed Sicily for food and money to fight Hannibal. Rapacious governors levied onerous taxes on the whole island except for five free cities. Roman officials also stole art and valuables at will. However, Rome generally permitted Greek cults, laws, and government as long as the province supplied the food and treasure that fueled Rome's expanding ambitions. As it conquered new lands around the Mediterranean Sea, Rome used its Sicilian policies as a generic model for provincial rule.

Hellenism had convinced Romans that they worshipped the same gods that Greeks worshipped, even though Romans knew the gods by different names. Like Greeks, Romans believed in divination and observed many simple superstitions. Yet, while Hellenistic Greek priests investigated theology, philosophy, and personal transformation, Roman priests concentrated mostly on performing unchanging rituals that valued the stern dignity of participants over other considerations. Distrusting fancy ideas, Romans repeated rituals without questioning them and accepted vague ideas about what happened to a soul after death without thinking the topic worthy of further consideration.

One can see the cultural differences between Romans and Greeks by comparing the coins they produced in the third century B.C. Figure 11-1 displays two coins minted in Syracuse, a Greek coin on top and a Roman coin below. Both coins portray Nike (winged Victory) decorating a military trophy on the reverse. On the obverse of the Greek coin, a Greek artist portrayed Persephone, a youthful female goddess of transformation and hope. On the obverse of the Roman coin, a Roman artist portrayed Jupiter, the Roman equivalent of Zeus, a male god of power and domination.

Agathocles, Tyrant of Syracuse and self-proclaimed King of Sicily, minted the top coin around the time he married a daughter of Ptolemy I, Soter (Savior), of Alexandria. From a time early in the Hellenistic Age, this artistic coin serves well as a metaphor for the best of Hellenistic philosophy, science, and religious practice. The goddess Persephone wears a royal diadem made of wheat. Worshipped as the

Figure 11-1. Coins that Compare Greek and Roman Culture on Sicily. Top Coin: Persephone and Nike, Sicily, Syracuse, AR Tetradrachm, 317–289 B.C. Bottom Coin: Jupiter and Winged Victory, Roman Sicily, AR Victoriatus, 211–208 B.C.

Mother of Wheat, the Goddess of Spring, and the Queen of the Dead, she offered possibilities for nourishment, renewal, and salvation for all mankind. On the reverse, Nike decorates a trophy in honor of enterprise, struggle, and achievement.

Minted less than a century after Agathocles' death, the lower coin reveals a cultural decline. Whereas Syracusans crafted the Greek coin with subtle and refined artistry, Romans minted the lower coin with, at best, a dull and efficient competence. The qualitative differences in the coins reflect qualitative differences that Romans brought to Sicilian life by the end of the third century B.C. As Greek dominance declined and Rome emerged as a world power, Romans believed their success proved the innate superiority of their stiff, brutal, and simple-minded moral code over Greek cleverness and culture.

Rome dominated Mediterranean regions focusing on the mechanics of profit and plunder. Successfully maximizing profit and control, Rome never noticed its increasing vulnerability to the Hellenistic cults that eventually transformed Roman society. Hellenized Eastern cults gained their easiest access to Rome through their established presence in Sicilian towns: Enna retained its status as a center for the Cult of Persephone; Akrai possessed a brand new open-air temple to Cybele and Attis; Tauromenion maintained a temple to Serapis; Syracuse built a new temple to Isis; and Elymians (honored by Romans as fellow descendants from ancient Troy) in the free city of Eryx maintained their celebrated Temple of Venus Erice (Syrian Aphrodite). Hellenistic ideas continued to evolve, presenting scarcely noticed long-term challenges to traditional Roman values and ways of life. Beginning in the second century B.C., the evolving story of Greek cults began to merge with the history of Rome.

Under Roman domination, Hellenized intellectuals continued to develop tools that shaped Christianity as well as Western civilization. Still, Romans tried to impose a classic cultural contradiction: They sought to dominate as much of the world as possible while maintaining the purity of their traditional culture, religious beliefs, and bloodlines, all of which were based on mythological history. Though resisting the education, Rome couldn't help learning much more from Greeks than merely tactics and strategy. The Second Punic War turned Rome into the shaper of circumstances in which Christianity developed in the West: Rome entered into a long, ambiguous relationship with Hellenism ultimately leading to Western domination of Judea by a Roman Empire in violent conflict with itself about Hellenistic cults and ideas.

PART FOUR

Venus Erice with Cruciform Earrings and Her Temple on Mount Eryx

IMPERIALISTIC, RELIGIOUS, AND CIVIL WAR

ORIENTING THE WEST TOWARD SALVATION

Rome's economic dependence on war set the stage for the emergence of Christianity in many complex ways: impoverishing Mediterranean multitudes, scattering salvation-oriented Hellenistic cults like seeds, empowering Rome's lower classes, and moving the Roman Republic inexorably through an escalating series of political crises.

CHAPTER
12

ADVERSARIAL VISION

SHAPING ROME'S EARLY INTERACTIONS WITH HELLENISTIC CULTS

Expanding rapidly in the second century B.C. through wars against Hellenistic societies, Rome struggled to preserve its culture, values, and traditions, unintentionally entering a long-term war against Hellenism and Hellenistic cults.

According to a popular saying, "If all you have is a hammer, everything around you looks like a nail." Toward the end of the third century B.C., this saying sums up the relationship between Rome and its Mediterranean neighbors: Dependent on war for the well-being of its economy, Rome generally viewed foreign lands either as sources of treasure or as strategic threats. Even when Rome entered alliances, the relationships usually progressed relentlessly toward complete Roman domination. As much as they could, Romans ignored foreign ideas, customs, and cults and clung to a simplistic "hammers and nails" perception of the world. However, Hellenistic cults subverted traditional Roman perceptions and values, particularly among the lower classes.

As Rome defended itself, invaded new territories, and ambitiously sought to dominate the Mediterranean region during the second century B.C., Hellenistic cults invaded Rome. Having successfully won numerous military battles, Rome nevertheless began losing a long war it could scarcely see. Broadly challenging traditional Roman understanding, Hellenistic philosophies and Eastern cults penetrated Rome despite every attempt to block them. Romans tried to preserve their traditional worldview, but sophisticated Hellenistic beliefs forced them to change, raising popular expectations about what cults could offer.

Strangely, the Cult of Cybele entered Rome by invitation during the Second Punic War. Other Hellenistic cults, like those of Dionysos, Atargatis, Sabazius, Yahweh (the name of God in Judaism), Isis, and so on, came to Rome during the second century B.C. Most of the cults arrived unnoticed accompanying newcomers, either those who came as entrepreneurs or those who were forced to serve Rome as slaves. In addition, at least one Roman emulated Eastern Diadochi by encouraging the development of a vanity cult based on his own military success, position, and personality.

THE STORY OF CYBELE'S PATRIATION TO ROME

Acceptance by the straight-laced culture of Republican Rome of an orgiastic Eastern cult like the Cult of Cybele took a remarkable confluence of miracles, prophecy, and politics across several centuries. In the sixth century B.C., Rome acquired its most sacred books, three books of prophecies written by a woman known only as the Cumaean Sibyl. Over time, the stature of the *Sibylline Books* increased such that, during the Second Punic War when strange events matched the Sibyl's prophecies in 205 B.C., Romans followed the books' recommendation and invited the Cult of Cybele to come to Rome.

Politics and natural events conspired miraculously to support an unprecedented transfer of the most sacred relic of the goddess: In a short time, a retinue of Galli[1] (priests) from the Anatolian city of Pessinus accompanied the baetyl of Cybele, a black meteorite regarded as the sacred home of the goddess, on a long journey to Rome. Afterward, despite the disquieting nature of the worship of Cybele to Western sensibilities, Rome experienced a remarkable century of successful growth, seemingly made possible by the divine favor of the goddess.

Rome's Acquisition of the Sibylline Books

Sometime before 509 B.C., the Cumaean Sibyl confronted Tarquinius Superbus, the last Etruscan[2] king of Rome. For an outrageously high price, she offered to sell him nine books that foretold the future of Rome. When the king declined her offer, she threw three of the books in a fire. The sibyl then offered six books of prophecy to Tarquinius Superbus at the original high price. He refused, and the sibyl threw three more books in the fire. The king finally bought the remaining three Sibylline Books for the same price that he could have purchased nine books.

Though Romans overthrew the Etruscan king and created a republic, they learned to respect the prophecies in the Sibylline Books. A college of priests charged with preserving and interpreting the books stored them in a vault under the Temple of Capitoline Jupiter. When miraculous events occurred, or when Rome experienced stressful times, the priests consulted the Sibylline Books searching for passages that helped illuminate divine will. Among their most famous prophesies, the books described events that would bring the Idaean Mother of Pessinus (Cybele) to Rome.

Mythologically, a prophecy that mentioned Cybele made sense to the people of Rome. The progenitor of the Roman race, Aeneas (a child of the goddess Venus and the Trojan prince Anchises), had grown up in Troy[3] not far from Mount Ida. Also, Roman entrepreneurs

---

[1] See Chapter 10.
[2] Etruscans (from Anatolia?) first appeared in Tuscany around 800 B.C.
[3] The Palladium (statue of Minerva/Athena) carried by Aeneas (the progenitor of Rome's founders) from Troy to Rome may originally have been understood as a statue of Cybele, a goddess worshipped by many Greeks in the Western Anatolian region associated with ancient Troy. See Chapter 7.

encountered this militaristic goddess (and Phrygian[4] goddesses like her) while pursuing business interests anywhere in the Anatolian Peninsula. In the light of Hellenism's tendency to identify goddesses in different lands as Greek goddesses known by different names, Cybele was just a foreign name for Venus (the goddess known as Aphrodite by Greeks), Aeneas' mother.

The Land of Cybele in the Hellenistic Age

Philetaerus, a Macedonian eunuch, established the Pergamene Kingdom during the wars after the death of Alexander the Great. Loosely dominated by the Seleukid Empire, the Pergamene Kingdom served as a buffer state between Seleukia and Macedon. Philetaerus built a Hellenistic capital city at Pergamon and named Athena (known as Minerva in Rome) the city's patron goddess. The most militaristic goddess on Mount Olympus, Greek Athena closely resembled the militaristic Phrygian mother goddess Cybele.

All but one of the Attalids[5] put Philetaerus' portrait on their coins, yet none of them could claim him as an ancestor. Accounts differ regarding how the ruler lost his manhood, but Philetaerus ruled well and founded a worthy line of succession. King Attalus I, called "Savior" by his subjects, ruled the Pergamene Kingdom from 241 B.C. to 197 B.C. and minted the coin in Figure 12-1. On the obverse of the coin, Philetaerus, the founder of the Attalid dynasty, stares resolutely to the right. On the reverse, Athena sits on a throne and crowns Philetaerus' name with a victory wreath. Even though the coin in Figure 12-1 appears at first to have nothing to do with Cybele, the Hellenistic citizens of the Pergamene Kingdom would have associated the goddess on the reverse with Cybele as much as Athena. Philetaerus accompanied the goddess on the coin like a castrated priest attending Cybele.

---

[4]Mother Goddesses from the region of Phrygia (Central Anatolia) often governed war as well as fertility. Worshippers thought that pain purified the soul and provided access to prophecy and divine ecstasy. From their cults came pagan and Christian ecstatic religious practices involving confession of sins and physical punishment.
[5]From 282 B.C. to 129 B.C., the Attalid dynasty ruled the Pergamene Kingdom from its capital city, Pergamon. After founding the kingdom, the Diadochus, Philetaerus, passed control of the kingdom to his nephew, Eumenes I, in 263 B.C. Attalids continued to rule the Pergamene Kingdom until Rome seized it in 129 B.C.

Figure 12-1. Philetaerus and Athena. Pergamene Kingdom, AR Tetradrachm, 241–197 B.C.

Politics Connecting Rome with the Pergamene Kingdom

In the face of Roman expansion after the First Punic War, Greeks divided into two camps: The first camp comprised Ambitious Philip V[6] of Macedon and his allies who viewed Rome as a threat to Greek culture and a roadblock to Macedonian intentions of building a Mediterranean empire; and the second camp consisted of less ambitious Greeks who saw Philip V as a greater threat than either Rome or Carthage. Most Greek states watched the Carthaginian invasion[7] of Rome in 218 B.C. with apprehension, feeling that, once victorious, either party could become a serious threat to their security. However, Hannibal's early victories coupled with direct competition between Philip V and Rome in northwestern Greece prompted Philip to form an early alliance with Carthage.

Rome began looking for Greek allies against Macedon and Carthage in 212 B.C., just as Greek allies known as the Aetolian League[8]

---

[6]Philip V ruled Macedon from 238 B.C. to 179 B.C. Although he was an ally of Rome during his later years, he constantly looked for ways to increase the power of Macedon. He executed his younger son, Demetrius, for helping Rome too much.

[7]The Carthaginian general, Hannibal, crossed the Alps with foot soldiers, cavalry, and war elephants to invade Northern Italy, starting the Second Punic War in 218 B.C.

[8]All Greek city-states on the Greek peninsula outside of Attica joined the Aetolian League, including Locris, Phocis, Acarnania, part of Thessaly, and Greek tribes called Malis and Dolopes.

began to increase their activity against Philip V. Greek states joined the league from locations as diverse as Illyria, the Peloponnese Peninsula, and Anatolia (King Attalus I). Convinced of Rome's rising fortunes by its defeat of Syracuse—and greatly in need of Rome's naval capabilities—the league welcomed Rome's participation in the alliance. Rome nevertheless had too many troubles of its own to focus on preserving league members from jeopardy.

Among Rome's new allies, King Attalus I of Pergamon ruled a kingdom that contained Pessinus and Mount Ida, places central to the worship of Cybele. (See map of the Roman Mediterranean region in Figure 12-2.) The king's emergence as the principal leader of the Aetolian League against Philip V forced the Pergamene Kingdom into a continuing alliance with Rome as Philip V slowly came to dominate Aetolian League member states on the Greek peninsula.

Roman Desperation during the Second Punic War

Over the course of the Second Punic War from 218 to 202 B.C., Rome first suffered grave defeats and then entered a prolonged period of widening war, stalemate, and increasing desperation. After its first catastrophic losses, Rome could make progress against Hannibal only by destroying crops in his vicinity or by attacking the Italians who helped him. In 214 B.C., the war widened as Syracuse and Macedon allied with the Carthaginians. Rome also acquired new allies and held its own against Carthage, but Roman citizens suffered from an atmosphere of constant threat.

Attempting to prevent Italians from joining the Carthaginian invaders, Rome minted gold coins like the one in Figure 12-3 to pay its Italian allies. The obverse of the coin shows the Dioscuri, the Gemini twins, in a composite bust like Janus, the two-faced God of Borders. On the reverse, a man kneels with a pig in his arms. Jointly declaring sacred oaths, two soldiers touch the pig with the points of their swords. The soldier on the left wears a military costume of Italy while the soldier on the right wears a Roman uniform. The coin declares that sacred duty binds Romans and Italians together to rid their lands of the Carthaginian invader.

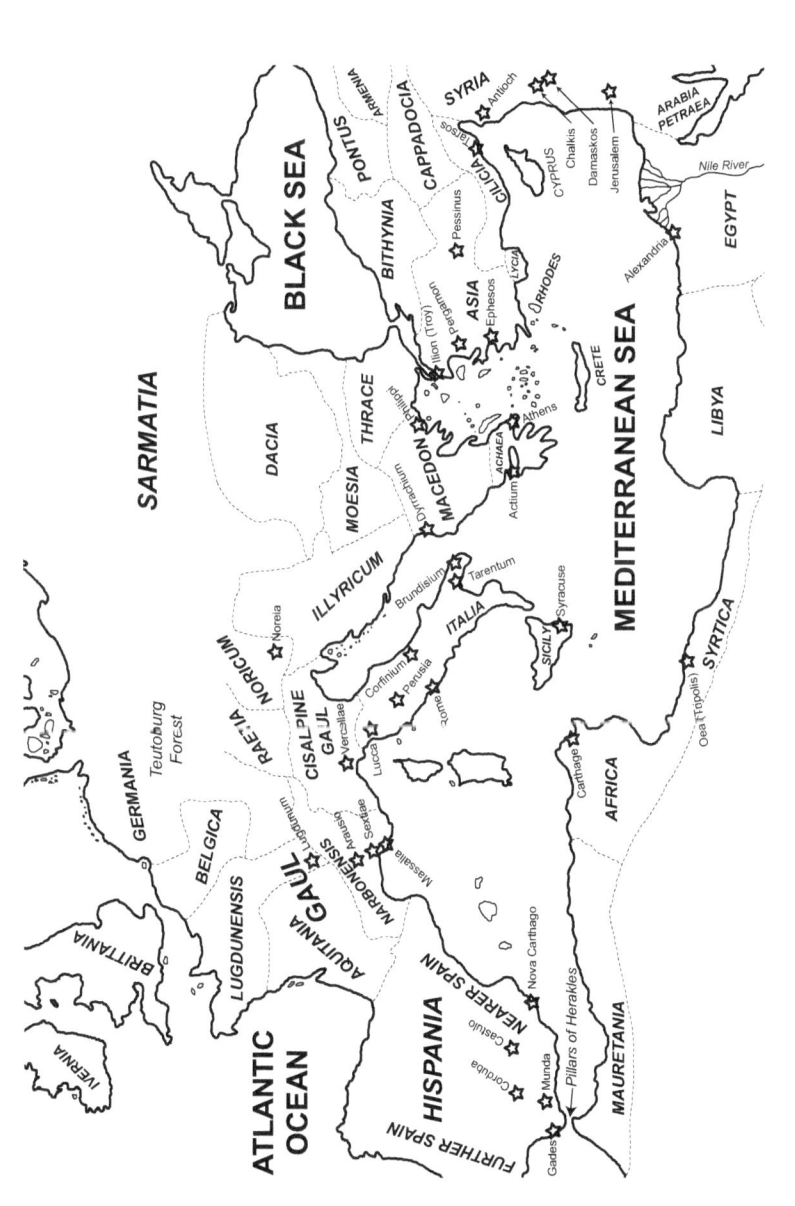

Figure 12-2. Map of Roman Mediterranean Region of the Mid-First Century B.C.

Figure 12-3. Coin with Janus Bust and Punic War Oath-Taking Scene. AU Stater, 225–212 B.C.

Rome expanded the fight against the Carthaginians to distant battlegrounds. Although unable to defeat Hannibal in Italy, Rome won victories in Spain, Sardinia, and Africa. In 207 B.C., Roman forces critically weakened the Carthaginian invaders by defeating Hannibal's brother, Hasdrubal, in central Italy. Hannibal's army continued fighting in Southern Italy, and Hannibal's other brothers, Mago and Hanno, attacked northern Italy. By 205 B.C., Rome was making steady progress against Carthaginians in Spain, Italy, and Sicily. However, far too dangerous and far too close for comfort, the forces under direct command of Hannibal still threatened Rome.

By 205 B.C., too many years of hard fighting against a skilled foe who slaughtered whole armies had reduced Romans to superstition and spiritual desperation. Attempting to prevent sacrilege from influencing the course of the war, the Roman senate ordered everyone who possessed written prayers, books of prophecy, or instructions for foreign religious rites to surrender those materials to the government. Further, the senate forbade unusual religious practices, sacrifices, and even ordinary prayers in public. When rocks (a shower of meteorites?) fell from the sky, Rome searched for a spiritual explanation. Consulting prophets, priests, and ancient writings, officials finally found an answer in the Sibylline Books: When rocks fell from the sky, Romans would succeed in expelling an invader from the Italian peninsula only if the Idaean Mother of Pessinus (Cybele) came to live in Rome.

Bringing Cybele to Rome

Rome sent envoys to the Oracle of Delphi to verify the prophecy about Cybele in the Sibylline Books. The oracle confirmed the prophecy and added the condition that the "Best Man of Rome" must welcome the goddess to the city. Still, it seemed unlikely that the Anatolians who lived in Pessinus would give up their goddess easily.

Roman envoys met with King Attalus and asked for permission to remove the black meteorite from Cybele's shrine in Pessinus and carry it to Rome. Initially, King Attalus (whose name reflects a connection with Cybele's consort, Attis) rejected this request. Then the earth rumbled beneath King Attalus' feet (a small earthquake shook Pergamon), and Attalus changed his mind. Attalus affirmed that an ancient bond of brotherhood connected the Pergamene Kingdom with the Romans, and he agreed to allow them to transfer the stone, along with attending priests (Galli), to Rome.

Miracles and profound spiritual experiences touched everyone who sailed with the goddess and Galli to Rome. A miracle even greeted the ship's arrival. Upon reaching Rome's port, Ostia, on April 4, 204 B.C., the ship carrying the goddess ran aground on a mudbank. A Roman matron, a descendent of Atta Clausas (the Sabine founder of the Claudian line whose name associated him with Attis), removed her girdle, tied it to the ship, and easily pulled the ship free from the mud.

Romans chose Publius Scipio Nasica, a nephew of Scipio Africanus (the general who ultimately defeated Hannibal—see Figure 12-4) to represent them as the "Best Man of Rome." After the ship docked, Publius Scipio Nasica piously welcomed the stone, lifted it, and passed it to a waiting line of noble matrons. Dressed in exotic costumes, the Galli danced and played sacred instruments: timbrels, tambourines, horns, flutes, and drums. Roman matrons passed the stone hand-to-hand in

Figure 12-4. Portrait of Scipio Africanus on First Coin Depicting a Living Roman. Spain, Carthago Nova, Roman Occupation. AR Shekel, ca. 209 B.C.

a long line, each matron desiring to touch the stone and receive its blessings. In this way, surrounded by incense, music, and celebration, the goddess traveled to her temporary home in the Palatine Temple of Victory (the Greek goddess Nike).

On April 10, 191 B.C., Rome consecrated the Palatine Temple of Cybele. Near the earliest foundation of the temple, archaeologists found terracotta votive deposits[9] (probably buried by Anatolian slaves) that indicate the worship of Attis, Cybele's consort. The votive deposits testify to the presence in Rome during the early second century B.C. of people who worshipped a savior called the Good Shepherd (an appellation of Attis[10]). Artists installed the black stone as the face of the goddess, and Romans began to refer to Cybele as the Black Virgin.

The Benefits of Cybele's Presence in Rome

After Cybele's arrival, Rome's circumstances improved dramatically. That year, Roman farms produced abundant harvests, and many matrons who had touched the stone became pregnant. Within two years, Carthage ordered Hannibal to return to Africa to defend

---

[9] See *The Cults of the Roman Empire* p. 37 by Robert Turcan.
[10] Worshippers of Attis celebrated his resurrection in late March, even decorating evergreen trees. When Jesus called himself the "Good Shepherd" (see *John* 10:14 and 11:11), he compared himself directly with Attis. Also, see *Cybele, Attis and Related Cults: Essays in Memory of M. J. Vermaseren* pp. 39–40, edited by Eugene Lane.

Carthage. Then, in October of 202 B.C., Scipio Africanus brought an end to the Second Punic War by defeating Hannibal at the Battle of Zama, which fully confirmed the prophecy in the Sibylline Books.

Throughout most of the second century B.C., Rome prospered and its forces won new territories in military adventures to distant Mediterranean shores. Republican forces enjoyed a prolonged series of victories against Africans, Gauls, Greeks, and Seleukids, ensuring a steady inflow of treasure and slaves. Roman entrepreneurs harnessed newly won lands and cheap slave manpower to build multinational enterprises. Slaves served every function needed by Romans, from teachers and administrators in wealthy Roman households to field hands in vast agricultural plantations like those on Sicily.

Roman Discomfort with Cybele

Nobody doubted that Cybele had brought good fortune to Rome, but many Romans found the practices for worshipping the goddess disturbing. Romans usually worshipped their gods with public games, solemn ceremonies, and family offerings at home. To participate in traditional religious ceremonies, a Roman had to be whole, healthy, and virtuous—physically and morally without blemish. With their heads covered, Romans sacrificed and prayed modestly, sometimes accompanying their prayers with a little flute music.

But the priests of Cybele—the Galli—committed themselves to her service by castrating themselves in violent ecstatic orgies and offering their own flesh on her altar. Even normal worship consisted of music and wild dancing. Priests and priestesses routinely lashed themselves with whips, slashed their arms and chests with swords, and splashed their blood on the altar. Romans scorned this barbarous and bloody worship, just as they scorned the castrated Galli in their gaudy, effeminate costumes. To many conservative Romans, the sacred story[11] of Cybele, Agdistis, and Attis comprised only immoral fantasies and inspired only repugnance. Nevertheless, Rome committed itself to long-term support of the Cult of Cybele, importing foreign priests because Roman law forbade Roman citizens from mutilating themselves.

---

[11]While Chapter 10 describes an early version of the story of Cybele, Agdistis, and Attis, cult details varied from place to place and from century to century.

Limiting Roman Worship of Cybele

From the beginning, the Roman senate and the Pontifex Maximus (the supreme religious authority in the Roman Republic) strictly regulated the Cult of Cybele. No Roman citizen could enter the priesthood of the Great Mother, and Roman law confined all foreign priests and priestesses to the temple compound. Virtually imprisoned, the Galli conducted ceremonies to Cybele mostly in private. Rome allowed only a few annual celebrations to publicly honor the goddess who had preserved Rome.

Once a year in late March, playing timbrels, cymbals, trumpets, and flutes, priestesses and Galli escorted the enthroned goddess to the banks of the Almo River. Worshippers lined the path to the river to shower the goddess with flower petals and coins as she passed in a chariot pulled by heifers. Wearing a purple robe and a gold crown, the high priest bathed the goddess in the river. Then he washed the instruments used in her worship.

On April 4 and April 10, Roman citizens celebrated anniversaries of the arrival of Cybele in Rome and the dedication of her temple. On these two days, Romans carried gifts inside the temple compound and offered them directly to the goddess. Between April 4 and April 10, Romans honored the goddess with the Megalesian Games. During this brief period, priests and priestesses worshipped the goddess outside the compound. They played music, danced in the streets, performed obscene passion plays, and begged door-to-door for contributions. Bearing a platform on their shoulders, the Galli carried their enthroned goddess in public parades just as Italian Catholics carry enthroned effigies of the Virgin Mary during modern Christian festivals.

THE FIRST ROMAN TO INSPIRE A HELLENISTIC VANITY CULT

After Alexander the Great died, a number of Eastern Hellenistic rulers declared themselves divine, sometimes requiring their subjects to sacrifice to them in temples as they would to a god. Most Romans regarded claims of divine status by men as examples of absurd vanity,

Figure 12-5. Second Numismatic Portrait of a Living Roman. Chalkis(?), AU Stater, T. Quinctius Flamininus, ca. 196 B.C.

but the Hellenistic idea that a man might achieve divinity attracted some ambitious Romans. At the beginning of the second century B.C., one Roman inspired the brief emergence of a Hellenistic cult that affirmed his personal divinity.

After concluding the Second Punic War in Africa, Rome professed a need to preserve the freedom of Greece against Macedonian interference: Rome declared war on Macedon in 200 B.C. Within three years, the Roman consul, Titus Quinctius Flamininus, forced Philip V to withdraw all his forces from Greece and return home. To celebrate Rome's victory, Titus issued Greek coins with his own portrait in a style reminiscent of images of Hellenistic rulers. (See Figure 12-5.) The obverse of this coin, only the second coin ever to portray a living Roman, lacks devices indicating royalty or divinity. However, the coin's reverse portrays Nike crowning Titus' name with a victory wreath.

A lover of Greek culture, Titus tried to create a new kind of relationship between Rome and Greece, that is, different from Rome's brutal treatment of Sicily. He implemented a lenient, mutually beneficial stewardship of Rome over Greece based more on respect and cooperation than on domination. At the Ithsmian Games of 196 B.C., he announced that European Greeks would continue to enjoy unrestricted freedom under Roman rule. Titus enjoyed great popularity in

Greece. Some Greek states proclaimed that he was a divine savior and offered sacrifices to him as to a god.

Of course, nobody in Rome regarded Titus as divine, but the example of Alexander the Great always attracted the most capable of Rome's leaders. Many dreamed of matching or exceeding Alexander's military accomplishments; however, Rome expanded only incrementally at first. Further, even if a truly great general had emerged at this time, Roman Society was not yet sufficiently Hellenized to accept the idea that a human being could become a god.

THE CULT OF DIONYSOS: PLUMBING THE DEPTHS OF ROMAN XENOPHOBIA

At the beginning of the second century B.C., Hellenistic mystery cults like the Eleusinian Mysteries and the Cult of Dionysos thrived in many forms throughout the Western world. In Thrace and Macedon, Greeks participated in mysteries of a child or brother of Dionysos named Sabazius (the God of Beer). Throughout the Mediterranean region, devotees also worshipped mysteries of Orpheus,[12] claiming that he had helped create the Eleusinian Mysteries but had been murdered treacherously during sacred rites. Numerous variants of mystery cults existed in Hellenistic lands from Seleukia and Egypt in the East to Greek colonies in the West.

In Egypt, Ptolemy IV wore a tattoo of ivy leaves to express his devotion to Dionysos. Concerned about the quality of mystery initiations in Egypt, Ptolemy IV issued a proclamation sometime between 221 and 205 B.C. requiring all teachers of mysteries—whether Dionysian, Orphic, Sabazian, or any other type—to come to Alexandria within three days of their arrival in Egypt. There, they were required to identify the genealogy of their teachings going back three generations, submit sacred objects for inspection, and deliver a sealed copy of their sacred texts with their name written on it.

---

[12]Orpheus, a semi-divine hero who could charm savage beasts with his singing, visited Hades intending to restore his dead lover to life. Mystery cults of Orpheus appear to have been similar to mystery cults related to Dionysos, Persephone, and Demeter.

Interest in Dionysos in Rome

The city of Rome grew more cosmopolitan as more soldiers returned from foreign wars, as more nouveau riche Romans grew increasingly dependent on foreign slaves, and as the wealth of Rome attracted foreign traders with exotic goods. Newcomers from distant lands wanted to worship foreign gods not previously recognized in Rome, something forbidden by Roman law. However, Hellenistic Greeks soon recognized that Dionysos was a different name for Bacchus, the Roman God of Wine.

Hellenistic mysticism also began to interest common Romans. Encouraged partly by leftover angst from the times when Hannibal dominated the Roman countryside and partly by the official presence of the Cult of Cybele, more Romans wanted to investigate what foreign cults had to offer. However, because laws against foreign religious rituals remained in effect from desperate times during the Second Punic War, worship of foreign cults in Rome occurred only within private homes and protected spaces.

Early, Clandestine Rites of Bacchus

Since the laws of Rome prevented the overt worship of cults that originated in foreign lands (with the exception of the Cult of Cybele), many foreigners in Rome worshipped Hellenistic cults in secret. Tending to live close to one another, worshippers of mystery cults from different traditions relied increasingly on the discretion of their neighbors. In the *Urbs* (a mixed, working-class district of Rome that attracted new immigrants), a Hellenistic community practiced multicultural Dionysian rites, ostensibly worshipping Bacchus, the Roman equivalent of Dionysos. The full participation of families suggests that the rites supported family values. However, by 186 B.C., this growing community began to celebrate its rites too openly.

At the conclusion of each initiation, two matrons ran with flaming torches from the Temple of Ceres (the Roman name for the Greek goddess Demeter) in the Urbs to the nearby Tiber River. Accompanied by a boisterous crowd, the women thrust their torches (secretly burning a mixture of chalk and sulfur) into the water, extinguishing

Figure 12-6. Portrait of Demeter and Cultic Torches. Sicily, Menaion, AE Trias, after 212 B.C.

them. The matrons then raised the torches, which quickly reignited and burned brightly once again. The crowd greeted the new flames with shouts and music, jubilant that the torches still burned.

The matrons represented Demeter searching for her daughter, and the torches symbolized the triumph of eternal life over death. Circulating on Sicily around 186 B.C., the coin in Figure 12-6 portrays Demeter and her torches. Dionysian cults brought courage and optimism to marginalized Hellenistic people in Rome. Because of the increasing popularity of these Dionysian cults, particularly among the lower classes, Rome's ruling consuls perceived an emerging political threat.

The First Roman Religious Persecution

Apprehensive about the increasing influence of cults of Dionysos, authorities searched for an excuse to take action. They needed a scandal to galvanize public opinion, and one soon developed. Close examination of surviving statements suggests that one of the consuls manufactured the scandal with help from family friends who lived in the Urbs and badly needed money.[13] The consul must have planned the scandal

---

[13] See *The Cults of the Roman Empire* pp. 302–306 by Robert Turcan.

with trusted staff who bought witnesses and coached testimony, and the plan worked. Rome established a general model for persecuting a foreign cult that would emerge repeatedly in centuries to come:[14]

1. Having learned of a perverted and sacrilegious cult, innocent locals sought help from the highest government authorities and begged for protection from murderous cult officials.
2. Authorities investigated the cult and announced the discovery of evidence that confirmed instances of murderous, depraved, and sacrilegious cultic practices.
3. Authorities warned the public of its grave danger: Spreading like an unseen cancer, a horrifying cult was working toward nothing less than complete destruction of the moral fabric of society.
4. Through a combination of martial law, secret informants, and torture, authorities identified and captured suspects whose guilt was accepted without question.
5. Authorities encouraged broad participation in punishing suspected cult members, formally executing many in public while abandoning others to murderous abuse by hysterical mobs.
6. Authorities formally outlawed the cult and ordered the expulsion of surviving cult members.

In 186 B.C., the people of Rome learned about danger from the Cult of Dionysos when a young couple, desperately fearful for their lives, informed a consul about murder and sacrilege in the Urbs in the name of a foreign god. They said that a Greek from Etruria had established a gang operating undercover as a mystery sect that sought to corrupt and destroy Roman society. Supposedly, the gang lured impressionable Roman youth into secret orgies of perversion disguised as religious rituals, but the problem didn't end there. The orgies acted as a cover for criminal racketeering that profited by murdering wealthy Romans and forging their wills in favor of the cult. Forced into complicity with the gang's plots, new initiates swore allegiance to sacrilegious priests in the pursuit of numerous illegal and immoral plots against Rome. Noisy

---

[14]For examples of Gentile propaganda that inspired numerous similar persecutions of Jews, see *Gentile Tales: The Narrative Assault on Late Medieval Jews* by Miri Rubin.

initiatory celebrations corrupted innocent Romans while drowning out the screams of uncooperative victims of ritual murder. The two young witnesses testified that this pernicious and obscene conspiracy already had corrupted at least seven thousand people. Apparently, under the noses of honorable Romans, a sacrilegious army bent on Rome's destruction was massing unnoticed in Roman streets.

Encouraging mass hysteria with sanctimonious speeches and proclamations, the Roman government publicly investigated the cult and rounded up suspects. The government issued emergency orders that restricted gatherings at night, forbade fires, and controlled traffic through the gates of Rome. Many cultists escaped from the city. Others, faced with interrogation and torture, committed suicide rather than implicate friends or reveal the mysteries of their cult. Regardless, the government succeeded in capturing thousands of cultists.

Releasing women and children to undergo family justice, Roman authorities nevertheless executed at least two thousand men and sentenced many others to lesser punishments. All through Italy, city authorities prosecuted worshippers of Dionysiac cults. Far south of Rome, the city of Tarentum arrested and sentenced seven thousand cultists. Within a year, Rome destroyed all Bacchic shrines on the Italian peninsula except for those with an unquestionable Roman pedigree. Rome also instituted new religious laws: No more than five people (two men and three women) could assemble to perform sacrifices, and nobody could collect and hold community funds in trust. Large cities posted bronze copies of the senate's proclamation against the worship of Bacchus. (See Figure 12-7.) Fear of the cult persisted for decades.

SLAVES: A MAJOR SOURCE OF HELLENISTIC CULTS IN ROME

Seleukid wars contributed a steady stream of Chaldaeans, Zoroastrians, Jews, and followers of the Syrian Goddess (Atargatis) into the general pool of slave labor. However, whether from the East, West, South, or North, slaves flowed through Delos, the hub of the Mediterranean slave trade. One of the Cyclades Islands just below Greece,

Figure 12-7. Senatus Consultum Proclamation Concerning the Scandalous Cult of Bacchus. Pergamon Museum, Berlin, Germany.

Delos acquired fame as a supplier of slaves as well as place where anyone, free or enslaved, could worship gods from a wide variety of Eastern cults. Island facilities for the cults of Isis, Serapis, and Cybele were particularly noteworthy. In general, goddess worshippers accepted Isis as representing any female goddess; so Isis of Delos represented Aphrodite, Artemis, Atargatis, Tanit, Fortuna, Nemesis, Victory, Justice, and so on. Ancients referred to Isis as the Goddess of Many Names, the Virgin, Our Lady of the Waves, and the Great Mother of the Gods. On Delos, every enslaved worshipper of a goddess could expect a compassionate hearing from Isis.

Jewish Slaves from the Wars of Antiochus IV

In the East, Seleukids, Egyptians, and other kingdoms fought among themselves and apprehensively watched Rome expand its control of lands around the Mediterranean Sea. King Antiochus IV[15] conquered Egypt twice, once in 170 B.C. and again in 168 B.C., but both times

---

[15]Antiochus IV ruled the Seleukid Empire from 175 B.C. to 164 B.C.

fear of Rome prevented him from incorporating the conquered land completely into his empire. Instead, Antiochus installed Egyptian puppets who owed their primary allegiance to him. On the eastern edge of his empire, Antiochus battled the emerging Parthian empire, mostly Chaldaeans and Zoroastrians. North of Egypt, only Jews continued to fight Antiochus.

Minted in the East during these times, the coin in Figure 12-8 recalls wars fought by the arrogant Seleukid emperor, Antiochus IV. On the obverse, a diademed bust portrays King Antiochus. On the reverse, seated Zeus holds the goddess Nike, who crowns him. The inscription to the right and left of Zeus proclaims an epiphany, the revelation of King Antiochus' divinity.

Antiochus captured Jerusalem, and he slaughtered and enslaved many of its inhabitants. His laws against Jews—compelling them to abandon circumcision and Sabbath worship and to offer sacrifices only to him in the Jerusalem temple—inspired the Maccabees to rebel against Seleukid domination. After Judah Maccabee and his followers successfully defeated a Seleukid army, Antiochus led a force toward Jerusalem declaring his intention of slaughtering every Jew. Before he could carry out this threat, however, he died of natural causes. Jews struggled against the Seleukids for another generation before finally achieving independence. Judaism continues to celebrate successful Jewish resistance against King Antiochus IV with the December festival of Hanukkah. However, by the time that the Maccabees obtained independence from the Seleukids, the Mediterranean slave trade had scattered Jewish captives, the seeds of future Jewish communities, to every shore of the Mediterranean Sea.

Carthaginian Slaves from the Third Punic War

While Carthage chafed under treaty restrictions after losing the Second Punic War, the wealth of former Carthaginian colonies flowed into Rome. Rome expanded its control over Greece and parts of Spain and North Africa. Still, Carthage managed to grow stronger. In 149 B.C., before the North African city-state could grow too strong, Rome manufactured an opportunity to declare war.

Figure 12-8. Diademed Bust and Seated Zeus with Text Proclaiming the Divinity of King Antiochus. Seleukid Empire, Antiochus IV, AR Tetradrachm, 175–164 B.C.

Unprovoked, Rome sent an army to Carthage and demanded the surrender of weapons and hostages. Scarcely believing that any power could be so unjust, the Carthaginians did not fight back. Instead, they surrendered their weapons and delivered 300 aristocratic Carthaginian children to the Romans. The Roman army then demanded that the Carthaginians vacate their city and move at least ten miles inland.

Forced to choose between a hopeless war and a peace that meant the destruction of their city as well as the end of their sea-going way of life, the Carthaginians stopped negotiating with the Romans. They precipitated the Third Punic War simply by closing the city gates. It took the Romans three years to capture Carthage. They burned it, demolished the city wall, and sold all 50,000 surviving Carthaginians into slavery. After this victory, no sophisticated foreign enemy ever again seriously threatened the Roman Republic. Few states within reach of Rome's army and navy could offer substantial resistance to the nation's growing power. However, largely unnoticed by Romans, Carthaginian slaves brought cultic worship of the solar deity Baal-Hammon, into numerous Roman homes. Beginning in the middle of the second century B.C., some Roman households began tolerating celebrations of a savior's birth on December 25.

THE CULTS OF HELLENISTIC ENTREPRENEURS

Regional wars generated business opportunities as well as slaves. The money spent on wars and the surfeit of cheap slave labor generated an abundance of new businesses around the Mediterranean Sea. Wherever Rome maintained good relations, Romans developed international trade and Roman wealth generated new businesses. From the Pergamene Kingdom, new priests and priestesses dedicated themselves to Cybele and then traveled to Rome to serve her baetyl. Entrepreneurs and clients from the Pergamene Kingdom also flowed into Rome. Some of these foreigners worshipped Cybele, some worshipped Sabazius, and some worshipped Yahweh, the god of the Jews.

Accomplished people from all over the world came to Rome and to Italy. Businessmen from Alexandria traded especially with Pozzuoli and Naples in southern Italy. These cities, as well as certain inland towns in southern Italy, built sanctuaries of Isis in the second century B.C. Astrologers, Jews, and educated Babylonians found their way to Rome via Alexandria as well. Fueled by slaves, freedmen, returning soldiers, and foreign entrepreneurs, Rome developed a cosmopolitan atmosphere that inevitably clashed again with Rome's conservative government and priesthood.

PROACTIVE EXPULSION OF CULTS: SABAZIANS, JEWS, AND CHALDAEANS

The events surrounding the persecution of Hellenistic cults of Bacchus cast a long shadow. After a few decades, conservative Romans again grew fearful of the varied and complex religious ideas circulating in their city streets. Charged with preserving public morality, officials rarely could make fine distinctions between dangerous and harmless beliefs, but by 139 B.C., officials knew once again that something had to be done.

In many parts of the West, followers of Sabazius had acquired an unpleasant reputation for creating violent and excessive festivities. In Rome, Sabazist clubs conducted initiations that sometimes violated acceptable standards of behavior. Rather than risk a repetition of the xenophobic hysteria that accompanied the eradication of the Cult of Bacchus fifty years earlier, a Roman praetor[16] issued a decree of expulsion for all followers of Sabazius. For unrecorded reasons, the praetor also expelled Chaldei and Jews.

By Chaldei, the decree probably meant newcomers who foretold the future, sold magic charms, and advertised the ability to invoke angels and demons—in short, anyone who charmed vulnerable Romans out of their money with fancy ideas about magic, souls, and astrology. However, the reason for expelling Jews seems more mysterious.

Perhaps Rome expelled Jews because officials could identify them easily and because Jews had a bad reputation in Rome: They possessed a written work that spoke of magical activities by people like Moses; they violated Roman laws against mutilation (that is, circumcising male babies); and they followed Jewish laws (for example, Kosher food laws and Sabbath observance) regardless of inconvenience to Romans. However, a persistent historical association of Jews with the worship of Jupiter Sabazius[17] also hints that some Jews from Asia Minor associated their god with Sabazius, a deity involved with mysteries of death and resurrection. Expulsion of the followers of Sabazius generally didn't bother anybody, but worshippers of the Syrian goddess Atargatis formally objected to the expulsion of Chaldei and Jews.

Approximately a year after the decree of expulsion, Rome minted the coin in Figure 12-9. The obverse displays a draped bust of Mars (the Roman name for Ares). In an oath-taking scene on the reverse, a kneeling man holds a pig and two soldiers touch the pig with the tips of their swords. This design recalls the gold coin in Figure 12-3 minted eighty years earlier during the Second Punic War. Then, one of the soldiers wore Italian armor and one wore Roman armor. That coin urged Italians and Romans to work together to expel Hannibal. Minted in a period relatively free from military threat, the coin in Figure 12-9

---

[16]The office of Praetor sometimes designated an appointed official and sometimes designated an elected official. A praetor served as a military commander, a judge, a governor, or a magistrate wielding special authority.

[17]For an example, see *Factorum et Dictorum Memorabilium Libri Novem* 1.3.2 by Valerius Maximus. Pergamene Jews, an independent community with its own cultic and literary traditions, may have viewed Jupiter Sabazius and Yahweh as equivalent.

Figure 12-9. Bust of Mars and Oath-Taking Scene. Rome, AR Denarius, 137 B.C.

portrays two Romans, one bearded without armor and one beardless with armor, making an oath to fight some common cause. The date of this issue suggests a religious interpretation: The coin urged all Romans to protect their country vigilantly against the corrupting influence of foreign Hellenistic cults.

ROMAN TOLERATION OF THE CULT OF ATARGATIS

Despite official policies against foreign Hellenistic cults, Rome generally tolerated the worship of the Syrian Goddess under her various names: Atargatis, Venus of Erice, Astarte, Asherah, Great Mother of Syria, the Syrian Aphrodite, and even Tanit. Temples to this goddess usually established themselves on the outskirts of towns. There, prostitutes (popularly known as wolves) associated with the temple could prowl and signal their availability with "wolf-whistles" without upsetting official morality.

In Rome and the Italian countryside, small groups of Atargatis worshippers roamed from place to place seeking religious offerings. Comprising mostly poor freedmen and slaves, the groups emphasized the similarities between their goddess and the official Cult of Cybele.

Romans described followers of the Cult of Atargatis as half-starved Greeks with flutes and timbrels who carried effigies of their goddess from house to house. Sometimes the worshippers knocked on doors and held out the goddess' hands begging for contributions; sometimes, dancing wildly in exotic costumes and violently swinging swords and axes, they shrieked and muttered prophecies; and sometimes they cut themselves with swords or lashed themselves with whips. Because groups like these provided opportunities for Syrian merchants and slaves to worship the goddess of their homeland, appreciative audiences offered coins for these devotions.

The Cult of Atargatis on Sicily

The Cult of Atargatis thrived, particularly on Sicily. No laws there prohibited foreign cults, and long-time worshippers arrived by the boatload to work the fields of Roman masters. In the city of Eryx, Romans, Elymians, and other Sicilians worshipped a goddess equated with Atargatis on top of a mountain at the Temple of Venus Erycina. Roman tourists and Sicilian natives enthusiastically participated in the worship of this goddess by dancing, sacrificing, and enjoying her cult of sacred prostitution. The obverse of the Roman coin in Figure 12-10 portrays Venus, the Goddess of Eryx; the reverse displays a city gate and Mount Eryx with a temple on top. Minted in 57 B.C., just before Rome transitioned from a republic to an empire, the coin shows the goddess wearing a curious cruciform earring, perhaps borrowed from the Egyptian cross (ankh) of Isis. In association with this goddess, a cross symbolized fertility as well as possibilities for salvation and eternal life. Earlier Sicilian Greek coins usually portrayed the Goddess of Eryx as a seated Syrian Aphrodite holding a sacred dove. (For an example, see Figure 4-4.)

A Dangerous Sicilian Prophet of Atargatis

In 135 B.C., on a large Sicilian estate near Enna, a Sicilian slave named Eunus began to speak in the name of Atargatis. Already regarded as a magician and a holy man, Eunus claimed that the goddess came to him in his dreams. Wild-eyed, he prophesied that the slaves of Sicily would

Figure 12-10. Bust of Venus Erice (Syrian Aphrodite) and View of Temple on Mount Eryx. Rome, AR Denarius, 56 B.C.

rise against their cruel masters. Atargatis would grant freedom to the slaves and Eunus would rule as their king.

He crafted a small device inside a nutshell that fit inside his mouth. This allowed him to blow powdered sulphur over a hot ember so that sulphurous sparks of divine fire flew from his mouth when the goddess spoke through him. Inspired by this fire-breathing prophet, approximately four hundred slaves picked up farm implements and attacked the community of Enna. They seized and beheaded their notoriously cruel master, and they threw his wife off one of the cliffs surrounding the city. The rebels killed most of the free inhabitants of Enna but preserved some to work as slaves.

Eunus crowned himself King Antiochus, and he chose a former slave woman as his queen. However, recognizing his own limitations, he appointed another man, Cleon, to lead the slave army. Within three days more than six thousand slaves joined Antiochus' army mostly carrying makeshift weapons like hooks and sharpened sticks. In the following weeks and months, the slave rebellion grew until it engulfed the entire island. Approximately 70,000 men, not all of them slaves, joined the army of King Antiochus.

During three years of rebellion, General Cleon led slaves to victories against four Roman armies. Their success inspired other slave rebellions throughout the Mediterranean. Pockets of Syrian slaves attempted to rebel in Rome and even on Delos. Eventually, Rome crushed the rebellion on Sicily, killing Cleon and capturing Eunus. Eunus died before the Romans could sentence him, but Rome crucified approximately 20,000 of his followers. The first of three major slave rebellions against Rome, this conflict underscored the vulnerability of a slave-dependent Roman society as well as the power of religious beliefs to unify and inspire a downtrodden people.

A CENTURY OF DRAMATIC CHANGE FOR ROME

Depending on whether they associated a cult more with a hammer or more with a nail, Rome treated foreign cults differently. After suffering at the hands of Hannibal, Rome found a spiritual way to strengthen its hammer: importing the Cult of Cybele, a goddess associated with Trojans, Rome's mythological progenitors. After successfully dominating Greeks in many lands, Rome suddenly awakened to find numerous varieties of the Cult of Dionysos sticking up like nails in working-class foreign communities in Rome. Further, having grown dependent on its slaves, Rome's worst fears materialized when agricultural slaves rebelled on Sicily: Imported from the East, the slaves united around their common faith in Atargatis to bring about an island-wide rebellion.

Ultimately, the importation of Hellenistic cults helped aggravate tensions between the upper classes and the lower classes of Roman society. Generally, Roman nobility continued to see everything foreign and different as corrupt, but many Romans who came into daily contact with worshippers of Hellenistic cults thought otherwise. Working-class Romans rubbed shoulders with freed slaves and foreign merchants who generally occupied the lower rungs of society. Also, simultaneously perceived as necessary workers and potential rebels, slaves brought Hellenistic cults into the homes of the most powerful people in Rome.

As the end of the second century B.C. approached, Rome had successfully dealt with threats in distant lands for a long time. Throughout the century, valiant Roman soldiers had been returning home from years of foreign service immersed in cultures that believed in Hellenistic philosophies and gods. Some Hellenistic beliefs had been designed by Greek soldiers (for example, Skepticism by Pyrrho who had fought in Alexander's army), and some (for example, Mithraism) took form in the second century B.C. explicitly serving Hellenistic populations engaged in extended struggles against Rome. Long-term contact of Roman soldiers with sophisticated Hellenistic ideas and cults proved the most insidious and unstoppable way of all to challenge the nature of Rome: Once Roman soldiers understood certain Hellenistic points of view, the soldiers viewed their universe differently.

CHAPTER
13

THE HELLENISTIC CULT OF MITHRAS

SHAPING WESTERN UNDERSTANDING OF GOD AND THE UNIVERSE

Inspired by Zoroastrian beliefs and Hellenized by Anatolian Greeks centuries before Christianity existed, the Cult of Mithras attracted military men and popularized new ideas about salvation.

In the East, Alexander the Great identified Ahura Mazda, the god of the Zoroastrians, with the Greek god Zeus. After Alexander's death, however, Hellenists connected Zoroastrian spirituality and the worship of Greek Olympic gods with only limited success. Even after Berosus made many Zoroastrian beliefs accessible to Greek philosophers,[1] Zoroastrian cultic worship failed to resonate well with Greek worshippers, with one important exception: Persian Zoroastrians and Anatolian Greeks both worshipped a divinity named Mithra.

---
[1] See Chapter 10.

An invocation of Mithra in a treaty[2] that dates to the fifteenth century B.C. shows that the deity was worshipped in Syria at a time that predated the arrival of Zoroastrianism. After entering Zoroastrianism as one of the first three spirits generated by Ahura Mazda,[3] Mithra was identified as a disembodied enforcer of contracts, a spiritual judge, and a protector of kings. Portrayals of Mithra as a man began appearing on Anatolian coins when Persians dominated the region in the fifth century B.C.

During the third and second centuries B.C., Hellenistic Greeks reinterpreted Zoroastrian beliefs, which resulted in the emergence of the Hellenistic Cult of Mithras. However, Western literature ignored the new god until the Hellenized name (*Mithras* instead of Mithra) finally appeared in a biography of Pompey the Great: In the first century A.D., the Roman biographer, Plutarch, wrote that the Cilician pirates worshipped mysteries of the Cult of Mithras.[4] By the time that Pompey encountered the Cilician pirates during the first century B.C., Hellenizing Greeks had merged Zoroastrian beliefs, Greek mythology, Stoic philosophy, and advanced scientific discoveries into a mystery cult. Much more than a Zoroastrian cult honoring a disembodied spirit, the Hellenized Cult of Mithras presented its god as an eternally dying and resurrecting savior who could mediate between humanity and powerful deities like Jupiter,[5] Saturn, and Cybele.

The new cult contained a mixture of science and religion because little conflict existed between science and religious beliefs during Hellenistic times. Before the development of Christianity, most Hellenistic Greeks easily tolerated scientific discoveries, even those that changed how people understood the universe. Hellenism presupposed that learning about nature and the universe revealed information about god. Increased knowledge about nature brought one closer to the

---

[2]A treaty between the Mitanni and the Hittites invoked the gods Mithra, Varuna, Indra, and Nasatya (Ashvins). See "The 'Aryan' Gods of the Mitanni Treaties," *Journal of the American Oriental Society* 80, 1960, pp. 301–17, by Paul Thieme.
[3]As the first step toward creating the universe, Ahura Mazda divided into Mazda, Varuna, and Mithra. See Chapter 7.
[4]For information about the defeat of the Cilician pirates by the Roman general, Pompey the Great, see Chapters 16 and 17.
[5]This chapter mostly uses the Roman names of Olympic gods because most surviving descriptions of the Cult of Mithras come from its later stages among Romans.

creator. Each new discovery enhanced the quality of one's spirituality and potentially brought insight about fate, free will, souls, and destiny.

Before Rome began to expand into the East during the second century B.C., Hellenistic schools had struggled to choose between two competing models of the universe: the sun-centered model of Aristarchus and the Earth-centered model of Hipparchus. By 128 B.C., the discovery of precession of the Earth's equinoxes by Hipparchus, one of the greatest achievements of Hellenistic science, clinched victory for the Earth-centered model and strengthened philosophical support for astrology. Quick to take advantage of the new understanding, Hellenistic scholars in the Anatolian region of Cilicia encoded an astrological interpretation of Hipparchus' discovery in the Cult of Mithras.

ZOROASTRIAN BELIEFS ABOUT MITHRA

Zoroastrian ideas about Mithra were closely linked with beliefs that Ahura Mazda created the universe to destroy his evil twin, Angra Mainyu. At the beginning of time, Ahura Mazda generated three spirits: Mazda, the spirit of wisdom; Varuna, the spirit of the spoken word; and Mithra, the spirit of covenant. Directed by Mazda, Varuna uttered a word that generated the universe. The sky took shape as a hard shell, and earth and water collected at the bottom. In the sky, the light of Ahura Mazda emanated from the sun, which was fixed in its noontime position above the Earth and shining down on one plant, one bull, and one man.

Mithra helped create all living things by performing the first sacrifices.[6] Through him, the first plant was harvested and crushed, the first bull was sacrificed, and the first man was sacrificed as well. The heavens then began to turn, and the machinery of seasons, weather, life, and death began to move. From the sacrifice of the plant came all living plants, from the sacrifice of the bull came all living animals, and from the sacrifice of the man came all humanity. The spirits of the sacrificed man and bull returned joyfully to their creator: Having

---

[6]For a discussion about the roles of Mithra during creation and in the world, see *Zoroastrianism: Its Antiquity and Constant Vigour* pp. 54–57 and 69–70, by Mary Boyce.

willingly offered themselves for the benefit of all unborn life, the souls of the bull and the man established the path that future righteous souls would follow to heaven.

As the spirit of covenant, Mithra acted as a judge and vigilantly oversaw the terms of all agreements. If a person were accused of breaking an agreement, the Zoroastrian community invoked Mithra to judge the person in a trial by fire: Based on a person's guilt or innocence, the spirit of Mithra within the fire would protect or gravely harm the person under trial. When two tribes entered a dispute, Mithra judged the matter as a spirit of war.

As a spirit inherent in fire, covenant, judging, and war, Mithra played important roles for both the living and the dead. Among the living, the spirit of Mithra protected kings and inhabited speech denoting commitment and relationship. In service to the dead, Mithra joined Sraosa (the spirit of hearkening to god) and Rasnu (the spirit of the act of judging) at Mount Hara on the fourth day after death when they judged the fate of each newly released soul. Eventually, at the End of Days, Mithra would participate in the resurrection and final judgment of all humanity.

Every year on the vernal equinox, around March 21 on our modern calendar, ancient Zoroastrians celebrated the first day of the first month of their new year. They named the seventh month after Mithra and they considered the sixteenth day of every month as sacred to him. The sixteenth day of the seventh month was doubly sacred to Mithra.

According to Zoroastrian beliefs, Mithra watched over humanity like the sun. Public inscriptions sometimes described Persian rulers as sharing their throne with Mithra. An ally as well as an aspect of Ahura Mazda (the good God of Light), Mithra carried a thunderbolt feared by Angra Mainyu (the evil God of Darkness) as well as by mortal breakers of contracts.

THE HELLENISTIC CULT OF MITHRAS

To make Zoroastrian beliefs about Mithra more palatable to Greeks, Hellenistic scholars added an enhanced Olympic pantheon to the Zoroastrian creation story and focused on the role of Mithras as a redeemer. Possessing much of the character of the original Mithra, the Hellenistic Mithras mediated between imperfect mortals and unfathomable gods, generally intervening on behalf of mankind as a savior. The cult incorporated Stoic ideas about the soul and the latest scientific discoveries about the Earth-centered universe, connecting the ideas with astrological iconography that associated Mithras with the Greek hero, Perseus.

Structured as a hierarchy of mysteries, the cult guided worshippers through a sequence of seven initiations to seven levels of knowledge named, from lowest to highest: Crow, Bridegroom, Soldier, Lion, Persian, Sun-Runner, and Father. The seven levels of knowledge in Mithraism corresponded to the seven planetary spheres of the Stoics.[7] Initiation into successive levels of Mithraism revealed keys to heavenly gates that gave access to higher spiritual realms. As with all Greek mystery cults, worshippers kept cult mysteries secret from outsiders.

In honor of the seven planetary spheres, worshippers of Mithras adopted a seven-day astrological week: Sun Day (Sunday), Moon Day (Monday), Mars Day (Tuesday), Mercury Day (Wednesday), Jupiter Day (Thursday), Venus Day (Friday), and Saturn Day (Saturday).[8] In the first century A.D., the innovation of the seven-day astrological week[9] began spreading throughout the Roman Empire. Astrological correspondences for the days of the week even reached China by the fourth century A.D.[10] Most of the modern world still uses astrological names for the days of the week without suspecting their Stoic and Mithraic origins.

Abandoning the incorporeal spirituality of Zoroastrianism, Hellenistic worshippers of Mithras replaced Zoroastrian spirits with

---

[7]Some Stoic philosophers, for example, Posidonius of Apamea, attributed moral qualities to the seven planetary spheres, which connected astrologically to parts of the soul.
[8]The correspondences between modern names for the days of the week and planet names can be seen more clearly in Romance languages than in English.
[9]Before adopting the seven-day astrological week, Rome used an eight-day week, numbering the days with the letters: A, B, C, D, E, F, G, and H. Rome adopted the seven-day astrological week in stages well after the crucifixion of Jesus. See *The Seven Day Circle: The History and Meaning of the Week*, pp. 45–46, by Eviatar Zerubavel.
[10]The days of the week in China (Star Period Day and Star Period 1 through 6) and Japan (Sun Day, Moon Day, Fire Day, Water Day, Wood Day, Gold Day, and Earth Day) express correspondences in terms of Chinese and Japanese astrology identical to the planetary correspondences of the Western astrological week.

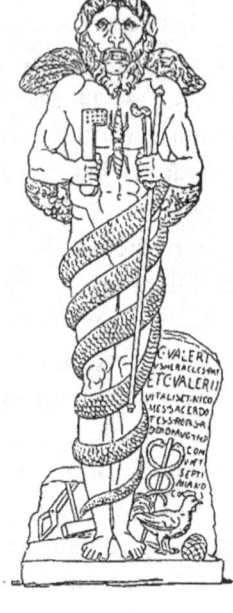

Figure 13-1. Etching of Vatican Sculpture, the Unbegotten Father (Saturn), Originally from Mithraeum in Ostia.

Olympian gods. Saturn (Cronos) ruled infinite time. Pluto (Hades) and Hecate (the goddess of witchcraft) ruled tormenting demons in fiery hell. Jupiter (Zeus, equivalent to Ahura Mazda) ruled the sky, Juno (Hera) ruled the Earth, Neptune (Poseidon) ruled the sea, Vulcan (Hephaistos) ruled fire, and Bacchus (Dionysos) ruled cultivation of the plant from which the sacred drink (usually identified as wine) was made. Diana (Artemis) and Luna (Selene, the moon) ruled processes for purifying one's soul, for example, baptism[11] and flagellation.

However, the Cult of Mithras modified Olympian iconography and conflated Olympian and Hellenistic deities. Mithraic Saturn usually appeared as a nude, lion-headed man wrapped by six coils of a giant snake. (See Figure 13-1.) Worshippers identified Mithras with

---

[11]Greeks used the word baptism, a synonym of cleansing or washing, to describe Eastern rituals of spiritual purification. Egyptian, Jewish, and Zoroastrian cults used water to cleanse worshippers spiritually. Hellenists appropriated the word to describe initiation ceremonies that required dipping or submersion in water, for example, initiation ceremonies into the cults of Mithras and Isis.

Chapter 13 | The Hellenistic Cult of Mithras 271

Figure 13-2. Anatolian Gods with Phrygian Caps, on Coins Clockwise from Top Left: Mithras, Mên and Sabazius, Attis, and Mên. Respectively from: Pontus, Trapezus, Lucius Verus, AE 29, 161 A.D.; Thrace, Pantikapaion, AE 31, ca. Second–First Century A.D.; Mysia, Kyzikos, Electrum Stater, ca. Fifth–Fourth Century B.C.; and Pisidia, Antiochia, Caracalla, 198–217 A.D.

the sun, but Helios (the sun) also existed separately, which allowed Mithras to be distinguished as the unconquered sun (Sol Invictus). Hellenists identified many Anatolian deities who wore Phrygian caps as equivalent to Mithras, for example, Sabazius,[12] Mên, and Attis. Also, Mithraists used the names Minerva, Venus, and Cybele as equivalent appellations of a single goddess of war and fertility.

Figure 13-2 portrays numismatic images of Mithras, Sabazius, Mên, and Attis revealing closely similar cult iconographies. On the reverse of the top left coin, Mithras wears a solar crown in addition to his characteristic Phrygian cap. On the top right coin, the obverse portrays a bust of Mên beneath a crescent and star; the reverse portrays Sabazius, holding grapes like his relative Dionysos, . The reverse of the lower left coin portrays Mên next to a rooster.[13] Mên stands in front of a crescent moon, his left foot resting on the skull of a bull, his right hand holding a scepter, and his left hand carrying a globe surmounted

---
[12]When Rome expelled worshippers of Sabazius in 139 B.C., the expulsion may have included a few Hellenistic worshippers of Mithras. (See Chapter 12.)
[13]Commonly associated with Saint Peter in Christianity, the rooster (a solar symbol) also served as a Mithraic symbol. For example, a rooster appears to the right of Saturn in Figure 13-1.

by Nike bearing a trophy. Close examination of Nike's trophy reveals that it combines features of an *ankh* (cross of Isis) and a Roman cross. The obverse of the coin on the lower right portrays a bust of Attis over a tuna fish. Christian cults adopted symbols associated with all four gods: For example, early Christians used the solar crown as an attribute of Jesus, they represented the Virgin Mary with the crescent and star, they associated the rooster with Saint Peter, they used both the ankh and the Roman cross to represent the crucifixion of Jesus, and they used a fish as a covert symbol of the Christian movement.

Originating in Greek Anatolia, the Hellenistic Cult of Mithras spread throughout the Roman Empire and flowered briefly in the third century A.D. as one of the most important cults in the Western world. Relatively little information about its mythology, its rituals, and its mysteries has survived. Nevertheless, scholars have pieced together information about the cult[14] by analyzing remnants of shrines, brief inscriptions of dedications, and criticisms by early Christian opponents of the cult.

The Hellenized Creation Story of Mithras

Although similar to the Zoroastrian creation story, Mithraic creation included many Hellenistic adjustments. In the beginning, Saturn (described as the unbegotten father) created a universe comprising the sky (Jupiter, equivalent to Ahura Mazda), Earth (Juno), hell (Pluto, equivalent to Angra Mainyu), and four elements (fire, earth, air, and water). Saturn gave thunderbolts to Jupiter, symbolically transferring dominion over the universe. Establishing his court on Mount Olympus, Jupiter married Juno and produced more gods, spiritual entities, and even humans. Connected by fate to the seven spheres of the universe, the Olympian gods ruled the universe from Mount Olympus and simultaneously lived as active principles in the world—for example, Vulcan lived as fire.

Ruling an unpleasant realm deep inside the Earth, Pluto conceived an army of demons (snake-legged giants) through impure relations

---

[14]See *The Mysteries of Mithra* pp. 105–149 by Franz Valery Marie Cumont.

with Hecate. Pluto then led his demons in an unsuccessful rebellion against Jupiter, who cast all of them back into hell. Eventually, the demons escaped and wandered the Earth spreading pestilence, misery, and corruption. Demons forced humanity to worship them.

In this time of need, Juno gave birth to the savior Mithras, who emerged from a rock beneath a sacred tree next to a river. Wearing a Phrygian cap, armed with a knife, holding a torch, and otherwise naked, Mithras hid in the branches of a fig tree. He ate figs and made clothing from fig leaves. While tending their flocks on a nearby mountain, shepherds witnessed the miraculous birth and quickly came to worship Mithras and bring him gifts.

However, sometime later, a disaster occurred that caused the first plants, creatures, and humans to disappear. Mithras reestablished divine control over an unruly universe by battling the sun. In victory, Mithras placed a radiant crown on the sun's head and directed the sun to follow a regular daily and annual path. Becoming good friends and allies, the two gods rode together in the solar chariot and they sometimes dined together. The top four panels of the etching in Figure 13-3 portray adventures of Mithras and the sun.

To restore life to the Earth, Jupiter created a single magnificent bull. Ordered to capture the bull, Mithras seized its horns, jumped on its back, and rode it until it tired. He then dragged the bull by its hind legs down a difficult path to a cave. To the worshippers of Mithras, carrying the bull served as a metaphor for suffering in life. Mithras did not harm the captive bull, and it eventually escaped.

The sun then sent a divine raven to bring a message to Mithras, a forwarded command from Jupiter to sacrifice the bull. Wearing a cape of stars and a Persian cap, Mithras pursued the bull with the help of a divine dog. They reached the bull just as it sought refuge in the same cave from which it had escaped. Adopting an iconic position (see Figure 13-4), Mithras seized the bull's nostrils with his left hand forcing the Bull to raise its head. Then, pressing his right leg and knee against the bull, Mithras plunged his dagger into the place where the bull's neck joined the shoulder.

Attending the scene, the crow watched from above, the dog leaped against the bull's flank, and a snake and scorpion attacked the belly

Figure 13-3. Etching of Mithraic Art Portraying Scenes from the Story of Mithras and Sol.

and genitals of the bull. Sent by Pluto, the snake and scorpion tried to poison the miracle of new life emerging from the sacrificed bull, but their efforts failed. All earthly life came from the bull: Useful plants came from his body, wheat came from his spinal cord, the sacred drink of mysteries (wine) came from his blood, and all useful animals came from his semen. The divine dog escorted the soul of the bull to the sky where both can be seen as constellations (Taurus and Canis Minor).

Creating the current race of human beings after the bull's death, Jupiter ordered Mithras to protect them. When Pluto attempted to

Chapter 13 | The Hellenistic Cult of Mithras   275

Figure 13-4. Mithraic Fresco in Marino, Italy, Showing Ladders to Heaven.

extinguish life by causing a prolonged drought, Mithras shot arrows into a stone, which made water gush from it. (See the lowest complete panel in Figure 13-3.) When Pluto sent a great flood to drown humanity, the gods advised one man who saved his family and his beasts by building an ark. When Pluto sent a great fire to burn the world, the gods intervened again, saving both good and bad creatures.

The gods confined Pluto in hell, which prevented further attempts to destroy mankind. To symbolize both the divine source of life and salvation from the gods, Mithras conducted a last supper on Earth. Helios and other gods joined him. From the bull's body, they drank wine and ate bread, which worshippers commemorated in their services with a Mithraic Eucharist ceremony. Then Mithras ascended into the sky with Helios, and all the gods returned to their heavenly home. From the sky, Mithras continued to participate in the lives of mortals, protecting those who served him faithfully.

The Fate of Human Souls

Worshippers of Mithras believed as Stoics did that a soul incarnated by passing through celestial gates in the same order as the days of the astrological week, Sunday to Saturday: first the gate of the Sun, and then the gates of the Moon, Mars, Mercury, Jupiter, Venus, and Saturn. After death, a soul returned to heaven by passing through the same gates in reverse order. Mithraic shrines used ladders as symbols for the path by which souls descended and ascended through a sequence of seven gates in seven heavenly spheres. Ladders appear on the left and right sides of the Mithraic fresco in Figure 13-4.

The duties of a worshipper of Mithras mostly involved being true to military virtues, for example: actively fighting evil, resisting sensuality, and cultivating strength and courage. In addition, worshippers abstained from certain foods and cleansed themselves spiritually by punishing themselves for sins and by undergoing purification ceremonies like baptism. Worshippers believed that one's actions while living mattered because souls maintained conscious survival after death and the purity of one's soul determined its subsequent fate.

When a soul separated from a body after death, spirits of heaven and spirits of darkness gathered waiting for Mithras to judge which realm possessed the soul. Spirits of light carried virtuous souls through the heavenly spheres to live in a realm of bliss. However, an evil soul could be condemned to reincarnate as beast, or spirits of darkness might drag it to hell to suffer torture.

At the End of Days, the gods again will allow Pluto to end all life on Earth. Jupiter will create a new divine bull, Mithras will descend from the sky, and all humanity will resurrect physically and emerge from their tombs. Mithras will sacrifice and immolate the divine bull, mixing a portion of its fat in consecrated wine. Every virtuous person will obtain immortality by drinking some of the wine. Then divine fire will fall from heaven, annihilating Pluto, Hecate, every demon, and every evil person. Only the virtuous will remain, blissfully inhabiting a universe cleansed of evil.

To worshippers of Mithras, his sacrifice of the divine bull promised eventual salvation for all virtuous humanity. Further, evidence of the promise glowed in the clear night sky: Anyone with sufficient knowledge could see Mithras as the constellation, Perseus, astrologically suspended above Taurus, the sacrificed bull. Commenting on the miraculous results of slaying the bull, an inscription found in the Santa Prisca Mithraeum in Rome says, "And you have saved us by shedding eternal blood."

The Myth of Perseus

In some parts of Anatolia, people added stories of gods like Mên, Attis, and Sabazius to the cult of Mithras, but Greeks from the Stoic school of Tarsos contributed stories of Perseus to the cult. Tarsians identified Mithras with Perseus because they believed that Perseus had founded their city. Further, centuries of Persian domination had taught them to associate Perseus and Baal of Tarsos with the Zoroastrian spirits, Mithra and Ahura Mazda. Many modern scholars credit Tarsian philosophers for systematically Hellenizing the cult by incorporating myth, philosophy, and science. By directly connecting Perseus to astrological mysteries of the Hellenistic Cult of Mithras,[15] Stoics connected Mithras to constellations long associated with the founder of Tarsos: Perseus, Cepheus, Cassiopeia, Ketos, Andromeda, Pegasus, and Pisces.

The story of Perseus begins with King Acrisius of Argos consulting an oracle to learn if he would beget a male heir. The oracle told him that he would die without an heir, killed by the son of his beautiful daughter, Danae. To ensure that Danae never conceived a child, Acrisius locked her in a cave. However, Zeus fell in love with Danae and came to her in the form of a golden shower. (See Figure 13-5.)

Concealing her pregnancy for nine months, Danae gave birth to Perseus and attempted to raise him in the cave. Eventually, King Acrisius discovered the child, but couldn't kill him without violating sacred law against killing family members. However, the king could transfer responsibility for the fate of Danae and Perseus to the gods: He locked both mother and son in a large trunk and cast them adrift on the sea.

Surviving with his mother on an island, Perseus matured and eventually took on numerous challenges, for example: slaying Medusa with the same weapon used by Saturn to castrate Uranus, saving a maid

---

[15] See *The Origins of the Mithraic Mysteries* pp. 25–27 and 40–45 by David Ulansey.

278 Part Four | Imperialistic, Religious, and Civil War

Figure 13-5. The Miraculous Conception of Perseus. Red-Figured Calyx-Krater from Attica by the Triptolemus Painter, ca. 490 B.C., Hermitage.

named Andromeda from a horrible sea monster, and affirming the authority of a virtuous fisherman over a corrupt aristocracy. One can see a number of parallels between stories about Perseus and stories related to Christianity:

- Ancient Greeks portrayed the miraculous conception of Perseus using iconography that appears metaphorically equivalent to Christian images of the Annunciation. For example, compare the ancient portrayal of the miraculous conception of Perseus in Figure 13-5 with the Renaissance painting of the Annunciation in Figure 13-6.
- The virgin, Danae, gave birth to Perseus, and Virgin Mary gave birth to Jesus.[16]
- King Acrisius tried to murder Perseus, just as King Herod tried to kill the infant, Jesus.

---

[16]Popular allegations about the virgin-birth of Mithras arise from his association with the Greek hero, Perseus, as well as from Greek beliefs about the perpetually renewed virginity of Earth goddesses.

Figure 13-6. The Annunciation. Central Panel of Triptych by Jean Bellegambe (1470–1534), Hermitage.

- Perseus passed kingly authority to a fisherman just as Jesus gave spiritual authority to Saint Peter, a fisherman who had become a "fisher of men."[17] The reverse of the coin in Figure 13-7 portrays Perseus telling his fisherman stepfather, Dictys, that he will be raised to a king.
- The killing of a sea-monster by Perseus recalls early Christian portrayals of Saint George and the dragon.

Further, the myth of Perseus provides insight into one of the few surviving descriptions[18] of mysteries of Mithras. A Christian critic of the cult stated that every year at Easter (that is, on a day near the vernal

---

[17]See *Matthew* 4:19.
[18]See *On the Error of Profane Religions* 8.2 by Julius Firmicus Maternus, a Christian who wrote about the Cult of Mithras in the fourth century A.D.

Figure 13-7. Perseus Bestowing Kingship on His Fisherman Father. Cilicia, Tarsos, Caracalla, AE 34, 198–217 A.D.

equinox), Mithras died and was buried by worshippers in a cave in the form of stone. He then rose in a day or two amidst much rejoicing, and a lamb or young ram was slaughtered.[19] Comparing the mysteries of Mithras with the birth of Perseus, Danae (confined deep within a cave) metaphorically represented an Earth goddess at the beginning of Spring. Perpetually a virgin, the Earth goddess attracted Zeus who magically fertilized her with rain. Mithras then was born from rock, emerging every year as a promise of fresh new life, which worshippers celebrated by slaying a symbolic gift of "first fruits" offered by the shepherds who witnessed his first miraculous birth.

Numismatically, one can see many connections between the Hellenistic Cult of Mithras and iconography associated with Perseus, particularly on Roman coins from Tarsos during the third century A.D., the peak of the cult's popularity in Imperial Rome. For example, the reverse of the coin in Figure 13-8 portrays Perseus and Apollo shaking hands just as Mithras and the sun shook hands after their battle. (See the center panel of the etching in Figure 13-3.) One also can find

---

[19]Throughout the Mediterranean region, kosher animals like sheep and cattle were sacrificed to sky gods, while pigs (non-kosher animals—even kids boiled in their mothers' milk) were sacrificed to chthonic deities. Recent excavations at Bethsaida by Dr. Ami Rav have suggested that Jews abandoned the slaughter and consumption of non-kosher animals after committing themselves to exclusive worship of God the Highest.

Figure 13-8. Perseus and Apollo (God of the Sun) Shaking Hands. Cilicia, Tarsos, Maximinus I, AE 37, 235–238 A.D.

earlier Greek coins from Anatolia that connect Perseus and Mithras. Minted under King Mithradates VI of Pontus, unofficial commander of the Cilician pirates, the coin in Figure 13-9 displays Athena (Cybele) on the obverse and Perseus (legendary ancestor of the Royal House of Pontus) on the reverse. Holding Medusa's head in his left hand and a hooked sword (harpé) in his right, Perseus looks slightly to his left as if apprehensive of an attack by Medusa's sisters.[20] Behind him, Medusa's headless body lies on the ground. Contemporaneous with warfare between Rome and Cilician pirates, the depiction of Athena and Perseus by a king named after Mithras provides evidence of a longstanding connection between Perseus and Mithras in Anatolia.

COMPETING HELLENISTIC IDEAS ABOUT THE NATURE OF THE UNIVERSE

To understand the scientific ideas that Stoic philosophers built into the Hellenistic Cult of Mithras, one must understand a little about competing beliefs that Hellenistic philosophers held about the nature of the universe. After the death of Alexander the Great, two famous

---

[20]For the story of Perseus and Medusa, see Chapter 2.

Figure 13-9. Bust of Athena Facing Right, and Perseus Holding Medusa's Head and a Harpé. Pontus, Amisos, Mithradates VI, 85–65 B.C.

astronomer-mathematicians advocated the most important models: Aristarchus of Samos (310–230 B.C.) proposed that the sun occupied the center of the universe and Hipparchus of Rhodes (190–120 B.C.) championed the more popular belief in an Earth-centered universe. Generally, Stoic philosophers preferred the Earth-centered model because it validated the central importance of humanity.

Aristarchus of Samos believed that observational evidence pointed to the Earth and planets moving around the sun in circles approximately in the same plane,[21] an idea which allowed him to use geometry to measure distances from the Earth to the moon and sun.[22] The third Chief Librarian of Alexandria, Eratosthenes of Cyrene (276–195 B.C.), refined the model of Aristarchus and accurately determined the tilt of the Earth's axis as well as the length of the year.[23] In addition, history credits Eratosthenes for measuring the circumference of the Earth with approximately 90 percent accuracy.

---

[21]We call the plane that contains the Earth's orbit the *ecliptic*. All planets in our solar system revolve around the sun traveling the same direction as the Earth. The orbits of the planets lie close to the ecliptic, diverging by fewer than three and a half degrees.
[22]Aristarchus came close to the correct Earth–moon distance, but his measure of the Earth–sun distance was only a twentieth of the correct value. See *On the Sizes and Distances of the Sun and the Moon* by Aristarchus of Samos.
[23]The work of Eratosthenes contributed to the *Canopic Decree* issued by Ptolemy III in 238 B.C., which temporarily gave Egypt a modern calendar with a 365-day year and a leap day added every four years. See Chapter 10.

Although Aristarchus' model largely matches our modern understanding of the universe, Hellenistic scholars overwhelmingly preferred Hipparchus' model, which dominated Western thought for almost two thousand years. Stoic philosophers connected Hipparchus' model to the Cult of Mithras, which spread religious ideas about the Earth-centered universe throughout the West. Filtering out impractical and unreasonable Greek ideas like those of Aristarchus, Roman society embraced Hipparchus' model as well as the Cult of Mithras. The Earth-centered model shaped features of Western life as fundamental as the number and names of the days of the week. Religious beliefs connected with Hipparchus and the Cult of Mithras eventually entered Christianity, which accepted them as unquestionable truth.

Aristarchus' Sun-Centered Model of the Universe

Aristarchus understood that astronomical observations and measurements fit a sun-centered universe much better than they fit an Earth-centered model. A slight tilt of the Earth's polar axis explained the seasons, and different periods of revolution for the planets explained their complicated motions from the Earth's point of view. His measurements suggested that the distance from the Earth to the sun measured millions of miles. Further, he realized that distances from the Earth to the stars must be vastly greater than the Earth's distance to the sun.

The sun-centered model of the universe explained the Earth's seasons exactly as we understand them today. The Earth rotates daily around its polar axis, which tilts approximately 23.5 degrees from vertical to the plane of the *ecliptic*, the plane of the Earth's orbit. As the Earth revolves around the sun, the Northern Hemisphere and the Southern Hemisphere alternately tilt toward and away from the sun: The hemisphere facing the sun experiences Summer; and the hemisphere facing away from the sun experiences Winter. Figure 13-10 portrays the Earth in four important positions of its counter-clockwise revolution: *winter solstice*, *vernal equinox*, *summer solstice*, and *autumnal equinox*, which we know as the beginnings of Winter, Spring, Summer, and Fall respectively in the Northern Hemisphere.

However, as scholars considered the geometry of a sun-centered universe, they saw a problem: The positions of the stars should shift

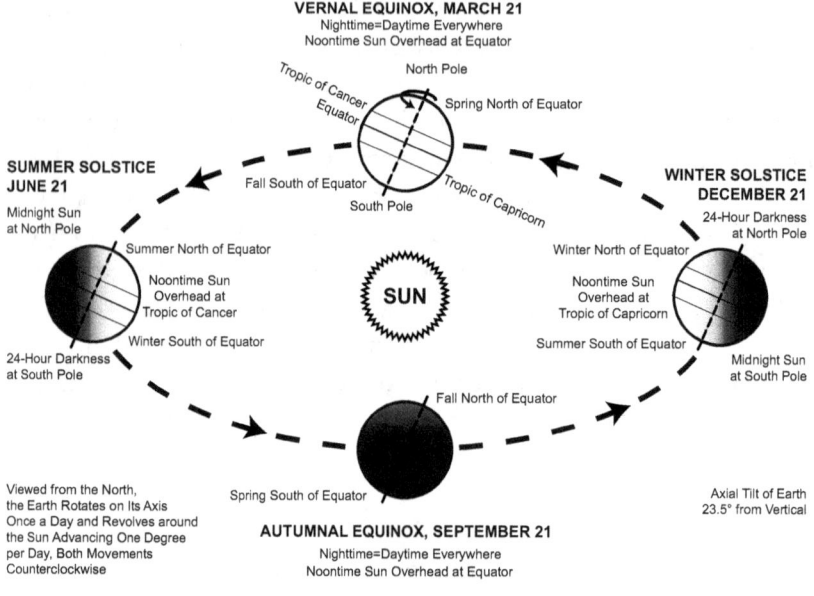

Figure 13-10. Sun-Centric View of Positions of the Earth Corresponding to Northern Hemisphere Seasons.

relative to each other as the Earth changed its position around the sun, but scholars could not detect any shift. To be true, the ideas of Aristarchus required enormous distances from the Earth to the stars, distances that seemed too large for practical consideration. Believing that a sun-centered universe failed a fundamental test of reasonableness, most scholars adopted the sophisticated Earth-centered model described by Hipparchus of Rhodes.

Hipparchus' Earth-Centered Model of the Universe

Hipparchus proposed a model of the universe in which a spherical Earth rested inside seven concentric planetary spheres, all surrounded by a rigid sphere of stars. From the Earth's point of view, the entire universe revolved around the Earth once a day, and the sun, moon, and planets moved slowly against a rotating shell of stars over the course of a year. The sun, moon, and planets always stayed on or near the ecliptic passing through a sequence of twelve constellations: Aries, Taurus,

Chapter 13 | The Hellenistic Cult of Mithras   285

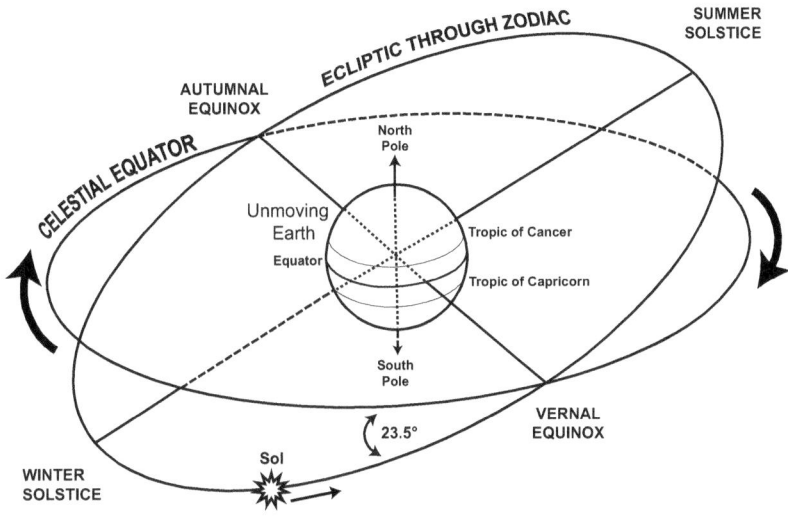

Figure 13-11. Earth-Centric View of Ecliptic, Celestial Equator, Equinoxes, and Solstices.

Gemini, Cancer, Leo, Virgo, Libra, Scorpio, Sagittarius, Capricorn, Aquarius, and Pisces. We call the broad path of the sun, moon, and planets through these constellations the *zodiac*.[24]

Over the course of a year, the sun travels east along the ecliptic, passing through each of the zodiacal constellations. The moon also travels east, sometimes above the ecliptic and sometimes below it, but the moon circles the zodiac once a month. The motions of the planets are more complicated: Mostly they advance west through the zodiac, but sometimes they briefly retreat east, which is called *retrograde* motion.

Figure 13-11 identifies important features of Hipparchus' model of the universe. From an Earth-centric point of view, the Earth's equator occupies a plane that splits the Earth in two. Extending this plane marks the *celestial equator* on a spherical sky. Two circles lie parallel

---

[24]On Earth-centered models, a band whose width extends nine degrees north and south of the ecliptic represents the zodiac, the region through which the sun, moon, and planets can travel.

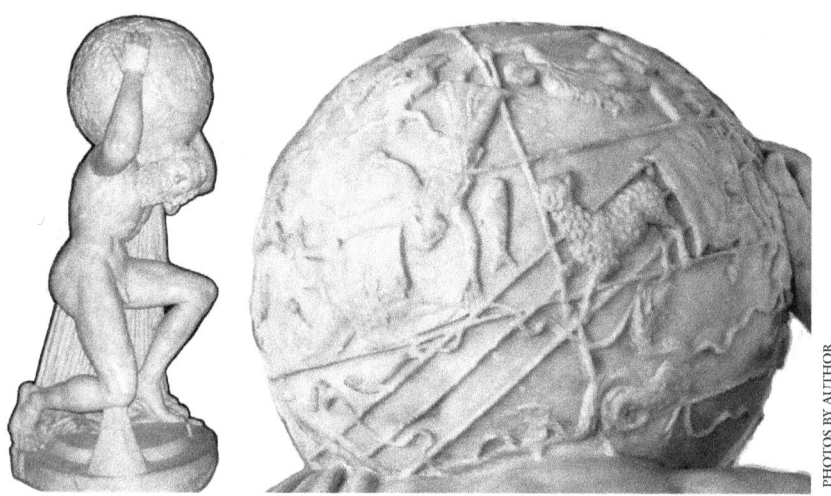

Figure 13-12. Distant and Close-Up Views of Farnese Atlas. Museo Archaeologico Nazionale in Naples, Italy, ca. 150 A.D., from a model by Hipparchus, ca. 128 B.C.

north and south of the celestial equator: the *Tropic of Cancer* and the *Tropic of Capricorn*. The ecliptic defines a plane that intersects the celestial equator at an angle approximately equal to 23.5 degrees. Four equidistant points on the ecliptic mark the sun's positions on the zodiac during the summer solstice, the winter solstice, the vernal equinox, and the autumnal equinox. The ecliptic and the celestial equator intersect at endpoints of a line segment that connects the vernal equinox and the autumnal equinox by passing through the center of the Earth. Philosophers in ancient times described the narrow cross (X-shape) formed by the intersection of the ecliptic and the celestial equator, particularly at the vernal equinox, as the fundamental structure of the soul of the universe.[25]

Figure 13-12 provides distant and close-up views of a Roman statue called the Farnese Atlas, portraying the Titan Atlas carrying the universe, a star-studded sphere of constellations, on his shoulders. Not visible through the outer sphere of stars, a spherical Earth rests in the center of seven concentric planetary spheres, one each for the sun,

---

[25]Around 360 B.C., the Greek philosopher, Plato, described the building of the universe by a god identified as the Creator. See *Timaeus* 8.36b and c by Plato.

moon, and five traditional planets (Mars, Mercury, Jupiter, Venus, and Saturn), a plan consistent with ideas proposed by Hipparchus. On the external globe of stars, three closely spaced parallel lines pass through Aries, the ram, representing the ecliptic and boundaries of the broad path traveled by the planets through zodiacal constellations. The line just above the ram's head represents the Tropic of Cancer. A line that passes through all four of the ram's legs represents the celestial equator, and, below it, a parallel line represents the Tropic of Capricorn. The sculptor also added a great circle passing through the poles and intersecting the celestial equator near the equinoxes on the celestial sphere.

Even though the model of Hipparchus was wrong in the light of modern knowledge, he compiled the world's first trigonometric tables and built improved astronomical instruments. With these tools, he laid the foundations of modern astronomy: improving technology for estimating the sizes and distances of the sun and the moon, making the first accurate predictions of solar eclipses, and publishing a famous star atlas that listed the positions and brightness estimates of approximately eight hundred stars.

PRECESSION OF THE EQUINOXES AND ITS IMPLICATIONS FOR THE CULT OF MITHRAS

Approximately two thousand years ago, the twelve zodiacal constellations bore a close relationship with the classical divisions of the zodiac in Figure 13-13. As represented in classical astrology, the noonday sun shone directly overhead on the Tropic of Capricorn when the sun moved from Sagittarius to Capricorn at the winter solstice. Similarly, the noonday sun shone directly overhead on the Tropic of Cancer when the sun moved from Gemini to Cancer at the summer solstice, which explains why mapmakers delimited the *tropics* (all parts of the Earth where the sun can appear directly overhead) with lines of latitude called the Tropic of Capricorn and Tropic of Cancer. The sun entered Capricorn at the beginning of Winter, Aries at the beginning of Spring, Cancer at the beginning of Summer, and Libra at the beginning of Fall. Similarly, a person born between May 22 and June 21 had his sun in Gemini, which meant that pointing at the sun between May

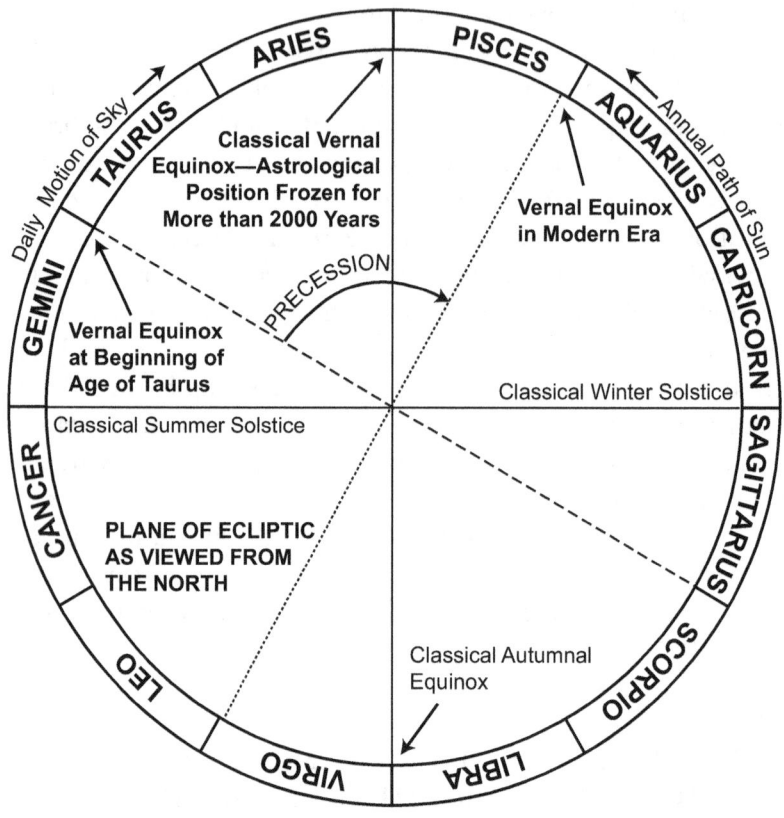

Figure 13-13. Directions of Daily, Annual, and Precessional Motions with Respect to Constellations of the Zodiac.

22 and June 21 also pointed directly toward stars in the zodiacal constellation, Gemini. That's no longer true, neither for Gemini nor for other astrological sun signs whose dates appear in horoscope listings.

Modern astrologers still use the classical zodiac, which associates twelve equally spaced divisions along the ecliptic with the twelve zodiacal constellations, but common practice ignores that the sky has shifted considerably in the past two thousand years. Today, we know that precession has shifted zodiacal constellations, but we don't know for sure how the original classical positions were established: We don't know when the original positions were mapped, nor do we know the boundaries of zodiacal constellations as Hellenistic astrologers mapped

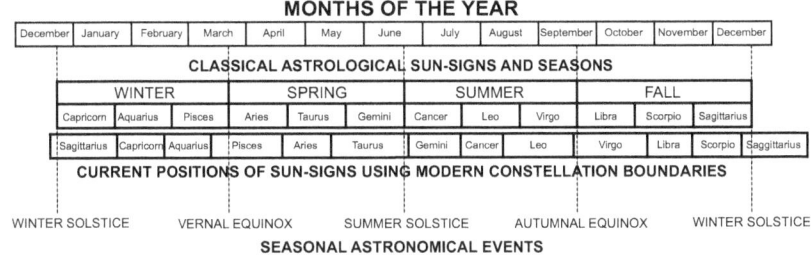

Figure 13-14. Modern Months, Seasons, and Classical Astrological Sun-Signs Compared with Positions of Modern Zodiacal Constellations.

them. One can illustrate both issues by comparing traditional astrological positions of the zodiacal constellations (unchanged for at least two thousand years) with current astronomical positions of the zodiacal constellations. For example, using the boundaries of constellations as we currently define them and adjusting their positions because of precession, Figure 13-14 reveals that the modern winter solstice happens shortly after the sun enters the constellation Sagittarius. The modern summer solstice happens while the sun occupies the last degrees of Taurus. Astronomically, we should rename the Tropic of Capricorn the Tropic of Sagittarius, and we should rename the Tropic of Cancer the Tropic of Taurus. The modern use of terms like Tropic of Cancer and Tropic of Capricorn refers to fossilized solar positions from ancient astronomy, positions that still exist in our speech and on our maps but not in our skies. Similarly, the traditional system of astrology still used in modern times employs fossilized positions of the constellations that haven't reflected reality since Hellenistic astrologers first mapped the sky over two thousand years ago.

Thus, the dates corresponding to sun-signs in modern horoscope listings do not reflect actual zodiacal positions of the sun. If the listings identify a reader's sun-sign as Aries, in all likelihood, the sun actually occupied Pisces on that reader's birthday. For a reader identified as a Gemini, the sun most likely occupied Taurus on that reader's birthday. By comparing modern positions of the constellations with the traditional system of astrology that Alexandrian scholars formalized in Ptolemaic Egypt, one can see that something has shifted the entire sky almost 30 degrees in two thousand years.

In 128 B.C., comparing astronomical data from the ancient East with the skies of his time, Hipparchus of Rhodes discovered that *precession of the equinoxes* had shifted the equinoxes slowly through the constellations of the zodiac: The vernal equinox had been moving through Aries for thousands of years and was slowly approaching the constellation, Pisces. One can see the effects of precession in the simplified Earth-centered model in Figure 13-13. As portrayed in classical astrology, the vernal equinox occurs when the sun enters Pisces and the autumnal equinox occurs when the sun enters Virgo, which determined the beginning of our current age, the *Age of Pisces*. In the next age, called the *Age of Aquarius*, the vernal equinox will be in Aquarius and the autumnal equinox will be in Leo. During an earlier age, the *Age of Aries*, the vernal equinox was in Aries and the autumnal equinox was in Libra. Before the Age of Aries, there was an *Age of Taurus*, an *Age of Gemini* before that, and so on.

With the advantage of Newtonian physics, we now understand that the rotating Earth behaves like a spinning top. The annual revolution of the Earth around the sun causes the tilted axis of the Earth to circle an axis perpendicular to the plane of the ecliptic. The axis of the Earth makes one full rotation around the perpendicular every 25,700 years, which causes both equinoxes to move 360 degrees through the zodiacal constellations. On average, the vernal equinox stays in each constellation approximately 2140 years before moving to the next one.

Stylistic elements reveal the Farnese Atlas to be a Roman copy (ca. 150 A.D.) of a Hellenistic original. One can determine the date that the original statue was designed by noting where the ecliptic and the celestial equator intersect. The detailed view of the statue in Figure 13-12 reveals that they intersect in a narrow cross toward the end of the constellation Aries, almost at the beginning of the constellation, Pisces. The position of the intersection establishes a design date around 128 B.C., which suggests that data from a lost star catalogue of Hipparchus helped artists create the original sculpture.

Although he detected the precession of the equinoxes, Hipparchus did not possess data as accurate as today's. His data suggested that a complete cycle of precession took somewhere between 30,000 and 40,000 years. At the beginning of the third century B.C., Berosus of

Babylon had written about the Chaldaean *Great Year*, which lasted 432,000 normal years. The Great Year began when all the planets gathered in Cancer and fire cleansed the Earth. Then, 216,000 years later, all the planets gathered in Capricorn and the Earth experienced a great flood. Because one twelfth of a Great Year (a *Great Month*) took 36,000 years, Hipparchus adopted 36,000 years as the length of his newly discovered cycle. To Hipparchus of Rhodes and his Stoic compatriots in Tarsos, it seemed that observation and measurement had confirmed the most profound cycle of the universe.

The Importance of the Age of Taurus to Hellenistic Scholars in Tarsos

Modern scholars have long known about the close association of the Hellenistic Cult of Mithras with the city of Tarsos and the Cilician school of Stoic philosophy. To Stoics, the discovery that something unseen had shifted the sun's path meant that something was influencing the astrological machinery of human fate by moving the whole universe. Through his discovery of precession of the Earth's equinoxes, Hipparchus gave Hellenistic philosophers the first concrete evidence that an unseen god controlled the universe on both human and cosmic scales. Dominating Hellenistic philosophy in the late second century B.C., the Stoics of Tarsos believed that Hipparchus' discovery confirmed the central importance of Earth and humanity. They saw the universe as an enormous living machine: The sun, moon, and planets moved in concentric heavenly spheres guiding human lives in an ongoing spiritual war between good and evil.

Hipparchus gave Hellenistic scholars tools like the Farnese Atlas to explore astrological implications of moving the vernal equinox from the beginning of the Age of Taurus to the end of the Age of Aries. Astronomical data revealed that the vernal equinox had moved from the tail to the forepart of Aries (the ram) over many centuries. To the rear of Aries in Figure 13-12, the forepart of Taurus (the bull) charges toward Atlas' right thumb. Above Aries and Taurus, half-naked Perseus (the ancestor of the Persian race) raises a sword above his head. As Hellenistic scholars contemplated the long-term movement of the equinoxes, they realized that the vernal equinox must have occupied Taurus before reaching Aries. They could estimate when the vernal equinox changed signs from Taurus to Aries and correlate the event with Greek mythology. Further, they could estimate the beginning of the Age of Taurus from the rate of movement of the vernal equinox through Aries.

Modern astronomers estimate that the Age of Taurus lasted from 4525 B.C. to 1875 B.C., and that the Age of Ares lasted from 1875 B.C. to 100 B.C. Hellenistic scholars would have estimated an earlier beginning for the Age of Taurus, which broadly matched the period that Greeks associated with the complete history of the universe.[26]

No Greek city was better prepared than Tarsos to project its symbolic history onto the Age of Taurus. Believing that Perseus, a savior associated with both Greeks and Persians, founded their city, Tarsians associated him with their most powerful deity, the sky god Baal of Tarsos. Confirming the importance of Perseus, northern constellations related to the myth of Perseus (Perseus, Cepheus, and Cassiopeia) circled Polaris (the Pole Star) and never set in the Greek sky.

After Hipparchus made it possible to think about skies during the Age of Taurus, philosophers discovered more connections between Tarsos and divinity. Tarsos had represented itself with the symbol of a lion attacking a bull since the city's earliest days. In the Age of Taurus, Leo and Taurus occupied the summer solstice and vernal equinox. Looking south at night during the winter solstice, the first Iron Age man in Tarsos would have seen Leo dominating the highest point of the zodiac and Taurus resting on the western horizon. Perseus and the Milky Way hung just above Taurus, and all constellations circled a dark region of sky just above the tail of the Great Bear.[27]

Speculation about souls coming from the Milky Way began to make sense: During the Age of Taurus, the Milky Way stretched directly from the vernal autumnal equinox through Perseus to Taurus and the vernal equinox. Souls began entering a gate in the vernal equinox to be born into the world. Then, after death, the souls returned to the celestial spheres through a gate in the autumnal equinox. Perseus, the divine

---

[26]See Chapter 8.
[27]The constellation of the Great Bear is often described in modern times as the Big Dipper. The tail of the Great Bear is the handle of the Big Dipper.

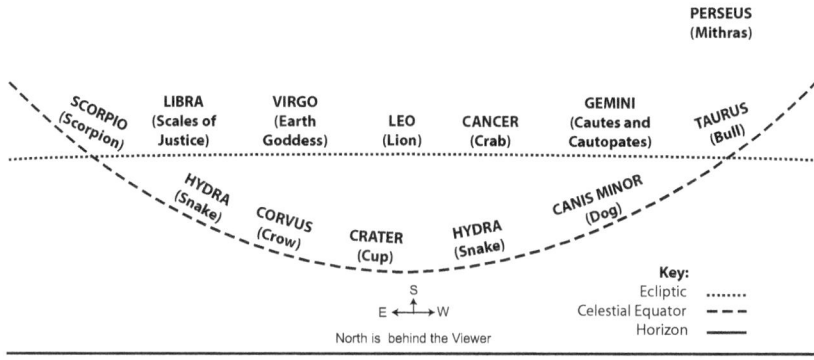

Figure 13-15. Constellations along the Zodiac and Ecliptic during a Winter Solstice Night at the Beginning of the Age of Taurus.

hero of Tarsos, must have had something to do with the processing of souls because the Milky Way passed through his constellation.

The Astrological Code of Mithraic Shrines

Many Western shrines of Mithras have been discovered, all of them incorporating similar iconography. Scholars estimate that the original model was carved by an artist from Pergamon during the second century B.C.[28] However, the astrological key to the Cult of Mithras and its relationship to the work of Hipparchus were discovered only recently.[29]

In every age, the celestial equator passes through different constellations. Figure 13-15 portrays a winter solstice view of the southern sky during the Age of Taurus. At night, the zodiac and the celestial equator formed two arcs in the southern sky. From right to left, animal constellations important in Mithraic iconography rest on the celestial equator: a bull (Taurus, the zodiacal constellation marking the vernal equinox), a dog (Canis Minor), a snake (Hydra, which extends from the left of Corvus to the right of Crater), a crow (Corvus), and

---

[28]For example, the head of Mithras found in a Mithraic shrine on the Capitoline Hill in Rome reflects artistic stylings of a "Dying Alexander" of a type known from a group of sculptures made in Pergamon during the second century B.C. See *The Mysteries of Mithra* p. 192 by Franz Valery Marie Cumont.
[29]See *The Origins of the Mithraic Mysteries* by David Ulansey.

a scorpion (Scorpio, the zodiacal constellation marking the autumnal equinox). On the ecliptic, Gemini refers to the twins Cautes and Cautopates in Mithraic shrines, Libra refers to the function of Mithras as a judge, and Virgo refers to the mother of Perseus (Mithras).[30] Even Cancer (the crab), Leo (the lion), and Crater (the cup) had Mithraic analogues: Philosophers thought that souls began their journey to Earth where Cancer touched the Milky Way, and a lion and cup existed as paired symbols in some Mithraea referring to the solstices in Leo and Aquarius (the water-bearer) during the Age of Taurus.[31] Representing Mithras, the constellation Perseus shone directly above Taurus, which lay just above the horizon. The Milky Way arched high across the sky from Taurus through Perseus, all the way to Scorpio. A slightly milky area (the Pleiades, an open star-cluster) sparkled on the bull's shoulder, symbolically marking the flow of blood from a wound.

Meeting in natural caves or cave-like structures, Hellenistic worshippers of Mithras congregated around a consistent and striking iconography. (See Figure 13-16.) Astronomical correspondences provide the key for understanding the Mithraic shrine as a representation of a night sky during the Age of Taurus. Symbolically related to the constellation, Gemini (the twins who stand next to Taurus in the zodiac), two torchbearers illuminate the sacrifice of the bull. The left torchbearer, Cautes, points his torch up, and the right torchbearer, Cautopates, points his torch down. Cautes represents the East where the sun rises, and Cautopates represents the West where the sun sets. Wearing a Persian cap and a cloak of stars, Mithras (the constellation, Perseus) thrusts a sword into the shoulder of Taurus, the bull, at a spot marked by the Pleiades. Above Mithras, the sun looks down from a station on the ecliptic that corresponds with the constellation, Virgo, the virgin. Below the bull, a dog, a snake, and a scorpion appear in the same order as their corresponding constellations (Canis Minor, Hydra, and

---

[30]One scholar suggests that the Mithraic importance of Virgo lies in the identification of its brightest star, Spica, as an ear of wheat, and that the importance of Libra lies in its placement as an equinox during the Age of Aries when Hipparchus discovered precession. See *The Origins of the Mithraic Mysteries* pp. 15 and 77, by David Ulansey.
[31]See *The Origins of the Mithraic Mysteries* pp. 53, 61, and 91, by David Ulansey. Conveniently, the lion and bull were important numismatic symbols on coins of Tarsos.

Figure 13-16. Mithraic Shrines. Third Century A.D., Museo Nazionale Archaeologico, Palermo, and Kunsthistorisches Museum, Vienna.

Scorpio) on the celestial equator. Mithras gazes over his shoulder in the direction of both Corvus (the crow) and the sun, the spiritual entities that forwarded the command from Jupiter to sacrifice the sacred bull. With few variations, the design of central shrines in Mithraea remained consistent across thousands of miles and hundreds of years.

With great art and subtlety, Tarsian Stoics had used elements from an Age of Taurus view of a winter solstice midnight sky to craft an astrological metaphor symbolizing the beginning of humanity, which included Perseus sacrificing Taurus the bull, releasing a flow of souls into the Milky Way, souls entering and exiting the world through gates in the vernal and autumnal equinoxes, and a scorpion, dog, snake, and crow from the celestial equator attending the scene.

Initiates in the Mysteries of Mithras learned to see spiritual processes in the natural cycles around them. Symbolically born again during initiations, worshippers emerged from Mithraea to see dark night as an extension of the cave of Mithras. The god's cape of stars billowed across the sky from his shoulders in the circumpolar constellation, Perseus. Next to the god, a ghostly stream of life emerged from the Pleiades, the faint glow that marked the wound in Taurus the bull's shoulder. Having shared bread and wine (the body and blood of the bull) they felt a connection between their lives and the soft glow of the Milky Way, the source and ultimate destination of all human souls.

Similarities between Christianity and the Hellenistic Cult of Mithras

The Hellenistic Cult of Mithras contained many features that ultimately attached to early Christian cults. Some features came to both cults separately. For example, both systems adopted beliefs previously held only by Zoroastrians: a heaven where good deeds are rewarded, a hell were evil deeds are punished, and a time when humanity will resurrect physically and experience a last judgment. Christianity adopted some Greek features whose inclusion in Mithraic mysteries is debated, for example, the virgin birth of Jesus. However, strong evidence suggests that some of the most cherished practices and beliefs in Christianity came directly from the Cult of Mithras.

Often called the Father of the Latin Church, Tertullian of Carthage wrote in the early third century A.D. that Mithraism parodied Christianity. Mithraism celebrated the birth of Mithras on December 25, the same date that Christians celebrate Christmas. Mithraism associated the sacrifice of the bull with the vernal equinox around the same time that Christians celebrate Easter. Mithraic priests wore robes and used incense during services in ways reminiscent of Orthodox Christian services. Worshippers of Mithras underwent baptism, and they even performed a ceremony that closely resembled the Christian ceremony of the Eucharist. The Mithraic ritual even used wording similar to that in Christian gospel:[32] Blood transformed to wine, and body transformed to wheat. Tertullian complained that the Devil inspired Mithraism to mimic the Christian ceremony[33] even though Mithraism existed long before Christianity. That the Devil could see the future and craft such a pernicious mockery before Christianity existed merely underscored the depth of his evil designs.

---

[32]In *First Apology* lxvi, Justin Martyr said that the Mithraic Eucharist ceremony used the same words that Jesus used in Luke 22:19–20.
[33]Indeed, the *Didache*, an early second century Christian manual (the earliest known), prescribes wording for the Eucharist ceremony that blesses wine and bread without mentioning the consumption of Jesus' blood and body. Professor James Tabor of the University of North Carolina at Chapel Hill has pointed out that it is unlikely that Jesus would have violated strong Jewish feelings against even symbolic cannibalism by creating the ceremony of the Eucharist as currently practiced. For the complaint, see *The Prescription Against Heretics* Chapter 40 by Tertullian.

Christians and worshippers of Mithras possessed equivalent understandings of the nature of the universe. Saturn gave the keys of heaven and hell to Jupiter, just as Jesus gave equivalent keys to Saint Peter.[34] Instead of holding the seventh day[35] sacred as prescribed by Jewish law, Christians honor Jesus on Sunday, the same day that Hellenistic worshippers honored Mithras. Christians even emphasized Semitic iconography that was similar to Mithraic iconography. For example, Christians developed iconography about the striking of a rock by Moses[36] to produce water because of its similarity to Mithraic iconography about shooting arrows at rocks to save humanity from dying of thirst.

The most intimate expression of the relationship between Christianity and the Hellenistic Cult of Mithras lies in the location of the Holy See,[37] the seat of the Pope and the center of the Catholic Church. A person who achieved the highest level of initiation in the Cult of Mithras was called Pater (Father). The supreme father was called the Pater Patrum. In the Roman Empire during the third and fourth centuries, the house of the Pater Patrum was located somewhere on Vatican grounds. One scholar has suggested that the Sistine Chapel occupies the location of the house of the Pater Patrum (abbreviated as Pa-Pa, the Latin word for pope) and, further, that the chair honored as the seat of Saint Peter, the Cathedra Petri, originally served as the chair of the Pater Patrum[38] of the Cult of Mithras. Bearing sixteen ivories with astrological signs, images of the labors of Herakles, and other symbols associated more with the Cult of Mithras than with Christianity, the chair appears more Mithraic than Christian.

However, as a mystery cult, the Hellenistic Cult of Mithras never could have become the only authorized religion in the West. In general, Greek mystery cults did not serve everybody: The Cult of Mithras

---

[34]A Mithraic statue of Saturn holding two keys stands at the north end of the Galleria della Biblioteca in the Vatican.
[35]The seventh day, or *Sabbath*, is equivalent to Saturday in Semitic law and tradition.
[36]See *Numbers* 20:7–11. Also, see Figure 25-5 for an example of a Christian image of Moses striking a rock.
[37]The term *Holy See* generally refers to the Vatican. The term derives from Sancta Sedes (holy chair).
[38]See "Cults, Christianity, and the Vatican: New Thoughts on Old Mysteries" by Nigel McGilchrist in *Current World Archaeology Magazine*, Issue 49, pp. 58–62.

explicitly served only men, usually only those who served in the army. Also, although Mithraic rituals included many practices similar to those in Christianity, the cult tolerated neither public observation nor the presence of women.

A HELLENISTIC CULT DESIGNED FOR WARRIORS

Mixing Zoroastrian beliefs, Greek mythology, Hellenistic philosophy, exotic iconography, and Eastern practices like baptism, the Hellenistic Cult of Mithras emerged as a masterful combination of old and new, East and West, and religious and scientific. The cult affirmed an Earth-centered model of the universe over a sun-centered model: Belief that the Earth occupied the center of a tiny spherical universe imbued elements of the sky (for example, the zodiac, equinoxes, and solstices) with divine meaning. In the first century A.D., Pliny the Elder[39] said that no man did more than Hipparchus to prove that man is related to the stars and that the human soul comes from heaven.

Certainly, no philosophers did more to encode the discoveries of Hipparchus in myth and ritual than the Stoics of Tarsos. From their school, a Hellenized Cult of Mithras blended astrological fatalism and Zoroastrian duty into salvation-oriented mysteries for Anatolian warriors. If worshippers of the Hellenistic Cult of Mithras came to Rome in the second century B.C., they were not noticed. However, for most Romans, Mithraists would have been indistinguishable from worshippers of the outlawed cult of Sabazius.

After Rome encountered the worshippers of Mithras among Cilician pirates in the first century B.C., the cult began attracting Roman interest. Former Cilician pirates kept their faith even while serving as Roman slaves, and some Roman soldiers who spent years in Anatolia became early Roman converts. Hidden from history, the cult traveled throughout the Mediterranean region among Rome's legions until, eventually, it suddenly seemed to blossom everywhere in the first few

---

[39]Pliny the Elder was a famous Roman general and naturalist in the first century A.D. He died, overcome by poisonous gases, while trying to save people during the eruption of Mount Vesuvius in 79 A.D.

centuries A.D. When the first Christian cults developed, they competed directly with the Cult of Mithras in the early Roman Empire. By comparing the features of modern Christianity with ancient Mithraism, one can see that Christianity gained ascendency only after adopting important beliefs and practices from the Hellenistic Cult of Mithras.

Hellenistic philosophy encoded in the Cult of Mithras helped shape the West's dominant understanding of the universe for more than 1500 years. After abandoning the sun-centered model in the second century B.C., the West would not see it again until Copernicus[40] developed his theory of a sun-centered universe in 1514. However, by the sixteenth century A.D., the Earth-centered model was considered Christian dogma. Copernicus did not dare publish his theory until 1541, just before he died.

By the end of the second century B.C., the traditional Roman practices that had fueled a century of rapid expansion had reached their effective limit. The next stage toward the development of the Roman Empire required big changes in Roman government, politics, defense, and culture. As always, Rome changed only in the face of existential challenges, which obligingly emerged.

---

[40]Nicolaus Copernicus was a Polish scholar, physician, astronomer, and Catholic Cleric who proposed a heliocentric model of the universe during the Renaissance.

CHAPTER
14

THE LIFE AND TIMES OF GAIUS MARIUS

RETOOLING THE ROMAN WAR MACHINE AND SHARPENING THE GAME OF POLITICS

Gaius Marius protected Rome, raised the wealth and status of its common man, and helped direct Roman attention toward Hellenistic kingdoms in the East.

One of Rome's greatest generals, Gaius Marius defended the Roman Republic during times of great danger. He changed Rome's army from an aristocrats-only rainy-day militia to a disciplined standing army open to lower-class Romans. Without the leadership of Gaius Marius, Rome may not have survived long into the first century B.C., but his changes ultimately doomed the Roman Republic: Men with military experience strengthened Rome's lower classes and merged Rome's external struggle against Hellenism with an internal struggle between wealthy conservatives and innovative poor.

Toward the end of the second century B.C., a series of catastrophes confronted Rome. Rebels murdered Romans in foreign lands and barbarians from Western Europe destroyed whole armies of noble Roman youth, which forced the constitution of Rome's legions to change from landed gentry to lower-class Romans and Italians. Slowly, the influence of Hellenistic cults began to increase as men relatively open to Eastern ideas built military careers that included long campaigns in foreign lands. Changes in military recruitment and support brought training, money, and greater familiarity with Hellenistic cults to common Romans, which ensured that the first century B.C. would be the most tumultuous and influential century of Roman history.

A hundred years before the birth of Jesus, Rome's circumstances during the life of Gaius Marius provide contrast, showing how much the world had yet to change to prepare the West for Christianity. For example, Rome needed to become a much bigger empire. With a population of approximately 150,000 people, Rome retained the character of a relatively small provincial city. Without a standing army, it had extended its authority to approximately half of all Mediterranean shores, but not far inland from most of them. However, a century after the death of Gaius Marius, Rome governed every shore and had become a sophisticated world capital; the city had a population of more than a million people representing every known culture and ethnicity.

Before it could adequately nurture early Christianity, Rome needed to develop a richer mix of religious beliefs. During the time of Gaius Marius, the ruling class that dominated Rome remained highly suspicious of foreign cults. Traditional Roman religious beliefs retained a distinctly conservative character despite the naturalization of the Cult of Cybele and the presence of worshippers of Hellenistic cults, mostly among Rome's slaves and visiting foreigners. In other parts of the Mediterranean region, non-Romans commonly believed in cults that offered spiritual salvation, but few people in Rome believed that a pleasant life after death lay within the reach of any ordinary person.

Regarding Jewish beliefs, Jews and Romans were just getting to know each other. A few Jews lived in Rome and a few adventurous Romans had traveled to Judea. However, like Romans, not all Jews believed in life after death toward the end of the second century B.C.

While Gaius Marius enacted military reforms to defend Rome, Jews were writing the last canonical books associated with the *Old Testament*.[1] Further, Jewish monastic movements like the Essenes[2] of Judea and the Therapeutae[3] of Egypt began evolving into movements that gave rise to teachers like John the Baptist and Jesus. Sharing a religious perspective that separated them from Hellenistic peoples in the East, neither Jews nor Romans believed that a man could become a god.

Rome transformed into a world empire mostly because of the efforts of a few great republican generals, beginning with Gaius Marius. However, change never came easily to Rome. Its political system already reflected centuries of warfare between "haves" and "have-nots." As responses to existential dangers that appeared far too often and unexpectedly, militaristic Roman traditions fostered rapid growth while simultaneously treating new beliefs and ideas with suspicion. During the life of Gaius Marius, however, existential threats weakened Rome's attachment to its traditions: Roman politics acquired new flexibility, and Hellenistic cults strengthened their hold on the city, particularly in the lives of common Romans of the lower classes.

AN INTRODUCTION TO ROMAN POLITICS

Throughout its history, the Roman Republic struggled to balance power between its privileged nobles, called *patricians*, and its less privileged majority, called *plebians*. The Roman Republic began in 509 B.C. with a government completely controlled by the patricians. However, by 133 B.C., plebians had established a parallel system of government capable of checking patrician control.

Political struggle between patricians and plebians often expressed itself in conflicts between Rome's two main political parties, *Optimates* and *Populares*. Optimates generally favored policies designed to preserve or increase the power, wealth, and privileges of patricians;

---
[1] The texts known as *1 Maccabees* and *2 Maccabees*, canonical for the Eastern Orthodox church, were written approximately a century before the life of Jesus.
[2] See *The Jewish War* 2.119 by Josephus.
[3] See *The Contemplative Life* 1.2 by Philo.

and Populares generally favored policies advantageous to lower-class Romans. However, not all patricians were Optimates, and not all plebians were Populares.

Optimates favored traditional Roman beliefs and practices and respected old forms of Roman worship, which included the carefully restricted Cult of Cybele from Asia Minor. At their best, Optimates pushed for a strong, moral, and safe republic. At their worst, they facilitated the plunder of the lower classes by the wealthy.

Less attached to Roman traditions, Populares sought to change Rome in ways that improved life for common people. The party drew support from a wide range of Romans, from progressive patricians to the newest citizens of Rome—including Italians, Greeks, and barbarians who originally came to Rome as slaves. At their best, Populares represented a wide variety of religious beliefs, occupations, customs, and sensitivities, helping Rome meet new challenges effectively as it grew. At worst, however, Populares allied themselves with gangs and criminal interests making life in Rome less secure.

Elections and Offices

In 133 B.C., Rome divided itself in two different ways, by wealth and by "tribe," to vote for two different types of magisterial offices, those traditionally open only to patricians and those explicitly open only to plebians. The winners of elections to magisterial offices automatically acquired lifelong membership in the Senate (subject to restrictions). Otherwise, terms of office generally lasted a year.

Divided into 183 "centuries" based on wealth, citizens voted once a year to fill important offices: two consuls, six praetors, two curule aediles, and two censors. During normal circumstances, the two consuls shared executive responsibility for the Roman Republic, each consul assuming primary responsibility every other month. Consuls served as commanders-in-chief of the army and executive heads of the main legislative, electoral, and military assembly called the *Comitia Centuriata*. Praetors[4] served as legal officers and lesser generals. Curule aediles

---

[4]After completing their terms in Rome, former consuls and praetors served as "proconsuls" (governors of important provinces) and "propraetors" (governors of less important provinces).

served as city managers of Rome. Censors controlled issues related to the census, divided Romans into centuries and tribes, selected replacements for vacant seats in the Senate—there were approximately 300 sitting senators at a time—and supervised public morality. The Senate and Comitia Centuriata best served the interests of Optimates, generally the wealthiest of Romans. Patricians competed with each other to pass through a traditional sequence of public offices: quaestor, curule aedile, praetor, and consul.

Divided into 35 tribes (a division based on citizenship and membership in hereditary voting districts), citizens elected members of the *Comitia Tributa* or popular assembly of ten tribunes of the plebs, two plebian aediles, and twenty quaestors. Tribunes of the plebs made laws, vetoed laws and actions of the Senate and Comitia Centuriata, and exercised powers of protection and punishment in the best interests of the people of Rome. Plebian aediles controlled matters related to record keeping, operation of temples, disbursement of grain (food supply), running the plebian games, and so forth. Quaestors served as financial officers in charge of mints, disbursement of funds, and similar functions. The Tribunate of the Plebs and public assemblies provided the only official avenues for balancing the interests of common people against those of Roman aristocrats.

The right to vote extended only to Roman citizens as identified in an official census taken every five years. Voting scenes sometimes appeared on coins. The obverse of the coin in Figure 14-1 displays Roma, a personification of Rome, along with astronomical symbols representing the watchful guidance of the goddess Venus. On the reverse, one Roman citizen receives a ballot from an election official and another citizen deposits his ballot into a ballot box.

Political Currents Late in the Second Century B.C.

Two brothers, Gaius and Tiberius Gracchus, played an important role in defining the issues between Optimates and Populares during the last century of the Roman Republic. In 133 B.C., they noticed that Rome was changing from an insular, small-time capital controlled by a few aristocrats into a cosmopolitan city characterized by ever-increasing numbers of foreign slaves, urban poor, and members of an emerging

Figure 14-1. Personification of Rome with Crescent Moon and Star, and Voting Scene. AR Denarius, P. Nerva. 113–112 B.C.

working class. Powerful advocates for the Populares, the brothers tried to implement progressive social reforms that would best serve Rome as it expanded in size and complexity.

Gaius Gracchus introduced tax farming as an efficient method of collecting taxes without burdening the Roman Republic with an ever-expanding army of petty bureaucrats. Instead of funding tax collectors, the Senate entertained bids by wealthy Romans to pay the taxes for a region. By paying the tax, the highest bidder (called a *publican*) obtained the right to administer a region and extract as much wealth as he could for a specific term of office. While this method of collecting taxes worked reasonably well close to Rome, avaricious publicani easily abused the system in foreign provinces.

The brothers also pushed populist issues like extending Roman citizenship to Italians, ensuring distributions of subsidized grain to the poor, and confiscating land from wealthy nobles and redistributing it to peasants. However, before the Gracchi succeeded in implementing these reforms, conservative Romans assassinated both brothers.

The Political Path to Extreme Wealth

Common Romans sometimes achieved wealth without help from family privilege and nobility, and privileged Roman families sometimes lost their wealth. However, Rome pioneered the harnessing of republican politics for greatly increasing personal wealth. Successful politicians allocated large, profitable state contracts among themselves and found ways to add public lands to their private agricultural holdings. After the innovation of tax farming, wealthy nobles also began systematically extracting wealth from foreign provinces. Without representation in the Senate, foreign populations could do little to protect themselves from the most rapacious practices of Roman publicani.

In particular, Rome's expansion into Asia helped some Romans amass stupendous personal fortunes. During the second century B.C., Rome's relationship with the Pergamene Kingdom, the original land of Cybele, grew increasingly close. Without an heir, King Attalus III of Pergamon foresaw that, after his death, ambitious men in his kingdom would assert connections with the royal family and attempt to seize the throne. Attempting to forestall the possibility of civil war,[5] King Attalus willed his kingdom to Rome. However, he never foresaw the devastating effects of ruthless Roman tax farming. From his bequest, the Roman Senate created Asia Province in 129 B.C. The Anatolian land that had prospered so much from its alliance with Rome then suffered greatly from the plundering of robber-publicani.

For example, Manius Aquillius (the elder), the first Proconsul of Asia Province, acquired immense personal wealth by selling the Roman territory of Phrygia, formerly part of the Pergamene Kingdom, to Mithradates V of Pontus. Accused of maladministration of Asia Province when he returned to Rome, Manius Aquillius easily escaped conviction by bribing Roman judges. The Senate even granted him a triumph for winning battles in Asia that he never fought. Family wealth and influence then helped the son of Manius Aquillius (possessing the same name as his father) to progress easily through the cursus honorum. The younger Manius Aquillius became a loyal friend of Gaius Marius, achieved a consulship of Rome, and then attempted to follow his father's example, eventually becoming a consular legate of Asia Province. Like his father, the younger Manius Aquillius acquired a reputation for greed in Asia.

---

[5]Despite the precautions of King Attalus III, a man named Aristonicus claimed to be the king's brother, fomented rebellion, and successfully seized the throne. It wasn't until 129 B.C., four years after King Atallus' death, that a Roman army defeated Aristonicus and asserted control over the Pergamene Kingdom.

A Convenient Alliance between Rome and Judea

The period just before the acquisition of Asia Province by Rome coincided with establishment of the first diplomatic relations between Rome and Judea. As described in the biblical text, *1 Maccabees*, the Hasmonean (Maccabean) King Hyrcanus I ruled Judea as a semi-independent vassal of the Seleukids. Taking advantage of a period of Seleukid weakness, Hyrcanus I took strong steps to strengthen the kingdom of Judea: He forcibly converted Idumeans (ancestors of Herod the Great) to the Jerusalem Temple Cult, he conquered the Samaritans of Shechem and destroyed their temple (a competing temple cult) on Mount Gerizim, and he sent a gold shield to Rome offering an alliance.

More valuable than a gold shield, an alliance with Jews promised ongoing opportunities for Rome to continue expanding east by involving itself militarily anywhere that Jews lived in conflict with non-Jewish neighbors. In 136 B.C., only three years after expelling many of its own Jews, Rome announced its alliance with Judean Jews to numerous rulers of territories with large Jewish communities, including Egypt, Cyrenaica, Seleukia, Cappadocia, Parthia, Mysia, Sparta, Delos, Sicyon, Caria, Samos, Pamphylia, Lycia, Rhodes, Cos, Phoenicia, Crete, and Cyprus. Giving notice to the Mediterranean world, Rome expressed a willingness to involve itself militarily if territories persecuted Jewish inhabitants, made war against Judea, allied with countries making war against Judea, or harbored criminals as defined by the Judean government.[6] Of particular note, Egypt harbored a large Jewish community at Leontopolis (modern Tell-el-Yahudya) on the Nile Delta whose inhabitants built a temple because they could not accept a Jerusalem Temple Cult dominated by Hasmoneans.[7]

Accepted as canonical by some modern Christians, the *1 Maccabees* and *2 Maccabees* express differing points of view and show that a variety of antagonistic Jewish cults existed by the beginning of the first century B.C. Written in Hebrew by a Judean, *1 Maccabees* portrays the Hasmoneans as legitimate inheritors of the kingdom of King David and mentions that many "lawless" Jews welcomed Hellenistic culture

---

[6]See *1 Maccabees* 15:16–24.
[7]See *Antiquities of the Jews* 13.1–3) and *The Jewish War* 7.2–4 by Josephus.

and beliefs.[8] The book affirms traditional Jewish beliefs and practices without promising resurrection or survival after death. However, written in Greek by a North African Jew familiar with Hellenistic culture, *2 Maccabees* affirms Pharisaic teachings[9] that later were adopted by the Catholic Church, for example, physical resurrection, prayer as a means of freeing the dead from sin, and the intercession of saints (martyrs). Representing a type of Judaism different from that espoused by Hasmonean priests of the Jerusalem Temple Cult, *2 Maccabees* expresses great disapproval for a common practice of yet another cult of Jews: carrying amulets of "Idols of Jamnia."[10]

Surviving examples of the amulets show that they were connected to a Gnostic[11] variety of Judaism, possibly associated with spiritual healing.[12] Iconography on the amulets related to Egyptian gods worshipped along with Yahweh in the Jewish community on Elephantine Island[13] near modern Aswan. For example, the top left amulet in Figure 14-2 portrays a lion-headed serpent labeled CNOUMIS in Greek on the obverse and a three-part Egyptian symbol of the god Khnum on the reverse. The lion-headed god with solar rays recalls Jewish traditions about the Saraph, or fiery bronze serpent, that Moses used to cure Israelites of snakebite.[14] The amulet on the top right portrays an anguipedal (snake-footed) deity associated with Yahweh by Jews,[15]

---

[8] See *1 Maccabees* 1:11–15.
[9] Commonly represented as antagonists of Jesus in the gospels of the New Testament, Pharisees affirmed a popular, legalistic Jewish cult in Judea that had no control of the Jerusalem Temple Cult. Sadducees, Jews who didn't believe in an afterlife, controlled the Jerusalem Temple Cult. See Chapter 25.
[10] For Pharasaic teachings, see *2 Maccabees* 12:42–45 and 15:11–17. For Idols of Jamnia, see *2 Maccabees* 12:39–42.
[11] Not directly connected with any specific Jewish cult, Gnostic Jews relied on oral transmission of religious teachings—generally characterized as philosophical, mystical, and ascetic—from master to student.
[12] For images and discussion of more of these amulets, see *The Masks of God: Occidental Mythology* pp. 274–275 by Joseph Campbell.
[13] Jews on Elephantine Island worshipped Yahweh along with other deities. See "What Happened to the Cult Figurines? Israelite Religion Purified After the Exile" by Ephraim Stern. *Biblical Archaeology Review*, July/Aug 1989, pp. 22–29, 53–54. Egyptians considered the island sacred to Khnum, Satis, and Anukis.
[14] See *Numbers* 21:4–9.
[15] Commonly labeled as Yahweh on gems and amulets, the anguipedal deity recalls Greek stories about Typhon in Egypt and Roman stories about Yahweh being a multifaced, anguipedal relative of Typhon.

Figure 14-2. Gnostic Gems of a Type Associated with "Idols of Jamnia" Referenced in *2 Maccabees*.

with various gods (for example, Set and Cnoubis/Khnum[16]) by Egyptians, and eventually with a solar deity called Abrasax by Christians. The lower amulet portrays the three Nile River gods associated with Elephantine Island as a crocodile, an ithyphallic baboon, and a young child. After the emergence of Christianity, Gnostic Jewish symbols continued to be used by Gnostic Christians.[17]

During the centuries immediately preceding the birth of Jesus, Jewish communities were dispersed throughout the Mediterranean world, and many adjusted Jewish literature and teachings to fit Hellenistic society. Most Hellenistic variants of scripture have been lost, but analysis of documents found at Qumran proves that different Jewish literary

---

[16] For an examination of the relationship between Jewish and Egyptian iconography, see *From Jewish Magic to Gnosticism* pp. 61–78 by Attilio Mastrocinque.
[17] For an example of a Gnostic Christian amulet, see the Figure 25-6.

centers had different approaches to canonization of Jewish scripture.[18] No single authority determined acceptable Jewish practices, beliefs, and literature for all Jews, but Hasmoneans expressed a rabid intolerance of Jewish beliefs different from their own and could be counted on to identify Hellenistic Jews as sacrilegious criminals. An alliance with Hasmonean Jews promised to facilitate Roman expansion into Hellenistic lands, but Rome didn't recognize that its long period of successful expansion was about to be tested.

The Increasing Importance of Isis in Roman Politics

Many of the gangs in Rome had specific cultic orientations because gangs often formed to protect worshippers and shrines of specific foreign cults in the Urbs (a working-class neighborhood of Rome). During the second and first centuries B.C., increasing Roman involvement in Africa had resulted in increasing numbers of worshippers of Isis in Sicily, Italy, and Rome. Many gangs in Rome cooperated to protect sanctuaries of Isis because priests of Isis generally supported the worship of all goddesses, domestic and foreign.

As a consequence of Gaius Marius' military and political successes, previously unimportant worshippers of Isis acquired military training, entered gangs, and began to influence politics. Anyone with sufficient money could purchase the services of gangs. Politicians found it increasingly effective to assert power through gangs.

Provincial coins often honored Isis, and her symbols started appearing on coins minted in Rome around 90 B.C. However, nobody knows whether Rome's moneyers intentionally used Isis symbols in their designs or if slaves and workers at the mints added the symbols as personal expressions of devotion. From Roman Katane on the island of Sicily, early in the first century B.C., the coin in Figure 14-3 displays symbols related to the Cult of Isis. On the obverse, rays of light emanate from the head of Serapis. On the reverse, Harpokrates stands next to his mother, Isis. A crown of Isis and a sistrum (a metal rattle used in Isis worship) help identify the goddess.

---

[18]See "Tracing the Evolution of the *Hebrew Bible*" by Adam S. der Woude, *Bible Review*, Feb 1995, pp. 42–45.

Figure 14-3. Radiate Bust of Serapis, and Harpokrates and Isis with Sistrum. Sicily, Katane, AE 25, first century B.C.

EMERGING THREATS TO ROME

Toward the end of the second century B.C., Rome came into increasing contact with powerful cultures that had little respect for Roman civilization or military capabilities. Having successfully expanded Roman control for decades, a largely seasonal Roman military composed of landed aristocrats soon found itself unable to defend Roman interests. Not recognizing that its institutions were no longer adequate to their burden, Rome entered a period of great danger. A series of threats emerged from Africa, Western Europe, Sicily, Italy, and Asia Minor:

- The destruction of Carthage in 146 B.C. gave Rome free use of its new Africa Province to build wealth. Africa provided an abundance of slaves, food, and exotic products. After a quarter century, however, threats from the neighbors of Africa Province placed Roman interests in jeopardy.
- From Europe, the Italian peninsula always had suffered periodic invasions of barbarian tribes of Gauls and Germans. Though no invasion had come for more than a lifetime, fear of the next invasion lurked in the background of everyday life in Rome and Italy.
- Reliance on slave-operated farms on Sicily for grain production placed a significant portion of Rome's food supply at risk to

problems on the island. With courage and faith in Atargatis, Syrian slaves started a second great slave rebellion against Rome.
- Suffering sometimes from barbarians and always from Roman policies, Italians increasingly resented Rome. Their resentment slowly evolved into a war waiting to happen.
- Somewhat naive about political relationships in Asia Minor, Rome slowly created new ways to siphon the wealth from Asia Province while ignoring the long-term need to protect the Romans who lived there. As in Africa, threats to Eastern Roman interests emerged from the actions of neighboring kingdoms.

The first hint of the emerging challenges came from Africa. In Numidia, a client-kingdom adjoining Rome's Africa Province, a brilliant rogue named Jugurtha overthrew a government run by his cousins in 118 B.C. A surviving cousin ran to Rome for help, but Roman military leaders were more interested in gaining wealth for themselves than in fighting one barbarian for the benefit of another. Jugurtha bribed the Romans to support a quick settlement that divided Numidia into two parts: a western kingdom controlled by Jugurtha and an eastern kingdom controlled by Jugurtha's cousin. Afterward, Africa remained quiet for a few years.

A Devastating Invasion of Germans in the North

During the lifetime of Gaius Marius, barbarous warlike tribes controlled the Western European lands of Gaul and Germany. Ever since 387 B.C., when Gauls sacked Rome and then plundered its territory for seven months, Romans feared that the barbarians would return. Even though Rome had soundly repelled invasions early in the second century B.C., the ever-present possibility of invasion by European tribes remained one of Rome's worst nightmares.

From Rome's point of view, little distinguished Gauls from Germans: The barbarians spoke different languages and came from different parts of Europe, but they looked equally threatening when they invaded Roman territory. On the battlefield, tall, blond Gauls and Germans often wore nothing but gold ornaments and spiked hairstyles. Carrying small shields and large swords, they all fought like madmen.

In 113 B.C., two Germanic tribes, the Cimbri[19] and the Teutones, invaded the new Roman province of Transalpine Gaul. The patrician consul, Gnaeus Papirius Carbo, speedily organized an army to fight them. According to custom, Carbo enrolled only landowners wealthy enough to bring their own armor and supplies into the army. Inadequately trained and overly impressed with their own nobility, 180,000 of the best men of Rome marched north with Carbo to Noreia. Only 20,000 men returned. The Germans might well have killed more, but a violent storm prevented them from catching everybody. For a long time afterward, all Rome lived in fear that the Germans would march south. However, inexplicably, the barbarians turned away from Italy.

Intolerable Murders of Romans in the South

Roman businessmen in North Africa had obtained escalating profits from an increasing flow of products and slaves into Rome. However, local politics in the African kingdom of Numidia quickly affected Roman interests when Jugurtha started a new war against his cousin. Rome sent an army to confront the Numidian king, but Jugurtha merely bribed the Roman commander to sign a peace treaty and go away. Jugurtha easily captured his cousin's kingdom and then executed the cousin and his allies—including Roman and Italian businessmen.

Rome declared war on Numidia in 111 B.C. Contemptuous of Roman morals and incompetence, King Jugurtha either bribed or defeated the armies that Rome sent against him. Influenced greatly by Roman corruption, the first years of the Jugurthine War caused little damage to Numidia.

Another Northern Disaster

In April of 109 B.C., word reached Rome that Germans (Cimbri) again had invaded Transalpine Gaul. Rome's senior consul (Marcus Junius Silanus) quickly organized an army of 50,000 soldiers, which left Rome around the end of May. On their way north during mid-June, Silanus and his soldiers observed the new moon glide past four planets

---
[19]Some scholars classify the Cimbri as Gauls.

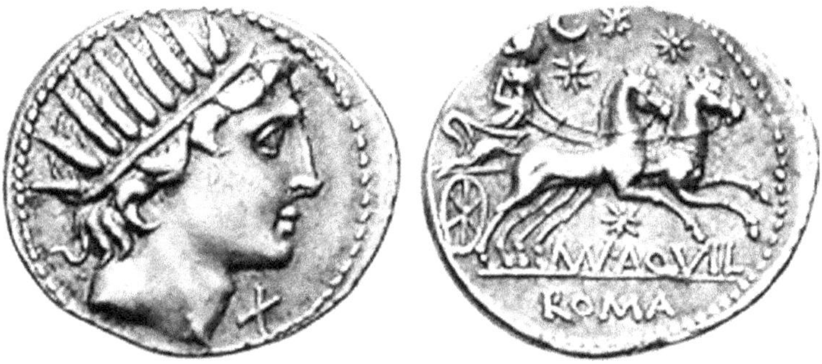

COIN IMAGES COURTESY OF THE CLASSICAL NUMISMATIC GROUP, INC.

Figure 14-4. Radiate Bust of Sol, and Luna Riding through Conjunction of Many Planets. Rome, Manius Aquillius, AR Denarius, mid-June 109 B.C.

grouped in the evening sky: Jupiter, Mars, Venus, and Saturn. The soldiers probably interpreted the configuration of moon and planets as an omen of good fortune and glory to come.

The massing of so many planets attracted the attention of common people, augurs, prophets, and astrologers. Speeding along the path of the cursus honorum, the younger Manius Aquillius minted the coin in Figure 14-4 in the Summer of 109 B.C. to affirm the common belief that the gathering of the moon and planets promised victory against the Germans. The coin's obverse portrays Sol (the sun) wearing his radiate crown. The reverse represents Luna (the moon) as a woman riding in her chariot among star-like planets.

When confronted, the Germans asked Silanus for permission to settle in Transalpine Gaul and even offered to fight for Rome, but Silanus haughtily refused them. Insulted, the Germans attacked, killing more than 30,000 Roman soldiers. The surviving Romans scattered, and the Germans traveled elsewhere. Weeks later, Rome heard that Germans again had destroyed a noble Roman army.

THE FIRST CAREER OF GAIUS MARIUS

Born in Latium south of Rome in 157 B.C., scarcely thirty years after citizens in the region acquired voting rights, Gaius Marius began pursuing political office in his early twenties. From a well-to-do family but without patrician ancestry, he built a career on devotion to Rome and to the well-being of its citizenry. Outstanding military talent brought victory in his first election as a special military tribune. Afterward, he successively won elections for quaestor and plebian tribune, acquiring a reputation as a strong supporter of the Populares. He lost an election for the office of aedile because his causes alienated important patricians in Rome, but he successfully won a close election for praetor. Opponents in his strongly polarized constituency soon charged him with corruption, so he accomplished little more than defending himself during his term as praetor. He then obtained a governorship of the province of Further Spain. There, at the age of 44, he achieved military and financial success, but his lack of noble ancestry gave him little chance of ever capping his career with a consulship of Rome.

In 110 B.C., Gaius Marius rejuvenated his political viability by marrying Julia,[20] a daughter of the Julian family (the family that gave rise to Julius Caesar). One of the most ancient and noble families in Rome, the Julians had declined in wealth and influence, becoming too poor to participate successfully in the cursus honorum. Through this marriage, Gaius Marius acquired a trace of nobility. In return, the Julian family acquired funding to support their own reentry into Roman politics.

The Julians claimed direct descent from Aeneas, the son of Anchises and the Trojan goddess that Roman mythology equated with Venus. A practical and straightforward military man, Gaius Marius worshipped the goddess of Rome in all her aspects: Venus Victrix, the protector of Rome; Cybele, the Great Mother of Pessinus (near Troy) who had granted victory to Rome in the war against Hannibal; Aphrodite Erice, the goddess who guarded the grave of Anchises; and Atargatis, the Syrian Aphrodite. By marrying Julia, Gaius Marius married into a noble family that descended directly from Venus.

A marital connection with the Julian family gave Gaius Marius enough nobility to gain access to Rome's highest political office. Over time, he won more consulships than any other Roman, a total of seven: 107 B.C., 104–100 B.C., and 86 B.C. Around 103 B.C., a member of the Julian family minted the coin in Figure 14-5 to celebrate the family's connection with Gaius Marius, popularly recognized as one of

---

[20]In 110 B.C., Gaius Marius was 47 years old and Julia was 20 years old.

Figure 14-5. Bust of Mars, and Two Cupids Pulling Venus in a Chariot, Symbols Associating Military Successes of Marius with the Julian Family. Rome, L. Julius Caesar, AR Denarius, 103 B.C.

Rome's greatest leaders. Referring to Marius' military achievements, the obverse of the coin displays a bust of Mars, the Roman God of War. The reverse refers to the divine origins of the Julian family: Venus rides a chariot pulled by two eroti (cupids), and a lyre refers to music played during the worship of Venus.

The First Consulship of Gaius Marius

Responsible for prosecuting the North African war against Jugurtha in 109 B.C., a patrician consul of Rome asked Gaius Marius to join the campaign as a senior military advisor. However, under the consul's leadership, the war followed a torturous, slow, and unsuccessful course. Gaius Marius abandoned the campaign in 108 B.C. and returned to Rome, determined to win a consulship so he could take charge of the war.

Having risen to wealth and prominence through his own brilliance and hard work, Gaius Marius never would have won a consulship if Rome had not suffered scandals and disastrous defeats under noble fools. In 107 B.C., tired of disasters from incompetent leadership, Rome elected Gaius Marius consul. Without delay, he seized responsibility for prosecuting the Jugurthine War.

Military adventures under arrogant Roman aristocrats had greatly reduced the number of Rome's noble youth. To build a new army strong enough to fight Jugurtha, Gaius Marius changed policies for recruiting and funding Roman legions. The new consul recruited non-Roman Italians and Rome's poor, illiterate, and unskilled to fill his army; and he paid for their horses, equipment, and training with funds from the Roman treasury.

Supporting the army with public funds and standardizing equipment and training, Gaius Marius built Rome's first professional army. From a previously disenfranchised multitude, trainable soldiers emerged who saw the military as a desirable career. Highly motivated, his men worked hard and eagerly acquired the discipline and skills necessary to win battles. When he was satisfied that his army was ready, Gaius Marius transported it to Africa.

Nevertheless, it took deft political maneuvering and lots of help from powerful friends in Rome for Gaius Marius to preserve his command long enough to defeat Jugurtha. After three years of hard fighting, the Roman army achieved victory in Africa in 105 B.C. Notably, a crafty young quaestor named Lucius Cornelius Sulla assisted brilliantly in the war.[21]

Two More Disasters at the Hands of Celts

From 107–105 B.C., Gaius Marius brought Rome its only military victories. When aristocrats criticized him and attempted to make light of his successes, they succeeded only in diminishing their own reputations. Two more serious defeats of patrician generals underscored patrician incompetence as well as Rome's helplessness to threats from the north.

While Gaius Marius recruited, trained, and transported an army of commoners to North Africa to fight Jugurtha, the patrician co-consul of 107 B.C., Gaius Cassius Longinus, led an army of Rome's remaining noble youth to deal with unrest in Roman Gaul. Unfortunately,

---

[21]Chapter 15 describes the remarkable career of Lucius Cornelius Sulla.

Tigurine Celts met him on a battlefield near modern Bordeaux, killing Longinus and most of his army. A surviving senior officer prevented complete slaughter by surrendering Roman supplies and accepting terms to march his soldiers under the yoke[22] of the Celts.

Then in 105 B.C., the arrogance and incompetence of another patrician general led to another mass slaughter of Roman soldiers. This time, 80,000 Romans and 40,000 auxiliaries, servants, and camp followers died at the hands of Germans near Arausio in Southern Gaul. Comparing the defeats in Gaul with the victory in North Africa, Rome stopped supporting incompetent leaders from Rome's privileged nobility. Gaius Marius easily won election as consul of 104 B.C., and he continued winning consulships for an unprecedented five consecutive terms. He did not leave office until after his sixth term in 100 B.C.

Slave Revolt and Religious Persecution in Sicily

After winning the public's confidence in 104 B.C., Gaius Marius took care not to lose it. He dedicated himself to preparations against the serious threat in the north and delegated lesser problems to men that he trusted. Still, a new threat affecting Rome's food supply challenged his resolve.

From 104–102 B.C., Syrian slaves again rebelled on Sicily. This time, slaves in eastern Sicily chose a flute player of Atargatis named Salvius as their leader; they called him King Tryphon. An astrologer (formerly a bandit) named Athenion simultaneously initiated a slave rebellion in western Sicily. Athenion organized his forces into a capable army, won control in the west, and then offered his services to King Tryphon.

Focused on preparing for the next invasion by Germans, Gaius Marius sent a loyal friend, the younger Manius Aquillius, to put down the rebellion on Sicily. It took two years, but Manius Aquillius finally broke the rebellion. Although pockets of slave resistance persisted on the island for two more years, Gaius Marius rewarded Manius Aquillius with a joint consulship in 101 B.C.

---

[22]Copying a Roman practice, the Celts forced the Romans to march beneath a "yoke" of spears while suffering jeers and humiliation.

Marius, Martha, and the Northern Threat

Gaius Marius respected Rome's traditions, but he didn't hesitate to go against traditional practices when circumstances demanded it. From 104–102 B.C., all of Rome believed that only he could revive the army and protect the city when the Germans returned. Taking care not to squander time, resources, and public confidence, he focused on building and maintaining an army trained specifically to deal with invading Germans. The army needed to be ready for the next attack, but no one knew when the next attack would come.

Sometime during these preparations, a Syrian prophetess named Martha tried to address the Roman Senate. She said that she had visions about the next German invasion, but the Senate expelled her without a hearing. Regardless, Martha soon acquired a reputation among the women of Rome as a person who could foretell and influence the future.

Perhaps Gaius Marius sought out Martha. Perhaps Martha obtained access to Marius through his wife, Julia. However it happened, Martha soon became Gaius Marius' personal prophetess. He gave her money, slaves, and a litter to ride. In return, she told him about the future and advised him how to sacrifice to the Syrian Goddess to ensure good fortune. Martha told Gaius Marius that Rome would elect him consul no fewer than seven times. He completed his sixth consulship at the end of 100 B.C., the year of Julius Caesar's birth. It took him fourteen more years to achieve his seventh and final consulship in 86 B.C. However, as the first great leader of Rome to worship Atargatis (the Syrian Goddess), Gaius Marius legitimized the presence of the goddess in Rome and strengthened her association with Cybele.

Events Surrounding the Last Invasion of Germans

Germans invaded Italy in 102 B.C. during the fourth consulship of Gaius Marius. With all of Rome praying for victory, he marched his greatly outnumbered force of 50,000 soldiers (eight well-prepared legions with auxiliaries) north. During the consul's absence, the High Priest of Cybele announced in Rome's Forum that the Great Mother in her sanctuary had granted victory to Gaius Marius and to Rome.

Chapter 14 | The Life and Times of Gaius Marius   321

In his gaudy and effeminate clothing, the priest began to harangue his audience: The Great Mother also demanded public expiations to restore the sanctity of her temple.

Calling the priest a charlatan, a tribune named Pompeius Aulus physically drove the priest away while the crowd laughed and shouted insults after him. Immediately, however, the tribune lost his voice and a burning fever came upon him. The tribune died three days later. The next time the High Priest of Cybele walked through the Forum, citizens of Rome greeted him deferentially and pressed expensive gifts into his hands.

Capably leading a force of six legions, and utilizing every tactic and advantage offered by the terrain, Gaius Marius proved that the High Priest of Cybele had prophesied the truth. With true mastery, he defeated more than 100,000 warriors of the Teutones and Ambiones tribes at Aquae Sextiae on the Rhone River. After the battle, the surviving barbarians shocked the Romans: Before Marius could capture them, many German women murdered their children and then killed themselves. Gaius Marius arranged to guard the few remaining survivors and then quickly marched to Vercellae to support the legions under his co-consul, a bitter rival whose force already had been compelled to retreat. The combined legions ended the threat of German tribes by slaughtering 100,000 Cimbri warriors. Altogether, the Romans captured and enslaved approximately 80,000 barbarians.

Minted around this time, the obverse of the coin in Figure 14-6 displays a bust of Cybele not terribly different from images of the Syrian Goddess. Appearing for the first time on a Roman coin, the obverse abbreviation represents "Ex Argento Publico," which means "From the Public Reserves." Victory rides in a chariot on the reverse. Bearing the first image of Cybele on a Roman coin, this denarius reflects Gaius Marius' new approach for funding the Roman army as well as the public's association of Cybele with divine military assistance. The image of Cybele may also represent public expiation to the goddess.

Rome celebrated a triumph for Gaius Marius' defeat of the Germans in 101 B.C. One of the rare numismatic depictions of living Romans during the Republican era, the reverse of the coin in Figure 14-7 portrays Gaius Marius in a triumphal chariot and his young son riding alongside on a horse. The obverse of the coin portrays Roma.

Figure 14-6. Cybele Facing Right, and Victory Riding a Chariot. Rome, AR Denarius, 102 B.C.

An Unpopular Sixth Consulship and Then Retirement

Even though Gaius Marius saved Rome during his fourth consulship in 102 B.C., his popularity waned in his fifth consulship and reversed completely in 100 B.C. during his sixth consulship. These years saw a resurgence of conflict between Optimates and Populares, particularly regarding reforms reminiscent of those of the Gracchi.

Gaius Marius had recruited, trained, and led men based on their ability instead of their birth. In preserving Rome from foreign threats, he created a generation of well-trained soldiers who had served capably in the Roman army against Africans and Germans and then returned to their disadvantaged lives in Italian cities and among Rome's lower classes. Commoners who had learned about war under Gaius Marius transformed local politics and shifted the regional balance of power, which spawned new long-term threats for Rome.

When Optimates blocked attempts by Gaius Marius to allocate African land as payment to veterans for their service in recent wars, he formed an alliance with powerful members of the Tribunate of the Plebs. The alliance succeeded in allocating African land and then pursued a larger populist agenda. Their goals included allocating more lands (for example, in Greece, Macedonia, Sicily, and Cisalpine Gaul) as payment for veterans, lowering grain prices in Rome, and increasing the power of the Tribunate of the Plebs. The entire platform angered Optimates, but they considered attempts to shift the balance of power

Figure 14-7. Gaius Marius in a Triumphal Chariot with His Son, Publius, Riding a Horse Alongside. Rome, C. Fundanius, AR Denarius, 101 B.C.

from the Comitia Centuriata toward the Comitia Tributa as nothing less than treason.

In 101 B.C., a plebian leader further angered patricians by exposing a plot by envoys of King Mithradates VI[23] of Pontus to bribe the Senate. For ruining a lucrative relationship with the East, patricians tried to punish the plebian leader. The plebian successfully obtained protection by appealing to the public. However, relations between Optimates and Populares continued to deteriorate.

During Gaius Marius' sixth consulship in 100 B.C., violence broke out between Optimates and Populares over a proposed law to decrease the price of grain in Rome. When a plebian hired a gang to kill a patrician politician on the day of his election, the Senate ordered Gaius Marius to defend Rome from radical Populares. Despite his broad sympathy for Populares and populist causes, the consul confronted rioters in the Forum and defeated them in pitched battle. Capturing the leaders, he assured them that their lives would be spared and took them to the Senate to face justice. However, Optimates climbed to the roof of the Senate and killed many defendants by stoning them with roof tiles. Losing his taste for Roman politics, Gaius Marius completed his term as consul, announced his retirement, and traveled to the East.

---

[23]King Mithradates VI was the last Hellenistic ruler to challenge Roman dominance of the Mediterranean Sea.

A NEW PERIOD OF INTERNAL AND EXTERNAL DANGERS

Gaius Marius proved himself an inspired leader in military campaigns in Spain, Africa, and Gaul. A dedicated advocate of the common man, he also tried to improve the lives of Italians and lower-class Romans. However, his best efforts only seemed to aggravate entrenched political antagonisms on the Italian peninsula, and disaster soon threatened on two fronts, internal and external. By 91 B.C., a series of escalating political crises resulted in the Social War between Romans and Italians, and Rome again relied on Gaius Marius to defend the Republic. As Rome struggled with a civil war, the Anatolian king, Mithradates VI of Pontus, challenged Rome's growing interests in Anatolia. As foretold by the prophetess, Martha, Gaius Marius eventually obtained his seventh consulship in 86 B.C. at the age of seventy-one, one of the darkest periods in Roman history. He spent the last few weeks of his life preparing to lead a Roman army against King Mithradates VI.

The Long-Term Threat in Anatolia

While Rome focused on events in North Africa, Sicily, and Transalpine Gaul, Mithradates VI slowly added bits of Scythia, Bithynia, and Armenia to his kingdom. He acquired control over most of the territories around the Black Sea, successfully consolidating a small empire. In Roman Asia, patrician governors had concentrated on siphoning wealth from Rome's new Asia Province but they began to suffer from the activities of Cilician pirates. In 100 B.C., Rome attacked the home territory of the pirates and annexed Cilicia,[24] which increased Rome's holdings in Anatolia. Officially, Rome took little notice of the expansionist policies of Mithradates VI until he interfered in the affairs of Galatia and Cappadocia, territories that had become protectorates of Rome. After 100 B.C., Gaius Marius, recently retired from his sixth consulship, traveled where he wanted and formed his own ideas about events and political forces in Asia Province.

---

[24]Many people in Cilicia believed in the Hellenized Cult of Mithras.

When Mithradates VI sent an Armenian force to depose King Ariobarzanes of Cappadocia in 96 B.C., Rome's Proconsul of Asia Province[25] immediately marched a Roman army to intervene. This time, Mithradates VI's army backed down and King Ariobarzanes regained his throne. However, the political climate throughout Asia Minor was shifting strongly against Rome.

Rome's friend, Nicomedes III of Bithynia (east of Pontus), died in 94 B.C. and willed the throne of Bithynia to his son, Nicomedes IV. Again, Mithradates VI tried to expand his empire, attempting to depose King Nicomedes IV in favor of one of the king's more cooperative brothers. Mithradates also tried again to gain control of Cappadocia by deposing King Ariobarzanes, also replacing him with a submissive brother.

The Social War

Italian veterans who had served Rome well wanted the privileges and benefits of Roman citizenship. Also, common Romans who were veterans of Gaius Marius' legions wanted more than merely second class citizenship. After Gaius Marius' disastrous sixth consulship, demagogues inflamed the passions of Italians and Rome's lower classes such that social order became increasingly volatile. Armed gangs of former soldiers increased the threat of violence in the streets of Rome, and politics became a particularly dangerous profession.

Gaius Marius returned to Rome from the East but did not get involved in the Italian struggle for citizenship. In 95 B.C., Rome expelled all non-citizens from the city. Then in 91 B.C. a plebian tribune pushed for immediate citizenship for all free men of Italy. Optimates attempted to punish the tribune politically by rendering all his previous bills invalid for religious reasons, and then someone assassinated him.

Soon after the assassination, an open rebellion began in Asculum, a city in the mountains of central Italy. Italians rose at a prearranged moment and murdered every Roman within the city's walls. Because a

---

[25] The proconsul happened to be Lucius Cornelius Sulla. See Chapter 15.

Figure 14-8. Personification of Italia, and Oath Ceremony of Italian Tribes against Rome. Corfinum, Marsic Confederation, AR Denarius, 90–88 B.C.

majority of surviving soldiers from the recent wars had come from Italian tribes, Rome suddenly faced a serious threat from a large army of experienced fighters. History remembers the conflict between Romans and Italians from 91–88 B.C. as the Social War.

Figure 14-8 displays a coin minted during the Social War in the name of Italian tribes described as the Marsic Confederation. The coin uses the same symbolism that Rome used in the war against Hannibal. The obverse of the coin displays a personification of Italia. On the reverse, Italian tribes swear a sacred oath to unite against Rome. Tribal representatives touch their swords to a pig that will be sacrificed to seal their vow of unity. The Latin state, Venusia, changed the name of its capital city from Corfinium to Italia and minted coins like this to pay Italian soldiers.

Gaius Marius left retirement to command Roman legions against Italians. As had happened in his first career, he entered the war as an adviser but acquired full command of his legions following losses by incompetent patrician generals. Unfortunately, his involvement in the war diminished because of illness, possibly a stroke.

The war entered its most critical moments in 90–89 B.C. A member of Gaius Marius' family, Lucius Julius Caesar,[26] became consul and

---

[26]The consul, Lucius Julius Caesar, was a distant cousin of Julius Caesar whose exploits are described in Chapter 17.

succeeded in passing a law that granted full Roman citizenship to all Italians who lived in cities that had not taken up arms against Rome. Effective as a conciliatory gesture, the new law shortened the war. By 88 B.C., only small groups of hardened revolutionaries still fought against Rome.

The Assignment of Manius Aquillius, the Younger, to Roman Asia

In 90 B.C., all Rome suffered from the hardships of war, but local politics continued to reflect antagonisms between Optimates and Populares. Nevertheless, something needed to be done about Mithradates VI who had installed puppet governments in the Roman protectorates, Bithynia and Cappadocia. The Senate dispatched the younger Manius Aquillius as a consular legate to go to Anatolia and address issues related to Mithradates VI.

Accepting the assignment almost as a family birthright, Manius Aquillius acted boldly to solidify the rule of Nicomedes IV in Bithynia and reinstall King Ariobarzanes in Cappadocia. Then, reputedly motivated by greed, Manius Aquillius attempted to provoke a wider war. Blinded by arrogance, he failed to recognize the weakness of his position compared with Mithradates' strength. Under the direction of Manius Aquillius, Nicomedes IV conducted raids on the Pontic Kingdom in a misguided attempt to goad Mithradates into declaring war.

A New Disaster in the East

For some time, Mithradates VI quietly endured Bithynian raids and insults from Manius Aquillius, but the King of Pontus carefully monitored the course of the Social War on the Italian peninsula. In July of 89 B.C., Mithradates VI finally decided to move against the Roman presence in Anatolia: He again deposed King Ariobarzanes and seized control of Cappadocia. When Rome's provincial army organized sufficiently to challenge Mithradates VI, he defeated it, captured Manius Aquillius, and seized control of the entire province of Roman Asia. As a cure for Roman greed, Mithradates VI executed Manius Aquillius by pouring molten gold down his throat. In May of 88 B.C., to commit himself and his fledgling empire against Rome, Mithradates VI ordered the execution of every Roman in Anatolia. Tens of thousands of Romans and Italians[27] died almost as quickly as word could spread.

Mithradates VI then contacted Greek leaders in Athens and Macedonia and invited them to join a Hellenistic rebellion against Rome. With support from Mithradates VI, an Athenian named Aristion overthrew Athens' Roman magistrates and formally allied the Greek city-state with Pontus. Mithradates VI then sent an army under General Archelaus to Greece, intending to liberate the remainder of Greece and Macedonia from Rome. In spite of losses against the Pontic army, the Roman governor of Macedonia maintained control over most of his province. Still, the long-term prospects for preserving a Roman presence east of Italy looked grim.

Minted in Athens nine years before Rome's war with Mithradates VI, the coin in Figure 14-9 proves the longstanding relationship between Aristion and Mithradates VI. The coin's obverse shows Athena in her war helmet. On the reverse, her sacred owl stands on an amphora of olive oil. More tellingly, however, the coin names Aristion as magistrate and displays Pegasus, a symbol connected with Perseus, the divine ancestor of Mithradates VI.

PRESERVING ROME IN A DANGEROUS WORLD

During the life of Gaius Marius, Romans lived as both victims and victimizers in a dangerous world. No one could have foreseen Rome's rise to complete dominance of the Mediterranean world by the time of Jesus only one century later, yet fate seemed to mold the psyche and guide the footsteps of Romans. Years of disasters, political unrest, and war gradually drove an increasing number of Romans to embrace the politics of the Populares. As the party acquired more power, it brought changes that improved the lives of common Romans. Also, even though Italians lost the Social War, Rome gave citizenship to Italians,

---

[27]Appian of Alexandria, a historian who wrote in the second century A.D., said that 80,000 Italians died in the massacre. If Anatolians had not killed these expatriates, the Hellenistic Cult of Mithras may have spread to Rome much earlier than it did, changing the course of religious history.

Figure 14-9. Bust of Athena, and Pegasus (a Symbol of Mithradates VI) next to Owl and Oil Jar. Athens, AR Tetradrachm, 97–95 B.C.

which suddenly placed new interests, languages, and cultures under the umbrella of the Roman Republic. However, despite the intensity of issues on the Italian peninsula, the activities of King Mithradates VI firmly drove Rome's attention to the East.

Romans began to expect more out of both life and death because of Gaius Marius. His rise empowered Italians and lower-class Romans, and his support for Eastern cults, like those of Atargatis and Cybele, opened Romans to new religious ideas. Metaphorically, Mithradates VI stood before Rome as the last roadblock before Jerusalem. After crushing Anatolian resistance, Rome acquired control over biblical lands and impoverished millions of Easterners, people already familiar with the benefits of Hellenistic cults like those of Mithras, Mên, Cybele, Attis, Atargatis, Isis, and others. Harsh conditions imposed by Rome produced desperate subjects yearning for hope and salvation.

Hellenistic cults shaped Western expectations of religion, and Roman history and involvement with the East set the stage for events described in the gospels. The decades surrounding the death of the Roman Republic and the birth of the Roman Empire eventually prepared the West to understand, receive, and nourish the earliest Christian cults. However, Rome had to dig itself out of a hole first.

CHAPTER
15

LUCIUS CORNELIUS SULLA

HERO, DICTATOR, AND CREATIVE MASTER OF WAR

> Lucius Cornelius Sulla preserved Rome by defeating it, ensured the Hellenization of Rome by affirming traditional Roman values, and strengthened the Republic so much that it could not survive for long.

In some ways the opposite of Gaius Marius, Lucius Cornelius Sulla possessed nobility by birth, poverty by family circumstance, and debauchery by personal inclination. However, the two men also shared important characteristics: Both men worshipped goddesses, their leadership preserved Rome at key moments in history, and they played important roles in establishing conditions surrounding the birth of the Roman Empire. Sulla possessed a natural brilliance in military tactics and strategy that outshone even the genius of Gaius Marius. By pursuing a remarkable career as a military commander and dictator of Rome, Sulla framed initial conditions that nourished early Christianity, especially in Anatolia.

Both men created brilliant military careers but they differed politically: Whereas Gaius Marius successfully defended his country's interests and raised the status of Italians and lower-class Romans, Lucius Cornelius Sulla valued hereditary nobility over relationship with any person or cause. Gaius Marius continually proved his nobility through acts of devotion to his country and his people; but Lucius Cornelius Sulla entered politics as a birthright, pursued goals that he judged worthy, and manipulated others to do as he wished. Enormously talented, Sulla shaped Rome while enjoying a peculiar mix of fear, respect, loathing, and admiration from Roman citizens.

Intending to strengthen Rome, Sulla restructured Republican government and naturalized his favorite Hellenistic cults. The changes ensured continuing upper-class political domination of the Republic and momentarily arrested the flow of new Hellenistic cults into Rome. However, Sulla made Rome's government too inflexible and too insulated from popular opinion to prevent collapse under the stress of rapid growth. In addition, instead of halting Roman interest in Hellenistic cults, the naturalization of select cults gave Romans a stronger thirst for Hellenistic approaches to salvation and prophecy.

SULLA'S EARLY CAREER

Although born to a noble family, Sulla lived a dissolute youth in which he maintained himself cheaply, partied as much as he could, and obtained sufficient money to enter politics by charming older women.[1] Nothing in his early life pointed toward the success he eventually achieved. However, as a nobleman, he easily obtained the office of quaestor in the legions of Gaius Marius during the Jugurthine War.

Sulla distinguished himself as a natural military leader in Africa. Responsible for camp administration, he soon acquired a reputation for performing his duties well. He also exhibited a remarkable degree of initiative and creativity as he engaged personally with the Jugurthine War. In 106 B.C., as the strategic successes of Gaius Marius diminished political support for King Jugurtha, Sulla found ways to cultivate the

---

[1] See *The Life of Sulla* 2 by Plutarch.

trust of King Bocchus of Mauretania,[2] a father-in-law of King Jugurtha. An unreliable ally, King Bocchus continually balanced risks and benefits in his conflicting relationships with Rome and King Jugurtha. Sulla succeeded in tipping the balance in favor of Rome and hatching a plot to capture King Jugurtha. Sulla informed Gaius Marius of the plan only after it was ready for execution.

Early Military Achievements

At the age of thirty-two, Sulla exhibited courage, diplomatic skill, and tactical mastery as he personally led the raid that captured King Jugurtha of Numidia—a grandstand finish to the hard-fought Africa campaign of Gaius Marius. Afterward, King Bocchus made the most of his freshly clarified political situation by commissioning a gilded equestrian statue of Sulla and sending it to Rome as a memorial. The Senate installed the statue in the Forum even though Gaius Marius deserved the credit for bringing the Jugurthine War to a successful conclusion.

Sulla continued to serve capably under Gaius Marius after they returned to Rome in 104 B.C. and began preparations for the next German invasion. However, fortunately for Rome, Sulla transferred to the legions under Gaius Marius' co-consul by 101 B.C. Modern historians believe that Sulla played a key role in the preservation of the legions under the patrician co-consul, an incompetent leader who was disinclined to cooperate with Gaius Marius. In this context, Sulla deserved much of the credit for Rome's victory when the combined forces of Gaius Marius and his co-consul met the Cimbri at Vercellae in 101 B.C.[3]

Service as Proconsul of Cilicia

As a well-known war hero, Sulla acquired a praetorship in 97 B.C., a position just under consul. A year later, successful service as a praetor enabled him to obtain an assignment from the Senate as Proconsul of Cilicia. There, with less than a single legion at his command, Sulla

---
[2]The ancient kingdom of Mauretania comprised territories corresponding with modern Morocco and western Algeria.
[3]See Chapter 14.

Figure 15-1. Tigranes II of Armenia, and Atargatis with River God, Orontes. Armenia, Tigranes II, AR Tetradrachm, 95–56 B.C.

exercised his political and military skills by engaging powerfully with neighboring Anatolian rulers from 96–92 B.C.

In 96 B.C., at the direction of Mithradates VI[4] of Pontus, Tigranes II of Armenia deposed King Ariobarzanes of Cappadocia, which was a protectorate of Rome in central Anatolia. The tetradrachm in Figure 15-1 portrays Tigranes II (the Great) wearing the distinctive crown of ancient Armenia. On the reverse, a mother goddess[5] similar to Cybele extends a branch to the river god Orontes. Even before reaching his new command, Proconsul Sulla marched his legion to Cappadocia and easily expelled the larger force of Armenians.

Sulla restored Ariobarzanes to power and personally crowned him King. Nonplussed by the quick defeat of the Armenian army, Mithradates VI chose not to press the issue any further. Sulla met with ambassadors sent by Parthia and Pontus to discuss territorial boundaries and diplomatic relations, and he exhibited such diplomatic mastery that the outmaneuvered Parthian ambassador suffered execution after reporting the results of the meeting to his king.

---

[4] The name "Mithradates" means "Given by Mithras." Rome fought three Mithridatic Wars against Mithradates VI: Sulla dealt with two and Pompey the Great finished the third. See Chapter 16.

[5] Syrians called the goddess Atargatis and Romans called her the Syrian Aphrodite. However, she was known by a multitude of names throughout the East.

Besides getting to know the political landscape of the East, Sulla also learned about Eastern cults. A great Chaldean seer attended Sulla's meeting with the unfortunate Parthian ambassador and proclaimed that Sulla would become the greatest man in the world. Further, the seer predicted that Sulla would die at the height of his good fortune after living a life filled with honor.[6]

Prophets of Mâ, the Great Mother of Cappadocia, also communicated with Sulla. Though Mâ resembled Cybele, Romans generally identified her with the Roman Goddess of War, Bellona. In services of the goddess, black-costumed priests and priestesses danced to music from horns and drums and they slashed themselves with sharp weapons—particularly the bipennis, a double-headed axe. Delirious and bleeding from wounds, prophets spoke to Sulla about his destiny.[7]

When he returned from Cilicia to Rome, Sulla allied himself with Optimates and worked against the popular policies of Gaius Marius. Optimates opposed granting citizenship to Italians and, instead, advocated policies designed to ensure the continuing domination of Rome by its patrician class. As the political situation deteriorated between Rome and Italy Sulla believed he was divinely chosen to lead Rome in the oncoming war.[8]

Winning the Social War

From 91–88 B.C., Sulla distinguished himself in the Social War between Romans and Italians. He assumed command of all Roman forces south of Rome in 90 B.C. Visitors to Pompeii can still see evidence of Sulla's siege next to the Vesuvian gate: Scars in the walls date from his capture of the Italian city from Oscan[9] forces in 89 B.C. At nearby Nola, Sulla won the highest honor that the Roman military could bestow: His legions gave him the Grass Crown, a decoration given only to a commanding general whose personal bravery had saved a whole army.

---

[6]See *The Life of Sulla* 5.5–6 and 37.1 by Plutarch.
[7]A meeting between Sulla and a prophet of Bellona is described in *The Life of Sulla* 27 by Plutarch, and the process a prophet used to enter an inspired state is described in *Elegies* I.6.45–50 by Tibullus.
[8]See *The Life of Sulla* 6.6–7 by Plutarch.
[9]Italian peoples called Oscans, Umbrians, and Samnites occupied territories mostly east and south of Rome, and all spoke variants of the Oscan language.

Popularly credited with turning the Social War in Rome's favor, Sulla married into a prominent noble family, conceived twins, and easily won election as Consul of Rome in 88 B.C. Outside Rome, he continued defeating the last pockets of Italian resistance, and inside Rome, he participated in bitter arguments between Optimates and Populares about issues like extending citizenship to even more Italians. Once, after Sulla blocked pro-Italian legislation, a gang of Populares attacked him in a meeting. He ran to the house of Gaius Marius for refuge, but before Marius opened his gates, he demanded that Sulla pledge support for the legislation.

Squaring Off against Gaius Marius

From 89–88 B.C., Rome suffered a series of increasingly grave insults to its dominion in Asia Minor: another takeover of Cappadocia, the loss of Asia Province, the execution of Manius Aquillius, and the murder of thousands of Romans and Italians. Sulla and Gaius Marius both wanted to lead a war against Mithradates VI. Both men had spent time in the East and knew that they could defeat the army of Pontus. Although he was old and sick, Gaius Marius wanted the glory of saving Rome one more time. He also wanted the seventh consulship promised to him years earlier by Martha, the prophetess of Atargatis. In the prime of his life, Sulla similarly wanted glories promised to him by a Chaldean seer and by prophets of Bellona and Mâ. However, as the end of 88 B.C. approached, conflict between Populares who supported Gaius Marius and Optimates who supported Sulla plunged Rome into political turmoil.

Consistent with the ancient tradition of a current consul leading the Republic to war, the Senate assigned Sulla and his legions to fight Mithradates VI. As he prepared to leave, Sulla camped with his legions well away from Rome. In the city, however, a small army of thugs invaded the streets. The Tribunate of the Plebs (the voice of the Populares) officially revoked the Senate's action and transferred responsibility for the war to Gaius Marius. To sweeten this edict for common Romans, the Tribunate of the Plebs passed additional laws, for example, the cancellation of all debts. Tribunes raced on horseback to Sulla's camp with orders to transfer control of his legions to Gaius Marius, but soldiers loyal to Sulla stoned the tribunes to death.

Ever since his term as Proconsul of Asia Province, Sulla had worshipped the militaristic mother goddess Mâ. That night, he dreamed that Mâ visited him in a garden with winged Victory at her side. The goddess urged Sulla to strike his enemies. Naming the leaders of the Populares one by one, Gaius Marius chief among them, Mâ gave Sulla thunderbolts to use as weapons. The next morning, he summoned his six most loyal legions and led them against the city of Rome.

He easily seized control of Rome. The gladiators and thugs of the Populares stood no chance against disciplined soldiers. Sulla captured and executed many troublemakers, but Gaius Marius and some of his closest supporters escaped. In the following weeks, Sulla restructured the government of the Roman Republic, especially eliminating laws that gave too much power to lower-class Romans. He increased the power of the Senate and reduced the power of the Tribunate of the Plebs. Pressing his reconfigured government into service, he left orders to find Gaius Marius and other leaders of the Populares and execute them all. Then he and his legions departed for Greece to fight the First Mithridatic War.

The Seventh Consulship of Gaius Marius

As Sulla departed for Greece, seventy-year-old Gaius Marius hid from pursuers in the countryside. Eventually, he arranged passage to Africa Province, joined with his son and loyal friends, and prepared his own force to march on Rome. Riots erupted in Rome as Populares and Optimates continued to battle each other. Late in 87 B.C., Gaius Marius led his small army to Rome and captured the city. Then, for five days, his soldiers prosecuted a vengeful reign of terror, murdering Romans sympathetic to Sulla and mounting their heads on spears in the Forum.

The Senate named Gaius Marius as the new commander of the Eastern war and condemned Sulla to exile. At the beginning of 86 B.C., a politically cleansed Rome elected Gaius Marius to his seventh consulship. However, only a few weeks after the election, the old general suffered a stroke and died.

Still, a Populares government hostile to Optimates maintained power in Rome, issued new laws and decrees, and pretended that Sulla didn't matter. Eventually, the Senate assigned command responsibility for the Eastern war to a new consul named Flaccus. With orders to relieve Sulla of his command, the consul prepared new legions and departed for Greece.

SULLA IN EXILE

In the Spring of 87 B.C., while Optimates and Populares struggled for control of Rome, Sulla began executing his strategy for winning the First Mithridatic War. With a relatively small army and an indeterminate situation in Rome, he alone made the difference between winning and losing. Huge challenges stood in his way: He had to convince both provincial Romans and nonaligned Greeks to support him; he had to capture the renegade city of Athens, which was well defended by fortified walls and well provisioned by the Pontic navy; and he had to defeat the spirited and numerically superior Pontic army in Greece.

In northern Greece, also threatened by the Pontic army and with little prospect of receiving any support from Rome other than Sulla, the proconsul of Macedonia gladly sent as many soldiers as he could spare for Sulla to command. Sulla then met with representatives from the major city-states of Greece and convinced them that he would answer any Greek opposition with utter ruthlessness. Sulla's record of successes in war spoke for itself: In Greece, only Athens and the Pontic army dared to oppose him.

Throughout the First Mithridatic War, neither Roman nor Pontic commanders shrank from committing sacrilege. The Pontic general, Archelaus, looted the temple treasuries of Delos, and Sulla looted the temple treasuries of Epidauros, Olympia, and Delphi.[10] Near Athens the Romans cut down a sacred grove and built siege engines from the wood. Sulla maintained that Apollo gladly contributed the sacred treasures. Preserving a small gold statue of Apollo from Delphi, Sulla wore

---
[10]See *The Life of Sulla* 12.3–6 by Plutarch.

it like an amulet and sometimes made a point of praying to it publicly before a major battle.[11]

The Siege of Athens

Like Persians and Spartans[12] before him, Sulla placed Athens under siege. The siege lasted from the Summer of 87 B.C. to early Spring in 86 B.C. Warships of the Pontic navy occupied Piraeus (Athens' port city) and struggled to resupply their allies, but Sulla successfully prevented food from reaching Athens. Militarily outmatched and slowly starving, Athenians nevertheless shouted insults from behind the walls that Sulla methodically sought to weaken. During the siege, reports of recent events in Rome—the murder of his friends, the proclamation of his exile, and the death of Gaius Marius—reached Sulla from Optimate refugees who escaped Rome and joined his camp.

Reduced to eating grass and leather, Athenians maintained their haughty disposition toward Sulla. However, Sulla eventually discovered a weakness in a section of the city wall. Successfully collapsing the wall at night, he led a merciless midnight raid that left rivers of blood flowing in the streets of Athens. After witnessing the capture of Athens, the navy of Pontus abandoned Piraeus and Sulla burned the port city to the ground.

The coin in Figure 15-2 resembles standard Athenian coins minted early in the first century B.C., but Sulla minted this coin, not Athens. Some scholars maintain that the monogram on the reverse indicates that silver for the coins came from the famous silver mines of Laurion.[13] However, others expand the monogram to MAPKOY TAMIOY (Marcus quaestor), representing Sulla's younger brother, Marcus, who bore responsibility for minting Sulla's coinage at Athens. A large part of the silver for Sulla's coins came from the plundered treasuries of Greek temples.

---

[11]See *The Life of Sulla* 29.6 by Plutarch.
[12]King Xerxes of Persia captured Athens in 480 B.C., and Spartans placed Athens under siege during the Peloponnesian War, which lasted from 431–404 B.C.
[13]A monogram that indicated the Laurion mine as the source of the coins' silver would have reassured Greeks that feared spiritual pollution from Sulla's blasphemous acts.

Figure 15-2. Athena, and Owl on Amphora. Athens, Sulla, AR Tetradrachm, ca. 86–84 B.C.

The Battle of Chaeronea

After capturing Athens, Sulla marched his army, 40,000 strong, north to intercept the smaller of two enormous Pontic armies in Greece: the army of Taxiles, a force of approximately 120,000 men. Nominally in charge of Mithradates VI's forces in Greece, Archelaus led a larger army of approximately 140,000 men. Archelaus wanted Taxiles to surround Sulla's army and starve it to death, but Mithradates VI sent orders for Taxiles to defeat Sulla in battle. Using inspired tactics, Sulla crushed the forces of Taxiles at Chaeronea. Only 10,000 of Taxiles' men survived while Sulla's army suffered only minor losses.[14]

After his victory over Taxiles, Sulla met with Flaccus, the consul that the Populares government of Rome had sent to take over the war. Sulla declined to accept Flaccus' order to stand down, and Flaccus chose not to insist. The two armies remained near each other until Flaccus realized that men from his army were deserting to join Sulla's. Toward the end of 86 B.C., General Flaccus decided to strike out on his own. He abandoned Greece and lead his army to Anatolia, bringing the war directly to Mithradates VI.

---

[14]Sulla claimed that he lost only fourteen men in the battle and later found that two of those had survived. See *The Life of Sulla* 19.4 by Plutarch.

The Battle of Orchomenos and an Abrupt Peace Agreement

General Archelaus tried to delay a decisive encounter, hoping that Sulla's position in Greece would weaken. Nevertheless, in 85 B.C., Sulla enticed Archelaus (now with 150,000 men) into battle near Orchomenos on an open battlefield that appeared to favor the Pontic cavalry. However, by employing trench-warfare tactics,[15] Sulla trapped Archelaus' men and massacred them. Archelaus fled and soon tried to contact Sulla to negotiate a treaty. In little more than two years, Sulla had secured the Greek peninsula for Rome by demolishing a Pontic army ten times larger than his own.

Having secured the Greek peninsula, Sulla considered how best to proceed with Rome in the hands of Populares and with antagonistic Roman legions making progress in Anatolia. Because Rome still suffered from violent conflicts between Optimates and Populares, new patrician refugees arrived regularly at Sulla's camp. Also, disturbing reports reached Sulla from Anatolia. Flaccus had scarcely reached Asia when he came to a bad end. His first officer, a man named Fimbria, led a successful mutiny and killed the consul. Generally much more capable than Flaccus, Fimbria led punishing raids against Asian cities that had betrayed Rome in alliance with Pontus and began winning major victories against Mithradates VI.

Balancing concerns about political events in Rome with the military successes of Fimbria's army in Asia, Sulla offered relatively generous terms for reconciliation to Mithradates VI. If the king withdrew all his forces from Roman territories, paid a substantial sum as reparations, and donated a fully equipped navy of seventy ships to Sulla, Mithradates VI could keep his kingdom. Underscoring the consequences of refusing these terms, Sulla began pacifying rebellious tribes of Macedonia by depopulating entire regions. Under pressure from Fimbria and facing a broad loss of confidence in Anatolia, Mithradates VI met with Sulla and agreed to his terms.[16]

---

[15]Some of Sulla's inspired tactics were not used again until World War I.
[16]Not affected by the peace agreement, Cilician pirates increased their activities on the Mediterranean Sea at the urging of Mithradates VI. Ostensibly privateers, they served as an unofficial navy of Pontus.

Settling the East

After concluding an agreement with Mithradates VI, Sulla shifted military operations to Asia, located Fimbria, and camped near him. Fimbria tried valiantly to prevent his soldiers from deserting to Sulla and even hatched an unsuccessful assassination plot. Yet, as Sulla's soldiers began constructing an earthwork around Fimbria's position, Fimbria's soldiers fraternized with Sulla's and helped with the construction. Sulla sent a message that he wouldn't bother killing Fimbria if he abandoned his army and immediately left for Rome. Unable to obtain promises of loyalty even from his closest aides, Fimbria realized that his dreams of redeeming himself with glorious victories in Asia had evaporated. He could not defeat Sulla, nor could he ever return to Rome. Fimbria fell on his sword and his leaderless soldiers joined Sulla.

After successfully concluding the First Mithridatic War, Sulla reconstituted Roman administration of Asia Province in 84 B.C. He restored the system of Roman magistrates and levied harsh penalties against the rebellious cities of Asia Province. Because Mithradates VI also had siphoned treasure[17] from these cities, Asia Province suffered for decades under a heavy burden of debt.

DICTATORSHIP, CONSULSHIP, AND RETIREMENT

Sulla returned to Italy in 83 B.C. but had to fight his way to Rome. As Rome's consuls organized armies against Sulla, ambitious young Optimates like Crassus and Pompey[18] swarmed to join his ranks. The armies of the Populares broke against those loyal to Sulla like waves against rocks. In early 82 B.C., two more consular armies formed, one of them

---

[17]Before exiting Roman territories, Mithradates VI robbed city treasuries. He tried to create civic disturbances by canceling all debts, freeing all slaves, and extending full citizenship to all resident aliens. He also purged personal enemies, particularly officials who had attempted early negotiations with Sulla.

[18]Crassus became the wealthiest man in Rome, and Pompey became the next great Roman general after Sulla. See Part Five for more information about these men.

commanded by the son of Gaius Marius. Fearing that Sulla would revoke liberties granted after the Social War by Rome's Populares government, Italians eagerly joined the legions against him. Regardless, Sulla defeated all opposition.

By the end of 82 B.C., Sulla marched into Rome as a victorious conqueror and the Senate obligingly appointed him dictator. For two years, Sulla ruled Rome with absolute power. Implementing a new reign of terror, he executed approximately 1500 aristocrats[19] and many times that number of common Romans. Adding to the terror, if someone tried to help a condemned man escape, Sulla executed that person as well. He even banned the sons and grandsons of proscribed persons from ever holding political office in the future.

While dealing effectively with enemies, Sulla proved that he also knew how to treat friends who might become enemies. Noting Pompey's ability and ambition, Sulla showered the young general with honors for his victories. Further, Sulla arranged a marriage between his daughter and Pompey and then sent Pompey to fight forces loyal to the Populares in Sicily and Africa. Restoring control over distant territories kept Pompey busy and extinguished any temptation he might have felt to rebel against Sulla.

Regarding Roman government, Sulla did his best to cripple the Tribunate of the Plebs. For example, after Sulla's reforms, the Tribunate could no longer initiate legislation nor could it veto legislation approved by the Senate. The only bills the Tribunate could consider were those that had been introduced with the Senate's permission. To prevent ambitious men from seeking office in the Tribunate, he forbade ex-tribunes from obtaining any other political office. Sulla doubled the number of Senators, increased the number of courts, codified the cursus honorum, and established a number of rules intended to prevent any future Roman from following a career like his own or like that of Gaius Marius.

---

[19]Young Julius Caesar was one of the nobles that Sulla ordered to be executed; however, the intervention of a vestal virgin saved Caesar's life. From 83–82 B.C., Sulla effectively launched the military careers of Pompey the Great, Crassus, and Julius Caesar, the first triumvirs of Rome. See Chapter 18.

An Inconsequential Second Mithridatic War

Scarcely noticed by most Romans and Anatolians, a second Mithridatic war came and went from 83–81 B.C. An ambitious young commander in Asia Province disobeyed Sulla's orders to leave Mithradates VI alone. Hoping to win fame and wealth through aggressive action, the commander manufactured an excuse to attack Pontus but Mithradates strongly repelled the attack. A practical and cynical man, Sulla enticed the young commander to Rome by promising him a triumph and then replaced him with a more seasoned commander. Following Sulla's orders, the new commander renewed the peace agreement with Mithradates VI.

Religious Reforms

The most important religious organizations in Rome were the *College of Pontifices* and the *College of Augurs*. The College of Pontifices comprised the *Pontifex Maximus* (the highest religious authority in Rome), four to six *vestal virgins* (priestesses of Vesta), eight *flamines* (priests of official Roman cults), and the *Rex Sacrorum* (a priest who performed official sacrifices). The College of Augurs comprised nine priests that were responsible for interpreting signs and determining the will of the gods. Sulla increased the number of flamines and augurs to fifteen.

The term *Pontifex Maximus* is still used to describe the Pope of the Catholic Church, but Christian use of the term has not been attested earlier than the fifteenth century A.D. Nevertheless, many practices and much of the administrative structure of the Catholic Church evolved from Roman state religious administration, which recognized Christianity as the official religion of the Roman Empire beginning in the fourth century A.D. In the Roman Republic, the Pontifex Maximus and the College of Pontifices defined the nature of spiritual entities, determined acceptable religious practice, and distinguished true religious beliefs from falsehoods, powers currently claimed in the Catholic Church by the Pope and his college of Bishops.

Besides leading the College of Pontifices, the Pontifex Maximus supervised the vestal virgins, priestesses of Vesta (Goddess of the

Hearth) whose cult ensured the security and well-being of Rome. Young girls between six and ten years of age entered the service of Vesta for a period of thirty years: ten years of education and preparation, ten years of service, and ten years as teachers. While their primary duty was to keep a sacred fire burning, they also fetched water from a sacred spring, prepared sacred food used in religious rituals, cared for sacred objects, and maintained an archive of wills. Vestal virgins had the power to save the life of a condemned man. They remained celibate as long as they served their goddess, but they were free to leave the priesthood and marry after fulfilling their full term of service.

Sulla had obtained initiation into the Eleusinian Mysteries in Greece and he had learned to respect the goddess cults of Anatolia. Breaking with a tradition of Roman prejudice against Hellenistic cults, he increased the number of flamines to formally naturalize the cults of Cybele, Aphrodite of Eryx, and Asclepius. Sulla also informally welcomed other cults. For example, Sulla personally approved arrangements for priests of Isis[20] to practice their cult in Rome even though the cult had suffered official condemnation for more than a century.

Sulla hadn't forgotten the goddess who had promised him so many victories. While visiting Aphrodisias, he had donated a gold crown and a fine bipennis (double-headed axe) to the local Temple of Aphrodite,[21] which honored a warlike goddess similar to Mâ and Cybele. Dedicating these gifts to the goddess, he thanked her for helping him since she first visited his dreams years earlier as he camped outside Rome. The obverse of the coin in Figure 15-3 shows a picture of the Goddess of Aphrodisias, and the reverse displays her characteristic double-headed axe. Two palm branches cross on the haft of the axe.

Consistent with Sulla's reforms, Rome minted a few coins with symbols of Hellenistic cults during the last years of Sulla's life. The obverse of the coin in Figure 15-4 displays a representation of Juno Sospita, an ancient Roman goddess representing Juno as the Savior of Women. Behind her, one can see the first headdress of Isis to appear on a Roman coin. On the reverse a young virgin feeds a snake. Portraying

---

[20] See *Metamorphoses* (*The Golden Ass*) 11.30.5 by Apuleius.
[21] See *Civil Wars* 1.97.455 by Appian.

Figure 15-3. Aphrodite of Aphrodisias, and Sacred Bipennis—Two-Headed Axe Used in Worship. Caria, Aphrodisias, AE 18, First Century B.C.

a snake (like a divine Egyptian cobra), a virgin (like Isis), and a headdress of Isis, this coin signified increased toleration of the Hellenistic Cult of Isis in Rome.

Sulla's devotion to goddesses helped ensure the lasting importance of Hellenized goddess cults in Rome. Christians usually consider the Cult of Mary, which became an official part of Christianity at the Council of Ephesos in 431 A.D., as something completely different from barbaric goddess cults worshipped by pagans. However, Mary retains many titles of earlier goddesses (for example, the Mother of God, the Queen of Heaven, and the Great Mother) as well as the merciful character and motherly iconography that characterized Isis.

More representations of Atargatis also began to appear on coins. Romans recognized Atargatis as the same Middle Eastern goddess that they worshipped in the Elymian Temple of Venus in Eryx, Sicily. In Syria as well as on Sicily, Romans participated in complex musical ceremonies of the cult as well as in acts of sacred prostitution. Romans knew the Syrian religious triad—Atargatis, Hadad, and Adonis—as Venus, Jupiter, and Mercury. In the East, a city's local Goddess of Prosperity was called Tyche and was represented by an image of Atargatis holding a rudder and a cornucopia. Without an association with a specific city, the goddess was called Fortuna and represented generic

Figure 15-4. Juno Sospita in Goatskin Headdress, and Virgin Ritually Feeding a Snake. Rome, AR Denarius, after 78 B.C.

good luck. Scholars have shown that even the famous *Venus de Milo* in the Musée du Louvre in Paris originally portrayed Tyche. Devices lost with the statue's arms probably included city symbols like a rudder and a cornucopia. Many goddess cults west of the Tigris and Euphrates rivers had features in common with the Cult of Atargatis, for example, frequently appearing among a triad of ruling gods, designating fish and doves as sacred animals, and affirming that souls of the dead lived in an underground location.

Sulla's naturalization of the Cult of Cybele eventually resulted in the recognition of a serious religious problem: How could an intact Roman pontifex rule over a cult that required priests to be castrated? The castration requirement for priests of Cybele precluded Roman citizens from entering the priesthood because mutilation of citizens was illegal. Naturalization of Cybele implies the creation of ceremonies that made it possible for intact Roman citizens to enter her priesthood,[22] but the form of these ceremonies during the dictatorship of Sulla is unknown.

---

[22] By 160 A.D., Romans who wanted to become priests of Cybele entered her service through baptism in bull's blood, a ceremony called a taurobolium. Whether castrated or intact, former priests of Cybele sometimes became Christian fathers, and many Christian practices emphasizing devotions to Mary previously belonged to cults of Hellenistic goddesses like Cybele and Isis.

Sulla's Second Consulship

Two years after he'd started, Sulla finished cleansing Rome of enemies and restructuring its government and constitution. Much to everyone's surprise, he then resigned his dictatorship toward the end of 81 B.C. After restoring consular government and dismissing his legions, he ran in a normal election for the office of consul. He won the election and served as one of the two consuls of Rome in 80 B.C.

Sulla completed his relatively uneventful second consulship and then retired. In his retirement speech, he publicly acknowledged a notorious actor and female impersonator as his lover and then withdrew from public life to complete writing his memoirs. He dedicated his memoirs to Lucius Licinius Lucullus, a friend and great Roman general. Sulla died a particularly horrible death in 78 B.C. from symptoms characteristic of liver failure or a ruptured gastric ulcer.[23] His will named Lucius Licinius Lucullus as the guardian of Sulla's young son, Faustus.

SULLA'S LEGACY

Emerging from a debauched youth, Sulla acquired fame for spectacular heroism: for example, bringing an end to the Jugurthine War in 105 B.C. by personally capturing King Jugurtha. Once his career was launched, he continued to advance politically and militarily. Among his greatest achievements, he solidified Roman control over the Italian peninsula and temporarily arrested the ambitions of Mithradates VI, Rome's last great Hellenistic threat. Sulla won two consulships, marched his army against Rome twice, ruled once as dictator, and voluntarily relinquished dictatorship at the height of his power.

The financial burden that Sulla placed on the cities of Roman Asia was one of many hardships imposed by Rome on Asia Province over several generations. Long familiar with promises from Hellenistic cults about life after death and spiritual salvation, Anatolians met suffering with a willingness to consider religious innovations. By the time that early Christians came to Anatolia in the first century A.D., they found many poor people eager to listen to stories about Jesus.

---

[23]See *The Life of Sulla* 36–37 by Plutarch.

Politically, Sulla attempted to roll back changes in the government of Rome to recreate the Roman Republic of the previous century. Sometimes restoring old laws and sometimes creating new ones, he attempted to secure the lion's share of political power for Rome's nobility. Recognizing the huge increase in Rome's population, he extended Rome's official boundaries, thereby doubling the city's size. However, because he failed to realize that Rome's new scale and diversity had fundamentally changed the nature of Rome, he succeeded only in postponing another crisis.[24] Rome and the world had changed a great deal in a hundred years, and not even Sulla could force Rome to operate for long as it had during the good old days.

The passing of Lucius Cornelius Sulla inaugurated an age when common Romans pursued Hellenistic promises of life after death and Roman generals pursued the Hellenistic possibility of personal deification. Inclined to use the power of their legions to enforce personal agendas and exaltation, Roman generals competed ruthlessly among themselves: demonizing their opponents, harnessing public disaffection to their careers, and arraying their followers like opposing armies. Eventually, aristocratic control conflicted irreparably with the progressive agenda of Rome's burgeoning lower-class population. After Sulla's reforms, the collapse of the Roman Republic was only a matter of time.

---

[24]The Roman Republic did not survive the next big crisis. After Julius Caesar became Dictator for Life, radical republicans assassinated him and Rome's political system lurched from a republic toward an imperial monarchy. See Part Six.

PART FIVE

Venus and Symbolic Apotheosis of Julius Caesar

BECOMING A STAR
How Julius Caesar Obtained Popular Recognition as a God

Competition between the last great generals of the Roman Republic shaped the greatest apotheosis story in the Western world.

CHAPTER
16

JULIUS CAESAR AND THE FIRST TRIUMVIRATE

> The activities of Crassus, Pompey, and Caesar prepared for increasing economic, military, and political control by Rome over the Western world.

By marching on Rome, defeating foreign armies much larger than his own, and relating personally with foreign goddesses, Sulla launched a period of extraordinary opportunity and danger for the Roman Republic. He started the careers of the greatest generation of Roman generals, he showed how a disciplined Roman Army could take apart the defenses of territories less focused on war, and he demonstrated that stories about a general's relationship with a divinity could strengthen an army's resolve. By hardening Rome, he created a brittle state that could not change without being broken, and by exemplifying strong leadership he created generals willing to destroy Rome in order to save it.

Sulla personally touched the lives of the first triumvirs of Rome: Marcus Crassus, Pompey the Great, and Julius Caesar. Sometimes controlling, sometimes teaching, and sometimes opposing them, Sulla gave each man a combination of challenge and opportunity that helped him become one of the greatest men of his time. Under Sulla, Marcus

Crassus learned to exploit business opportunities created by war and became the wealthiest man in Rome; Pompey the Great obtained the military education he needed to expand Rome's foreign influence to every Mediterranean shore; and Julius Caesar received pressure to obtain martial, engineering, and political skills that he combined so powerfully that, for a while, he made Romans believe that anything was possible and the whole world lay within their grasp.

Of course, new possibilities for Rome brought new possibilities for Rome's enemies. Rome's dependence on slaves inspired a Thracian gladiator named Spartacus to lead a rebellion, and Hellenistic rulers like Mithradates VI sought to create new Hellenistic empires at Rome's expense. In such an environment, the limitations of borders, traditions, and morality dissolved, from time to time placing increased stress on traditional religious beliefs. Throughout the West, the ordinary men who marched and struggled to build their leaders' dreams returned home bringing new ideas about themselves and their universe.

THE ORIGINS OF THE MEMBERS OF THE FIRST TRIUMVIRATE

The dictatorship of Sulla launched the careers of three important generals: Marcus Licinius Crassus, Gnaeus Pompeius Magnus (Pompey the Great), and Julius Caesar. (See the timelines in Figure 16-1.) Each embodied a different combination of personality and abilities, but for thirty years after the death of Sulla, these three generals extended Roman control to every territory on the Mediterranean Sea. By cooperating, they found a new way to control Roman politics: forming an alliance called the *First Triumvirate*. By dominating Rome, they dominated most of the known world.

Marcus Licinius Crassus: The Embodiment of Lust for Wealth

Marcus Licinius Crassus was born to a noble family in 116 B.C. He was twenty-three years younger than Sulla, but nine years older than Pompey and sixteen years older than Julius Caesar. Even though his father served as a consul in 97 B.C., Crassus exhibited little interest in

Chapter 16 | Julius Caesar and the First Triumvirate

Figure 16-1. Timelines Comparing the Lives of Marcus Licinius Crassus, Gnaeus Pompeius Magnus (Pompey the Great), and Julius Caesar.

pursuing a military career until Gaius Marius marched on Rome in 87 B.C. Marian partisans persecuted Roman aristocrats, including murders of the brother and father of Marcus Licinius Crassus and confiscation of his family's wealth. Crassus survived by fleeing to Spain and living in a cave.[1] In 84 B.C., after learning that Sulla was returning to Italy and that an unruly mob of soldiers had murdered Cinna,[2] Crassus emerged from hiding, publicly announced his presence, and quickly gathered a pro-Optimate army.

Crassus led his army against Populares in Spain, but some accused him of having greater interest in acquiring plunder than in furthering the Optimate cause.[3] He joined other Optimates in North Africa and then led his force to Italy where he supported Sulla. Crassus served Sulla well but lacked the initiative and imagination of his younger competitor: Sulla conspicuously heaped honors on young Pompey and denied them to Crassus. However, Crassus successfully commanded Sulla's right wing during the Battle of the Colline Gate, the decisive battle that gave Sulla control of Rome toward the end of 82 B.C.

During the years before Sulla's last consulship, Crassus exhibited two distinguishing personality traits: jealousy of Pompey's leadership ability and a compulsive striving to acquire wealth.[4] As Sulla executed enemies and cleansed Rome of Populares leaders, nobody profited more from the acquisition of dead men's property than Crassus. From the days that he hid in a cave to the end of his life, he focused so successfully on acquiring money (especially through war profiteering) that he became the richest man in Rome.

The character of Crassus is evident in one surviving story about charges laid against a Vestal Virgin for having criminal intimacy with him. Crassus defended the Vestal saying that he courted the woman only because he wanted to buy her property at a good price. Because of his reputation, the Roman court believed Crassus and acquitted the Vestal Virgin. However, Crassus refused to stop bothering the woman

---

[1] See *The Life of Crassus* 4.1 by Plutarch.
[2] Lucius Cornelius Cinna served as the co-consul of Gaius Marius during his disastrous seventh consulship. See *Cinna and His Times: A Critical and Interpretative Study of Roman History During the Period 87–84 B.C.* p. 61 by Harold Bennett.
[3] See *The Life of Crassus* 6.1 by Plutarch.
[4] See *The Life of Crassus* 6.2–7 by Plutarch.

until she finally sold her property to him.⁵ After Sulla restored Optimate dominance in Rome, Crassus focused less on military and political pursuits and more on increasing his wealth. However, from time to time, he sought leadership positions in war and politics, but mostly as means for increasing his wealth.

Pompey the Great: The Embodiment of Lust for Glory

Born in 106 B.C., Pompey the Great was the first Roman general to acquire renown throughout the Western world. He began his professional military career during the Social War in 89 B.C., leading Roman soldiers against Italian rebels. During the last decades of the Roman Republic, he played an important role in shaping borders and international relations throughout the Mediterranean region.

From Picenum on the Adriatic coast of Italy, Gnaeus Pompeius Strabo, the father of Pompey the Great, lacked official Roman nobility. His contemporaries described him as ruthless, greedy, and duplicitous. Nevertheless, following a path toward Roman respectability first trod by Gaius Marius, Pompey's father ascended through Rome's cursus honorum,⁶ passing successively through the offices of quaestor (104 B.C.), praetor (92 B.C.), and consul (89 B.C.). Gnaeus Pompeius Strabo made sure that his son got the education and opportunities he needed to become a formidable military leader at an early age.

Even though Pompey's family came from Picenum, family traditions connected Pompey's ancestor, a shepherd named Faustulus, to mythical events related to the founding of Rome. Once, while walking near the Tiber River, Faustulus glanced in the direction of a woodpecker drumming persistently on a fig tree. Beneath its branches, he saw a she-wolf nursing Romulus and Remus.⁷ When the wolf went

---

⁵See *The Life of Crassus* 1.2 by Plutarch.
⁶The cursus honorum was a recognized sequence of political offices that ambitious aristocratic Romans followed to eventually become a consul, the highest political office in Rome. See Chapter 14.
⁷The Roman God of War, Mars, raped Rhea Sylvia, a Vestal Virgin who gave birth to Romulus and Remus. Rhea Sylvia's father (a descendant of Aeneas) buried his daughter alive and ordered her children to be exposed. A servant left the children in a basket near the Tiber River, which flooded and carried the basket to the branches of a fig tree. A she-wolf then found the children and nursed them.

away, the woodpecker fed the children. Recognizing the children's divine nature, Faustulus carried them back to his hut where he and his wife raised them to manhood.

Sextus Pompeius Faustulus, the paternal uncle of Pompey the Great, designed the coin in Figure 16-2 to commemorate his family's participation in the founding of Rome. The coin's obverse displays a personification of Rome, and the reverse portrays Romulus and Remus suckling from a she-wolf. Above the wolf, a woodpecker sits on a tree; and to the left of the wolf, Faustulus watches the children, wolf, and woodpecker in amazement.[8] True to Faustulus' mythological role as a protector of Romulus and Remus, Picenum allied itself with Rome against Hannibal during the Second Punic War and against Italians during the Social War. In the struggles between Optimates and Populares, Pompey's family identified with Optimates.

The Beginning of Pompey's Military Career. When his father became consul in 89 B.C., seventeen-year-old Pompey served as an officer in his father's legions. While stories about other Roman generals often emphasized religious sacrifices, prophecies, and omens, the stories about Pompey emphasized his character, military prowess, and administrative ability. People compared his character, talent, and appearance with historical descriptions of Alexander the Great.[9] Like Alexander, Pompey made a point of extending honorable and fair treatment even to vanquished enemies. Later in life, he obtained Alexander's cloak and wore it while celebrating a triumph in Rome,[10] and he minted coins[11] that symbolically associated him with Alexander.

After serving his father during the Social War, which ended in 88 B.C., Pompey visited Rome where he was prosecuted for misappropriating Italian plunder. Coincidentally, the judge who tried the case had a daughter of marriageable age. Upon agreeing to marry the judge's daughter, Pompey won acquittal in the trial.

---

[8]Romans considered the woodpecker and the wolf as sacred to Mars, the God of War.
[9]See *The Life of Pompey* 1.3–2.2 and 46.1 by Plutarch.
[10]See *The Mithridatic Wars* 12.17 by Appian.
[11]See Figures 17-3 and 17-11.

Figure 16-2. Discovery of Romulus and Remus by Faustulus near Tiber River. Rome, Sextus Pompeius Faustulus, AR Denarius, ca. 137 B.C.

Pompey's father died, either from disease or a lightning strike,[12] during the siege of Rome by Gaius Marius in 87 B.C. At the age of nineteen, Pompey inherited his father's wealth, estates, military reputation, and authority in Picenum. In 83 B.C., when Sulla returned to Italy after concluding the First Mithridatic War, Pompey raised three Picenean legions and marched to the aid of the Optimate general.

Sulla's Treatment of Pompey. Sulla welcomed support from a general who commanded sufficient wealth and reputation to raise three legions at the age of twenty-three. However, Sulla also recognized the long-term threat posed by such a talented young man. Sulla pandered to Pompey's ego by calling him *Imperator* (a term for a military commander whose successes warranted public recognition) and tried to cement an alliance by offering his daughter in marriage. Pompey accepted, but Pompey had to divorce his wife and Sulla's pregnant daughter had to divorce her husband before the marriage could take place. After the marriage, Sulla granted the precocious young general's request for greater responsibilities: Sulla sent Pompey far away from Rome to fight rebel Populares in Sicily and in Africa Province.

---

[12]See *Civil Wars* 1.9.80 by Appian.

Pompey defeated the Populares in Sicily in 82 B.C. and in Africa in 81 B.C. When he returned to Rome he demanded that Sulla, the dictator, grant him a triumphal procession through Rome. Respect for Pompey's talent didn't prevent Sulla from having fun at Pompey's expense. At first, Sulla refused: A private citizen didn't deserve a triumph by defeating other Roman citizens. Then Sulla granted the request for a triumph and encouraged Pompey to make it as grand and spectacular as possible.

Sulla scheduled three triumphs on the same day—first came Sulla's, then another general's, and then Pompey's. When the time finally arrived for Pompey to march, he discovered that the grandest parts of his procession wouldn't fit through Rome's triumphal arch. Citizens who had cheered the first two triumphs found comic relief in the third as Pompey frantically attempted to reconfigure his procession. Taking keen delight in using Pompey's own ego against him, Sulla jokingly referred to the young prodigy as "Pompey the Great," and the name stuck. Regardless, even though Pompey seemed to crave adulation too much, he served for decades as Rome's greatest general.

Julius Caesar: The Embodiment of Brilliance and Daring

Born in mid-July of 100 B.C. into the Julian family, Gaius Julius Caesar[13] grew up in a working-class neighborhood of Rome. The Julian family, one of the noblest Roman families, descended directly from Iulus, the son of Aeneas, which made Iulus the grandson of Anchises (a Trojan prince) and an Anatolian goddess that Rome identified as Venus. During the war with Hannibal, Rome learned other appellations of the Anatolian goddess, like Cybele and the Pessinian Mother.[14]

Little information about the childhood of Julius Caesar has survived, but many people thought well of the young man. A Gaul educated in Alexandria tutored Julius Caesar during his early years, and one can see the quality of both student and teacher in Julius Caesar's writings. To the extent that Caesar studied Homer, history, and mythology, he learned about relatives of the Julian family: For example, King Priam

---

[13]Julius Caesar was the fourth member of the Julii Caesares to be named Gaius Julius Caesar. His father, grandfather, and great-grandfather all had the same name.
[14]See Chapter 12.

of Troy, Alexander the Great, and Herakles all connected with the mythical genealogy of the Julian family. To the extent that Julius Caesar associated with his famous uncle, Gaius Marius, he learned about leadership, battlefield tactics, military strategy, and planning.

From 87–86 B.C., the Julian family suffered at the hands of both Optimates and Populares. Close friends with Gaius Marius' wife, the immediate family of Julius survived purges by both Optimates and Populares. However, in 87 B.C., just a few years before the terrible seventh consulship of Gaius Marius, Populares killed Lucius Julius Caesar, Julius Caesar's distant relative who had served as consul in 90 B.C.

When Julius Caesar was fifteen years old, in 85 B.C., his father died one morning while dressing himself for the day. Gaius Marius took an interest in the family's welfare and arranged marriage and a career for Julius Caesar beginning the very next year. Julius Caesar married Cornelia, the ten-year-old daughter of the consul Cinna, and entered the priesthood as high priest of Capitoline Jupiter,[15] normally a life-long position. Cornelia bore a daughter (Julia) to Julius Caesar in 82 B.C.

Antagonistic toward everything accomplished during the period that Populares controlled Rome, Sulla confiscated the wealth of Julius Caesar in 81 B.C., terminated his appointment as high priest of Capitoline Jupiter, and ordered him to divorce Cinna's daughter. Julius Caesar obeyed in every way, except he refused to divorce Cinna's daughter. Sulla declared that he saw "many Mariuses" in the young man and ordered his execution. However, after Vestal Virgins and numerous Optimates pleaded for mercy, Sulla reluctantly canceled the execution.[16] Aware that the dictator might easily change his mind, Julius Caesar left his young wife in the care of his mother and fled the Italian peninsula toward Anatolia.

Winning the Civic Crown. As the Second Mithridatic War wound down, nineteen-year-old Julius Caesar joined the Roman army in Asia Province. Far from Rome, he lived the adventurous military life that he craved, a way of life forbidden to a high priest of Capitoline Jupiter.

---

[15]The grandest and most important temple on the Capitoline Hill, the high defensible heart of the ancient city, honored Jupiter, King of the Gods.
[16]See *The Life of Julius Caesar* 1.3–7 by Plutarch and *The Life of Julius Caesar* 1.2–3 by Suetonius.

By the end of the war in 81 B.C., he served on the staff of Rome's Governor of Asia Province.

After the Second Mithridatic War ended, fighting continued in Asia Province. Certain islands off the coast of Asia Province (for example, Lesbos) asserted their independence from Rome, and the Roman army needed ships to reach them. The Governor of Asia Province sent young Julius Caesar to the court of King Nicomedes IV in Bithynia to negotiate the use of ships from the king's fleet. Julius Caesar took so long accomplishing his mission that jealous soldiers invented ribald stories that described causes for the delay.

The stories didn't describe the difficulties a young soldier might encounter negotiating with an old king, nor did they include the details of preparing a fleet of ships for war. Instead, the stories described young Caesar languishing in the Bithynian court as a lover of Nicomedes IV. From time to time throughout Julius Caesar's life, opponents defamed him by claiming that he serviced King Nicomedes as Ganymede serviced Zeus.[17] During triumphs, legions commonly sang insults about their triumphal general as a way to avert the evil eye and remind the general of his mortality. During Caesar's triumphal celebrations, his victorious legions sang that he once played queen to a foreign king.[18]

While in Bithynia, Julius Caesar encountered money like the tetradrachm in Figure 16-3. The obverse of Nicomedes IV's tetradrachms portrayed a bust of Nicomedes' immensely popular grandfather, Nicomedes II, the first Bithynian king to form an alliance with Rome. The reverse of the coin displays images of Zeus and an eagle. Text on the coin proclaims a revelation of the divinity of King Nicomedes, a common conceit of Hellenistic kings in the East.

After returning to Asia Province with Bithynian ships, Julius Caesar participated in the siege of Mytilene on Lesbos in 80 B.C. He fought courageously and well, winning the Civic Crown, an award equivalent to the Medal of Honor today. This achievement greatly enhanced his

---

[17]As mentioned in Chapter 4, Ganymede replaced Hebe (Goddess of Youth) as the cupbearer of Zeus and also served as Zeus' catamite.

[18]Among many parallels with Julius Caesar, allegations of homosexual behavior also surfaced about Jesus from followers of Carpocrates of Alexandria in the second century A.D., apparently based on the controversial text known as *Secret Mark*.

Figure 16-3. Bust of Nicomedes II, and Zeus with Eagle. Bithynia, Nicomedes IV, AR Tetradrachm, 94–74 B.C.

political prospects in Rome.[19] After leftover hostilities from the Second Mithridatic War ended, Julius Caesar's commander again posted the twenty-year-old hero to the court of Nicomedes IV in Bithynia, this time to serve as an ambassador. There, Julius Caesar learned details about Anatolian politics and the activities of Mithradates VI of Pontus, the dangerous neighbor of Bithynia.

Exhibiting Uncommon Nerve. After he learned of Sulla's death in 78 B.C., Julius Caesar returned to Rome at the age of twenty-two. His sixteen-year-old wife, Cornelia, took care of their four-year-old daughter, Julia. Julius Caesar earned a living for his family as a lawyer, particularly as a prosecutor of notoriously wealthy and corrupt governors of foreign provinces. He quickly acquired fame for his eloquent speeches and populist stands.

Ambitious and striving to hone his political skills, Julius Caesar left Rome in 75 B.C. to study rhetoric on the island of Rhodes; but

---

[19]Sulla's constitutional reforms gave winners of the Civic Crown the right to enter the Senate and sit among the senators. The reforms also required that winners of the crown wear it to public meetings. Participants in the meetings were required to rise to honor men who had won the award.

pirates captured him on the way and held him for ransom. When the pirates told him how much ransom they intended to ask, he laughed and declared that his worth was far greater than that. He insisted that the pirates increase the ransom demand.

While he waited for the ransom to be paid, Julius Caesar made friends with his captors. He amused them by promising that, after they received the ransom and freed him, he would capture and crucify them all. True to his word, after the pirates released him, Julius Caesar organized a small naval force. He located the pirates, defeated them in battle, and crucified all the survivors.

A TUMULTUOUS PERIOD OF TOO MANY WARS

In the decade after Sulla's death, war threatened Rome in the West, East, and even in the heart of Rome itself. Aware that Sulla's reconfigured Rome was unlikely to grant them amnesty, rebel Populares gathered in Spain to cast their lot with a rebel general named Sertorius. Other Mediterranean wars also developed: Mithradates VI launched the Third Mithridatic War, slaves rebelled in Rome bringing about the Third Servile War, and Cilician pirates harassed Roman shipping and coastal towns throughout the Mediterranean Sea.

Minted in 75 B.C., the coin in Figure 16-4 served as a recruiting tool for Rome during an age of too many distant wars. The obverse of the coin portrays a crowned personification of Liberty facing right. The reverse portrays Mars, the God of War, inviting a citizen to climb aboard a war chariot.

The Sertorian War

After Sulla died in 78 B.C., the conflict between Populares and Optimates continued in distant Spain.[20] There, General Sertorius, a former colleague of Gaius Marius, threatened to establish his own empire. The

---

[20]The two consuls of 78 B.C., Marcus Aemilius Lepidus and Quintus Lutatius Catalus, also fought in Italy in 77 B.C. Lepidus wanted to nullify Sulla's reforms, but Catalus preserved them by defeating Lepidus. In Cisalpine Gaul, Pompey defeated and executed Marcus Junius Brutus (the father of Julius Caesar's assassin), an ally of Lepidus.

Figure 16-4. Liberty, and Mars Helping a Roman Citizen Mount a War Chariot. Rome, L. Farsuleius Mensor, AR Denarius, ca. 75 B.C.

Senate asked Pompey to help put down the rebellion, but he refused unless the Senate granted him proconsular imperium.[21] Proconsular *imperium* would give Pompey, a young man in his twenties, command authority equal to that of the former consul who served as the provincial governor of Further Spain. Refusing for years to accommodate the demand of the young general, the Senate finally granted him extraordinary imperium only when the loss of Spain seemed imminent.

After he obtained the authority that he wanted from the Senate, Pompey happily marched his legions to Spain in 77 B.C. Once there, however, he discovered that he had underestimated his opponent. Pompey's fresh legions helped greatly, especially in battles against allies of the rebel general, but Pompey achieved only a stalemate against forces commanded directly by Sertorius. Pompey learned hard lessons about the difficulty of confronting guerilla warfare and about the creative application of battlefield tactics by a rebel general who had mastered his craft under Gaius Marius. Pompey made little progress against the rebels in Spain until 72 B.C., and then only after a traitor in the rebel camp assassinated Sertorius.

After the death of Sertorius, Pompey succeeded in defeating the rebel army by luring it into an ambush. It was during the rebuilding

---

[21]Different levels of office along the cursus honorum gave different levels of imperium, the power to command. Pompey wanted equality with the proconsul of Spain.

of Rome's administrative infrastructure in Spain that Pompey's true genius emerged: He possessed extraordinary talent for organization, administration, and generation of policies that worked for governors as well as for the governed. He reorganized Rome's Spanish provinces to serve Rome's Spanish subjects efficiently and fairly while operating profitably and transparently for Rome. He granted citizenship to many supporters of Rome and expelled die-hard rebels from Spain to southwestern Gaul.

The Beginning of the Third Mithridatic War

While learning rhetoric in the East, Julius Caesar found opportunities to develop other skills as well. In 74 B.C., King Nicomedes IV of Bithynia, Rome's most important ally in Anatolia, died and willed his kingdom to Rome. In the neighboring kingdom of Pontus, Mithradates VI chose this moment to invade Bithynia, which began the Third Mithridatic War. The widespread slaughter that initiated the First Mithridatic War had occurred only fourteen years earlier. Far from Rome and possessing few regular military resources, Romans in Asia Province feared for their lives. Julius Caesar leaped at the opportunity to raise and lead an army in Asia Province.

As Winter approached, he organized and trained a provincial militia. Leading his army of hastily trained volunteers, Julius Caesar confronted an army allied with Mithradates VI and drove it out of Asia Province, which delayed Mithradates from campaigning in Asia Province until the Spring of 73 B.C. The delay saved many Roman lives and provided time for the Senate to assign responsibility for the war to Lucius Licinius Lucullus,[22] Rome's best available military commander, and for Lucullus to assemble and transport sufficient men and resources to Roman Asia to prosecute the war.

Julius Caesar joined the staff of the praetor, Marcus Antonius,[23] and served briefly in a campaign against Cilician pirates along the Anatolian

---

[22]Lucullus served under Sulla during the First Mithridatic War. See Chapter 15.
[23]A relative of Julius Caesar, Marcus Antonius was the father of Marc Antony, Julius Caesar's future lieutenant. See Chapter 17.

coast. However, Caesar soon learned that the College of Pontifices in Rome had chosen him to fill a position as pontifex vacated by the death of his mother's cousin.[24] Selection as a pontifex enticed Julius Caesar to return to Rome and enter politics.

Once in Anatolia, Lucullus fought brilliantly for years. Carefully and effectively he led his vastly outnumbered army against Mithradates' massive war machine, disassembling it one piece at a time. Without assistance from Rome, Lucullus made steady progress against the forces of Pontus for six long years.

The Third Servile War

While Rome's most accomplished generals were fighting wars in Spain and Anatolia, twenty-seven-year-old Julius Caesar returned to Rome in 73 B.C. Shortly afterward, a Thracian gladiatorial slave named Spartacus and approximately seventy gladiators like him escaped from a training facility in Capua. They quickly gathered more slaves and sparked a rebellion remembered as the Third Servile War.

A worshipper of the god Sabazius, Spartacus led fellow Thracians as well as slaves from other parts of the Mediterranean in an effective military campaign against Rome. His forces grew from seventy escaped gladiators to approximately 120,000 liberated slaves—men, women, and children—who plundered towns up and down the full length of Italy. Reminiscent of the days of Hannibal, Spartacus' army repeatedly defeated Roman forces led by arrogant and incompetent generals.

Sabazius (the Thracian god equivalent to Dionysos and Bacchus) guided Spartacus by speaking through a prophetess in his camp. The Thracian coin in Figure 16-5 portrays Sabazius on the reverse. Like Dionysos, Sabazius holds grapes in his right hand and a *thyrsus* (a staff of fennel, grapevines, and a pine cone used in initiation ceremonies) in his left; a panther crouches at his feet. The worship of Sabazius often connected to the worship of other gods, particularly Zeus, Dionysos,

---

[24]Julius Caesar took the pontifex position vacated by the death of Gaius Aurelia Cotta, a relative who had served as consul in 75 B.C. See Chapter 15 for a description of Roman priestly offices.

Figure 16-5. Portrait of Mên (Thracian God of the Moon), and Sabazius Holding Grapes and Thyrsus. Thrace, Pantikapaion, ca. Second to First Century B.C. Also, Hand of Sabazius from the Vatican Collection.

Bacchus, Attis, Mên, Mithras, and even Yahweh, God of the Jews.[25] On the obverse of the coin, the moon god Mên wears a conical cap of stars next to a crescent and star. To the right of the coin, a Roman "Hand of Sabazius" symbolizes the god's role as a creator of life. With the hand, positioned in the ancient Sabazian gesture of blessing (a gesture still used by the Catholic Church), humans, plants, and animals magically emerge from the wrist, palm, thumb, and fingers. Thracian worshippers also portrayed Sabazius on horseback battling a divine serpent, reminiscent of images of Saint George and the Dragon.[26]

The wealthy Optimate businessman, Marcus Licinius Crassus, craved military glory and repeatedly asked the Senate for authority to prosecute the war against the slave rebellion of Spartacus. As it had done with Pompey, the Senate refused Crassus until no other viable option remained. When the Senate finally granted him command

---

[25] See the *Nine Books of Memorable Deeds and Sayings* 1.3.2 by Valerius Maximus, and *Symposiacs* 4.6 by Plutarch. Although scholars dispute Roman associations of Yahweh with Typhon and Sabazius, numismatic depictions of Jupiter Sabazius in Syria and of Typhon in Samaria lend credence to the assertions of ancient historians.

[26] Other mythic iconography—Perseus and Ketos, and Bellerophon and the Chimaera— also prefigured Saint George and the Dragon. A hero on horseback killing a monster was a common icon in cults throughout the West.

responsibility in 72 B.C., Marcus Licinius Crassus launched the methodical campaign that eventually crushed the rebellion.

Coincidentally, Julius Caesar won election to the post of military tribune[27] in 72 B.C. Although no record survives about his participation in the Third Servile War, it's difficult to imagine him standing idly by when he could have served on the staff of Marcus Licinius Crassus. In Rome, the war against Spartacus surpassed all other military considerations.

By the end of 71 B.C., Crassus had forced the army of Spartacus into an untenable position in the toe of Italy. Word reached Rome that Pompey was returning triumphantly from Spain, so the Senate sent him orders to march south and help Crassus. Fearful that Pompey would steal credit for defeating Spartacus, Crassus successfully forced a decisive battle with the slave army.[28] His legions killed most of Spartacus' forces and captured many as well. Crassus returned the captured women and children to slavery, but he made an example of the men: To discourage future slave rebellions, he crucified six thousand men on wooden crosses along the Appian Way between Rome and Capua.

Approaching Rome as Crassus crushed the last resistance from Spartacus' army, Pompey encountered five thousand former slaves fleeing north to escape the slaughter. Pompey captured these runaway slaves and executed them without fanfare. He then sent a letter to the Senate claiming that he had ended the slave rebellion.

Although the wars fought by both men were over, Pompey and Crassus refused to disband their armies. Nervous Romans elected both men as consuls of Rome. The Senate rewarded Crassus for his hard campaign against Spartacus with a simple ovation in the privacy of the Senate chamber. In contrast, on December 31, 71 B.C., all Rome celebrated Pompey's triumph for his Spanish victories. The public honored Pompey for his foreign victories as well as for saving Rome from Spartacus. For a long time, Crassus hated Pompey for stealing credit and winning public acclaim.[29]

---

[27] High ranking officers, most military tribunes in a legion won their position by election.
[28] See *The Life of Crassus* 11.2 by Plutarch and *Civil Wars* 1.119 by Appian.
[29] See *The Life of Crassus* 11–12 by Plutarch.

A DECADE OF STRUGGLE AND MAKING NEW CONNECTIONS

Although Sulla had shaped Rome as a monument to Optimate power, the political pendulum soon began to swing the other way. Pompey and Crassus were both Optimates but they cooperated poorly as consuls. Also, they both craved popularity and good reputation, each especially at the expense of the other. In a political climate characterized by the inability of Optimates to get anything done, spokesmen for Populares began to enjoy increased popularity, the currency so ardently desired by Crassus and Pompey. Crassus tried to buy popularity by providing a great feast and a free three-month's supply of grain to citizens.[30] However, Pompey found more political ways to pander to the common majority of Rome. Breaking from his aristocratic background, Pompey allied with Populares to increase the power of Rome's lower classes: He weakened Sulla's laws and restored power to the Tribunate of the Plebs.[31] As Pompey continued to search for new ways to win glory and popularity, Crassus returned his focus toward making money.

Julius Caesar acquired a reputation for caring about common people and for fighting corruption: He continued to prosecute former governors who had used their authority in foreign lands for personal gain. In addition, as a young priest with substantial experience in the East, he took steps to restore tolerance of the Cult of Dionysos/Bacchus in Rome. Archaeological evidence supports history in that the number of Roman artifacts related to the Mysteries of Bacchus suddenly increased beginning around 70 B.C.[32]

Orienting Julius Caesar toward Populares Causes

Julius Caesar reentered politics in 69 B.C. and won election to the office of quaestor (in this case, a judicial magistrate) posted in Further Spain. Just before he left for Spain, two important family members died: his aged Aunt Julia (the widow of Gaius Marius) and his

---
[30]See *The Life of Crassus* 12.2 by Plutarch.
[31]See *The Life of Pompey* 22.3–6 by Plutarch.
[32]See *The Cults of the Roman Empire* pp. 306–7 by Robert Turcan.

young wife, Cornelia. Julius Caesar delivered public funeral orations for both women. For his aged Aunt Julia, he spoke of her ancestors, both kings and gods, and he included effigies of Gaius Marius and his son, Publius, in her funeral procession. Some supporters of Sulla complained, but supporters of Marius shouted them down, grateful that Julius Caesar had resurrected the honor of heroic Populares. Regarding Cornelia, the act of honoring a young woman with a funeral oration defied convention but earned popular respect for Julius Caesar for being tender-hearted.[33]

During his service as quaestor for Rome's governor of Further Spain in the circuit court of Gades (Cadiz), Julius Caesar visited a local Temple of Herakles/Melqart, famous for producing oracular dreams. While gazing at a statue of Alexander the Great in this temple, Julius Caesar suddenly realized that he had accomplished nothing, while, by the age of thirty-one, Alexander already had conquered the world. That night, Julius Caesar slept in the temple and dreamed that he had raped his mother. Temple staff interpreted his dream to mean that he, too, would conquer the world.[34]

Ancient Cadiz was located in a region known as the land of the Gadarenes in ancient times. Figure 16-6 portrays a coin of ancient Gadir, which helps provide an impression of the statue that moved Julius Caesar to take charge of his life. The obverse of the coin portrays Herakles/Melqart in a portrait style reminiscent of numismatic images of Alexander the Great. (For example, see Figure 9-9.) The reverse portrays a Punic legend and two fish on either side of a crescent and star symbol.

Toward the end of 68 B.C., Julius Caesar decided to leave Spain and aggressively pursue his ambitions: military success, wealth, and fame. He obtained a discharge and immediately headed for Rome. On his way, he met with leaders of Cisalpine Gaul and listened to their complaints about supporting Rome without enjoying the benefits of Roman citizenship. He expressed sympathy and soon attracted the

---

[33] See *The Life of Julius Caesar* 5.1–5 by Plutarch. Around this time in Alexandria, Egyptians learned of the birth of a daughter to their ruler, Ptolemy XII. Named Cleopatra VII, this daughter became the queen who bore Julius Caesar's only known natural son.
[34] See *The Life of Julius Caesar* 7.1–2 by Suetonius.

Figure 16-6. Herakles/Melqart Wearing Lion Skin Headdress, and Fishes with Crescent and Pellet. Spain, Gadir (Gades), AE 26, Second Century B.C.

attention of government officials. Concerned that the meetings would precipitate a rebellion, the Roman governor of Cisalpine Gaul charged Julius Caesar with treason but failed to convict him.

Galvanizing Pompey against the Cilician Pirates

In the East, Lucullus continued to make slow and steady progress against the land armies of Pontus in the Third Mithridatic War. However, as semi-independent allies of Mithradates VI, Cilician pirates operated with relative impunity throughout the Mediterranean Sea. More than merely ocean-going thieves, the pirates comprised Cilician nobility and regular naval forces that attacked anyone allied with Rome. Cilician pirates attacked Roman ships, raided coastal cities of Italy, and even interrupted the international slave trade by sacking the island of Delos.

In 68 B.C., Cilician pirates directly challenged the security of Rome by attacking Ostia, Rome's port city. They plundered and burned the city, they stole Roman grain, and they murdered and kidnapped Roman citizens. Continuing to attack Roman ships and cities, the pirates even raised the specter of hunger by interrupting the flow of agricultural products from Sicily to Rome.

In Rome, Julius Caesar had worked assiduously to acquire renown and obtain political office. He championed popular causes in the Senate and married advantageously to Pompeia Sulla (the granddaughter of Sulla, the dictator) in 67 B.C. In 66 B.C., he volunteered to work as curator for the Appian Way.[35]

To deal with the pirates, Pompey requested authority over the entire Mediterranean Sea and fifty miles inland from every coast. Roman aristocracy generally opposed the granting of such unprecedented authority. However, Pompey's friend, Aulus Gabinius, won election to the Tribunate of the Plebs and succeeded in passing a law known as *Lex Gabinia*, which gave Pompey the authority he had requested to fight the Cilician pirates. Having once been abducted by pirates, Senator Julius Caesar successfully rallied senatorial support for Pompey, who got everything that he wanted.

At the peak of his abilities in 68 B.C., Pompey spent months planning and preparing his campaign against the pirates. He then took only forty days to sweep the pirates from the Mediterranean Sea, from the Pillars of Herakles in the West to the pirates' Anatolian stronghold in the East. After chasing the pirates to their homes, he offered generous terms to persuade them to surrender, which prevented a long war of attrition along the Cilician coast.

Pompey's Vanity and Opening Rome to the Cult of Mithras

Because Alexander the Great founded many Alexandrias, Pompey wanted to found at least one city named after himself. In 66 B.C., he forcibly relocated Cilician pirate communities to the vacant site of an ancient city destroyed a decade or so earlier by the Armenian King, Tigranes II. On the ruins, Pompey built a new city named Pompeiopolis. Minted in Pompeiopolis, the bronze coin in Figure 16-7 displays a bust of Pompey on the obverse and Nike holding a victory wreath on the reverse.

By organizing Roman Cilicia and founding Pompeiopolis, Pompey established a place where ideas and practices from Judaism, Hellenistic

---

[35]Responsibility for the Appian Way gave Julius Caesar engineering experience.

Figure 16-7. Pompey, and Nike Holding Palm and Presenting Victory Wreath. Cilicia, Soli-Pompeiopolis, AE 20, ca. 66–27 B.C.

Mithraism,[36] and other pagan cults could mix and influence Roman citizens. Located between the Cilician Gates and Pompeiopolis, nearby Tarsos had long possessed a rich tradition of philosophical inquiry and a large multicultural community of Jews.[37] Pompey built a Roman road through the Cilician Gates, established Tarsos as the capital of Roman Cilicia, and assigned leaders of the Cilician pirates as provincial administrators. For example, the Cilician pirate Tarkondimotos[38] helped Rome rule Cilicia for more than thirty years. A heavy flow of travelers, trade goods, and ideas passed between the Cilician Gates in the North and Anatolian ports like Pompeiopolis in the South, and they all mixed freely in Tarsos.

Bearing a portrait of Tarkondimotos, the coin in Figure 16-8 preserves the features of a pre-Christian worshipper of the Hellenistic Cult of Mithras. In combination with historical testimony that Cilician

---

[36] The use of Mithraic philosophical and religious terminology in the *New Testament* (particularly in the letters of Paul and the gospel of *Mark*) underscores the influence of Hellenistic Mithraism on Christianity. For example, in *2 Corinthians* 12:1–4, Paul referred to multiple heavens.

[37] Archaeological evidence has been found for both Samaritan and Jerusalem Cult Jews in Tarsos. See "How to Tell a Samaritan Synagogue from a Jewish Synagogue" by Reinhard Pummer, *Biblical Archaeology Review*, May/Jun 1998, pp. 24–35.

[38] The Roman triumvir, Marc Antony, appointed Tarkondimotos as King of Cilicia in 39 B.C.

Figure 16-8. King Tarkondimotos of Eastern Cilicia (a Former Cilician Pirate), and Zeus Holding Nike, AE 22, ca. 39–31 B.C.

pirates worshipped Mithras,[39] the coin provides evidence of a pre-Christian time and place where Roman provincial military personnel encountered the Hellenistic Cult of Mithras. Nevertheless, because Mithraism and Christianity shared many important features, some scholars question that Hellenistic Mithraism existed before the end of the first century A.D.[40]

However, even though Hellenistic Mithraism did not enter the historical record until 66 B.C., widespread use of Mithraic iconography on Hellenistic coins minted before the birth of Jesus proves the antiquity and influence of the cult. There is little reason to doubt that Mithradates VI, the sixth Hellenistic ruler of Pontus to be named after Mithras, was familiar with syncretic Hellenistic ideas about Mithras. The coinage of Mithradates VI often employed mythological symbols related to the Hellenistic Cult of Mithras. The obverse of the coin in Figure 16-9 displays a diademed bust of Mithradates VI facing right. The reverse uses symbols related to his ancestor, the Greek hero

---

[39]See Chapter 13.
[40]The issue is important because proof that Hellenistic Mithraism existed at least a century before Christianity begs an important question concerning the origins of Christian ideas and practices: How much of Christianity comes from Galilean Jews like Yochanan HaMatbil (John the Baptist) and Yeshua bar Yosef (Jesus, son of Joseph), and how much comes from Hellenistic cults?

Figure 16-9. Mithradates VI, and Royal Symbols (Crescent and Star, and Pegasus) Related to Perseus. Pontus, Mithradates VI, AR Tetradrachm, 120–63 B.C.

Perseus: A crescent and star represents the act of cutting off Medusa's head with a curved harpé and Pegasus grazes nearby, having emerged from Medusa's neck after she died.

Numismatics reveals that several Hellenistic kingdoms interpreted Mithras along Hellenistic lines: For example, while Pompey settled the East, the last remnant of a Hellenistic Greek kingdom located near the modern borders of Afghanistan, Pakistan, and northern India used coins like the one in Figure 16-10. The obverse of the coin portrays a supreme deity that possesses attributes of both Zeus and Mithras, which shows that the last members of Alexander's Eastern empire conflated Zeus and Mithras just as Saint Paul conflated Zeus and the Christian god. Adherents of the Christian god and Mithras both compared their deities with Zeus, and newly converted pagans brought their favorite beliefs, practices, and iconography into Christianity from classical Greek mythology and from Eastern cults like Mithraism.[41]

By chance, the city of Pompeiopolis rested on the foundations of the old city of Soli. The site was available when Pompey needed a place

---

[41]Chapter 25 provides examples of artifacts showing the use of pagan iconography in early Christianity.

Figure 16-10. Hellenistic Deity That Combined Attributes of Both Zeus and Mithras. Baktria, Indo-Greek Kingdom, Hermaios. AE Unit, ca. 90–70 B.C.

to settle Cilician pirates because Tigranes the Great had destroyed Soli in his campaign to build an Armenian Empire. The religious importance of this region can be seen in the words of a famous Stoic poet of Soli. In the third century B.C., Aratus of Soli wrote a pagan prayer in his most famous work, *Phaenomena*.[42] As famous in Hellenistic lands during the time of Pompey the Great as the *Lord's Prayer* is among modern Christians, the prayer, called the *Invocation of Zeus*, is the only pagan prayer quoted in the *New Testament*.[43]

Pompey's Winning of the Third Mithridatic War

By 66 B.C., the outnumbered Roman army in Anatolia had campaigned against Mithradates VI for six long years. During that time, Lucullus destroyed most of the fortified cities of Pontus and decimated the combined armies of Mithradates VI and Tigranes II. Still, his legions were

---

[42]Hipparchus, the discoverer of the precession of the equinoxes, wrote about the *Phaenomena* in his *Commentary on the Phaenomena of Eudoxus and Aratus*, the only work of Hipparchus that has survived to modern times.
[43]See *Acts* 17:28. In his speech before the Council of the Areopagus in Athens, Saint Paul quoted the *Invocation of Zeus* as he spoke of the Christian god, saying "We are all his children." Saint Paul implied that parts of the prayer were acceptable as Christian prayer and that Athenians should think of the Christian god as they thought of Zeus.

tired of long marches, endless campaigning, and countless hard-fought battles. Even though Mithradates VI stood at the brink of defeat, the Roman soldiers wanted only to go home.

At the same time, having just made his name a common household word on every shore of the Mediterranean Sea, Pompey had a large force in Southern Anatolia. While Pompey organized Rome's administration of former pirate domains, Julius Caesar urged the Senate to extend Pompey's mandate to winning the Third Mithridatic War. The Tribunate of the Plebs[44] passed a law that transferred responsibility for the war from Lucullus to Pompey. When the news reached Anatolia, much of Lucullus' hard work was undone as previously pacified territories reentered the war pledging new allegiance to Mithradates VI. Regardless, Pompey faced a worn-down and greatly reduced foe.

Pompey marched his army north and annihilated the remaining army of Pontus. Mithradates VI fled to Armenia for refuge, but Tigranes II withdrew support from Mithradates and sought peace with Pompey. Tigranes II expelled Mithradates VI from Armenia and allowed Pompey to march unopposed to Tigranocerta, the Armenian capital. Magnanimously accepting Armenia's complete surrender in 65 B.C., Pompey allowed Tigranes II to continue ruling his country, but only as far as its original borders. Pompey annexed the more desirable southern and western portions of Tigranes' empire as Roman territory.

Pompey continued to pursue Mithradates VI toward the Caucasus Mountains as far as the Fasis River (also known as the Fax or Rioni River). Strong resistance from local armies in Georgia eventually convinced Pompey to abandon pursuit and return west for more rewarding activities. Unknown to Pompey, Mithradates VI hid, terrified, in the nearby Caucasus Mountains. Fearful of imminent capture and completely abandoning hope, he soon committed suicide.

Julius Caesar's Ambitious Push into Politics

In 65 B.C., Julius Caesar obtained an opportunity to make himself known throughout Rome in a big way. He won an election for the post of curule aedile with responsibility for staging important public games:

---

[44]See Chapters 14 and 15 for information about the Tribunate of the Plebs.

April games honoring Cybele and September games honoring Capitoline Jupiter.[45] In this capacity, Julius Caesar borrowed huge sums of money to stage games more lavish than any previous Roman games.

In 64 B.C., he became a judicial officer in the criminal courts, and in 63 B.C., he borrowed more money to win election to the office of Pontifex Maximus, a life-long position. As Pontifex Maximus, the head of the College of Pontifices in Rome, he stayed permanently in the public eye no matter what else he did and no matter where else he served. Further, Julius Caesar and his family moved into the official residence of the Pontifex Maximus in the Forum in the heart of ancient Rome. Around this time he learned of the birth of his grandnephew, Octavian, the son of his sister's daughter.

Julius Caesar's Brush with Scandals in Rome

History associates the two biggest scandals during this period with a man named Catiline.[46] In 65 B.C., the first scandal[47] involved a vague plot to seize the consulship after murdering new senators on Election Day. Surviving descriptions of the plot—mostly contradictory rumors and accusations—provide few details that connect it with Catiline. Crassus persuaded the Senate to drop its inquiry into the matter, and, in 64 B.C., Julius Caesar's court accepted an accusation of murder against Catiline but acquitted him.

In 62 B.C., Julius Caesar won election as praetor, occupying the post when the second "Catiline Conspiracy" erupted in Rome. The political climate in Rome resembled the period of Sulla's absence during the First Mithridatic War: While Pompey was ending the Third Mithridatic War in the East, political discontent was growing in Etruria and Transalpine (Narbonese) Gaul. For a long time, foreign cults had woven inseparably into the fabric of everyday life in Rome, and politicians had

---

[45]Rome dedicated temples on the Capitoline Hill to Jupiter, Juno, and Minerva, who were referred to collectively as the *Capitoline Triad*.

[46]Lucius Sergius Catilina was a patrician whose tarnished reputation prevented him from winning a consulship. He was accused of committing adultery with a Vestal Virgin in 73 B.C., of abusing power during his governorship of Africa in 66 B.C., and of murder in 64 B.C., but he was never convicted of any of these crimes. He sought revenge by leading a rebellion against Rome in 62 B.C.

[47]Suetonius accused Julius Caesar and Crassus of originating the plot.

grown accustomed to employing cult-oriented gangs for political purposes, for example, to influence tribal votes or to ensure compliance by key political opponents.

Catiline tried to take political violence to a new level: He attempted to arrange a coup d'état in Rome while simultaneously organizing a rebellion in Etruria. After Cicero[48] revealed the conspiracy, Catiline denied involvement and fled. He then joined an army massing in Etruria and prepared to march on Rome. Cicero organized the speedy capture and execution of conspirators in Rome, news of which caused most of the rebel army in Etruria to desert. However, when Rome sent forces to put down the rebellion, approximately three thousand rebels fought to the last man. Catiline's participation in the rebellion against Rome in 62 B.C. caused Cicero to accuse him of involvement in the earlier plot as well.

Also in 62 B.C., a more personal scandal visited Julius Caesar's residence, the house of the Pontifex Maximus. During a celebration of the Mysteries of Bona Dea (Rome's virgin Goddess of Fertility and Healing), mysteries celebrated only by women, Caesar's mother discovered that Publius Clodius Pulcher (soon to acquire notoriety as a gang lord) had desecrated the mysteries by dressing as a woman and sneaking into the house of the Pontifex Maximus. Rumors spread that Publius Clodius had intended to pursue an affair with Pompeia Sulla. Proclaiming that his wife must be above suspicion, Julius Caesar divorced her.

Pompey's Expansion of Roman Control over the East

Without learning the fate of Mithradates VI, Pompey returned to Pontus in 64 B.C. and reorganized the country as a Roman province. Then he marched south into Syria. More ambitious than Lucullus, Pompey used his mandate, not just to end the war with Mithradates, but also to annex and organize the Levant under Roman administration. Pompey deposed Antiochus XIII[49] and declared Syria a Roman province.

---

[48]Marcus Tullius Cicero was a highly respected Roman statesman, philosopher, and orator who served as consul in 63 B.C.
[49]In 69 B.C., Lucullus restored Antiochus XIII Asiaticus to the throne of Syria, briefly reviving a last remnant of the Seleukid Empire.

Pompey advanced into Phoenicia, Coele-Syria, and Judea in 63 B.C. While in Judea, he settled a dispute about the rightful King of the Jews. Aristobulus II, the ambitious younger brother of Hyrcanus II,[50] had seized power in Jerusalem and awarded Hyrcanus an empty title in 66 B.C. Hyrcanus II tried to regain power by leading a rebellion, but failed. Both brothers presented their claims for kingship over the Jews to Pompey in Syria. Judging Hyrcanus II to be the weaker and more malleable of the two brothers, Pompey declared him the rightful ruler of the Jews and ordered Aristobulus II to surrender his power.

Aristobulus II pledged to do as Pompey commanded and then hurried to Jerusalem to prepare for war. Angered by Aristobulus' betrayal, Pompey placed Jerusalem under siege.[51] Within three months, he had killed approximately 12,000 residents of Jerusalem, captured the city, and imprisoned Aristobulus.[52]

To ensure that Hyrcanus II ruled only as a puppet of Rome, Pompey terminated the institution of Jewish kingship. He allowed Hyrcanus II to rule as leader of the Jews, but only as long as his rule proved agreeable to Rome. Minted under John Hyrcanus II, the coin in Figure 16-11 proclaims him "High Priest and Leader of the Council of the Jews." The reverse displays a double-cornucopia with a pomegranate between the horns. By ending the institution of Jewish kingship, Pompey focused Judeans on the prospects of anointing their next king, whom they referred to as a *moshiach* or messiah.

Julius Caesar's Acquisition of Spanish and Egyptian Wealth

In 61 B.C., Caesar again won assignment to Further Spain, but this time as proconsul (governor of the province). Having borrowed and spent freely since his election as curule aedile four years earlier, he left Rome well before his term began because he no longer could cover the

---

[50]Members of the Hasmonean dynasty, Hyrcanus II and Aristobulus II fought a war for the throne of Judea three months after Hyrcanus II inherited the throne in 66 B.C. By the time Pompey arrived in Syria, Aristobulus II had successfully retained the kingship of Judea for three years.
[51]During the rebellion in Jerusalem, Pompey learned of the death of Mithradates VI.
[52]Pompey also entered the Holy of Holies in the Jerusalem Temple, the first non-Jew ever to have done so.

Figure 16-11. John Hyrcanus II Described as "High Priest and Leader of the Council of Jews." Judah, Hasmonean Dynasty, 73–40 B.C.

payments on his enormous debts. During his governorship in Spain, however, Julius Caesar led successful and highly profitable military campaigns against independent Spanish tribes. He paid his creditors and acquired so much additional treasure that he and all his soldiers became rich. He even sent more money than expected to the public treasury in Rome. Julius Caesar's conquests in Spain made him so famous and influential that he attracted the attention of Ptolemy XII,[53] an Egyptian ruler who obtained important support from Rome by bribing effective Roman politicians and generals.

An illegitimate son of Ptolemy IX (known as "the Savior,"), Ptolemy XII lived most of his early life in exile in the court of King Mithradates VI of Pontus. The obverse of the Egyptian coin in Figure 16-12 portrays a realistic bust of Ptolemy XII, the father of Cleopatra VII. Text on the coin's reverse proclaims him King and identifies the coin as having been minted in Paphos, Cyprus, around 67 or 66 B.C.; Cleopatra VII was only one year old.

Ptolemy XII assumed the throne of Egypt in 80 B.C. after the death of the last legitimate male claimant of the throne. Known variously by the epithets "New Dionysos," "God Beloved of His Father," "God Beloved of His Brother," "the Flute Player," and "the Bastard," he married his sister according to the custom of Egyptian royalty and

---

[53]In 61 B.C., Ptolemy XII's daughter, Cleopatra VII (Julius Caesar's future consort) was eight years old.

Figure 16-12. Ptolemy XII, and Eagle. Egypt, AR Tetradrachm, 67–66 B.C.

secured his position by bribing influential Romans and maintaining pro-Roman policies. Pompey the Great and Julius Caesar benefitted greatly from bribes by Ptolemy XII, though he never paid all that he owed to Pompey for restoring his throne after his daughter, Berenike IV, expelled her father in 58 B.C.

By the time Ptolemy XII died in 51 B.C., he had acquainted Julius Caesar with Egyptian wealth and provided a legal excuse for him to come to Egypt. Ptolemy XII named Cleopatra VII (then eighteen years old) and her younger brother, Ptolemy XIII, co-regents of Egypt. Hoping to ensure Roman support for his children's rule, Ptolemy XII named the "People of Rome" as executors of his will.

THE BIRTH OF THE FIRST TRIUMVIRATE OF ROME

By the end of 62 B.C., Pompey finished structuring new Roman provinces in the Levant. He had taken care to establish good relations with other Eastern rulers, especially the Parthians who had seized most of the former Seleukid Empire. He returned to Rome in 61 B.C. and celebrated his third triumph on September 29, his forty-fifth birthday. Enjoying tremendous popularity and international renown, he promised distributions of land to his soldiers and then dismissed them in good faith. Having secured immense tax revenue and returning with the captured wealth of many nations, he expected the Senate to confirm his settlements and shower him with honor. However, Pompey found that, despite his success and honorable actions, he had too little political power to ensure the implementation of his commitments.

Pompey had not noticed that the Senate often chose to frustrate men of ability rather than honor them. The Roman Senate declined to confirm Pompey's Eastern settlements and refused to grant the land that Pompey had promised to his soldiers. The Senate also had refused to confirm tax-farming clients for Marcus Licinius Crassus, the richest man in Rome. Together, Pompey and Crassus represented tremendous capital in terms of honor and wealth, but they needed a practical politician to translate their strengths into political accomplishments.

In 60 B.C., forty-year-old Julius Caesar wanted Rome to acknowledge his military successes in Spain with a triumph, and he also wanted to run for election as consul. However, his political enemies passed laws that required him to choose one goal or the other: Either he missed the election and remained outside Rome waiting for approval of his triumph, or he abandoned his triumph and returned to run for consul. Even though it meant abandoning his triumph, Julius Caesar returned to Rome. Perceiving an opportunity to secure unprecedented control of Roman politics, he negotiated a mutually beneficial alliance with Pompey and Crassus—the First Triumvirate[54]—and easily won election as consul in 59 B.C. Pompey, Crassus, and Julius Caesar found just what they needed in each other: Pompey provided international credibility, Crassus provided money, and Caesar provided the political savvy to ensure that all three men achieved their goals in Roman politics. The First Triumvirate endured until 53 B.C.

In 59 B.C., the three triumvirs achieved a great deal. They arranged for Rome's election of Julius Caesar as consul to help further their agenda. Then, under triumviral leadership and influence, the Senate confirmed Crassus' tax farmers, approved Pompey's settlements and land grants, and recognized Ptolemy XII as the rightful ruler of Egypt—after he paid an enormous bribe to Julius Caesar.

---

[54] The Triumvirate had no official status but had immense power in Rome due to the combined influence of Pompey, Crassus, and Julius Caesar.

Chapter 16 | Julius Caesar and the First Triumvirate

Figure 16-13. Saturn with Harpé and Stone, and Victory Crowning Roma on Pile of Shields. Rome, M. Nonius Sufenas, AR Denarius, 59 B.C.

Enormously wealthy and successful, Julius Caesar acquired fame for giving extravagant gifts. For example, he gave an enormous black pearl worth six million sesterces (a year's salary for four thousand people) to Servilia Caepionis, his favorite mistress. Julius Caesar maintained an on-again, off-again relationship with Servilia for many years. During Julius Caesar's consulship, Servilia's son, Marcus Junius Brutus (the future murderer of Julius Caesar) was twenty-five years old.

To cement his relationship with Pompey the Great, Julius Caesar gave his only daughter, Julia, in marriage to the famous general. Julius Caesar also obtained advantageous political connections by marrying Calpurnia Pisonis, a member of a powerful and respected Roman family. Regardless of opposition, he accomplished almost every political goal he chose to pursue. He exercised power in ways that served common Romans, rewarded his friends, and infuriated the Optimates.

As 59 B.C. drew to a close, the triumvirs arranged for the Senate to grant Julius Caesar three governorships for five years after his consulship: Cisalpine and Transalpine Gaul, and Illyricum. The triumvirs also arranged for agreeable politicians, Julius Caesar's father-in-law and a military comrade of Pompey, to serve as Rome's consuls for 58 B.C. Through family relationships, Julius Caesar maintained at least a symbolic presence in Rome.

Minted in 59 B.C., the coin in Figure 16-13 offers an appropriate metaphor for this moment in Roman politics. On the reverse, Victory crowns Roma as she sits peacefully on a pile of shields. On the obverse a bust of Saturn, a harpé, and a stone recall the Greek creation story when Saturn (Cronos) castrated his father, Uranus (Sky), with a harpé. Saturn then ate his children by Rhea (Cybele), but she fed him a stone wrapped in swaddling clothes in place of baby Jupiter. The use of this imagery hints that, during relatively peaceful times in Rome, religious conflict and internecine violence lay just beneath the surface.

CHAPTER
17

AMASSING POWER

JULIUS CAESAR'S CONQUEST OF GAUL AND DEFEAT OF POMPEY THE GREAT

Pursuing glory in Gaul, Julius Caesar achieved his goals and produced unequaled tales of adventure and conquest; however, tragic losses of family and friends ultimately placed him at odds with Pompey the Great in a war over who would dominate the Western world.

While a consulship was the pinnacle of careers to most Romans, Julius Caesar's first consulship marked only the beginning of his. More than any previous consul, he planned to use foreign governorships as a springboard to greater achievements. He saw that conquering Gaul would permanently secure Rome's northern borders and bring Gallic wealth and slaves to Rome. Having been tutored by a Gaul and having grown up in a population whose greatest nightmare was invasion by Gauls, Julius Caesar saw opportunities to translate transalpine Roman governorships into military conquests, public adulation, and personal wealth.

With a careful eye on the future, Julius Caesar embraced his opportunities while taking great care to nurture his partnership with the other two triumvirs as well as his relationship with the Roman people. By scrupulously honoring his commitments to Pompey and Crassus, he nurtured their trust and helped promote the well-being of Rome. Also, by sending well-crafted reports to Rome from the field, he gave common Romans a sense of personal involvement with the Gallic wars.

Cultivating the ability to lead his legions successfully regardless of circumstances, Julius Caesar nevertheless was unable to preserve the triumvirate. One triumvir died because of his overreaching ambition and the other triumvir allied with privileged friends and turned against Julius Caesar. After successfully conquering Gaul, Julius Caesar found himself deprived of honors, pushed away from Rome, and portrayed as criminal, regardless of his popularity among the lower classes in Rome. In the end, pursuing greatness meant making war against Pompey—formerly Julius Caesar's colleague, family member, and trusted friend—and pursuing the interests of the Roman Republic meant taking his legions to distant corners of the Western world.

JULIUS CAESAR, THE GALLIC WARS, AND TROUBLING POLITICAL EVENTS IN ROME

As Julius Caesar ended his term as consul, he prepared to assume the governorships of Illyricum, Cisalpine Gaul, and Transalpine (Narbonese) Gaul for a period of five years beginning with 58 B.C. In the Roman Republic, foreign governorships always offered rich opportunities for ambitious men; and Julius Caesar wanted to achieve enough international renown and wealth of his own to rival the extent of those qualities already possessed by Pompey and Crassus. Knowing that war provided the quickest path to glory and wealth, he involved himself deeply in the affairs of his provinces.

Figure 17-1. Ring Money of Helvetii, Perhaps Representing Lugh, the Celtic Sun God.

The Excuse that Julius Caesar Needed

Searching for opportunities to take sides in inter-tribal conflicts, Julius Caesar soon found himself in the right place at the right time. Under pressure from Germanic tribes in the North, a Celtic tribe from Switzerland called the *Helvetii* began to migrate west toward Transalpine Gaul. Figure 17-1 displays a type of wheel money used by the Helvetii of Switzerland during their migration west. The wheel was one of many symbols associated with the Celtic sun god Lugh, the most powerful god in the Celtic pantheon.

Julius Caesar declared that the planned migration path and settlement of relatively vacant lands in Gaul, all well outside Roman provincial borders, somehow posed a threat to Roman interests. Quickly raising new legions and auxiliary forces to augment his four experienced provincial legions, Julius Caesar marched against the Helvetii. He defeated them, killing up to 250,000 people in two engagements. Then he forced the survivors to return to their homeland. He placed Helvetii territory under the administration of Transalpine Gaul and proactively searched for additional opportunities to continue and expand the war.

Launching the Gallic Wars

All of Gaul heard about Julius Caesar's defeat of the Helvetii. At first, many Gauls perceived him as a savior because he prevented the arrival of new, unwanted neighbors. Numerous Gallic tribes sent representatives to his camp to express their respect and gratitude. A council of chieftains then approached him with a request to help defend Gaul against marauding Germans from the North.

The Germans who were the subjects of Gallic complaints previously had established diplomatic relations with Rome and had won the title, "Friends of the Roman People." On behalf of Gallic chieftains, Julius Caesar began to negotiate with the Germans, provoking them while pretending to play the role of an honest broker. By antagonizing a powerful tribe, he caused a number of allied German tribes to mobilize against him, which was a dangerous situation. Nevertheless, his legions confronted the Germans and defeated them, temporarily halting their flow into Gaul. When the Roman legions wintered in Gaul from 58–57 B.C., they enjoyed great respect from Gallic tribes. However, when Julius Caesar returned to Cisalpine Gaul to take care of provincial administrative duties, he prepared new plans for the conquest of Gaul.

Early in 57 B.C., Julius Caesar carefully launched his invasion of Gaul. At first, he led his legions against regional troublemakers, but he began strategically attacking additional tribes with the goal of bringing all of Gaul under Roman control. He quickly conquered a host of Gallic tribes—*Aduatuci, Atrebates, Suessiones,* and many others—all but the south and the west of Gaul. (See the map of Gallic tribes in Figure 17-2.) As the campaign season of 57 B.C. ended, Julius Caesar left his legions securely encamped in Gaul. He then speedily traveled to Cisalpine Gaul to deal with issues regarding all his provinces as well as to monitor current events in Rome.

Unfavorable Political Events in Rome

Immediately after Julius Caesar left Rome at the beginning of 58 B.C., political friction began to increase between Optimates and Populares. Together, the triumvirs had represented the interests of both parties: Pompey and Crassus supported the interests of Optimates, and Julius

Figure 17-2. Map of Gaul Showing Locations of Selected Tribes and Cities during the Mid-First Century B.C.

Caesar supported interests of Populares. In the absence of Julius Caesar, common Romans rallied around Publius Clodius[1] (the uncrowned king of Rome's street gangs[2]) and supported him as leader of the Populares. He influenced Roman politics using a broad spectrum of techniques: When legitimate methods failed, gang commandos (often worshippers of foreign gods like Isis) enforced his will, which inspired increasingly harsh political opposition from Optimates.

---

[1] See Chapter 16 for the involvement of Publius Clodius in religious scandal.
[2] See Chapter 14 for a discussion of the emergence of Roman gangs associated with the Cult of Isis.

The Senate initiated a minor war against the Cult of Isis as an indirect way of tackling the problem of gangs in Rome. Local worshippers of the goddess maintained sacred statues and altars in several locations in the heart of the city.[3] In 58 B.C., the Senate ordered the images and altars of Isis demolished on the Capitoline Hill. Gangs of Isis worshippers re-erected devotional sites almost immediately. In addition, the gang-lord Publius Clodius kidnapped a priest of Cybele and auctioned him publicly as a slave.

As public dissatisfaction increased with the deteriorating political situation in Rome, Optimates rallied particularly around Pompey. As a measure of Optimate respect for Pompey, Sulla's son minted the coin in Figure 17-3 in 56 B.C. The obverse of the coin portrays Pompey cloaked in a lion skin like Hellenistic images of his hero, Alexander the Great. On the reverse, three wreaths commemorate the three triumphs Pompey celebrated for campaigns in Africa, Spain, and against the Cilician pirates. A fourth wreath recalls a gold diadem that Aristobulus of Judea gave Pompey as a bribe. Pompey donated the crown to Jupiter Capitolinus with the inscription, "The gift of Alexander, King of the Jews." The year this coin entered circulation in Rome, the gangs of Publius Clodius created disturbances during the games of Cybele, desecrating them. Soon, Cybele expressed her anger by making the Italian countryside rumble and shake.[4]

A RENEWAL OF THE TRIUMVIRATE RESULTING IN TRAGEDY

During the Winter of 56 B.C., Julius Caesar realized that political developments in Rome and the increasing power of his enemies might pose a threat to his campaign in Gaul. He arranged to meet with Marcus Crassus and Pompey the Great in Lucca, northern Italy, in May to discuss long-term issues and to renew their triumviral agreement.

---

[3]Three surviving inscriptions, datable to 90–60 B.C., indicate the existence of an *Iseum Capitolina* (a Temple of Isis on Rome's Capitoline Hill).
[4]See *The Cults of the Roman Empire* p. 39 by Robert Turcan.

Figure 17-3. Pompey Portrayed as Alexander the Great in Lion Helmet of Herakles, and Four Crowns Won by Pompey. Rome, F. Cornelius Sulla, AR Denarius, 56 B.C.

Crassus and Pompey brought 120 Roman senators to the meeting, representing a significant portion of Rome's government expected to help implement triumviral goals.

The triumvirs agreed that Pompey and Crassus would hold joint consulships in 55 B.C. Then, at the end of their terms, both men would acquire long-term foreign governorships: Pompey would govern Spain, and Crassus would govern Syria. In return, Julius Caesar would retain control of Gaul for another five years. To help deal with the emergent problem of gangs, Julius Caesar also agreed to send a thousand battle-hardened soldiers under Publius Crassus, the son of Marcus Crassus, to Rome.

A Weakening of Triumviral Bonds

Efforts to force Rome's government to implement provisions of the new triumviral agreement increased political tensions in Rome. Nevertheless, Pompey and Crassus acquired a second joint consulship in 55 B.C. and ruled more successfully than they had during their first consulship together in 70 B.C. Massive bribery produced the legal

Figure 17-4. Venus, and Cavalry Warrior with Horse, Armor, and Persian Headdress. Rome, Publius Licinius Crassus, AR Denarius, 55 B.C.

resolutions that the triumvirs desired. In particular, Pompey built Rome's first public theater, a grand multi-faceted entertainment structure that included shops and gardens. However, triumviral reliance on corruption resulted in political opposition and general social unrest.

Publius Crassus returned to Rome leading a thousand Gallic soldiers, who quickly dealt with problems related to gangs and civil disturbances. He also served as a moneyer in 55 B.C. while his father served as consul. Publius minted coins like the one in Figure 17-4. The obverse of the coin portrays a bust of Venus with her characteristic diadem and cruciform earrings.[5] On the reverse, a female figure stands next to a horse and military equipment. She wears a headdress that resembles a Persian military hat called a *kyrbasia*, which refers to the ambitions of Marcus Crassus to lead a successful campaign against the Parthians in the East.

Pompey's beloved wife, Julia, had become pregnant during her husband's consulship. Tragically, she died giving birth and her child died a few days later, which completely severed the familial connection between Julius Caesar and Pompey. Julius Caesar offered his fifteen-year-old grandniece, Octavia,[6] to fifty-one-year-old Pompey. Julius

---
[5]See note 18 of Chapter 10.
[6]Octavia's brother, Octavian, was eight years old.

Caesar even offered to marry Pompey's daughter. However, Pompey declined both offers. With Marcus Crassus soon to travel East (scorning all help and good advice), the strength of the triumviral agreement in Rome depended increasingly on the good will of Pompey the Great.

The Tragic Deaths of Marcus and Publius Crassus

When his consulship ended at the beginning of 54 B.C., Marcus Crassus intended to use his governorship of Syria to achieve military glory and even greater family wealth. He hoped to match the achievements of Alexander the Great by conquering Parthia and marching all the way to India. Marcus Crassus and his son, Publius, prepared to transport fresh Roman legions to Syria.

Every step of the way, pessimistic omens warned Marcus Crassus against his Parthian expedition. In Rome, political opponents tried unsuccessfully to stop his departure: A tribune publicly damned Crassus' legions as well as the whole overly ambitious enterprise. In Brundisium, the port of departure, Marcus Crassus ignored signs that warned against his legions departing by sea. On arriving in the East, he declined reinforcements from King Artabazes of Armenia that would have doubled the size of his army. In Syria, a storm broke part of a bridge that soldiers had to cross, and lightning struck the army's campsite. Once, while performing a religious sacrifice in front of his soldiers, Marcus Crassus accidentally dropped the entrails of an animal. Despite numerous divine warnings, he invaded Parthia in 53 B.C. with a force equivalent to ten legions—including a detachment of Gauls under his son, Publius.

The day before engaging the Parthians in battle near Carrhae, Crassus accidentally dressed in a black robe early in the morning, which signified mourning or death, but he quickly changed into a scarlet robe when he realized what he'd done. More importantly, Crassus ignored good advice from his quaestor, Gaius Cassius Longinus,[7] to secure a base at the Euphrates River before attacking the Parthians. The next three days brought devastation to the expedition as a numerically

---

[7] Gaius Cassius Longinus and Marcus Brutus became the ringleaders of the plot to assassinate Julius Caesar in 44 B.C.

inferior Parthian force continually rained arrows down on the Roman position. During the night, just before the last battle, Gaius Cassius Longinus and a detachment of cavalry abandoned Crassus. In all, the Parthians killed half of Crassus' army and captured a quarter. The remaining soldiers escaped and made their way back to Syria.

After destroying the Roman legions, the Parthians beheaded Marcus Crassus and his son. Regarding Publius Crassus, even though the Parthians executed him, they treated him honorably because of his bravery. However, Marcus Crassus had earned regional contempt for his arrogance, avarice, and incompetence. One account[8] says that the Parthian general, Surena, preceded the decapitation of Marcus Crassus with execution by pouring molten gold down his throat, as Mithradates VI had done to Manius Aquillius.[9] General Surena informed King Orodes II of Parthia about the victory by arranging for actors to use Crassus' head as a prop during a production of the king's favorite play, *The Bacchae* by Euripides.[10]

The obverse of the coin in Figure 17-5 displays a bust of King Orodes II of Parthia surrounded by stars (planets) and the crescent moon. The king took great pride in the growth on his forehead, a hereditary family symbol. On the coin's reverse, blundered Greek letters describe Orodes as King of Kings and a great benefactor. An anchor behind him, King Arsakes I (the founder of the Parthian Empire) sits on a throne and holds a bow.

JULIUS CAESAR'S CONTINUING CAMPAIGN

After the meeting in Lucca, Julius Caesar returned to the campaign in Gaul. He led his legions to the Atlantic coast and built boats to conquer the sea-going tribes of the West, which introduced Julius Caesar to naval warfare. Discovering that tribes in Britain supported the Gallic sea-going tribes, he resolved to invade Britain sometime during the

---

[8] See *Roman History* 40.27 by Cassius Dio.
[9] See Chapter 14.
[10] See *The Life of Crassus* 33.2–5 by Plutarch. Orodes II eventually executed General Surena because of his numerous successes and increasing popularity.

Figure 17-5. King Orodes II with Moon and Stars, and King Arsakes I Enthroned. Parthia, Orodes II, AR Drachm, 58–38 B.C.

coming year. By the end of 56 B.C., he had conquered most of Gaul south of the Rhine River, including Belgica, Celtica (Lugdunensis), and parts of Germania.

In 55 B.C., Julius Caesar turned his attention to solidifying Gaul's northern border. To discourage German tribes from crossing the Rhine into Gaul, he destroyed a German tribe that he caught having done so. Then he built a bridge across the Rhine at the modern location of Mainz. His field reports described how he bridged the Rhine River in just ten days. By marching across that bridge into Germania, accepting a few surrenders, and making some token conquests, he made his point: German tribes should not enter Gaul unless they intended to give Julius Caesar an excuse to conquer Germania as well. After returning to Gaul with his legions, he destroyed the bridge.

Two Invasions of Britain

Some Celtic tribes (for example, the Atrebates) maintained a presence in Britain as well as in Gaul. Julius Caesar interviewed Gauls about the land and people of Britain, and the answers that he got deepened his curiosity about the land across the English Channel. When word reached British tribes about the interest of Julius Caesar, tribal rulers attempted to dissuade him from invading Britain by sending him pledges of friendship and offerings of goods and hostages, but Julius Caesar decided to cross the channel anyway.

His bold exploration of Britain produced the first historic descriptions of British Celts in field reports that captivated the Roman public's imagination. Britain seemed like an exotic and distant land with scarcely human inhabitants. Julius Caesar wrote that Britons shaved their bodies (except for their heads and upper lips), dyed their bodies blue, and shared their wives—particularly among brothers, fathers, and sons.[11] He visited Britain twice: a brief expedition with two legions in 55 B.C. and a more extended exploration involving five legions and cavalry in 54 B.C. Both times he landed on beaches north of the Dover cliffs near the modern towns of Deal and Walmer. In between, he wintered in Cisalpine Gaul, as usual, but he also made a Winter dash to Illyria, quickly settling a conflict between tribes and impressively traversing large distances in short periods of time.

Though he conquered only a tiny portion of the Britain's southeast corner, Julius Caesar obtained Rome's first reliable information about the island, its tribes, and their leaders. Two British tribes, the Trinovantes and Catuvellauni,[12] surrendered hostages. Julius Caesar brought the hostages with him when he returned to Gaul.

Minted by the Trinovantes tribe, the coin in Figure 17-6 displays a mysterious spiral design on its obverse with six arms emerging from three crescent moons. The frequent occurrence of trinities in Celtic cults suggests that the crescents may represent three aspects of a Celtic moon god. The coin's reverse portrays a horse running to the right above a cornucopia. Circles like the ones to the left and right of the horse often represented the sun.

Dark Times for Julius Caesar

Julius Caesar gained nothing substantial in Britain. By the end of 54 B.C., he decided to abandon attempts to subdue the island. Then, before his planned departure from Gaul for the Winter, he received a series of nasty shocks. News reached him about the death of his

---
[11] See the *Gallic Wars* 4.33, 5.12, and 5.14 by Julius Caesar.
[12] See the *Gallic Wars* 5.21–23 by Julius Caesar.

Figure 17-6. Six-Armed Spiral from Crescent Moons, and Horse with Cornucopia and Solar Symbols. Celtic Britain, Trinovantes and Catuvellauni. Addedomaros, AU Stater, ca. 40–30 B.C.

daughter, Julia, and her child. Julius Caesar also learned that his own mother had died. Pompey rejected renewing a familial alliance and Crassus left for Syria. Julius Caesar's influence waned in Rome.

In addition, rebellious Gauls had not remained idle during Julius Caesar's adventures in Britain. A tribal king in northern Gaul executed carefully planned surprise attacks that exploited weaknesses of the Roman legions' Winter camps. The Gauls succeeded in destroying almost two full legions, roughly a quarter of Julius Caesar's forces.

That Winter, Julius Caesar stayed in Gaul and quashed the northern rebellion, but he suffered losses. To strengthen his position, he recruited two new legions and asked Pompey to send another. Pompey responded favorably and sent one legion to Gaul, which was the last active support he ever provided to Julius Caesar.

The Beginnings of Rebellion in the North

To Gauls, the first significant Roman losses revealed vulnerability, which inspired a gathering general rebellion against Julius Caesar. Over three years beginning in 53 B.C., all of Gaul rebelled. However, not all of Gaul rebelled at the same time.

The first regional rebellion immersed the Romans in a hard, bloody, and merciless war. King Ambiorix of the *Eburones* cobbled together a rebel coalition of northern tribes, including the *Treviri*. Allied with the Treviri, German tribes crossed the Rhine to help fight Romans. The Treviri minted coins like the one in Figure 17-7, which may have been used to purchase support for their campaign against Julius Caesar. Mysterious triskeles appear on both sides of the coin. On the obverse, a triskeles surrounded closely by a circle of dots refers to a deity (perhaps Lugh, the sun god) that possessed three aspects.

Julius Caesar briefly crossed the Rhine into Germania and convinced his German allies to raid the German tribes that supported the rebellion in Gaul. He then returned to Gaul and spent the rest of the campaign season annihilating Gallic resistance. By the end of 53 B.C., not a single building of the Eburones remained standing. History never again mentions the existence of the tribe.

Learning of Pompey's Alliance with Enemies in Rome's Worsening Political Environment

When he finally returned to Cisalpine Gaul in the Winter of 53 B.C., Julius Caesar heard about the deaths of Marcus and Publius Crassus in the disastrous campaign against the Parthians. Further, Julius Caesar learned that Pompey the Great had formed an alliance with a man who had led Optimate opposition against Julius Caesar, a man named Quintus Caecilius Metellus Pius Scipio Nasica (QCMPSN).[13] Pompey had comforted the widow of Publius Crassus, a beautiful and talented woman named Cornelia Metella who was the daughter of QCMPSN. After a suitable period of mourning, Pompey married Cornelia and QCMPSN became Pompey's father-in-law.

Politics grew more polarized than ever in Rome and public dissatisfaction often resulted in violence. As part of its continuing efforts against gangs, the Senate ordered the destruction of all images and altars of Isis in the city, including those in private chapels. However, workmen didn't dare touch the rebuilt altar of Isis on the Capitoline Hill.

---

[13]As a loyal Optimate, Quintus Caecilius Metellus Pius Scipio Nasica (hereafter identified by his initials, QCMPSN) opposed Julius Caesar's political positions and sought to reduce his influence as a triumvir.

Figure 17-7. Triskeles within Pearled Wreath, and Horse with Wolf and Triskeles. Northern Gaul, Treviri, AU Quarter Stater, Second Century B.C.

Powerful gangs protected the altar, and simple contractors couldn't afford to act against them. The altar remained standing until a consul[14] attacked it with a large hammer.

The politics of Populares grew more complicated as gang lords competed for political power: Publius Clodius[15] ran for praetor[16] and a gang-lord named Milo ran for consul. In December, battles broke out in the streets between their two gangs, preventing completion of the elections for 52 B.C. The conflict was not resolved until the gangs met outside the city on the Appian Way.

The gangs fought until Publius Clodius got hurt. His men retreated and, hoping to nurse him back to health, carried him to a nearby tavern. That night, however, Milo's gang came to the tavern and murdered Publius Clodius. Supporters of Publius Clodius carried his body into the Senate building (*Curia*), placed him on top of a large mound of benches, scrap wood, and cloth, and set fire to it all, burning the Senate building of Rome in the funeral pyre of Publius Clodius.

As the strongest leader in town, Pompey dealt quickly and effectively with the problem of gang violence. He put trained soldiers on the streets of Rome who restored civil order and shut down gang

---

[14] A consul and auger, Marcus Valerius Messalla Rufus probably committed this act.
[15] See Chapter 16.
[16] See Chapter 14 for a discussion of Roman political offices.

operations. Fearing that Pompey would declare himself a dictator, the Senate temporarily appointed him as Rome's only consul. Pompey then appointed QCMPSN as the second consul for 52 B.C.

News of the events in Rome reached Gaul not long after they reached Julius Caesar. Gallic tribes perceived Julius Caesar as a weakened leader and began to agitate for a broad rebellion. Obtaining intelligence of energetic preparations for rebellion among Gauls, including opportunistic murders of Roman citizens, Julius Caesar sent a request to Rome for additional reinforcements. Pompey abandoned all pretense of maintaining the triumviral agreement. He refused to send reinforcements and began working with QCMPSN to enact legislation specifically targeted against Julius Caesar.[17] Facing a gathering rebellion in Gaul, Julius Caesar understood that he could expect no further assistance from Rome.

Julius Caesar's Worst Defeat

At the beginning of the campaign season in 52 B.C., Julius Caesar faced grave challenges. A new leader named Vercingetorix emerged among the *Arverni* tribe (from the modern Auvergne Region in France) and built a coalition of central and western tribes. More skillful than any previous Gallic leader, he waged war against the Romans with a combination of shrewd politics, careful strategy, and ingenious tactics. Vercingetorix began the year by attacking Gallic tribes that had expressed reluctance about joining the rebellion, which encouraged tribes to declare allegiance and greatly increased the size of the rebel army. Julius Caesar countered immediately by punishing tribes that declared against him. Then, Vercingetorix attempted to weaken the Romans by reducing their food supply: Some Gauls harassed Roman supply trains, while others set fire to lands around Roman camps and ambushed foraging Roman soldiers.

---

[17]Pompey implemented a law that enabled prosecution of Julius Caesar for bribery related to his election as consul in 59 B.C. Pompey also restored an old law that prevented Julius Caesar from running for consul unless he left his legions and returned to Rome as a private citizen. If Julius Caesar arrived in Rome as a private citizen, his enemies intended to prosecute him for abuses of office and corruption. With Pompey's assistance, the enemies of Julius Caesar stood a good chance of convicting him.

By the end of the Summer of 52 B.C., Vercingetorix had succeeded in making life so difficult for the Romans that Julius Caesar offered the option of retreat to his soldiers. However, demonstrating complete faith in their general, the soldiers chose to stay and fight. Julius Caesar finally cornered a Gallic force at Avericum (modern Bourges), a capital city that the Gauls didn't want to burn. The Roman legions captured the town and wreaked vengeance, slaughtering 40,000 inhabitants of Avericum including women, children, and the infirm. Only eight hundred Gauls managed to escape. Skillfully making the best of the defeat, Vercingetorix used Julius Caesar's treatment of Avericum to convince more Gauls to join the rebellion.

Julius Caesar's legions chased the army of Vercingetorix to a powerfully situated hillfort named Gergovia, camped on a hill opposite, and waited. The Romans expected reinforcements, but news soon arrived that the *Aedui* (a tribe that had promised to send 10,000 soldiers) no longer intended to supply reinforcements. Julius Caesar immediately took four legions from his camp to discuss this matter with the Aedui. Tribal leaders fled in advance of the Romans, and messages soon arrived that Vercingetorix had attacked the legions remaining at Gergovia. Marching twenty miles at night, Julius Caesar and his legions raced back to camp.

From a variety of factors—exhaustion, confusion caused by difficult terrain, and even overconfidence—the legions failed to respond correctly to Julius Caesar's battlefield commands. Vercingetorix's forces killed almost one thousand Romans and forced the remainder to retreat. Still, after giving up their camp, Julius Caesar's disciplined troops assembled on level ground and held their position. Over the next couple of days the Roman forces regrouped, challenged Vercingetorix to attack, and then resolutely marched away.

After Julius Caesar's defeat, the Aedui fully supported Vercingetorix. A number of hard-fought battles followed, and both Romans and Gauls found it difficult to obtain sufficient food. Still, Julius Caesar's German allies never deserted him. The Roman legions captured the rebellious leaders of the Aedui tribe and never again lost a battle.

When the Aedui tribe betrayed Julius Caesar, they used coins like the one in Figure 17-8. The obverse of the coin mimics Roman coins that

Figure 17-8. Gallic Coin Similar to a Roman Quinarius. Central Gaul, Aedui, AR Quinarius, ca. 100–50 B.C.

portrayed a helmeted personification of Roma. On the reverse, circular ornaments (Celtic solar wheels?) appear above and below a galloping horse. The similarity of the coin in size and design to a standard Roman quinarius reveals a longstanding history of tribal cooperation with Romans.

Julius Caesar's Most Brilliant Victory

In September of 52 B.C., Vercingetorix and a force of 80,000 Gauls camped in the strongly fortified town of Alesia, increasing its population from 90,000 to 170,000. Julius Caesar's force of 60,000 soldiers camped outside Alesia and immediately began building a wall around the town. Julius Caesar intended to isolate the overcrowded town and starve the Gauls into submission. Vercingetorix tried to stop the wall's construction by attacking its builders, but Alesia's own fortifications posed a logistical problem: The city's narrow gates allowed too few soldiers to attack quickly enough to seriously harm the Romans. Even worse, Julius Caesar's German cavalry cut the Gauls to pieces when they retreated because the narrow gates prevented Gauls from entering the city quickly enough to find safety.

Effectively locked inside the town, the Gauls watched Julius Caesar's legions build eleven miles of wall, protected by ditches and booby traps, completely around Alesia. Before the wall's completion, Vercingetorix's entire cavalry emerged from Alesia. Pretending to attack, the horsemen broke through an unwalled stretch of ground and scattered in all directions. Each horseman raced to his home tribe to summon reinforcements to help defeat Julius Caesar.

As quickly as they could, the legions completed the fortified siege wall. Then they built a matching walled system just outside the first, but with trenches and booby traps facing away from Alesia. The second wall protected the legions between the walls from external attack. While some soldiers labored to complete the walls, others foraged for food and collected water. In this way, the Romans accumulated a 30-day supply of provisions in the narrow camp between the two walls.

Inside Alesia, food supplies quickly began to dwindle. To harass the Romans and help preserve food stores, Vercingetorix expelled helpless members of the local Mandubii tribe—old men, women, and children. Trapped between Alesia and the Roman wall, these people suffered and fruitlessly begged the Romans for food and water. Dwindling supplies increased hunger and hardship inside the town, but the suffering and deaths of expelled Mandubii just outside added new levels of horror.

However, Gallic reinforcements soon began to arrive. Eventually, as many as 250,000 warriors assembled around Julius Caesar's outer wall. Believing they had trapped the Romans, Gauls inside and outside Alesia called to each other, eagerly anticipating the slaughter of the Roman legions to the very last man.

The final struggle for Alesia reached a climax in three battles over several days. The first battle began when Gallic archers assembled outside the exterior wall. They fired arrows at Romans on the wall the instant any portion of any man became visible, but Julius Caesar's German cavalry surprised the Gauls by suddenly charging outside the wall through special gates. The cavalry drove the Gauls back, encircled the archers, and killed them. Gauls on horseback attacked, but the German cavalry defeated the Gallic cavalry. Roman foot soldiers then drove the Gauls all the way to their camp, well away from the Roman fortifications. From Alesia, Vercingetorix's troops attacked the interior Roman wall whenever they heard an attack on the outer wall, but they failed to penetrate Roman defenses.

The second attack began during a moonless night. Gauls attacked the exterior wall with ladders and iron hooks, but the Romans defended the wall successfully. Roman ballistas and booby traps killed thousands of the attackers.

In the third and final battle, 60,000 Gauls focused on a weak point on the exterior Roman wall as Gallic forces inside and outside simultaneously attacked the full length of both Roman walls. Exhibiting extraordinary heroism and discipline, the Romans not only preserved the integrity of the walls, but they also mustered an attack against the Gauls outside. The Romans forced the Gauls to retreat and slaughtered fleeing Gauls by the thousands. Julius Caesar wrote that he believed his men could have killed all the Gauls if his soldiers hadn't suffered so much from exhaustion.

The third battle broke the siege by Gauls against Julius Caesar. Outside Alesia, surviving Gauls fled homeward. Starved into submission, Vercingetorix and all the Gallic leaders within Alesia surrendered unconditionally.

Imposing Peace on Gaul

Continuing into 51 B.C., spontaneous rebellions erupted from place to place throughout Gaul. Julius Caesar punished each rebellion by encouraging his troops to rape, pillage, and plunder without limit. Roman forces captured Gallic treasure and sold thousands of Gauls into slavery.

Finally, Julius Caesar decided to make an example out of a rebellious town named Uxellodunum (near modern Puy D'Issolu). First, he destroyed the water supply, forcing the town's unconditional surrender. Next, he ordered amputation of the hands of all the thousands of men in Uxellodunum who had borne arms against him. He then transported the disabled survivors of Uxellodunum throughout Gaul to serve as living reminders that he would deal with further rebellion without mercy.

After the horrific treatment of the men of Uxellodunum, an enduring peace finally came to Gaul. Julius Caesar negotiated terms for establishing cooperative administrative structures in the new Roman provinces of Belgica, Aquitania, and Lugdunensis. He also imposed a tribute of 40 million sesterces on Gaul. For three provinces the size of Gaul, this relatively small amount reflects Caesar's mercy as well as the region's impoverishment after ten years of brutal war.

Julius Caesar sent Vercingetorix to Rome to be placed in secure confinement until the time came for celebration of a triumph for the Gallic War. The obverse of the Roman coin in Figure 17-9 displays a bust of Vercingetorix in front of a Gallic shield. On the reverse, a naked warrior brandishes a shield and spear on a war chariot driven by another Gaul. During his ten years in Gaul, Julius Caesar orchestrated the killing of more than a million Gauls and the enslavement of a million more. He also captured vast amounts of Gallic treasure—gold and silver for the people of Rome. When the time eventually arrived for Rome's celebration of Julius Caesar's victories, few celebrations in history could match it.

Provincial and Populares Support for Julius Caesar

In 50 B.C., fifty-year-old Julius Caesar completed the conquest and reorganization of Gaul. Then he began a long tour of the free cities in Transalpine Gaul, Cisalpine Gaul, and Illyricum to express gratitude for the provinces' support, to listen to their concerns, and to share a vision for how they might prosper under his continued leadership. Where he could, he placed trusted men from his legions in local leadership positions. He also ensured that the legions maintained battlefield readiness. Mindful that his provincial governorships would expire in the beginning of 49 B.C., Julius Caesar worked his way slowly toward Italy, consolidating a dependable power base behind him.

From a distance, Julius Caesar also tried to influence politics in Rome. He sent his cousin, Marc Antony, and another officer so both men could win election to the Tribunate of the Plebs. From the hands of Marc Antony (Julius Caesar's second in command on the battlefields of Gaul), Gallic wealth found its way into many politicians' pockets.

Figure 17-9. Vercingetorix, and Gallic Soldier on a Battle Chariot. Rome, L. Hostilius Saserna, AR Denarius, 48 B.C.

Marc Antony even bribed one of the consuls of 50 B.C., L. Aemilius Lepidus Paulus, the son of an old friend of Julius Caesar.

The common people of Rome loved Julius Caesar. They loved his glorious victories as well as the wealth and new territories he won for Rome. They also loved him because of his reputation for addressing the concerns of the common man.

The Hardening of Opposition against Julius Caesar in Rome

Gaius Claudius Marcellus Minor, Rome's consul in 50 B.C., had married Caesar's nineteen-year-old grandniece, Octavia; however, the consul passionately hated Julius Caesar and joined the Optimates in their anti-Caesar efforts. The Optimates knew that the people of Rome would elect Julius Caesar as consul if given half a chance, so they desperately attempted to block his access to power. They tried to terminate his governorships early and made laws to support trying him for corruption and punishing him with exile at least. Pompey the Great adopted the Optimates' agenda as his own. Using his influence and wealth to help anti-Caesar politicians attain public office, Pompey promised to use his legions to defend the Roman Republic from Julius Caesar, if necessary.

Provocatively, the Senate passed a resolution that ordered Pompey and Caesar each to supply a legion to fight the Parthians. Pompey donated the legion he previously had sent to Julius Caesar. Forced to supply two legions, Julius Caesar discharged Pompey's legion in Cisalpine Gaul, which allowed members of the legion to return to Pompey if they chose to do so. Then he ordered one of his own legions to march toward Rome, but before they left, he gave each soldier 1000 sesterces[18] on top of the soldier's earnings from the immensely successful Gallic campaign. When the legions arrived at their base near Rome—Caesar's legion arrived first, then members of Pompey's legion trickled in—the Senate placed both legions under the command of Pompey just outside Rome.

Julius Caesar tried to negotiate a compromise with the Optimate-controlled Senate. Several times, he asked either for an extension of his governorships or permission to run for consul in absentia. He even said that he would settle for an agreement that he and Pompey both disband their legions at the same time. The Optimates controlling the Senate not only refused to compromise, but they also nullified contrary decisions from the popularly controlled Tribunate of the Plebs. The Optimates branded Julius Caesar a criminal and pushed resolutions that led inevitably to civil war. Even Pompey ignored personal communications from Caesar attempting to negotiate peace. Ultimately, the Roman government's disregard of decisions made by the Tribunate of the Plebs gave Julius Caesar the legitimate excuse he needed to march into Italy.

THE CIVIL WAR BETWEEN JULIUS CAESAR AND POMPEY THE GREAT

Like Hannibal, Julius Caesar led an army of battle-hardened veterans across the Alps toward Rome. In early 49 B.C., Julius Caesar led a single legion across the Rubicon River, the border between Cisalpine Gaul and Italy. By taking a military force across this boundary without

---

[18] 1000 sesterces was more than eight months' pay for a legionnaire.

senatorial permission, Julius Caesar committed an illegal act, which all Romans understood as a declaration of civil war.

Rome learned about the crossing several days later. Almost immediately, reports followed of cities surrendering to Julius Caesar and of Roman soldiers deserting to join Caesar's cause. Because no armed force existed in Rome that was capable of challenging Julius Caesar's legions successfully, Pompey and the forces loyal to him hastily prepared to leave Rome and the Italian peninsula.

Upon hearing numerous reports about Julius Caesar's progress and expecting more legions to enter Italy, Pompey the Great abandoned Rome before nightfall. Other members of the Optimate government soon followed. Strangely, Pompey and the Optimates abandoned Rome with its treasury intact in the Temple of Saturn.

Julius Caesar sent four legions to secure Sicily even before he reached Rome. Within a month, he controlled the Italian peninsula, the city of Rome, and the wealth of the Roman Republic. In fact, he barely missed catching Pompey; Julius Caesar and his legions arrived in the port city of Brundisium just hours after Pompey had sailed.

Minted during Julius Caesar's slow advance toward Italy, the coin in Figure 17-10 displays religious implements on the reverse and an elephant treading on something usually identified as a snake on the obverse. The religious implements (cullullus, aspergillium, axe, and apex) referred to religious offices held by Julius Caesar, including pontifex maximus[19] and high priest of Jupiter Capitolinus. Numismatists usually explain the elephant as a multilingual pun related to Julius Caesar's name: Because North Africans used the word *cesai* for elephant, Julius Caesar may have used the elephant as a graphic symbol for himself and his army. The elephant tramples an object to the right that resembles both a Gallic trumpet (*carnyx*) and a snake, which allowed Julius Caesar to portray himself simultaneously as the conqueror of Gaul and a killer of treacherous creatures. The coin proclaimed that, with full religious authority, he was marching like Hannibal into Italy with sufficient force to crush his enemies.

---

[19]Many features of the government of the Roman Catholic Church come directly from ancient Rome. For example, the Pope cointinues to use the title, pontifex maximus.

Figure 17-10. Elephant Trampling Snake or a Gallic War Axe, and Priestly Implements. Rome, Military Mint, Julius Caesar, AR Denarius, 49–48 B.C.

The War in the West

Aware that the illustrious career of Pompey made it possible for him to seek support from clients in Spain, North Africa, and almost anywhere throughout the East, Julius Caesar could not afford the luxury of waiting to see where Pompey would go. Spending less than a week in Rome, Julius Caesar installed a provisional government, obtained funding from the treasury, and then marched overland toward Spain, either to meet Pompey there or to deprive the Optimates of a Western support base. On the way, Julius Caesar discovered that Optimates had bribed citizens in the fortified city of Massalia (modern Marseille) to declare loyalty to Pompey. To keep a lid on this opposition, Julius Caesar split his forces. First, he paid all his legions well. Then, leaving enough soldiers to keep Massalia under siege, he led the rest of his forces toward Spain. He left strict orders for his soldiers not to take Massalia by force.

Entering Spain, Julius Caesar assigned some legions to secure passage through the Pyrenees and then quickly marched south to challenge two generals loyal to Pompey. Julius Caesar prosecuted the war methodically, taking care to minimize casualties on both sides. Many Iberian tribes declared loyalty to Julius Caesar. Still, a vicious game of hide-and-seek ensued. Whenever Pompeian forces stopped to fight, they lost, and, on at least one occasion, Pompeian soldiers met with Caesar's and talked without fighting, which angered the Pompeian commander. In the end, the Pompeian forces slowly ran out of food and negotiated surrender. In fewer than forty days, Julius Caesar won the war in Spain with a minimum of bloodshed. He disbanded the Pompeian legions and installed a loyal Governor of Spain.

Julius Caesar quickly marched back to Massalia. The city negotiated surrender as soon as Julius Caesar returned. He spared the city but revoked the rights of its population for citizenship.

Preparing for a Showdown

While in Massalia, Julius Caesar learned that the Roman Senate had declared him dictator. He quickly returned to Rome and terminated his dictatorship after only eleven days. In speedily arranged consular elections for 48 B.C., Rome elected Julius Caesar to his second consulship along with P. Servilius Isauricus, the son of an old friend. Caesar then focused the government on the most pressing problems of the Republic: food distribution, the economy, and the high level of debt.[20] Learning that Pompey had recruited a powerful army in Greece, Julius Caesar immediately began preparing an expeditionary force to go to Greece and confront the Optimate army.

Bad news soon reached Rome that the commander whom Julius Caesar had posted to Sicily had taken two legions—half of Caesar's army on Sicily—to fight Pompeian forces in North Africa. Allied with King Juba of Numidia, the Pompeian forces had greatly outnumbered Julius Caesar's legions and had quickly defeated them. To avoid disgrace, Julius Caesar's men had fought to the death rather than surrender.

In Greece, Pompey the Great had assembled eleven legions, four thousand auxiliaries, and seven thousand cavalry. Important allies, including his father-in-law, QCMPSN, scoured the East with small armies and arranged a steady flow of money and supplies to

---

[20]Julius Caesar also assigned Octavian (Julius Caesar's sixteen-year-old nephew) as a priest in the College of Pontifices in Rome, just as sixteen-year-old Julius Caesar had been appointed to the post of High Priest of Capitoline Jupiter in 84 B.C., thirty-six years earlier. See Chapter 16.

Pompey. Further, a Pompeian navy commanded by a competent admiral patrolled the sea between Italy and Greece.

Pompey minted coins like those in Figure 17-11 to pay his soldiers in Greece and to reminded people of his virtues and accomplishments. The top coin portrays a bust of Apollo on the obverse and devices associated with Herakles (a lion skin, a club, a bow and arrows) on the reverse. Pompey used Herakles' lion skin and club to symbolize a metaphorical association with Alexander the Great, who also represented himself on coins with Herakles' devices. The lower coin bears symbols that refer specifically to a few of Pompey's great accomplishments: The obverse portrays Jupiter Terminus, a personification of borders, which refers to special proconsular powers that transcended borders that the Senate granted only to Pompey; and the obverse bears a dolphin referring to his victory over the Cilician pirates, an eagle referring to his defeat of Mithradates VI on land, and a scepter referring to Pompey's extension of Roman dominion, particularly over the East.

The War in Greece

Julius Caesar believed that fortune always favored quick and decisive action.[21] With fewer ships than he needed to carry all his legions, he transported seven legions from Brundisium to Greece in January of 48 B.C. He then sent the ships back to bring the remaining five legions, cavalry, and supplies, but the ships didn't return. Pompey's navy found them and burned thirty of the ships at sea, forcing Julius Caesar to begin a protracted campaign in Greece with too few soldiers and hardly any supplies.

Julius Caesar marched his legions to a friendly city and camped on the south bank of the Apsus River. To deny Caesar access to another potentially friendly city, Pompey marched his forces to the north bank of the Apsus River. That Winter, the soldiers of Julius Caesar and Pompey often spoke to each other from opposite banks of the river.

During this time, Optimate expatriates gathered in Pompey's camp, mostly greedy old aristocrats who caused nothing but problems. They argued among themselves, divided into factions, and alienated

---

[21]For example, see *The Life of Julius Caesar* 32.8 by Plutarch.

Figure 17-11. Coins Minted by Pompey the Great in Greece. Military Mint, Cnaeus Pompeius Magnus, AR Denarii, 49–48 B.C.

Pompey's allies in the East. The funding efforts of Pompey's father-in-law, QCMPSN, alienated Eastern rulers further by resembling acts of thievery and extortion more than negotiation. Just as QCMPSN prepared to plunder the Temple of Artemis at Ephesos, however, time ran out. Pompey sent word for QCMPSN to cease his fundraising and bring his forces immediately to Greece.

Minted in Rome in 48 B.C., the coin in Figure 17-12 celebrates that pressure from Caesar prevented the Pompeian forces from plundering the Temple of Artemis at Ephesos. On the obverse, a bust of Gallia, the female personification of Gaul, faces right. A carnyx, or Gallic trumpet, stands behind her. On the reverse, Diana stands like Artemis of Ephesos holding a spear in one hand and a deer, her sacred animal, in the other.

In early Spring of 48 B.C., Marc Antony successfully brought reinforcements and supplies to Greece. Four legions and seven hundred

Figure 17-12. Gallia, and Artemis of Ephesos with Spear and Her Sacred Deer. Rome, L. Hostilius Saserna, AR Denarius, 48 B.C.

cavalry landed just north of Pompey so that his camp briefly had enemies on opposite sides. Both Julius Caesar and Pompey then began to maneuver their forces to better positions around Dyrrachium.[22]

Two soldiers defected from Julius Caesar's camp and took valuable information to Pompey. Pompey attacked advantageously, and the battle raged back and forth for two days. During the second day, Julius Caesar's battle line crumbled and Pompey could have won the battle if he'd pressed the attack. However, afraid of a trap, Pompey held back. Julius Caesar lost approximately one thousand men, but he quickly regrouped his forces.

After the battle, more soldiers joined Pompey until his army outnumbered Julius Caesar's two to one. Meanwhile, the Caesarean forces continued to suffer from having too little food. Aristocrats in Pompey's camp began to argue among themselves about how to divide the plunder after Pompey defeated Julius Caesar.

The decisive battle between the generals finally took shape near Pharsalos in central Greece. The two armies met on level ground. With both sides well trained and well equipped, and with clear numerical superiority on Pompey's side, the battle starkly revealed Julius Caesar's superiority as a battlefield commander. The Caesarean army slaughtered

---

[22]The modern Albanian city of Durres is built on top of the ancient city of Dyrrachium.

Pompey's. By midmorning, Pompey abandoned the field as lost. He disguised himself, grabbed a few possessions, and fled secretly toward Egypt. Many of his officers, including Brutus,[23] fled as well.

The next day, Julius Caesar asked Pompey's four remaining legions to surrender. Kneeling before Caesar, the men begged for mercy, and Caesar pardoned them all. He ordered his soldiers neither to harm Pompey's men nor to take any of their possessions. Brutus sent a letter asking for pardon, and Julius Caesar happily pardoned Brutus as well.

To pay his legions, Julius Caesar minted coins that referred to his victories in the West. In Figure 17-13, for example, the goddess on the obverse of the coin (commonly identified as a personification of Clemency) wears a victory wreath. On the reverse, a ceremonial axe stands next to a military trophy comprising a Gallic shield, helmet, uniform, and Gallic battle trumpet. The LII (52)[24] on the obverse refers to Julius Caesar's age when he defeated Pompey at Pharsalos.

Julius Caesar promoted Marc Antony to Master of Horse, which gave him the authority to rule on Julius Caesar's behalf, and sent him to Rome to manage the government. Then, leaving other generals and most of his soldiers to consolidate victory in Greece, Julius Caesar took a small force—twenty ships and four thousand soldiers—to chase after Pompey. Ironically, in Rome, the Senate again ordered the destruction of altars and images of Isis that had re-emerged on the Capitoline Hill.

Pompey's Flight to Egypt

Running for his life, Pompey escaped Greece by ship. Though he badly needed money and soldiers, hot pursuit by Julius Caesar once again prevented plunder of the Temple of Artemis of Ephesos. Pompey considered asking for an alliance with the King of Parthia, but Egypt still owed money for assistance that Pompey had given to Ptolemy XII.[25]

---

[23]Julius Caesar thought of Brutus almost as a son because he was the son of Julius Caesar's favorite mistress. Yet, Brutus followed Pompey, even though Pompey had unjustly executed Brutus' father in 77 B.C. (a year after Sulla died) when Brutus was a seven-year-old child.
[24]Note that this coin, the first Roman coin ever to carry a date of issue, is dated year 52 after the birth of Julius Caesar (52 A.J.C.).
[25]See Chapter 16.

Figure 17-13. Clementia, and a Gallic Trophy. Rome, Military Mint, Julius Caesar, AR Denarius, 48–47 B.C.

Stopping briefly at the island town of Mytilene to pick up his wife and children, Pompey set sail for Egypt.

However, Ptolemy XII had died three years earlier. Civil war had erupted recently in Egypt between Ptolemy's heirs (Ptolemy XIII and Cleopatra VII) during the third year of their marriage and joint reign. The army of Ptolemy XIII, a fourteen-year-old child, had driven twenty-one-year-old Cleopatra VII's forces from Egypt into southern Judea. Firmly in control of most of Egypt, Ptolemy XIII and his advisors wanted only to strengthen their position.

All of Egypt knew about the war between Pompey the Great and Julius Caesar. Ptolemy's advisers wanted to ensure an Egyptian alliance with the winning side, but they didn't want to bring the Roman civil war to Egypt. The advisors soon recognized an opportunity to help forge a strong new relationship between Ptolemy XIII and Rome.

On his fifty-eighth birthday, September 29 by the Roman calendar and seasonally toward the end of July, 48 B.C.,[26] Pompey the Great anchored his ship near an Egyptian royal camp approximately fifty miles east of Alexandria. A boat containing Egyptian government

---

[26] The Roman calendar during Republican times lost an average of ten days per year. Romans adjusted their calendar at irregular intervals, frequently related to political concerns, for example, arranging for longer or shorter terms of political office.

representatives and two former Roman officers came to meet him; one of the Romans was an old acquaintance of Pompey's. Pompey stepped into the small boat, which then made its way to the shore. From the ship, Pompey's wife and children watched: As Pompey stood to get out of the boat, the two Romans killed him. After the assassination, Pompey's ship immediately lifted its anchor and sailed away.

THE CONSEQUENCES OF JULIUS CAESAR'S WARS

It was inevitable that some ambitious general would win control of the Roman Republic. However, the way that Julius Caesar climbed to the pinnacle of power left an indelible mark on Western history. By being a true friend of powerful men, by concerning himself with the well-being of common Romans, and by achieving his goals with flair and imagination, his soldiers and fellow Romans began to think of him as something more than an ordinary man. By defeating Pompey the Great, the most successful and well-known general in the Mediterranean region, he attracted interest throughout the West: Everyone wanted to know more about him.

In all ways, Julius Caesar raised the art of influencing the world to new heights. Taking a deep interest in people and their circumstances, Julius Caesar wrote about the Gallic Wars, preserving a valuable record of notable events, personalities, politics, religion, military tactics, and natural history. The reports that he sent to Rome with exciting stories of Gallic conquests enhanced his reputation among his contemporaries and survived to modern times to be respected as examples of the best of ancient literature. He pioneered speedy travel and communications: To manage his governorships, which stretched from the English Channel to the Dalmatian Coast, he maintained pony-express style way stations on well-constructed Roman roads, which allowed him to obtain information while it was still relevant and to travel long distances with great speed. In addition, he communicated with the public by minting coins that told about himself and his victories in exciting new ways.

However, some of the ways that Julius Caesar influenced the West were barely noticed by history. For example, he brought Roman culture to Gaul and placed Romans, Celts, and Germans in close contact. He wrote little about religious beliefs in Gallic societies except that Germans worshipped the sun and Celts believed in the transmigration of souls.[27] However, information about Gallic religion that survived in Celtic myths and place names reveals that Celtic religious beliefs greatly influenced Roman soldiers over the long term.

The capital of Gaul, Lugdunum, was named after a Celtic solar deity called Lugh. Celts celebrated sacred holidays when the sun occupied cardinal points along the zodiac, the summer and winter solstices, and the vernal and autumnal equinoxes; and symbols related to Lugh often appear on Celtic coins. In addition, Celtic myths related to Lugh strongly resembled Greek myths of Perseus.[28] For example, Lugh was raised by a foster family of gods because of a prophecy that he would kill his grandfather. After obtaining a spear of victory and a divine horse, Lugh performed heroic deeds and led other gods in battle. Like Perseus, Lugh eventually killed his grandfather.

With perspective supplied by numismatics, archaeology, and history, we now can see that Roman soldiers simultaneously came in contact with the Cult of Mithras in the East and the Cult of Lugh in the West. In Anatolia, Roman officers learned about Mithras from Cilician administrators; and, in Europe, Roman foot soldiers learned about local solar cults from Celtic and German auxiliaries in Roman forts. Both cults honored important dates of the solar year and both offered personal salvation and survival after death. Contact with foreign soldiers in the East and the West who believed in solar cults predisposed many Roman soldiers favorably toward solar deities.[29]

---

[27] Most of Julius Caesar's commentary on Celtic and German religious beliefs can be found in his work, *The Gallic Wars* 6:13–14, 16, 18, and 21.

[28] Lugh's grandfather was named Balor. See *Balor With The Evil Eye: Studies In Celtic And French Literature* by Alexander Hagerty Krappe.

[29] The exposure of Roman soldiers to solar cults from 50 B.C. to 50 A.D. was very important for the development of Christianity. For example, see information about the Dacian Rider Cult in Chapter 25. The Dacians were Romanian Celts who merged their cultic beliefs with those of Hellenistic Mithraism.

After the First Triumvirate crumbled, Julius Caesar obtained a huge boost in his international reputation by defeating Pompey the Great and winning absolute control of Rome. In two short years, Julius Caesar had won a war that he fought in Italy, Sicily, Africa, Spain, and Greece. After Pompey's death in Egypt, Julius Caesar was recognized as the greatest living general: a single personality who dominated the Western world. However, Julius Caesar eventually achieved an even higher level of reputation: It wasn't long before some people believed that he had become a god.

CHAPTER 18

JULIUS CAESAR'S JOURNEY TOWARD APOTHEOSIS

By the end of Julius Caesar's life, his unparalleled accomplishments convinced many in the Western world that he was a god.

Julius Caesar wanted to conquer the world, or at least as much of the world as Alexander the Great had conquered. Long after the death of Alexander, Hellenistic kingdoms minted coins that portrayed him as a divinity. Sometimes they portrayed him as Herakles and sometimes as Zeus/Amon/Ra, however, no Cult of Alexander ever attracted a following. Eastern Hellenistic rulers frequently claimed to be divine. A few even maintained priests who officiated over sacrifices as part of the rulers' cults, but the cults never endured for long after the rulers died. In this respect, at least, Julius Caesar surpassed Alexander the Great and Eastern pretenders to divinity: The cult established around Julius Caesar lasted for centuries.

The second part of Julius Caesar's life began when he crossed the Rubicon River and prosecuted a civil war against Pompey the Great. Eventually, Pompey fled to Egypt and Julius Caesar followed, only to discover that Egyptians had murdered Pompey by cutting off his head. Julius Caesar then began a new life traveling throughout the Western world, winning victories, instituting reforms to help the poor and oppressed, and conceiving a child with Cleopatra VII, a ruler widely recognized in the East as the living incarnation of Isis. Four years after the death of Pompey the Great, Julius Caesar was betrayed by people whom he trusted and was fatally stabbed.[1]

Having restructured Rome to benefit common Romans, Julius Caesar died at the hands of men committed to preserving their privileged positions in Roman society. However, once common Romans obtained a sample of a better life, they generated a political force that could not be stifled. People who had learned to expect miracles from Julius Caesar found that their faith in him continued after his death. In addition, working-class foreigners in Rome, Jews prominent among them, joined the thousands of Romans who flocked to cultic services that venerated Julius Caesar after his death. When a bright comet appeared during Julius Caesar's funeral games, believers in Julius Caesar recognized that he had sent the comet to signal his apotheosis.

Ambitious leaders struggled for power by serving the population that revered Julius Caesar and opposing his exiled murderers. Forming a partnership called the *Second Triumvirate*, the three most powerful leaders (Marc Antony, Octavian, and Lepidus) found a previously unimaginable way to cater to the people's wishes: They arranged for the Senate to recognize Julius Caesar's deification, they constructed his temple, and they started operating his cult. All that remained was to clarify who would emerge as the strongest among them, that is, who would rule Rome as the single legitimate successor to a man who had become a god.

JULIUS CAESAR'S MOST PRESSING ISSUES AFTER THE DEATH OF POMPEY

In 48 B.C, in the beginning of October by the Roman calendar (seasonally, the end of July), fifty-two-year-old Julius Caesar arrived in Alexandria just days after the assassination of Pompey the Great. Accompanied by 3200 footsoldiers and 800 cavalry, Caesar met with

---

[1] Julius Caesar's career corresponds symbolically with that of Jesus, from the crossing of the Rubicon River and the beheading of Pompey (corresponding to the baptism of Jesus and the beheading of John the Baptist) to betrayal and death. See Chapter 24.

an Egyptian delegation comprising King Ptolemy XIII, royal advisors, and bodyguards. When the Egyptians presented Pompey's head preserved in honey to Julius Caesar, he wept.[2] He ordered his soldiers to gather Pompey's remains and deliver them to Pompey's wife, Cornelia. Then he announced that he had come to Alexandria to fulfill the terms of Ptolemy XII's will, which did not please the Egyptian delegation.

Outside Egypt, recalcitrant Optimate enemies of Julius Caesar were scattering to Spain, Africa Province, and Asia, hoping to rekindle resistance to his control of Rome. As a tremendous source of wealth and grain, Egypt held such strategic importance that Julius Caesar had to safeguard it from Optimate hands; yet Egypt was wracked by civil war between thirteen-year-old Ptolemy XIII and his twenty-one-year-old sister/wife, Cleopatra VII. To calm and control Egypt, Julius Caesar had only his wits and the relatively small military contingent that had sailed with him from Greece.

Most of Ptolemy's army still engaged the forces of Cleopatra east of Alexandria. The Egyptian military that remained in Alexandria could not prevent Julius Caesar's small force from occupying the fortified district of the royal palace and securely holding the king and his advisors. Intending to end the Egyptian civil war in some way favorable to himself, Julius Caesar also planned to settle Ptolemy XII's debts to Rome, ensuring that Egypt paid him instead of any Optimate claimants. An Egyptian artifact from precisely this period of time, the coin in Figure 18-1 was minted in 49/48 B.C. The obverse bears a feminized portrait of Ptolemy I. On the reverse, a headdress of Isis appears to the left of the eagle's legs[3] and the date above it indicates year three of the reign of Cleopatra VII and Ptolemy XIII.

While the Romans hurriedly prepared to defend the fortified district of Alexandria, a Sicilian servant of Cleopatra VII smuggled the queen into the palace inside a rug and presented her to Julius Caesar. Queen Cleopatra's audacity must have impressed him because he began an affair with the queen immediately.[4] The next morning, he summoned Ptolemy XIII to begin a formal reconciliation of the two rulers.

---
[2] See *The Life of Pompey* 80.5 by Plutarch.
[3] Ptolemy XII first used the headdress of Isis on Ptolemaic tetradrachms in 54 B.C., and Cleopatra VII continued the practice until her death in 30 B.C.
[4] See *The Life of Julius Caesar* 49.3 by Plutarch.

Figure 18-1. Coin from the Time of the Egyptian Civil War. Alexandria, Cleopatra VII and Ptolemy XIII, Year 3, AR Tetradrachm, 49–48 B.C.

When Ptolemy XIII discovered his sister in the palace, he threw a fit, stormed outside, and began to foment a riot. Julius Caesar skillfully calmed the crowd. Then he read Ptolemy XII's will in the presence of members of the Egyptian court and the assembled people of Alexandria. The will stated that Ptolemy XIII and Cleopatra VII should rule jointly over Egypt and provided detailed provisions for Rome's role as a guarantor.

The impromptu event gradually turned into a ceremony that proclaimed Ptolemy XIII and Cleopatra VII, brother and sister, the joint married rulers of Egypt. For weeks afterward, it seemed as if Julius Caesar had ended the Egyptian civil war. Regardless, friction continued between the retinue of Ptolemy XIII and everyone else in the palace. His advisors summoned the Egyptian military to Alexandria, and violence soon erupted.

The Alexandrian War

Ptolemy XIII's most skilled general led 20,000 Egyptian soldiers into Alexandria to eliminate the Romans. Arsinoe IV (the younger sister of Cleopatra VII) further complicated the situation by leading a military faction that also attempted to seize the Egyptian throne. Vastly outnumbered, but using a variety of creative tactics, Julius Caesar defended the palace fortress against attacks by all Alexandrian forces.

In numerous battles over four months, Julius Caesar lost approximately four hundred men. During one engagement, he had to leap into the harbor and swim to avoid being captured. During another, a Roman commando operation set fire to Egyptian ships, but the blaze spread to shore and burned the Library of Alexandria.[5] Still, conflict among competing Alexandrian factions reduced their effectiveness against the Romans. Julius Caesar expelled Ptolemy XIII from the palace to help increase confusion among opposing leaders.

As secretly prearranged by Julius Caesar, reinforcements from Asia Province and Syria Province eventually neared Alexandria. Greatly strengthened with fresh reinforcements,[6] the Roman legions directly engaged the Egyptian forces of Ptolemy XIII and Arsinoe IV. By mid-January of 47 B.C., Julius Caesar had defeated the Egyptian army, killed Ptolemy XIII, and imprisoned Arsinoe IV.

The Aftermath of the Alexandrian War

Julius Caesar enjoyed a special relationship with the Jews of Alexandria. During the war, Jews helped Julius Caesar at critical moments. Grateful for their assistance as well for the assistance of Jews among the reinforcements from Syria Province, he granted rights to Alexandrian Jews equal to the rights of Alexandrian Greeks and Egyptians.

To establish a legal and customary framework for Cleopatra to rule Egypt, Julius Caesar oversaw her marriage to Ptolemy XIV, her twelve-year-old brother. Julius Caesar then accompanied Cleopatra VII[7] on a Nile cruise. Historians disagree about whether the cruise was a three-month vacation or merely a quick trip to Memphis to participate in traditional pharaonic coronation ceremonies.[8]

---

[5]Although some historical accounts say that the fire destroyed the Library of Alexandria, the fire probably burned a warehouse that stored library scrolls for export.
[6]The reinforcements included Jewish forces under Antipater, the father of the future King Herod the Great.
[7]Although *The Life of Julius Caesar* by Suetonius indicates that Cleopatra VII was pregnant with Julius Caesar's son during the cruise, some modern historians believe that the son was not born until several years later, shortly after the death of Julius Caesar.
[8]See *Cleopatra: Beyond the Myth* p. 28.

Figure 18-2. Large Egyptian Coin with Portrait of Cleopatra VII. Alexandria, AE Diobol, 51–30 B.C.

During the reign of Cleopatra VII, most Egyptian coins carried her image.[9] For example, Figure 18-2 displays her portrait on the largest bronze denomination in the standard set of Alexandrian coins. Traditional Egyptians viewed Cleopatra not only as their ruler, but also as the living incarnation of their principal goddess, Isis. For Egyptians and for worshippers of Egyptian cults throughout the Mediterranean world, Julius Caesar gained a new aura of divinity from his close relationship with the Queen of Egypt.

Distant Concerns Calling Julius Caesar Out of Egypt

While Julius Caesar remained in Egypt in early 47 B.C., Optimate leaders prepared to oppose him. Pompey's sons, Cnaeus and Sextus, traveled to Spain and began to reconstitute their father's legions. Also, two enemies of Julius Caesar, Marcus Portius Cato[10] and Quintus Caecilius Metellus Pius Scipio Nasica (QCMPSN, Pompey's father-in-law[11]), began to organize Optimate resistance in North Africa in alliance with King Juba of Numidia.

---

[9]Cleopatra VII put her image on more denominations of Egyptian coins than any other Egyptian ruler, which emphasized her claim of divinity to her subjects.
[10]Cato took an immediate dislike of Julius Caesar when they first met in the Senate early in their careers. After the establishment of the First Triumvirate, Cato helped lead political opposition against it.
[11]See Chapter 17.

In Asia Province, a foreign enemy emerged hoping to take advantage of Rome's political confusion. After most of the Roman legions in Asia Province had marched south to help Julius Caesar in the Alexandrian War, Pharnaces, the son of Mithradates VI, saw an opportunity to seize Roman Asia. Pharnaces murdered the Roman administrators of Pontus and captured much of Bithynia and Cappadocia, which resurrected a large portion of his father's Pontic Empire. Reports of Pharnaces' effrontery quickly reached Julius Caesar in Egypt.

Dealing with the Levant and Anatolia

Sometime toward the middle of 47 B.C., leaving half of his forces to secure Cleopatra VII and Ptolemy XIV as King and Queen of Egypt, Julius Caesar marched several legions north toward Anatolia. Along the way, he paused to cement good relations with Eastern rulers, to pardon Romans previously loyal to Pompey, and to secure commitments of funds for Rome. Notably, Julius Caesar met young Herod the Great (the future King of Judea) and pardoned Gaius Cassius Longinus,[12] the Roman governor of Syria Province. Often expressing a high regard for Jews and gratitude for Jewish assistance, Julius Caesar settled many regional issues in ways favorable to Jewish interests.

He then sailed from Syria to Tarsos to meet with a gathering of Anatolian leaders. Noting that Julius Caesar had pardoned a ruler formerly allied with Pompey, Pharnaces sent a letter asking for pardon. Julius Caesar replied that he would not befriend anyone who had killed innocent Romans for gain. However, he would consider granting a pardon if Pharnaces paid reparations and abandoned Pontus.

Promising to do as Julius Caesar asked, Pharnaces sent a gold crown as a peace token but did nothing further. In early August of 47 B.C., Julius Caesar confronted Pharnaces near Zela, a location where Mithradates VI once defeated a Roman army. Julius Caesar ordered his legions to build fortifications in preparation for battle, but Pharnaces' army attacked the Romans before they could complete their preparations. The battle lasted approximately one hour, and mopping up took three more hours. Julius Caesar's legions destroyed the Pontic

---

[12]Commonly known as Cassius, he later led a conspiracy to murder Julius Caesar.

army and chased Pharnaces until he escaped by ship on the Black Sea. Julius Caesar reconstituted the Roman provinces in Anatolia and sent his famous message to the Roman Senate: "*Veni, vidi, vici,*" meaning "I came, I saw, I conquered."

Resolving Issues in Rome

When Julius Caesar returned to Rome in October of 47 B.C., he found that Marc Antony had allowed discontent to increase in Rome, resulting in street fighting and martial law. Quickly establishing order, Julius Caesar restarted the economy with money obtained by auctioning the properties of his dead enemies. He returned the government to working order and conducted elections for offices that began the following year. Rome elected Julius Caesar and Marcus Aemilius Lepidus as consuls for 46 B.C. In Rome for little more than a month, Julius Caesar took advantage of this brief opportunity to get to know his sixteen-year-old grandnephew, Octavian.

Unexpectedly, the general also had to deal with a mutiny by his favorite legion. Julius Caesar had promised much to the Tenth Legion over the years. Soldiers in the legion saw long, hard service followed by a period of inactivity and unpaid salaries. Sudden orders to prepare for a new campaign in Africa pushed the legion to the threshold of rebellion. The soldiers marched on Rome, killing two senators on the way. Julius Caesar allowed the soldiers to enter Rome unhindered, and then he walked alone to meet them. He listened to all their grievances. To their surprise, he agreed with them, called them citizens, and promised to pay the salaries he owed them. He even assigned land to them on the spot from his personal holdings as well as from state land. When he finally asked who among them wanted to join his Africa campaign, the soldiers rushed forward to volunteer.

Paying Attention to Symbols and Defeating Opposition Forces in Africa

Julius Caesar consolidated his Africa invasion force on Sicily at the port of Lilybaeum. From there, he and his legions sailed to Africa on December 24, 47 B.C. As usual, Caesar paid meticulous attention to

Figure 18-3. Coins Related to the War between Julius Caesar and Optimate Forces in Africa, 47–46 B.C. Left Coins: Julius Caesar, Sicily and Africa, AR Denarii. Right Coins: Q. Caecilius Metellus Pius Scipio Nasica, AR Denarii.

prophecies and omens. Because QCMPSN (the S stands for Scipio) commanded the Optimate forces and a prophecy said that no Scipio could fail in Africa, Julius Caesar added a soldier named *Scipio* Sallutio to the general staff of the invasion force. When he landed in Africa, Julius Caesar tripped as he stepped on shore. Transforming a bad omen into a good one, he kissed the ground, clutched the earth, and shouted loudly, "Africa, I hold you."

Both sides of the conflict in Africa used symbols to attract support for their cause. Figure 18-3 displays Julius Caesar's coins on the left and Optimate coins on the right. The coins of Julius Caesar portrayed gods as members of his family. The coins of Optimates emphasized their intention to preserve Rome as a republic; however, they also made oblique references to Pompey the Great as a general who enjoyed divine favor.

Julius Caesar's Proconsul of Sicily, Aulus Allienus, oversaw production of the top left coin at Lilybaeum. The obverse of the coin portrays Julius Caesar's ancestor, Venus, a goddess born from the sea. On the reverse, Trinacrus, an enigmatic Sicilian son of Neptune,[13] stands with one foot on the prow of a ship and holds a *triskeles*, the ancient symbol of Sicily. Julius Caesar's military mint in Africa portrayed the general's

---

[13]Venus was Neptune's aunt. See Chapter 2.

divine ancestry on the lower left coin. On the obverse, Venus gazes right. On the reverse, Aeneas (the child of Venus and Anchises) carries his mortal father and the sacred *Palladium*[14] as they flee the fallen city of Troy. In Rome, the Vestal Virgins guarded the Palladium as a sacred token of Rome's divine origins. Julius Caesar's coins symbolized that divine members of his family were directly involved in guiding the fate of Rome.

Marcus Portius Cato and QCMPSN minted the two coins on the right of Figure 18-3 to pay an army of Roman Optimates and North Africans. The obverse of the top right coin asserts Optimate piety by portraying Jupiter (Zeus), King of the Gods, facing right. On the reverse, scales, wheat, a cornucopia, and a consular chair promise abundance through Republican justice administered by Optimate consuls. The obverse of the coin on the lower right personifies Africa as a divine personage wearing an elephant hat. On the reverse, Herakles leans on his club, reminding the Numidians that Herakles (either Phoenician Melqart[15] or a similar African deity) fathered their race. The symbols on the lower coin also refer obliquely to Pompey the Great through numismatic associations of his hero, Alexander the Great, with Herakles and with personifications of Africa.[16]

In early 46 B.C., the Africa campaign had lasted approximately three and a half months. As usual, the Caesarean forces spent much of the campaign vastly outnumbered and with too little food. However, Julius Caesar won battles that lesser generals would have lost. Many soldiers defected to his side from the Optimate legions. The campaign finally concluded in April with a few skirmishes and a gruesome suicide by the Optimate leader, Marcus Portius Cato.[17] Julius Caesar spent several months reorganizing the administration of Roman Africa and collecting fines from African cities that had opposed him. He returned to Rome by the end of July.

---

[14]The Palladium was a cultic statue from Troy, originally representing Cybele or some other militaristic Eastern Aphrodite, but generally identified by Romans as representing the warlike goddess, Minerva (Athena).
[15]See Chapter 4.
[16]Ptolemy I minted tetradrachms that portrayed Alexander the Great as semi-divine, sometimes wearing a lion helmet like Herakles and sometimes wearing an elephant helmet like Africa.
[17]See *Cato the Younger* 70.5–6 by Plutarch.

JULIUS CAESAR'S EXTENDED STAY IN ROME

When Julius Caesar returned to Rome in July of 46 B.C., the Senate declared him dictator for ten years. In addition, the Senate showered him with many new and unusual honors, including the following:

- The right to speak first in the Senate.
- The right to sit in a curule chair with the consuls.
- The right to appear in a triumphal chariot drawn by white horses and accompanied by lictors.
- The right to start all races in the Circus Maximus.

The Senate also appropriated funds to place a statue of Julius Caesar on the Capitoline Hill facing the statue of Capitoline Jupiter.

Italy, Gaul, Egypt, Syria, Asia, and Africa seemed stable for the moment, even though Pompey's sons still led significant rebel armies in Spain. Julius Caesar sent two generals to pacify Spain, but neither proved equal to the task. After receiving numerous requests for help from the generals, he realized that he would have to deal with Pompey's sons himself.

Still, Julius Caesar succeeded in spending approximately five months in Rome. Away from the hardships of war, he took time to improve the city and the lives of its citizens. He began the construction of a new Forum including a new temple to honor his ancestor, Venus Genetrix. Again remembering the assistance he received from Alexandrian and Syrian Jews, he awarded official rights for Jews to worship within Rome's sacred boundaries. He also planned and prepared an enormous ten-day party in September, 46 B.C., a time for all Rome to celebrate his triumphs over Gaul, Egypt, Pontus, and Africa.

Cleopatra VII in Rome

Julius Caesar invited both Cleopatra VII and Ptolemy XIV[18] to Rome to participate in the triumphal celebrations. They soon arrived with a large retinue and moved into Julius Caesar's garden estate across

---

[18]Fourteen-year-old Ptolemy XIV was recognized as the co-ruler of Egypt when he accompanied his sister/wife, Cleopatra VII, to Rome.

the Tiber River from Rome.[19] From the beginning, Queen Cleopatra VII captivated Rome's attention. Because she ruled Egypt as the living Isis, devotees of Egyptian gods in Rome considered her at least partly divine. Romans flocked to see the exotic queen, and young Roman women copied her hairstyle, clothes, and mannerisms. In addition, Cleopatra's relationship with Julius Caesar provided fuel for endless curiosity and speculation.

One of the many controversial aspects of the life of Cleopatra concerns the birth year of Caesarion, her son by Julius Caesar. One popular source[20] implies that Cleopatra gave birth to Caesarion in June of 47 B.C., scarcely nine months after Julius Caesar's arrival in Egypt, which appears inconsistent with information from other sources. If Cleopatra had given birth to Caesarion in 47 B.C., she would have brought him to Rome in 46 B.C. and many Romans would have commented about him and his religious role as an incarnation of the god Harpokrates. However, no source mentions the child's presence in Rome in 46 B.C. Documentary and numismatic evidence[21] favors the year 44 B.C. for Caesarion's birth soon after his father's death, which allows for a consistent reading of all sources.[22]

Four Grand Triumphs

When September 46 B.C. arrived, Julius Caesar inaugurated ten days of lavish celebrations of the triumph over Gaul. The sounds of Gaulish horns echoed throughout Rome as legions escorted captives and cartloads of weapons and treasure through the streets. Soldiers led Vercingetorix in chains to the *Tullianum*,[23] Rome's oldest official prison located at the northwestern corner of the Forum. There, Julius Caesar halted his triumphal procession while soldiers took Vercingetorix inside. Custom required a triumphal general to wait in front of the

---

[19]See *The House of Ptolemy: A History of Egypt Under the Ptolemaic Dynasty* p. 368 by Edwyn Bevan.
[20]See *The Life of Julius Caesar* 49.20 by Plutarch.
[21]See the discussion in Chapter 19 of Figure 19-1.
[22]See *Cleopatra: Beyond the Myth* pp. 32–4 by Michel Chauveau, for a brief outline of an argument for Caesarion's birth in 44 B.C.
[23]The Tullianum is also called by its medieval name, the Carcere Mamertino (Mamertine Prison).

Tullianum while the executioner strangled notable enemies of Rome. When he received word that Vercingetorix was dead, Julius Caesar continued his triumphal procession. The axle of his chariot broke just as he passed the Temple of Fortune. Still, the triumphal activities progressed relentlessly to their climax: After dark, illuminated by forty torches held in the trunks of forty elephants, Julius Caesar climbed the steps of the Temple of Capitoline Jupiter on his knees.

In the triumph over Egypt, soldiers led Arsinoe IV in golden chains. Because the Roman crowd responded sympathetically to her youth and courage, Julius Caesar granted her the opportunity to seek asylum. She left Rome and found refuge in Asia Minor serving as a priestess of Artemis at Ephesos.

In the triumph over Pontus, soldiers carried a painting that portrayed Pharnaces running away from Julius Caesar. Other soldiers carried signs that said, "Veni, vidi, vici." The legions also sang a ribald song about young Julius Caesar's service as a queen to King Nicomedes IV of Bithynia.

In the triumph over Africa, King Juba's four-year-old son walked, delighted, through the celebrating streets of Rome. Julius Caesar not only spared the child from harm, but also arranged for his care and education. When the young boy grew up, Juba II served Rome as a Client-King, first of Numidia (comprising territories in Western Tunisia and Eastern Algeria), and then of Mauretania (Western Algeria and Morocco). He acquired enduring fame as an enlightened ruler and noteworthy scholar.

In every triumph, Julius Caesar's designated heir, young Octavian, rode in a chariot just behind the general. These months in Rome gave Julius Caesar important opportunities to teach Octavian how to lead an army and a nation. However, Julius Caesar still hoped to conceive his own son and make him an heir in preference to Octavian.[24]

For ten days, Julius Caesar provided grandiose spectacles, gladiator fights, and even a mock sea battle. He also gave a feast for all of Rome, distributing 22,000 dining couches throughout the city and arranging for the preparation, delivery, and replenishment of food. He gave each citizen 400 sesterces as well as free oil and grain. To each soldier in his

---

[24]See *The Life of Julius Caesar* 52 by Suetonius.

Figure 18-4. Coins Displaying the Face of a Prophetess and a Sphinx with Features of Cleopatra VII. Rome, T. Carisius, AR Denarius, 46 B.C.

legions, Julius Caesar gave 20,000–80,000 sesterces, depending on the soldier's rank.

Minted in 46 B.C. for the triumph over Egypt, the coins in Figure 18-4 portray a prophetess (associated with either the Syrian Mother or Isis) on the obverse and a sphinx on the reverse. The female sphinx's features on the top coin portray an insulting caricature of Cleopatra, but the sphinx on the bottom coin bears a more flattering portrait. The differences between these coins recall some of the fascination and controversy inspired by the Egyptian Queen during her time in Rome. At one point during celebrations, Caesar unveiled a gold statue of Cleopatra in the new Temple of Venus Genetrix.

Improving the Lives of Common Romans

In the months before Julius Caesar left for Spain, the triumphs and their preparations helped the Roman economy enormously. This sharing of his success with common citizens greatly increased his public support. He worked hard to improve the lives of Rome's citizens in a variety of other ways as well. For example, he established an improved system of criminal courts, and—importantly—he made it possible for every citizen to obtain land.

The civil war between Julius Caesar and Optimate rebels left many lands vacant in Italy, and recent expansions of Rome's dominion added vast new territories for colonization. Julius Caesar used this opportunity to legislate an allocation of land, not just for his soldiers, but also for the poor in Rome. To encourage settlement of the land and growth of agriculture, he simultaneously halved the monthly grain allowance to Rome's poor.

As his most enduring accomplishment, Julius Caesar changed the Roman calendar. In late Republican times, a calendar year regularly contained 355 days, which conformed poorly to the actual length of a year and created opportunities for political corruption: The pontifex maximus arbitrarily adjusted the calendar over the years, sometimes to restore months to their appropriate seasons and sometimes to extend the term of a rich consul who needed extra time in office. With advice from the scholar, Sosigenes of Alexandria, Julius Caesar added sixty-seven days[25] to the year 46 B.C. Further, he lengthened the standard year to 365 days and provided for an additional day to be added every four years. After the establishment of the Julian calendar, nobody adjusted the Western calendar again for more than 1600 years.

DEFEATING REBELS IN SPAIN AND PREPARING FOR PEACE

Just before launching his new Spanish expedition, Julius Caesar presided over Rome's elections for 45 B.C. At the recommendation of Marcus Aemilius Lepidus, Rome elected Julius Caesar as sole consul for the year. The Senate had awarded the same honor to Pompey the Great in 52 B.C.

Julius Caesar and his legions left for Spain sometime during the forty-five days added between November and December to adjust the

---

[25]In 46 B.C., twenty-two days were added to February, and then two special months, Intercalaris Prior (twenty-three days) and Intercalaris Posterior (twenty-two days) were added between November and December.

Figure 18-5. Coin of Cnaeus Pompey Used to Pay Pompeian Forces in Spain. Spain, AR Denarius, 46–45 B.C.

calendar in 46 B.C. The late timing of the invasion gave him the element of surprise, but his soldiers still had to find shelter and food at a bad time of the year. They succeeded in winning a few battles and in securing barely adequate food and shelter. Julius Caesar suffered from illness for much of the campaign.

A general who formerly served under Julius Caesar in Gaul joined forces with Pompey's sons, Cnaeus Pompey and Sextus Pompey. With local support and funding, the Pompeians paid their legions with silver coins like the one in Figure 18-5. The obverse of the coin displays a bust of Roma. On the reverse, a female personification of Spain holds two spears and a shield as she extends a palm branch to Cnaeus Pompey, the eldest son of Pompey the Great. With competent leaders and capable legions, the well-provisioned Pompeian forces held their own against the hungry forces of Julius Caesar. The fighting was bitter, and neither side took prisoners.

Battles at Munda and Corduba

The decisive battle of the campaign in Spain occurred on March 17, 45 B.C., coincidentally the date of the annual festival of Bacchus. Cnaeus Pompey led thirteen legions and six thousand light troops, cavalry, and auxiliaries against Julius Caesar's eight legions and eight thousand cavalry. Outnumbered and hungry, Julius Caesar's army faced a well-trained, well-fed, and well-led enemy on the plains near the Spanish city of Munda (near modern Osuna).[26] Both armies struggled for advantages of terrain and tactics. Both sides prosecuted vicious warfare, man-to-man and sword-to-sword. At the age of fifty-five, Julius Caesar fought alongside his men, urging them always to greater effort.

His disciplined soldiers and masterful use of battlefield tactics once again gave Julius Caesar victory in one of the hardest battles of his career. Although Cnaeus Pompey escaped, his losses totaled approximately 29,000 soldiers. Approximately one thousand of Julius Caesar's men died. As a temporary measure to prevent treachery from the inhabitants of Munda, Julius Caesar barricaded the city gate with a giant wall of dead Pompeian soldiers. He then marched to Corduba (modern Cordova) to deal with the forces of Sextus Pompey.

Supporters of Julius Caesar met him outside Corduba's walls and surrendered. He spared these people. His legions then attacked Corduba, captured it, and slaughtered all 22,000 soldiers and residents who had remained inside the city walls. However, Sextus Pompey escaped. After the defeat of Cordoba, a few Pompeian forces and towns continued to fight, but Julius Caesar brutally crushed them, expunging the last Pompeian resistance from Spain.

Julius Caesar's soldiers found Cnaeus Pompey hiding in a cave. They killed him, cut off his head, and stuck it on a pike in the center of Gades (modern Cadiz). Sextus Pompey survived, but he left Spain for a hard life of shifting fortunes.

Building a New Multicultural Roman Society

Octavian came to Spain to learn practical lessons about leadership as his uncle reestablished Roman administration over the two provinces of Spain. Julius Caesar founded new colonies for his soldiers and he reshaped the region's economy and cultural focus to support peace

---

[26]The territories where Julius Caesar battled Pompey's sons were known by residents of Anatolia as the land of the Gadarenes, which helps explain some of the contradictions and strange details in descriptions of Jesus' travel to the land of the Gadarenes in the synoptic gospels. See *Mark* 5:1–9, *Matthew* 8:28–34, and *Luke* 8:26–39. Also, see Chapter 24.

instead of war. When he finished organizing Spain, he traveled through the provinces of Gaul where he continued to found colonies. Sometimes he granted citizenship to cities, groups, and individuals. He even enrolled capable men from Gaul as Roman senators. As he had desired many years earlier, Julius Caesar finally granted Roman citizenship to all the residents of northern Italy.

Unrecorded by history, a foreign cult gained its first entry into Spain. Among Julius Caesar's soldiers, a few had acquired initiation into the Hellenistic Cult of Mithras: some from transplanted Cilicians in Italy and others from traditional cultic centers during service in Anatolia. These early seeds of the Cult of Mithras eventually found fertile soil in Spain and Gaul among the Roman soldiers in Julius Caesar's new colonies. In addition, a significant number of Jews began to settle on Spanish shores.

Rome's Urge to Venerate Julius Caesar

In Rome, the Senate heard about the defeat of rebels in Spain and began to grant Julius Caesar even more unusual and extreme honors. The Senate authorized an issue of coins with his portrait, the first official coins of Rome to honor a living Roman like a god.[27] The Senate also funded the creation of several significant new statues. In religious processions, a new ivory statue of Caesar accompanied statues of the gods in processions through the streets of Rome. In the Temple of Quirinus (the deified Romulus), a new statue of Caesar bore the inscription, "To the Invincible God."[28]

The most controversial of the new statues joined a collection of eight other statues on the Capitoline Hill. There, seven statues portrayed the early kings of Rome, and an eighth statue portrayed one of the first consuls of the Roman Republic: Lucius Junius Brutus, the man who killed the last King of Rome in 509 B.C. Igniting controversy,

---

[27]Previously, only foreign mints, one in Spain and one in Greece, had produced coins with large, realistic portraits of living Romans. See Figures 12-4 and 12-5.
[28]This Latin text mimics the Greek inscription on a statue of Alexander the Great in Athens. For descriptions of both statues, see *Roman History* 43:45.3 by Cassius Dio, and *Against Demosthenes* 5:32 by Hyperides.

the Senate placed a statue of Julius Caesar next to the statue of Lucius Junius Brutus.

JULIUS CAESAR'S FATEFUL RETURN HOME

Julius Caesar returned home from his protracted Spanish expedition and extensive travels through Gaul early in September 45 B.C. Resting at his estate at Lavicum, he wrote his will and considered his next moves. As the fifty-five-year-old leader made plans for the next several months, he knew that many of his strongest supporters, Rome's poor, had abandoned Rome to enjoy new lives as landowners in new colonies. He also understood that the honors showered upon him by the Senate made him a target for jealous men. As always, Roman politics remained volatile.

A brave and realistic man, Julius Caesar suffered periodically from grand mal epileptic seizures: He lived constantly with the possibility of losing his self-control in public. Though he hid his malady as best he could, the likelihood of suffering a seizure in public approached certainty over time. At the height of his accomplishments, his search for ways to achieve more glory for himself and Rome began to resemble a search for ways to die with his honor intact.

The challenge of conquering Parthia held the same fascination for Julius Caesar as it had for Crassus. Alexander the Great, the West's greatest conqueror, had achieved unparalleled renown by defeating the Persian Empire. Occupying the same territory that previously constituted the core of Persia, Parthia represented a strategic threat to Eastern lands already controlled by Rome: Anatolia, Syria, and Egypt. Unable to resist an opportunity to secure Roman interests while matching the achievements of Alexander the Great, Julius Caesar planned to invade Parthia during the campaign season of 44 B.C.

A prophecy in the *Sibylline Books*[29] said that only a great king could defeat the Parthians. Julius Caesar always looked for creative ways to bend prophecies and omens in his favor, but Rome had violently

---
[29]See Chapter 12 for a discussion of the *Sibylline Books*.

rejected rule by kings in 509 B.C. Stalwart Optimate Republicans might acquiesce as the Senate fawned over Julius Caesar and awarded him bizarre honors, but many Roman aristocrats would die before they would accept anyone as King of Rome. In this context, Caesar's last five and a half months in Rome acquired a strained atmosphere of flattery, cynicism, and foreboding.

Toxic Honors

After resting at his estate, writing his will, and planning his next campaign, Julius Caesar formally reentered Rome in the beginning of October of 45 B.C. Against custom, he resigned his sole consulship and appointed two other men as consuls. By appointing the consuls instead of arranging an election, he demonstrated his absolute power over the Roman Republic and offended aristocratic Romans. Many feared that the Roman Republic was dead and that only an image of the Republic continued to exist. Julius Caesar offended aristocratic Romans even further by celebrating a triumph for his victory in Spain over Optimate rebels. Custom reserved triumphs for victories over foreign enemies, and Julius Caesar's victory in Spain had come by winning battles against Roman citizens.

However, the Senate continued to flatter Julius Caesar. It declared him consul for the next ten years and gave him extraordinary powers to shape the government and appoint office-holders as he saw fit. The Senate proclaimed his birthday a national holiday and renamed the month of Quintillius to July in his honor. Implicitly elevating Julius Caesar to godhood, the Senate appointed Marc Antony as High Priest of the Cult of Julius Caesar and appropriated funds to build a temple in his honor.

In February of 44 B.C., the Senate named Julius Caesar Dictator for Life. On the obverse of the coin in Figure 18-6 (minted in February or March of 44 B.C.), a bust of Julius Caesar wears a victory laurel. The surrounding text identifies him as "Perpetual Dictator." On the reverse, Venus Victrix holds a scepter in her left hand next to a shield. In her right hand, she carries a small Goddess of Victory.

Figure 18-6. Julius Caesar Wearing Laurel Crown, and Venus Victrix with Symbols of Dominion and Victory. Rome, Sepullius Macer, AR Denarius, Feb.–Mar. 44 B.C.

Treacherous Death

While mobilizing resources for his campaign against the Parthians, Julius Caesar also prepared Rome for his extended absence. To reinvigorate the troubled economy, he made populist laws that seemed calculated to serve common Romans and to anger aristocrats. One law required that at least one-third of the workforce consist of free men. Another law canceled one-quarter of all debts. He appropriated funds to build public showpieces in Rome, including new temples, a huge public library, and a new Senate building called the Curia Julia. He also funded projects that greatly improved the quality of life in Rome, for example, draining and filling in nearby marshes. He ran official advance elections covering the next three years, the expected duration of his Eastern campaign.

Two well-respected Romans, Cassius[30] and Brutus,[31] led a conspiracy to murder Julius Caesar before the Senate could make him a king.

---

[30] Gaius Cassius Longinus was a well-respected military man who had served under both Crassus and Pompey the Great.
[31] Marcus Junius Brutus the Younger was the son of Servilia Caepionis, Julius Caesar's favorite mistress before Cleopatra VII.

The participation of Brutus in particular lent an aura of respectability to the plot. Brutus was a descendant of Lucius Junius Brutus, the man who murdered the last King of Rome in 509 B.C. Brutus proudly cultivated a reputation for defending the Republic as well as for doing what was right instead of what was convenient: For example, he had fought against Julius Caesar in Greece under Pompey the Great[32] even though Pompey had executed Brutus' father.[33] Julius Caesar had enjoyed a long relationship with Brutus' mother and often had expressed respect and affection for Brutus as well. Nevertheless, Brutus chose to ignore his personal relationship with Julius Caesar because of the threat that the dictator posed to the Roman Republic.

As many as sixty Optimates participated in the conspiracy, which had to act before March 18, the scheduled departure of the army for the East. Many omens warned Julius Caesar about the plot to kill him. A prophetess told him to "beware the Ides of March," and his wife, Calpurnia, dreamed of her husband's death and begged him not to go to the Senate on March 15.

While contractors worked on the new Senate building (the Curia Julia), the Senate occupied the Theater of Pompey. On March 15 (the Ides of March), Julius Caesar walked without a bodyguard to the Theater of Pompey. While conspirators engaged his friends with manufactured distractions, Caesar entered the Theater of Pompey alone. There, a crowd of conspirators pulled out knives and attacked him.

Julius Caesar fought his attackers, but they overpowered him and stabbed him numerous times. Before succumbing, he expressed surprise at seeing his lover's son, Brutus, among the murderers. Covering his face so no man could see him die, Julius Caesar collapsed and expired next to a statue of Pompey the Great.

The Funeral of Julius Caesar

Self-righteously asserting that they had preserved the Roman Republic from subjugation by a new dynasty of tyrant kings, the conspirators acted as if they expected Rome to honor them as heroes. However,

---

[32] Julius Caesar pardoned Brutus after defeating Pompey in Greece. See Chapter 17.
[33] Brutus was eight when his father was executed in Cisalpine Gaul in 77 B.C.

common Romans understood that the conspirator's true interests lay in securing their families' wealth and privileges against Julius Caesar's reforms. To ensure their own safety in the rapidly deteriorating political environment, the conspirators kidnapped and held hostage the sons of Marc Antony and Marcus Aemilius Lepidus.

While common Romans increasingly expressed grief and outrage about the murder of Julius Caesar, the conspirators persuaded the Senate to continue operating and to grant amnesty to everyone involved in the plot. Attempting to calm the public, the Senate also ratified all of Julius Caesar's acts. However, when the feelings of common Romans proved difficult to tame and violence threatened to erupt in the streets, the Senate quickly assigned the conspirators to administrative positions in foreign provinces.

At first, the people of Rome seemed disinclined to pursue the matter further. However, the general mood shifted strongly against the conspirators after the public reading the will. Julius Caesar bequeathed each Roman citizen 300 sesterces, and he provided for the creation of a public park. Despite political uncertainty in Rome, many thousands of Romans attended his funeral.

Before the assembled mourners, Marc Antony read a proclamation by the Senate that granted Julius Caesar all honors, divine and human. Marc Antony then delivered a stirring eulogy. Viewing the mangled body, the angry crowd surged forward and carried it to the Forum. There, they built a funeral pyre out of wooden benches, tables, and branches. Miraculously, two divine beings[34] ignited the pyre. Mourners fed the flames with offerings of jewels, weapons, robes, and even the robes of their children. As the fire died down, people seized flaming brands and ran to set fire to the houses of the conspirators. Those conspirators who had remained in Rome quickly left town.

From the ashes, freedmen from Julius Caesar's household gathered his charred bones and interred them in his family cemetery. Mourners continued to come to the site of the funeral pyre for many days

---

[34]See *The Life of Julius Caesar* 84.3 by Suetonius. Consistent with this text, some numismatists interpret the coin in Figure 18-7, minted in 44 B.C., as representing the apotheosis of Julius Caesar in the presence of two "divine beings," Victory (or Thanatos, the Angel of Death) and Venus (or Luna). On the coin, the upright torch above Julius Caesar's head symbolizes resurrection.

afterward. Jews came especially.[35] Someone built an altar at the site, and mourners began to offer sacrifices and perform devotions to Julius Caesar as if he were a god.

Julius Caesar's Legacy and the Second Triumvirate

Cleopatra was approximately six-months pregnant when Julius Caesar died.[36] His will never mentioned his son, Caesarion, by name, but it made provisions for "the son who might be born to him."[37] In addition, Julius Caesar explicitly gave Cleopatra permission to name her child after him, and he had left orders for a law to be enacted after he left for Parthia, which would allow a bequest from his estate to his child by a foreign woman.[38] Some Romans considered Cleopatra divine, some saw her as an expendable pawn in a political game of chess, and some regarded her as a witch who had ruined Julius Caesar and threatened to ruin Rome. Yet, hugely pregnant with Julius Caesar's child, she delayed her departure from Rome for another month.

Cleopatra gave birth to Caesarion in Greece in early May.[39] News of the birth arrived in Rome by May 11,[40] but produced little reaction. Marc Antony tried to use the information to prevent Octavian from inheriting Julius Caesar's estate but was unsuccessful: Existing Roman law did not recognize Roman bequests to children of foreign women.

The will named Octavian as Julius Caesar's adopted son and heir. From July 20–23, 44 B.C., Octavian publicly affirmed his inheritance with games honoring both Venus and Julius Caesar. During the games, a comet suddenly appeared, shining so brightly that it was visible even in the daytime sky, and it continued shining for seven days. Few doubted that this comet came as a special sign: It confirmed Julius Caesar's divinity and expressed his approval of the games.

In 44 B.C., a moneyer named L. Aemilius Buca, a staunch supporter of Julius Caesar, minted an enigmatic coin. (See Figure 18-7.) On the

---

[35]Thousands of Jews lived in Rome at this time.
[36]See *Cleopatra: Beyond the Myth* p. 32 by Michel Chauveau.
[37]See *The Life of Julius Caesar* 83 by Suetonius.
[38]See *The Life of Julius Caesar* 52 by Suetonius.
[39]See *Cleopatra: Beyond the Myth* p. 33 by Michel Chauveau.
[40]See *Ad Atticum* 14:20:2 by Cicero.

Figure 18-7. Venus, and a Scene Reminiscent of Both Sulla's Dream and the Apotheosis of Julius Caesar. Rome, L. Aemilius Buca, AR Denarius, 44 B.C.

coin's obverse, the diademed head represents Venus, symbolizing the goddess who gave birth to the Roman race as well as the Eastern Aphrodite who brought good fortune to Sulla. Modern scholars disagree about the meaning of the coin's reverse,[41] but the year that the moneyer was active (44 B.C.), the subject matter of the moneyer's other coins (all portray images of Julius Caesar), and the poses of the figures speak to the popular perception in Rome that Julius Caesar died and then resurrected as a god: The prone figure represents Julius Caesar waking from death, the god bearing the upraised torch portrays either Victory or Thanatos (the Angel of Death) signaling resurrection, and the goddess on the right represents Venus coming to welcome her descendent as a god.

Rome suffered another volatile political period as opposing Roman factions struggled for power. At first, Marc Antony blocked Octavian from power, but Julius Caesar's legions rallied to support eighteen-year-old Octavian and chase Marc Antony and Marcus Aemilius Lepidus out of Rome. The Senate then cooperated with Octavian and declared Marc Antony and Marcus Aemilius Lepidus enemies of the state. In exile, they traveled toward Gaul to recruit their own legions.

---

[41]Some scholars describe the scene as Nike holding a torch, Sulla dreaming (see Chapter 15) in a garden, and Mâ approaching to name his enemies. Others describe the scene as Cupid lighting a tryst between Luna and a sleeping shepherd named Endymion.

Urging the Senate to ignore Octavian, Cicero[42] tried to restore honor to Julius Caesar's murderers and Optimate enemies. Under Cicero's leadership, the Senate assigned control of the Roman navy to Sextus Pompey and granted extraordinary powers in the East to Cassius and Brutus. Outraged, Octavian used Julius Caesar's legions to threaten the Senate.

The Senate appeased young Octavian by granting him a consulship. Octavian then marched his legions to Gaul to confront Marc Antony and Lepidus. Instead of fighting, however, the three men negotiated an agreement to join forces. Octavian, Marc Antony, and Marcus Aemilius Lepidus created the Second Triumvirate in November of 43 B.C. The triumvirs then drew up a proscription list and began executing enemies: former conspirators against Julius Caesar as well as current enemies of the Second Triumvirate.

The obverse of the Ephesian coin in Figure 18-8 displays busts of the triumvirs: Marc Antony, Octavian, and Lepidus. The reverse portrays a cultic statue of Artemis of Ephesos. Technically, the Second Triumvirate lasted for two five-year terms, from 43–33 B.C.

THE APOTHEOSIS OF JULIUS CAESAR

A staunch defender of the Roman Republic who had supported Pompey the Great and opposed Julius Caesar, Cicero had advised Rome, "Let no one have separate gods, either new or foreign, unless they are officially allowed."[43] However, by mid-December of 43 B.C., Cicero was dead. The Second Triumvirate had quietly arranged his assassination.

The Eastern idea that a great man might become a god finally achieved formal expression at the highest levels of Rome: On January 1, 42 B.C., Rome passed legislation that proclaimed Julius Caesar had become a god. The Senate also formally proclaimed Octavian, Caesar's

---

[42] A philosopher and former consul, Marcus Tullius Cicero tried to maintain the Roman Republic by restoring the respectability of Julius Caesar's assassins and treating Marc Antony as a dangerous enemy. The Second Triumvirate proscribed and then quietly murdered Cicero.

[43] See *Laws* 2.19 by Cicero.

Figure 18-8. Conjoined Busts of Marc Antony, Octavian, and Lepidus—the Second Triumvirate. Ionia, Ephesos, AE 15, 43–33 B.C.

adopted son, the *Divi Filius* or Son of God. A brand new temple served as the center of the Cult of Julius Caesar in Rome. Octavian participated in a formal ceremony acknowledging his adoptive father's apotheosis, and Marc Antony officiated as the cult's high priest.

The obverse of the coin in Figure 18-9 portrays a bust of Octavian encircled by a legend that proclaims him the "Son of God" and one of the triumvirs of the Republic. On the reverse, the coin bears an image of the temple that Rome dedicated to Julius Caesar. On its pediment, the temple portrays the *Sides Iulium*, or star of Julius Caesar (the comet that appeared during his funeral games). To the left of the temple, an altar supports garlands and offerings. A statue inside the temple portrays Julius Caesar as the pontifex maximus holding a *lituus* (an augur's tool). As high priest of the Cult of Julius Caesar, Marc Antony organized a program of devotional ceremonies in the temple.

Although traditional Roman society objected to elevating a man to kingship, many noble families had long revered small images of their ancestors as much as they revered statues of their household gods. Julius Caesar possessed qualities that tested the limits of humanity. Nevertheless, general acceptance in the West that a man might die and become a god marked a fundamental departure from previous religious beliefs in the region.

Figure 18-9. Octavian Caesar as the "Son of God," and Temple of the Divine Julius. Rome, AR Denarius, ca. 36 B.C.

Julius Caesar's accomplishments—numerous, revolutionary, and far-reaching—placed him in a class that confused Roman citizens. For example, after vanquishing Pompey the Great, he had traveled to Egypt and almost miraculously reduced it to a vassal state of Rome. He treated Cleopatra, the living Isis, as his mistress, but he also honored her as a goddess by placing her statue in a Temple of Venus Genetrix. Although traditional Roman society frowned on the worship of foreign gods, particularly Egyptian gods,[44] the Egyptian Cult of Isis had become a powerful force in the streets of Rome. In December of 43 B.C., the Second Triumvirate took advantage of the popularity of Egyptian religious beliefs by publicly announcing their intention to erect a Temple of Isis and Osiris in Rome.[45]

Julius Caesar had quickly defeated the forces that opposed him in Pontus, Africa, and Spain; and he had restructured Roman society: He granted citizenship to underprivileged Roman subjects, he gave land to his soldiers and to the poor, he created a library, he initiated a program of urban renewal, and he redefined the calendar according to precise movements of the stars. Having lived a controversial life without fear, Julius Caesar seemed more than human to his contemporaries. His

---

[44]During the first century B.C., Marcus Terentius Varro (116–29 B.C.) wrote critically against the worship of Alexandrian gods.
[45]Politics later interfered with the construction of this temple.

supporters had tried to crown him king and he had kept his true ambitions unclear and ambiguous during the last months of his life. Then, at the height of his fame and influence, some of his closest associates betrayed him, resulting in his brutal murder.

For the first time in history, social conditions, religious beliefs, politics, and astronomical chance conspired to make common Roman citizens believe that a human being had become a god. Romans heaped honors on the living man, proclaiming him Dictator, extending his dictatorship forever, and finally offering to make him King of Rome. Although, by modern standards, Julius Caesar resembled a war criminal more than a deity, the influx of Eastern ideas to the Italian peninsula had prepared common Romans to accept him as a god. After he died, Julius Caesar left every citizen a substantial amount of money, touching their lives as profoundly as a divine blessing. When the comet appeared in the sky during his funeral games, common Romans believed that Julius Caesar had sent a star to confirm his apotheosis.

In the power vacuum after Julius Caesar's death, ambitious leaders manipulated every circumstance, struggling to grasp political power and striving ultimately to take the place of the divine Julius Caesar. For a while, nobody in Rome cared much about the evil influence of new gods and foreign cults. Attracting ambitious entrepreneurs from all the nations in the known world, Rome had grown from a cultural backwater during the early Republic into a cosmopolitan mega-city with a population of several million. Foreigners in Rome worshipped cults from their distant homelands without hindrance while members of the Second Triumvirate looked for ways to take advantage of foreign religious beliefs to acquire more power.

Previously unimagined possibilities emerged in the game of politics: Ruling Rome brought power, wealth, and divinity as well. Octavian, the adopted son of Julius Caesar, began using the title, "*Son of God*,"[46] which immediately promoted the idea that he had inherited at least a spark of divinity from Julius Caesar. Using words and symbols in powerful ways, Octavian pioneered important new techniques for inspiring loyalty and influencing Western masses.

---

[46] *New Testament* gospel writers spoke of Jesus as the "Son of God" largely in contrast to earlier use of the same title by Octavian.

PART SIX

Victory Awarding Dominion over the Universe to Octavian, Son of God

THE CULT OF THE EMPEROR
RULE OF THE WEST SUPPORTED BY SYMBOLS AND LANGUAGE OF DIVINITY

Competing with Marc Antony and Cleopatra, Octavian/Augustus found it increasingly useful to assume a mantle of divinity as he acquired power, eventually portraying his ascendance over the Western world as the birth of a new spiritual age.

CHAPTER
19

THE ALLIANCE OF MARC ANTONY AND CLEOPATRA

HOW THE NEW DIONYSOS AND THE LIVING INCARNATION OF ISIS CAME TO OPPOSE THE SON OF GOD

> Some gods are born divine, some achieve divinity, and others have divinity thrust upon them.

In a sense, Cleopatra VII was born divine. Egyptians customarily regarded their pharaoh and his queen as gods. Since the death of Alexander the Great, Ptolemaic pharaohs had identified themselves with deities and sometimes claimed the title of *savior*, but none placed as much emphasis on their divine role as Cleopatra. In the West, her relationship with Julius Caesar enhanced her status as the living incarnation of an Egyptian goddess, and giving birth to Julius Caesar's only son directed continuing international attention toward a child whom many regarded as the incarnation of the savior Harpokrates.[1]

---
[1] See Chapter 10.

Eventually, Cleopatra established a relationship with Marc Antony and found new opportunities for expanding Egypt's power and influence. Surpassing all previous Hellenistic emperors in expression of divine conceits, she used her identification with Isis to associate herself with Eastern goddesses[2] like Astarte, Artemis, and Aphrodite in many regions far from Egypt.

As Julius Caesar's second-in-command, Marc Antony had matured during times when Rome still resisted cults from other parts of the world. After Julius Caesar's death, he expected that his military experience and popularity would propel him to leadership over Rome. However, new respect for Eastern ideas and spirituality in Rome brought an unpleasant surprise: Many Romans chose to follow Octavian, a youthful Son of God, in preference to a seasoned military commander. Beginning with his first struggles against Octavian, Marc Antony began to learn important lessons about the power of religious symbolism, which moved him eventually to find creative ways to claim his own divinity.

As people in the West embraced the Eastern notion that a man who had lived among them had become a god, a relationship with divinity was thrust upon Octavian Caesar through formal adoption. The comet that appeared in the night sky during Julius Caesar's funeral games affected Octavian deeply: He stated that the comet had come into being for him, and that he was coming into being in it.[3] In modern terms, he felt born again and the comet symbolized his rebirth. Because the comet appeared every day just as the constellation Capricorn rose on the eastern horizon,[4] Octavian afterward considered Capricorn his true birth sign.[5] After the Senate declared Julius Caesar's apotheosis, Octavian's natural talent for political spin and self-promotion moved him to popularize his official title, *Son of God*.

---

[2] The ability of Isis to represent any goddess in the Western world was so well-known that she was called *Isis the Many-Named*. See Chapter 10.

[3] See *Natural History* 2.93–94 by Pliny the Elder.

[4] See *The Comet of 44 B.C. and Caesar's Funeral Games* p. 15 by John T. Ramsay and A. Lewis Licht.

[5] Before he was "born again," Octavian's original birth sign was Virgo, the virgin. Ancient astrologers referred to Capricorn as the *Gate of Souls* because the sun underwent rebirth in that constellation every December 25. See *The Comet of 44 B.C. and Caesar's Funeral Games* p. 151 by John T. Ramsay and A. Lewis Licht.

Octavian had no illusions about his own mortality: He suffered from asthma and occasional grave illnesses over the course of his life. However, he used the astrological sign of Capricorn as a symbol to promote the idea that he had inherited divinity from Julius Caesar. Reflected divinity from Julius Caesar gave Octavian the power to compete with Lepidus and Marc Antony as an equal, enabling the creation of the partnership called the Second Triumvirate. Nevertheless, enormous problems confronted Octavian Caesar as a triumvir: If he survived the immediate economic, political, and military threats in Italy, then he would be forced inevitably to face challenges regarding the long-term ambitions of the other triumvirs.

By leading the Second Triumvirate to victory against Brutus and Cassius, the murderers of Julius Caesar, Marc Antony acquired the status of senior triumvir. Afterward, when the triumvirs carved Rome into separate domains for each triumvir to pursue separate ambitions, he chose the East, which offered the lion's share of opportunities for acquiring wealth and military glory. Tracing his descent from Herakles and exploiting the god's longstanding connection with the savior Dionysos,[6] Marc Antony publicly announced that he was the New Dionysos. He portrayed his Roman wives as the goddesses, Victory and Persephone. In addition, he obtained powerful support for military adventures against the Parthians by establishing a relationship with Cleopatra VII: In celebration of his relationship with the Egyptian queen, he minted coins that bore both their portraits and that described Cleopatra as "the youngest goddess."

With hard work and a little luck, Marc Antony had every reason to expect that he would accumulate so much wealth and military success that no one could prevent him from eventually dominating the West as the sole ruler of Rome. However, he never fully appreciated the power of public relations as a weapon, nor the talent of Octavian in wielding it. He allowed Octavian, uncontested, to characterize his triumviral relationship with Marc Antony as Western virtue against Eastern corruption, which slowly turned the tide of Roman opinion against Marc Antony and made East and West increasingly polarized.

---

[6] See Chapter 5.

ASSERTING EGYPT'S STATEGIC POSTURE TOWARD ROME

When Cleopatra abandoned Rome in mid-April 44 B.C., she had a lot more on her mind than merely her own safety. She began a journey with stops related to the long-term security of Egypt. She sailed first to Greece,[7] a land noted for excellent medical care, where she gave birth to Caesarion in early May. After that, Cleopatra focused on less immediate concerns, particularly those regarding her sister, Arsinoe, and her brother/husband, Ptolemy XIV.

When Julius Caesar released Arsinoe in 46 B.C., she found refuge at the temple of Artemis of Ephesos in Anatolia. From there, Arsinoe pursued long-distance intrigues hoping to resurrect an Egyptian faction dedicated to making her the Queen of Egypt. As long as Arsinoe lived, she posed a threat to Cleopatra's rule of Egypt. Similarly, even though Ptolemy XIV was young and stayed always close to Cleopatra's side, his ability to threaten Cleopatra's power would only increase over time. To Cleopatra, the threats represented by both siblings called for permanent solutions.

A Stopgap Measure against Arsinoe

After recuperating from childbirth, Cleopatra traveled to Cyprus, an island that her father had given to Rome and that Julius Caesar restored to Egypt in 48 B.C. Cyprus was important because it minted most of the coins used in Egypt. Further, the island offered excellent possibilities for Arsinoe to establish a territorial foothold and gain control of substantial Egyptian wealth. While nursing young Caesarion, Cleopatra VII came personally to assert Egyptian authority and to counter intrigues by her sister to seize control of the island. Cleopatra gave responsibility for governing Cyprus to Serapion, a trusted member of her retinue. Having assured herself that a loyal man had taken charge and made the island secure, Cleopatra sailed home, arriving in Alexandria in July.

---

[7]For a description of Cleopatra's voyage to Alexandria, see *Cleopatra: Beyond the Myth* pp. 32–4 by Michel Chauveau.

Chapter 19 | The Alliance of Marc Antony and Cleopatra   457

Figure 19-1. Egyptian Coins Related to Caesarion. Cyprus AE Diobol, and Alexandria AR Tetradrachm, ca. 44–43 B.C.

The bronze coin of Cyprus at the top of Figure 19-1 commemorates Cleopatra's successful visit to Cyprus in 44 B.C. The obverse of the coin portrays Cleopatra and young Caesarion. To worshippers of Hellenistic Egyptian cults, the images of the woman and child on this coin represented Isis and Harpokrates. Egyptians with more traditional backgrounds interpreted the images as Isis and the young god-king, Horus. Romans saw Venus and Cupid, and Hellenistic Greeks saw Aphrodite and Eros. Coins like this served to remind everyone of Julius Caesar's affair with Cleopatra and the birth of Caesarion—facts that helped confirm Julius Caesar's divine nature as well as ignite new interest in Egyptian cults throughout the Mediterranean region. Over the long term, the existence of Caesarion offered possibilities for Egypt to wield increasing leverage in its strategic relationship with Rome.

Permanently Dealing with Ptolemy XIV

Fifteen-year-old Ptolemy XIV, the only surviving brother of Cleopatra VII (ostensibly, her husband) also posed a long-term threat for the throne of Egypt. Egypt had relied for centuries on incestuous relationships between its kings and queens as a means of maintaining the purity and divinity of its rulers: Gods always mated with parents, siblings, and children.[8] However, Ptolemy XIV was necessary only as long as no other Ptolemy existed for Cleopatra to marry.

The birth of Caesarion, also named Ptolemy XV, eliminated the need for a fictitious relationship with Ptolemy XIV. Once she had returned to Alexandria, Cleopatra made sure that her brother never would challenge either herself or Caesarion for the throne of Egypt. Although his specific fate remains unknown, Ptolemy XIV disappeared from history. Cleopatra then declared Caesarion co-regent of Egypt.

Affirming Divinity of the Egyptian Line of Julius Caesar

Familiar with all the important players in Roman politics (men like Octavian, Marc Antony, Lepidus, Brutus, Cassius, Sextus Pompey, and others), Cleopatra VII received regular reports from her spies about the evolution of Rome's political situation. After a comet appeared in the sky in July 44 B.C., Cleopatra learned about the popular Roman belief in Julius Caesar's divinity. Learning that Rome had built a temple to Julius Caesar as a god, Cleopatra decided to do the same in Egypt: She ordered the building of the *Caesareum*,[9] a temple larger and more magnificent than even the enormous Serapeum[10] in Alexandria. The Egyptian temple affirmed the relationship between Julius Caesar and Caesarion as symbolically equivalent to the divine relationship between Osiris and Horus.[11]

Mindful of her long-term dependence on good relations with Rome, Cleopatra waited for an opportune moment to send emissaries

---

[8] See Chapter 2.
[9] Filled with admiration and praise for this temple, the Alexandrian Jew, Philo, describes the Caesareum in *Legatio ad Baium* 15.
[10] Recently uncovered, the foundations of the Caesareum supported walls 2.5–3.5 meters thick.
[11] See Chapter 10.

to ask for Rome's recognition of Caesarion's official status. At a delicate moment in 43 B.C., as Octavian, Marc Antony, and Lepidus maneuvered for ascendance of the Second Triumvirate over the murderers of Julius Caesar, she sent a formal request for Rome's recognition of the new rulers of Egypt. Facing difficult problems in Rome, none of the triumvirs wished to foster additional problems with Egypt. The Second Triumvirate officially recognized Cleopatra and Caesarion as co-rulers of Egypt in November 43 B.C.

Cleopatra marked her achievement by minting a coin that identified 43 B.C. as year one[12] (LA) of the new reign. (See the bottom coin in Figure 19-1.) The star on the coin's obverse represents the comet that appeared in the sky during Julius Caesar's funeral games. Having ensured a position of increasing strength in Egypt's strategic relationship with Rome, Cleopatra carefully avoided becoming embroiled in Rome's civil war between the triumvirs and Cassius and Brutus. Instead, she focused on dealing with the day to day issues of Egypt: In fact, a bad omen occurred in the form of severe famine, which caused her to return mostly to dating Egyptian coins from her own accession to the throne in 51 B.C. Nevertheless, she returned once again to minting coins with a star and the new dating system several years later, just before she gave birth to twins by Marc Antony in 40 B.C.

DEALING WITH THE ENEMIES OF THE SECOND TRIUMVIRATE

Generous, energetic, affable, and generally competent, Marc Antony had an enviable record of leading Roman legions to victory in hard-fought battles. In peacetime, however, he sometimes shirked his responsibilities, occasionally abandoning all reason and dignity.[13] He wanted power, but he was quick to forgive, and he had counted many

---

[12]This controversial dating system was first suggested in the mid-nineteenth century by W. Dittenberger in *Orientis Graeci Inscriptiones Selectae*, No. 194. See discussion in *The House of Ptolemy: A History of Egypt under the Ptolemaic Dynasty* p. 370. Numismatics lends credence to this conjectural dating system because these coins, dated year one and four, strongly resemble Egyptian tetradrachms minted in Cleopatra's regnal years eight and eleven during the years 44–43 B.C. and 41–40 B.C.

[13]For examples of Antony's bad behavior, see *The Life of Antony* 9:3–6 by Plutarch.

of the murderers of Julius Caesar among his friends.[14] Nevertheless, he welcomed the opportunity to eliminate long-time enemies like Cicero, a family enemy whose writings had proved both personally embarrassing and politically damaging.[15]

At first, the triumvirs bargained among themselves about who to enter on the proscription list. Attempting to protect their kinsmen and kill their enemies, they traded one name for another. That all changed, however, when the military demanded that Octavian and Marc Antony establish a familial bond between them, which was possible only through Fulvia, Marc Antony's wife.

Marc Antony had married Fulvia[16] after he returned to Rome from the Gallic Wars. Extraordinarily ambitious and energetic, she helped Marc Antony in his quest for power after the death of Julius Caesar. During the negotiations for Octavian to marry Claudia, her fourteen-year-old daughter, Fulvia, entered wholeheartedly into the proscription process: three hundred names suddenly found their way onto the Second Triumvirate's list.[17] Opponents disappeared and the triumvirs soon acquired sufficient power to declare Cassius and Brutus enemies of the state. However, arguments with Fulvia eventually persuaded Octavian to end his relationship with her daughter.

Marc Antony placed Sextus Pompey's name on the list of proscribed Romans early in 42 B.C. By then, Sextus had assumed command of a Roman fleet based in Massalia. When news of his proscription reached him, he used the fleet to rescue other proscribed Romans, escaped slaves, and anyone else willing to join him. He brought numerous supporters to Sicily and established a pirate base from which he began to blockade the western coast of Italy.

---

[14]As ambitious aristocrats like Cassius organized the plot against Julius Caesar and Brutus, contributing an aura of legitimacy to the cause, it's even possible that Marc Antony knew about the plot in advance and acted as a provocateur by repeatedly offering a king's crown to Julius Caesar. See *The Life of Julius Caesar* 79.2–80.1 by Suetonius.

[15]See *The Life of Antony* 2.1 and 17.1 by Plutarch.

[16]Entering her third marriage as well, Fulvia previously had married Publius Clodius Pulcher, the notorious gang lord of Rome. After Milo's gang murdered Clodius, Fulvia married the unfortunate commander that Julius Caesar posted in Sicily. Her second husband led the disastrous expedition from Sicily to Africa in 49 B.C. and died fighting Roman Republicans and King Juba's Africans. See Chapter 17.

[17]For indications of Fulvia's participation, see *The Life of Augustus* 62.1 by Suetonius and *The Life of Antony* 20.1 by Plutarch.

Chapter 19 | The Alliance of Marc Antony and Cleopatra   461

Figure 19-2. Civil War Issue with Bust of Brutus, Daggers, and Pileus. Northern Greece, Military Mint, Brutus, AR Denarius, 42 B.C.

Preparations by Brutus and Cassius for a Showdown in Greece

As the triumvirs solidified their control over Rome, Cassius and Brutus traveled through Greece and Syria (at first with strong Senate support) gathering money, allies, and soldiers to fight a new civil war. Coordinating their efforts, they successfully raised substantial armies. When Brutus defeated antagonistic tribes in Thrace, his legions praised him as *imperator*, or conqueror. Also, the combined legions of Brutus and Cassius defeated the Lycians and Rhodians, owners of large navies that the rebels wanted to prevent from entering an alliance with the triumvirs. As an expression of commitment to each other and to the Republican cause, Brutus and Cassius made a pact to commit suicide if they lost the approaching war against the triumvirs.

Brutus paid his legions with coins like the one in Figure 19-2. The obverse displays a proud bust of Brutus and proclaims him a conqueror. The reverse glorifies the murder of Julius Caesar by displaying two daggers, one belonging to Brutus and the other belonging to Cassius. The cap (*pileus*) between the daggers portrays the type of hat that Roman masters gave slaves when granting them freedom. The inscription on the reverse names the date of Julius Caesar's murder, the Ides of March.

The Battle of Philippi

In the Summer of 42 B.C., the triumvirs arranged to transport an army to Greece to fight the rebels. Marc Antony and Octavian led the triumviral legions to Greece while Lepidus remained in Rome. However, Octavian spent much of the campaign incapacitated by ailments of various kinds.

Near Philippi in northern Greece, two battles in the beginning of October 42 B.C. decided the fate of the latest Roman civil war. Symbolic of Julius Caesar's presence, a comet[18] appeared in the night sky before hostilities. Early in the first battle, the triumvirs' legions seemed to be winning. However, Brutus achieved a draw against the forces of Marc Antony and Octavian with a strong last-minute effort. Unfortunately, Cassius misinterpreted the course of the battle and thought his side had lost: He committed suicide before he could learn differently.

Several weeks later, Brutus fought Marc Antony and Octavian again. This time, Brutus' army appeared stronger at the beginning of the battle, but Marc Antony reversed the battle's momentum and routed Brutus' legions. Brutus fled on horseback. A few days later, he fulfilled his pact with Cassius by killing himself with the same dagger he'd used against Julius Caesar. One account says that Marc Antony gave Brutus a respectful funeral, burned his body, and sent his ashes to his mother in Rome. However, a different account[19] says that Octavian decapitated Brutus and sent his head on a ship to Rome.[20] Octavian intended to throw the head at the foot of Julius Caesar's statue. Instead, superstitious sailors tossed the head overboard during a storm.

TRIUMVIRAL MANEUVERS: COMPETING AND COOPERATING TO DOMINATE THE ROMAN WORLD

After the Battle of Philippi, the triumvirs divided Rome into three parts among themselves. Marc Antony obtained control over Greece and Asia, and he began to think about extending Rome's dominion even further east. Lepidus went south to govern the important, relatively

---

[18]See *Roman History* 47.40.2 by Cassius Dio and *Astronomica* 1.907 by Manilius.
[19]See *Roman History* 47.49.2 by Cassius Dio.
[20]See *Marcus Brutus* 52.1–53.4 by Plutarch.

stable areas of North Africa and Spain. Twenty-one-year-old Octavian returned to Rome alone to face critical challenges in Italy, and Gaul.

The enormous problems afflicting the central portion of the Roman world presented Octavian with few opportunities for gain and a high likelihood of disaster. If he failed to solve Rome's problems, a wealthy and powerful Marc Antony eventually might return from the East, wrest control from Octavian, and enjoy a savior's welcome. With Rome suffering from a naval blockade, Octavian's most critical problem was making sure that an adequate supply of food reached the city.

Octavian's Nemesis: Sextus Pompey

By using his ships to steal goods bound for western Italy, Sextus Pompey drastically reduced Rome's food supply. Octavian launched a fleet toward Sicily to destroy Sextus and his pirates, but Sextus destroyed Octavian's fleet instead. Acutely aware that calling himself the Son of God brought only the opportunity to rule Rome and that he needed to improve Rome's food supply soon, Octavian desperately searched for ways to secure his position.

Increasing his own strength at the expense of Octavian, Sextus began calling himself the *Son of Neptune*. He minted coins like the one in Figure 19-3. The obverse portrays Sextus' father, Pompey the Great. On the reverse, Neptune poses with several nautical symbols: a rudder, an *aplustre* (decoration for ship's stern), and a ram. On either side of Neptune, the Sicilian Katanean brothers, Amphinomus and Anapias,[21] carry their parents away from an eruption of Mount Aetna. Proscribed Romans that were similarly rescued by Sextus, including refugees from the Battle of Philippi, eagerly joined their savior on Sicily.

Marc Antony's Introduction to the East

Introducing himself to his Eastern subjects with celebrations reminiscent of Hellenistic conceits, Marc Antony established control over the East in 42–41 B.C. in new and extravagant ways. He entered important Eastern cities as a visiting deity. For example, he entered Ephesos

---

[21]See Chapter 4.

Figure 19-3. Coin of Sextus Pompey with a Bust of Pompey the Great, and with Neptune with Katanean Brothers. Sicily, AR Denarius, ca. 42–40 B.C.

dressed as Dionysos incarnate preceded by Pans, Satyrs, and *Bacchantes* (frenzied female worshippers) dancing to the music of flutes and pan-pipes. Ephesos proclaimed Marc Antony the "New Dionysos, bringer of joy and source of peace."

To honor his wife, Marc Antony changed the name of a Phrygian city from Eumenia to Fulvia. The city then minted bronze coins with his wife's portrait (see the top coin in Figure 19-4), the first known images of a non-mythological Roman woman on coins. Wings at her shoulder identify her as the Goddess of Victory.

Fulvia's War against Octavian

While Marc Antony traveled in Greece and Anatolia, Fulvia stayed in Rome and busied herself with political intrigues with Lucius Antonius, Marc Antony's brother. Lucius served as consul while Octavian, the triumvir, struggled to negotiate the settlement of 100,000 discharged soldiers in eighteen cities in Italy. Together, Lucius and Fulvia exploited Octavian's absence from Rome by attempting to undermine his power: They publicly maligned him and obtained permission from the Senate to wage war against him.

In 41 B.C., Lucius and Fulvia raised eight legions to prosecute a war against Octavian. Before initiating hostilities, they attempted to

Chapter 19 | The Alliance of Marc Antony and Cleopatra   465

Figure 19-4. Coins of Marc Antony's wife, Fulvia. Phrygia, Eumenia, AE 18, ca. 41–40 B.C., and Gaul, Lugdunum, AR Quinarius, ca. 43–42 B.C.

summon additional legions from Gaul that Marc Antony kept as his own reserve against Octavian. However, even though Marc Antony paid his Gallic legions using small silver coins with Fulvia's portrait (see the lower coin in Figure 19-4), the legions declined to join Lucius and Fulvia in Italy without Marc Antony's explicit authorization.

Supported by an enlarging pool of talented and loyal friends, Octavian reacted quickly. Summoning legions from Spain, Octavian confronted Lucius and Fulvia at Perusia (modern Perugia), placed the town under siege, and forced them to surrender in February 40 B.C. Octavian executed Perusian senators and burned the city of Perusia. However, to reduce the possibility of precipitating a war against the allied forces of Lepidus, Sextus, and Marc Antony, he did not harm Lucius and Fulvia. Octavian appointed Lucius to an unimportant position in Further Spain and allowed Fulvia to depart Italy for Athens, Greece. Both Lucius and Fulvia died of natural causes within a year of their defeat by Octavian, however, Fulvia met one last time with Marc Antony before she died.

A Divine Interlude Badly Interrupted

In the Summer of 41 B.C., Marc Antony moved to Tarsos. He sent orders to Egypt for Cleopatra to appear and explain Egyptian support of Brutus and Cassius[22] during the civil war. Slow to respond, Cleopatra arrived in Tarsos in the Fall of 41 B.C. Three years after Julius Caesar's murder, twenty-eight-year-old Cleopatra (outfitted like the Goddess, Venus) sailed into the harbor at Tarsos. Her ship gleamed with sunlight sparkling from gilded wood and gold-embroidered fabrics. Young men in Cupid costumes swarmed the deck, and young women resembling Nereids (sea nymphs) and Graces sat on rower's benches and pulled silver oars. In Tarsos, people described the event as Aphrodite visiting Dionysos.[23] Captivated at the prospect of a divine affair, Marc Antony abandoned his responsibilities in Tarsos.[24] He accompanied Cleopatra to Alexandria and spent the Winter at her palace.

Early in 40 B.C., unexpected events interrupted Marc Antony's delightful interlude: The Parthians invaded Syria. Taking an Alexandrian astrologer with him,[25] Marc Antony sailed to Tyre, a center of resistance against the Parthians. There, Marc Antony learned about the rebellion that Lucius and Fulvia had led in Italy and of Octavian's victory at the Battle of Perusia.

Distracted from prosecuting the war against Parthia, Marc Antony sailed from Tyre to Athens and met with Fulvia. He scolded her bitterly and then traveled to Italy with soldiers and ships to sort out his relationship with Octavian. Although Marc Antony arrived ready for war, Octavian preferred negotiating to fighting; and friends of both men easily reconciled the two.[26] Lepidus joined them in Brundisium and all three triumvirs began discussing the terms of their agreement.

---

[22]Roman legions left Egypt and joined Cassius. Also, Cyprus' ruler, Serapion, sent ships to support Cassius. Cleopatra claimed that famine, pestilence, and bad winds had prevented her ships from delivering support to Marc Antony and Octavian. However, it's likely that she provided intentionally ambiguous support to protect Egypt regardless of who won the civil war.
[23]Hellenistic Greeks often paired Aphrodite and Dionysos.
[24]As evidence of the price Marc Antony paid for an intimate relationship with Cleopatra, Roman soldiers murdered Arsinoe in Ephesos around this time.
[25]See *The Life of Antony* 33 by Plutarch.
[26]See *The Life of Antony* 30:3–4 by Plutarch.

Renegotiating the Second Triumvirate

With assistance from his Alexandrian astrologer, Marc Antony negotiated with Octavian and Lepidus to resolve their differences and modify their triumviral agreement. They declared Italy a shared territory and reaffirmed assignment of the East to Marc Antony and the West to Octavian. Octavian also acquired Spain at the expense of Lepidus who then ruled only North Africa.

While still in Brundisium, Marc Antony learned of Fulvia's death in Greece. Greeting her loss as an opportunity, he arranged to bind himself closer to Octavian by marrying Octavia, Octavian's older sister. Marc Antony remained in Italy after the marriage and enjoyed a prolonged honeymoon. Octavia soon became pregnant.

Having successfully improved his relationship with Marc Antony through marriage, Octavian reconsidered his approach toward resolving his biggest problem: Sextus Pompey. The pirate had directed his attacks only against Octavian and Italy. Approaching the problem with renewed flexibility and creativity, Octavian married Scribonia, a niece of Sextus Pompey. Then, with Marc Antony's approval in 39 B.C., Octavian succeeded in negotiating a deal: Sextus Pompey could control Sicily, Sardinia, Corsica, and Achaea if he lifted the blockade against Italy and supplied grain to Rome.

Events in the East Calling to Marc Antony

In the East, the Parthians successfully captured more Roman territory. Having supported Rome's administration in Syria Province as Ethnarch of Judea, young Herod barely escaped from the Parthians with his life. He fled embattled Syria Province and arrived in Egypt in the latter part of 40 B.C. Hugely pregnant by Marc Antony, Queen Cleopatra VII granted Herod an audience. She listened to his report of the Parthians' successes and offered him an Egyptian army, but he declined. Instead, he asked only for passage to Rhodes. She granted his request, and he departed.

Once in Rhodes, Herod found passage to Rome where he obtained Marc Antony's support. The Senate honored Herod for his faithfulness

Figure 19-5. Bust of Marc Antony Imitating Dionysos, and Bust of Octavia with Snakes and Cista Mystica. Ionia, Ephesos, AR Tetradrachm, Summer/Fall 39 B.C.

to Rome and proclaimed him King of the Jews. Around the same time in Egypt, Cleopatra gave birth to fraternal twins by Marc Antony, a girl named Cleopatra Selene and a boy named Alexander Helios.

Toward Summer's end in 39 B.C., Marc Antony and Octavia left Rome and set up their household[27] in Athens. Octavia soon gave birth to a baby girl named Antonia. During this period, Marc Antony ruled the Roman East as a loyal friend of Octavian.

Minted in Ephesos a year after the Treaty of Brundisium, the coin in Figure 19-5, celebrates the marriage of Marc Antony and Octavia. The obverse of the coin portrays Marc Antony surrounded by his titles and wearing a diadem of ivy like the god Dionysos. The reverse carries a bust of Octavia (representing Persephone) on a *cista mystica* (a basket that contained sacred objects for conducting initiations into the Bacchic or Dionysiac mysteries). Snakes, also used during initiations, surround the cista mystica.

---

[27] If Marc Antony's other children accompanied them, the household would have included children by Fahdia, his first wife, a daughter (Antonia) by Antonia, his second wife, and two boys (Marcus Antonius Antyllus and Iullus Antonius Creticus) by Fulvia, his third wife.

Cooperating to Resolve Rome's Biggest Problems

From Athens, Marc Antony directed the efforts of his military staff to liberate Roman territories occupied by the Parthians. Once his generals successfully repatriated Roman territories, Marc Antony personally led a force that crushed the small kingdom of Commagene ruled by Antiochos, the last pretender to the throne of the Seleukid Empire. Antiochos had strongly supported the Parthians.

However, Parthian power continued to threaten Roman interests in Asia. Marc Antony intended to mount a campaign to finish the Parthians once and for all. First, however, he needed to renew the triumviral agreement for a period long enough to encompass the campaign, so he and his family returned to Italy.

Octavian's alliance with Sextus Pompey hadn't lasted. Having suffered continuing piracy, Octavian reinitiated the war against Sextus just one year after making peace with him. Octavian sent another fleet against Sextus, who again destroyed it. Octavian divorced Scribonia the same day that she gave birth to Julia, his only natural child, and he soon married Livia Drusilla.[28]

In December 38 B.C., Marc Antony, Octavian, and Lepidus again met in Tarentum, to discuss extending the Second Triumvirate. Marc Antony needed legions to fight a land war against the Parthians, and Octavian needed ships to fight Sextus Pompey. Marc Antony gave 120 ships to Octavian in exchange for Octavian's promise to send 20,000 soldiers to Marc Antony. The Treaty of Tarentum extended the triumvirate for a second five-year term until December 33 B.C.

COMMITTING TO AN ALLIANCE WITH CLEOPATRA

Returning East in the Fall of 37 B.C., Marc Antony and Octavia crossed the Adriatic Sea to Corfu. Then, because of apprehensions about his wife's pregnancy, Marc Antony arranged for her to return, slowly and

---

[28]Octavian obtained special approval from Rome's pontifices to marry Livia because she was pregnant with her second child by her first husband, Tiberius Claudius Nero. For the peculiar circumstances surrounding the marriage, see *Roman History* 48.44 by Cassius Dio.

carefully, to Rome while he continued toward Antioch. After reaching Rome, Octavia gave birth to their second daughter, Antonia Minor.

In Antioch, Marc Antony struggled with the problem of administering Rome's territories in the East, a difficult region plagued with an abundance of incompatible ethnicities, cults, and sensibilities.[29] He couldn't begin a campaign against the Parthians unless he had reliably secured the administration and control of the Roman East during his absence. Further, he had to establish his administration in the face of well-deserved antagonism inspired by longstanding, rapacious Roman policies that drained the wealth from Rome's foreign provinces.

Attempting to create a new, enlightened administrative model, Marc Antony abandoned direct administration of the East by Romans. Instead, he divided the East into large territories governed by local client rulers loyal only to him. Elevating talented men with no connections to previous dynasties, he divided most of Asia Minor into three territories: Galatia ruled by Amyntas (a secretary of the former king), Pontus ruled by Polemon (son of a local politician), and Cappadocia ruled by Archelaos (son of a former mistress of Marc Antony). Marc Antony already had stabilized Judea by placing it under King Herod, but other areas in Cilicia, Syria, and Phoenicia remained problematic. Some regions, like Chalkis (an ancient city-state halfway between Beirut and Damascus), had enthusiastically declared allegiance to the Parthians in the recent war. As Marc Antony considered how to resolve his remaining issues, he began to see his relationship with Cleopatra as the key for giving him what he needed to pursue his ambitions in the East.

A Second Meeting with Cleopatra

In the Winter of 37 B.C., Marc Antony summoned Cleopatra to Antioch. She brought the twins, Cleopatra Selene and Alexander Helios, to meet their father. Conveniently merging political and personal interests, Marc Antony and Cleopatra rekindled their romance. Whether or not he actually married her, Marc Antony reaffirmed Cleopatra's possession of Cyprus and he offered her control over all the territories he considered problematic. Egypt previously had ruled

---

[29]Similar issues still confront modern rulers in this region.

Figure 19-6. Bust of Marc Antony, and Diademed Bust of Cleopatra VII Wearing a Pearl Necklace. Antioch or Other Eastern Mint, AR Tetradrachm, 36–33 B.C.

these lands during the height of the Ptolemaic Empire. By offering her a chance to rule the empire of her ancestors, Marc Antony ensured Cleopatra's strong support. In return, he obtained freedom to focus on preparations for war against the Parthians.

Marc Antony used Cleopatra's connection to the traditional gods of Egypt to elevate his reputation throughout the East and to legitimize his regime. For example, he struck a new issue of large silver coins like the tetradrachm in Figure 19-6. On the coin's obverse, the legend around Cleopatra's portrait describes her as both a queen and the youngest goddess. On the reverse, the legend around Marc Antony's portrait proclaims him a triumvir, declared for the third time. Around Cleopatra's neck, a pearl necklace (a traditional wedding gift) advertises an otherwise unrecorded marriage between Marc Antony and Cleopatra VII, symbolically representing their relationship as a divine marriage between Dionysos (Osiris/Bacchus) and Isis (Aphrodite/Venus).

Cleopatra's Role as Marc Antony's Enforcer

After settling plans with Marc Antony, Cleopatra toured her new territories with a substantial contingent of Marc Antony's forces and masterfully asserted control. She visited Chalkis first. Lysanias, the ruler of the city-state, had notoriously defected from Rome at the

Figure 19-7. Coins Related to Cleopatra's March against Lysanias. Bronze Coins of Chalkis, ca. 36 B.C.

first opportunity and fought on the side of the Parthians in the recent war. In Figure 19-7, the top left coin from Chalkis is *countermarked* (stamped) with a small bust of Cleopatra[30] on the obverse approximately at six o'clock. (A bust of Zeus on the obverse is upside-down.) Coins with this countermark come from all the Eastern territories that Marc Antony granted to Cleopatra. Countermarked bronze coins often served as temporary military pay tokens that soldiers could exchange for camp supplies.

Minted before Cleopatra's arrival, the beautiful coin on the upper right of Figure 19-7 bears a realistic portrait of Lysanias, the self-styled King of Chalkis. His monogram appears just above Athena's shield on the coin's reverse. As Cleopatra and her borrowed legions approached Chalkis, its king had good reason to dread their arrival. When she arrived, the queen summarily executed him and brought Chalkis under the direct control of Egypt.

After the execution of Lysanias, the Chalkis mint produced coins bearing Cleopatra's portrait and Egyptian symbols, but the earliest depictions of Cleopatra on coins of Chalkis rank among her ugliest portraits. For example, the obverse of the lower coin in Figure 19-7 portrays a strong-chinned Cleopatra VII instead of weak-chinned

---

[30]The attribution of this countermark to Cleopatra VII is controversial but her territories correspond well with the geographical distribution of countermarked coins.

Lysanias. The reverse of this coin bears two cornucopias to the right of Lysanias' monogram. Ominously, the monogram appears crossed out beneath a large X. The cornucopias (common devices on Alexandrian coinage) assert Egyptian domination of Chalkis, and the treatment of Lysanias' monogram reflects Cleopatra's treatment of Lysanias. These coins served to warn rulers of nearby regions that resistance to Egyptian control would not be tolerated.

Marc Antony's Disastrous Invasion of Parthia

With Cleopatra VII administering problematic regions, Marc Antony spent the beginning of 36 B.C. making preparations for the conquest of Parthia. He amassed an invasion force of approximately 100,000 men, a third of them provided by Eastern allies. Although Octavian had promised to send 20,000 additional soldiers in exchange for Marc Antony's ships, the soldiers never arrived. Marc Antony chose not to wait longer for Octavian's legions because the time seemed right for action: Parthia had entered a civil war; Phraates IV of Parthia had assassinated his older brother, Orodes II; and a group of Parthian nobles had assured Marc Antony that they would support the Roman invasion.

With all his client rulers reporting firm control over the Roman East, Marc Antony launched his expedition against Parthia. Ambitious and optimistic, he attempted a vast flanking movement, first leading his forces northeast through Armenia and then south toward the Parthian heartland. On the way, he also intended to conquer the kingdom of Medea. Unfortunately, the campaign suffered from planning mistakes, bad luck, and naked treachery by the King of Armenia.

By October of 36 B.C., Marc Antony had succeeded only in establishing an unproductive siege of the capital of Medea. Because approaching Winter threatened his army's survival, he abandoned the siege and struggled to march his legions back to Roman territory. A third of his men died in numerous attacks throughout the retreat, and he saved the rest only through heroic effort and outstanding leadership. When he finally reached the Mediterranean Sea, just south of modern Beirut, Marc Antony sent to Cleopatra for help.

It took time for Cleopatra to gather resources to help thousands of starving and wounded Roman soldiers. In addition, she had just reached full-term in her second pregnancy by Marc Antony. When she arrived with her ships bearing food and medicines, she also displayed their new son, Ptolemy Philadelphus.

The End of Octavian's Need for Support from Marc Antony

While Marc Antony unsuccessfully battled Parthians and Armenians in the East, Octavian finally defeated Sextus Pompey. Even though Sextus had damaged Octavian's fleet in August 36 B.C., Agrippa, Octavian's best military commander, destroyed Sextus' navy in September. Having learned much from hard experience, Agrippa achieved victory using all Octavian's legions in concert with a navy augmented by Marc Antony's ships. The defeat of Sextus Pompey eliminated Octavian's single greatest obstacle toward consolidating power.

However, defeat at the hands of Agrippa did not immediately bring an end to Sextus Pompey. Escaping capture once again, he sailed east where he intended to build a new pirate navy. As his father had years before, Sextus considered forming a partnership with the Parthians. However, Marc Antony's forces held firm control over the East, and Sextus had to watch his step.

Lepidus brought fourteen legions to Sicily from North Africa, ostensibly to help Octavian fight Sextus. Instead, Lepidus tried to steal control of Sicily. After disposing of Sextus' navy, Agrippa landed Octavian's legions on Sicily and confronted Lepidus, whose legions promptly defected. Octavian expelled Lepidus from the triumvirate and placed him under guard. Still, Octavian did not allow himself the luxury of ill-considered vengeance. He merely stripped Lepidus of all his honors and titles but one—Pontifex Maximus. Lepidus continued to serve Rome as Pontifex Maximus until his death almost a quarter century later.

Preparing the Roman World for War between East and West

While Marc Antony recovered from his disastrous setback, Octavian basked in his first great military success. For the first time, he could concentrate on ruling Rome without an enemy actively attempting to defeat him. Also, because of Lepidus' ill-conceived attempt to steal

Sicily, Octavian acquired control over North Africa. He soon felt confident enough to initiate a new kind of campaign against Marc Antony.

Unexpectedly, Marc Antony began to experience the sting of a war of ideas and words coming from Rome. While Marc Antony might prove Octavian's superior commanding equal forces on a battlefield, Octavian demonstrated unrivaled mastery over spin and public relations. Marc Antony soon found himself at a disadvantage in a propaganda war. Octavian publicly criticized Cleopatra for taking too long to bring help to Marc Antony and his defeated soldiers. Also, damning Marc Antony in comparison, Octavian made sure that equal praise was heaped on Marc Antony's disastrous campaign against Parthia as on Agrippa's success against Sextus Pompey.

Octavian even pretended to fulfill his obligation to provide military assistance to Marc Antony against the Parthians. For Marc Antony's campaign against land-locked Parthia, Octavian finally returned seventy ships, a heavily used remnant of the 120 ships Marc Antony originally loaned to Octavian. To man the ships, Octavian provided two thousand soldiers, one-tenth the number he had promised. As Octavian's masterstroke in delivering this assistance, he sent Octavia in the Spring of 35 B.C. to lead the fleet to her husband and to redeem him from his infidelity with Cleopatra.

Neither stupid nor cowardly, Marc Antony nevertheless found no way to fight against the remorseless campaign against his reputation in Rome. Short of civil war, his only hope for retaining power came from the wealth of Egypt and his relationship with Cleopatra. From Alexandria, Marc Antony sent a letter to Octavia in Athens: He ordered her to return to Rome but to send the ships and soldiers east. The written insult to Octavia committed Marc Antony to Cleopatra and gave Octavian fresh ammunition for intensifying his propaganda campaign.

TOO MANY GODS

Three people dominated the Western world in the first decades after the death of Julius Caesar: Cleopatra VII, Octavian Caesar, and Marc Antony. Cleopatra possessed great wealth, brilliance, and courage, but her single-minded focus on the welfare of her country distanced her at first from the cutting edge of world politics. Eighteen-year-old Octavian quickly seized significant power in Rome: Although he seemed too young and inexperienced to succeed in the long term, he demonstrated a precocious ability to comprehend, calculate, and act with a masterful grasp of political tactics and strategy. Marc Antony, an experienced veteran of war and Roman politics, easily commanded Roman respect and popularity, but he sometimes acted intemperately and committed blunders. These three people gathered strength during the confusion following Julius Caesar's death in 44 B.C. until they dominated all other competitors for power. All three enhanced their abilities to influence public opinion by representing themselves as divine.

In Rome, Julius Caesar's adopted son, Octavian, won increasing recognition as a worthy heir by applying himself vigorously to solving Rome's problems. His situation improved slowly through a sequence of stages: struggling for survival, maintaining equilibrium, credibly sharing power, seizing advantage, and then carefully orchestrating the overthrow of his competitors. After Agrippa defeated Sextus Pompey, Octavian easily marginalized Lepidus and began taking aim against Marc Antony.

In the East, Marc Antony squandered his opportunities, not through lack of imagination, energy, or good ideas, but through overconfidence and acting without making effective contingency plans. If he had been less sure of victory against Parthia in the beginning, his campaign might have succeeded and he might have been remembered for equaling or surpassing Alexander the Great. Instead, he suffered a grave defeat and lost respect in Rome through Octavian's attacks on his public image.

Approximately thirty years before the birth of Jesus Christ, Octavian, Cleopatra, Marc Antony, and Sextus Pompey framed the political competition for power over the Western world as a struggle among gods. Marc Antony foolishly gave generous material support to Octavian whom he mistakenly judged to be an honorable ally. In return, Octavian successfully characterized his rivalry with Marc Antony as a clash between East and West: While portraying Marc Antony as having been corrupted by Eastern luxuries and immorality, Octavian maintained a reputation for virtue as he lied, reneged on commitments, and acted freely according to his own best interests. He even used his sister as a political pawn, pretending that Marc Antony's negotiated partnership with Cleopatra, a relationship never recognized as a marriage in Roman terms, was an insult to Western womanhood.

However, the source of Octavian's claim to divinity was nothing compared to the deep historical roots that nourished the incarnate gods of Egypt. As Isis, Cleopatra had borne a child by the martyred god Julius Caesar,[31] whom a spectacular temple in Alexandria honored as Osiris, the god who made eternal life possible. Allied with Antony against Octavian, Cleopatra attracted international support based solely on her association with important regional goddesses throughout the East.

Even though Marc Antony failed dramatically in his bid to conquer the Parthians, his relationship with Cleopatra lent credibility to his continuing identification with Dionysos, a divine savior of humanity. In addition, Egypt's wealth gave him more than merely a second chance to field an army: With the wealth of Egypt, his enhanced status as the consort of Cleopatra VII, his demonstrated leadership ability, and his years of military experience, Marc Antony had every right to expect that he would easily win if outright hostilities ever developed with Octavian.

Of course, the existence of Caesarion, Cleopatra's natural son by Julius Caesar, made the development of hostilities inevitable. To Egyptians, the child provided assurance of continuing divine rule in Egypt. However, to Octavian, Caesarion represented an increasing threat over time. The more Octavian succeeded as the Son of God, the more he had to lose when Caesarion, the real son of Julius Caesar, appeared on the world stage. The threat that had seemed insignificant in 43 B.C. when the Second Triumvirate accepted Caesarion as co-ruler of Egypt would prove insurmountable in the form of a brilliant young man with the features and deportment of Julius Caesar.

---

[31] Even though Cleopatra lost the struggle against Octavian, the image of Isis nourishing Horus/Harpokrates became an iconic symbol of piety in the West.

CHAPTER
20

A CIVIL WAR PORTRAYED AS A CLASH OF GODS FOR CONTROL OF THE UNIVERSE

> Octavian's masterful use of propaganda and Agrippa's brilliant execution of a deadly first strike attack convinced the East to abandon Marc Antony and Cleopatra and declare allegiance to Octavian.

In 35 B.C., the two remaining triumvirs, Octavian and Marc Antony, worked on strengthening their respective domains: Octavian struggled to coax the economy of the Roman Republic back to functional health while Marc Antony harnessed the wealth of the East to support a gigantic military machine. Although many bonds still connected the two men—years of triumviral partnership, common friends, and familial relations—increasing friction between them forced people to choose one side or the other. Many powerful friends of Marc Antony served in the Roman Senate, and many common Romans remembered him as Julius Caesar's dashing and powerful cousin who had served as second-in-command during the Gallic Wars. However, as the relationship between the triumvirs grew strained, it became increasingly unhealthy in Rome to express positive sentiments about Marc Antony.

The last great struggle for power over the Roman Republic initiated a brief period when both East and West united in the conviction that mortals might become gods. Regardless of which triumvir won the war, it was inevitable that a Roman Empire would emerge ruled by a mortal who had made serious claims of divinity.[1] Influenced by state propaganda, East and West became increasingly polarized and interactions between the two triumvirs increasingly resembled stylized relations between virtue and vice in a morality play.

By partnering with Cleopatra and pursuing an independent agenda in the East, Marc Antony gave ample ammunition for assassination of his character to Octavian. Regardless of whether Marc Antony succeeded or failed at achieving his goals, Octavian's propaganda turned the result into a moral fault: When Marc Antony failed to conquer Parthia, Octavian portrayed him as corrupt and weakened by Cleopatra; but when Marc Antony defeated Armenia, Octavian portrayed him as obsequiously using the benefits of his victory to purchase favors from his domineering Egyptian mistress. By finally divorcing Octavia and appearing to found an Eastern dynasty, Marc Antony communicated acceptance that he and Octavian eventually must go to war.

However, strong bonds of affection connected Rome and Marc Antony. His love and patriotic respect for Roman institutions and values disinclined him from attempting to seize Rome like a conqueror. Instead, he chose to prepare for war, but not to start it. He waited for Octavian to take the dishonorable step of beginning the war.

With an immense army and all the wealth of the East at his disposal, Marc Antony didn't see his weaknesses. He failed to anticipate Octavian's first deadly thrust and neglected to pay the cost of saving himself while he had a chance. He and Cleopatra survived their first major engagement with Octavian's forces, but were too weakened afterward to build a credible defense of the East. Their last year together has become a frequently retold story of dramatic love and loss. However, in the more important terms of Octavian's religious propaganda, the old gods died in Egypt and the East, and a Son of God from the West began to rule the universe.

---

[1] Precedents like Julius Caesar, Octavian, and Marc Antony made it easier for many Romans eventually to accept that a human named Jesus had become a divine savior.

THE POLARIZATION OF EAST AND WEST

Governing a territory that suffered from having too much political division and too little money and food, Octavian used persuasion, propaganda, and force to keep his government running from day to day. Few details survive about the expediencies Octavian used to ameliorate his difficulties. However, because he won the civil war, the world remembers his side of the story: He succeeded in making the world better than it used to be because of Western virtues and divine intervention. Octavian's histories comprise stories that condemn Marc Antony and Cleopatra for weakness and corruption, characterizations that support Octavian's story that he built a moral and vastly improved empire by using Western virtues to overcome Eastern vices.

However, many Romans preferred Marc Antony's military experience and traditional manliness to Octavian's manipulative intellect and tendency toward ill health. If Octavian had died in 35 B.C., Rome would have embraced Marc Antony as its ruler. He would have shaped the emerging Roman Empire and we would remember him much differently than we do.

Believing that time was on their side, Marc Antony and Cleopatra concentrated on recovering from the Parthian misadventure and consolidating their control over the East. Neither wanted trouble with Octavian, and both wanted to enhance their lives in the East. While Octavian restricted support for Marc Antony in Rome, Marc Antony tried to recreate Roman traditions in Egypt: For example, he created a way to celebrate triumphs in Alexandria. Cleopatra, on the other hand, busied herself trying to resurrect the Ptolemaic Empire.

First Steps toward Setting East and West in Opposition

From 35–34 B.C., Octavian Caesar waged a successful campaign against Illyrian tribes along the northern Adriatic Sea, thereby gaining valuable experience working with his generals. Instead of celebrating a military triumph after winning the Illyrian War, he publicly honored his wife and sister, Livia and Octavia, crediting their Roman virtues for the victory and implicitly contrasting them with the Eastern vices of Cleopatra.[2] Marc Antony's relationship with the Queen of Egypt served as a constant and easy target for Octavian's propaganda. Playing to Roman fears that Eastern immorality would weaken Western civilization, Octavian portrayed himself as Rome's savior, a guardian of morality divinely appointed to preserve the Roman Republic. However, events proved that he would do anything to achieve unrivaled power in Rome, and he would never relinquish power once he had grasped it firmly.

Cleopatra advised Marc Antony to ally with Sextus Pompey against Octavian. Marc Antony dispatched one of his generals to meet the rebel, neutralize his forces if necessary, and escort him to Alexandria. However, Sextus Pompey didn't cooperate: He invaded northwestern Anatolia and, when chased, fled inland toward Armenia. A wily commander, he fought vigorously and refused to surrender. He finally was captured attempting to conduct a raid that came close to inflicting serious losses on his pursuers. For exhibiting unrelenting antagonism, he was taken to Miletus on the west coast of Anatolia and executed.[3] Although the historical record vacillates about Marc Antony's personal responsibility in the death of Sextus Pompey, the execution allowed Octavian to criticize Marc Antony for failing to extend mercy to a worthy Roman citizen.

Cleopatra's Role in Solidifying Marc Antony's Control over the East

Marc Antony slowly regained his optimism in Alexandria as he recuperated from the failed Parthian expedition. He still intended to expand his territories eastward. When a conflict developed between Medea and Parthia, the King of Medea expressed willingness to go to war against Parthia in alliance with Marc Antony.

Partly to exact revenge and partly to eliminate another possibility for treachery against a future campaign, Marc Antony marched against Armenia in the Spring of 34 B.C. Cleopatra VII accompanied Antony's

---

[2] See *Roman History* 49.38.1 by Cassius Dio.
[3] For information related to this episode, see *Roman History* 49.18.1–5 by Cassius Dio, *Civil Wars* 5.133–144 by Apian, *Geographica* 3.2, p. 141 by Strabo, and *Roman History* 2.79.5 by Velleius.

legions as far as the Euphrates River,[4] and then returned slowly toward Alexandria. As she conducted a long inspection tour of her expanded empire, she made a point of visiting King Herod of Judea, a relatively independent client-king who reported directly to Marc Antony.

By 34 B.C., King Herod and Cleopatra VII hated each other: Cleopatra hated King Herod because he governed Judea, a land that she wanted to add to her restored Ptolemaic Empire; King Herod hated Cleopatra because she actively sought to depose him—he even discovered that she was plotting against him with one of his mothers-in-law.[5] Only partly protecting King Herod from Cleopatra, Marc Antony gave Cleopatra control over Jericho's profitable production of *balsam oil*.[6] To King Herod—a man who murdered members of his own family when they crossed him[7]—a long-term threat like Cleopatra deserved a well-planned assassination. Still, the King of the Jews welcomed his visiting rival with the generous hospitality due the consort of Marc Antony.[8]

In 34 B.C., all the Roman territories subject to Cleopatra VII began to mint coins that affirmed her association with local gods and goddesses. These coins generally bear a date referencing 37 B.C.—the year Marc Antony first gave her control of the territories—as year one of the new Ptolemaic Empire.[9] Some coins paired her portrait with that of Marc Antony, implicitly recognizing him as her consort deity, while other coins portrayed only Cleopatra. Figure 20-1 shows the obverses and reverses of three examples of these coins. All of the examples bear the queen's portrait, but they indicate her divinity in different ways: The first implicitly identifies her as the consort of a local male deity; the second implicitly identifies her as a local female deity; and the third calls her a goddess without specifying which one.

---

[4] See *Antiquities of the Jews* 14:96 and *The Jewish War* 1:362 by Josephus.
[5] See *Cleopatra: Beyond the Myth* pp. 57–58 by Michel Chauveau.
[6] The plant that produced balsam oil is now extinct. The oil was heavier than water and was important in ceremonies for anointing (Moshiach) Jewish Kings.
[7] See *The Jewish War* 1.22 by Flavius Josephus.
[8] See *Antiquities of the Jews* 15:4:2 by Josephus. The accusation that Cleopatra attempted to seduce Herod lacks credibility. See *Cleopatra: Beyond the Myth* p. 58 by Michel Chauveau.
[9] See *Cleopatra of Egypt: From History to Myth* p. 235 edited by Walker and Higgs, *Porphyry of Tyre* in *Die Fragmente der griechischen Historiker* no. 260, F 2.17 by F. Jacoby, and *Cleopatra: Beyond the Myth* p. 52.

Figure 20-1. Imperial Coins of Cleopatra VII, 36–31 B.C. Top Left: Phoenicia, Orthosia, AE 21, ca. 36–35 B.C. Top Right: Syria, Damascus, AE 25, ca. 37–36 B.C. Bottom: Syria, Chalkis, AE 20, ca. 32–31 B.C.

From the coastal Phoenician city of Orthosia, the first (top left) coin portrays Cleopatra on the obverse and Baal of Orthosia in a chariot pulled by griffins on the reverse. Composite animals, griffins resemble the Cherubim that attended the Jewish God in the Jerusalem Temple's Holy of Holies. Providing archaeological confirmation for the iconography of this coin, an inscription in the Temple of Isis in the Phoenician city of Tripolis explicitly equates Isis with Artemis of Orthosia, the consort of Baal of Orthosia.

From Damascus, the second (top right) coin portrays Tyche on the reverse. Syrians in Damascus identified Tyche with Atargatis, the principal Goddess of Damascus at this time. The coin implicitly identifies Cleopatra as an incarnation of Atargatis.

From Chalkis, the third (lower) coin explicitly proclaims Cleopatra as queen and "youngest goddess." Because the coin portrays both Marc Antony and Cleopatra, it symbolizes their union as a divine marriage of Dionysos and Isis. Nevertheless, the legends on both sides of the coin speak only about Cleopatra and fail to mention Antony at all.

The Donations of Alexandria: Proclaiming an Eastern Empire

Marc Antony and Cleopatra both returned to Alexandria by late Summer of 34 B.C. Having crushed Armenian resistance, Marc Antony brought Armenia's King Artabazes in chains. The successful campaign against Armenia impressed the King of Medea so much that he agreed to a future marriage between his only daughter and the six-year-old son of Marc Antony and Cleopatra, Alexander Helios.

In the Fall, Marc Antony and Cleopatra honored the victory with a special Eastern-style triumph. Celebrating a triumph in Alexandria instead of Rome declared Marc Antony's complete independence from the West. Crowned with ivy and carrying a thyrsus like Dionysos, Marc Antony began the celebration by parading Armenian captives before Cleopatra who sat like a goddess on a golden throne.

Later, in the Great Gymnasium of Alexandria, Marc Antony conducted a ceremony remembered by history as the "Donations of Antony."[10] On top of a tall silver platform, Marc Antony, Cleopatra, and Cleopatra's four children sat on gold thrones before the people of Alexandria. Marc Antony declared that Cleopatra was "Queen of Kings" and ruler of Egypt, Cyprus, Libya, and central Syria. Next, he declared Caesarion to be the rightful son of Julius Caesar and named him "King of Kings." Wearing Persian robes and a tiara, Alexander Helios, the six-year-old fiancé of the Princess of Medea, was declared the sovereign of Armenia and of all the lands beyond the Euphrates River as far as India. Wearing the purple robe, cap, and diadem of a Macedonian king, two-year-old Ptolemy Philadelphus was declared King of Syria, Phoenicia, and much of Asia Minor as far as Byzantion (modern Istanbul). Lastly, Marc Antony declared Cleopatra Selene the Queen of Cyrenaica (modern Libya) and parts of Crete. Marc Antony retained sovereignty only of Greece, Macedonia, and Roman Asia.

While celebrating the Donations of Alexandria, Marc Antony distributed coins like the denarius in Figure 20-2 to Egyptian citizens. On the obverse of the denarius, the legend[11] and the Armenian tiara behind Marc Antony's head refer to his conquest of Armenia. The legend on the reverse describes Cleopatra as the "Queen of Kings whose sons are kings" and a ship's prow honors her contributions to Marc Antony's war chest.

---
[10]See *Roman History* 49:40:3–4 and 49:41:1–3 by Cassius Dio, *The Life of Antony* 54 by Plutarch, and *Cleopatra: Beyond the Myth* pp. 58–61 by Michel Chauveau.
[11]The legends on this coin are written in Latin so Romans could read them.

Figure 20-2. Coin Related to Marc Antony's Triumph in Alexandria. AR Denarius, Armenia Devicta, 34 B.C.

PREPARING FOR CIVIL WAR

After Marc Antony's significant defeat of Armenia, Octavian dared not speak about military prowess lest his own meager victory over Illyria suffer in comparison. However, the two men started to exchange increasingly bitter letters. When Octavian accused Marc Antony of immoral behavior for sleeping with Cleopatra, Marc Antony replied with a long list of the names of Octavian's mistresses. Marc Antony offered a moderate proposal for reconciling their differences: He suggested that they restore the Republic by both relinquishing their triumviral powers simultaneously. Of course, he made this proposal knowing full well that Octavian never would agree.[12]

While conducting a state visit to Medea toward the end of 33 B.C., Marc Antony received a letter in which Octavian rejected the possibility of ever sharing power in Rome. This refusal to honor his legal obligations toward Marc Antony affirmed the inevitability of war once the triumviral agreement expired in December of 32 B.C. Marc Antony started preparing for a defensive campaign against Rome. He

---

[12]See *Cleopatra: Beyond the Myth* p. 64 by Michel Chauveau.

established a military headquarters at Ephesos and sent instructions for Cleopatra to join him. Soon, Cleopatra arrived in Ephesos accompanied by two hundred ships loaded with provisions, soldiers, and large amounts of gold and silver.[13]

Marc Antony's Well-Supplied but Chaotic Base in the East

In January of 32 B.C., the beginning of the last year of the triumviral agreement, Rome elected two consuls loyal to Marc Antony with the ability to make trouble for Octavian. Octavian immediately sent armed partisans into the streets of Rome. Fearing for their lives, the consuls and two hundred pro-Antony senators fled the city. In a short time, like Pompey the Great fifteen years earlier, Marc Antony found his camp in Ephesos burdened with a Roman government in exile.

Marc Antony spent freely, purchasing goods and services that he needed for war. In addition, he paid his soldiers with legionary denarii made from Cleopatra's silver. All legionary denarii portray a ship on the obverse and military standards on the reverse: Of the two examples in Figure 20-3, the lower coin honors the Third Legion and the upper coin honors Marc Antony's spies. Coins like these paid wages to 30 legions, crews of 500 warships, 25,000 auxiliary infantry, and 12,000 cavalry. The coins flooded the economies of the East where they continued to circulate well into the first century A.D.

Octavian's Preparations for War

In poverty compared to Marc Antony, Octavian used spin, propaganda, and political manipulation to damage Marc Antony's reputation while delaying the start of the war. Struggling to fund an army and build ships, Octavian pretended that he had sent Marc Antony's senators and consuls to negotiate an alternative to civil war. Not wanting to provoke Marc Antony into invading Italy, Octavian focused his propaganda mostly against Cleopatra at first. Yet, when Marc Antony announced his divorce of Octavia and sent orders for her to leave his

---

[13]See *The Life of Antony* 55–56 by Plutarch.

Figure 20-3. Coins Related to Marc Antony's Preparations for Civil War. Top: AR Denarius, Patrae, Chortis Speculatorum, ca. 32–31 B.C. Bottom: AR Denarius, Patrae, Legion III, ca. 32–31 B.C.

house in Rome,[14] Octavian launched an unbridled campaign of slander against both Marc Antony and Cleopatra.

Unconstrained by decency, law, or religious beliefs, Octavian found useful propaganda in unusual places. For example, even though the Vestal Virgins[15] guarded Marc Antony's will, Octavian obtained it and publicly revealed a shameful provision: Marc Antony wanted to be buried in Alexandria with Cleopatra.[16] Further, Octavian's stooges, defectors from Marc Antony's forces among them, testified that Marc Antony intended to conquer Rome and give it to Cleopatra to rule.

---

[14] See *The Life of Antony* 57 by Plutarch.
[15] The College of Vesta comprised eighteen Vestal Virgins: six in training, six functioning as priestesses of Vesta, and six older members who served mostly as teachers. Their most important function was to make sure that a fire always burned in the sacred hearth of Vesta in Rome. Their responsibilities also included guarding wills and sacred religious objects, for example, the Palladium that Aeneas brought from Troy.
[16] See *The Life of Antony* 58 by Plutarch.

Gossips spoke of Marc Antony wearing woman's clothing and being dominated by Cleopatra, just as Omphale once had dominated Marc Antony's ancestor, Herakles.[17] Stories that circulated about Cleopatra's sorcery and depravity tested the limits of both the imagination and credulity of the Roman public.

Despite Octavian's effective use of propaganda, many Romans continued to support Marc Antony. His supporters sent a messenger to tell him that, by renouncing Cleopatra and returning to Rome, he easily could rally Romans to his cause and overthrow Octavian. In Egypt, Cleopatra discredited the bearer of this message[18] as well as other friends of Marc Antony who expressed similar beliefs.

Octavian's military strength paled in comparison with that of Marc Antony. Few historians doubt that if he had marched against Rome during the Summer of 32 B.C., no force in Italy could have stopped him.[19] Instead of attacking, however, Marc Antony occupied the moral high ground: He chose not to begin a war against Rome, but to wait until war came to him.

Waiting for Octavian to Strike

In Ephesos, some of Marc Antony's commanders asked him to distance himself from Cleopatra and send her back to Egypt. They argued that her presence in a military camp seemed to confirm Octavian's propaganda. Instead, Marc Antony followed advice from his Chief of Staff who believed that Cleopatra should stay in Ephesos to remind the legions that their main financial supporter—the provider of so many ships and soldiers—had committed the wealth and well-being of herself and her nation to their success.[20]

In the Spring of 32 B.C., with war preparations largely complete, Marc Antony and Cleopatra began a tour of major Eastern cities. The cities welcomed them lavishly. On Samos, for example, the couple enjoyed a festival run by the richest Dionysiac guilds of Greece and Asia. During the opulent religious celebrations, visiting Eastern leaders

---

[17]See *Comparison of Demetrios and Antony* 3 by Plutarch. Also, see Chapter 6.
[18]See *The Life of Antony* 59 by Plutarch.
[19]See *Cleopatra: Beyond the Myth* p. 66 by Michel Chauveau.
[20]See *The Life of Antony* 56 by Plutarch.

Figure 20-4. Greek Coin Honoring Cleopatra VII as Isis. Achaia, Patrae, Hexachalkon, ca. 32–31 B.C.

filled every spare moment with expressions of commitment and loyalty to the royal couple.

Marc Antony and Cleopatra reached Athens in the Summer. Cleopatra tried to erase Athenians' memories of Octavia by hosting spectacular events and giving generous public donations. In gratitude, the Athenians installed statues of Marc Antony and Cleopatra on the Acropolis among statues of the gods.[21]

By Fall, Marc Antony had prepared a chain of fortified ports to protect the sea route all the way from Actium (anchorage for Marc Antony's fleet) on the eastern coast of Greece to Alexandria. He and Cleopatra then wintered on the northern Peloponnese in Patrae, which honored Cleopatra by minting the coin in Figure 20-4. This bronze coin bears an attractive bust of the queen on the obverse and a crown of Isis on the reverse. At Patrae, Marc Antony's mint continued to churn out large quantities of legionary denarii.

As an example of bitter historical irony, the Achaean town of Aegira (near Patrae) minted coins with crude obverse portraits also intended to resemble Cleopatra: The town placed Cleopatra's features, including the addition of a feminine bosom, to their numismatic portrait of

---

[21] See *Roman History* 50:15:2 by Cassius Dio.

Chapter 20 | A Civil War Portrayed as a Clash of Gods

Figure 20-5. Crude Coin That Associates Cleopatra with Iphigenia Minted while Antony and Cleopatra Wintered in Greece. Achaia, Aegira, AE Tetrachalkon, 32–31 B.C.

Iphigenia. (See Figure 20-5.) The Temple of Artemis in Aegira contained a famous statue of Iphigenia, a noble and beautiful daughter of Agamemnon. At the beginning of the Trojan War, Iphigenia had willingly allowed her father to sacrifice her to Artemis so that the goddess would allow the Greeks to launch their ships for Troy. In the gathering storm between Marc Antony and Octavian, many Greeks would have seen a resemblance between Cleopatra's unstinting support of Marc Antony and Iphigenia's support of Agamemnon. Yet, after the battle of Actium, Octavian's propaganda criticized Cleopatra precisely because she did not allow herself to be sacrificed.[22]

THE PROGRESS OF THE WAR

At the end of 32 B.C., Octavian ordered the Senate to declare war on Egypt. By design, the Senate declared war only on Cleopatra and her supposed intention of enslaving Rome. Regarding Marc Antony, the Senate declared that his term as a triumvir had expired, but he could return to Rome as a private citizen if he chose: He need only renounce

---

[22] See *The Life of Antony* 66 by Plutarch.

his connection with Cleopatra. In the Spring of 31 B.C., Octavian's forces (well commanded by Agrippa) began a systematic sweep down the coast of Greece from Corfu. Agrippa captured isolated cities and islands and landed troops at strategic locations.

Overconfident, Marc Antony had failed to perceive the impossibility of defending a long supply chain between Alexandria and Greece. After learning of Agrippa's activities, he hurried north to Actium where the largest concentration of vessels in his fleet lay anchored in the Gulf of Ambrakia. Agrippa's fleet arrived just in time to blockade the mouth of the gulf and prevent Marc Antony's fleet from leaving. Then, the opposing navies fought indeterminate skirmishes for months in the gulf while Agrippa's land forces gradually captured Antony's bases of support on land.

The Battle of Actium

Marc Antony grew more desperate as his land support dwindled and his fleet grew more vulnerable. Perceiving themselves at a long-term disadvantage, his soldiers began to desert and join Octavian. Shaken by the defections, Marc Antony could have altered his situation by abandoning his ships and transferring his operations completely to land. However, he decided against scuttling the ships and losing the huge investment they represented.

Octavian's propagandistic history emphasized Cleopatra's cowardly flight toward Egypt and Marc Antony's passionately mad race to catch her.[23] However, using the same facts, a different story could be told: Marc Antony placed all his hopes on a desperate gamble that failed because he placed too much trust in his friends and subordinates. Believing that his best remaining option was to run the blockade, he hoped to free as much of his navy as he could, regroup his forces on land, and continue the war from Asia Province after. He ordered the bulk of his land forces to begin marching overland toward Asia Minor and then he gambled on freeing critical resources in a naval battle.

During the Battle of Actium on September 2, 31 B.C., Marc Antony struggled to liberate as much of his navy as possible to escort

---

[23]See *Cleopatra: Beyond the Myth* p. 69 by Michel Chauveau.

Cleopatra's treasure ship carrying the remainder of her gold and silver back to Alexandria. Agrippa's navy captured or sank more than 170 ships, killing more than five thousand soldiers including ships' crews. Fewer than sixty of Marc Antony's ships escaped. On land, Marc Antony's Chief of Staff prepared to march his army east, but emissaries brought an alternative proposal from Octavian: an attractive offer that allowed the army to change sides and avoid risking further loss or hardship in battles of Romans against Romans.[24] Reconsidering their loyalty to an absent leader who had blundered so badly, all of Marc Antony's land forces in Greece defected to Octavian.

Rapidly Shifting Fortunes

Once free from Octavian's blockade, Marc Antony and Cleopatra sailed to a port west of Alexandria and then divided the fleet. Cleopatra sailed immediately for Alexandria to deal with possible treason and rebellion in Egypt while Marc Antony sailed to Cyrenaica (Libya) to gather four legions he had stationed there. He soon discovered that all four legions had abandoned him and declared allegiance to Octavian.

Before they deserted Marc Antony, the Cyrenaican legions minted coins like the lower coin in Figure 20-6. The obverse portrays a bust of Zeus Amon, and the reverse portrays the Goddess of Victory. This coin was the last ever minted that expressed loyalty to Marc Antony.

Upon returning to Egypt, Marc Antony learned that all his legions had turned against him except the few that still remained in Alexandria. Further, the Asian cities that previously had sworn to support him had rushed to declare allegiance to Octavian. All the alliances, all the armies, and all the ships purchased with the wealth of Egypt had disappeared like smoke on a windy day.

However, not all of his former supporters benefited during the mass defection. After the Battle of Philippi years earlier, Marc Antony had pardoned Decimus Turullius, one of the original murderers of Julius Caesar. Earning recognition as a trusted military commander, Decimus minted the top coin in Figure 20-6 during the Summer of 31 B.C. The obverse of the coin portrays a smiling bust of Marc Antony surrounded

---

[24]See *Cleopatra: Beyond the Myth* p. 70 by Michel Chauveau.

Figure 20-6. The Last Coins Minted During Marc Antony's Campaign. Top: Actium, AR Denarius, Decimus Turullius, ca. 32–31 B.C. Bottom: Cyrene, AR Denarius, Amon and Nike, Summer, 31 B.C.

by his titles, among them *Augustus* or "Revered One," a title that the Roman Senate later granted to Octavian. The reverse of the coin portrays the Goddess of Victory, implicitly ready to crown Marc Antony for defeating Octavian. After the battle of Actium, Agrippa captured Decimus and executed him on the island of Cos.

Languishing in Alexandria, Marc Antony succumbed briefly to depression while Cleopatra energetically searched for opportunities for survival. She investigated possibilities for rebuilding Egyptian defenses as well as for retreating to India or Spain. Although her efforts finally roused Marc Antony, they both soon gave up hope. Cleopatra, Marc Antony, and their loyal friends began to call themselves "those who would die together." They worked, they feasted, and they lived one day at a time. Cleopatra minted a final set of tetradrachms commemorating the twenty-second year of her reign.

Before the war, King Amyntas of Galatia, one of Marc Antony's client-rulers, had minted bronze coins with goddess images that

Chapter 20 | A Civil War Portrayed as a Clash of Gods   495

Figure 20-7. Images of Cleopatra VII (Top) and Livia (Bottom) as Artemis on Coins Minted by King Amyntas of Galatia. AE 19, 37–25 B.C.

resembled Cleopatra. Variations among these coins show that the king adjusted images of the goddess on the coins according to the progress of the war. Minted early in the campaign, the top coin in Figure 20-7 portrays Artemis with the strong features commonly associated with Cleopatra VII. On later specimens of these coins, for example, the lower coin in Figure 20-7, Artemis looks more generic and more like Octavian's second wife, Livia. These coins confirm the special collaboration that existed between politics and religious convictions during these times: The gods remained the same, but their faces changed to reflect dramatic shifts in power.

Octavian's Slow Advance toward Alexandria

Even after achieving overwhelming victory, it took Octavian another year to finish the war. He stayed in the East long enough to accept declarations of loyalty from Antony's former clients and to obtain initiation into the Eleusinian Mysteries. Then he hurried back to Rome to put down a festering rebellion of discontented veterans. While preparing for the war, he had risked everything by relentlessly abusing credit and good will. Although his success at Actium dramatically improved his prospects for repairing the problems he had created, he could not afford to weaken himself further. He consolidated his victory slowly and carefully because only complete victory could secure the revenues he needed from the East. When he finally launched an invasion of Alexandria, half of his fleet advanced toward Alexandria by way of Cyrenaica while he accompanied the other half by way of Greece, Asia Minor, and Syria.

With all Marc Antony's forces and allies declaring allegiance to Rome, Octavian adjusted his propaganda. He minted the top coin in Figure 20-8 portraying himself as a divine conqueror. On the obverse, an Apollonian bust of Octavian gazes left. On the reverse, the Goddess of Victory stands on a globe[25] that bears lines marking the ecliptic and the celestial equator as they appeared on Hipparchus' model of the universe.[26] The goddess extends her arm holding a victory wreath over text that proclaims Octavian *Caesar Son of God*. Symbolically, Octavian used this coin to announce that he, the Son of God, had achieved mastery over the universe. When Marc Antony's legions in Cyrenaica switched allegiance, they minted the lower coin in Figure 20-8 announcing to the world that they had abandoned Marc Antony to serve Octavian Caesar. Crudely executed, the obverse of the coin portrays an extended hand offering friendship while the reverse expresses support for Octavian's view of his role as ruler of the universe.

Shortly after the battle of Actium, King Herod of Judea hurried to Rhodes, taking a prominent place among Marc Antony's clients rushing to declare allegiance to Octavian, which successfully preserved the life and kingship of Herod. Afterward, he continued to use every opportunity he could find to eliminate any remaining doubts about

---

[25]The coins in Figure 20-8 reveal remarkable similarities between symbols surrounding the birth of the Cult of the Emperor under Octavian and symbols used later by Christians: Christians also honored a Son of God; Nikes evolved into angels; and victory wreaths changed into halos. Christian emperors also used globes as symbols of power and dominion, but they forgot that globes originally represented the shapes of the Earth and the universe.

[26]See Chapter 13.

Figure 20-8. Coins Proclaiming the Victory of Octavian Caesar over Marc Antony and Cleopatra VII, 31–30 B.C. Top: Italian Mint, AR Denarius, Octavian, ca. 32–29 B.C. Bottom: Cyrene, AR Denarius, 31 B.C.

his loyalty to his new master. As Octavian advanced carefully toward Alexandria, Herod greeted Octavian in Syria with an elaborate display of loyalty toward Octavian and Rome.

The Fall of Alexandria

Some of the most storied, yet uncertain events in the lives of Marc Antony and Cleopatra happened during their last days.[27] On the evening of August 1, 30 B.C., a ghostly Dionysiac procession left Alexandria through the Canopic Gate, just one day before Octavian's forces

---

[27]For descriptions of these days, see *Roman History* 51:10–17 by Cassius Dio and *The Life of Antony* 76–87 by Plutarch.

entered Alexandria through the same gate. Marc Antony organized resistance against Octavian's invading army. However, Cleopatra barricaded herself, a few servants, and supplies inside her fortified mausoleum. After false news about Cleopatra's death reached Marc Antony, he attempted suicide. Loyal supporters of Marc Antony carried their mortally wounded leader to the mausoleum where, tragically, he died in Cleopatra's arms.

Octavian captured Cleopatra, held her under armed guard, and personally interviewed her. Yet, somehow, Cleopatra and all her attendants successfully committed suicide. In death, Cleopatra's body lay on a golden bed, her hands holding both Macedonian and Pharaonic royal symbols. Using text comparable to *New Testament* descriptions of events after the crucifixion of Jesus,[28] the historian, Cassius Dio, said that, "comets were seen and dead men's ghosts appeared, the statues frowned, and Apis bellowed a note of lamentation and burst into tears."[29] Embellishing stories of people's deaths with miracles was a common literary device that emphasized their greatness and, in this case, added a sense of dramatic inevitability to Octavian's victory—the old gods died and then the new god took over.

Considering the strength of Marc Antony's support in Rome and the double-edged prospect of parading Cleopatra in chains in a triumph in Rome, Octavian may have played an active role in helping Cleopatra die. In addition, significantly less drama and far fewer details survive in descriptions of the deaths that Octavian ordered for two teenagers: Julius Caesar's only natural son, Caesarion; and Marc Antony's oldest son by Fulvia, Marcus Antonius Antyllus.

Octavia assumed the responsibility of raising at least four of Marc Antony's surviving children by other women. Besides caring for her own children by Marc Antony (Antonia Major and Antonia Minor), Octavia found room in her Roman household for his younger son by Fulvia (Iullus Antonius Creticus), and all three of Marc Antony's children by Cleopatra—the ten-year-old twins, Alexander Helios and Cleopatra Selene, as well as seven-year-old Ptolemy Philadelphus.

---

[28]See *Matthew* 27:51–54 and *Luke* 23:44–46.
[29]See *Roman History* 51:17:4 by Cassius Dio.

THE END OF AN AGE

The victory of Octavian over Marc Antony in 30 B.C. brought an end to a brief period when Western leaders masqueraded as gods as they competed for control over the Western world. The Ptolemaic Empire died along with its deified rulers, and the only human god left standing was the adopted son of Julius Caesar. Octavian never gave up the power he wielded at the moment of the Roman Republic's greatest victory. Instead, his success precipitated the end of the Roman Republic.

The Ptolemaic Empire was the last of the Hellenistic empires spawned by Alexander the Great. By enabling diverse cultures to communicate freely, Hellenism had brought about a cultural Springtime, a great flowering of civilization that produced great empires. However, extending itself to every shore of the Mediterranean Sea, Rome harvested the wealth of Hellenistic lands and spent it on military domination. Sophisticated Eastern cults began to deteriorate along with the cultures that made them, and great cultural centers like Pergamon, Babylon, and Alexandria began to wither in a cultural Fall. For many people in the East, the collapse of the Ptolemaic Empire recalled prophecies that a savior would be born when the last Hellenistic empire fell and the End of Days would soon follow.[30]

Marc Antony died at the age of fifty-three and Cleopatra died at the age of thirty-nine. Most of the story of their lives reached modern times only through the filter of Octavian's propaganda. Octavian said that Marc Antony celebrated his triumph in the East, not because Octavian would have marginalized him in Rome, but because Marc Antony wanted to deprive Roman citizens of a share in the spoils. Further, the distribution of Roman lands to Antony's children by Cleopatra happened, not because Egypt funded and supported Marc Antony, but because Cleopatra had bewitched him into committing high treason. Octavian never spoke of Marc Antony's declaration of Caesarion as the legitimate son of the god Julius Caesar. While Caesarion lived, he presented a continuing and grave threat to Octavian, exposing him eventually as only an unnatural pretender.

---

[30]See Chapter 7.

At the young age of thirty-two, Octavian Caesar enjoyed undisputed mastery of Rome and all her territories. His administrative talent and the wealth of Egypt combined well to bring good times to Rome. Skillfully employing his gift for spin and propaganda, he continued to strengthen his position until his power, success, and longevity served as conclusive arguments for his divinity. The first ruler of the Roman Empire, he inspired a persistent belief in the divinity of Rome's emperor and his propaganda provided the symbols that clothed a rapidly developing Cult of the Emperor.[31] As just one measure of Octavian's effectiveness, the family name of Caesar has survived two thousand years as a title for rulers and kings (for example, *Kaiser* and *Tsar*).

In 30 B.C., the Roman Republic was not yet dead. It would take time for Octavian to persuade Rome to press power and honors upon him as if it were Rome's idea. Some historians say that the Roman Republic died in 27 B.C. when Octavian ostensibly gave up his powers to restore the republic: That's when the Senate renamed him Augustus and gave his powers right back. Some say the republic died in 19 B.C. when Augustus (previously Octavian) received consular power for life. Regardless, the republic was certainly dead by 2 B.C. when the Senate proclaimed Augustus Caesar "Father of His Country." During his later years, he cultivated a dignified image, gravely managing the empire while frantically searching for an heir. Within a few decades, the Roman Republic that would not tolerate a king died so gradually that no one knows for sure when the death occurred. Throughout this period, Octavian/Augustus used his talents for propaganda to precipitate a spiritual renewal and to create a new combination of political and religious sensibilities in Romans. By the time of Augustus' death, Romans accepted rule by him and his heirs as though by a divine family.

---

[31]Beginning under Octavian/Augustus, Romans commonly built temples for worshipping members of the imperial first family, living and dead, as divine beings.

CHAPTER
21

THE INAUGURATION OF A NEW SPIRITUAL AGE

> During his long reign over Rome—forty-one years—Octavian skillfully transformed himself from the adopted son of a god into a cult deity.

Although Rome's transition from a republic to an empire did not happen all at once on a specific date, most historians place the event sometime between 27 B.C. and 19 B.C. In January of 27 B.C., the Senate proclaimed a new name for Octavian, *Augustus*,[1] which means sacred or revered, because he gave up the absolute powers he had wielded over the Roman Republic since 33 B.C. However, the Senate granted Augustus numerous specific powers, largely restoring the powers he had given up, and continued granting him more powers over time. As the transfer of power to Augustus made republican institutions irrelevant, people eventually recognized in retrospect that he had become the first emperor of Rome. By the time that the Senate granted Augustus consular powers for life in 19 B.C., the last possibilities for resurrecting the Roman Republic effectively had died.

---

[1] When discussing the first emperor of Rome, the name Octavian is used in discussions of events before 27 B.C.; and the name Augustus identifies the same man in discussions of events after 27 B.C.

During the four decades that Augustus ruled, many stories accumulated about him. Some said that he had been divinely conceived, that he had performed miracles as a young child, and that during important moments of his life he had enjoyed divine favor. Throughout his reign, coins circulated with images that supported the identification of Augustus as well as members of his extended family as divinities. By the end of his reign, Romans were accustomed to living in an empire in which peace and prosperity were nurtured by a divine ruler.

Under Augustus, Romans freely enjoyed Hellenistic cults. Although the Cult of Isis, which had been closely associated with Queen Cleopatra, suffered some regulation, religious beliefs from every corner of the known world met and mingled on Roman streets. Romans became increasingly familiar with many different types of Eastern cults, among them, cults of solar deities (gods born or reborn at moments related to cardinal points of the Earth's orbit around the sun[2]) like Mithras, Dusares, and Zeus Ouranios (Jupiter, God of the Sky).

Paying close attention to harmonizing religious symbolism with imperial rule, Augustus renewed Rome's relationship with all the gods, ensuring continuing domination of the Mediterranean world. As part of a grand scheme to found a dynasty of divine emperors, Augustus established a tradition of *Secular Games* beginning in 17 B.C. to inaugurate a new spiritual age. In modern times, we associate the word "secular" with separation from religion. However, in ancient Rome, "secular" meant once in a generation. Secular Games described grand ceremonies associated with the renewal of Roman spiritual life, which occurred only once in the life of an entire generation.

In the years following the first Secular Games, the most cherished friends and relatives of Augustus began to die. The deaths of Agrippa and Octavia—the best friend and the devoted sister of Augustus—hit him particularly hard. Augustus had no male children of his own and he agonized over whom he could trust to inherit power over Rome. For the remainder of his life, he worried about whom he could adopt to succeed him. Regardless, by the end of his reign, the Cult of the Emperor was firmly established and a combination of dominion and divinity was inherently associated with ruling the Roman Empire.

---

[2]See Chapter 13.

Chapter 21 | The Inauguration of a New Spiritual Age 503

PREPARING ROME FOR RULE BY A DIVINE EMPEROR AND HIS EXTENDED FAMILY

Finding creative ways to assert his divinity, Octavian Caesar at first seemed merely to continue traditional conceits of Hellenistic rulers in the East. However, by continually associating himself with the Divine Julius Caesar, Octavian parlayed his successful acquisition of power over Rome into broad public veneration of the emerging dynastic cult. Imperial historians publicized that numerous signs had foretold Octavian's birth and divine status. Further, Octavian's propaganda convinced Rome that his reign marked the spiritual transition from an age of evil and immorality to an enlightened age when divine Roman rulers would bring virtue and spiritual renewal to the world.

As Rome gradually acquired the stature of a cosmopolitan imperial capital, religious symbols, practices, and metaphors began to mingle from one cult to another throughout the empire. Facilitated by the prolonged peace of Augustus' reign, religious leaders in the Western world reshaped local cultic traditions by infusing them with exotic ideas and rituals derived from Hellenistic traditions and first-century philosophical fashions. The fastest-growing cults in Rome came from the East and used Greek language. Their iconographies readily entered Roman culture through its passion for Greek images.

Examples of Miracles that Indicated Octavian's Divinity

In the century after Augustus died, historians[3] collected miraculous stories that foretold the ruler's greatness and divinity. Recorded as facts, some of the stories grew out of Octavian's propaganda campaigns and others emerged spontaneously as urban legends. After the death of Augustus, Romans increasingly believed in his divinity. For example, they venerated the exact place of his birth, maintaining that miracles continued to occur there.[4]

---

[3]Suetonius, a Roman historian who lived approximately from 69 A.D. to sometime after 130 A.D. recorded the signs and miracles presented in this section as well as many more in *The Life of Augustus*. Many of the signs and miracles that Suetonius associated with Augustus appear similar to those associated with Jesus in the *New Testament*.
[4]See *The Life of Augustus* 5–6 by Suetonius.

An ancient prophecy from Velitra, the city of Octavian's birth, foretold that a native of the city would rule the world. Also, an Annunciation of sorts occurred nine months before the divine birth of Octavian. His mother, Atia, the daughter of Julius Caesar's sister, Julia, participated with other married friends in a midnight service at a Temple of Apollo. After the service, she and others fell asleep in their litters. A snake crawled into Atia's litter, entered her, and then crawled away. On waking, Atia purified herself as after sex, but the event left a mark on her skin shaped like a snake. Because of this mark, Atia never again bathed publicly.

Gods sent dreams to Octavian's parents that foretold their divine child's destiny. Atia dreamed that her intestines rose into the sky and hung over all the lands and seas of the Earth. Octavian's father, Octavius, dreamed that the sun rose from between Atia's thighs.

A few months before Octavian's birth during the month of *Sextilis*[5] in 63 B.C. (while Pompey campaigned in the East), omens warned the Senate of the birth of a new king of Rome. The Senate disapproved of this possibility so strongly that it voted to outlaw the rearing of any male child for a year. A group of senators with pregnant wives prevented a massive "*massacre of innocents*"[6] by blocking registration of this senatorial decree as law.

On the day of his son's birth, having waited until the birthing completed successfully, Octavius entered the Senate late. When told the exact time of Octavian's birth, an astrologer (*magus*) in the Senate proclaimed, "The ruler of the world is now born." Later, while traveling in Thrace, Octavius came to a sacred grove of Dionysos and asked the priests about his son's destiny. When the priests poured wine over the altar, a flame shot higher than the roof of the temple. The priests told Octavius that this sign had not occurred since Alexander the Great sacrificed at the same altar as a young man. That night, Octavius dreamed of his son riding a chariot pulled by twelve brilliant white horses. His son wore a solar crown and carried the thunderbolt, scepter, and regalia of "Jupiter, Best and Greatest."

---

[5]Although Sextilis eventually was renamed Augustus (August) in honor of Augustus Caesar, the anniversary of his birth occurs on September 23 on a modern calendar.
[6]The threat of a Roman "massacre of innocents" parallels the biblical massacre of young children in Bethlehem. See *Matthew* 2:16–18.

Once, Octavian's nurse placed the sleeping infant in his cradle. In the morning, she found the cradle empty. The entire household searched frantically for baby Octavian. They finally found him lying alone on top of a tall tower, his face turned toward the rising sun. Later at his grandfather's country house, just after Octavian had learned to talk, frogs started a loud chorus of croaking. The little boy told the frogs to stop; locals claimed that no frog ever croaked there again.

While still a child, Octavian once ate lunch next to a forest near the Appian Way. As he held a crust of bread, an eagle swooped down and snatched it from him. The eagle carried the crust into the sky and then glided back and returned it.

Famous Romans who never before had seen young Octavian sometimes dreamed of him just before meeting him. Responsible for refurbishing the city of Rome, Quintus Catulus dreamed that Capitoline Jupiter held a young boy in his lap and called him Rome's savior. Cicero dreamed of a young boy lowered from the sky by a golden chain to a temple where Capitoline Jupiter handed him a whip. Both Quintus Catulus and Cicero, after seeing young Octavian for the first time, identified him as the very boy who had appeared in their dreams.

After he came to power in Rome, Octavian persistently and unabashedly employed propaganda to encourage acceptance of his divinity. Symbols of his divinity often appeared on his coins. For example, the obverse of the coin in Figure 21-1 carries an attractive bust of winged Victory, and the reverse displays Octavian in the aspect of a god (naked) holding the prow of a ship in one hand and a scepter in the other. Octavian's right foot rests on a globe that represents the universe. Crossed circles on the globe mark celestial pathways: the ecliptic and the celestial equator. The legend on the coin identifies Octavian as "Caesar, Son of God."

Divine omens shaped and framed the life of Octavian/Augustus: they directed Julius Caesar to claim Octavian as his heir; they told Octavian the results of his major battles at Philippi, Sicily, and Actium; and they eventually predicted his death and apotheosis. During the unusually long and peaceful reign of Octavian/Augustus, stories of the magnificent successes of Julius and Octavian Caesar—sanctified by numerous signs and nurtured by skillful manipulation of public opinion—slowly gave rise to a persistent Cult of the Emperor of Rome.

Figure 21-1. Victory, and Octavian with Aplustre and Scepter Dominating the Universe. Rome, AR Denarius, ca. 31–30 B.C.

Opening Rome to Selected Hellenistic Cults

After the suicides of Antony and Cleopatra, Octavian arranged for temple sacrifices at the Hellenistic Cult of Serapis in Alexandria. However, Octavian declined to have anything to do with other Egyptian cults, especially those of Isis (too strongly associated with Cleopatra) and the Apis Bull at Memphis. Regarding Judaism, also practiced in Alexandria, Octavian similarly expressed little regard for the god worshipped by the Jerusalem Temple Cult.

As power drained away from its republican institutions, Rome abandoned its struggle against invading Hellenistic cults. Throughout the Mediterranean world, Hellenized institutions scheduled festivals according the Greek liturgical year in preference to the Roman calendar. In Latin communities, Hellenized cults frequently performed religious ceremonies in Greek. The Roman Empire opened to Hellenistic ideas and the resulting Hellenization of Rome helped promote empire-wide acceptance of Augustus as divine.

Goddess cults remained important in the Roman Empire. Temples to the Syrian Aphrodite enjoyed philosophical and astrological support because Hellenistic astronomy had placed Atargatis' parents (divine fish) in the heavens as the constellation, Pisces. The prophetess who warned Julius Caesar to "beware the Ides of March" drew from the same tradition as the seeress of the Syrian Aphrodite who advised Gaius Marius.[7] During the peaceful rule of Augustus, Syrian merchants carried their goddess cult with them even to Africa and Gaul, and cities everywhere began to represent their good fortune as Tyche, a generic symbol associated with the Syrian Aphrodite.

Under Augustus, the worship of Cybele acquired new importance because of the connection between the Julian family and the Great Mother of Pessinus. Augustus encouraged worship of Cybele as an alternative to worshipping Isis. His house stood next to the Palatine Temple of Cybele, a temple that he proudly renovated in 3 B.C. During his reign, Roman artists sometimes carved images of Livia wearing Cybele's crown and robes.[8]

Art and traditions associated with Cybele merged with those of ancient Roman goddesses like Juno Sospita, Rhea, and Venus. Priests of Cybele in Rome also facilitated the worship of other Eastern goddesses (like Isis and the Syrian Aphrodite) as aspects of Cybele. Thus, traveling Egyptians, Syrians, or Italians could send prayers and offerings to their home goddess by visiting the Temple of Cybele in Rome.

By making it illegal for citizens to mutilate themselves, Roman law generally prevented Romans from entering the priesthood of Cybele. After Sulla normalized the cult by inducting the High Priest of Cybele into the College of Pontifices, the cult needed a mechanism for validating the authority of uncastrated Romans over Anatolian eunuchs. Sulla and Augustus both helped naturalize the Cult of Cybele, a process that culminated in the use of the *taurobolium*,[9] a ritual baptism in the blood of a sacrificed bull. Augustus even authorized freed slaves from his own household staff to enter Cybele's service.[10]

Beneath Vatican land today, the architectural remains of a taurobolium mark where a prospective Roman priest (pontifex) of Cybele would descend into a sunken cage with its roof level with the ground.

---

[7] See Chapter 14.
[8] See *The Cults of the Roman Empire* p. 43 by Robert Turcan.
[9] Although the earliest archaeologically attested use of taurobolium in Italy occurred in 134 A.D. (an inscription in Puteoli), some scholars suggest that the practice originated as a means of entering the priesthood of Cybele without castration. *Criobolium*, baptism in lamb's blood, also was used. Christian hymns unconsciously memorialize criobolium through references of being "washed in the blood of the lamb."
[10] See *The Cults of the Roman Empire* p. 43 by Robert Turcan.

At the climax of each taurobolium ceremony, priests slaughtered a bull on top of the cage so that fresh blood drenched the person inside. Baptized in bull's blood, the priest emerged from the cage, physically intact but born again, spiritually purified for the service of Cybele.

Controlling Undesirable Cults instead of Forbidding Them

Of all the foreign cults in Rome, Octavian restricted only those cults associated with Egypt, particularly the Cult of Isis. In 28 B.C., for example, Octavian prohibited Egyptian cults inside the *Pomoerium* (the sacred boundary of Rome). However, private underground chapels of Isis flourished. Possessing its own multicultural challenges, Octavian's home contained a Chapel of Isis that served the needs of household staff and the children of Marc Antony and Cleopatra VII. Household worshippers even scratched Isiac graffiti on the walls.[11]

Elsewhere in the Roman Empire, people freely worshipped Egyptian deities and local coins portrayed Egyptian symbols, although Augustus sometimes encouraged tweaks to the designs. For example, minted sometime after 27 B.C., the coin in Figure 21-2 uses Egyptian religious symbols to promote the Cult of the Emperor. This silver cistophorus from Pergamon affirms the worship of Egyptian cults in Roman Asia by portraying a female sphinx. Consistent with imperial interests, the head of this sphinx uses numismatic conventions associated with portraits of Livia, but the sphinx must have looked uncomfortably similar to Cleopatra: On other specimens of this coin type, the ambiguity was eliminated by placing the head of Octavia on the sphinx.

Religious Symbols Used by Augustus

Augustus focused on making laws that encouraged public morality and preserved traditional Roman family values. He also issued many types of artfully propagandistic coins. Bearing images that spoke to the common person, Augustus' coins financed the beautification of Rome while simultaneously affirming Roman values and the special status

---
[11]See *The Cults of the Roman Empire* p. 88 by Robert Turcan.

Chapter 21 | The Inauguration of a New Spiritual Age   509

Figure 21-2. Augustus Caesar and Sphinx with Head of Livia. Pergamon Mint, AR Cistophorus, after 27 B.C.

of Augustus as the Son of God. Over time, the Cult of the Emperor acquired qualities of a loyalty cult: To be a loyal Roman, one had to worship Augustus.

He relentlessly associated himself and his office with religious symbols. For example, Figure 21-3 shows his creative use of religious symbols on coins. While ostensibly promoting a return to traditional values, he used religious symbols in new ways. With great variety, the coins of Augustus affirmed his piety, trumpeted his military successes, and associated him with divinity as the son of the god Julius Caesar. Most of the images on the coins refer directly or indirectly to the Cult of the Emperor:

- They all portray obverse busts of Augustus larger than the symbols of divinity on the coin's reverses.
- Legends on the coins almost always refer to Augustus as the Son of God (for example, both coins on the left).
- Members of the imperial family sometimes appear as minor deities (for example, Livia as Pax on the lower left coin).
- The coins sometimes carry important new symbols associated explicitly with the Cult of the Emperor (for example, the Capricorn on the lower right coin).

Figure 21-3. Religious Symbols on Coins Minted in the Roman Empire during the Reign of Octavian/Augustus, 32 B.C.–14 A.D. Top Row: AR Denarii from Italian Mints. Bottom Row: AR Cistophoric Tetradrachms from Eastern Mints (Ephesos and Pergamon).

Augustus used important Roman symbols in attractive and meaningful ways. For example, on the top left coin in Figure 21-3, Venus Victrix, the ancestor of Augustus, walks naked among pieces of armor. Similar to a warlike Eastern goddess (for example, Cybele or a Syrian Aphrodite), she carries a scepter and gazes at a military helmet. Behind her, a shield bears the star of the Divine Julius.

As another characteristic theme in his propaganda, Augustus never let Rome forget about his come-from-behind victory over Marc Antony and Cleopatra. The top right coin in Figure 21-3 refers indirectly to both the victory as well as Augustus' divinity. On the reverse, Apollo of Actium (a feminine-looking musician) gratefully offers a sacrifice on an altar ornamented with anchors and ships' rams, which shows that even Apollo worshipped Augustus.

The lower left coin in Figure 21-3 portrays a *cista mystica* (ritual basket) and a snake, symbols emblematic of Dionysian cults. Looking older than usual, his wife Livia represents Pax (Peace) and carries a *caduceus*, Hermes' staff, a symbol associated with victory as well as commerce. The Mysteries of Eleusis maintained their prestige throughout the changing times of the early Roman Empire. However, while Eleusis performed initiations only twice a year (lesser mysteries in

March and greater mysteries in September), imitation Dionysian cults provided more accessible, though less venerable salvation throughout the Roman Empire. Out of reverence for the cult, Augustus allowed the worship of Dionysos, Bacchus, and Sabazius in Rome without restrictions. During these times, Romans became familiar with Dionysian initiation stories, for example, with the story of Dionysos turning water into wine at a sacred wedding.[12] Recorded only in the gospel of *John*,[13] a similar miracle of Jesus changing water into wine at a wedding in Cana reflects direct competition between early Christian and Dionysian cults.

The lower right coin in Figure 21-3 affirms that the stars foreordained the greatness of Augustus. During the his reign, Hellenized magi provided astrological services regardless of a client's cult or nationality. Just as a modern politician reveals details about his federal taxes, Augustus published his birth chart to prove his legitimacy in ruling Rome as well as to quell rumors about his early death.[14] The astrological symbol of the constellation Capricorn refers to Augustus' rebirth into divinity. In the last years of his life, Augustus banned the popular practice of consulting astrologers—not because he didn't believe in astrology anymore, but because he worried that people would use astrological predictions about his death to their advantage.[15]

Throughout the Roman Empire, cities minted coins with obverse portraits of Augustus and reverse portrayals of local religious symbols. In Anatolia, Aphrodisias minted coins of Augustus that bore images of their goddess's sacred bipennis (double-headed axe). Phoenician coins portrayed Augustus with Baal. Some cities even portrayed Augustus with Egyptian symbols related to Isis.

---

[12]To ancient Greeks, Dionysos presided over the miraculous transformation of water through fermentation of "grapes' blood" into wine. See *The Adventures of Leucippe and Clitophon* 2:2:8:2 by Achilles Tatius. Dionysos regularly made wine fill empty water vessels or gush from water springs, especially at his temples on Elis and Andros. See *Library of History* 3.66.1–2 by Diodorus Siculus, and *Natural History* 2.106 and 31.13 by Pliny the Elder. Dionysos' transformation of water into wine was featured prominently as an element of chthonic marriage celebrated during initiations into mysteries. See "The Miracle of the Wine at Dionysos' Advent; On the Lenaea Festival" by J. Vürtheim in *The Classical Quarterly*, Vol. 14, No. 2 (Apr., 1920), pp. 92–96.
[13]See *John* 2:1–11.
[14]See *The Star of Bethlehem: The Legacy of the Magi* p. 160 n. 9 by Michael Molnar.
[15]See *Roman History* 56.25 by Cassius Dio.

Other Cults under Augustus

Other minor foreign cults thrived under Augustus and even migrated to Italy, although few ever spread beyond small immigrant communities. For example, as early as 54 B.C. in Pozzuoli, Italy,[16] Nabataeans installed an altar to an Arabian solar deity named Dusares. Worshippers restored this altar during the time of Augustus in 5 A.D. The central story of the cult of Dusares involved a virgin named Khabu or Khaamu who gave birth to Dusares on December 25. The earliest Roman descriptions of Nabataean (Arabian) cults say that Arabs worshipped stones—sometimes irregularly shaped, sometimes round, and sometimes cubic: In ancient Petra (in modern Jordan), Nabataeans worshipped Dusares as a black cubic *baetyl*;[17] while in Arabia, ancient coins represent Dusares and Khabu as baetyls in a variety of sizes and shapes. Modern veneration by Muslims of the Ka'aba, a cubic granite structure in Mecca that houses a meteorite, derives in part from ancient worship of Dusares and Khabu.

Though the Cult of Mithras had not yet emerged into public Roman discourse, the cult grew rapidly during the reign of Augustus, especially in the colonial towns founded by former legionaries who had served in Cilicia.[18] As in other Eastern cults, the followers of Mithras used Greek for the names of their offices and initiatory grades. Adopting a seven-day astrological week, worshippers congregated on Sundays, purified themselves in sacred pools, and honored their savior (a god born of a virgin on December 25) by breaking bread and drinking wine in a ceremony similar to the Eucharist[19] (Holy Communion).

THE SLOW DEATH OF THE ROMAN REPUBLIC

After the deaths of Marc Antony and Cleopatra in 30 B.C., the Roman Senate showered honors on Octavian: triumphal arches, games, special powers, and so on. The Senate pleased him most by formally closing

---

[16] See *The Cults of the Roman Empire* p. 186, by Robert Turcan.
[17] For information about baetyls, see Chapter 7.
[18] Marc Antony minted coins that explicitly referred to Eastern solar cults. For example, see denarii 496 and 533 in *Roman Republican Coinage* by Michael Crawford.
[19] See Chapter 13, especially notes 32 and 33.

the doors of the Temple of Janus.[20] Closing the temple doors symbolized that Rome was at peace with the world, something unusual for Rome: The doors had been closed only twice before in history.[21]

Octavian portrayed his victory over Egypt as a triumph of traditional Roman virtue over Eastern corruption. In 29 B.C., he celebrated a triple triumph for the defeat of Illyria, the battle of Actium, and the annexation of Egypt. Then, having learned from the example of his Uncle Julius, Octavian chose not to dominate Rome directly. Instead, he solidified his hold on power through propaganda, political manipulation, and artful control while carefully avoiding overt political actions that appeared to threaten the Roman Republic.

On January 13, 27 B.C., Octavian restored the Roman Republic by ostensibly relinquishing the absolute powers that the Senate had granted to him in 33 B.C. to prosecute war against Egypt. He formally transferred most of his power to the Senate and the people of Rome. However, he kept his office as consul along with personal control of the provinces of Gaul, Spain, Egypt, and Syria—including their legions. Within three days, the Senate granted him the new title, Augustus, along with numerous special powers, permanently restoring most of the powers that he had temporarily given up.

Augustus never took his power for granted. He used it responsibly and nurtured it with care and insight. When he finally resigned his consulship in 23 B.C., the Senate granted him the power of the Tribunate for life.[22] The Senate also offered him a dictatorship, but he declined. In 19 B.C., the Senate granted him consular powers for life.

Appointing Divine Rulers from the Extended Family: Juba II and Cleopatra Selene in Africa

A chaste and modest personification of Roman feminine virtues, Octavia raised many children—some hers, some Antony's, and some hostage children seized from royal foreign families after Roman victories. Among the graduates of Octavia's nursery, Juba II had come from

---

[20]See *Augustus* p. 44 by A. H. M. Jones.
[21]The doors of the Janus Temple were closed once under King Numa Pompilius, said to have reigned from 715–673 B.C., and once under the consul, Titus Manlius, in 235 B.C.
[22]Many historians consider 23 B.C. as the year that Rome ceased to be a republic.

Africa after Julius Caesar defeated the allied forces of Pompeian rebels and Juba I in 46 B.C.

In the years since he had marched as a young child in Julius Caesar's African triumph, Juba II acquired a formidable education. Writing well in both Latin and Greek, he completed several important scholarly works by his early twenties, among them a book on Roman archaeology.[23] Juba II and Octavian Caesar formed a close, lifelong bond of friendship and mutual respect. In 25 B.C., Augustus solidified his control over Mauretania, an amorphous territory in western North Africa, by naming Juba II as the country's client-king. Sometime between 25 B.C. and 19 B.C., Cleopatra Selene, the daughter of Marc Antony and Cleopatra, also graduated from Octavia's care and married Juba II, which made her Queen of Mauretania.

Egyptian religious images on the North African denarii of Juba II testify to his wife's strong connection to her heritage as daughter of the living Isis of Egypt. Juba II supported Cleopatra Selene's divine pretensions, representing her on coins as an alligator, an Isis-crowned cow, and even a divine personification of Africa. The coins on the left in Figure 21-4 connect Cleopatra Selene with symbols of Isis: a crescent and star,[24] a crown of Isis, and a special rattle called a *sistrum*.

Acutely sensitive to the power of symbols, Augustus nevertheless tolerated a small show of independence from the rulers he'd known as children inside his own household. The coins on the right in Figure 21-4 show that Juba II also expressed symbolic loyalty to Augustus' divine administration by minting coins with Capricorn and elephant reverses. Modern North Africa—Morocco and Algeria in particular—fondly remembers Juba II as the "Scholar King."

Early Concerns about Succession

After he suffered a severe illness in 25 B.C., Augustus increasingly began to worry about who would succeed him as the second emperor of Rome. He wanted a son to succeed him, but never succeeded in

---

[23] See *The World of Juba II and Cleopatra Selene* p. 2 by Duane Roller.
[24] The crescent and star represented pagan goddesses (like Isis), then Mary the mother Jesus, and eventually connected with Islam. See "Crescent and Star and Related Images: A Historical Perspective" by David Wray in *The Celator* Vol. 18, No. 2, February 2004.

Figure 21-4. Coins of Juba II and Cleopatra Selene. Mauretania, AR Denarii, 25 B.C.–23 A.D.

fathering one. Augustus' second wife, Scribonia, had given him a daughter (Julia), but his marriage with Livia (his third wife) had failed to produce any children of their own. His first choice for succession, Marcellus (the son of Octavia and Marc Antony) married Augustus' daughter, Julia, in 25 B.C., but Marcellus died in 23 B.C. also without producing a child.

After Augustus recovered from another serious illness in 23 B.C., he looked for a way to encourage his daughter, Julia, to bear acceptable male heirs. In 21 B.C. at the insistence of Augustus, Agrippa divorced his second wife (a daughter of Octavia by her husband before Marc Antony) and married Julia. Hoping for a grandson by his daughter and his best friend, Augustus left Rome in the care of Agrippa and traveled for several years through Sicily, Greece, and Asia.

While traveling, Augustus helped manage the Empire's interests by maintaining communication with Agrippa, his loyal and capable best friend. Augustan religious policies continued without interruption. Agrippa expanded the official proscription against the Cult of Isis beyond the Pomoerium to nearby suburbs of Rome. However, around the same time, Julia decorated Agrippa's home in Rome with scenes from Egyptian mythology.[25]

---

[25]See *The Cults of the Roman Empire* p. 88 by Robert Turcan.

SHAPING HIS LEGACY

In 20 B.C., while Augustus wintered at Salamis, he received a fresh reminder of the power of religious beliefs. King Poros of India sent an ambassador to Augustus, a Brahmin Hindu priest named Zarmaros. The ambassador met with Augustus and engaged in discussions about gods and philosophy. To honor India's ambassador, Augustus arranged an out-of-season initiation for Zarmaros in the Eleusinian Mysteries. At the normal conclusion of initiations at Eleusis, new initiates emerged from the grand hall at night to the illumination of a great bonfire. Beyond the bonfire, a multitude of townspeople waited to celebrate the ambassador's initiation. Unexpectedly, Zarmaros emerged from the grand hall and walked deliberately into the bonfire, immolating himself in the presence of Augustus and shocked onlookers.[26] After this event, Augustus found little reason to inquire further into religious beliefs and philosophies of India and the Far East.

However, the experiences of Augustus while traveling in the East deepened his understanding about the power of religious language and symbols. Throughout the Eastern Mediterranean region, astrologers, philosophers, and priests discussed the imminent arrival of a new age. Astrologers debated the meaning of the Vernal Equinox passing from the constellation Aries to the constellation Pisces. In Tarsos, Jerusalem, and Alexandria, Jews expected a militaristic savior, called the *Moshiach* (Messiah), to liberate them from Rome. Farther east, the demise of the Ptolemaic Empire, the last of the Hellenistic empires, that formed after the death of Alexander the Great, caused Zoroastrians to predict the arrival of the *Saosyant*, a spiritual savior born of a virgin whose coming would precipitate the End of Days.[27]

The Cult of the Emperor

By referring to himself as the Son of God throughout his reign, Augustus amassed and used religious devotion as political capital. As a side effect, he increasingly became accepted as a divinity. In distant

---

[26]See *Geography* XV, 1:73, by Strabo, and *Roman History* 54.9 by Cassius Dio.
[27]See Chapter 7.

provinces of the new Roman Empire (for example, Spain, Croatia, Turkey, and Israel), sycophantic client-rulers like King Herod of Judea built temples to the living Augustus as if he were a god. At least sixteen Temples of Augustus are known to have existed in Italy alone,[28] but few (if any) of these were built during his lifetime.

While spending time in the East, Augustus began thinking of ways to extend his influence for generations: Merging political and religious language in ways that prefigured the language of Christianity and using symbols to associate himself and his family with deities throughout the Roman Empire, he intended to characterize himself as the savior of the world and founder of a new age. For example, consider the language in the following proclamation issued in 9 B.C. in large cities in Roman Asia Province: "Since the Providence which has ordered all things and is deeply interested in our life has set in most perfect order by giving to us Augustus, whom she filled with divine power that he might benefit mankind sending him as a savior (*soter*), both for us and for our descendants, that he might end war and arrange all things, and since he, Caesar, by his appearance [excelled even our anticipations], surpassing all previous benefactors, and not even leaving to posterity any hope of surpassing what he had done, and since the birthday of the god Augustus was the beginning of the world of the gospel (*euangelion* or good news) that came by reason of him, therefore, let all reckon a new era beginning from the date of his birth, and let his birthday mark the beginning of the new year."[29] The proclamation shows that, before the birth of Jesus, people in Roman Asia Province were discussing the "gospel of Augustus" using religious language similar to language used later by Christians.

Beginning with Augustus, emperors ruled Rome while the Senate concerned itself with lesser issues. However, the Senate acquired an important new power regarding the new state cult: The Senate voted to decide whether or not to recognize a recently deceased dynastic member as a god.

---

[28]See *Emperor Worship and Roman Religion* p. 338 by Ittai Gradel. Oxford Classical Monographs, Clarendon Press, 2002.
[29]This inscription, dated 9 B.C., was found in Priene, Roman Asia Province. See *Backgrounds for Early Christianity* p. 46 by Everett Ferguson. Prof. James Tabor's online translation is posted at http://religiousstudies.uncc.edu/people/jtabor/divine.html.

Inaugurating a New Spiritual Age

Freshly convinced of the timeliness and importance of Rome's imperial cult in managing Rome's Eastern possessions, Augustus returned home armed with new knowledge. Invigorated, he applied his talent for manipulating Roman society toward strengthening the religious role of the Cult of the Emperor. With encouragement from Augustus, Roman historians and poets found (or manufactured) evidence that Rome had celebrated Secular Games in 456, 348, 236, and 146 B.C.[30] Since more than a century had passed since the last Secular Games, Augustus proclaimed that the time had arrived once again for Rome's spiritual renewal. In 17 B.C., he proclaimed the inauguration of a new age with the rebirth of an ancient tradition of Secular Games.

During the Secular Games from May 25 to June 12 of 17 B.C., Augustus honored every official cult of the Roman Empire. Purification rites and offerings of first fruits occurred from May 26 to May 30. From May 31 to June 3, Augustus orchestrated grand events of sacrifice and prayer by day and of Latin and Greek theater by night. Additional games continued through June 11. The last day, June 12, featured an animal hunt and circus games. Throughout the Mediterranean world, everyone received the good news that the Son of God had consecrated the beginning of a new spiritual age.

Augustus minted many new coins to publicize the Secular Games and beginning of the new age. The obverse of the top coin in Figure 21-5 portrays a bust of Augustus crowned with laurel like Greek portraits of the god Apollo. On the reverse, a legend affirms the divinity of Julius Caesar accompanied by one of antiquity's most magnificent illustrations of a comet—the *Sides Iulium*—the comet that confirmed the deification of Julius Caesar. The lower coin in Figure 21-5 portrays a herald who walked through the streets of Rome during May in 17 B.C. This herald announced the beginning of the Secular Games, celebrations like no living human had ever seen. The legend on the lower

---

[30]See "The Origin of the Ludi Saecularies" in *Studies in Roman Literature Culture and Religion* p. 193 by H. Wagenvoort, E.J.Brill-Liden, Netherlands, 1956, and *Roman Religion and Roman Empire–Five Essays* pp. 101–106 by Robert Palmer, University of Pennsylvania Press, 1974.

Figure 21-5. Coins of Augustus Proclaiming the Beginning of a New Spiritual Age. Rome, AR Denarii, 17 B.C.–14 A.D.

coin identifies Augustus, the Son of God, as the sponsor the games. For good measure, the coin's reverse displays a bust of Augustus surmounted by a comet.

The Impact on Augustus of Tragedies Involving Friends and Family

After inaugurating a new age, Augustus adopted the two sons of Julia and Agrippa, Lucius and Gaius, as heirs. He then focused on strengthening and expanding the Roman Empire in the West. However, the closest family members and friends of Augustus began dying around him. The old triumvir, Lepidus, died around 13 B.C. Halley's Comet appeared in the sky for two months after Agrippa died in 12 B.C, and Octavia died in 11 B.C.

Trying to obtain more heirs of his bloodline, Augustus forced Julia to marry Livia's son, Tiberius. However, neither Julia nor Tiberius could stand each other. Rather than endure his wife at home, Tiberius left Rome at every opportunity to fight in frontier wars.

In 6 B.C., disgusted with Julia, Augustus, and Rome's sycophantic Senate,[31] Tiberius abandoned Rome and began a self-imposed exile on Rhodes. During the years that he lived on the island, Tiberius studied under a famous astrologer named Thrasyllus. When an aristocratic army friend named Quirinius came to Rhodes, he had opportunities to join Tiberius and Thrasyllus in their discussions about astrology.[32] Most Christians believe that the Star of Bethlehem appeared in the sky and Mary gave birth to Jesus Christ sometime during this period.

In Rome, Julia rebelled after Tiberius deserted her. Having dutifully followed her father's orders all her life, she finally acted as she pleased. Roman gossips described her as a loose woman who enjoyed the attentions of any man who would have her. Most upsetting to Augustus, however, Julia took Iullus Antonius (the son of Marc Antony and Fulvia) as a lover and openly caroused with him in the Forum. The Senate acclaimed Augustus the father of his country in 2 B.C. That same year, he arrested his daughter for adultery and treason. Generously allowing Iullus Antonius to commit suicide, Augustus nullified Tiberius' marriage to Julia and exiled her. Augustus condemned his daughter to live on a small island[33] in the Tyrrhenian Sea, never again to know a life of privilege and luxury.

Unfortunately, the adoption of Gaius and Lucius in 17 B.C. failed to resolve the issue of succession. Both young men died just as they began maturing into serious heirs. At the age of nineteen, Lucius died of disease in Gaul in 2 A.D. Briefly governing Syria Province with help from Juba II and Quirinius, Gaius died in Lycia at the age of twenty-four from wounds received in a military campaign in Armenia. Gaius survived Lucius by only eighteen months.

---

[31] In 8 B.C., the Roman Senate honored Augustus by renaming the month Sextilis to Augustus (August).
[32] According to *Luke* 2:2–3, Quirinius oversaw the Judean census related to the nativity of Jesus. Quirinius' interest in astrology figures prominently in Roman coins that depict an astrological event related to the Star of Bethlehem. See Chapter 22.
[33] Known in ancient times as Pandataria, the island of Ventotene is 25 nautical miles from the town of Gaeta on the Italian coast.

Figure 21-6. Coin Honoring Tiberius as Co-ruler of the Roman Empire. Lugdunum, Tiberius, As, 13–14 A.D.

The marriage of Julia and Agrippa produced two other children: an ill-favored son and a daughter. Neither child developed into a suitable heir. Augustus exiled both of them after he caught them plotting against him, which left no better candidate than Tiberius as a successor.

The Adoption of Tiberius

Tiberius ended his self-imposed exile on Rhodes after Augustus exiled Julia and sent word to Tiberius of his divorce. Having meritoriously served Rome in wars in Pannonia and Germany, Tiberius no longer could be ignored. Augustus grudgingly adopted Tiberius and acknowledged him as his imperial heir and successor. In 12 A.D., Augustus raised Tiberius to the status of co-ruler. Minted in Lugdunum around 13–14 A.D., the coin in Figure 21-6 honors Tiberius as a successful general and the son of Augustus. The reverse of the coin portrays the famous altar dedicated to Augustus and Rome in Lugdunum (modern Lyons), the ancient capital of Gaul.

A quarter century earlier, Tiberius' younger brother, Nero Claudius Drusus, dedicated the altar on the same day that his wife (Octavia Minor, a daughter of Marc Antony and Octavia) gave birth to his son, the future emperor, Claudius. The famous altar carried the names of sixty Gallic tribes, figures of heroic (nude) males, and a *corona civica* (the Roman equivalent of a Medal of Honor) flanked by laurel branches. Claudius' six-year-old brother, Germanicus, was barely old enough to attend the altar's dedication ceremony. In a last attempt to ensure a succession by his family's bloodline, Augustus forced Tiberius to adopt Germanicus publicly as an imperial successor ahead of Drusus, the natural son of Tiberius by his first wife, Vipsania.

The Last Years of the Reign of Augustus

Roman legions suffered terrible military disasters during the later years of Augustus. In 6 A.D., Pannonia[34] rebelled. Although Roman legions largely subdued the rebellion in 9 A.D., trouble persisted in the region. Also in 9 A.D., a blundering general, Publius Quinctilius Varus, led three Roman legions[35] into a trap in the Teutoburg Forest in Germany. The German King Arminius ambushed and slaughtered all three legions almost to the last man—though not all of them died immediately. Evidence of Arminius' creative executions remained visible for years. After this disaster, Augustus abandoned his attempts to expand the Roman Empire into Germany.

In the end, a blood-red comet foretold the death of Augustus.[36] At first, he tried to ignore the ailment that killed him. However, when he finally realized that his death was near, he called his friends and family together and asked them to applaud the role that he had played in life. He passed away on August 19, 14 A.D., at his family estate in Nola in the same room where his father had died. The Senate honored Augustus with a public funeral and grand tomb. After his cremation, a man of praetorian rank swore under oath that he saw the spirit of Augustus emerge from the funeral pyre and ascend toward the sky. Approximately one month later, the Senate formally proclaimed that Augustus was a god.

---

[34]Ancient Pannonia was a region equivalent in modern times to western Hungary and parts of Austria, Croatia, Serbia, Slovenia, and Bosnia and Herzegovina. The rebellion of 6 A.D. is known to history as the *Great Illyrian Revolt*.
[35]The legions had just arrived in Germany from Roman Syria Province where Publius Quinctilius Varus had served as Governor.
[36]See *Roman History* 56.29.3 by Cassius Dio.

AUGUSTUS AND THE BIRTH OF JESUS

By the end of the reign of Augustus Caesar, everyone in the Roman Empire knew how to identify a human being who might become a god: The mother would experience a divine conception; a special astrological sign would attend the child's birth; the growing child occasionally performed miracles; and a divine hand would guide the prospective divinity throughout his life. Regarding what would happen after such a person died, Rome had experienced two possibilities: Either false friends would murder the man who then would resurrect as a god, or the man would peacefully ascend to heaven at the end of his life after presiding over a remarkable period of peace and prosperity.

Augustus attempted to reestablish traditional values in Rome by declaring spiritual renewal and dedicating a new spiritual age. However, nobody transformed Roman society more than Augustus, and nothing could stop Roman society's evolutionary drift away from the old ways. Opening Rome to Hellenistic cults and connecting politics with religious imagery brought a period of rapid religious evolution to the West. The period was so important that our current Western dating system begins with year 1 during the reign of Augustus Caesar.

The Roman Republic died, and the Cult of the Emperor emerged from the lives of Julius and Augustus Caesar. By declaring a new age and creating the Secular Games, Augustus invented an important new Roman tradition. Also, beginning with the death of Augustus, the Senate determined which rulers of Rome became gods and which ones remained human after their death. However, people living on the edge of the Roman Empire, especially in the East, had their own religious traditions about the development of a new age. To many, the emergence of the Cult of the Emperor was a straw-man waiting to be overthrown when the real savior arrived.

Jesus was born just before the first millennium, although the day and year of his birth are unknown. The apparition of Halley's Comet at the death of Agrippa in 12 B.C. marks the earliest of the known celestial events that some people associate with the *Star of Bethlehem*, the astrological sign that marked the birth of Jesus. The death of King Herod of Judea in 4 B.C. marks the latest possible date for the biblical "massacre of innocents,"[37] which occurred after Jesus was born. Therefore, Jesus must have been born sometime between 12 B.C. and 4 B.C. He must have been at least eighteen years old when Augustus died.

The roots of Christianity emerged from a confluence of Western and Eastern trends: as much from the long history of politics and religious innovations involving Eastern cults in the West as from the historic development of political and religious tensions in the Levant during the lifetime of Jesus. By presiding over the West during the birth and childhood of Jesus, Augustus developed powerful symbolic messages that projected ancient political and religious metaphors centuries and millennia into the future. Sometimes Augustan propaganda combined powerfully and well with foreign influences, and sometimes foreign traditions reacted powerfully in opposition to Augustus as the Son of God. In the East, the most important shaper of political and religious circumstances in Judea immediately before and after the birth of Jesus was Herod the Great, King of the Jews.

---

[37] See *Matthew* 2:16–18.

PART SEVEN

Star of Bethlehem Coin Minted during the First Census of Judea

INFLUENCES ON THE BIRTH, LIFE, AND CRUCIFIXION OF JESUS CHRIST

Among the many Jewish responses to Rome's tightening grip over Judea, spiritual revolutionaries began a movement dedicated to fighting foreign influences: a movement later reinterpreted according to political and religious influences in early Christian communities, resulting in gospel stories that shaped history as much as recording it.

CHAPTER
22

HERODIAN JUDEA

THE NATIVITY OF JESUS

Political movements, religious controversy, and violent events in Judea framed the birth and early childhood of Jesus.

King Herod ruled Judea from 37 B.C., a time when Marc Antony controlled the East, until 4 B.C., soon after the birth of Jesus during the reign of Augustus. Herod's kingdom comprised a patchwork of ethnicities and sensibilities that reflected a complex history of foreign conquests and diverse cultic expressions in the region. Originally, ethnic groups known as Idumeans, Galileans, Samaritans, Moabites, Ammonites, Phoenicians, and Nabataeans, to name a few, participated in local religious cults as well as in cults that originated in distant regions like Greece, Anatolia, Parthia, and Egypt. However, a century of *Hasmonean*[1] theocracy from 160 B.C. to 63 B.C. had purified Jewish religious beliefs, expanded the Jerusalem Temple Cult to previously non-Jewish populations, and pressed most Jews in the region to adopt a conservative Jewish viewpoint focused on strict interpretation of

---

[1] The Hasmonean dynasty was founded by Maccabees whose liberation of Jerusalem from Seleukid Greeks is celebrated in the Jewish festival of Hanukkah. See Chapter 12.

Jewish scriptures. However, regional and ethnic differences persisted among Jews. In addition, cults that survived the Hasmoneans, or that reentered Judea after the Hasmonean dynasty fell, flourished in protected ethnic and Hellenistic enclaves under King Herod.

Before Pompey ended the Hasmonean dynasty and the institution of Jewish kingship in 63 A.D., Jews who found Hasmonean religious beliefs unacceptable either preserved their beliefs secretly among like-minded people in remote communities or they abandoned Judea for life in the *diaspora*[2] (the dispersed Jewish community outside Judea). By the time King Herod came to power, the Hasmonean theocracy cast a long and complicated shadow in Judea: For example, forced conversions of Idumeans and Galileans turned previously non-Jewish population into staunch advocates of the Jerusalem Temple Cult; however, central Judean Jews looked down on religious converts from Idumea and Galilee as Jews of questionable quality. Money, geography, and politics organized the multitude of Jewish ethnicities and religious understandings into four broad categories: businessmen and religious officials invested in the status quo, messianic seekers of Jewish independence, Eastern regional patriots who advocated closer ties with Parthia, and Hellenizers who generally wanted closer ties with the West.

King Herod emerged as a strong and multi-dimensional leader during particularly difficult times when Rome and Parthia aggressively competed for dominance in the Levant. He harnessed his career and the welfare of Judea to the rising power of Rome, facilitating regional prosperity as opportunities for business and trade proliferated under Augustus. Herod survived as King of Judea by embracing Augustan claims of divinity, which offended many Jews. Yet, under King Herod, Jewish diversity expressed itself freely and non-Jews lived comfortably in Hellenistic cities in the Jewish Kingdom. However, peace, prosperity, and tolerance came at a price: King Herod ruthlessly murdered anyone who opposed him. After the death of King Herod, conditions

---

[2]The dispersed Jewish community west in Mediterranean coastal regions, east in the Parthian Empire, north in Anatolia, and south in Africa generally became known as the diaspora. In the absence of focused archaeological research, particularly regarding Jewish history in Muslim countries, evidence of the great variety of Jewish beliefs in the diaspora survives primarily in isolated references in ancient literature.

in Judea deteriorated: Poverty, factional strife, and Roman interference with Jewish life increased.

Jesus was born during times when many leaders of the Jerusalem Temple Cult began growing comfortable with their regional alliance with Rome. However, in 4 B.C., Jews antagonistic to the leadership of the Jerusalem Temple Cult interpreted the death of the king and the failure of his son to succeed to the throne of Judea as revelations of divine judgment against King Herod, against the legitimacy of a Herodian dynasty, against Roman influence, and against the leadership of the Jerusalem Temple Cult. Chaos ensued as different Jewish leaders rebelled and attempted to acquire control over pieces of the kingdom. Forced to intervene, Rome pacified the citizenry, partitioned the kingdom, and placed parts of it under direct Roman control.

The gospels in the *New Testament* portray King Herod as a particularly evil Jewish ruler of Judea who connived to murder Jesus immediately after learning of his birth. However, the gospels fail to give a clear picture for understanding the social context of events and even what actually happened. The two accounts of the *nativity* (the birth of Jesus) in the *New Testament* contradict each other on almost every detail. Regardless, modern analysis of these stories in the light of ancient beliefs about astrology clarifies some details and helps explain the confusion: The gospels preserve an interpretation of events and circumstances that reflects political and spiritual understandings when the gospels were written, not what actually happened in the context of the times that the gospels ostensibly describe.

NUMEROUS JEWISH CULTS IN THE ROMAN WORLD

In the Hellenistic Age, a Jewish diaspora had developed to the north, south, east, and west of the Levant built by a combination of Jewish slaves (and their free descendants), expatriates, and merchants: The Seleukids exported Jewish slaves during many conflicts, many Jews fled Judea because they disapproved of Hasmonean rule, and Jewish merchants joined the wave of Syrians that moved goods between the East and the West during Hellenistic and Augustan times. Unoppressed by

Hasmoneans, Jews outside the Levant experimented with every possible Jewish point of view.

During the reign of King Herod, Jews in the diaspora distinguished themselves largely by their relationship with the Jerusalem Temple Cult and by the degree to which they accepted or rejected local Hellenistic influences. Under direct control of the Roman emperor, Alexandria contained the largest population of Hellenistic Jews outside of Judea; however, Rome, Pergamon, and many other cities surrounding the Mediterranean Sea also contained large Jewish populations. For the most part, only a few details about Jewish community life outside Judea, including hints of variant beliefs and practices, have survived to modern times.[3]

However, the Jewish population in the Mediterranean region increased dramatically during the peaceful times of Augustus. Finding prosperity under an umbrella of peace enforced by Rome, many Jews in the Western diaspora conscientiously tried to prove themselves good Roman citizens, which sometimes meant adapting their political and religious beliefs to suit local circumstances. Whether they supported the Jerusalem Temple Cult or not, Jews thrived throughout the Mediterranean world.

Differences between Judeans and Other Types of Jews

History identifies the most important types of Judean Jews as *Sadducees* and *Pharisees*. Sadducees comprised families descended from Hasmonean leaders who dominated the Jerusalem Temple Cult: Generally, they did not believe in an afterlife. Pharisees also originated in Hasmonean times, and they believed in an afterlife: Some believed in resurrection during the End of Days, some believed in survival of the soul after death, and some believed in the transmigration of souls through many lifetimes. However, despite their disagreements, both Sadducees and Pharisees agreed about the importance of the Jerusalem Temple Cult: Faithful operation of the cult and the performance of prescribed cult sacrifices ensured a good relationship with God, survival of cult, and general good fortune for all Jews.

---

[3] See Chapter 9.

Sadducees considered all other Jews as inferiors. After Pompey ended the Hasmonean dynasty, many Sadducees nursed hopes of expelling Roman influence and restoring Jewish kingship. Some looked east for help from alliances with Parthia. However, Rome expelled the Parthians who interfered and punished the Jews who had joined them. As an Idumean, King Herod got little respect from Judean Jews. However, he successfully courted Hasmonean support as he rose to power in Judea, ultimately marrying a Hasmonean princess to affirm his legitimacy as king. Under the administration of King Herod, Sadducees learned to appreciate their connection with Rome: They grew wealthy and secure in their positions by maintaining positive relations with Roman businessmen and leaders.

Pharisees, like most Jews other than Sadducees, believed in survival after death in one form or another. Judean Pharisees shared Sadducean beliefs that other ethnicities and other types of Jews were inferior. However, they advocated legalistic interpretation of Jewish scriptures, an activity appropriate to their positions as businessmen and as middle-managers in the operation of the Jewish society.

Beyond Sadducees and Pharisees, the kingdom of Judea under King Herod accommodated many different kinds of Jews: Each little region identified itself as a different ethnicity with its own relationship with the Jerusalem Temple Cult as well as with regional centers of power: Roman, Egyptian, Parthian, Seleukid, and Anatolian. In Herod's kingdom, many Jews viewed Sadducees and Pharisees as corrupt because they generally supported Herodian and Roman power structures in central Judea. The easiest way to refer to Sadducees and Pharisees was to call them "Judeans" (*Judaioi*).

Samaritans and Criticisms of Judaioi

After Hasmoneans destroyed the last competing (Samaritan) temple sometime between 129 B.C. and 110 B.C.,[4] the Hasmonean belief in the centrality of the Jerusalem Temple Cult achieved unrivaled dominance among Jews in the Mediterranean region. Most Jews outside

---

[4]The destruction of Samaria's capital and temple by the Hasmonean John Hyrcanus I (134–104 B.C.) earned undying hatred of the Jerusalem Temple Cult from Samaritans, whether they lived in Herodian Judea, Egypt, Greece, or other Mediterranean regions.

Jerusalem craved a more spiritual faith than the Sadducean priesthood offered. Nevertheless, as the last Jewish temple to survive,[5] the Jerusalem Temple strongly influenced all Jews. However, perceiving themselves as the last believers in the true religion of Moses, Samaritans strongly disapproved of Sadducees and Pharisees and consistently opposed the Jerusalem Temple Cult.

Having suffered the destruction of their temple by Judean Jews, the Samaritans built the first known synagogues outside the Levant.[6] Within King Herod's Judea, Samaritans generally occupied the northern territory called Samaria where they expressed unrelenting antagonism to the Jerusalem Temple Cult. Nevertheless, King Herod extended freedom of worship to all Jewish cults in Judea, and he honored all Jewish religious leaders—as long as they behaved and did as they were told. Encouraging tolerance between different types of Jews, King Herod took a Samaritan wife. However, the breach between Samaritan and Judean cults resisted the balm of royal marriage.

Jews in regions like Samaria and Galilee had good reasons for referring negatively to the Judaioi. Non-Judean Jews generally perceived the Jerusalem Temple Cult as corrupted by foreign influences. Samaritans believed that the corruption occurred centuries earlier when Jerusalem Jews were taken to Babylon. Galileans believed that Rome was actively corrupting the Jerusalem Temple Cult with money and foreign influence. An alliance between Samaritans and Galileans was unlikely: Neither group could stand the other.

Christian gospels preserve the criticisms of Samaritans, Galileans, and other types of Jews against Judean Jews. The criticisms reflect one group of Jews calling another group of Jews unfaithful to Jewish law. However, by the time that the *New Testament*[7] was assembled as a canonized collection of separate Christian documents, the term Judaioi simply meant Jews to Christian readers. Ironically, Christians eventually used Jewish criticisms against "Judaioi" to justify attacks by Christians against all Jews.

---

[5]For brief discussions of other Jewish temples and cults, see Chapters 9 and 14.
[6]The oldest known synagogue, a Samaritan synagogue on the island of Delos, was built sometime from 150–128 B.C.
[7]In this context, the Christian *Bible*'s anti-Judean rhetoric, originally written by Jewish Christians, has been misunderstood and used to justify immoral persecutions of Jews throughout history.

Other Types of Jews

During the early first century A.D., even Judea contained a multitude of Jewish cults, some named and described in historical documents and some whose names and details remain unknown to history. The *New Testament* refers to Sadducees, Pharisees, Samaritans, and Zealots; and other sources speak of Essenes, Therapeutae, and Sicarii. However, even these broad categories contained numerous splinter groups. Some Jews, like the Essenes who hid the Dead Sea Scrolls in caves near Qumran, measured time using a solar calendar.[8] Other Jews, Pharisees among them, used an older and more traditional lunar calendar. Some Jews like Therapeutae in Egypt taught philosophy and healing, and other Jews like Zealots and Sicarii defined themselves in terms of violent opposition to foreigners and foreign influences. Poor, homespun Galilean Jews clung to cults shaped by reactionary leaders who fiercely condemned foreign influences, while wealthy Jerusalem Sadducees collaborated with Rome and embraced a certain amount of Hellenization.

Sacred Jewish texts generally consisted of the *Torah*, the *Prophets*, and the *Writings* (*Torah*, *Neviim*, and *Ketuviim*—the three parts of the *Tanach*, or *Hebrew Bible*), as well as other, cult-specific rules documents. Judean Jews and Jews in the Eastern diaspora (for example, Parthia, Adiabene, and Armenia) mostly used Hebrew and Aramaic scriptures, while Egyptian and Western Jews generally used a Greek version of these scriptures, collectively called the *Septuagint*. As demonstrated by the wide variety of previously unknown writings found at Qumran, many cults possessed their own scribal traditions, often embracing variant or additional sacred texts used only by them.

Some Jews strictly enforced narrow interpretations of their scriptures. Others interpreted their scriptures flexibly, integrating them with the most advanced philosophies of their day. However, almost all ancient Jews lived according to a core set of Jewish laws—for example, eating only kosher foods, praying with *tallit* (Jewish prayer shawls)

---

[8]References to use of a solar calendar by Essenes can be found in *I Enoch* and in *The Book of Jubilees*. See the *Handbook of Biblical Chronology: Principles of Time Reckoning in the Ancient World and Problems of Chronology in the Bible* p. 44 by Jack Finedan, revised edition (1998), Hendrickson Publishers, Inc., Peabody, Massachusetts, and *Calendars in the Dead Sea Scrolls: Measuring Time* p. 55 by James C. Vanderkam, Routledge, London.

and *phylacteries* (small calf-skin boxes containing scripture worn on the forehead or left arm as commanded by *Deuteronomy* 6:8), maintaining the sanctity of the Sabbath, and paying the annual *temple tax*.[9] In addition, most Jews in Herod's kingdom (including Samaritans) wished that they could eradicate foreign cults and Hellenistic influences from all regions associated with the ancient kingdoms of Judah and Israel; it's just that they sometimes perceived each other as no better than foreign cults and Hellenistic influences. Jews battled among themselves about politics and religious practices even more ferociously than they battled with foreigners.

Jewish Messianic Expectations

Consistent with the general Eastern response to centuries of domination by Hellenistic rulers, Jews believed that God would not allow an evil age of foreign domination to continue. God would send a savior—known by different names in different traditions—whose coming would bring the End of Days. Judean Jews generally believed that their savior would be a militaristic king called the *messiah* because he would be anointed (*moshiach*) as King of the Jews in Jerusalem.

The ancient Jewish concept of the messiah was based on a vision of Balaam, a seer, whom King Balak of Moab ordered to curse the Israelites after their *exodus* (departure) from Egypt. Instead, Balaam blessed them and prophesied, "A star from Jacob takes the leadership. A scepter arises from Israel. It crushes the brows of Moab, the skulls of all the sons of Sheth."[10] Balaam's prophecy appealed to Jewish hopes for self-determination by referring to the well-known Egyptian visual metaphor of a conquering pharaoh crushing the skulls of his defeated enemies. Figure 22-1 displays an example carved on an ancient temple wall in Luxor, Egypt. Metaphorically, Balaam's prophecy predicts that a Jewish king someday would conquer all the enemies of the Jews. Other

---

[9]The *New Testament* (*Matthew* 17:24–27) refers to the tax paid to the Jerusalem Temple, one half-shekel (two drachms) per male per year. Samaritans did not pay this tax unless forced to do so.

[10]See *Numbers* 24:17. The biblical passage describes a time shortly after the exodus when King Balak of Moab commanded the seer Balaam to curse the invading Israelites. Instead, he blessed them.

Chapter 22 | Herodian Judea 535

Figure 22-1. Pharaoh Seti I Crushing the Skulls of Defeated Syrian Enemies. Luxor, Egypt.

biblical passages clarify that the king would be a descendant of the first Jewish king, David.[11] Because of widespread distribution of the *Septuagint*, biblical prophecies about the messiah became known throughout the Hellenistic world.

Well before the reign of King Herod, some Jews earned reputations as possible messiahs by performing miracles. For example, a righteous Jew named Honi the Circle-Maker[12] led a small Jewish cult early in the first century B.C. He prayed to God, calling him father, and demonstrated miraculous control over weather. Although Jewish religious literature reports that God carried Honi directly to heaven, other historical writings say that he died during the Jewish power struggle between Pharisees (led by John Hyrcanus II) and Sadducees (led by Aristobulus) arbitrated by Pompey the Great in 63 B.C.: Pharisees under John

---
[11]See *Psalms* 132:11 and *Jeremiah* 23:5–6.
[12]See *Mishnah Ta'anit* 3:8 and 23a. Also, see *Antiquities of the Jews* 14.2.1 by Josephus.

Hyrcanus II executed the miracle worker by stoning.[13] However, when Pompey ended the institution of Jewish kingship, he unintentionally increased Jewish interest in prophecies and signs about the coming of the messiah.

The widespread expectation of the imminent arrival[14] of the Jewish messiah encouraged a proliferation of new Jewish cults. Jewish religious leaders competed by developing their own particular teachings about the messiah. It was important for Jews to follow the correct teachings because only true followers of God would fare well when the messiah came. Alternative Jewish cults grew stronger in relation to perceived corruption and sacrilege in the Jerusalem Temple Cult. Traditional Jews disliked their Idumean king (Herod), the increasing Roman presence in Jerusalem, and the priests of the Jerusalem Temple who paid more attention to money and power than to righteousness.

Increasing Jewish interest in messianic prophecy even changed Jewish burial customs: Jews who believed in physical resurrection at the End of Days began to plan for it. While poor Jews almost always were buried individually in shallow trench graves, well-to-do Jews had long practiced *charnel burial*: Dead bodies were placed on stone benches in family burial chambers until the flesh disappeared; then the bones were swept in a disarticulated mass into a large pit.[15] Around 10 B.C., well-to-do Jews began collecting the bones of individuals (or as many as a few close family members) and placing them in small stone boxes called *ossuaries*. The ossuaries then were placed in smaller chambers, called *loculi*, which were cut into the sides of the main burial chambers.[16] For wealthy Jews who believed in physical resurrection, *ossilegium* (burial in ossuaries) seemed like a good way to facilitate the

---

[13] Pompey the Great gave kingship of Judea to John Hyrcanus II in preference to his stronger brother Aristobulus II. See Chapter 16.

[14] Written during the second century B.C., the book of *Daniel* (especially chapters 7–9) in the *Old Testament* was thought to predict the coming of the messiah around the time of Herod's death. *Daniel* 12 prophesies the End of Days, and *Daniel* 9:24–27 indicates a time frame.

[15] See "What Did Jesus' Tomb Look Like?" by Jodi Magness in *Biblical Archaeology Review* Jan/Feb 2006, pp. 38–49, 70.

[16] The funerary practice of using ossuaries continued until the destruction of the Jerusalem Temple in 69 A.D.

awakening of their family when the time came to join the righteous of all generations at the Jerusalem Temple.

Whether seeking to live righteously or yearning to devote themselves to an invincible leader, Jews searched passionately for evidence of their messiah. Writings in the first century B.C. supported divergent points of view: For example, one "Dead Sea Scroll"[17] speaks in spiritual terms about a messiah establishing an eternal kingdom populated by righteous Jews resurrected from the dead. Other Jewish literature[18] explicitly called for a militaristic messiah to cleanse Jerusalem and its temple of non-Jews and spiritual impurities. Of particular concern to central Judean government and temple leaders, the popular Jewish search for a righteous military leader frequently expressed itself as anti-Roman civil unrest. Believing that a messiah soon would guarantee their liberation, Jews throughout Judea grew increasingly willing to confront Romans and all purveyors of Hellenistic influences. Early in the first century A.D., Romans quickly learned to see potential Jewish messiahs as agitators for violent rebellion.

KING HEROD AND ROMAN CONTROL OF JUDEA

Herod's mother was a princess of Nabataea, a nearby country whose people worshipped a pantheon that included the solar deity Dusares. Herod's father, an Idumean, came from a territory that Hasmonean Jews had taken from Nabataea in the second century B.C. and forcibly converted to the Jerusalem Temple Cult. Herod's father raised his son as a Jew, but close relatives in his mother's family celebrated the virgin birth of the savior Dusares on December 25. Having obtained the best Hellenistic education that his parents could buy, Herod developed into a capable, even brilliant leader. Further, with familial connections to

---

[17]Found in a cave near Qumran, the document *4Q521* refers to a messiah using the same terminology that Jesus used in *Matthew* 11:4–5 and *Luke* 7:22–23.

[18]For example, see the *Psalms of Solomon* 17:20–26 as well as *I Enoch* 46:1–4, 48:2–7, and 69:26–29.

two different religious traditions, Herod demonstrated a tolerance of opposing religious beliefs that was unusual among Jews in Judea.

When Herod was twenty-five years old, his father led a Jewish army to help Julius Caesar in Alexandria during the winter of 48–47 B.C.[19] Julius Caesar rewarded Herod's father by naming him Chief Minister of Judea with the right to collect taxes. In the new political climate, rapidly improving for Jews, Herod's father assigned governorships to his sons. He gave Herod the governorship of Galilee.

Over the next few years, Herod married, had a son, and acquired a reputation as a tough man capable of holding his own in a difficult neighborhood. In 43 B.C., regional Roman military leaders extorted monetary support from Herod's father for the Republican legions of Cassius and Brutus. Political unrest increased in Judea as different Jewish factions searched for advantage in alliances with different external powers. A local conspiracy murdered Herod's father and tried to take over his government, but Herod enforced a regional status quo.[20] With Roman assistance, he even arranged the assassination of the instigator of his father's murder.

At a time when ambitious Romans began looking for paths to deification, messianic Jewish kingship loomed as a possibility in Herod's future. Falling in love with a beautiful woman who just happened to descend from Judean kings, Herod entered negotiations to take the Hasmonean Princess Mariamne as his bride. Even though he legally could have taken multiple wives, he banished his first wife and son. Carefully, he prepared for his marriage with Mariamne as if making her the focus of all his aspirations for kingship.

Symbolic Messianic Claims by King Herod

During Rome's Second Triumvirate,[21] Herod won the trust of Marc Antony and Octavian by serving as tetrarch (one of four regional rulers) of Galilee. While Marc Antony wooed Hellenistic populations with claims of semi-divinity and made long-term plans to defeat the

---

[19] See Chapter 18.
[20] Generally, Sadducees supported Herod and Pharisees opposed him.
[21] See Chapter 18.

Parthians, Herod continued to serve as a trusted client in the evolving patchwork confederation of loyal Eastern rulers. The Parthians actively pursued their ambitions as well: They lured Jewish leaders with promises of military support for expelling Rome from the East. In the Winter of 40 B.C., while Marc Antony dallied with Cleopatra VII (the living Isis) in Alexandria, Parthians helped Mariamne's uncle (the Hasmonean pretender to the throne) seize large portions of the ancient kingdom of Judea. Herod fought the invaders as long as he could, but he eventually fled south to Egypt.

Refusing a generous offer of military assistance from Cleopatra, Herod traveled to Rome and presented detailed information to the Senate about Parthian activities. He won such favor that the Senate proclaimed Herod, "King of the Jews." Herod served Rome well. Within three years, Marc Antony had expelled the Parthians and executed Jewish rebels.[22] Then, in 37 B.C., the high priest of the Jerusalem Temple anointed Herod *King of the Jews*. Having finally obtained a title worthy of a messiah, Herod further legitimized his position by marrying Princess Mariamne.

From the moment that Herod assumed the kingship of Judea, he began minting coins that referred to messianic prophecy. The top coin in Figure 22-2 portrays a star above a military helmet, which recalls Balaam's prophecy of a militaristic "Star from Jacob." The obverse portrays an incense burner with the date (year 3) on the left referring to the year of his reign that Herod acquired political control over Judea. To the right of the incense burner, a monogram[23] comprising the Greek letters Chi (X) and Rho (P) represents the the first two letters of the word *christos*, which means anointed in Greek just as messiah (*moshiach*) means anointed in Hebrew. Jewish expectations of a holy man anointing the messiah's head with sacred balsam oil were confronted with coronation ceremonies that involved the high priest of the Jerusalem Temple anointing King Herod.

---

[22]Herod helped Rome recapture Judea, deposing the anointed Hasmonean King (Mattathius Antigonous) who had supported the Parthians. Mattathius Antigonous was the only anointed "King of the Jews" (messiah) to be scourged and executed by Romans. Sources differ concerning the manner of his execution: crucifixion or beheading.

[23]This monogram bears a striking resemblance to the Chi-Rho symbol that Christianity began to adopt late in the reign of Constantine the Great.

Figure 22-2. Messianic Symbols on Coins of King Herod. AE Eight Prutot, Samaritan Mint, and AE Two Prutot, Jerusalem Mint, ca. 40–4 B.C.

Like Augustus, King Herod used religious symbols on coins to broadcast his status. The obverse of the lower coin in Figure 22-2 portrays a round symbol that represents Herod's royal diadem. The X in the center of the diadem is the Greek letter Chi,[24] which refers to the anointing of King Herod using only the first letter of the word *christos*. Christians later transformed symbols of diadems and victory wreaths into angelic halos. On its reverse, the coin portrays a tripod for supporting religious offerings flanked by palm branches, Jewish symbols of victory associated by Christians with the story of the entry of Jerusalem by Jesus on Palm Sunday. These symbols numismatically portray King Herod as *christos*—that is, the anointed King of Judea—with messianic symbols that referred to Jewish expectations about the arrival of the messiah.

---

[24]The cross also had meaning for Jews because it resembled the Semitic letter Tau. In *Ezekiel* 9.4, the cross (Tau) is a symbol of righteousness. Although most scholars believe that the cross did not become a symbol of Christianity until the fourth century A.D., Tertullian, a Church Father who lived during the second and third centuries A.D., criticized Ebionites (Jewish Christians) for putting crosses on their foreheads.

Ruling His Kingdom with Strength and Moral Flexibility

Ascending to power six years before Octavian's defeat of Marc Antony, Herod reigned with a combination of brutality, treachery, and power politics. Mariamne soon learned to hate her husband, and the hatred only deepened over time. When Mariamne pressed Herod to install her seventeen-year-old brother as High Priest of the Jerusalem Temple, Herod reluctantly agreed; but, within a year, he arranged for the young man's murder. He further antagonized Mariamne by leaving orders with trusted staff that, if he died, they must kill Mariamne immediately. According to Herod, he loved her so much that he couldn't bear to be parted from her, even by death. In addition, Mariamne's mother, the principal negotiator of the marriage with Herod, quickly turned to plotting against him with Cleopatra VII. Still, he maintained Marc Antony's favor by scrupulously delivering whatever Marc Antony wanted. However, as Antony and Cleopatra moved ever closer to a confrontation with Octavian, Herod focused mostly on local issues. Once, he fought a brief war against Nabataea (his mother's kingdom), an ambitious endeavor that risked antagonizing Marc Antony.

After the battle of Actium in 31 B.C., Herod preserved his power and maintained his connection to Rome by skillfully realigning with Octavian. He gambled with his life by rushing to Rhodes to meet personally with Octavian and declare loyalty. The gamble paid well: Octavian decided not to punish Herod for previously supporting Marc Antony. Further, Herod retained kingship over Judea with minimal interference from Rome.

The same year that Octavian defeated Antony, a powerful earthquake rocked Judea. As Client-King of Judea under Octavian (whose name changed to Augustus in 27 B.C.[25]), Herod repaired damaged cities, constructed aqueducts, and acted vigorously to improve the lives of his subjects. Because of Herod, Jews had access to healthful water, they ate during times of famine, and their quake-damaged cities re-emerged in better condition than before. He even rebuilt the Jerusalem Temple on a grand scale. Although Herod earned the right to be called "the Great," he also earned hatred and condemnation from his subjects: He enforced his will with harshness and brutality, he built

---

[25]See Chapter 21.

temples to foreign gods, and he was quick to execute priests, righteous men, and members of his own family.

Of the ten women he married, he banished the first and executed the second (Mariamne, the wife he loved the most). Of his nine sons, he executed at least three. He also killed numerous relatives for getting involved in assassination plots. Once, Augustus ordered reconciliation between Herod and two of his rebellious sons, but Augustus' efforts merely delayed the inevitable. Herod eventually executed both sons. Commenting on the executions as well as on Herod's adherence to Jewish law, Augustus punned in Greek that, "It's safer to be Herod's pig (*hus*) than his son (*huius*)!"

To many Jews, King Herod seemed more Roman or Greek than Jewish. He used the taxes that he collected to support restarting the Olympic Games in Greece as well as to build pagan temples and opulent palaces in Judea. After he completed the massive reconstruction of the Jerusalem Temple, he placed a gold statue of a Roman eagle above the temple's main gate. He even portrayed this eagle on his coinage. (See the reverse of the coin in Figure 22-3.) Shortly before his death, a crowd of Jews pulled down the eagle and destroyed it, attempting to cleanse the Jerusalem Temple of foreign religious symbols; but King Herod ordered soldiers to attack them. The soldiers captured at least forty members of the crowd and executed them—burning some of them alive. During the night after the deaths, a lunar eclipse turned the sky blood-red.[26]

Among those executed for destroying the gold eagle, at least two men were identified by contemporaries as possible messiahs.[27] One of them, an Essene named Menahem, had won royal favor by prophesying correctly many years earlier that Herod would be anointed King of the Jews.[28] However, by abandoning his favored status and giving his life in an attempt to purify the Jerusalem Temple, Menahem was

---

[26]A phenomenon commonly associated with red skies, a lunar eclipse occurred on March 13, 4 B.C. See *Antiquities of the Jews* 17.6.4 by Josephus. Also, see *Messiahs and the Resurrection in 'The Gabriel Revelation'* p. 47 by Israel Knohl.

[27]See *The Messiah before Jesus: The Suffering Servant of the Dead Sea Scrolls* pp. 51–68 by Israel Knohl.

[28]See *Antiquities of the Jews* 15.372–379 by Josephus (quoted in *The Messiah before Jesus: The Suffering Servant of the Dead Sea Scrolls* pp. 54–55 by Israel Knohl).

Figure 22-3. Image of the Gold Eagle Installed by King Herod on the Gate of the Jerusalem Temple. AE Lepton from the Jerusalem Mint, 40–4 B.C.

popularly recognized as an embodiment of the Hebrew meaning of his name—that is, comforter or spirit of truth.[29]

King Herod's health suddenly took a horrible turn for the worse. Pious Jews believed that God had cursed him for his association with Rome and for enforcing the sacrilegious presence of foreign gods and idols in Judea.[30] In this time of hardship and political turmoil, Jews clung to the prophecy that a messiah would come. Jews everywhere believed that the time of the messiah must be close at hand. King Herod suffered madness and an excruciating death in Jericho in 4 B.C.

The Partitioning of Judea after the Death of King Herod

Herod's kingdom comprised many small regions: Iturea, Decapolis, Judea, Samaria, Idumea, Galilee, Perea, Panias Gaulanitis (Golan), Batanea, Aurantis, and Trachonitis. (See Figure 22-4.) As a largely autonomous king, he ruled and taxed all these regions until he died. Herod's will named one of his sons, Herod Archelaus, as King of Judea, but Augustus chose not to approve the terms of the will.

---

[29]See Chapter 24 and *The Messiah before Jesus: The Suffering Servant of the Dead Sea Scrolls* pp. 68–71 by Israel Knohl.
[30]See *Antiquities of the Jews* 17.9.1 by Josephus.

Figure 22-4. Kingdom of Judea during the Reign of Herod the Great.

Having decided to end the institution of Jewish kingship, Augustus ordered Governor Varus to reorganize Judea. The governor placed Iturea under Roman control as part of Syria Province and also gave a large measure of autonomy to a group of Hellenistic cities in the region known as the Decapolis[31]—the city governments in this region reported directly to Rome's provincial administration in Antioch.

---

[31]Although literally meaning "ten cities," the Decapolis actually included at least nineteen: Damascus, Philadelphia, Raphana, Scythopolis, Gadara, Hippos, Dion, Pella, Gerasa, Canatha, Heliopolis, Abila, Saana, Hina, Lysanias, Capitolias, Edrei, Simulis, and Scythopolis.

Varus divided the rest of the kingdom of Judea among three of King Herod's sons, as follows:

- Herod Archelaus ruled as *ethnarch* (national leader) of central Judea, Samaria, and Idumea. (Bethlehem was in central Judea.)
- Herod Antipas ruled as *tetrarch* (a title that means one of four rulers) of Galilee and Perea. (Nazareth was in Galilee.)
- Herod Philip ruled as tetrarch of Panias, Gaulanitis (Golan), Batanea, Aurantis, and Trachonitis.

By the time of King Herod's death in 4 B.C., his family had fully assimilated into the upper class of Hellenized Roman society. Family members employed agents in Rome to lobby the Senate on behalf of Jewish interests, pursued cordial relations with Roman aristocrats and imperial government officials, and maintained connections with Hellenized leaders of Jewish communities throughout the Roman Empire. At least two of Herod's daughters married leaders of the Hellenistic Jewish community in Alexandria.

All three Judean rulers minted coins for use in their separate regions. Since the purification of Jewish religious beliefs during the Hasmonean dynasty, Jews radically opposed the use of non-Jewish religious symbols or images of animals and people in predominantly Jewish territories. As the sons of King Herod and a Samaritan queen, Herod Archelaus and Herod Antipas both minted coins designed to avoid offending the religious sensibilities of the traditional Jewish populations in their regions. However, inheriting an amalgam of his father's most difficult regions with a long history of contentious relationships—Samaria, Idumea, and central Judea—Herod Archelaus combined symbols that asserted his military strength with relatively inoffensive agricultural images. In Figure 22-5, the obverse of the top coin portrays grapes and a vine leaf[32] while the reverse portrays a military helmet with a caduceus, a symbol representing Herod Archelaus as victorious in battle; the obverse of the lower coin bears a double cornucopia, a symbol of abundance, while the reverse portrays a Roman warship.

As tetrarch of two militantly Jewish regions, Herod Antipas minted coins that bore agricultural symbols directly relevant to Jewish ritual.

---

[32]Although agricultural, grapes and vine leaves also symbolized Dionysian mystery cults.

Figure 22-5. Coins Minted under Herod Archelaus as Ethnarch of Judea. AE Prutahs from the Jerusalem Mint, 4 B.C.–6 A.D.

For example, the obverse of the coin in Figure 22-6 portrays a palm branch, not only symbolic of victory but also a component of a *lulav*, a ritual object used during *Sukkoth*, called the *Feast of Tabernacles* in the *New Testament*. The coin's reverse bears an inoffensive inscription of the name of the Emperor of Rome, Tiberius, surrounded by a wreath.

As tetrarch of Panias, Gaulanitis, Batanea, Aurantis, and Trachonitis—regions whose populations consisted mostly of non-Jews and Hellenized Jews—Herod Philip freely used human faces and pagan temples on his coins. For example, the obverse of the top coin in Figure 22-7 portrays the face of Tiberius and a laurel branch. The reverse portrays an *Augusteum*, a temple for the worship of Augustus. The obverse of the lower coin bears a portrait of Livia, and the reverse portrays a hand holding three stalks of ripe wheat, which commonly represented mystery cults related to Demeter and Persephone.

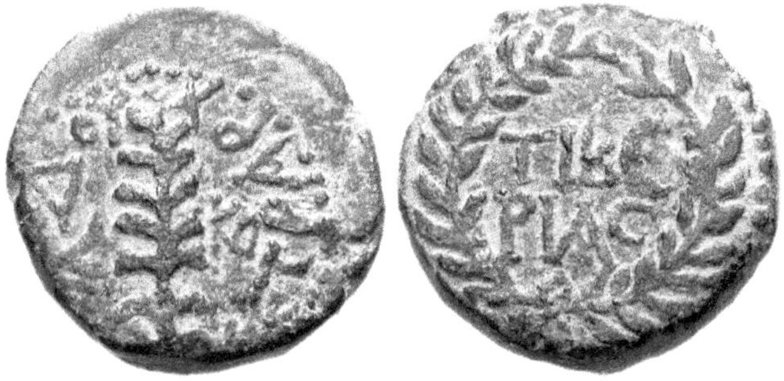

COIN IMAGES COURTESY OF THE CLASSICAL NUMISMATIC GROUP, INC.

Figure 22-6. Coin Minted under Herod Antipas as Tetrarch of Galilee and Perea. AE 24 from the Tiberias Mint, 19–20 A.D.

Jewish Rebellions during the Childhood of Jesus

Beginning immediately after the death of King Herod in 4 B.C., Judean patriots fought to depose Herod Archelaus and resurrect the messianic position, "King of the Jews," ideally with someone who claimed descent from Jewish royalty. Espousing open rebellion, violent messianic figures arose throughout Judea representing a variety of regional cultic traditions:

- Judas, son of Hezekiah,[33] led a rebellion of Jewish malcontents and thieves based in Sepphoris in Galilee.
- A former slave of King Herod named Simon of Perea[34] crowned himself with a royal diadem and led a band of rebellious Jews in central Judea.
- A shepherd named Athronges[35] crowned himself with a diadem and led a rebellion west of Jerusalem.

In support of Herod Archelaus, the Roman Governor of Syria Province, Publius Quinctilius Varus,[36] moved swiftly to crush these

[33]See *Antiquities of the Jews* 17.271–272 by Josephus
[34]See *The Jewish War* 2.57–59 and *Antiquities of the Jews* 17.273–277. Also, see *The Histories* 5.9 by Tacitus.
[35]See *Antiquities of the Jews* 17.278–284, by Josephus.
[36]Varus led three Roman legions to extinction thirteen years later in the Teutoburg Forest in Germany.

Figure 22-7. Coins Minted during the Reign of Herod Philip as Tetrarch of Panias, Gaulanitis, Batanea, Aurantis, and Trachonitis. AE 21 and AE 15 from Panias Mint, 30–31 A.D.

rebellions. Under his command, Roman soldiers crucified two thousand Jewish rebels.[37] While dealing with Judas, son of Hezekiah, in Galilee, the Romans destroyed the city of Sepphoris only four miles from Nazareth.

Among King Herod's sons, Herod Antipas played the most important role in the development of Christianity. Burdened with the task of raising Galileans from ignorant traditionalism to sophisticated Hellenization, he rebuilt Sepphoris[38] (the largest town near Nazareth) as the Hellenistic "Ornament of Galilee." When Jesus mentioned *hypocrites*[39] (actors) in the *canonical gospels* (the four authoritative gospels

---

[37]In comparison, fewer than two thousand Christians were killed in all the persecutions during the first three centuries of the first millennium, as estimated in *The Decline and Fall of the Roman Empire* 1:16 by Gibbon, who suggested that many deaths of Christian martyrs be considered a type of suicide.

[38]Romans destroyed Sepphoris defeating the Galilean rebellion of Judas, son of Hezekiah, after the death of King Herod.

[39]Hypocrites were actors in Hellenistic theaters. See *Matthew* 6:1–6, 7:1–5, and 15:1–9 in the *New Testament*. In the four gospels of the *New Testament*, Jesus used this word twenty-four times.

that appear in the *New Testament: Matthew, Mark, Luke,* and *John*), he spoke from direct experience of Hellenistic theater in Sepphoris just four miles from his home.

The rebellion in Perea strongly influenced Jesus. A recently discovered "Dead Sea scroll on stone"[40] dates from a time shortly after King Herod's death and bears a text called *Gabriel's Revelation*. The text refers metaphorically to Herod's slaughter of pious Jews in Jerusalem as well as to the defeat by Rome of three rebel leaders referred to as "shepherds." The artifact refers to two messiahs, a military leader called a "son of David" and a pious "son Joseph" who would suffer and die. One of the translators speculates that the artifact refers to the brutally executed rebel leader, Simon of Perea, as the suffering messiah.[41]

Gabriel's Revelation documents an emerging belief system called *catastrophic messianism*.[42] Faced with continuing murders of pious Jews and messianic leaders, some Jews began to believe that the End of Days would come only after enough pious blood had been spilled. In particular, foreigners would murder the messiah and leave his unburied body to lie like dung on the earth, but he would resurrect spiritually after three days. No mortal hand would kill the tyranical leader of the foreigners. Instead, the blood of the last messiah would precipitate overt action in the world by God: overthrowing tyranny, resurrecting righteous souls, and establishing God's eternal kingdom.[43]

The death of King Herod also encouraged the development of another messianic movement: A former high priest of the Jerusalem Temple started a Cult of King Herod to help calm public turmoil. Called Boethusians after their founding Sadducee priest, members of the cult did not believe in immortality of the soul nor did they believe

---

[40] The stone also is called the "Jeselsohn Stone," named after its owner, David Jeselsohn, a Swiss antiquities collector. In 2008, Israeli scholars Ada Yardeni and Israel Knoll published information about this artifact in "A New Dead Sea Scroll in Stone?" *Biblical Archaeology Review* Jan/Feb 2008, pp. 60–61.

[41] In his book *The Jesus Dynasty: The Hidden History of Jesus, His Royal Family, and the Birth of Christianity*, James Tabor discusses a thematic Jewish belief that two messiahs would usher in the Kingdom of God, one from the line of David and another from the line of Aaron, and that many Jews would have considered Jesus and John the Baptist as messianic equals.

[42] For information about catastrophic messianism, see *Messiahs and the Resurrection in 'The Gabriel Revelation'* pp. 38–39 by Israel Knohl.

[43] See the analysis of the Jeselsohn Stone inscription in *Messiahs and the Resurrection in 'The Gabriel Revelation'* pp. 22–30 by Israel Knohl.

in physical resurrection at the End of Days. However, they believed that King Herod was the messiah foretold by Jewish scripture. Surprisingly, the cult persisted for at least two centuries.[44]

The First Roman Census of Judea

With all the rebellions and crucifixions in Judea, the ethnarch, Herod Archelaus, never succeeded in obtaining the good will of his subjects. He ruled and taxed Judea, Samaria, and Idumea, and Jews despised him at least as much as they had despised his father. In 6 A.D., Augustus awarded the governorship of Syria Province to Publius Sulpicius Quirinius (an old friend of Tiberius) and ordered him to settle the unrest in Judea. Governor Quirinius deposed Archelaus, oversaw the transfer of his wealth to the Roman treasury, and exiled him to Gaul. As part of the annexation of Herod Archelaus' ethnarchy into Syria Province, Governor Quirinius ordered a census of central Judea, Samaria, and Idumea.

Placing Archelaus' troubled region under direct Roman control, Quirinius installed the first prefect of Roman Judea in a new administrative center in Caesarea, King Herod's Hellenistic showcase city. The prefect governed only central Judea, Samaria, and Idumea. The two remaining sons of King Herod who ruled portions of their father's kingdom continued to enjoy a large degree of independence from Rome: Herod Antipas continued to rule Galilee and Perea; and Herod Philip continued to rule Panias, Gaulanitis (Golan), Batanea, Aurantis, and Trachonitis.

The political chaos, the census, and the imposition of Roman taxes in central Judea caused many Jewish families (not just Joseph, Mary, and Jesus) to leave central Judea and move to Galilee, a comparatively peaceful and predominantly Jewish region capably ruled by Herod Antipas. However, to Romans, Galilee continued to earn a reputation as a source of troublemakers. Originally from Galilee, Judas of Gamala[45] led a new rebellion explicitly against Rome and the census of

---

[44]See *Adversis Omnes Haereses* 1:1 by (pseudo?) Tertullian.
[45]See *Antiquities of the Jews* 18:1 by Josephus.

central Judea. During the rebellion, Judas helped found a new Jewish cult whose members, called *Zealots*,[46] dedicated themselves to the violent expulsion of Romans from the Holy Land. From their beginning in 6 A.D., Zealots steadily increased in numbers.

Details about the defeat of Judas of Gamala have not survived. Regardless, Roman legions quickly imposed peace, and public unrest generally subsided as Judea briefly experienced improved conditions under direct Roman rule. The first few Roman prefects generally ruled conscientiously and well.

THE CHRISTIAN NATIVITY STORIES IN THE CANONICAL GOSPELS

While Christianity did not yet exist, the story of Jesus, son of Joseph (Yeshua bar Yosef), begins sometime between the last years of King Herod and the earliest years of Roman control over Judea. Written in Greek, the four canonical Christian gospels tell similar but contradictory stories about the life of Jesus.[47] Of these gospels, only *Matthew* and *Luke* describe the nativity. Both gospels associate the birth of Jesus with an astronomical event, but *Matthew* says that the event occurred before the death of King Herod in 4 B.C. and *Luke* says that the event occurred during the first Roman census of Judea in 6 A.D.

Christian tradition says that a disciple of Jesus wrote the gospel of *Matthew*, but modern scholars generally agree that the author was a Jewish Christian who wrote the gospel sometime toward the end of the first century A.D., several generations after the time of the disciples of Jesus. Early church fathers said that a non-Jewish (Greek or Syrian)

---

[46]Zealots played a dominant role in the Jewish revolution against Rome from 66–70 A.D., which resulted in the second destruction of the Jerusalem Temple. Contrasting sharply with the Zealot movement in Judea, Jews in Rome (up to 30,000 in 11 different synagogal communities during the first century A.D., not counting slaves) strove to prove themselves loyal Romans.

[47]Professor Julie Glambush of the College of William and Mary points out in her book, *The Reluctant Parting: How the New Testament's Jewish Writers Created a Christian Book*), that, "If it had been vital to the early Christians to have a literally accurate picture of Jesus, they wouldn't have kept all four gospels."

physician, a companion of Paul of Tarsos, wrote the gospel of *Luke*, also composed sometime around the end of the first century. Both gospels provide a general understanding that a young virgin named Mary (Miriam) became pregnant while she was engaged to a day-laborer (*tekton*) named Joseph (Yosef). Joseph married Mary even though he had not fathered her child,[48] and Mary gave birth to Jesus (Yeshua) in Bethlehem (Beit-Lechem), either in a cave or in the first-floor stable of a traditional Jewish four-room house.

The Nativity in the Gospel of *Matthew*

In the gospel of *Matthew*, the Holy Spirit impregnated Mary. When Joseph learned she was pregnant, his first inclination was to cancel their marriage. However, an angel counseled Joseph in a dream to accept Mary and instructed him to name the child Jesus (*Yeshua* means "Yahweh saves") because the child would bring salvation to his people. Joseph married Mary, but chose not to have intercourse with her, at least until after the birth of Jesus.

Mary gave birth to Jesus in Bethlehem during the reign of King Herod, but *Matthew* does not explain how the family arrived there. Wise men from the East, the *magi*, followed a star and brought gifts to the newborn savior. Herod then tried to kill Jesus by ordering a massacre of innocent children in Bethlehem, but an angel warned Joseph just in time for him to take his family to Egypt. Joseph, Mary, and Jesus remained in Egypt until after King Herod died and Herod Archelaus assumed the ethnarchy of Judea. Joseph and his family then returned, but they chose to avoid the political troubles afflicting Judea. Instead, they settled in a village called Nazareth in Galilee, a region peacefully ruled by Herod Antipas.

Except for the virgin birth of Jesus, the nativity story in *Matthew* resembles stories from the Jewish tradition of writing *midrash* or

---

[48]Giving a sense of Mary's anguish and her predicament in a small Jewish community, several sources preserve gossip that identified the natural father of Jesus as a Sidonian auxiliary named Pantera who served Rome in the forces of Governor Varus. See *The Jesus Dynasty: The Hidden History of Jesus, His Royal Family, and the Birth of Christianity* pp. 64–72 by James Tabor.

religious fiction. That is, it resembles a fictional story that metaphorically recalls sacred scripture for purposes of contemplation and discussion. Recalling several chapters in the *Torah*,[49] Herod represents King Balak, the magi represent Balaam, and the star recalls Balaam's prophecy about the coming of a messiah.

The Nativity in the Gospel of *Luke*

In the gospel of *Luke*, Joseph and Mary lived in Nazareth in Galilee, but they traveled to Bethlehem in Judea to register during the tax-related census conducted by Governor Quirinius when he took control over Judea in 6 A.D.[50] When Mary gave birth to her first-born son in Bethlehem, shepherds witnessed the "heavenly host" and came to see baby Jesus. At least thirty days after the birth, Joseph and Mary took Jesus to the Jerusalem Temple for the ceremony of *Pidyon Ha' Ben* (redemption of the first-born son).[51] Then the family returned home to Nazareth.

As one might expect in a document written by a non-Jewish Greek or Syrian influenced by philosophy from Tarsos, the gospel of *Luke* describes Jesus' birth in the context of a Hellenized Zoroastrian struggle between a good god of light and an evil god of darkness.[52] In addition, the gospel reveals symbolic connections with Hellenistic religious ideas in many references, for example: demons leaving a person and entering swine;[53] the mission of the seventy-two disciples; signs expected in the sun, moon, and stars; and so on.

---

[49] See *Numbers* 22–24.
[50] This assertion in *Luke* begs the question: Why would a poor resident of Nazareth in Galilee volunteer to pay taxes in Roman Judea?
[51] The poverty of the holy family is revealed by the sacrifice of two doves at the Pidyon Ha' Ben ceremony. See *Luke* 2:24 and *The Jesus Dynasty: The Hidden History of Jesus, His Royal Family, and the Birth of Christianity* p. 87 by James Tabor. The first description of Joseph as an old man appears in the *Infancy Gospel of James* (or *Protoevangelium of James*). In the marriage between Mary (a young pregnant woman) and Joseph (a poor old man), many genealogists recognize the common predicament that forces a young woman to take an old man as a husband to give her child at least a small degree of legitimacy.
[52] See Chapter 7.
[53] See Chapter 5.

Understanding the "Virgin Birth" of Jesus

The important description of the "virgin birth" in the nativity of *Matthew* conforms with the collection of Ptolemaic translations of Jewish scriptures called the *Septuagint*, the version of the *Old Testament* propagated by Alexandrian scholars to pagans throughout the Western world. The Hebrew for "young girl" in *Isaiah* 7:14–17 appears as the Greek word for "virgin" in the *Septuagint*.[54] Existing Hebrew versions of *Isaiah* use this passage poetically to describe how long it will take for threats from Assyria to pass—enough time for a young woman to conceive, give birth, and begin teaching her child about the difference between right and wrong. Altering this passage from "young woman" to "virgin" changed its meaning for Hellenistic readers from merely indicating a time frame into prophesying the birth of God's son. Further, the passage helped non-Jewish Westerners connect prophecy about a Jewish messiah with beliefs about other Hellenistic saviors born of virgins.[55]

No surviving Hebrew prophecy outside the *Septuagint* foretells that a virgin will bear the messiah. However, mistranslation might not provide the only explanation for this passage. Even though Jewish scribes have demonstrated an amazing ability to transmit Hebrew text faithfully across millennia, different Jewish cults used different versions of Hebrew Scriptures. The *Septuagint's* version of *Isaiah* may accurately reflect a lost variation of *Isaiah* associated with an extinct Jewish cult. To modern readers, it still seems strange that the Greek gospels of *Matthew* and *Luke* trace Jesus' descent from David (an important ancestor of the true messiah) through Joseph. If he never had sexual relations with Mary, his lineage has nothing to do with Jesus. However, early Christians may have had good reasons for relating both genealogies to Jesus: One was the genealogy of Joseph and one was the genealogy of Mary; and Mary's genealogy avoided an ancient Judean curse.[56]

---

[54]Also, see *Genesis* 34:3 of the *Septuagint*: After Shechem had sex with Jacob's daughter Dinah, he continued to describe her using the word *parthenos*, Greek for virgin, clearly meaning only that she was female and young.
[55]For example, see Chapters 6 and 13.
[56]In *The Jesus Dynasty: The Hidden History of Jesus, His Royal Family, and the Birth of Christianity* pp. 44–58, James Tabor analyzes the different genealogies of Jesus in *Matthew* and *Luke* and identifies them as genealogies of Joseph and Mary, respectively.

Connecting the Nativity Stories in *Matthew* and *Luke* with History

The nativity of *Matthew* connects better to the history of Judea and Galilee than the nativity of *Luke*. For example, the gospel of *Luke* contradicts itself by associating the birth of Jesus simultaneously with two different historical events separated in time by at least twelve years:

- A decree of Augustus around 8–6 B.C. that ordered a census of the Roman world.
- A census of Judea ordered by Governor Quirinius of Syria in 6 A.D.

The gospel of *Luke* identifies Jesus' age at the beginning of his ministry as approximately thirty years. If Mary gave birth to Jesus during the governorship of Quirinius, Jesus would not have reached the age of thirty by the time of his crucifixion (30–33 A.D., the most commonly accepted range of dates). Birth during the governorship of Quirinius would have made Jesus no older than twenty-seven and possibly as young as twenty-four at the time of his death.

Jesus and the First Roman Census of Judea

Compiled in all territories directly administered by Rome, the census ordered by Augustus in 8–6 B.C. helped forecast tax revenues as the empire moved away from the early Republican practice of tax farming. Before 4 B.C., King Herod, a semi-independent client-king of Judea, ruled and taxed central Judea and Galilee directly. At the time of Jesus' birth, the order to conduct a census of Roman-administered territories simply did not apply to Herod's kingdom.

Before the death of King Herod, Mary and Joseph never had a reason to leave Nazareth (Galilee) for Bethlehem (central Judea) to register for a census related to Roman taxation. Rome did not tax central Judea until after the exile of Herod Archelaus in 6 A.D. Further, Rome did not tax Galilee directly until Syria Province annexed that territory toward the end of the first century A.D. Therefore, history contradicts the nativity story in the gospel of *Luke*: Augustus' order for a census affected neither central Judea nor Galilee during the most likely period for Jesus' birth. Did the author of *Luke* make a historical mistake?

Both *Matthew* and *Luke* identify the location of Jesus' birth as Bethlehem, the birthplace of King David. Even King Herod's advisors knew that the messiah had to come from Bethlehem. *Matthew* then says that Joseph and Mary then fled to Egypt to avoid persecution by Herod. Looking only at when and where Joseph, Mary, and Jesus are said to have traveled, most of their travel can be explained only as a way to avoid Roman taxes associated with the decree of Augustus' in 8–6 B.C. After Herod's death, the family would have returned to Bethlehem from Egypt to avoid the tax-related Egyptian census of 3–2 B.C.[57] The family then avoided Bethlehem (Judea) and went to Nazareth (Galilee) to escape political unrest in Judea under Herod Archelaus, and they stayed in Nazareth to avoid Roman taxation imposed after the annexation of Judea. If the gospels of *Matthew* and *Luke* had fully presented and accurately explained the movements of the holy family, they would have served as a bad example of Roman civic responsibility. Did someone ensure that the text of *Luke* portrayed the family of Jesus as good, tax-paying Roman citizens?

THE IMPORTANCE OF ASTROLOGICAL SIGNS

To modern readers, the nativity stories in the gospels of *Matthew* and *Luke* both describe strange astronomical miracles that announced the birth of Jesus: a wandering star followed by wise men in *Matthew* and a "throng of heavenly host" visible to shepherds in *Luke*. While Jews around the time of Jesus looked for signs in the sky, few understood astrology. However, many of the first Christian readers of the gospels of *Matthew* and *Luke* understood sophisticated Hellenistic astrology.

Non-astrological English translations of *Matthew* don't make sense (for example, how could magi travel west by following a star in the East?), but the contradictions vanish when one examines the gospels in terms of the expectations of ancient astrologers. Both *Matthew* and *Luke* use Greek words with precise astrological meanings. One can understand what the authors of *Matthew* and *Luke* meant about the

---

[57]For details about the relationship betweeen census and taxes in Egypt, see "The Beginnings of the Roman Census in Egypt" by R. S. Bagnall in *Greek, Roman, and Byzantine Studies* 32, pp. 89–90, 1991.

miraculous star, the "throng of heavenly host," the wise men, and so on, only in terms of ancient knowledge: To astrologers late in the first century A.D. (when the gospels of *Matthew* and *Luke* were written), a specific, rare astrological event had indicated the birth of a god-like king in Judea.

The gospel of *Matthew* says that an unknown number (tradition identifies three) of wise men (magi) came to Bethlehem because a star in the East told them that the King of the Jews was born.[58] Two thousand years ago, the term *magi* referred to astrologers from the East, commonly Zoroastrians. A modern analysis[59] of the nativity stories in *Matthew* and *Luke* in terms of ancient astrology points to one specific astrological configuration that matches the events described in both gospels: Regardless of when the birth of Jesus actually occurred, astrologers who lived two thousand years ago would have identified one specific date for the birth of the Jewish messiah. Surprisingly, ancient astrology also explains the contradictions between *Matthew* and *Luke*, especially how early Christians associated the nativity with the census in Judea during the governorship of Quirinius in 6 A.D.

Scholars easily discredit modern suggestions that identify the Christmas star with a spectacular comet or planetary conjunction: The true event could not have appeared too spectacular because, according to *Luke*, no one in Judea noticed the star except a few shepherds. Also, many Jews expected the imminent arrival of the messiah, yet *Matthew* says that only a few Hellenistic astrologers from the East knew that the birth had happened—and they needed to ask King Herod where to find the baby.

Using Hellenistic Astrology to Identify the Messiah's Date of Birth

Ancient astrological texts identify one specific astronomical configuration that would have announced the birth of the Jewish messiah to Hellenistic astrologers. The most appropriate and explicit indications came from the *Mathesis*, a text written by a fourth century Sicilian

---

[58] See *Matthew* 2:1–2.
[59] A professional astronomer and historian, Dr. Michael Molnar presented his analysis of the Christmas miracle in his book: *The Star of Bethlehem: The Legacy of the Magi*.

Christian astrologer named Julius Firmicus Maternus.[60] Key passages from the *Mathesis* point to important astrological signs of kingship and divinity. Maternus describes important aspects of Jupiter in the birth of "unconquerable generals," referring at least in part to elements related to the birth of Augustus, which was published in 11 A.D. to dispel rumors of his imminent death.[61] However, Maternus identifies stronger aspects of Jupiter and other astrological indicators of the birth of a person with an especially "divine and immortal nature," apparently referring to Jesus:[62]

> (**WARNING:** Descriptions of these signs use concepts and terms that only people familiar with astrology will understand.)
> - Close conjunctions of the moon and Jupiter indicated a king's birth, and Jupiter appeared as a royal *Star of the East* by rising in the morning sky exactly twelve degrees ahead of the sun (Jupiter's heliacal rising).
> - The sun was exalted in Aries (close to the planets Jupiter and Saturn that ruled Aries)—a constellation associated with Judea—and the moon was moving toward Jupiter.
> - Other characteristics of planetary position, rulers of constellations, cardinal points, attendants, and maleficent planets were well-situated at the birth.

Although the above information appears obscure, its importance toward understanding what people saw in the sky at the nativity emerges simply and elegantly: The tiniest visible crescent moon rose like an axe blade centered just above the planet Jupiter on the last day that the moon was visible before the New Moon and the first day that Jupiter was visible in the early morning sky. Further, observation verified that the moon *occulted* Jupiter. In modern terms, the moon passed in front of planet Jupiter in the sky. To less sophisticated viewers, the

---

[60]The historian Theodor Mommsen estimated that Maternus published the *Matheses* in 336 A.D., a couple years before publishing *On the Error of Profane Religion*, a work that attacks non-Christian religious beliefs.
[61]See Chapter 21.
[62]For a careful analysis of the astrological aspects that ancient astrologers associated with the birth of a Jewish messiah, see *The Star of Bethlehem: The Legacy of the Magi* pp. 65–108 by Michael Molnar.

event looked like the moon, shaped like a mouth, was trying to swallow a bright star.

Consistent with the gospel of *Matthew*, ancient astrologers calculated the possibility that the crescent moon would occult the heliacally rising Jupiter in the constellation Aries, but they needed to observe the relative positions of Jupiter and the moon in the early morning sky to verify that the occultation actually occurred. Such a propitious occultation in the morning sky happened only once during the lifetimes of King Herod and Jesus: April 17, 6 B.C. Consistent with the date of this configuration, Clement of Alexandria[63] said in the second century A.D. that some people identified the birthday of Jesus as April 20 or 21.

Astrological Interpretation of *Matthew* and *Luke*

One can imagine a group of learned Hellenistic astrologers, perhaps in Babylon, noting that astrological conditions appeared suitable for the birth of the Jewish messiah. Early in the morning on April 17, 6 B.C., they peered into the East anticipating their first view of Jupiter at its heliacal rising. They saw Venus and Saturn rise, and then they saw the crescent moon and Jupiter rise so close together that they seemed almost like a single object: The moon and planets were a beautiful sight in the morning sky.[64] (See Figure 22-8.) The magi joyously observed that the crescent moon soon would occult Jupiter, which meant that Jupiter would disappear behind the bright blade of the crescent moon in a matter of hours.

Observation of the crescent moon occulting Jupiter (a bright "star") in the East might well have moved the magi to travel west to Judea to find the newborn king. Preparations for travel and the travel itself would have taken a long time. Jupiter advanced westward

---

[63]Clement of Alexandria was a Christian theologian who headed the Catechetical School in Alexandria, Egypt. He lived approximately from 150 A.D. to 215 A.D. and is remembered as the teacher of Origen, one of the most important writers in the early Christian Church.

[64]The astronomical software *Starry Night Pro Plus* can be used to model the appearance of the sky over Babylon and Bethlehem on April 17, 6 B.C. Other software packages may not have the precision to calculate the motions of the moon and planets accurately enough to portray an event that happened so long ago.

Figure 22-8. Eastern View of the Sky from Bethlehem in the Early Morning of April 17, 6 B.C.

through the last degrees of Aries and passed into Taurus on June 20, but the planet stopped its direct motion through the ecliptic around August 23. (See Figure 22-9.)

Because the earth revolves once around the sun in one year and Jupiter revolves once around the sun in slightly less than twelve years, the earth makes a close approach to Jupiter once every thirteen months or so. From the moment that earth reaches its closest approach to Jupiter, the bright planet appears to move backward (eastward) through the zodiac for approximately four months. In English, we say the planet becomes retrograde. The Hellenistic astrological term equivalent to "retrograde" appears in the gospel of *Matthew* in English translation as "went before."

As a retrograde "star," Jupiter reentered Aries on October 7. If the magi had randomly searched Judea—unsuccessfully—they might finally have met with Herod in November or December of 6 B.C. Directed to Bethlehem by Herod's advisors, the magi would have watched Jupiter as it "went before" them in the night sky until Jupiter stopped again, or "stood over" them just as they entered Bethlehem in mid-December 6 B.C. Within seven days, Jupiter resumed direct

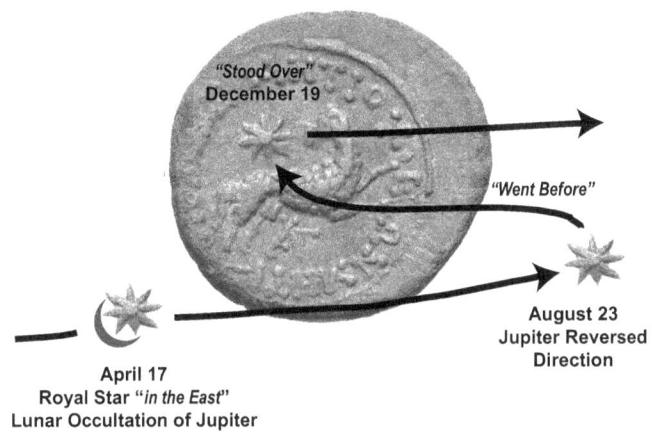

Figure 22-9. Representation of the Passage of Jupiter Through the Constellation Aries in 6 B.C.

motion westward until it left Aries completely. Jupiter didn't return to Aries until more than a decade later in 5 A.D., not long before the first Roman census of Judea.

The Historical and Astrological Context of the Nativity

Learned Hellenistic seers like the magi would have had little difficulty obtaining an audience with King Herod. From the rare occultation of heliacally rising Jupiter by the moon in Aries, the magi knew only that a new King of the Jews had been born. In *Matthew*, the magi met with King Herod, a notoriously paranoid and treacherous ruler, and naively revealed their purpose of honoring someone greater than the king. The king's advisors didn't know about the meaning of the planets in the morning sky because they didn't practice astrology. However, King Herod respected the Hellenistic art and worried that a newborn king would supplant, not just his Herodian dynasty, but also his personal desire for recognition as the messiah.

Steeped in Jewish prophecy, King Herod's advisors told the magi to look for the newborn king in Bethlehem, the ancestral home of King

David. Herod asked the magi to return after they found the child so that Herod could honor the child as well. However, the magi understood that King Herod really wanted to kill Jesus.

When the magi failed to return, King Herod decided to kill all the children who someday might claim to be King of the Jews. To be sure of killing the correct child, he had to kill all the male children born since Jupiter first appeared in Aries. Because Jupiter could stay in an astrological sign for a year or longer before moving completely to the next sign, Herod ordered his soldiers to kill all the children of Bethlehem two years old and younger. Modern scholars estimate that Herod's soldiers might have murdered a dozen children or so.[65]

Mentioned briefly in the gospel of *Matthew*, the "massacre of the innocents" does not appear in any other historical source from these times—possibly for good reason. Jews of the time would have considered the killing of a few children in a remote village as a relatively minor event: It affected only a small number of people in comparison to other events during Herod's terrible last years. For example, his high-profile executions of important Jewish leaders and his Roman-inspired flirtation with idolatry at the Jerusalem Temple were much more noteworthy.

Reconciling Contradictions in the Nativities of *Matthew* and *Luke*

Using ancient astrology to understand the Star of Bethlehem explains contradictory statements in the gospel of *Luke* and simultaneously provides a glimpse of late first-century Christianity. Christians in Antioch wrote both *Matthew* and *Luke* at least two generations after the crucifixion of Jesus. In *Matthew*, Hellenistic astrologers confirmed the importance of Jesus' birth using the vocabulary of ancient astrology. Reluctant to associate the nativity with Hellenistic astrology, the author of *Luke* replaced the magi with stargazing shepherds. Even so, *Luke* also used important astrological terminology.

The astrological birth chart in Figure 22-10 shows the relative positions of planets and the sun around sunrise on April 17, 6 B.C. On the

---
[65]See *The Star of Bethlehem: The Legacy of the Magi* pp. 117–118 by Michael Molnar.

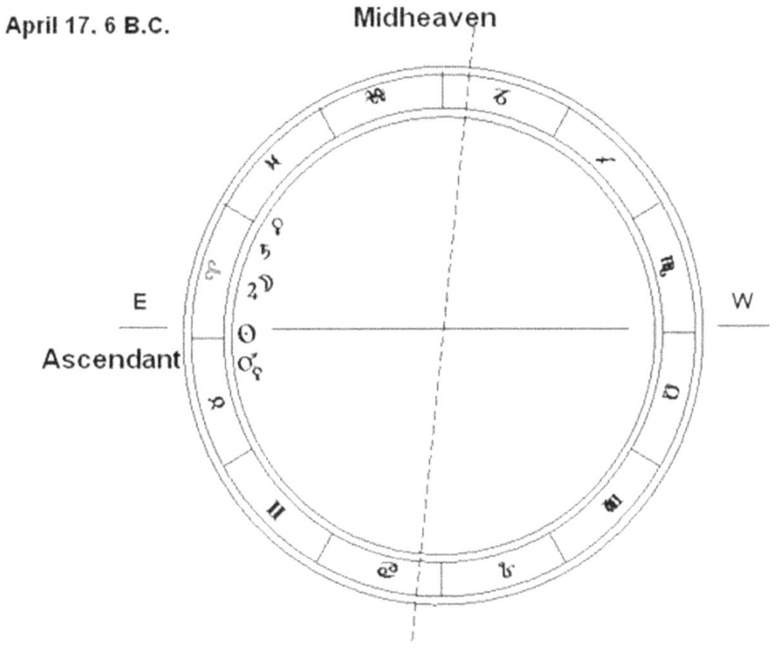

Figure 22-10. Calculated Planetary Positions for April 17, 6 B.C., and a Corresponding Birth Chart of a Jewish Messiah Born on That Day.

birth chart, the symbol of the sun (☉) appears on the Ascendant (the horizontal radius on the left side of the birth chart). The planetary symbols above the sun—from closest to the horizon to highest in the sky, Jupiter (♃), moon (☽), Saturn (♄), and Venus (♀)—represent planets that appeared in the night sky just before sunrise. The two planetary symbols below the Ascendant—from close to the horizon to farther away, Mars (♂) and Mercury (☿)—represent planets that appeared in the evening sky just after sunset.

Many ancient astrological portents affirm the special nature of this birth chart. The three planetary rulers of Aries (♈)—the Sun, Jupiter and Saturn—all occupy Aries, the astrological sign of Judea. The moon, also in Aries, occulted the planet Jupiter shortly after its heliacal rising. Venus and Saturn precede the Sun in a relationship that ancient astrologers called *spear-bearers*. Similarly, Mars and Mercury serve as *attendants*. The planets that usually harm birth charts, Mars and

Saturn, occupy particularly favorable positions: Mars occupies Taurus (♉), a constellation ruled by Mars; and Saturn occupies Aries, a constellation ruled by Saturn. Close to the other planets, Venus occupies Pisces (♓), a sign that Venus rules. *Luke* says that, "There was with the angel a multitude of the *heavenly host* praising God." To modern ears, these words sound like a poetic description of angels singing in the sky. However, they were an astrological technical description in ancient times: The term "heavenly host" referred to planets clustered together in the sky, particularly in their aspect as "morning stars." Ancient astrologers would have referred to this close grouping of sun, moon, and planets as a multitude of the heavenly host proclaiming the birth of a divine being.

Jupiter left Aries early in 5 B.C. and did not return to the constellation until 5–6 A.D., precisely the time when Governor Quirinius prepared Judea for direct Roman rule. His recent discussions of astrology with Tiberius on Rhodes[66] inspired the governor to represent Rome's takeover of Judea on coins using astrological symbols. Quirinius began minting coins in Antioch like the one in Figure 22-11. The coins display Zeus on the obverse and the symbol of a planet in Aries on the reverse. A few generations later, early Hellenistic Christians in Antioch believed that these coins commemorated the same astrological event as the one that heralded the birth of Jesus. Because he connected historic events related to these coins with astrological events related to the nativity, the author of the gospel of *Luke* mistakenly set the birth of Jesus during the census of Quirinius.

Connecting Hellenistic Astrology to a Jewish Sign

In the context of astrological evidence about the nature of the Star of Bethlehem, it's intriguing to speculate how Jews responded to the occultation of Jupiter by the moon on April 17, 6 B.C. Jews didn't calculate Hellenistic astrology charts, but they looked for signs involving the sun, moon, and planets, especially in the morning sky toward the end of the moon's cycle. Every month, Jews everywhere noted the death of the moon in the morning sky and, a few days later, celebrated

---

[66]See Chapter 21.

Figure 22-11. Star of Bethlehem Coin Minted under Governor Quirinius. Syria, Antioch, AE 21, 5–6 A.D.

the birth of the moon (the first day of the new month) in the evening sky, calling the event *Rosh Chodesh*. Jews who noticed the occultation of Jupiter at the death of the moon on April 17, 6 B.C., would have remembered it as a remarkable sign: Jupiter hovering just in front of the crescent moon as if about to be swallowed by a beast. The crescent moon soon disappeared as well, and then reappeared several days later at Rosh Chodesh, a series of events metaphorically associated with the story of Jonah and the whale.

The moon occulted Jupiter in the middle of the zodiacal constellation, Aries. On the Farnese Atlas in Figure 13-12, the constellation Aries is portrayed as a ram running along the zodiac right next to the intersection of the zodiac and the celestial equator. The beast below the ram is Ketos, a bird-headed sea-monster after which whales were named. (See Figure 7-5.) With mouth agape, Ketos looks as if he is about to bite the ram on its belly, the location where the occultation of Jupiter occurred in 6 B.C.

Born around 6 B.C., Jesus didn't remember events related to his birth, but he heard about them. When magi entered Bethlehem looking for a newborn child who was destined to rule as King of the Jews, Mary welcomed them as a way to counteract the gossip about her pregnancy and the speculation about her child's father. Everyone in the village of Bethlehem wanted to know details about what the astrologers saw that made them travel so far. They recognized that the magi had seen an authentic sign and they probably gave the sign a name. They did not call the sign the "Star of Bethlehem," nor did they refer to it as the "Christmas Star."

Developments in astrology after the death of Jesus suggest that the occultation of April 17, 6 B.C., was known to his followers as the Sign of Jonah.[67] During the first few centuries of the first millennium, Roman astrologers integrated the Egyptian concept of decans[68] into their astrological toolkit. A decan is one of thirty-six ten-degree sections of sky. Each astrological sign comprises three decans, and each decan is identified by a name and has a planetary ruler. In the names of decans used by Roman astrology, an unknown Christian astrologer encoded a "Gospel of Jesus Christ," in the names of decans beginning with decans of Aries and ending with decans of Pisces.[69] The name of the middle decan of Aries was Ketos, the Whale, and it was ruled by the sun. Referring to the portion of sky in which the sign of the "Star of Bethlehem" had occurred, the name shows that Christian astrologers close to the time of Jesus connected this decan simultaneously with symbolism related to the birth of Jesus, the story of Jonah and the whale, and Christian ideas about the death and resurrection of Jesus, particularly connected with the sun.

HEROD'S JUDEA: A CULTURAL AND IDEOLOGICAL BATTLEGROUND

The story of King Herod reveals a mixture of positive and negative aspects of his rule over Judea. History remembers King Herod as *Herod the Great* for all the good that he accomplished: He preserved his kingship under opposing Roman regimes; he maintained order in a complex, multi-ethnic kingdom; he completed building projects of unprecedented scale and magnificence; and he generally presided over

---

[67]See Chapter 24.
[68]Egyptians began using decans as part of their calendar around 2100 B.C. The concept formed the basis of the solar calendar that Julius Caesar introduced to Rome toward the end of his life.
[69]See "The Witness of the Stars" by Gerardus D. Bouw in *Biblical Astronomer* Vol. 12, No. 100, pp. 47–50, Spring 2002.

a period of peace, economic prosperity, and relatively free expression of diverse Jewish religious beliefs. On the negative side, he brutally suppressed all opposition; he murdered members of his own family for real or imagined offenses; and he periodically offended devout Jews by committing acts that many regarded as sacrilegious.

Ruling Judea during a period when strong rulers sought recognition as divinities, King Herod symbolically pursued his own claim to be a messiah. Powerfully suppressing local competitors, he increased the pressure of competing ideologies in Judea the way a lid increases pressure in a pressure-cooker. When he died in 4 B.C., the lid came off Judean society. Rome divided the kingdom into four parts—three controlled by sons of King Herod and one (the Decapolis) controlled by the Roman provincial government—and Rome eliminated Jewish kingship, unintentionally heightening Jewish expectations about the coming of a militaristic messiah.

Minor rebellions erupted that threw poorly trained Jewish civilians in combat against professional legionnaires. The Roman soldiers hunted down the rebels and brutally murdered them. It was during this time, the early childhood of Jesus, that catastrophic messianism emerged as a mature ideology: Jews combined belief in the spiritual resurrection of a messiah three days after his death with the necessity of spilling a quantity of righteous blood sufficient to force God to establish his eternal kingdom.

Under Herod Archelaus, numerous Jewish leaders sought to purify local worship, which increased participation in militaristic Jewish cults. Eastern prophecies about the End of Days instilled a new sense of urgency among Jews struggling to put themselves on the right side of God. Failing to rule effectively, the administration of Herod Archelaus lost Rome's confidence because of its inability to deal with corruption, festering discontent, and continuing public disorder. He succeeded only in giving Rome an excuse to expel him and assume direct control over central Judea. Then, consistent with the policies of Augustus Caesar, Rome conducted a census of central Judea as a step toward implementing direct Roman rule and taxation.

Jesus grew up in a time and place in which bitter religious conflict was unavoidable. Religious symbols employed so painlessly and effectively in Rome to communicate a renewal of spiritual life created outrage among conservative elements in the shattered pieces of Herod's kingdom. Western and Eastern points of view collided and mixed: Some enlightened Hellenistic Jews focused on building a prosperous multicultural society under Rome while messianic Jews built movements dedicated to expelling foreign influences and purifying traditional religious institutions. Everyone searched for the messiah, some wanted to be the messiah, and whole generations of Jews began to consider that it might be necessary to die for their religious beliefs.

Scholarly analysis of the nativity stories in the gospels of *Matthew* and *Luke* in terms of ancient astrology offers insight into the historic core of the nativity stories of Jesus. The gospels document rapidly shifting social conditions, tensions between Hellenism and traditional Jewish beliefs, and non-Jewish religious ideas encoded in ancient metaphors and technical language, the significance of which has become lost or misinterpreted over two millennia. The ideological battles of the past were vastly different from what most modern readers of the *Bible* would like to believe.

In the widespread peace during the dominion of a Roman Son of God, righteous Jewish leaders emerged willing to battle the *Cult of the Emperor*[70] (also known as the *imperial cult*) on all levels. Romans saw Jewish messianic movements as weeds growing in Rome's Eastern garden, and many feared that discontent in Judea might rapidly spread to Jewish populations everywhere. The first dynastic transfer of imperial power from Augustus to Tiberius brought harsh changes to Rome's relationship with Judea. To appreciate the context of the life of Jesus and the earliest emergence of Christianity, it's important first to understand how Tiberius Caesar, the successor of Augustus, spread disillusion in the imperial cult throughout the Roman World.

---

[70]See Chapter 21.

CHAPTER
23

THE REIGN OF TIBERIUS

THE LIFE AND MINISTRY OF JESUS

Politics during the reign of Tiberius distracted Rome from troubles in Judea and shaped a diverse lower-class of Jewish and Hellenistic seekers of salvation distributed throughout the empire.

For Jews living in the Roman Empire, the last decade of the reign of Augustus (4–14 A.D.) and the first decade of the reign of Tiberius (14–24 A.D.) marked a period when improving conditions reached a peak. Free Jews lived in major cities on every Mediterranean shore and positive aspects of the way they lived—for example, relatively high literacy, good behavior consistent with a written moral code, and the enviable observance of a day of rest every week—attracted interest and imitation from non-Jews who were collectively known as *Judaizers* or *Godfearers*. Jewish beliefs became so popular that many non-Jews formally converted, even though conversion meant undergoing circumcision (for men) and adopting a *kosher* lifestyle—for example, giving up pork, praying daily, and learning to follow unfamiliar laws. Scholars estimate that, by the middle of the first century A.D., as much as one-tenth of the population of the Roman Empire consisted of Jews, Jewish converts, and Godfearers.[1]

Generally associating Jewish beliefs with Egyptian cults, Augustus and Tiberius both expressed personal distaste for the Jerusalem Temple Cult. Also, most Jews in Judea objected to foreign influences, whether Hellenistic or Roman, that accompanied Roman soldiers into Jewish territories. The transition from Herodian rule to Roman rule in central Judea resulted in several regionally based rebellions that Roman legions put down quickly and brutally. Subsequently, many Roman officials began to see the widespread distribution and increasing population of Jews throughout the Mediterranean region as a potential source of trouble. Needing to ensure that Jewish unrest did not spread, Tiberius sanctioned policy changes that signaled a shift toward worsening conditions for Jews. In Rome, Tiberius initiated the first civil action against Jews since the punishment of Jews for worshipping Jupiter Sabazius in 139 B.C.[2]

Prior to his death in 14 A.D., Augustus established the first dynasty of the Roman Empire, which history remembers as the *Julio-Claudian dynasty*,[3] by arranging for Tiberius to become the first hereditary emperor of Rome. Augustus wanted the dynasty to continue through Germanicus, a grandson of Marc Antony and Octavia[4] who also was a nephew of Tiberius, instead of continuing through Drusus, the son of Tiberius. In addition to being a descendent of Octavia, Germanicus had married Agrippina the Elder, the daughter of Agrippa and Julia (the daughter of Augustus). Augustus forced Tiberius to adopt Germanicus and name him as the official imperial successor. Forced to favor his nephew over his son, Tiberius automatically assumed a position of blame should any harm prevent Germanicus from inheriting the empire. The death of Germanicus in 19 A.D. contributed significantly to Rome's dissatisfaction with Tiberius, and the death of Tiberius's son

---

[1] See "Population" by Salo W. Baron in the *Encyclopaedia Judaica* 13 (1971), p. 869.
[2] See Chapter 12.
[3] The Julio-Claudian dynasty lasted only until the death of Nero in 68 A.D. After Augustus and Tiberius, all the Julio-Claudian emperors were descendants of Marc Antony and Octavia Minor, the sister of Augustus.
[4] Germanicus was the grandson of Marc Antony and Octavia Minor through their daughter Antonia Minor who married Drusus, the brother of Tiberius.

Drusus in 23 A.D. contributed significantly to the fading of Tiberius' interest in governing Rome.

The reign of Tiberius divides easily into three parts: 14–26 A.D. when he struggled to cope with the adversarial relationship that developed between himself and the people he governed, 26–31 A.D. when he placed the day-to-day administration of the Roman government in the hands of a notorious underling named Sejanus, and 31–37 A.D. when he again took personal charge of Rome and tried to make up for some of the wrongs committed by Sejanus. Throughout most of the adult life of Jesus of Nazareth, Roman prefects ruled central Judea in a competent and non-partisan fashion. However, most Jews still wished that a messiah would declare himself and liberate Jerusalem from Roman control. When Tiberius abandoned personal involvement in the governing of Rome in 26 A.D., Sejanus used his position to implement anti-Jewish policies wherever he could. It was Sejanus who assigned Pontius Pilate as prefect of Judea, which resulted in a sudden deterioration in relations between Jews and Romans in Judea. Beginning soon after the arrival of Pontius Pilate, the ministry of Jesus continued until his arrest, trial, and crucifixion in Jerusalem sometime during the years 30–33 A.D.

Unpopular in Rome from the beginning, Tiberius Caesar was responsible for official Roman policy during the period that Christian scripture says that Jesus Christ established himself as a religious teacher, taught compassion to the multitudes, and died on a Roman cross. For almost two thousand years, Western historians have contrasted the evil reign of Tiberius with the virtuous life of Jesus. However, in the light of modern analysis concerning the prejudices and agendas of ancient historians who first wrote about Tiberius, a more nuanced picture of his reign is emerging.

THE RELIGIOUS AND POLITICAL CLIMATE IN ROME

Tiberius generally tolerated all cults while showing little interest in any. However, he expressed distaste for Egyptian cults and for Jewish cults, apparently considering them connected or at least equally bad.⁵ Also, Tiberius was aware of problems in Judea. As prefects of central Judea collected taxes, maintained order, and extended respect to all Jewish cults, their most vexing problems concerned Jewish intolerance. Jews hated Jews with different beliefs and Jews hated non-Jews for bringing foreign cults into Judea.⁶ Tensions among Jewish cults or between Jews and Romans in Judea had the potential of infecting Jewish populations elsewhere. In addition, Hellenistic Jews contributed to the common Roman misunderstanding that Egyptian cults and Jewish cults were connected: Hellenizers experimented with combining Jewish and Egyptian religious beliefs, sometimes describing Moses as the child of Sophia (wisdom) in a religious relationship that ran parallel to the relationship between Harpokrates (Horus) and Isis.⁷

Astrology and Roman Cults under Tiberius

Astrology entered its golden age in Rome under the patronage of Tiberius who studied astrology, promoted interest in the art throughout the Roman Empire, and encouraged practitioners' attempts to improve its reliability. His interest in astrology contributed to the increasing popularity of astrology among all segments of Roman society, including Godfearers and Jewish Christians who recorded astrological accounts of the nativity in the gospels of *Matthew* and *Luke*.⁸

Astrology brought new understanding of the universe, the soul, and divinity, which changed popular perceptions about the location where souls would experience life after death: While Greek and Roman traditions dictated that common humans passed into the underground realm of Hades, Julius Caesar and Augustus Caesar both had risen into the sky to join the gods. An astrological poet wrote about the birth chart of Tiberius saying that he was destined to rule the universe from the sky.⁹ Influenced by Hellenistic interpretations of Zoroastrianism,

---

⁵See *The Cults of the Roman Empire* p. 88 by Robert Turcan.
⁶Either because few Parthian sources have survived or because of similarities between Jewish and Zoroastrian beliefs, there are few records of Jewish intolerance of Parthian religious beliefs.
⁷See *The Jesus Mysteries: Was the "Original Jesus" a Pagan God?* p. 182 by Timothy Freke and Peter Gandy. Also, see Chapter 10.
⁸See Chapter 22.
⁹See *Astronomica* 4.548 by Manilius.

astrology, and Eastern cults of sky gods like Baal and Zeus-Ouranios, common Romans began to believe that even their souls could ascend to heaven after death, as long as they lived virtuous lives.

In combination with astrology, Hellenized Eastern beliefs widely influenced philosophy, popular culture, and cultic practices throughout the Roman Empire. In their everyday lives, Romans began believing in spiritual ages, angels, demons, magic, and miracles. Investigating the sources of moral law, Stoic Philosophers spoke of virtue and vice in Zoroastrian terms of light opposing darkness.[10]

During the reign of Tiberius, influence from the Hellenistic Cult of Mithras emanated mostly from southern Anatolia in general and from Tarsos in particular. Romans who joined the cult believed that they were participating in a divine struggle between good and evil: They washed away their sins with ritual baptism and symbolically reenacted their divine covenant by sharing sacred meals of bread and wine. Representing their savior with images of Sol Invictus (the unconquered Sun), devotees in the Roman legions began spreading their cult to distant places throughout the Roman Empire.

Unlike Augustus, Tiberius expressed little interest in cults that offered personal salvation—for example, the Cult of Eleusis and the Hellenistic Cult of Mithras. However, throughout the Roman Empire, mystery cults offered salvation, healing, and miracles. Many of these cults portrayed their savior as a dying and resurrecting god symbolized by the apparent reversal in the sun's motion at the winter solstice or the return of fertility to nature at the vernal equinox.[11] Minted in Egypt in 20–21 A.D., the lower left coin in Figure 23-1 portrays Tiberius on the obverse and Augustus on the reverse. The emperors' busts match each other in size, but Augustus wears a radiate "solar" crown like the sun god, Sol, which betrays at least a symbolic confluence between the Cult of Mithras and the Cult of the Emperor, also known as the *imperial cult*.

During the reign of Tiberius from 14 A.D. to 37 A.D., iconographic differences between humans and divinities changed on Roman

---

[10]For example, in *Moral letters to Lucilius, Letter 50* by Seneca, the first century Stoic philosopher describes evil as natural darkness within us that must be illuminated by teaching about virtue.

[11]See Chapter 13.

Figure 23-1. Tiberius as a Mortal and Augustus as a Solar Deity. Egypt, Billon Tetradrachm, ca. 20–21 A.D.

provincial coins: Human busts grew proportionally larger until they appeared bigger than or equal to the size of busts of gods. Often, only one or two divine symbols distinguished a deity from a mortal. For example, the obverse of the North African coin in Figure 23-2 portrays Tiberius as larger and more imposing than the feminine-looking Apollo Citharoedus on the reverse. In addition, only the *cithara* (a musical instrument like a harp) and a diadem distinguish the god from the human. Regarding Apollo's indeterminate gender, images of Apollo sometimes represented Baal (male) and sometimes Tanit (female) in lands strongly influenced by the Phoenicians.

In Rome, relatively few overt religious symbols appeared on coins. Whereas Augustus artfully placed numerous religious symbols to coins attempting to project an aura of piety and influence public opinion, Tiberius used symbols that affirmed his rightful, divine inheritance from Augustus but did little else. For example, the coin in Figure 23-3 portrays a bust of Tiberius ringed by text that explicitly calls him the son of the divine Augustus. On the reverse, Livia sits on a throne as the personification of Peace. The legend around her indicates that Tiberius holds the office of Pontifex Maximus. Tradition remembers this coin, among the most common minted under Tiberius, as the *Tribute Penny*

Figure 23-2. Comparing Human and Divine Portraits on a Coin from the Reign of Tiberius Caesar. Syrtica, Oea, AE 29, ca. 22–29 A.D.

referred to by Jesus when he said, "Render unto Caesar the things which are Caesar's, and unto God the things that are God's.[12]"

However, Roman coinage continued using symbols that claimed a heritage of divinity in the royal family. Minted after 16 A.D., the obverse of the coin in Figure 23-4 portrays Livia, Tiberius' mother, as a goddess. A crescent Moon above her head, a globe beneath her neck, and the words "Genetrix Orbis" identify her as "Venus, Mother of the World." On the coin's reverse, Augustus wears a solar crown that identifies him as a solar deity, metaphorically connecting him with the dawning of a new spiritual age. A star above Augustus' head represents the comet of Julius Caesar, the symbolic source of the imperial cult.

Although he supported the Cult of the Emperor, Tiberius waited eight years before minting coins that explicitly commemorated the deification of Augustus. In 22 A.D., the Rome mint began striking coins like the one in Figure 23-5. On the obverse, Augustus' crown identifies him as a solar deity and a legend proclaims him father (of the country and of Tiberius). The reverse of the coin displays an altar used for sacrifices to the Divine Augustus.

---

[12] See *Matthew* 22:21. The images and text on the coin underscored the distinction that Jesus made between political and spiritual obligations while ironically comparing Jesus and Augustus as "Sons of God."

Figure 23-3. Example of a "Tribute Penny" Minted during the Reign of Tiberius. Lugdunum, AR Denarius, ca. 15–18 A.D.

Scandal Involving the Cult of Isis and a Rogue Named Decius Mundus

After Germanicus died in 19 A.D., Tiberius tried and convicted Gnaeus Calpurnius Piso, the accused murderer, and generously allowed him to commit suicide. However, many Romans persisted in believing that Tiberius had arranged the murder of Germanicus. As Tiberius sought ways to turn Rome's attention away from highly charged speculations, a Roman citizen approached the emperor with a complaint: A Roman knight named Decius Mundus had corrupted a priest of Isis to obtain sex from a virtuous Roman matron.

Of all cults, Tiberius liked the Cult of Isis least, so he leaped at the opportunity to distract the public by investigating an illicit combination of religion and sex. Sophisticated Romans lived in world characterized by openness, deceit, faith, and naiveté. Surviving details about the scandal provide a fascinating psychological portrait of religious beliefs among people in the highest levels of Roman society.

Decius Mundus fell in love with the husband's wife, a virtuous and noble lady named Paulina; and he offered her 200,000 denarii to spend one night with him—but she refused. Disconsolate, Decius Mundus stopped eating. Aware that the Lady Paulina worshipped Isis, a freedwoman from the household of Decius' father approached Decius

Figure 23-4. Augustus and Livia Portrayed as Gods during the Reign of Tiberius. Colonia Romula (Seville) AE 33, ca. 16–37 A.D.

Mundus with an offer: The freedwoman said that she could arrange for him to have sex with Paulina for only 50,000 denarii. Decius Mundus quickly agreed.

Especially popular among women in Rome, the Cult of Isis offered salvation through confession of sins, sincere repentance, and spiritual purification by washing in sacred Nile water. Worshipping Isis simultaneously as a merciful mother and an eternal virgin, supplicants crawled on their knees begging her forgiveness. However, the worship of Isis also featured grand celebrations, for example, the exuberant festival of *Carrus Navalis* (the forerunner of the Christian festival *Carnival*), which marked the annual arrival of Isis by sea at the beginning of the sailing season.

Familiar with cult operations, the freedwoman of Decius Mundus bribed the senior priest of the *Iseum* (Temple of Isis) in Rome to help trick Paulina. The priest approached the matron and told her that the Egyptian god Anubis had selected her for a special ceremony involving a meal and a night of sacred marriage. Thrilled, Paulina went home and told her husband. Confident of his wife's piety and virtue, Paulina's husband gave full consent for her participation in the ceremony.

On the designated evening, Paulina went to the Iseum in her finest clothes. She ate a meal in the presence of the priest who wore a jackal-headed mask of Anubis, and she prepared for a night of sacred

Figure 23-5. Commemoration of the Deification of Augustus. Rome, AE As, ca. 22–30 A.D.

marriage. At a key moment, Decius Mundus took the place of the priest of Isis and enjoyed enthusiastic sex with Paulina.

Delighted with the honor bestowed on her, Paulina bragged to all her friends about the experience. Similarly pleased with himself, Decius Mundus bragged as well. Soon, Paulina heard that she'd been tricked. Distraught, Paulina confessed all that had happened to her husband, who brought the matter to the attention of Tiberius.

Acting quickly and decisively, Tiberius sent soldiers to close Rome's Iseum. They smashed its statue of Isis into pieces and threw them into the Tiber River. Tiberius punished the freedwoman and all the priests of Isis with death by crucifixion, however, Decius Mundus suffered only exile.

As the affair concluded, Tiberius became aware of troubles involving Jews and decided to deal with both religious populations at the same time. He ordered all Isiac and Jewish religious paraphernalia seized and burned, and he made new laws against both communities. He then exiled many worshippers of Isis and approximately four thousand Jews to Sardinia.

Within four years, however, Tiberius began to make amends for his harsh treatment of worshippers of Isis. He made a significant donation to the Cult of Isis after Drusus died in 23 A.D. In honor of his son, Tiberius funded the carving of a nativity scene in the Holy of Holies of the Iseum at Philae close to Aswan, Egypt. (See Figure 23-6.) The

Figure 23-6. Nativity Scene of Isis and Horus/Harpokrates Made in 23 A.D. The Roman Emperor, Tiberius, Appears among Dignitaries Bringing Gifts.

carving portrays Isis nursing Horus/Harpokrates shortly after giving birth to him. Several divine and mortal visitors, including Tiberius Caesar, attend the scene bearing gifts for the goddess and her child: incense, precious objects, and food. Another carving at Philae portrays Tiberius, like a Pharaoh from Egypt's distant past, grasping his enemies by their hair with one hand and raising a stone mace with the other as if to crush their skulls.[13]

THE REIGN AND INFLUENCE OF TIBERIUS CAESAR

In 14 A.D., the Senate acclaimed Tiberius as emperor in Rome's first hereditary transfer of power in over five hundred years. At the age of fifty-four, Tiberius accepted power with a false modesty that annoyed the Roman senators. Much maligned by history and popular opinion,

---

[13] Chapter 22 discusses this Egyptian image as an element of messianic prophecy.

Tiberius ruled Rome for twenty-three years until his death in 37 A.D., a period that encompassed the adult life, ministry, and crucifixion of Jesus as well as the first years of Christianity.

Throughout the Roman Empire, few people approved of Tiberius' elevation to emperor. In Germany, the Roman legions threatened mutiny. Fundamentally a competent, boring, and unappealing administrator, Tiberius sent his popular adopted son, Germanicus (the father of the future emperor, Caligula), to appease the legions in Germany and to busy them by launching a new offensive. Germanicus successfully led the legions and won their respect and affection. In 17 A.D., Tiberius recalled Germanicus to Rome to celebrate a triumph and to share consulship for a year. From this time forward, however, jealousy and paranoia characterized Tiberius' actions toward Germanicus.[14]

In 19 A.D., Tiberius again sent Germanicus on a mission, this time to take care of important business in Asia. However, shortly after arriving in Antioch, Germanicus suffered a fatal case of indigestion. Many people in Rome believed that Tiberius had arranged for Syria's governor, Gnaeus Calpurnius Piso, to murder Germanicus so the line of imperial succession would pass to Tiberius' son, Drusus. Harsh accusations of Tiberius by Agrippina the Elder (the granddaughter of Augustus who had married Germanicus) outraged Rome. The uproar forced Tiberius to bring Gnaeus Calpurnius Piso to trial. Found guilty, Piso conveniently killed himself before speaking publicly about his motives. The affair almost ruined Tiberius, but no proof ever connected him to the plot.

Regardless, effort to ensure Drusus' inheritance by murdering Germanicus was not fruitful. Sejanus, one of Tiberius' most trusted advisors, also burned with ambition to rule Rome. Scarcely four years after the murder of Germanicus, Sejanus seduced Drusus' wife (a granddaughter of Octavia) and conspired with her to kill Drusus with slow-acting poison. In this way, Tiberius' only son died in 23 A.D., but the role of Sejanus in the murder remained hidden until after the death of Sejanus in 31 A.D.[15]

---

[14]See *The Annals* 2.26.6 by Tacitus.
[15]See *Roman History* 58.11 by Cassius Dio and *Annals* 4.11 by Tacitus.

As Tiberius lost interest in governing after his son's death, Sejanus gradually acquired complete control of the Roman government. He appeared to serve Tiberius well, but he encouraged the emperor's worst prejudices and fears. Sejanus developed a network of spies and found creative ways to tighten his grip on power. For example, he began framing powerful Romans who opposed him, charged them with treason, and destroyed their lives. Slowly and carefully, he worked toward the day when he would replace Tiberius as emperor. In the rapidly deteriorating political climate, Sejanus chose a new prefect for Judea who could be counted on to treat Jews harshly: Pontius Pilate headed east in 26 A.D., just in time for the beginning of Jesus' ministry.

Giving Power to Sejanus and Taking It Back

In 26 A.D., Tiberius abandoned his responsibilities as emperor and moved to Capri. Living in a palatial home called the Villa of Jupiter, he spent most of his time in avid pursuit of hobbies; for example, studying philosophy, history, mythology, and astrology. Sejanus took over all the top-level, day-to-day business of governing Rome. Informed by his private network of spies, backed by the full might of the Praetorian Guard, and complicit with Tiberius' blossoming paranoia, Sejanus quickly turned Rome into a police state.

From his villa on Capri, Tiberius encouraged Sejanus to root out traitors among the Roman aristocracy. Honest Roman citizens feared imprisonment, banishment, or worse because of Sejanus' ill will and jealousy. Sejanus even convicted Germanicus' widow, Agrippina the Elder, and her two older sons for plotting against Tiberius. All three died of starvation in prison. Grandmother Livia assumed responsibility for taking care of Agrippina's other children: young Caligula and his three sisters.

When Livia died in 29 A.D., Tiberius stayed on Capri rather than attend her funeral. He ignored the terms of her will and prevented her deification. Antonia Minor, the younger daughter of Mark Antony and Octavia, became the matriarch of the Julio-Claudians and assumed the responsibility of caring for Caligula and his sisters.

Eventually, Sejanus went too far. In 31 A.D., Antonia learned that her daughter was plotting with to overthrow Tiberius. Antonia then had to choose who would rule Rome: Tiberius, a man whom she believed responsible for the poisoning of her son (Germanicus), or Sejanus, a man actively involved in killing her grandchildren. She chose to inform Tiberius of the plot. Tiberius quashed the conspiracy so quickly—arresting, executing, and replacing Sejanus—that the people of Rome were shocked by the sudden change.

After Sejanus' death, Tiberius recognized that many Roman policies implemented in his name had been inappropriate and needed to be corrected. Atoning for the unjust punishment of Jews in 19 A.D., he lifted the ban on Jewish cults in Rome. He even forbade Roman officials from annoying Jews or disturbing Jewish services.[16]

No evidence indicates that Tiberius ever knew about the execution of Jesus. However, reports of Pontius Pilate's ruthless treatment of Jews trickled into Rome. Tiberius was just preparing to fix that problem when he died in 37 A.D. Regardless, having ruled with distaste as emperor for twenty-three years, he never succeeded in reversing the Roman public's bad opinion of him.

Tiberius' Reputation as a Pervert

Because Rome generally prospered and functioned well under Tiberius, modern historians suggest that much of his unpopularity came from his misplaced confidence in Sejanus. However, according to salacious gossip written during the Flavian dynasty,[17] Tiberius passed his time in Capri in notorious sessions of cruel and perverted pleasures.[18] When Tiberius' fancies became violent, he ordered his guards to throw condemned or damaged persons off the cliffs that flanked his villa. Below the cliffs, boatmen cleared the area of bodies, energetically applying boathooks to anyone unlucky enough to have survived the fall.

Ancient gossip also portrays Lucius Vitellius as a procurer of young aristocratic male prostitutes who served as erotic playmates for Tiberius

---

[16]See *On the Embassy to Gaius* XXIII–XXIV by Philo of Alexandria.
[17]The Flavian dynasty ruled Rome from 69 A.D. to 96 A.D. when Suetonius and Tacitus wrote histories of Tiberius' reign.
[18]See *The Life of Tiberius* 43–45 and 60–64 by Suetonius, and *Annals* I.6 by Tacitus.

and his guests. Lucius Vitellius even volunteered the services of his own son, the future emperor, Aulus Vitellius.[19] Tiberius rewarded the services of Lucius Vitellius by appointing him governor of Syria Province in 35 A.D. Once in Syria, Vitellius sent word to Tiberius that Pontius Pilate had acted with excessive cruelty against Jews. Vitellius then forcefully deposed Pontius Pilate and sent him to Rome in chains to face justice, which suggests that gossip masquerading as history has preserved overly harsh characterizations of both Tiberius Caesar and Lucius Vitellius.

Tiberius died on March 16, 37 A.D. Historical reports identify causes of death ranging from age-related illness to murder by suffocation orchestrated by Caligula with assistance from the Praetorian Guard.[20] The Roman Senate chose not to deify Tiberius. Roman citizens called for his body to be torn apart, but soldiers escorted the body of the dead emperor to Rome, cremated it, and interred the ashes in the Mausoleum of Augustus.

Rehabilitation of the Reputation of Tiberius in Modern Times

Tiberius' reputation as a sexual pervert is based primarily on information from two historians.[21] Both wrote that Tiberius sexually abused children, that he tortured and killed people for amusement, and that he practiced numerous other sexual perversions as well. Only in modern times have historians considered that the historians who maligned Tiberius may have had strong reasons to lie:[22] Portraying Julio-Claudian emperors (except Augustus) as evil made the authors' Flavian patrons look virtuous in comparison.

History paints an inconsistent portrait of Tiberius: He was prudish and depraved, disciplined and self-indulgent, remarkably competent, and morally weak. One numismatist has suggested that, independent of the emperor's personal behavior, an unusual series of coins (see

---

[19]See *The Life of Vitellius* 3.2 by Suetonius.
[20]See *On the Embassy to Gaius* IV.25 by Philo and *The Life of Tiberius* 73 by Suetonius.
[21]Writing in the second half of the first century A.D., Tacitus and Suetonius recorded malicious gossip about Tiberius.
[22]See "Tiberius, Vitellius, and the Spintriae" by C. L. Murison in *The Ancient History Bulletin* 1.4, pp. 97–99, 1987.

Figure 23-7. Erotic Spintriae of Tiberius. AE Tesserae, ca. 14–37 A.D.

Figure 23-7) helped inspire stories about the perversions of Tiberius.[23] Numismatists call these coins *spintriae*, the same name by which historians refer to the young male prostitutes that supposedly served the emperor and his guests on Capri.

Also referred to as *tesserae* (tokens of uncertain purpose), spintriae portray erotic scenes on one side and Roman numerals on the other. Since 1664, many scholars have associated the images on these coins directly with claims of immoral behavior by Tiberius.[24] Until the twentieth century, scholars always connected the use of the coins with sexual activities, for example, suggesting that the coins served as brothel tokens. However, the real purpose of the coins remains unknown. They might have served as gaming pieces, good-luck tokens, or even tickets to special events. Unlike ancient Greek coins with sexual themes, spintriae have no apparent relationship with religious beliefs.

---

[23]See "The Spintriae as a Historical Source" by T. V. Buttrey in *Numismatic Chronicle* 13 pp. 52–63, 1973.
[24]In 1664, Friedrich Spanheim discussed spintriae in his *Dissertatio De Praestantia et vsv Nvmismatvm Antiqvorvm*, a work that laid the foundation for modern numismatics.

Modern scholars confidently assert that Tiberius did not deserve his reputation as a perverted monster.[25] Suffering from a horrible skin condition on his face that made him reluctant to appear in public, he secluded himself on Capri and tried to live outside the public eye. Still, he frequently met with philosophers, jurists, and historians and pursued intellectual interests that contradict his bad reputation.[26] Some numismatists have suggested that Tiberius minted spintriae to serve as brothel tokens because he prudishly objected to people paying prostitutes with coins bearing images of the imperial family.[27]

A PERFECT STORM FOR THE LIFE AND MINISTRY OF JESUS

Many influences conspired to increase tensions in the territories that previously constituted Herod's kingdom of Judea. Cognizant of tendencies toward rebellion and inter-ethnic conflict in central Judea, the Roman provincial government was inclined to deal harshly with anyone who questioned Roman authority. However, Pontius Pilate sharply increased the number and severity of confrontations between traditional Jews and Roman authorities: He committed acts that flaunted Jewish sensitivities and then punished the Jews who objected. At the same time, many Jews grew increasingly inclined toward confrontation against foreign and Hellenizing influences: While many Jews accepted Hellenization in varying degrees, other Jews expected an imminent intervention by God, which turned religious disagreements among Jews into issues of spiritual survival.

---

[25] See "Notes on Suetonius" by John C. Rolfe in *Transactions and Proceedings of the American Philological Association* 45 pp. 35–47, 1914, and *A History of Rome under the Emperors* pp. 130 and 150, by T. Mommsen, London, Routledge, 1996. Mommsen said that Tiberius ruled conscientiously but people rewarded his hard work with hatred.
[26] See "The Spintriae as a Historical Source" by T. V. Buttrey in *Numismatic Chronicle* 13 pp. 52–63, 1973, and *Le Tessere Erotiche Romane (spintriae), Quando ed a che scopo sono state coniate* by B. Simonetta and R. Riva, Lugano: Gaggini-Bizzozero Sa. 1981.
[27] See "Tiberius, Vitellius, and the Spintriae" by C. L. Murison in *The Ancient History Bulletin* 1.4 pp. 97–99, 1987, and "The Spintriae as a Historical Source" by T. V. Buttrey in *Numismatic Chronicle* 13 pp. 52–63, 1973.

Among Galilean Jews, suspicions of corruption attached easily to Jerusalem's priestly councils and judges. Many Galileans found themselves increasingly uncomfortable supporting a Jerusalem cult controlled by Pontius Pilate, a prefect who actively promoted Rome's Cult of the Emperor in Judea. Issues related to the purity of the Jerusalem Temple Cult under foreign control eroded confidence in traditional religious authorities and encouraged the emergence of new Jewish leaders who opposed the Jerusalem priesthood.

Encouraging Hellenistic City Administrations in Judea

The territories previously ruled by King Herod contained a mixture of traditional Jewish and Hellenistic populations. Political and religious differences between these populations sometimes resulted in violent disagreements. However, under the Romans, urban centers were free to choose the style of local administration that best suited the predominant population: a traditional Jewish administration with priestly councils or a Hellenistic administration with elected officials as a Greek *polis* or free city. Romans and Hellenistic tetrarchs encouraged the adoption of Hellenistic administrations.

Traditional Jewish towns and villages governed themselves with priestly councils that tended to resist the influx of Hellenistic policies and institutions. In Jerusalem, a priestly council of seventy-one members called the *Great Sanhedrin* wielded as much power and authority as the Roman prefect would allow: It issued religious rulings, conducted trials, and dealt with appeals from lower courts. To govern a smaller Jewish city, Jews established a council of twenty-three priests, called a *Sanhedrin*, which served as judges overseeing the application of local religious law.

In a polis, citizens combined architecture and social organization to support Hellenistic life under Roman control, which included freedom to worship any god tolerated by the Roman Empire, freedom to participate in Greek-style athletic events, freedom to enjoy Greek and Roman arts like plays and literature, and responsibility for supporting state defense. Male citizens of a polis often elected government officials, and any citizen who met the requirements of office, like age, wealth, and morality, could run for election. Romans and Hellenistic rulers rewarded cities that adopted Greek-style democratic rule by funding the construction of Hellenistic architectural showpieces: theaters, temples, and so on.

In traditional Jewish culture, only males from certain families could hold priestly office and all laws and public decisions were based on local interpretations of religious scriptures. Roman and Hellenistic rulers tolerated priestly councils that maintained peace and responded appropriately to regional authority. However, throughout the Jewish homeland, many Jews believed that the Jerusalem Temple Cult had lost much of its legitimacy because of pollution by foreign influences. In the early first century A.D., many Jews looked for spiritual guidance from an emerging class of itinerant teachers, men like Jesus and John the Baptist who operated outside the official Jerusalem Temple Cult.

After deposing Herod Archelaus and annexing Judea in 6 A.D., Rome allowed the other sons of King Herod—Herod Antipas and Herod Philip—to continue ruling the tetrarchies that they had acquired after their father's death. Herod Philip's tetrarchy contained Hellenistic Jews and a large non-Jewish population. However, Herod Antipas ruled Galilee, a region well-known for religious conservatism and antagonism toward foreign influences.[28]

Traditional Jews expressed displeasure with the rule of Galilee by Herod Antipas, not because he failed to support Judaism but because he strongly espoused liberal Hellenism. He built and restored towns throughout his realm and attempted to modernize Galilean society by implementing Hellenistic architecture, organizations, and practices. Archaeologists have found important examples of his work in towns like Sepphoris (rebuilt after being badly damaged by Romans fighting the Galilean rebel Judas of Gamala in 6 A.D.), Livias (a city in Perea named after Tiberius' mother), and Tiberias (a new city named after

---

[28]Galileans generally regarded the Jerusalem Temple Cult as having been corrupted by Roman influence. In the gospels, some of the critical language against Jews (for example, *John* 7:1–9) originally came from antipathy between Galileans and Judeans. The *New Testament* helped foster generic anti-Jewish sentiment because, written in Greek, the text failed to distinguish between Jews and Judeans.

the Roman emperor). Offending traditional Jews, Herod Antipas built Tiberias over an ancient graveyard—a violation of Jewish law—and then forcibly relocated Jewish subjects to live there. Tiberias became the largest Hellenized polis in the Holy Land with a Jewish majority.[29]

The First Prefects of Judea

Conducting the census and dealing harshly with opposition, soldiers under Coponius, the first prefect of central Judea, oversaw the region's first collection of Roman taxes. Coponius also closely supervised activities of the Jerusalem Temple Cult on Mount Zion. He personally maintained possession of the vestments of the high priest and controlled the operation of the cult. Jewish priests maintained their positions in Jerusalem only as long as their service met with Roman approval.

When Jews resisted Roman control in Judea, Coponius dealt quickly with the troublemakers.[30] Regardless, an increasing number of traditional Jews committed themselves to the overthrow of their Roman masters. The *Zealots* and their even more radical splinter group, the *Sicarii*, began committing opportunistic acts of violence in Roman Judea just as terrorists do in many parts of the world today.

Coponius didn't last long as prefect, not because he couldn't deal effectively with Jewish terrorists, but because he underestimated the depth of ethnic and religious tensions between different Jewish cults in Judea. When Samaritan troublemakers entered the Jerusalem Temple and polluted the sanctuary with human bones,[31] Coponius barely prevented the eruption of a civil war between Jerusalem and Shechem.[32] The governor of Syria Province[33] removed Coponius from office in

---

[29]Ironically, during the troubled first centuries of the first millennium A.D., Hellenized Jewish cities played important roles in preserving the main branch of Judaism that survived to the present day. For example, the Jerusalem Talmud was compiled from teachings from Jewish schools in Caesarea, Tiberias, and Sepphoris.
[30]For example, he dealt effectively with the revolt of Judas of Gamala in 6 A.D., but the conflict gave birth to an organization of Jewish rebels called Zealots. See Chapter 22.
[31]Documented in *Antiquities of the Jews* 18:29–30 by Josephus, the event probably occurred in 9 A.D., the last year that Coponius held the office of prefect.
[32]Shechem was the ancient capital of Samaria.
[33]The name of the governor of Syria Province in 9 A.D. is unknown.

Figure 23-8. Bronze Coins Minted under the Prefects of Judea before Pontius Pilate, Clockwise from Top Left: Coponius, Marcus Ambibulus, and Valerius Gratus.

9 A.D because he failed to anticipate and prevent inter-ethnic provocations and because he dealt poorly with the resulting violence. The second prefect, a man named Marcus Ambibulus, did a better job controlling the simmering antagonisms among different Jewish cults. He capably governed Roman Judea, extracting taxes while artfully preventing rebellion.

Figure 23-8 displays coins minted under the authority of three of the first four prefects, clockwise from the top left: Coponius, Marcus Ambibulus, and Valerius Gratus. Representatives of Augustus Caesar, Coponius and Marcus Ambibulus, distinguished their administrations numismatically only by the dates on their coins, in this case, year 36 (6–7 A.D.) and year 41 (11–12 A.D.), respectively. Under Tiberius, Valerius Gratus slightly changed his coins; however, all coins minted by the first Roman prefects displayed only agricultural symbols designed not to offend Jews.[34] The obverses of all three coins portray palm branches.

---

[34] The most conservative Jews of this period objected to foreign religious symbols and images of animals and people, subscribing to a strict aniconic interpretation of biblical prohibitions against graven images. See *Exodus* 20:3–6, *Leviticus* 26:1, *Numbers* 33:52, and *Deuteronomy* 4:16 and 27:15.

The reverses of the first two coins portray date palms and the year of issue, and the reverse of the lower coin, minted by Valerius Gratus in 24 A.D., bears the legend, "Tiberius Caesar," surrounded by a wreath.

Religious Beliefs, Practices, and Symbols during the Life of Jesus

Throughout the West, Mediterranean cults included practices and beliefs that modern Christians associate exclusively with Christianity. People worshipped divine mothers who gave birth to dying and resurrecting gods on December 25. Saviors miraculously healed faithful followers and guided them to lead moral lives. Some cults baptized their followers, some passed their sins and inner demons to pigs, and some waited for a complete destruction of evil during the imminent End of Days. Then, as now, people argued whether the end would come by fire or water and whether many or few souls would be saved.

Numerous symbols and beliefs associated in modern times with Christianity already existed in pre-Christian Hellenistic cults: Madonna and child images, angels, God the Father, the cross as a symbol of life after death, and the gift of eternal life through the shedding of immortal blood. On temple walls, wise men offered gifts of incense and gold to newborn gods; and merciful mothers granted salvation to the poor in spirit who confessed, repented, and begged forgiveness for their sins. However, Jews generally rejected all these practices, symbols, and beliefs.

Some Jews believed in physical resurrection, and some did not. Some believed in eternal life, and some did not. For most Jews, however, a righteous life required the following of God's laws. If a Jew sinned against another man, no automatic forgiveness from God was possible. Forgiveness required acknowledgement of wrongdoing, restitution, and then forgiveness from the wronged party. Applying Jewish ethics to problems at the Jerusalem Temple meant recognizing the corruption within the priesthood, refusing to tolerate the evil rule of Rome, and giving one's life if necessary to precipitate the Kingdom of God. Just as God always had responded to the prayers of suffering Jews in the *Bible*, he would do so again. Soon he would send a messiah to deliver Jerusalem from the evil power of Rome and to cleanse Judea from the polluting practices of Eastern cults.

JESUS IN THE GOSPELS: CONFLICTING STORIES WITH AGENDAS

The authors of the gospels never intended to write biographies of Jesus as we think of biographies today. Other than the circumstances surrounding his birth and one story about his childhood,[35] the canonical gospels ignore the first thirty years of his life. Additionally, all the gospels[36] that survived to modern times offer information about Jesus in the context of furthering a variety of agendas,[37] some of which include:

- Proving that Jesus fulfilled *Old Testament* messianic prophecies and that other Jewish leaders (like John the Baptist) played only supporting roles for Jesus.
- Demonstrating that Jesus was more powerful than pagan saviors; for example, Dionysos, Asclepius, Pythagoras, Mithras, and so on.
- Presenting insightful and inspirational sayings[38] that communicate an understanding of Jesus, which varies from gospel to gospel.

---

[35]Only *Matthew* and *Luke* offer token information about the childhood of Jesus. (See Chapter 22.) However, stories about the childhood of Jesus can be found in non-canonical sources like the *Infancy Gospel of James* (also known as the *Protoevangelium of James*), the *Infancy Gospel of Thomas*, the *Gospel of Pseudo-Matthew* (also known as the *Infancy Gospel of Matthew* or *Birth of Mary and Infancy of the Saviour*), the *Syriac Infancy Gospel*, the *History of Joseph the Carpenter*, and the *Life of John the Baptist*.

[36]See *The Complete Gospels* edited by Robert J. Miller. However, Miller's collection is not complete. Ancient texts refer to other gospels (for example, the *Gospel of Barnabas*) that have not survived. Also, more gospels are being discovered all the time, for example, the recently discovered *Gospel of Judas*.

[37]For general discussion and examples of canonical gospel agendas, see *Misquoting Jesus: The Story behind Who Changed the Bible and Why* by Bart Ehrman.

[38]Biblical scholars generally agree that the first writings about Jesus consisted of collections of his sayings. Surviving examples of sayings gospels like include the gospel of *Thomas*, the *Secret Book of James*, the *Dialogue of the Savior*, and the gospel of *Mary*. Authors of the three synoptic gospels (*Matthew*, *Mark*, and *Luke*) are thought all to have used a lost source referred to by scholars as *Sayings Gospel Q*.

Not all stories in the canonical gospels come directly from the life of Jesus. Some gospel stories are creative combinations of recorded sayings by Jesus and prophetic passages from the *Old Testament*.[39] Stories generated this way easily helped prove that Jesus fulfilled biblical prophecies as the one and only messiah. However, not all of the stories connecting Jesus and prophetic passages were fabricated: As a proponent of catastrophic messianism, Jesus intentionally sought to fulfill prophecies and provoke his own crucifixion as a means of precipitating the End of Days.[40]

The nativity stories in *Matthew* and *Luke* say that a virgin[41] gave birth to Jesus in circumstances that identified him astrologically as a "star from Jacob.[42]" His genealogies validate his descent from King David.[43] Further, many stories in the gospels, especially those about his last days, provide numerous details showing that he fulfilled *Old Testament* prophecies: for example, his entrance into Jerusalem riding an ass,[44] his betrayal for thirty pieces of silver,[45] and his crucifixion among criminals.[46]

Nevertheless, the earliest writings about Jesus consisted mostly of sayings and did not address whether or not he fulfilled scriptures. The need to prove that Jesus was the messiah simply did not exist until after the End of Days failed to materialize in the generation after his death, around the time the first of the canonical gospels was written. The gospel of *Thomas*, which may have been written before the earliest canonical gospel,[47] serves as a good example of a *sayings gospel*. Significantly, it

---

[39] See *New Testament Apologetic: The Doctrinal Significance of the Old Testament Quotations* by Lindars Barnabas, London, SCM Press, 1973.
[40] See Chapter 22 and *Messiahs and Resurrection in 'The Gabriel Revelation'* pp. 90–91 by Israel Knohl.
[41] Christians interpret *Isaiah* 7:14 as prophesying that a virgin would bear the messiah. See Chapter 22.
[42] See *Numbers* 24:17–19.
[43] See *Matthew* 1:1–17, *Luke* 3:23–38, and *The Jesus Dynasty: The Hidden History of Jesus, His Royal Family, and the Birth of Christianity* pp. 49–55 by James Tabor.
[44] See *Zechariah* 9:9 and *Matthew* 21:5.
[45] See *Zechariah* 11:12, *Matthew* 26:15, and *Luke* 22:5.
[46] See *Isaiah* 53:12 and *Matthew* 27:35.
[47] The gospel of *Thomas* was discovered in Egypt in 1945 among a large cache of Gnostic documents. See *The Nag Hammadi Library* edited by James M. Robinson.

reflects a *Gnostic*[48] point of view that Roman Christianity had discarded as heresy by the time that the books in the *New Testament* were canonized in the fourth century A.D. Early Jewish Christians and followers of John the Baptist both incorporated Gnostic beliefs in their teachings,[49] which suggests that some sayings that appear only in the gospel of *Thomas* accurately reflect authentic teachings of Jesus.

The Relationship between John the Baptist and Jesus

One canonical gospel[50] provides details about the familial relationship between Jesus and John the Baptist[51] (known as Yohanan ha Matbil by his Aramaic-speaking, Jewish followers). Living in the Judean village of Ein Kerem, Elizabeth, the mother of John the Baptist, became pregnant six months earlier than Mary, the mother of Jesus. After the *Annunciation* (the divine conception of Jesus by the Holy Spirit,[52] an event mentioned only in the gospel of *Luke*), Mary visited her relative, Elizabeth. Suddenly, recognizing the proximity of the fetus (Jesus) inside Mary, the fetus (John) inside Elizabeth "leaped" in her womb.[53]

When he grew up, John the Baptist became a spiritual teacher who encouraged all Jews to live strictly according to the commandments in the *Torah*. Attracted to John by his reputation for piety and his courageous affirmation of traditional Jewish teachings, Jesus came to John

---

[48] Gnostics sought to live spiritual lives rather than being governed by physical concerns. Gnostic masters taught advanced spiritual teachings only to students ready for them.

[49] For example, Gnostics believed that John was a reincarnation of the prophet Elijah, an idea echoed in three canonical gospels: *Mark* 9:11–13, *Matthew* 11:13–14, *Luke* 7:27.

[50] See *Luke* 1.

[51] Technically, the gospel of *John* does not say that John the Baptist baptized Jesus, only that he identified Jesus as the "lamb of God" who will "baptize with the Holy Spirit." See *John* 1:19–34.

[52] In Christianity, the Holy Spirit is the third part of the three-part deity: God the Father, Jesus, and the Holy Spirit. The Annunciation is archetypally the same as the impregnation of Danae (the virgin mother of Perseus) by Zeus in the form of a golden shower. However, under close scrutiny, biblical references to the Holy Spirit and the doctrine of the Trinity frequently reveal themselves to be artifacts of translation. For example, see *The Messiah before Jesus: The Suffering Servant of the Dead Sea Scrolls* pp. 68–71 by Israel Knohl and *Misquoting Jesus: The Story behind Who Changed the Bible and Why* pp. 81–82 by Bart Ehrman.

[53] See *Luke* 1:41–42.

for a Jewish purification ritual (baptism) under John's spiritual authority. Most Christians understand the spiritual relationship between John the Baptist and Jesus in terms of Jewish prophecy: that Elijah would announce the coming of the messiah. Even today, Jews still believe that Elijah will announce the coming of the messiah.[54] However, Christians interpret John's baptism of Jesus more as an initiation than a purification ritual.

The recent discovery of a cave containing a *mikveh* (Jewish ritual bath) where John the Baptist performed baptisms has illuminated the origins of an important difference between the *synoptic gospels*[55] and the gospel of *John*. The gospel of *John* and the synoptic gospels differ significantly in character and content. In particular, the gospel of *John* describes Jesus washing the feet of his disciples,[56] a practice unattested in the synoptic gospels. However, the recently excavated cave of John the Baptist contains a unique footbath carved in stone, which confirms that followers of John the Baptist practiced the ritual washing of feet.[57]

Problems arose for John the Baptist because he publicly criticized wealthy Jews (especially Herod Antipas) for abandoning Jewish law and living Hellenistic lifestyles. While married to a princess of Nabataea, Herod Antipas fell in love with his niece Herodias,[58] the wife of his brother Herod Philip. As enlightened Hellenistic men of their day, Herod Antipas and Herod Philip both divorced their wives. Herod Antipas and Herodias then married each other. Ancient Jewish law did

---

[54]Christians combine the statement in *Malachi* 3:23 (also numbered 4:5) that God will send Elijah to announce the coming of the Messiah with Jesus' statement in *Matthew* 11:7–14 that John the Baptist was Elijah. Conditioned by Pythagorean teachings, Hellenistic followers of Jesus believed John the Baptist was a reincarnation of Elijah. However, modern Christians struggle to explain how a non-Jewish concept like reincarnation became an element of Christianity. Continuing to wait for the messiah and expecting Elijah to show up without reincarnating, Jews set a place at their table for the prophet at every Passover Seder.

[55]The synoptic gospels (*Matthew*, *Mark*, and *Luke*) are the three canonical gospels that tell mostly the same stories in the same order. They are called synoptic because one can lay them out next to each other and compare them visually, episode by episode.

[56]See *John* 13:5.

[57]See "John the Baptist's Cave" by Shimon Gibson and James D. Tabor, in *Biblical Archaeology Review*, May/Jun 2005, pp. 36–41, 58. Comparing archaeological evidence with canonical gospel accounts of the Last Supper, one sees that the gospel of *John* describes an archaeologically attested Jewish foot-washing ritual but the authors of the synoptic gospels transformed it into a Mithraic Eucharist.

[58]Herodias was a granddaughter of Mariamne, the Hasmonean wife of King Herod.

not condemn the marriage of Herod Antipas to his niece; however, it did forbid marriage between a man and his brother's wife as long as the brother still lived. John the Baptist spoke strongly and publicly against the marriage of Herod Antipas and Herodias.[59] Courageously condemning Herodias as a prostitute and her daughter (Salome) as a bastard, John stirred up so much public enmity against the ruling family that Herod Antipas arrested John and threw him in jail. Eventually, Herod Antipas even granted Salome's request to execute John.[60]

All four canonical gospels portray Jesus as superior to John; but John was a popular Jewish figure,[61] arguably much more famous as a messianic candidate than Jesus during the early part of the first century A.D. As proof of John's importance, the canonical gospels begin their accounts of the ministry of Jesus only after mentioning his encounter (that is, his baptism in the synoptic gospels) with John the Baptist. In itself, ritual immersion in water was not an unusual event for Jesus: As an observant Jew, he often would have immersed himself in the "living water" of a mikveh. For traditional Jews, immersion under John's authority cleansed them from the spiritual pollution of foreign religious influences; for example, Roman and Hellenistic influences that had corrupted the Jerusalem Temple Cult.

In contrast to Jewish use of immersion, Hellenistic cults used baptism primarily for initiations, as in the cults of Isis and Mithras. The canonical stories of John's baptism of Jesus speak more to pagan sensibilities than to Jewish ones, portraying the event as an initiation that transformed[62] Jesus. The synoptic gospels[63] emphasize the similarity of the baptism to an initiation by saying that Jesus went to the desert to fast and suffer temptation by the devil, aspects of initiation that worshippers of mystery cults would have recognized. However, the

---

[59] See *Mark* 6:17–19.
[60] The gospels of *Matthew* (14:3–11) and *Mark* (6:21–28) describe Salome's role in the execution of John the Baptist without mentioning her name. Salome's name is found in *Antiquities of the Jews* 18.5.4 by Josephus.
[61] See *Antiquities of the Jews* 18.116–118 by Josephus.
[62] Many early Christian cults differentiated themselves based on how they interpreted what happened at Jesus' baptism, for example, as a divine adoption, a transformation to divine being, a comingling of mortal and divine beings, an initiation, a cleansing from sin, and so on.
[63] See *Matthew* 4:1–11, *Mark* 1:12–13, and *Luke* 4:1–13. Accounts of the temptation of Jesus beg the question: Who witnessed and recorded the temptation of Jesus?

gospel of *John* tells a different story:[64] Virtually ignoring the baptism of Jesus, John the Baptist recognizes Jesus as a spiritual superior and Jesus immediately begins gathering disciples.

As one of the many ironies of religious history, Jesus' teacher, John the Baptist, died for condemning Herod Antipas for breaking Jewish laws and living a Hellenistic life. Yet Christianity built its ethical structure from Hellenistic philosophy in preference to Jewish law: The early church adopted the Hellenistic writings of Philo (a relative of Herod Antipas) as the philosophical basis of the early Christian Church. In his *Lives of Illustrious Men*, Saint Jerome[65] identified Philo, not as a Hellenistic Jew, but as an early Christian Father.

Proving Jesus Superior to Pagan Saviors

The canonical gospels tell numerous stories designed specifically to prove the superiority of Jesus to other cult figures. While the authors of gospels in the *New Testament* do not explicitly compare Jesus to other saviors, Hellenistic Christians easily recognized intended comparisons: By walking on water and calming a storm,[66] Jesus equaled or surpassed miracles performed by Pythagoras;[67] by changing water into wine for a wedding in Cana, Jesus demonstrated greater power than Dionysos, the god who first gave the miracle of wine-making to humanity; the miraculous healings performed by Jesus, especially of blindness and leprosy,[68] demonstrated that Jesus possessed healing powers superior to those of the healing god, Asclepius; also, by performing the first Christian *Eucharist* ceremony, offering wine and bread at the Last Supper, Jesus identified himself with an all-powerful source of life similar to that honored by the Cult of Mithras.

---

[64]See *John* 1:29–51.
[65]A Christian leader during the fourth and fifth centuries A.D., Saint Jerome translated the *Bible* into Latin, producing the *Vulgate Bible*. He is recognized as a saint by both the Catholic and Eastern Orthodox churches.
[66]See *Matthew* 14:22–33, *Mark* 4:35–40 and 6:45–52, *John* 6:16–21.
[67]See *The Life of Pythagoras* 29 by Porphyry.
[68]Originally from India, leprosy (Hansen's disease) is proven to have existed in Judea during the lifetime of Jesus. See *The Final Days of Jesus: The Archaeological Evidence* p. 34 by Shimon Gibson.

At first glance, the death and raising of Lazarus[69] also seems like an act of extreme healing. However, when Jesus announced the death of Lazarus, the disciple Thomas suggested to his fellow disciples, "Let us go too, and die with him." The story represents something different from ordinary healing or even simple resurrection. Some early Christians, for example, Gnostics, understood the raising of Lazarus metaphorically because they believed that scriptures used symbols to encode mysteries that only initiates could understand. To these Christians, the story of Lazarus spoke about the importance and power of initiation into Christian mysteries.

By driving demons out of a possessed man near Gadara[70] in the Decapolis, Jesus demonstrated the availability of greater power to Christians than to initiates of the highly regarded Eleusinian Mysteries.[71] The demons entered swine that immediately cast themselves in a lake near Gadara and drowned. Coins of Gadara carried images of the emperor (Tiberius) on the obverse and Tyche/Cybele/Atargatis on the reverse. (See Figure 23-9.) Used by Jesus and his followers, coins from the Decapolis preserve a symbolic record of pagan competition with Christian cults. Christians understood many gospel stories as declarations of the superiority of Christian worship over pagan practices.

The most explicit comparison of Jesus to a Hellenistic savior is presented by Jesus in the form of a parable. While in Jerusalem, Jesus spoke to a crowd of Pharisees and metaphorically compared himself to "the good shepherd" who has the power to lay down his life for his sheep as well as the power to come back to life again.[72] Hearing his words, Pharisees became agitated and wanted to stone Jesus for blasphemy. The accusation of blasphemy seems like an unreasonable overreaction until one realizes that, by calling himself "the good

---

[69] See *John* 11, especially *John* 11:14–16.
[70] Referred to in three of the four canonical gospels (*Matthew* 8:23–34, *Mark* 5:1–20, and *Luke* 8:26–39) the trip to the land of the Gadarenes sounds more like an extended sea voyage than a boat trip of a few kilometers on Lake Kinaret (the Sea of Galilee). Anatolian Christians would have seen echoes of Julius Caesar's travels to Spain in the mischaracterization of travel by Jesus to Gadara. See Figure 16-6.
[71] To prepare candidates for initiation, the Eleusinian Mysteries specified ceremonies that transferred a person's sins into a pig, which then was sacrificed. See Chapter 5.
[72] See *John* 10:1–31.

Figure 23-9. Coin Minted in the Decapolis near the Miracle of the Gadarene Swine. Gadara, AE 18, ca. 4–3 B.C.

shepherd," Jesus explicitly referred to himself using an appellation of the god Attis, the consort of Cybele that created the possibility of eternal life for humanity by dying an agonizing self-inflicted death and physically resurrecting.[73] Romans celebrated the resurrection of Attis during *Hilaria*, an eight-day celebration[74] centered on the vernal equinox—around the time that modern Christians celebrate Easter. At the time the gospel story was written, the parable served as a metaphorical bridge for potential Christian converts, offering a comfortable path for Roman and Anatolian worshippers of Attis to accept Christian beliefs.

Searching for Jesus in the Canonical Gospels

The search for the historical Jesus is fraught with difficulties. Two thousand years ago, people understood the universe differently from people in modern times. Sometimes an enormous gulf separates a modern reader's understanding of *New Testament* text from the meaning

---

[73] See Chapter 10.
[74] The first day, March 15, celebrated Attis' rescue as a baby from a basket in a reed sea by Cybele and marked the beginning of nine days of dietary restrictions. The festival resumed with the sacrifice of a ram on March 22, which included decorating and burying an evergreen tree during three days of mourning the death of Attis, and ended with four days celebrating the resurrection of Attis.

originally intended by the author: For example, when soldiers gave Jesus "wine mixed with gall," before the crucifixion, they offered mercy rather than insult because the described mixture contained opium.[75] The four canonical gospels confuse the picture further by presenting four completely different accounts of the life of Jesus.

In modern America, political candidates commonly profess to support Christian family values and numerous books profess to teach them.[76] However, what are "Christian family values?" Jesus said, "If any man comes to me without hating his father, mother, wife, children, brothers, sisters, yes and his own life too, he cannot be my disciple."[77] It hardly seems possible to incorporate this statement in any acceptable set of modern "family values." Yet Jesus also explicitly affirms the Jewish commandment to honor one's father and mother.[78]

Contradictions between Gospels. Contradictory statements by Jesus abound in the gospels. For example, in *Matthew* 12:30, Jesus says, "He who is not with me is against me," but in *Mark* 9:40, Jesus says, "Anyone who is not against us is for us." If one begins a logical argument assuming contradictory statements both to be true, the rules of logic allow one to prove almost anything, which means that demagogues can argue that Christian teachings support many contradictory positions. "It's a matter of interpretation" is a familiar pronouncement during heated theological disagreements, as if fault lay in the reader of contradictory scripture rather than in the contradiction itself.

The ability to use statements by Jesus in support of almost any ethical or political position has encouraged modern Christian communities to project how Jesus would have stood on current political issues, as if someone two thousand years ago could have opinions about issues like nuclear energy, gay rights, and sexism. However, during the life of Jesus, no one knew anything about nuclear technology, no one

---

[75] See *Matthew* 27:34–35. Regarding the identification of "gall" with opium, see "Opium for the Masses" by Robert S. Merrillees in *Archaeology Odyssey*, Winter 1999, pp. 20–29.
[76] For example, see *Building a Strong Christian Family Foundation* by Romy Baylon.
[77] See *Luke* 14:26–27.
[78] See *Matthew* 19:18–19.

imagined gay rights to be an issue, and no one believed in the equality of women. Often imagined to be a supporter of equal opportunities for women, Jesus never stated that men and women have equal rights. Instead, his position about the divinely ordained relationship between men and women emerges most clearly from his description how heaven would be governed when he finally sat on his divine throne: All twelve of his male disciples also would sit on thrones, each disciple raised as a judge over a tribe of Israel.[79] However, Jesus had nothing to say about the roles that women would play in divine government.

Living two thousand years ago Jesus had nothing to do with modern churches that preach a broad spectrum of theological and political doctrines in his name. He was not Catholic, Protestant, Orthodox, nor any other type of Christian. Regardless, modern Christian sects often claim that only they correctly understand ancient scripture about the intentions of God, which may be the only belief they truly share with apocalyptic Jewish cults during the lifetime of Jesus.

Each of the four canonical gospels provides a different understanding of Jesus. A reader is tempted to combine the facts in those stories into an expanded biography, but contradictions between the gospels prevent this. Not only are Jesus' words different—a problem easily explained as mistakes by listeners, but events unfold differently: sometimes happening in a different order, sometimes combining in different ways, and sometimes directly contradicting one another regarding details about what really happened. From reading the four gospels, one can build an understanding of the events during the life of Jesus only by ignoring the contradictions, which forces readers to construct individualized, custom-built life stories of Jesus.

Jesus as a Young Man. Jesus lived most of his life in Galilee under the rule of the tetrarch Herod Antipas. As mentioned previously,[80] the gospel of *Matthew* assumes that Jesus and his family lived in Bethlehem but moved to Egypt for a time,[81] barely escaping death when King

---

[79] See *Matthew* 19:28 and *Luke* 22:28–30.
[80] See Chapter 22.
[81] See *Matthew* 2:13–16.

Herod ordered the massacre of innocent children in Bethlehem. However, while the gospel of *Luke* says that Jesus visited Bethlehem[82] in time to be born there (in 6–7 A.D.), no gospel other than *Matthew* suggests that Jesus lived anyplace other than Nazareth until he began his ministry.

Jesus assumed adult responsibilities in his synagogue at the age of twelve after he demonstrated competence discussing scripture during a Passover visit to Jerusalem.[83] Like his stepfather Joseph,[84] Jesus earned his living as a *tekton*,[85] a Greek word that generally designates a poorly paid day laborer. The canonical gospels say nothing further about Jesus until sometime after he reached thirty years of age.

However, important structural aspects of the life of Jesus are mentioned briefly or implied. For example, Jesus had four brothers named James, Joses, Judas, and Simon. He also had at least two sisters, traditionally identified as Mary and Salome.[86] Because of Christian beliefs about the perpetual virginity of the Virgin Mary, it is frequently claimed that all the brothers and sisters of Jesus are by Joseph with a previous wife. However, this claim presents a problem in the context of Jewish law. The advanced age of Joseph[87] when he married Mary and his absence during the ministry of Jesus suggests that he died before Jesus reached full maturity. If Joseph died without having a child by Mary, Jewish law would have required that the brother of Joseph (Clophas)

---

[82] See *Luke* 2:1–39.

[83] During the life of Jesus, Jews assumed adult responsibilities in the synagogue when they demonstrated competence in scripture. This is the point of the story about Jesus and the rabbis in *Luke* 2:39–52, the only story about Jesus before he was thirty in any of the canonical gospels. The first historical Bar Mitzvah ceremonies for thirteen-year-old Jewish boys did not occur until the fourteenth century A.D.

[84] In a small town like Nazareth, Jesus must have suffered cutting remarks about having been conceived out of wedlock. One hears an echo of his childhood pain in saying 105 of the gospel of *Thomas*, "One who knows his father and his mother will be called the son of a whore."

[85] See *Mark* 6:3 and *The Jesus Dynasty: The Hidden History of Jesus, His Royal Family, and the Birth of Christianity* p. 90 by James Tabor.

[86] See *Mark* 6:3 and *The Jesus Dynasty: The Hidden History of Jesus, His Royal Family, and the Birth of Christianity* p. 73 by James Tabor. The apocryphal *History of Joseph the Carpenter* identifies the names of Jesus' sisters as Assia and Lydia.

[87] The apocryphal *History of Joseph the Carpenter* identifies the age of Joseph as ninety-two and the age of Mary as fourteen when they married. The work also claims that Joseph died at the age of one hundred and eleven when Mary was thirty-three.

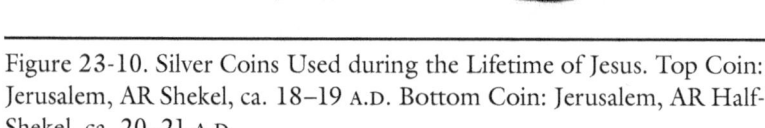

Figure 23-10. Silver Coins Used during the Lifetime of Jesus. Top Coin: Jerusalem, AR Shekel, ca. 18–19 A.D. Bottom Coin: Jerusalem, AR Half-Shekel, ca. 20–21 A.D.

attempt to have a child by Mary, which then would have been considered a child of Joseph.[88]

Figure 23-10 displays two silver coins minted in Jerusalem, a shekel[89] and a half-shekel, which circulated in Nazareth and Sepphoris during the life of Jesus. Bearing images standardized during times when Seleukids and Ptolemies ruled Judea, both coins display a bust of the Phoenician god Melqart on the obverse and an eagle (referring to Zeus) on the reverse. The shekel coin would have paid Jesus for four days of work.[90] Jews used coins like these to pay their annual tax, one-half shekel per male, to the Jerusalem Temple. Even though the coins

---

[88]See *The Jesus Dynasty: The Hidden History of Jesus, His Royal Family, and the Birth of Christianity* pp. 76–81 by James Tabor.
[89]Judas Iscariot would have received shekels like this as his thirty pieces of silver, the equivalent of four months' pay for a day laborer.
[90]See *The Jesus Dynasty: The Hidden History of Jesus, His Royal Family, and the Birth of Christianity* p. 91 by James Tabor. One half-shekel was equivalent to two denarii.

bear pagan images, no less-objectionable silver coins existed in Galilee during the lifetime of Jesus.

While still a teen, or perhaps in his early twenties, Jesus learned about the death of Augustus Caesar in 14 A.D. Eyewitness accounts that Augustus ascended from his funeral pyre into the sky like a god generally did not impress Galilean Jews. The transfer of power to a new emperor, Tiberius, had little direct impact on life in Galilee, even though Tiberius ruled the Roman Empire until 37 A.D., well after the crucifixion of Jesus. However, the arrival of Pontius Pilate in Jerusalem in 26 A.D. suddenly activated anti-Roman sentiment among Judean Jews. Around this time, Jesus traveled to Judea to visit his cousin, John the Baptist, and began preaching soon afterward.

The Ministry of Jesus. If the synoptic gospels existed alone, it would be possible to lay out a reasonable and familiar chronology of significant events during the ministry of Jesus, as follows.[91] After baptism by John and forty days of temptation in the wilderness by the devil, Jesus (approximately thirty years old) began proclaiming the imminent arrival of the *Kingdom of God*,[92] which meant the End of Days and a moral judgment of all humanity. Jesus preached to the public mostly in parables[93] and he performed miracles (for example, raising a man's daughter from the dead[94]) and exorcisms. Generally, audiences (including his disciples) didn't know what to make of him; however, the demons that he cast out and a few perceptive people recognized that Jesus was the messiah. When recognized by ordinary people, Jesus always cautioned them to say nothing about his real nature to anyone else. Eventually, Jesus took his disciples up a mountain and revealed his special relationship with divinity, an event popularly known as the *transfiguration*, but the disciples still didn't know what to think about Jesus. After a ministry that lasted only about six months, Jesus presided

---

[91]See *The New Testament: A Historical Introduction to the Early Christian Writings* by Bart D. Ehrman, Third Edition, p. 159.
[92]In the synoptic gospels, Jesus often declared that the Kingdom of God (End of Days) would arrive before the deaths of members of his audience. For example, see *Mark* 9:1.
[93]According to *Mark* 4:33–34, Jesus lectured in public only in parables.
[94]See *Mark* 5:21–43.

over a Passover supper in Jerusalem during which he inaugurated a Christian ceremony called the Eucharist: His followers ate bits of bread and drank wine—the bread was his body and the wine was his blood. Jesus then prayed in the garden of Gethsemane, asking God to change his immediate future so that he wouldn't undergo crucifixion. However, the difficulty of using gospels as historical sources becomes abundantly clear when one realizes that the ministry of Jesus in the gospel of *John* contains none of the foregoing synoptic elements.

In the gospel of *John*, John the Baptist testified to priests from Jerusalem that Jesus was the "lamb of God" who would "baptize with the Holy Spirit."[95] Instead of being tempted in the wilderness, Jesus started gathering disciples immediately, beginning a ministry that lasted almost three years.[96] In addition, throughout his ministry, he told one or two parables at most, he never cast out a demon, and he never proclaimed the imminent arrival of the Kingdom of God. From the beginning, many people immediately recognized him as the messiah.[97] Far from counseling silence about his divinity, Jesus not only confirmed that he was the messiah, but he also declared that he was God.[98] Rather than performing miracles in private as in the synoptic gospels (usually with only a few witnesses and often counseling secrecy), Jesus performed seven big miracles in front of huge crowds expressly for the purpose of proving his divinity:[99] turning water into wine,[100] healing a court official's son in Capernaum,[101] healing a paralytic by the pool of Bethsaida,[102] feeding five thousand people with five loaves and two fishes,[103] walking on water,[104] healing a man born blind,[105] and raising Lazarus from the dead.[106] Five of these miracles appear only in the gospel of

---

[95]See *John* 1:29–34.
[96]See *Jesus Interrupted: Revealing the Hidden Contradictions in the Bible (and Why We Don't Know About Them)* by Bart D. Ehrman, p. 42.
[97]See *John* 1:41.
[98]See *John* 10:30.
[99]*John* 20:30–31 says that Jesus performed many more miracles than just these seven.
[100]See *John* 2:1–11.
[101]See *John* 4:46–54.
[102]See *John* 5:2–9.
[103]See *John* 6:1–14.
[104]See *John* 6:16–21.
[105]See *John* 9:1–12.
[106]See *John* 11:1–44.

John. The only miracle that appears in all four gospels is the feeding of five thousand people with five loaves and two fishes, although walking on water appears in two of the canonical gospels.[107] In the gospel of *John*, the disciples of Jesus knew from the beginning that he was the messiah, so he never had to take them up a mountain and secretly reveal his nature.

Associated by scholars with the Essene community, the gospel of *John* places the *Last Supper*, the last meal of Jesus before his crucifixion, in a chamber owned by a community that had followed Menahem, the Essene leader executed during the last days of King Herod's reign.[108] Jesus did not perform the Eucharist ceremony, nor did he go to the garden of Gethsemane afterward to ask God to prevent his crucifixion. Instead Jesus washed his disciples' feet and said that, going forward, they all should wash each other's feet.[109] Jesus also spoke about Menahem as an example of a person sent by God to help a pious community. However, Greek translations of Jesus' words translate the name, Menahem, to its meaning in Hebrew, which appears in modern bibles as words like comforter or *Paraclete*, appellations of what became known to Christians as the *Holy Spirit*.[110]

Even when the canonical gospels share stories, they often differ regarding important details. For example, did Jesus cleanse the temple at the end of his ministry thereby attracting attention from city authorities as a troublemaker (as described in the synoptic gospels[111]), or did he cleanse the temple at the beginning of his ministry as described in the gospel of *John*? However, the problem of extracting history from the canonical gospels is bigger than merely reconciling differences between synoptic gospels and the gospel of *John*: Some gospel stories are fictional creations. For example, scholars have shown that the author of the gospel of *Matthew* fabricated the story called the *Sermon*

---

[107]See *Matthew* 14:22–33 and *Mark* 6:45–52.
[108]See Chapter 22.
[109]See *John* 13:1–20.
[110]See *John* 14:12–18 and *The Messiah before Jesus: The Suffering Servant of the Dead Sea Scrolls* pp. 68–71 by Israel Knohl. The appearance of the name Menahem in Syriac in the gospel of *Barnabas* is the source of Islamic claims that Jesus mentioned the prophet Muhammad—both names (Menahem and Muhammad) have the same Semitic root.
[111]See *Matthew* 21:12–17, *Mark* 11:15–19, and *Luke* 19:45–48.

on the Mount,[112] one of the most loved stories in all the gospels: Combining inspirational sayings by Jesus from different periods of his ministry, the author of *Matthew* created a single episode that analogously recalled the delivery of God's law by Moses on Mount Sinai.[113]

THE HISTORICAL SIGNIFICANCE TO JEWS AND CHRISTIANS

After Augustus died, control of the Roman Empire passed to Tiberius. While Augustus had made Romans feel good about supporting their emperor, Tiberius lacked the ability to cultivate good will and inspire affection. Tiberius supported the Cult of the Emperor, which easily coexisted with a wide variety of other popular cults in Rome, but he used it mostly to affirm the legitimacy of his rule. Nevertheless, Romans often voiced disapproval of Tiberius, and life throughout the empire became a little less pleasant.

Under Tiberius, the Roman Empire simmered Jews and Judaizers in a complex cultural soup. Eastern beliefs increased in popularity because they often were more hopeful, interesting, and flexible than traditional Roman cults. Popularizations of astrology, Skepticism, and other philosophical movements created an intellectual climate in Rome filled with trendy new ideas. Some Romans experimented with atheism, and many adopted Jewish beliefs.

In Judea, after the deposition and exile of Herod Archelaus[114] in 6 A.D., the first Roman prefects enforced peace and ruled the Jewish population with at least a modicum of cultural sensitivity. Prefects implemented effective controls over the operation of the Jerusalem Temple Cult but otherwise tried to maintain neutrality in religious disputes among Jews. Influenced by pro-Jewish Augustan policies that originated with Julius Caesar, Roman administrators maintained the peace. They captured bandits and quashed occasional rebellions

---
[112]See *Matthew* 5–7.
[113]See *The New Testament: A Historical Introduction to the Early Christian Writings* by Bart D. Ehrman, Third Edition, p. 101.
[114]See Chapter 22 for details about the troubled period when Herod Archelaus (a son of King Herod) ruled Judea.

while striking a balance between preserving the Judean economy and maximizing the extraction of taxes. However, Roman policies in Judea shifted drastically for the worse in 26 A.D.

If Tiberius had desired to ensure a continuation of the peaceful administration of Judea begun under Augustus, politics and personal concerns distracted the emperor. Petulantly empowering Sejanus, a power-hungry and immoral bureaucrat, Tiberius withdrew to Capri and wreaked vengeance on the Roman world by withholding his unrecognized ability to care. Under Sejanus, Pontius Pilate traveled to central Judea to serve as the region's new prefect.

In the highly charged political environment of Judea in 30 A.D., Jesus of Nazareth gathered followers in Galilee, central Judea, Perea, and the Decapolis. He conceived of a plan to bring the End of Days to the world. Depending on predictable responses from leaders of the Jerusalem Temple Cult and Pontius Pilate, Jesus implemented his plan, step-by-step, to its bitter conclusion. Beneath the contradictory and partisan descriptions of the last days of Jesus in the canonical gospels—through his arrest, trial, and crucifixion—one can glimpse the last moments in the life of a brilliant and courageous man, a Jew utterly committed to changing the world.

CHAPTER
24

PONTIUS PILATE'S ADMINISTRATION

THE CRUCIFIXION OF JESUS

In early first century A.D. Judea, Pontius Pilate broke trust with his Jewish subjects, and he aggressively pursued and executed messianic leaders.

In 26 A.D., while Emperor Tiberius closeted himself on Capri, his substitute in Rome Sejanus assigned Pontius Pilate as the new prefect of central Judea. After two decades of comparative peace under a series of four Roman prefects, Judea experienced changes that moved even poor Jews to action. Pontius Pilate implemented harsh new policies while largely ignoring Jewish sensitivities, which fostered widespread Jewish outrage during the critical years of Jesus' ministry. Freely dominating Jewish society for ten years until he was deposed in 36 A.D., Pontius Pilate caused the reactivation of dormant Judean revolutionary movements. Jews searched intensely for a messiah who would free their homeland from Roman rule. They looked especially in families believed to descend from King David.

Although Christian gospels portray Pontius Pilate in a sympathetic light, the historical record consistently portrays him as antagonistic toward Jews and prone to extreme violence. His anti-Jewish policies galvanized Jewish antagonism toward the corrupting influences of Roman rule. Priests in charge of the Jerusalem Temple Cult had little choice but to submit to the prefect and support his policies, which gave many Jews a sense of having suffered betrayal at the core of their spiritual life. During this complex period, the ministry of Jesus emerged as just one of many movements of disaffected Jews.

Written in Greek forty to sixty years after the crucifixion, the canonical gospels offer contradictory and anachronistic details[1] about Jesus. Ostensibly telling only about Jesus, the gospels often reveal less about his life and more about the circumstances when they were written and the communities that they served. Nevertheless, the gospels in combination with numismatics, archaeology, and non-biblical historical sources provide considerable insight into the competing forces within Judea toward the end of the life of Jesus.

THE HISTORICAL, POLITICAL, AND RELIGIOUS CLIMATE THAT AFFECTED JESUS

Throughout the Roman Empire, Augustus and Tiberius enforced social stability while generally promoting policies of tolerance and respect toward Jews. The reigns of both rulers earned praise from Jews for improving their status.[2] However, the Roman administration of central Judea took a sharp turn for the worse under Tiberius during the last years of Jesus.

In 6 A.D., Publius Sulpicius Quirinius (the new governor of Syria Province) annexed Judea, which meant placing the region firmly under military control, taking a census, and beginning the collection of taxes. Under Governor Quirinius, a Roman knight named Coponius implemented the annexation and ruled as the first prefect of central Judea.

---

[1]For example, scholars regard the *parable of the vineyard* (*Mark* 12:1–9) as an anachronistic description of political conditions related to Christian movements after 70 A.D.
[2]See *The Embassy to Caligula* 155–161 by Philo of Alexandria.

After some initial problems,³ he forcefully established a Roman administration that imposed peace while avoiding intentional violation of the norms of Jewish society. Subsequently, three more Roman prefects ruled central Judea, successfully achieving two decades of relative harmony comparable to the peace imposed during the reign of King Herod. However, in 26 A.D., central Judea's fifth prefect Pontius Pilate initiated policies that diverged significantly from those of his predecessors: Artifacts and history testify to his insensitive and merciless ten-year term of office.

New Policies toward Jews by Pontius Pilate

Before Pontius Pilate became prefect of Judea in 26 A.D., Roman prefects avoided Jewish unrest by keeping man-made depictions of humans and animals out of Jerusalem.⁴ However, when Pontius Pilate arrived in Judea, his first official act set the tone for a contentious relationship with his Jewish subjects: He sent soldiers into Jerusalem carrying images of Emperor Tiberius.⁵ Soon afterward, a crowd of Jews assembled near the Roman government headquarters in Caesarea to demonstrate against the images. In a dramatic encounter, Pontius Pilate led a detachment of soldiers to confront the Jews, but they refused to disperse. Instead, they exposed their throats to the Roman soldiers. Supposedly impressed that Jews would accept death more willingly than sacrilege, Pontius Pilate relented and ordered the images to be removed from Jerusalem.

Another source describes the incident differently,⁶ saying that conflict between Romans and Jews developed after Jews objected to the presence of votive shields inscribed with dedications to Roman gods. All sources agree that Pontius Pilate backed down during his first confrontation with a Jewish mob. However, the reason had more to do

---

³See Chapter 23.
⁴Although the *Bible* records that Jews have had an ambivalent relationship with idols at different phases of their history, Judean Jews during the time of Jesus (that is, after a century of Hasmonean religious purification) were strongly aniconic. Most Judean Jews associated images of gods, animals, and people with unacceptable Hellenistic influence.
⁵See *Antiquities of the Jews* 18:55–59, and *The Jewish War* 2:169–174, by Josephus.
⁶See *The Embassy to Caligula* 299–305 by Philo of Alexandria.

with strategic calculations than with compunctions against shedding blood: A temporary vacancy in the governorship of Syria Province had depleted the Roman legions in Syria, which meant that Pontius Pilate would have gone a long time without military assistance if the slaughter of a few suicidal Jews had caused a general rebellion.

Pontius Pilate collected taxes with greater zeal than earlier Roman prefects. He antagonized Jews by taking funds directly from the Jerusalem Temple's treasury to build an aqueduct for Jerusalem.[7] When Jews demonstrated against his misappropriation of temple funds, soldiers in plain clothes infiltrated the crowd. At Pilate's signal, the soldiers pulled bludgeons from their clothing and began to beat the demonstrators. Many people died, some clubbed to death and some trampled as terrified demonstrators struggled to save themselves in the sudden confusion. Afterward, Pontius Pilate offered a token sacrifice to Roman gods thanking them for his success. The gospel of *Luke* refers to this event when it says that blood from Galilean pilgrims mingled with Roman sacrifices to pagan gods.[8]

Also, unrecorded by history, Pontius Pilate built a temple dedicated to Tiberius as a god.[9] Archaeologists discovered the temple's dedication stone in excavations of Caesarea. Referring to Pontius Pilate by name and title, the stone is the only artifact ever found from the time of Jesus that unquestionably bears the name of a person mentioned in the *New Testament*.[10]

---

[7] See *Antiquities of the Jews* 18.3.2 and *The Jewish War* 2.9.4 by Josephus.
[8] See *Luke* 13:1. The presence of this passage in the gospel underscores that knowledge of the deep hostility between common Jews and Pontius Pilate persisted for generations.
[9] See *King Herod's Dream: Caesarea on the Sea* pp. 110–111 by Kenneth Holum, Robert Hohlfelder, Robert Bull, and Avner Raban.
[10] Discovered in 2008 by the IEASM archaeological mission in the Portus Magnus in Alexandria, a *lecanomancia* (*Bowl Cl_3557* in the Alexandria Maritime Museum), or "magic bowl," carries the earliest known inscription that mentions "Christ." Attributed to a date between the first century B.C. and the first half of the first century A.D., the inscribed bowl reads, "DIA CHRSTOU O GOISTAIS," which has been interpreted as, "The magician, by Christ," or, "By Christ, the magician." Ancients filled the bowl with water and then added a little oil. Then, a magus, perhaps invoking spiritual power from Jesus, attempted to see the future in the oil on the surface of the water. Alternatively, the bowl might relate to an unknown Alexandrian messiah or even to unknown Hellenistic religious ceremonies, perhaps even the "orgia kai christeria" (ceremonies and anointing) associated with an Alexandrian Jewish healing cult.

Chapter 24 | Pontius Pilate's Administration 613

Figure 24-1. Bronze Coins Minted under the Authority of Pontius Pilate from 29–31 A.D.

Judean coins minted during the administration of Pontius Pilate portray devices explicitly associated with non-Jewish cults, which shows that he abandoned the respectful numismatic policies of previous Roman prefects. For example, the obverse of the top coin in Figure 24-1 portrays a *simpulum*, or ladle used to offer sacrifices to Roman gods. The reverse portrays a container holding three ears of wheat, an agricultural symbol that acquires cultic significance in the context of the simpulum. The obverse of the lower coin shows a *lituus*, or augur's wand, which refers to Pontius Pilate's service as an *augur*, a priest who interpreted signs from pagan gods. Both coins bear inscriptions that refer to Tiberius as Caesar, and both coins carry dates: year 16 (top coin) and year 17 (lower coin) of Tiberius' reign. These dates correspond to 29–30 and 30–31 A.D., a period generally associated with the ministry and crucifixion of Jesus.[11]

---

[11] In 1980, Rev. Francis Filas, S.J., of Loyola University in Chicago and Michael Marx, an expert in classical coins, claimed to identify designs from coins like these on the eyes of the figure on the *Shroud of Turin*. They discovered these designs by carefully examining data obtained in 1978 when researchers used NASA's VP-8 3-D Image Analyzer to examine shroud images. However, the discovery remains controversial.

Arrest, Trial, Crucifixion, and Resurrection

From the Roman point of view, Jesus was just another troublemaker from Galilee. Conversely, we can see Jesus' opinions about Rome and Hellenism in his choice of associates. Jesus came to John the Baptist attracted by his traditional Jewish teachings about purity and righteousness. All of the early followers of Jesus came from traditional Jewish backgrounds. Among the disciples of Jesus, two names stand out: Simon the Zealot[12] and Judas Iscariot. Simon's name proclaims his belief in the violent ejection of Romans from Judea. Similarly, Judas' name "Iscariot" comes from "Sicarius," which means knife,[13] so that Judas Iscariot is another way of saying, "Judas, a member of the Sicarii." One can translate the names, Simon the Zealot and Judas Iscariot, in modern terms as "Simon the proponent of violent revolution" and "Judas the killer-terrorist."

The Arrest and Trial of Jesus. According to the synoptic gospels, Jesus came to the attention of Jerusalem authorities after he attacked the money changers at the temple. Money changers facilitated the purchase of animals for sacrifice for travelers from cities that used different money from that used in Jerusalem. In modern times and in a Christian context, this event would be comparable to attacking people who worked in a small monetary exchange bank that served tourists near the Vatican—especially if the facility served people on a Saturday or a Sunday.[14] Attacking a monetary institution, threatening businessmen with bodily harm,[15] and claiming a divine right to cause trouble easily branded Jesus to Roman and Temple authorities as another dangerous troublemaker from Galilee. Sadducee priests of the Jerusalem Temple Cult served in the Great Sanhedrin at the sufferance of Pontius Pilate. They investigated troublemakers like Jesus as the

---

[12]The apostles James, Jude, Simon, and Joseph all may have been brothers of Jesus. See *The Jesus Dynasty: The Hidden History of Jesus, His Royal Family, and the Birth of Christianity* p. 142 by James Tabor.
[13]See *Mark: A Reader-Response Commentary, Continuum International* (1998) p. 167 by Bastiaan van Iersel.
[14]The penalty for violating the Jewish Sabbath was stoning. See *Exodus* 31:14.
[15]In *John* 2:13–16, Jesus attacked the money changers with a whip designed to tear human flesh.

Roman prefect required, but descriptions of the arrest and trial of Jesus vary significantly among the gospels of *Mark*, *Luke*, and *John*.

In the gospel of *Mark*,[16] the ministry of Jesus culminates in a visit to Jerusalem for a celebration of *Passover*, a Jewish holiday that commemorates the escape of Jewish slaves from Egypt. During a Passover feast, Jesus announced his imminent betrayal and then conducted the first Christian Eucharist ceremony. Later that night, Jewish authorities seized Jesus while he was in anguished prayer in the garden of Gethsemane. The followers of Jesus briefly resisted arrest. One follower used his sword to cut off an ear from a servant of the high priest, but all of the followers ran away before the authorities could catch them. Jesus rebuked the authorities for coming to arrest him as if he were a thief, but they immediately took him to a kangaroo court of Sadducee priests that was illegally assembled in the middle of the night on a holy day. When questioned, Jesus declared that he was a divine messiah who would judge the priests upon the imminent arrival of the End of Days. Identifying this claim as blasphemy, the court condemned Jesus to death. Jewish officials bound Jesus and then delivered him to Pontius Pilate first thing in the morning. Uttering only a few words in his defense—"So you say"—Jesus underwent a quick trial in front of Pontius Pilate and Jewish leaders. Pontius Pilate meekly accepted the judgment of the priests against Jesus but still tried to find some way to free him. Deciding to place the fate of Jesus in the hands of a random gathering of nearby people, Pontius Pilate offered them a holiday gift: He would grant freedom to one Jewish prisoner, either Jesus or a murderous rebel named Barabbas. Coached by the Jewish leaders, the people called for Pontius Pilate to free Barabbas and crucify Jesus. Guilty only of fulfilling the will of other people, Pontius Pilate freed Barabbas and ordered the immediate scourging and crucifixion of Jesus, all before 9:00 A.M.

In the gospel of *Luke*,[17] immediately after the Passover feast and Eucharist ceremony, Jesus prepared for his upcoming arrest by ordering his followers to obtain swords. They found two, which Jesus said was enough, and they all went to the garden of Gethsemane. There, Jesus

---

[16]See *Mark* 14–15.
[17]See *Luke* 22:14–23:31.

calmly prayed[18] while all his followers slept. When authorities arrived to arrest Jesus, he allowed one follower to amputate the right ear of a slave of the high priest and then said, "No more of this." With a touch, Jesus miraculously restored the slave's ear. He rebuked the authorities, but they seized him, confined him in a cell in the high priest's house, beat him, blindfolded him, and insulted him. Early in the morning, guards presented Jesus before a council of illegally assembled Jewish priests and scribes. When questioned, Jesus confirmed that he was the son of God, which brought immediate condemnation by the council. The entire council then rose and took Jesus to the Roman prefect. Pontius Pilate asked Jesus if he claimed to be the King of the Jews and received a noncommittal reply. The prefect told the Jewish leaders that he found no basis for their accusation of wrong-doing, but the Jewish leaders insisted that their prisoner was seditious, inadvertently informing Pontius Pilate that Jesus was a Galilean. Pontius Pilate then sent Jesus to Herod Antipas, the Tetrarch of Galilee, who just happened to be in Jerusalem for the holiday. Herod Antipas had heard of Jesus and was delighted to get an opportunity to question him, but Jesus would not speak to Herod. Herod's court mocked Jesus, clothed him in an elegant robe (intended as a gift for the prefect), and returned him to Pontius Pilate. Having previously been enemies, Pontius Pilate and Herod Antipas then became friends. Pontius Pilate announced that, because he and Herod Antipas had questioned Jesus and found him innocent, Jesus would be flogged and released. However, the Jewish leaders objected. They demanded instead that Pontius Pilate release Barabbas (a man rightfully convicted as a murderous rebel) and crucify Jesus (an innocent man). Pontius Pilate tried two more times to release Jesus, but the Jewish leaders forced him to give in to their demands: Pontius Pilate ordered Barabbas to be released and Jesus to be crucified. Unique to the gospel of *Luke*, as weeping and wailing Jewish women followed Jesus, he told them not to weep for him but to weep instead for themselves and their descendants who would suffer more than he.

---

[18] The sentences in *Luke* 22:43–45, attributing agony and bloody sweat to Jesus, do not appear in all textual versions and seem to be a late addition to the text. Also, with all the followers asleep, who observed Jesus in agony?

In the gospel of *John*,[19] Jesus ate a normal dinner the day before the Passover feast. After eating, he inaugurated the ceremony of washing his disciples' feet, and he delivered long lectures to his disciples. Then, he went to a garden near a brook called Cedron. Temple priests and authorities soon came to arrest him. They asked if he was Jesus, and he answered, "I am he," which caused all the authorities to fall to the ground. Jesus then told the authorities to take him and to leave everyone else. Attempting to save Jesus, Peter used his sword[20] to amputate the ear of the high priest's servant, but Jesus rebuked Peter for attempting to prevent fate. Contented to arrest Jesus alone, the authorities took him to two quick meetings, first with Annas, father-in-law of the high priest, and then with Caiaphas, the high priest. Early the next morning, still the day before the Passover feast,[21] Caiaphas sent Jesus to the Roman hall of judgment, however, no Jews other than Jesus entered the hall because they needed to remain ritually pure for the approaching holiday. Pontius Pilate questioned Jesus only after learning that the priests wanted him executed. In the presence only of Romans,[22] they discussed whether or not Jesus was King of the Jews. Jesus said that his kingdom was not of this world, but he was born to bear witness to the truth. Pontius Pilate asked, "What is truth?" Leaving the hall of judgment, Pontius Pilate told the waiting Jewish authorities that he found no fault with Jesus and offered to free him in honor of Passover, according to local custom. The Jewish authorities rejected Pilate's offer and asked that he free a thief named Barabbas instead. Pontius Pilate returned to Jesus, had him scourged, and then dressed him in a purple robe and a crown of thorns. Taking Jesus outside the hall of judgment, Pontius Pilate said, "Behold, the man," and the Jewish authorities shouted, "Crucify him!" Saying that he "found no fault in this man," Pontius Pilate told the Jewish leaders to crucify Jesus, which they could not legally do. However, when the Jewish authorities said that Jesus had claimed to be the son of God, Pontius Pilate suddenly became afraid and brought Jesus back into the hall of

---

[19]See *John* 13–19.
[20]How many disciples routinely carried swords?
[21]For Jews, days begin and end with sundown.
[22]Who recorded the conversation?

judgment for more discussion. Jesus and Pontius Pilate talked about who had power over whom, and Jesus reassured the prefect that the sin of the Jewish authorities was greater than his. Pontius Pilate decided not to crucify Jesus and, taking him to the seat of judgment at a place called Gabatha, entered into an extended discussion with a crowd led by Jewish priests. Pontius Pilate tried to prevent the crucifixion of Jesus but the Jewish crowd demanded it. Around noon, Pontius Pilate gave up and handed Jesus over to the Jewish authorities and a Roman execution squad.

Responsibility for Condemning Jesus. The canonical gospels present contradictory accounts of the trial of Jesus, but they all affirm the popular Christian belief that Pontius Pilate allowed the execution of Jesus only because Jews wanted him dead. Numerous books discuss the irregularities in the trial of Jesus as evidence proving the depth of the Jewish conspiracy against Jesus.[23] Written by native speakers of Greek, intended for Hellenistic Roman communities comprised largely of pagan converts to Christianity, and presenting contradictory accounts with temple procedures that explicitly violated Jewish laws, the canonical stories about the trial of Jesus simply lack credibility.

Before the death of Jesus, his followers consisted of Jews who honored him as a righteous man, a miracle worker, and a spiritual teacher. The distinction between Jewish and non-Jewish Christians didn't exist until more than a decade after the crucifixion of Jesus. By the time the first canonical gospel was written—four decades after the crucifixion—Judean Jews had risen in a major revolution against Rome. Hundreds of thousands of Jews were killed and a hundred thousand enslaved. Jerusalem had been sacked and burned, and the original Jewish Christian community that followed Jesus had been decimated. The strongest growth of Christian cults was happening in Roman-controlled cities far away from Judea. In the context of Judean history of the first century A.D., it's not surprising that the canonical gospels express strong positive sentiments about Romans and strong prejudice against Jews.[24]

---

[23]For example, see *The Illegal Trial of Jesus* by Earle Wingo.
[24]See Chapter 25 for further discussion of this point.

Found only in the gospel of *Matthew*, one famous detail during the trial of Jesus seems particularly out of place: Pontius Pilate symbolically washed away guilt by washing his hands as a crowd of Jews condemned Jesus and claimed the guilt of his murder for them and all their children.[25] The act of washing hands to cleanse oneself from guilt is a Jewish act,[26] not a Roman one, which suggests that Roman Christians chose to canonize a gospel that transferred to Pontius Pilate an action originally performed by a Jewish priest—that is, washing away guilt from an execution he could not prevent.

Canonical gospels contain such sympathetic portrayals of Pontius Pilate[27] that the Abyssinian Church declared him a saint with his own feast day (June 25). However, despite protestations of Pilate's innocence in the canonical gospels, the execution of Jesus could have happened only with explicit authorization by the Roman prefect. Like many thousands of other Jews during the first century A.D., Jesus met his death at the hands of a Roman executioner. Pontius Pilate enjoyed a well-deserved reputation for energetically pursuing and executing potential troublemakers, especially candidate messiahs. When he captured leaders of Jewish movements, he either killed them outright or ordered their execution following the barest essentials of due process. He cared little about whether the men he killed presented real risks to Roman rule or not.

The Crucifixion of Jesus. While central to Christianity, accounts of the crucifixion, death, and resurrection of Jesus in the canonical gospel disagree considerably in their descriptions of what actually happened. Even the synoptic gospels tell different stories, differing not just in small details but also in major characterizations of events. Contradictions between the gospels reveal the distance of gospel authors from the events that they described.

In the gospel of *Matthew*,[28] Jesus suffered the torturous agonies of crucifixion, and then spectacular events—a violent earthquake, the

---

[25]See *Matthew* 27:24–26.
[26]See *Deuteronomy* 21:6 and *Psalms* 26:6.
[27]For examples, see *Matthew* 27:3, *Mark* 15:14, *Luke* 23:4, and *John* 19:4.
[28]See *Matthew* 27:45–58.

splitting of rocks, and the resurrection of righteous Jews who then walked among the people of Jerusalem—marked the moment of his death around 3:00 P.M. on the day of the Passover feast.[29] Only female followers of Jesus observed the crucifixion, and they watched it from a distance through darkness. However, the gospel records intimate details of events and conversations close to Jesus.

The gospel of *Mark*[30] provides the same general story as the gospel of *Matthew* except dramatic events like the earthquake, the splitting of rocks, and the resurrection of dead Jews somehow escaped notice. Again, the gospel records details of words and interactions close to the cross even though only female followers of Jesus observed the crucifixion from a distance through darkness. Jesus died by 3:00 P.M. after suffering horribly, but Pontius Pilate expressed surprise that Jesus died so quickly.

The gospel of *Luke*[31] never mentions the scourging of Jesus but otherwise agrees with other synoptic gospels that Jesus was crucified in the morning on the day of the Passover feast and that he died around 3:00 P.M. Compared to the gospels of *Matthew* and *Mark*, however, Jesus calmly endured crucifixion. Some versions of the gospel record that Jesus said, "Father, forgive them for they do not know what they are doing," and some versions do not.[32] A short time after telling one criminal that he would join Jesus that day in paradise, Jesus loudly commended his spirit to his father and then died. The gospel of *Luke* records a small amount of conversation around the cross, including a declaration of Jesus' innocence by a pagan centurion, but otherwise provides details consistent with a gathering of male and female acquaintances of Jesus viewing the crucifixion from a distance during the darkness of a miraculous eclipse.[33]

---

[29]For Jews, the day began the previous evening with a Passover feast.
[30]See *Mark* 15:23–44.
[31]See *Luke* 23:32–53.
[32]See *The New Testament and Other Christian Documents: A Reader* pp. 90–91 by Bart D. Ehrman. Such a statement by Jesus was controversial among early Christians because it could be understood as explicitly pardoning Jews.
[33]An eclipse of the sun would have been impossible at the beginning of Passover in the middle of the Jewish month of Nisan, a time that always occurs around the full moon. Solan eclipses happen only during a new moon.

Significantly different from the synoptic gospels, the gospel of *John* says that Jesus was crucified the day before the Passover feast,[34] going up on the cross around noon and dying well before evening. Only in this gospel, Pontius Pilate ordered soldiers to write, "King of the Jews," on a board in Latin, Greek, and Hebrew and to fasten it on the cross above Jesus' head. Jesus endured his suffering calmly, at one point arranging for the care of his mother by one of his followers, as family and friends came near to him. Just before death, Jesus said, "It is finished," and died. Unique to this gospel, a Roman soldier pierced the side of Jesus with a spear because he seemed to die too quickly.[35]

Generally ignoring the contradictions in the canonical gospels, modern Christians often think of the *passion of Christ* as an indiscriminate combination of dramatic details from multiple gospels: for example, that Jesus was scourged, condemned by Pontius Pilate (who then washed his hands), crowned with a wreath of thorns, and crucified during a total eclipse under a board with writing that said, "King of the Jews." Believing that the passion occurred like this is equivalent to believing that Jesus was crucified twice: once with scourging and once without, and once before the Passover feast and once afterward. In addition, popular portrayals of the passion usually include details that the canonical gospels do not contain. For example, most people assume that the Romans crucified Jesus on a cross shaped like a Christian crucifix, but the earliest written description of the cross[36] says that it was shaped like the capital letter T.[37]

The Entombment and Resurrection or Survival of Jesus. Gospel accounts of the entombment and resurrection of Jesus suffer from consistency issues already amply illustrated in the accounts of his birth, ministry, trial, and crucifixion. The one feature that all the canonical

---

[34]See *John* 19:16–38.
[35]The gospel also contains a special note assuring the reader that the piercing actually happened. See *John* 19:35.
[36]See the *Epistle of Barnabas* 9:7, a text included in the earliest known Christian Bible, the Codex Sinaiticus, but otherwise not canonized.
[37]Some early Christians understood both forms of the cross as a T, which stood for the Eastern solar deity Tammuz commonly represented as a beardless shepherd. Like Jesus, Tammuz combined attributes of Sol Invictus and Attis.

accounts have in common is that Mary Magdalene discovered the resurrection, which suggests that she was the very first Christian. Other than this one common feature, the canonical gospels differ significantly regarding who went to the tomb, what they saw when they got there, and what happened afterward.[38]

The likelihood that Jesus survived scourging and crucifixion is vanishingly small, but a number of sources, Christian and non-Christian, say that he did. Christian sources say that he survived by dying first and then resurrecting from the dead; after which, he could materialize and dematerialize wherever and whenever he wished, a power also attributed to other saviors.[39] However, non-Christian sources make a broad range of claims: Some say that it only appeared as if Jesus was crucified;[40] others say that Jesus barely survived his torture and abuse in Jerusalem,[41] and that he abandoned Judea as soon as he regained his health. Indian sources say that Jesus traveled to North India, a region he already had visited during his undocumented years between thirteen and thirty-seven years of age. Honored as a Hindu Saint in India, Jesus often told the story of his torture and crucifixion in Jerusalem and displayed his scars as proof. Indian sources also say that Jesus had a wife named Mary.

While in India, Jesus met with a young maharaja and counseled him wisely regarding fulfillment of his family obligations. Praising Jesus, the young man agreed to marry, which was a prospect that he had been resisting. Perhaps the maharaja named a son after Jesus or perhaps he minted coins specifically to honor of Jesus. Regardless, around the middle of the first century A.D., coins appeared in North India bearing inscriptions like, "Isamahisa," and, "Isamula," which can be translated

---

[38] See *Peter, Paul, and Mary Magdalene: The Followers of Jesus in History and Legend* pp. 227–229 by Bart D. Ehrman.
[39] For example, see the discussion of Apollonius of Tyana in Chapter 25.
[40] See the *Koran*, Sura 4:157–158.
[41] The presence of Hansen's disease (leprosy) in Judea during Jesus' lifetime proves that people travel between Judea and India. Possibly reflecting the arrival of a strong disciple of Jesus, someone identified as Jesus traveled to Northern India in the first century A.D. He acquired a reputation as a holy man and people called him Saint Issa. See *The Unknown Life of Jesus Christ* by Nicolas Notovitch and *The Fifth Gospel: New Evidence from the Tibetan, Sanskrit, Arabic, Persian and Urdu Sources about the Historical Life of Jesus Christ after the Crucifixion* by Fida Hassnain and Dahan Levi. It's interesting to speculate how stories about Buddha influenced early Christianity.

Figure 24-2. Coin Minted in India Honoring Isamula or "Jesus Spiritual Teacher." Sakas of Junnar, Pb, ca. Mid-First Century A.D.

as "Jesus great Jesus" and "Jesus spiritual teacher," respectively. Figure 24-2 shows an example of an Indian coin with the inscription "Isamula" above a lion on the obverse. The reverse portrays a bow and arrow over a symbol representing hills.

Historical accounts about the presence of Jesus in India are not trusted in the West in the absence of compelling evidence.[42] However, if historical accounts of Jesus traveling to India are untrustworthy, the canonical gospel accounts of his life, death, and resurrection are similarly suspect: Important details and even the fundamental nature of Jesus vary from gospel to gospel. In the gospel of *Mark*, a pathetic, generally misunderstood Jesus dies an agonizing death in despair after declaring that God had forsaken him;[43] yet a pagan centurion observing the crucifixion proclaimed, "Truly, this man was the son of God.[44]" In the gospel of *Matthew*, the beloved son of God[45] modestly, resolutely, and beautifully fulfilled every Jewish prophecy regarding the messiah, discovering along the way that non-Jews were more worthy

---

[42]Even if Jesus never went to India, it's possible for a numismatist to collect first century Indian coins related to Christianity. Beginning in 52 A.D., the apostle Thomas visited Indian cities and won numerous converts to Christianity.
[43]See *Mark* 15:34.
[44]See *Mark* 15:39.
[45]See *Matthew* 3:17.

of salvation than Jews.[46] In the gospel of *Luke*, Jesus never suffered doubt or pain: He first offered salvation to Jews but then transferred God's covenant to non-Jews because Jews rejected him and caused him to die. In the gospel of *John*, Jesus staged spectacular miracles attempting to convince Jews that he was and always had been their one-and-only almighty God; however, after realizing that only non-Jews could understand the salvation that he offered, Jesus ended his covenant with Jews and extended a new covenant to non-Jews.

THE HISTORICAL SIGNIFICANCE TO JEWS AND CHRISTIANS

Far from deserving sainthood, Pontius Pilate was a vicious mass-murderer. During his tenure as prefect of Judea, even Rome found his policies unacceptably cruel. The only writers ever to say anything good about him were Roman Christians trying to rehabilitate the role of a Roman prefect in the death of Jesus. By injecting first-century propaganda in the gospels to shift blame from Pontius Pilate to Jews, early Christians perpetuated conflict between Christians and Jews that rightfully should have ended at the conclusion of the Second Jewish Rebellion in 136 A.D.

Gospel authors similarly mischaracterized Jesus. By inserting magic into the stories about his life and death, they denied his existence as a brilliant, caring, and all-too-human Jew. For a man purposely to choose arrest, trial, shame, torture, and execution—even if he believed in his own spiritual resurrection—requires nerve and heroic commitment. For God, ruler of the universe, to do the same is like a bored child taking the identity of an imaginary avatar in a video game. Belief in magical religion encourages people to abdicate their responsibility in the world, expecting that God will magically clean up all of humanity's mess, instantly and effortlessly, sometime in the future.

As a believer in catastrophic messianism, Jesus intended to bring the End of Days by offering his own royal blood.[47] He pursued a carefully

---

[46]See *Matthew* 8:5–13.
[47]For an analysis of the last days of Jesus in the light of the "Gabriel Revelation," see *Messiahs and Resurrection in the 'Gabriel Revelation'* pp. 85–93 by Israel Knohl.

considered plan: fulfilling scriptures, provoking his own arrest, and enduring terrible suffering until he died. However, despite his best efforts, the End of Days did not come.

Ancient Jewish writings show that Jews of Jesus' time believed that a messiah would undergo spiritual resurrection after three days, even if his mutilated body remained unburied like "dung on the earth."[48] Even the *New Testament* documents early Christian beliefs about spiritual resurrection: The earliest Christian writings about resurrection (letters of Paul) make it clear that believers in Jesus expected resurrection of a spiritual body that would live forever, not of a natural body that is subject to death. More than a decade after the crucifixion, Paul wrote about an emerging belief in resurrection as corpse resuscitation, especially among Christians in communities outside Judea. He called the people who believed in the idea, fools.[49]

The Death of Judas Iscariot

A realistic appraisal of the events related to the arrest, trial, and crucifixion of Jesus begs a number of suppositions:

- Before his arrest, Jesus knew what Judas Iscariot would tell Jerusalem authorities because Jesus was complicit in arranging his capture in a safe place—that is, a place where his capture wouldn't provoke a riot.
- Judas Iscariot didn't know the full intentions of Jesus and negotiated an understanding with Jewish leaders that Jesus would not be passed to Pontius Pilate, thereby avoiding capital punishment.
- Judas believed that the arrest of Jesus would help mobilize Jerusalem Jews toward violent revolution against Rome.

If any of these suppositions are true, Judas was bitterly disappointed.

After the crucifixion of Jesus, Judas committed suicide at a place called Akeldama or field of blood.[50] However, Akeldama is more than

---

[48]See *Messiahs and Resurrection in the 'Gabriel Revelation'* pp. 7, 71, and 95–96 by Israel Knohl. Also, see Chapter 22.
[49]See *1 Corinthians* 15:34–50 and *2 Corinthians* 5:1–5. Also, see *The Jesus Discovery: The New Archaeological Find That Reveals the Birth of Christianity* pp. 192–193 by James Tabor and Simcha Jacobovici.
[50]See *Acts* 1:18–19 and *Matthew* 27:7.

just a convenient place to die. It contains some of the most splendid Herodian tombs ever discovered. Specifically, Akeldama contains tombs of the Annas and Caiaphas families, prominent priests in the gospel stories about the crucifixion.[51] One investigator has suggested that, by committing suicide on that site, Judas Iscariot was attempting to defile the family graves of priests who lied to him and conspired to murder Jesus.[52] Regardless, Christians remember Judas, often metaphorically conflated with Jews and Judaism, as the betrayer of Jesus.

The Tomb of Jesus

Some descriptions of activities related to the interment of Jesus can be trusted. For example, the Jews who knew Jesus saw him die on a Roman cross. With the arrival of a holy day at sunset, there was a need to place his body in a temporary tomb until it could be moved elsewhere. A sympathetic member of the Great Sanhedrin, Joseph of Arimathea, negotiated with Roman authorities, took charge of the body, and placed it in a nearby borrowed tomb.[53] Out of respect for Jesus and his lineage, Joseph of Arimathea intended to move the body to a fresh tomb located on his estate.[54] The next morning, when Mary Magdalene, a wealthy "companion"[55] of Jesus, came alone to the borrowed tomb to anoint his body, she found that it had been taken away, but a "messenger"[56] remained to speak with her.

Some descriptions of activities related to the interment of Jesus cannot be trusted. For example, in the gospel of *Mark* (the earliest

---

[51] See "Akeldama: Potter's Field or High Priest's Tomb?" by Kathleen and Leen Ritmeyer in *Biblical Archaeology Review*, Nov/Dec 1994, pp. 22–35, 76, and 78.

[52] This possibility emerged from a discussion between Simcha Jacobovici and Professor James Tabor in the video program, *The Naked Archaeologist*, Season 2, Episode 14, "Hangin' with Judas."

[53] See *Mark* 15:46.

[54] See *The Jesus Discovery: The New Archaeological Find That Reveals the Birth of Christianity* pp. 119–120, 126–127 by James Tabor and Simcha Jacobovici.

[55] The Gnostic *Gospel of Philip* (32 and 55) calls Mary Magdalene the companion of Jesus, which meant wife in the first century A.D. Also, a 4th century A.D Coptic fragment refers to the wife of Jesus. See *A New Coptic Papyrus* by Professor Karen King.

[56] Although we now understand the word angel as referring to a semi-divine winged protector, the ancient Hebrew and Greek words translated as "angel" literally meant "messenger." See *The Jesus Discovery: The New Archaeological Find That Reveals the Birth of Christianity* pp. 133–134 by James Tabor and Simcha Jacobovici.

canonical gospel), Mary Magdalene, Mary the mother of James, and Salome came to anoint the body of Jesus and they found the blocking stone "rolled away" from the entrance of the tomb.[57] Jews did not use tombs with round, roll-away blocking stones when Jesus died. That burial custom did not take hold among ordinary Jews until after the Jewish War[58] more than thirty-seven years after the crucifixion of Jesus. The description of the tomb with a round blocking-stone helps confirm that the gospel of *Mark*, the earliest of the canonical gospels, was not written until sometime after 70 A.D.

The gospel of *Mark* acknowledged a belief that Jesus was buried and his corpse did not come back to life, but the gospel called it a Judean lie, which was understood in Greek-speaking communities as a Jewish lie.[59] The first Jewish Christians in Jerusalem knew that Jesus died and was buried in a family tomb. In addition, they believed that he was the messiah, that he had resurrected with a spiritual body after three days, and that his sacrifice had ensured that God would bring the End of Days within one generation.

After the death of Jesus, surviving members of his family kept a low profile to avoid sharing his fate. Supporting the earliest Christian church in Jerusalem, the family of Jesus lived among Judeans who did not believe that the revivified corpse of Jesus had emerged from his family tomb, materializing and dematerializing at various locations in Judea and Galilee. The family of Jesus continued to play important roles in the Jerusalem church until 106 A.D. Then, the last known family member, a leader of the Jerusalem church, was crucified for being a descendent of the *House of David*.[60]

Evidence suggests that Jesus and close members of his family were interred in a tomb near Jerusalem: In 1980, a family tomb was discovered in Talpiot, Israel, that contained ossuaries bearing names associated with the family of Jesus, including an ossuary of "Jesus, son of

---

[57]See *Mark* 16:1–4.
[58]The gospels of *Mark* and *Luke* provide anachronistic descriptions of the tomb of Jesus, however text in the gospels of *Matthew* and *John* are consistent with the use of appropriately shaped blocking stones. See "Did a Rolling Stone Close Jesus' Tomb?" by Amos Kloner, *Biblical Archaeology Review* 25:5, Sep/Oct 1999, pp. 23–29 and 76.
[59]See *Matthew* 28:11–15.
[60]See *The Jesus Dynasty: The Hidden History of Jesus, His Royal Family, and the Birth of Christianity* pp. 284–293 by James Tabor.

Joseph."⁶¹ Using conservative assumptions, a peer-reviewed statistical paper estimated the probability that the recently discovered tomb was used by Jesus and the members of his immediate family as approximately 98 percent.⁶² When other information is factored into the analysis—for example, isotopic analysis indicates that the ossuary of James the brother of Jesus (who became the first known leader of the Jerusalem Church) was looted from the same tomb and rare spellings of the names on several ossuaries match spellings used in Christian texts for the names of the mother of Jesus (Maria), a brother of Jesus (Joses), and Mary Magdalene—the probability approaches certainty.⁶³ No one can prove that the Talpiot tomb is the final resting place of Jesus and members of his family, but no other known tomb provides a better example of what the true tomb of Jesus would look like. For convenience, people often refer to the tomb as the *Jesus family tomb*. See Figure 24-3.

The Sign of Jonah

In modern times, Christians generally believe that the *Sign of Jonah*⁶⁴ refers to the physical resurrection of Jesus. Interpreted this way at least since the Reformation, most discussions of the Sign of Jonah among Christians have occurred in the context of proving that Jews will be damned unless they believe in the physical resurrection of the corpse of Jesus. However, it is unlikely that the Sign of Jonah had the same meaning to the earliest followers of Jesus, all of whom were Jews.

Only the most astrological of canonical gospels, namely, *Matthew* and *Luke*, refer to the Sign of Jonah.⁶⁵ Early in the ministry of Jesus, Jews listening to him speak about his mission asked him for a sign. The

---

⁶¹See *The Jesus Family Tomb: The Evidence Behind the Discovery No One Wanted to Find* pp. 74–82 and 219–234.
⁶²See "Statistical Analysis of an Archaeological Find" by Andrey Feuerverger, *Annals of Applied Statistics* 2 (2008): 3–54, followed by six discussion papers and a rejoinder by Feuerverger, pp. 666–673 and 99–112.
⁶³See *The Jesus Discovery: The New Archaeological Find That Reveals the Birth of Christianity* pp. 106–118, 175–177, and 204.
⁶⁴See Chapter 22.
⁶⁵See *Matthew* 12:38–40 and *Luke* 11:29–30. Also, see Chapter 24.

Figure 24-3. The Entrance to the Jesus Family Tomb in Talpiot, Israel.

Jews were not asking Jesus to perform a miracle: The gospels of *Matthew* and *Luke* both describe Jesus performing miracles, for example, healing, resuscitation of the dead, and feeding a multitude of people with five loaves and two fishes. However, none of these miracles constituted a sign. Jesus responded to the request by saying, because the current generation is evil and adulterous, no sign would be given except, "The Sign of Jonah, the prophet who spent three days and three nights in the belly of the whale[66] (Ketos) just as the 'Son of Man' would spend three days and three nights in the heart of the earth."

When Jesus speaks about the Sign of Jonah in the gospels of *Matthew* and *Luke*, his followers don't question him; so at least something about the sign was already well known.[67] Scholarly analysis in terms of ancient astrology combined with textual evidence in the gospels of

---

[66] See *Jonah* 1:17.
[67] Either people knew about the sign that attended the birth of Jesus and spoke of it as the Sign of Jonah, or people understood that Jesus intended to force his own execution and spiritual resurrection (for example, attended by a lunar eclipse and blood-red sky after the death of Simon of Perea) as a sign that would precipitate the End of Days.

Matthew and *Luke* suggests that early followers of Jesus understood the Star of Bethlehem and the Sign of Jonah to be one and the same—a sign intimately associated with Jesus and the only sign that would be given to their generation.

Astrological Connection between the Sign of Jonah and the Crucifixion. According to the *Bible*,[68] a sign involves the sun, moon, planets, and stars. Non-Hellenistic Jews in the time of Jesus didn't believe in astrology, but they still believed in signs. Just as *Matthew* and *Luke* are the only canonical gospels that speak of the Sign of Jonah, they are the only canonical gospels that describe one indisputable sign involving the sun, moon, planets, and stars: the Star of Bethlehem. Connecting astrological details about the Star of Bethlehem with the biblical references about the Sign of Jonah suggests that an astrological understanding of the nature of Jesus[69] was important to the authors of *Matthew* and *Luke*.

The sign known as the Star of Bethlehem contains astrological elements that can be associated with the story of Jonah and the whale (Ketos), as follows:

- A divinely ordained swallowing occurred: The crescent moon occulted Jupiter in the sign of Aries such that two different objects became one.
- The event was associated with Ketos: The occultation happened at the beginning of the *decan of Ketos*, a place in the sky where the open mouth of the constellation Ketos appears to attack the belly of Aries the ram.
- A symbolic death and resurrection occurred over three days: The moon disappeared (died), only to reemerge (resurrect) three days later at the beginning of the new month.

Coincidentally, astrology connects the crucifixion of Jesus to the sign that occurred at his birth. The two most commonly identified dates for the crucifixion of Jesus are Thursday, April 5, 30 A.D., and Friday, April 3, 33 A.D. Both dates offer a peculiar astrological coincidence: The sun

---

[68] See *Genesis* 1:14.
[69] See Chapter 22.

occupied the same position in the sky—the beginning of the decan of Ketos (also called the *decan of death*)—that the crescent moon and Jupiter occupied during their conjunction on April 17, 6 B.C. If Jesus had known this fact, he would have understood it as confirmation that the "Sign of Jonah" that marked his birth also participated in his mission of precipitating the End of Days.

However, even if Jesus knew nothing about the astrological timeliness of his crucifixion, the first astrologers to convert to Christianity from the Cult of Mithras would have investigated astrological correspondences related to the birth and death of Jesus. Symbolically, the resurrection of Jesus in three days was foretold by the arrival of the new moon three days after the sign that attended his birth. Christian astrologers understood that the crucifixion of Jesus occurred when the sun occupied the same position as the conjunction of Jupiter and the moon on the day of his birth. Some early Christians believed that Jesus was an incarnation of Sol Invictus. Descriptions in the synoptic gospels of a total eclipse during the crucifixion referred to the monster Ketos swallowing the sun, metaphorically related to the swallowing of Jonah by a whale (called a *Cetacean* after Ketos). Consistent with the perception of Jesus as a solar deity, early non-Jewish Christians portrayed Jesus as a beardless figure, either radiate or with a *nimbus* (halo), like Sol Invictus. For example, in Figure 24-4, a funerary token from Palmyra (close to modern Aleppo in Syria) portrays Sol Invictus as a beardless radiate deity, which strongly resembles some of the earliest Christian images of Jesus.

The Sign of Jonah and the Interment of Jesus. Recent archaeological discoveries in Talpiot, Israel, lend credence to the astrological connection between the Star of Bethlehem and the Sign of Jonah. The earliest known depiction of the Sign of Jonah occurs on an ossuary in an unexcavated tomb in Talpiot located very close to the Jesus family tomb. Much grander in style than the Jesus family tomb, the second Talpiot tomb (commonly referred to as the *patio tomb*) has been tentatively identified as the family tomb of Joseph of Arimathea.[70] The

---

[70]See *The Jesus Discovery: The New Archaeological Find That Reveals the Birth of Christianity* by James D. Tabor and Simcha Jacobovici, pp. 119–128.

Figure 24-4. Funerary Token from Ancient Palmyra Portraying Sol Invictus in a Style Adopted by Early Christians for Images of Jesus.

patio tomb contains undisturbed ossuaries. In 2010, archaeologists conducted a visual exploration of the tomb with the assistance of remotely guided robotic cameras. They discovered that the ossuary in the most prestigious position in the tomb (occupying the front right *loculus* as one enters the tomb) bears an image used to represent the Sign of Jonah.[71]

The figure first was interpreted as a fish swallowing or disgorging a man because, to modern eyes, the symbol comprises a crude fish shape, badly drawn fish scales, and an unusually modern stick-figure man. However, the image is so poorly rendered that critics declared that it actually depicted an architectural column or a grave offering like an *unguentarium*, a container of scented oil. Then, archaeologists noticed that what looked at first to be exceptionally crude stick-figure arms and legs actually comprised Hebrew letters that spelled the name "Jonah." Figure 24-5 shows two hand-rendered sketches of the Sign of Jonah: one with and one without the Hebrew letters. One sees immediately that the image did not begin as a fish swallowing a stick-figure man. Instead, the image without the Hebrew text looks like a fish with a peculiar chevron-shaped head and a circular object stuck on its nose.

---

[71] See *The Jesus Discovery: The New Archaeological Find That Reveals the Birth of Christianity* p. 69 by James Tabor and Simcha Jacobovici.

Figure 24-5. Two Drawings of Earliest Jonah Symbol Found on Ossuary in the Patio Tomb in Talpiot: with Hebrew Label (Left) and without Hebrew Label (Right).

The Sign of Jonah from Talpiot is very different from images of Jonah and Ketos that appear in other early Christian contexts.[72] As the earliest known Christian Sign of Jonah, the shape of the symbol appears connected to the astrological event that appeared in the sky at the birth of Jesus (Figure 22-8) as well as to the symbol that appears on the entrance of the Jesus family tomb (Figure 24-3). Both symbols from Talpiot contain similar elements: a *chevron* (a V-shaped symbol) and an *annulet* (circular symbol) or *pellet* (a filled-in annulet). Also, in numismatics, the chevron can have many different meanings, but a chevron associated with a small circle or pellet usually represents a crescent moon and star.

Derived from the magnificent visual impression from close approaches of the crescent moon to a planet in the morning or evening skies, the crescent and star symbol traditionally represents a god or a goddess. For example, the Phoenician coin from Gadir in Figure 16-6 portrays a bust of Melqart on the obverse and two fishes and crescent

---

[72]For an example of an early Christian portrayal of Jonah and Ketos in a style more characteristic of non-Jewish Christianity, see Figure 25-5.

and star on the reverse. The crescent and star on the coin represents the Syrian Aphrodite (Atargatis); and the fishes, raised into the sky as the constellation Pisces, represent her step-parents who protected the egg from which the goddess was born.[73]

If one erased the posterior portion of the fish on the unlabeled Sign of Jonah, a chevron and circle would remain. One then could orient the unlabeled symbol at an angle such that the chevron and the circular object recall the relative positions of the crescent moon and Jupiter as they rose together above Bethelehem on April 17, 6 B.C. (See Figure 22-8.) An accomplished older man, Joseph of Arimathea was old enough to remember what the original sign looked like.

The Jesus family tomb in Talpiot is the only known Herodian tomb marked with a chevron and a circle above its entrance. To modern eyes, the symbol in Figure 24-3 looks like a slanted roof over a circular eye, reminiscent of old homes in New England bearing architectural elements that protect inhabitants against the *evil eye*.[74] However, the only buildings in Judea with slanted roofs during the time of Jesus were Roman temples, so the chevron does not represent a roof. It has been suggested that the circle represents a royal diadem indicating that the tomb houses descendants of a royal Jewish bloodline. Other possible interpretations also exist. From close examination of the photograph in Figure 24-3, it appears that the symbol originally contained at least one other horizontal component below the circle.[75] When combined with the chevron and circle and considered as a unified whole, the symbol begins to resemble an anchor, another symbol commonly used to represent Judean royalty. For example, minted by Alexander Jannaeus around 78 B.C., the coin in Figure 24-6 bears an anchor on the obverse and a poorly rendered inscription (proclaiming him king) on the reverse. However, in the context of the sign that occurred during the birth of Jesus, which metaphorically recalled the swallowing of Jonah by Ketos, the symbol on the Jesus family tomb combines

---

[73] See Chapter 9.
[74] Surviving from the days of polytheism, cultural beliefs about the evil eye refer to the possibility that one god might wish to destroy blessings granted by another god.
[75] Unfortunately, the Jesus family tomb has been buried so it is not currently possible to examine the tomb's entrance more closely than the picture in Figure 24-3 allows.

Figure 24-6. Royal Anchor Symbol on Lead Prutah of Alexander Jannaeus, King of Judea 103–76 B.C.

abstract elements that represent the crescent moon occulting Jupiter, a fitting symbol for the tomb of Jesus.

No matter how one interprets the symbol at the entrance of the Jesus family tomb—an anchor, a royal diadem, or a crude Jonah symbol—its components can be associated with a crescent moon and star. From the Jesus family tomb, the ossuary of "Jesus, son of Joseph" bears three symbols: a chevron, a star, and cross. Even the Jonah symbol on the ossuary from the patio tomb looks like it started as a representation of a crescent moon and star. Figure 24-7 brings all the symbols together so they can be easily compared: In the top row, the figure above the Jesus family tomb appears similar to both a Judean royal anchor and a Phoenician crescent and star; in the bottom row, the anterior portion of the earliest known Sign of Jonah recalls the appearance of the crescent moon and Jupiter as they rose over Bethlehem on the morning of April 17, 6 B.C. Carved during a time when the early followers of Jesus struggled to develop meaningful iconography, the symbols from the two Talpiot tombs appear related: They both attempt to represent the Sign of Jonah referenced in the gospels of *Matthew* and *Luke*.[76] Early followers of Jesus understood both symbols

---

[76]See Chapter 22.

636   Part Seven | Influences on the Birth, Life, and Crucifixion of Jesus

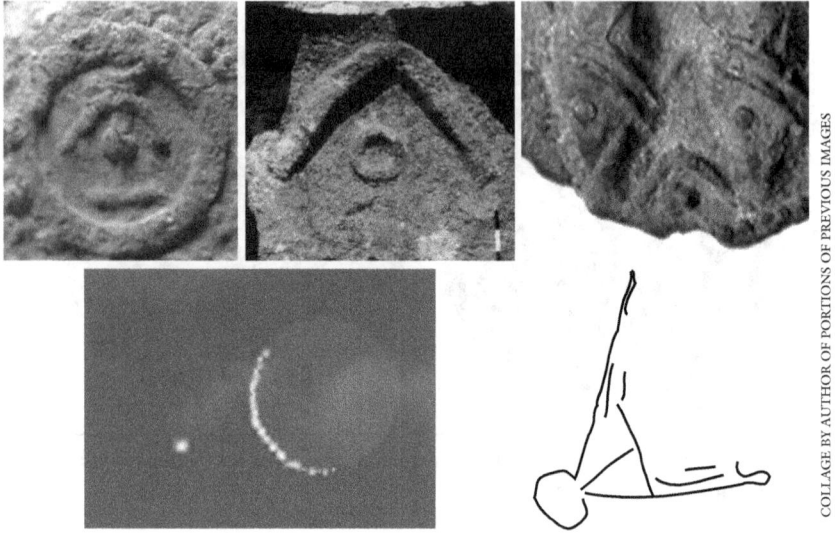

Figure 24-7. Symbol from Jesus Family Tomb (Top Center) with Hasmonean Royal Anchor (Top Left) and Phoenician Crescent Moon, Star, and Fish (Top Right). Also, Jupiter and Crescent Moon at Sunrise, April 17, 6 B.C. (Bottom Left), and Anterior Portion of Unlabeled Sign of Jonah from the Patio Tomb (Bottom Right).

as referring to the sign that marked the birth and the mission of their messiah.[77] Emerging from these first primitive expressions of the Sign of Jonah in the Talpiot tombs, the fish and the anchor became the earliest common Christian symbols.

The Expulsion of Pontius Pilate from Judea

Eventually, a violent attack on a self-proclaimed messiah and his followers ended the career of Pontius Pilate. In 36 A.D., a Samaritan who claimed to be the *taheb* (the Samaritan messiah) assembled a multitude of followers near Mount Gerizim. He asked the crowd to accompany

---

[77]See Figures 16-6 and 22-8. The crescent and star was a pagan symbol and then a Christian symbol until it was ceded to Islam in the Middle Ages. Turks adopted the crescent and star as a lucky symbol after they conquered Constantinople and found numerous crescent and star flags (Christian invocations for divine support) throughout the city.

Figure 24-8. Mount Gerizim (Left) and Mount Ebal (Right) above the Modern Town of Nablus (Ancient Shechem).

him to the top of the mountain where he would uncover sacred vessels deposited by Moses.[78] Many people followed him up the mountain.

Like Jerusalem, Shechem and the twin mountains on either side of it (see Figure 24-8) played important roles in Jewish history. Joshua pronounced his blessings on Mount Gerizim (left) and his curses on Mount Ebal (right). Priests of the northern kingdom claimed descent from Moses and priests from Judah claimed descent from Aaron.[79] Shechem, the ancient capital of the northern kingdom of Israel, held both Joseph's tomb and Jacob's well.

Having monitored the taheb's activities with spies, Pontius Pilate assembled detachments of cavalry and heavy infantry near Shechem. As the peaceful group of Samaritans ascended the base of Mount Gerizim, intending only to watch their leader dig for ancient religious artifacts, Pontius Pilate's soldiers attacked. The Romans slaughtered some, captured many, and put the remainder of the Samaritans to flight. Pontius

---
[78]See *Antiquities of the Jews* 18.85–87 by Josephus.
[79]See *Who Wrote the Bible* p. 42 by Richard Friedman.

Pilate then brutally interrogated his captives. He forced them to name every leader and every influential participant in the event, and then he captured and executed them all.

The Samaritans could do little but complain. They sent an embassy to the new Governor of Syria Province, Vitellius, the same man identified by history as both a procurer for Tiberius and the father of a future emperor of Rome. The embassy accused Pontius Pilate of mass murder. After carefully considering the Samaritan's complaints, Vitellius marched his legions to Caesarea, deposed Pontius Pilate, and appointed a new prefect to replace him.

Vitellius then sent Pontius Pilate to Rome to answer the charges of mass murder directly to Tiberius. However, before Pilate reached Rome, Tiberius died from natural causes.[80] Pontius Pilate then disappeared from the historical record.

FROM HISTORY TO LEGEND

His friends, family, and disciples called him Yeshua, but most people remember him by his Hellenized name, Jesus. As a circumcised Jew from Nazareth, he gathered disciples and preached an apocalyptic Jewish message in Galilee, Judea, and parts of the Decapolis. Believing that the spilling of royal Jewish blood would precipitate the End of Days within a short period of time, he sent his message only to Jews. He told his disciples, "Do not turn your steps to pagan territory, and do not enter any Samaritan town; go rather to the lost sheep of the House of Israel."[81] Reputedly a healer, a magician, and an inspirational speaker, he lived an enormously influential Jewish life four decades before Judea erupted in its first great revolution against Rome.

On a gloomy Spring day, sometime during the years 30–33 A.D., Roman soldiers acting under the authority of Pontius Pilate crucified Jesus. Surviving descriptions of the event speak of a total eclipse,

---

[80]See *On the Embassy to Gaius* 25 by Philo of Alexandria and *Antiquities of the Jews* 13.6.9 by Josephus.
[81]See *Matthew* 10:5–6.

an earthquake, the splitting of rocks, the opening of tombs, and the bodily resurrection of righteous Jews who walked among the living in Jerusalem.[82] Two thousand years ago, miraculous elements like these commonly appeared in Roman descriptions of the deaths of other great personages,[83] as well. Writers of the canonical gospels included events like these to emphasize the importance of Jesus and the crucifixion to non-Jewish audiences.

Providing the only official accounts of the life and death of Jesus, the gospel stories in the *New Testament* emerged as inspirational literature for communities under pressure. The canonical gospels speak meaningfully about how to live a good life, but details in the gospels sometimes tell more about Hellenistic Christians than about Jesus. With stories more relevant to faith than to history, the gospels lack credibility as primary historical documents.

The traditions that nurtured Jesus, the first followers of Jesus, and the first people to carry his message to the world all were Jewish, but non-Jews soon established cults of Jesus throughout the Western World, which sparked controversy about the need for them to adhere to Jewish laws. New Christian cults began to grow and differentiate themselves from other Christian cults. Eventually, *religion* as an overarching category of acceptable cults developed during the third century A.D. when Christians needed to distinguish true Christianity among a multitude of radically different cults.[84]

The Christian religion has evolved for almost two thousand years as cults grew, changed, and died in a Darwinian game of survival of the fittest. Beliefs outside the bounds of acceptable religion were purged with extreme prejudice. To many Christian leaders, Jesus was a loving god who wanted Christians to kill people who believed unacceptable beliefs. In one of history's cruelest ironies, Hellenistic Christians who did not follow Jewish law used stories about Jesus attempting to

---

[82]See *Luke* 23:44 and *Matthew* 27:51–54.
[83]For example, in *The Life of Caesar* 69, Plutarch reports that a comet appeared, a phantom spoke to Brutus, and the sun dimmed for a year after the death of Julius Caesar.
[84]See the Foreword, note 1. Also, see Chapter 25, note 73. The invention of the Christian religion simultaneously created religions called Judaism and Paganism.

eliminate Hellenism from Jewish beliefs and practices as a justification for persecuting Jews who clung to Jewish law. Novel Christian beliefs continue to emerge from time to time in Christianity's complex dance with politics, science, and spirituality.[85]

An authentic appraisal of Western religious history reveals a largely unacknowledged debt by modern Christianity to pagan religious beliefs. Transformational mystery cults, great leaders, evolutionary politics, existential wars, and important historical events shaped religious perceptions before, during, and after the life of Jesus. Enduring through difficult times, choosing what to keep and what to throw away, Christians combined a dynamic mix of old and new beliefs about salvation. Inspired by the brilliance, courage, and dedication that a remarkable Jewish man exhibited during the last few years of his life, the *New Testament* coalesced from writings by numerous authors into a valuable literary gift that powerfully shaped Western culture.

In modern times, literary analysis, historical scholarship, archaeology, and numismatics all contribute to uncovering the true story of lost Christian roots. One simply cannot understand the development of Christianity without understanding the world from which it grew. Emerging broadly and deeply from numerous sources, Christianity developed into a market-tested combination of best practices, metaphysical wisdom, and social innovations from a rich soup of Christian and pre-Christian philosophies and cults. Unconsciously nourished by lost and secret roots, Christianity continues to touch modern lives bringing hope and salvation to those who need it, offering powerful guidance in the struggle to live meaningful, loving, and compassionate human lives.

---

[85]For example, Christianity went through an iconoclastic phase in the eighth and ninth centuries A.D. that resulted in the destruction of important ancient art in Egypt and the Middle East. As a modern example, belief in the inerrancy of the Bible emerged among Christian fundamentalists in the late nineteenth century A.D.; the belief persists today among many Protestants even though important Reformation figures like Martin Luther and John Calvin knew such an extreme position to be false. See "Critical Biblical Scholarship—What's the Use?" by Ronald Hendel in *Biblical Archaeology Review*, Vol. 38, No. 4, July/August 2012, p. 22.

CHAPTER
25

THE BIRTH OF A THOUSAND CULTS

All the pieces of Christianity existed when Jesus died in 33 A.D., but it took centuries to combine a diverse assemblage of beliefs, traditions, and cults into a religion called Christianity.

By the time that Tiberius inherited the Roman Empire early in the first century A.D., Jews lived peacefully and well in every major city in the Roman Empire. The Roman provincial government in Judea had established a complex relationship with the Jerusalem Temple Cult, empowering priests who cooperated with Rome but upsetting Jews who saw the sanctity of their temple compromised. After 26 A.D., stories of sacrilegious and unjust rule by the controversial Roman prefect Pontius Pilate began spreading everywhere among Jews.[1] Apocalyptic leaders like Jesus attracted Jews in Galilee and Judea with the prospect of purifying Jewish worship, and many Romans saw that deteriorating relations among different groups of Jews were causing unrest in Jewish

---

[1] In Alexandria, Philo wrote that Pontius Pilate offended Jews by bringing shields dedicated to Tiberius into Jerusalem and that the prefect had a well-deserved reputation for "cruelty, violence, thefts, assaults, and executing prisoners without trial." See *On the Embassy to Gaius* 299 and 302.

communities throughout the diaspora. Concerned with precipitating the End of Days, Jewish apocalyptic movements sometimes provoked violence, which gave Jews a bad reputation among Romans, increasingly damaging relations between Jews and non-Jews throughout the Roman Empire.

After the crucifixion of Jesus sometime during the years 30–33 A.D., the *apostles* (the original disciples of Jesus, excluding Judas) urgently spread their message—at first only among Jews—that the End of Days would arrive within a generation.[2] Competing with other messianic movements of the day, the first Christians observed Jewish laws and holy days, and they clung to Jewish practices and traditions even though they abhorred the corruption of the Jerusalem Temple Cult. Some Jews, particularly those who benefitted under the *Pax Romana* (Roman-enforced peace), disapproved of Christians because veneration of an executed Jewish troublemaker was bound to cause problems with Rome—Romans generally could not distinguish Christians from other types of apocalyptic Jews. However, many Jews in Judea disapproved of Rome's presence in Jerusalem and interpreted the execution of Jesus as just another tragic injustice committed by Romans against an overly idealistic Jew.

Among Jews, there was plenty of tragedy to go around. The crucifixion of Jesus marked the beginning of a disastrous century that saw more than a million Jews killed and more than a hundred thousand Jews enslaved. The first recorded pogroms against Jews erupted in Alexandria in 38 A.D.[3] From 66–70 A.D., a major revolution called the *First Jewish War* resulted in the destruction of the Jewish Temple and raised questions about the widespread presence of Jews throughout the Roman Empire. From 115–117 A.D., a conflict called the *Kitos War* erupted between Jews and non-Jews in provincial Jewish communities, which resulted in the destruction of significant portions of the diaspora as well as more deaths in Judea. Then, from 132–135 A.D.,

---

[2] See *Mark* 13:30.

[3] For a description of the first pogrom, see *On the Embassy to Gaius* 119–131 by Philo of Alexandria. In addition, see "The first pogrom: Alexandria 38 CE" by Pieter van der Horst, *European Review* 10, pp. 469–484. Additional pogroms came to Alexandria in 68 A.D. See *The Jewish War* 2.487–498 by Josephus.

the second great Jewish war, called the *Bar Kokhba Revolt*, finally convinced Rome to take steps toward eradicating Jewish religious beliefs.

In Judea, Sadducean and Pharisaic authorities transferred their disapproval of Jesus to his followers, opportunistically opposing and persecuting Jewish followers of Jesus, which motivated Christians to begin separating themselves from the Jerusalem Temple Cult. Around the middle of the first century, the early church took a major step away from traditional Jewish worship by deliberately opening its membership to non-Jews. Then, as tensions between Romans and Jews increased, resulting in the First Jewish War in Judea, Christian separation from the Jerusalem Temple Cult transformed from an inconvenience to a matter of survival.

Throughout the Roman Empire, the political climate shifted profoundly against Jews. Many Jewish citizens of Rome felt a need to prove their loyalty to the emperor and disassociate themselves from the revolution in Judea. Christian cults offered a new identity for discomfited Jews in the diaspora as well as a way for non-Jewish *Godfearers*[4] to access the benefits[5] of Jewish religious practices without acquiring the appearance of traitors. Before long, the number of Christians had increased dramatically and the bulk of the Christian constituency had shifted from observant Jews to Hellenistic Greeks and Romans.

The canonical gospels give the false impression that Christians and Jews strongly opposed each other from the beginning.[6] Some Christians and some Jews opposed each other at various times, mostly because of localized political considerations. However, the gospels' inaccurate emphasis on conflict[7] between the two groups negatively influenced the relationship between Christians and Jews for millenia.

---

[4]Pagan admirers of Judaism who stopped short of converting to Judaism were commonly referred to as Godfearers. See *Acts* 13:16 and 13:26.
[5]Simply put, Jews got one day off every week, they only had to sacrifice to one god, they had a familiar and fairly self-consistent written history of the universe, and they had written rules that applied equally to every Jew, regardless of his wealth or position.
[6]Even though the gospels portray "Jews" negatively, no distinction between Jew and Christian existed until decades after the death of Jesus.
[7]During the first few centuries A.D., some Pharisaic Rabbis spoke well about Jesus and Christianity and many Jews helped Christians during persecutions. Jews even buried Christian martyrs in Jewish burial grounds. See *The Anguish of the Jews* p. 31 by Edward H. Flannery.

During the second half of the first century A.D., non-Jewish God-fearers mixed Christian beliefs with pagan sensibilities and developed a multitude of ideologically and geographically separate Jesus movements. Far from Jerusalem, the Christian understanding of God shifted from a solitary Jewish divinity concerned with the observance of laws to a Hellenistic solar deity commanding a multitude of other spiritual entities that helped him rule the universe. By the end of the first century A.D., Christian cults were well-entrenched in Syria, Anatolia, Greece, Egypt, and Rome and were spreading rapidly throughout the Roman Empire.

From early disagreements among Christian apostles, numerous Jesus movements emerged and developed. Acquiring regional and ethnic flavors, they inadvertently incorporated beliefs, practices, and iconography never previously associated with Jewish cults. Christian cults diversified and expanded until a Christian identity crisis blossomed during the second century A.D. Then, while competing for followers, regional leaders struggled to impose unprecedented ideological control over Christian communities.

The long-term struggle to distinguish acceptable worship from unacceptable heresies resulted in the invention of church government, which strengthened *Christianity* as a political entity. During the third century A.D., market forces and visionary leaders winnowed away the weakest and most malformed Christian cults, giving rise to broad agreement regarding the defining features of Christian religion. Successfully amalgamating under ever-larger umbrellas of administrative control, Christianity branded itself as a powerful and organized alternative to less-centralized paganism (equated by Christians with the worship of Satan[8]) and Judaism (generally unacceptable to Christians, but much more tolerable than Christian heresies). The increasing power of Christianity and its leadership signified a growing threat to pagan political leaders. From 303–311 A.D., pagan political leaders orchestrated persecutions[9] against Eastern Christian communities just

---

[8] See "Satan's Throne" pp. 26–39 by Adela Yarbro Collins in *Biblical Archaeology Review*, May/Jun 2006.
[9] As many as 20,000 Christians died in Diocletian's persecutions from 303–311 A.D., a number four to six times greater than all the Christians murdered during the first three centuries of the first millennium.

before Christianity acquired full legal status in the Roman Empire. Although worse than any previous persecutions that targeted Christians alone, the purges were only nominally comparable to the slaughter of Jews and Jewish Christians during the conflicts between Jews and Romans from 38–132 A.D.

By the fourth century A.D., Christianity had incorporated features from numerous pagan cults. Christian leadership had created effective methods for administering and controlling the new religion and had eliminated many of its least respected cults by successfully branding them as heresies. Christianity then achieved the greatest success of any Western religion: It established itself as a dominant political force and merged with Roman government. Church leadership controlled Christian communities so effectively that the Roman emperor, Constantine the Great (a devotee of Sol Invictus/Mithras), seized an opportunity to legalize the religion and harness its developing administrative hierarchy to strengthen his control over a new Roman Empire.

OTHER MESSIAHS MENTIONED IN THE *NEW TESTAMENT*

History records the emergence of many prospective messiahs in the first century A.D.—not all of them Jewish—from small-scale brigands to an unnamed "Egyptian Prophet"[10] who convinced 30,000 Jews to follow him in an ill-fated reenactment of the Exodus around 55 A.D. In addition to Jesus and John the Baptist, the *New Testament* mentions two other candidate messiahs by name: Apollonius of Tyana (a Pythagorean) and Simon Magus (a Samaritan). John the Baptist died before the crucifixion of Jesus, but Apollonius of Tyana and Simon Magus survived him, traveled widely, attracted large followings, and acquired reputations for performing miracles. Outside the *New Testament*, ancient writings about John the Baptist, Apollonius of Tyana, and Simon Magus confirm that they all achieved great fame during the first century A.D.

---

[10]See *The Jewish War* 2.259–263 and *Antiquities of the Jews* 20.169–171 by Josephus. The Egyptian prophet also is mentioned in the *New Testament* in *Acts* 21.38.

In contrast, ancient historians overlooked Jesus. Outside of the *New Testament*, only one uncontested mention of Jesus by a first-century historian[11] exists, and that reference mentioned Jesus incidentally while discussing the stoning of his brother, James the Just. Well-known ancient historians largely ignored Jesus because he taught only for a few years, because he confined his activities to Judea, Galilee, and the Decapolis, and because he preached only to Jews. However, many Jews knew Jesus well and might have written about him. Unfortunately, Jews of that time (for example, Simon the Zealot) often involved themselves with revolutionary movements in Judea. After the crucifixion of Jesus, Jews who opposed Rome faced reduced life expectancies, which diminished the odds that their writings would survive to influence future generations.

John the Baptist

Remembered by Christians as a holy man who proclaimed the coming of Jesus, John the Baptist built his career over many years, achieving a reputation for religious purity and for high-profile denunciations against powerful Hellenistic Jews. He acquired a large following among disaffected Jews in the early first century A.D., teaching ideas later espoused by *Ebionites* (Jewish Christians who followed Jewish laws) and Gnostic Christians.[12] After his death, his followers eventually gave rise to a cult called the *Mandeans*, which continues to exist in present day Iran and a few other countries.[13] Mandeans still recognize John the Baptist as a great prophet, but they believe that Jesus was a false messiah who corrupted John's message. Some Mandean teachings echo Gnostic beliefs; for example, that the material world enslaves our souls and death can free us, but only if we have acquired sufficient spiritual knowledge while living.

---

[11] See *Antiquities of the Jews* 20.9 by Josephus.

[12] One of the earliest Christian cults, Gnostics guarded spiritual mysteries, disclosing them only through initiation to worthy spiritual seekers. Gnostics believed that each person found salvation by discovering God within them.

[13] Since 1990, the 60,000 Mandeans that used to live in Iraq have emigrated under pressure to Syria, Jordan, Sweden, Australia, the U.S., the U.K., and Canada.

If Jesus originally included Gnostic teachings in his message, they had to be deemphasized or removed before Christianity could become the dominant religion in the West. Gnostic Christians valued celibacy too much for their cults to maintain popularity without a high rate of conversion. In *The Dialogue of the Savior*, a Gnostic text found at Nag Hammadi, disciples discussed a teaching by Jesus about the necessity of putting an end to the "works of the female," which meant that the world itself was evil and that salvation would come only after women stopped having children and humanity voluntarily achieved extinction. In *The Gospel of the Egyptians*, another text found in the Gnostic library at Nag Hammadi, Jesus explains to Mary Magdalene that human bodies are prisons for divine sparks.[14]

Apollonius of Tyana

Apollonius of Tyana[15] was an important, non-Jewish messianic figure from Cappadocia in Asia Minor. Born around the same time as Jesus, Apollonius lived from the very beginning to the very end of the first century A.D. Ancient literature records the same claims about Apollonius that the *New Testament* makes about Jesus; for example, an angel announced the forthcoming birth of Apollonius to a virgin daughter of one of the best families of Tyana, and Apollonius performed miracles, which included restoring life to a dead person.

As a young man, Apollonius traveled to Tarsos, studied Pythagorean mysteries, and adopted Pythagorean ethics, which included chastity and vegetarianism. He began his teaching career as a young healer at a Temple of Asclepius in Cilicia. Eventually, however, he traveled throughout the ancient world in search of wisdom. He traveled as far east as India and studied with magi, *gymnosophists* (naked philosophers), and Brahmins. He also traveled south to Egypt and west as far as Spain. Many ancient writers mentioned Apollonius, and he attracted numerous disciples. In the *New Testament*, Paul spoke of a meeting

---

[14]See *Peter, Paul, and Mary Magdalene: The Followers of Jesus in History and Legend* pp. 232–233 by Bart D. Ehrman.
[15]See *The Life of Apollonius of Tyana* by Flavius Philostratus.

with a saintly man in Corinth named Apollos[16] (a shortened form of the name Apollonius[17]). Apollos and Paul competed against each other to attract disciples. Affirming the desirability of his particular brand of spirituality, Paul reported that some disciples chose to follow him and some chose to follow Apollos.

Famous as a great sage and healer, Apollonius exorcised demons, healed the sick, and cured the insane. Among his numerous public miracles, he brought a Roman senator's daughter back to life at her funeral and he healed both a man and a dog of rabies. His followers said that he never died. Instead, he rose directly to heaven and, afterward, reappeared physically from time to time. Apollonius wrote many books about medicine, science, and philosophy, and his disciples wrote many books about his life. Little from these works has survived. In the centuries after his death, Christians actively sought to destroy all works that mentioned Apollonius of Tyana.

To a considerable extent, the known stories of Apollonius match many stories about Jesus and Saint Paul. In the fourth century A.D., a man named Sossianus Hierocles[18] argued with Eusebius[19] about the origins of certain miracle stories about Jesus. Sossianus maintained that early Christians created the stories about Jesus by plagiarizing stories about Apollonius.

Simon Magus

Not much is known about Simon Magus, another miracle worker who lived as a contemporary of Jesus and survived him. The *New Testament* treats Simon in contradictory ways, first using his good name to affirm the importance of Jesus and then attacking him with accusations of impiety. As recorded in the *New Testament*,[20] Simon converted to Christianity and then became the first heretic by attempting to buy the

---

[16]See *I Corinthians* 3:3–6.
[17]A manuscript of *I Corinthians* from the fifth century A.D. called *Codex Bezae* presents the name as Apollonius.
[18]Sossianus Hierocles was an aristocrat who held public office in Roman Syria in the late third and early fourth centuries A.D.
[19]Known as the "Father of Church History," Eusebius served as the Bishop of Caesarea from 313–339 A.D.
[20]See *Acts* 8:9–24.

secret of miraculous healing. In his honor, Christians named the sin of attempting to buy spiritual favors "simony."

Other sources[21] say that Simon (a Hellenized Samaritan Jew) performed miracles in his own right. He taught his own brand of mystery cult and founded a movement frequently identified as Christian (or proto-Christian) Gnosticism. Modern scholars continue to debate the relationship between Simon Magus and the early Christian Church.

A FIRST-CENTURY CHRISTIAN TIMELINE

Although scholars dispute every date for every Christian event in the first century A.D., a general timeline expressing the relative order of known events helps one think about the beginnings of Christianity. (See Figure 25-1.) Estimates for the birth of Jesus range from 12 B.C. to 7 A.D.; however, astrological events in 6 B.C. help clarify the association of visiting magi with his birth.[22] Estimates for the crucifixion usually range from 30–33 A.D. Gospel accounts suggest the beheading of John the Baptist occurred sometime from 27–32 A.D. However, underscoring the difficulty of dating events related to Christianity in the first century A.D., evidence from a non-biblical historical source[23] indicates that Herod Antipas executed John the Baptist just before the death of Tiberius in 36 A.D., at least three years after the crucifixion of Jesus.

The First Church Leadership

Nobody knows who led the followers of Jesus immediately after Jesus died, although suggestions usually focus on Peter, James the Just (the brother of Jesus), and John the son of Zebedee. Perhaps few Christians saw the need for a leader while Christianity comprised only a

---

[21]For example, see *Simon Magus: An Essay on the Founder of Simonianism Based on the Ancient Sources with a Re-evaluation of his Philosophy and Teachings* by G. R. S. Mead, part of the G. R. S. Mead Collection in the Gnostic Society Library.
[22]See Chapter 23.
[23]The controversial dating of John's death to 36 A.D. comes from a close reading of *Antiquities of the Jews* 18:5:1–3 by Josephus.

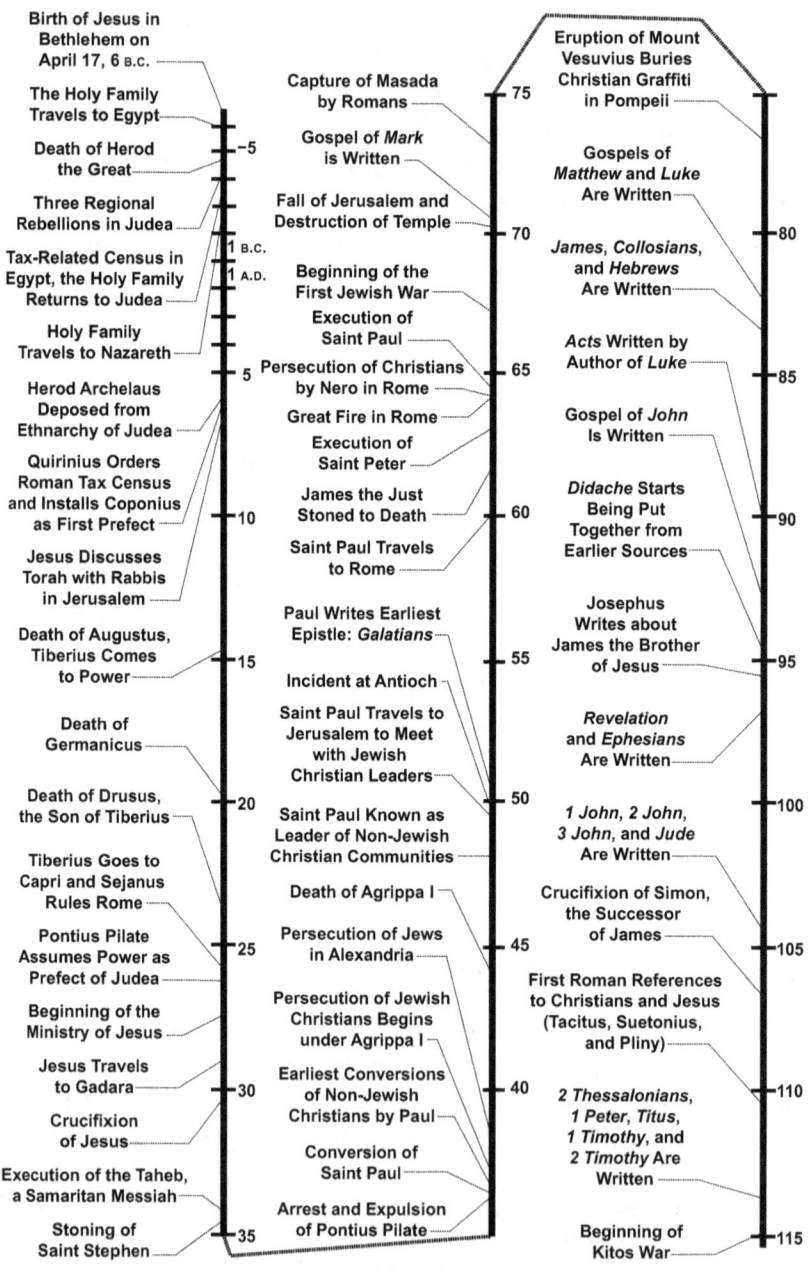

Figure 25-1. First Century A.D. Timeline of Events Related to Christianity.

small group of observant Jews; however, Christians definitely needed a leader when authorities from the Jerusalem Temple Cult began to attack them.[24] Around 34–35 A.D., following an ideological trail blazed by John the Baptist, a Christian named Stephen insulted priests of the Great Sanhedrin by proclaiming himself a witness of their infidelity to the laws of Moses as well as to their unjust treatment of Jesus, the true messiah. The Jewish officials convicted Stephen of sacrilege and ordered his execution by stoning.[25] At the time, the Greek word for witness was *martyr*. As the first person in the *New Testament* to die for his Christian beliefs, Stephen became Saint Stephen, thus beginning a shift in the meaning of martyr from a witness to someone who chose death instead of compromising his religious beliefs. As represented in the *New Testament*, Saul of Tarsos presided over Stephen's execution.[26]

A Hellenized Jew from Tarsos, Saul (renamed Paul) converted to Christianity around 36 A.D.[27] and led a hugely successful mission to the gentiles, which earned him the right to be known as Saint Paul. Operating for the most part independently from church leadership in Jerusalem, Paul became one of the most important leaders of the early Christian church. However, the various *New Testament* accounts of Paul's conversion are contradictory.[28] Some scholars question, not only the nature of Paul's role in the early Church, but also whether or not Paul ever really converted.[29]

Shortly after the stoning of Stephen and Pontius Pilate's removal from office, Caligula installed Herod Agrippa (a grandson of Herod the Great and Mariamne) as a client-king who ruled from 37–44 A.D. over

---

[24]Before Saint Paul (Saul of Tarsos) became a Christian, he was a Pharisee who assisted Jerusalem Temple authorities under the Sadducean priest Annas in the persecution of Christians. See *The Jesus Dynasty: The Hidden History of Jesus, His Royal Family, and the Birth of Christianity* pp. 260–261 and 284–287 by James Tabor.
[25]See *Acts* 7.
[26]See *Acts* 8:1.
[27]See *Jesus, the Rise of Early Christianity: A History of New Testament Times* p. 21 by Paul Barnett.
[28]See *Peter, Paul, and Mary Magdalene: The Followers of Jesus in History and Legend* pp. 96–100 by Bart D. Ehrman.
[29]For an unusual take on Paul's motives, see *Operation Messiah: St. Paul, Roman Intelligence and the Birth of Christianity* by Thijs Voskuilen and Rose Mary Sheldon. Also, see *James the Brother of Jesus: The Key to Unlocking the Secrets of Early Christianity and the Dead Sea Scrolls* by Robert H. Eisenman.

the same unified realm ruled by his grandfather, Herod the Great.[30] Having lived mostly in Rome since he was six—around the time his grandfather died in 4 B.C.—Herod Agrippa was a cosmopolitan, Hellenistic Jew who struggled to win the good will of his Judean subjects. Like a modern demagogue, he assumed a role as a patriotic defender of the Jerusalem Temple Cult and implemented policies against Jewish heretics, Christians among them.

Herod Agrippa started the world's first proactive persecution targeting Christians. One apostle lost his life[31] and many Jewish Christians abandoned Jerusalem because it grew too dangerous to worship there among non-Christian Jews. Some Jewish Christians went back to Jewish towns in Galilee, and some found new lives in Hellenistic cities like Antioch, Corinth, Damascus, Alexandria, and Rome, scattering like seeds among cities that nurtured future Christian communities. After Jerusalem, Jesus movements emerged first in Antioch and Corinth, cities associated with the leadership of Peter and Paul as well as with Jewish Christian refugees from Jerusalem. Among Christian Jews who remained in Jerusalem, leadership rested firmly with the brother of Jesus, James the Just.[32]

Opening the Church to Non-Jews

In Galilee and Judea, apocalyptic Jewish teachers like Jesus and John the Baptist had affirmed Jewish ideals and had taught their followers to resist the influx of Hellenistic culture and foreign cults. One of the earliest controversies of Christianity concerned whether or not to admit non-Jews without first requiring them to become observant Jews, that is, undergoing circumcision, purifying themselves in mikvehs, and committing to follow all Jewish laws. After declaring himself a Christian and taking his new name, the apostle Paul largely resolved this issue by initiating the first Christian mission to the gentiles. Without ever having met Jesus and without consulting Christian leaders in Jerusalem, Paul preached to pagans based solely on a vision he had while

---

[30] Herod Philip died in 34 A.D., and Caligula exiled Herod Antipas in 37 A.D.
[31] James the brother of John died "with the sword." See *Acts* 12:1–2.
[32] See *Peter, Paul, and Mary Magdalene: The Followers of Jesus in History and Legend* p. 81 by Bart D. Ehrman.

traveling on the road between Jerusalem and Damascus.[33] Paul never required pagan converts to become observant Jews.

Paul's mother originally came from Galilee, but Paul grew up in Tarsos, learning about spirituality in a Jewish community strongly influenced by Hellenistic culture and philosophy. Differences in the backgrounds of Jesus and Paul led them to seek different audiences. While Jesus of Nazareth had focused on delivering his message to Jews suffering under Roman domination, Paul, a Roman citizen, reinterpreted Christian spirituality in terms understandable to pagan audiences and preached mostly to non-Jews.

From the beginning, Paul's focus on preaching about Jesus to non-Jews was controversial.[34] Although any correspondence that existed between Paul and Christian leaders in Jerusalem has been lost, evidence shows that Jewish Christians were greatly concerned about Paul's activities.[35] In turn, Paul's letters (preserved in the *New Testament*) testify that even he had concerns about behaviors, beliefs, and practices of pagan converts in Hellenistic communities far removed from Jerusalem.[36]

Step by step during the years 37–50 A.D., competition among Christian leaders moved the Jerusalem church to make it easier for non-Jews to become Christians. Paul visited Jerusalem and began coordinating his activities with James the Just, and Peter also established a mission to the gentiles. However, establishing the most extreme position among the early Christian leaders, Paul exclusively solicited non-Jews for conversion and he required that non-Jewish converts to Christianity continue living non-Jewish lifestyles: Further, he explicitly forbade non-Jewish Christians from circumcising themselves and even from following Jewish purity laws. While visiting communities of pagan converts, Paul also "lived as if he were outside the law,"[37] which means that he, too, ignored Jewish purity laws.

---

[33]See the three differing accounts of Paul's vision in *Acts* 9, 22, and 26.
[34]See *Peter, Paul, and Mary Magdalene: The Followers of Jesus in History and Legend* pp. 112 and 164–165 by Bart D. Ehrman.
[35]See *Peter, Paul, and Mary Magdalene: The Followers of Jesus in History and Legend* pp. 89–90 by Bart D. Ehrman.
[36]See *Peter, Paul, and Mary Magdalene: The Followers of Jesus in History and Legend* p. 136 by Bart D. Ehrman.
[37]See *1 Corinthians* 9:21.

The disagreement among Peter, Paul, and James about how to deal with pagans who wanted to become Christians culminated in a historical confrontation known as the *Incident at Antioch*:[38] a violent argument between Peter and Paul about a directive from James. While the *New Testament* fails to show that the three leaders ever fully agreed, Paul's views prevailed if for no reason other than his letters on the subject survived while the letters of others were lost.[39] Eventually, even the Jerusalem church acknowledged that gentile Christians were not required to convert to Judaism.

Scholars largely disagree about the specific events that happened during this period—which leader did what, who decided important issues, and which laws actually applied to whom[40]—however, Jesus movements began spreading throughout the known world. In 47 A.D., the apostle Thomas began his mission to the East, which took him through Persia and eventually to India. In 49 A.D., the Roman emperor Claudius found it necessary to expel a number of "Jews" from Rome who "constantly made disturbances at the instigation of Chrestus."[41]

Jesus movements grew rapidly after 50 A.D. and Paul played an especially large role in establishing Christian communities that predominantly comprised non-Jewish converts. Preaching in Greek with the philosophical vocabulary of Tarsos, he taught about Christian ideas using terms connected to Mithraic beliefs and practices. To audiences familiar with salvation stories about Mithras sacrificing a divine bull, Paul taught a Jewish version of the story in which God offered his only son as an atonement sacrifice for all humanity.[42] With an urgency fueled by popular beliefs that the world soon would end, disenfranchised multitudes flocked to Christianity to obtain a share of the world to come. Even so, many Hellenistic converts to Christianity maintained affection for the pagan deities, practices, and iconography that they never completely abandoned.

---

[38] See *Galatians* 2:11–14.
[39] See *Peter, Paul, and Mary Magdalene: The Followers of Jesus in History and Legend* pp. 164–167 by Bart D. Ehrman.
[40] For example, see *Peter, Paul, and Mary Magdalene: The Followers of Jesus in History and Legend* pp. 58–60, 80–82, and 96–100 by Bart D. Ehrman.
[41] See *Lives of the Twelve Caesars, Claudius* 25:4 by Suetonius, and *Acts* 18:2.
[42] See *Peter, Paul, and Mary Magdalene: The Followers of Jesus in History and Legend* p. 143 by Bart D. Ehrman.

For downtrodden poorer classes throughout the Roman Empire, Paul lowered the bar for acquiring personal salvation by reducing the price of initiation. Just as Jews had democratized law centuries earlier by building a legal code beginning with *Ten Commandments* that applied equally to everybody, first-century Christians democratized salvation by requiring only a simple ceremony of baptism. Like worshippers of the Eastern cults of Dionysos, Atargatis, and Sabazius before them, Christians obtained strength from their faith and held fast to their beliefs even under the harshest persecutions.

When Paul traveled to Rome around 60 A.D., most members of the city's Christian community were non-Jewish converts.[43] Much of the canonized *New Testament* consists of *epistles*[44] (letters) written by Paul between 50 A.D. and 62 A.D. to largely non-Jewish congregations. By 62 A.D., when the Great Sanhedrin in Jerusalem found James the Just guilty of sacrilege and executed him by stoning, the growth of Jesus movements had slowed in communities of Jews and had accelerated in pagan communities.

Nero's Persecution of Christians and War in Judea and Galilee

In 64 A.D., Nero (the fifth Roman emperor) blamed Rome's Christian community for starting a fire that burned a significant part of central Rome. He began persecuting Christians, periodically arresting some and executing them in horrific ways. Hundreds died before Nero was deposed in 68 A.D.

According to tradition, Peter and Paul both died in Rome around 67 A.D. during one of Nero's persecutions. Roman officials beheaded Paul, executing him humanely because he was a Roman citizen; however, tradition says that they crucified Peter upside down. Today's Vatican was built over a tomb associated with Saint Peter, but his travel to Rome is far from certain. Some scholars deny that Peter ever visited

---

[43]See *Peter, Paul, and Mary Magdalene: The Followers of Jesus in History and Legend* pp. 81–83 by Bart D. Ehrman.
[44]Of the thirteen epistles associated with Paul in the *New Testament*, scholars generally agree that he wrote seven: *Romans, 1 Corinthians, 2 Corinthians, Galatians, Philippians, 1 Thessalonians,* and *Philemon*. See *Peter, Paul, and Mary Magdalene: The Followers of Jesus in History and Legend* p. 93 by Bart D. Ehrman.

Rome.[45] In 1953, an archaeologist discovered an ossuary labeled with Peter's true name, Shimon Bar Jonah, in an early Christian burial site[46] at a Franciscan monastery on the Mount of Olives in East Jerusalem. The site, called "Dominus Flevit" because of its identification as the place where Jesus wept about the fate of Jerusalem, also contained ossuaries with names associated with other famous characters from the *New Testament*, including Mary, Martha, and Lazarus.

Nero did not try to persecute Christians outside of Rome. However, in 66 A.D.,[47] more than thirty years after the crucifixion of Jesus, Jews rebelled against Rome in Judea, launching the First Jewish War. During this war, Judean rebels fought two equally vicious conflicts: one among different types of Jews and one between Jews and Romans. Generally, Jews saw themselves as patriots devoted to God. They fought other Jews over ideological differences and they fought Romans to expel impure foreigners from sacred soil. During the war, differences between Jews and Jewish Christians mattered so little that the activities of Jewish Christians were not distinguished as separate from the activities of other types of Jews.

Rome began prosecuting the First Jewish War by invading Galilee, a region famous as a source of Jewish resistance. For two years, Rome pacified Galilee by devastating it. In 68 A.D., surviving Jewish leaders fled south to Jerusalem where they intensified an already vicious, Jew against Jew, ideological war. During this second phase of the war, Roman legions focused on pacifying Judean coastal regions.

Roman politics delayed the ending of the First Jewish War. Nero committed suicide in 68 A.D., and four different men took turns being emperor in 69 A.D. The political situation of Rome was not resolved until the Roman legions in Judea acclaimed their commander, General Vespasian, as emperor. Leaving his son Titus in charge of finishing the

---

[45]See the review by James Dunn of *Petrus in Rom: die literarischen Zeugnisse. Mit einer kritischen Edition der Martyrien des Petrus und Paulus auf neuer handschriftlicher Grundlage* by Otto Zwierlein, Berlin: Walter de Gruyter, 2009, in the *Review of Biblical Literature* 2010.

[46]See *Gli Scavi del Dominus Flevit* by P. B. Bagatti and J. T. Milik, 1958, Tipografia del PP. Francescani, Jerusalem.

[47]See *The Jewish War* by Josephus.

war, he returned to Rome and successfully established the rule of a new dynasty (the *Flavians*) over the Roman Empire.

In early 70 A.D., Roman legions under Titus surrounded Jerusalem and placed the city under siege. Different Jewish factions prepared to defend Jerusalem in different ways: Jews who wanted to negotiate with Rome battled Jews who were committed to fighting Rome to their last breath. To prevent Jerusalem Jews from doing anything but fight, radical Zealots and Sicarii murdered less-radical Jewish leaders and destroyed caches of Jewish food supplies.

The Romans crucified everyone who tried to escape Jerusalem, as many as five hundred Jews a day for a period of six months. When the Romans finally overcame the last Jewish defenses at the end of July in 70 A.D., they tore down Jerusalem's famous temple and torched the city. In the chaos, the earliest Jewish Christian writings, perhaps documents written by Jesus, James the Just, and other Christian Jews mentioned in the *New Testament*, merely fed the flames. In the struggle for Jerusalem alone, over a million Jews died from famine, disease, and slaughter—many murdered at the hands of fellow Jews. The Romans sold approximately 100,000 Jews into slavery.

After the devastation of Jerusalem, a small group of Jewish rebels, possibly with Jewish Christians among them, occupied the Herodian fortress of Masada. There, they continued a token rebellion and succeeded in holding out against Rome for an additional three years. Eventually, all the Jews at Masada died.

During the chaos of the First Jewish War, the story of Jewish Christians in Judea was lost. No one knows how they divided themselves among different Jewish factions and nothing is known about who fought, where they fought, who didn't fight, and how their beliefs affected what happened to them. However, few Jewish Christians survived the war unless they fled early and found refuge in foreign lands. By the end of the war in 70 A.D., most members of the first generation of Jews who had followed Jesus and formed the backbone of the first Christian Church in Jerusalem were either dead or in exile.[48]

---

[48]Generally, 70 A.D. marks the end of the Jewish burial practice of ossilegium. See Chapter 22.

The Earliest Surviving Christian Gospels and Artifacts

Also during the years 67–70 A.D., somewhere in Roman Syria, a Hellenistic Christian with incomplete knowledge of Judaism wrote the gospel of *Mark*. Writing in Greek, his native language, and using information from sources that have not survived, the author generated a gospel for a non-Jewish audience that needed many Jewish terms and practices explained.[49] The earliest of the four canonical gospels, the gospel of *Mark* served as the principal source for the other two synoptic gospels: *Matthew* and *Luke*.

In 79 A.D., approximately 130 miles southeast of Rome, an eruption of Mount Vesuvius buried the town of Pompeii in volcanic ash and preserved the earliest known graffiti related to Christianity: an image of a man with an ass's head undergoing crucifixion, which apparently was intended to mock Christian faith in Jesus. The earliest known *SATOR Square* also was found. A rare symbol known from other examples at legionary outposts in Britain and Roman Syria, a SATOR Square combines symbols associated with both Mithraic and Christian cults.[50] SATOR Squares provide the earliest known evidence for the worship of Jesus as a solar deity among Christians in the Roman legions.

Most scholars estimate that the authors of *Matthew* and *Luke* wrote their gospels sometime between 80–85 A.D.[51] Scholars usually characterize the author of the gospel of *Matthew* as a Hellenistic, Greek-speaking, Jewish Christian who wrote for a predominantly non-Jewish audience, possibly in Antioch.[52] Scholars characterize the author of the gospel of *Luke* as a Hellenistic former pagan who wrote his gospel explicitly for a pagan Roman official, perhaps intending to persuade the official of the virtuous and harmless nature of Jesus movements.[53]

---

[49] See *The New Testament: A Historical Introduction to the Early Christian Writings*, Third edition, p. 81, by Bart D. Ehrman.
[50] See *Romans and Britons in North-West England. Lancaster: Centre for North-West Regional Studies* by David Shotter ([2004] 1993), and *The Mithraic Origin and Meanings of the ROTAS-SATOR Square* by Heinz Hofman and Walter O. Miller, (1973), in Gnomon 48 (1976), pp. 89–91.
[51] See *Jesus: Apocalyptic Prophet of the New Millennium* p. 48 by Bart D. Ehrman.
[52] See *The New Testament and Other Early Christian Writings: A Reader* p. 9 by Bart D. Ehrman.
[53] See *The New Testament and Other Early Christian Writings: A Reader* p. 60 by Bart D. Ehrman.

Both gospels are notable for connecting the birth of Jesus with astrological prophecy.

Written from 90–95 A.D., the gospel of *John* was the last canonical gospel to be written.[54] Distinctly different from the synoptic gospels, the gospel of *John* emphasized evidence that indicated Jesus was God. Scholars believe that the Hellenistic Christian who wrote the gospel was thoroughly familiar with Jewish culture. However, the gospel reflects a profoundly anti-Jewish (anti-Judean?) stance,[55] possibly related to a new round of persecutions. Domitian initiated persecutions during the later years of his reign from 95–96 A.D., either targeting Christians[56] or targeting Jews without distinguishing Christians as members of a separate cult. Either way, he focused primarily on persecuting upper-class Romans who had abandoned traditional pagan worship for what he described as believing in Jewish atheism and practicing Jewish customs.

New non-Jewish Christian communities developed their own understandings of what it meant to believe in Jesus. No authoritative Christian doctrine existed and no person or council specified the beliefs and practices that distinguished true Christian worship from heresy. Consistent with the changing demographics of Christians, Pagan beliefs, practices, and iconography changed the look and feel of Christian worship from something Jewish to something non-Jewish. During the first century A.D., few Jewish Christians illustrated Bible stories with pictures;[57] however, restrictions against images in Jewish law did not apply to pagan converts who already possessed a rich graphic language for expressing religious beliefs.

For example, the first century A.D. lead plaque in Figure 25-2 portrays iconography associated with a Celtic cult that had been worshipped for centuries along the Danube River. Jews never used Celtic iconography. However, the application of pagan iconography to Christian worship makes images on the plaque look remarkably Christian to modern eyes: The risen Jesus wears a solar crown, horsemen honor the

---

[54]See *Jesus: Apocalyptic Prophet of the New Millennium* p. 48 by Bart D. Ehrman.
[55]See *The Complete Gospels* pp.196–197 edited by Robert J. Miller.
[56]The claims mostly are based on conflicting interpretations of *Roman History* 67.14.1–2 by Cassius Dio.
[57]As an important exception, see Chapter 24, note 139.

Figure 25-2. Lead Votive Plaque for Cult of the Danubian Rider Cult. Roman, Early Imperial Period, First Century A.D. Artifact in the Museum of Fine Arts, Boston.

Virgin Mary, a Christian cross stands halfway between Jesus and the Virgin Mary, several fish represent Christianity, a group of worshippers attend a Christian meal, Adam and Eve walk naked in the Garden of Eden, Eve picks fruit from a tree at the bidding of a serpent-monster, and so on. Nevertheless, the plaque is not Christian. It expresses purely pagan iconography representing lost mythological stories from an influential Danubian cult that merged Celtic solar worship with the

Hellenistic Cult of Mithras.[58] At the beginning of the second century A.D., having incorporated images, concepts, and practices from pagan cults, Jesus movements were well positioned to grow and shatter into a thousand pieces.

INNOVATIONS IN CHRISTIAN STORY, ICONOGRAPHY, AND PRACTICE

Immediately after the death of Jesus, the first Christians worshipped as Jews and did not yet follow all the practices that eventually characterized Christian worship. As a Jew from Nazareth in Galilee, Jesus wore knotted fringes called *tzitzit* on his clothing and he sometimes prayed wearing special frontlets called *tefillin*,[59] but Christians eventually dropped these practices. By the end of the First Jewish War in 70 A.D., around the time when the earliest canonical gospel (*Mark*) was completed, most Christians understood that their survival depended on their identification as loyal Roman members of a non-Jewish cult. Jesus movements spread and shifted profoundly in character such that, by the end of the first century A.D., most Christians understood pagan cults better than they understood Jewish laws and traditions, and Christian worship had incorporated many pagan elements.

Rome dealt with additional Jewish rebellions from 115–117 A.D. and 132–135 A.D. During this terrible period, Jewish cults associated with Jesus—Jews who worshipped as Jesus did—largely died a violent death. Influenced by the horrific war of 66–70 A.D. that destroyed the Jerusalem Temple, a new generation of mostly non-Jewish Christians embraced writings that disassociated Christians from rebellious Jews in Judea. From 115–117 A.D., diaspora Jews rebelled in Cyrene, Cyprus, Egypt, and Mesopotamia (called the Kitos War), which further inflamed popular Roman opinion against Jews. Then, after the

---

[58]As early as 500 B.C., the Dacian Rider Cult used the icon of a horseman spearing a monster, which is recognizable to Christian eyes as an icon of *Saint George and the Dragon*. During the Hellenistic age (after 300 B.C.) the cult acquired Mithraic elements and developed the iconography that appears on the plaque.

[59]Biblical commandments to wear tzitzit and to pray wearing tefillin appear in *Numbers* 15:38 and *Deuteronomy* 6:8.

Bar Kokhba Revolt in Judea from 132–136 A.D., Rome attempted to expunge Jewish religious practices from the earth.[60] Judea was renamed *Syria Palaestina*, Jerusalem was re-founded as a Hellenistic polis, and Jews were forbidden to enter Jerusalem except on the day that commemorated the destruction of the Jerusalem Temple. For Christians, demonizing Jews was a better choice than clinging to Jewish roots.

Sometimes, pagans and Jews sided with each other against Christians, agreeing that Christians offended common decency with sacrilegious acts and words. To many pagans, Christians were only slightly different from Jews and the differences expressed themselves in unattractive ways: Christians often asserted that Roman gods actually were demons and that Jesus would return soon to conquer the Roman Empire. Also, to many Jews, claims by Christians about the divine status of Jesus sounded disturbingly like heresy.

However, Christians struggled to distance themselves from Jews and to appear more Roman. Gospel stories of Jesus portrayed his teachings as largely consistent with Roman life and values, emphasizing the differences between Christians and Jews and strengthening the case for Christians to ignore Jewish laws. To the extent that Jesus held negative opinions about Hellenized Roman culture, Christians failed to preserve them. Hellenistic images graphically reinterpreted biblical history, and Christian experiments with healing and magic attracted increasing numbers of non-Jewish pagans to the worship of Jesus.

Fabricating Scripture

Looking only at the four canonical gospels, many stories about Jesus bear internal evidence of fabrication by non-Jewish writers. For example, Jesus of Galilee would have quoted and debated passages from Hebrew scripture, but the canonical gospels show him quoting statements with peculiarities that appear only in the *Septuagint*.[61] Although it remains possible that Jesus used variants of Hebrew scriptures that

---

[60]In general, Christians suffered far less under Rome than worshippers of any other persecuted religious group. However, Jews suffered the most: In the century after the crucifixion of Jesus in 33 A.D., Romans killed more than a million Jews.

[61]See *The New Testament: A Historical Introduction to the Early Christian Writings*, Third Edition, p. 38, by Bart D. Ehrman.

have not survived to modern times, it's far more likely that Greek-speaking Christians—Hellenistic Jewish Christians and converted pagans—never intended the gospels to serve as factual archives of words and events related to the life of Jesus. Instead, each gospel expressed a living reinterpretation of Jesus suited to the time, place, and community for which the gospel was written.

By the time that Roman authorities canonized a set of Christian scriptures in the fourth century A.D., all the texts chosen for inclusion in the *New Testament* had undergone complicated processes of accidental and intentional adjustment. Modern scholarship has proven that whole books in the *New Testament* were forged by unknown authors who successfully passed their writings as if they carried the authority, for example, of Saint Paul.[62] Also, needing to differentiate their cults from opposing Christian cults, many early Christian leaders opportunistically adjusted *New Testament* texts to promote specific points of view.[63] Perhaps most troublesome of all, however, early Christianity's origins among a multitude of grassroots movements with many poorly educated followers meant that numerous poor copyists produced many flawed documents, which resulted in the creation of far more variations of surviving *New Testament*s than there are words in the *New Testament*.[64] Regardless of how the changes originally occurred, over time, the accumulated changes in gospels tended to reflect important long-term Christian agendas, such as diminishing the authority of women, sanitizing the role of Rome in the death of Jesus, and justifying the separation of Christians and Jews.[65]

While most textual differences reflect irrelevant spelling errors, others have shaped important Christian understandings. For example, the

---

[62]Many scholars believe that six of the thirteen books attributed to Paul in the *New Testament* were written by people who wanted to attach Paul's authority to their ideas. See *Forged: Writing in the Name of God—Why the Bible's Authors Are Not Who We Think They Are* pp.92–93 by Bart D. Ehrman.
[63]See *Misquoting Jesus: The Story Behind Who Changed the Bible and Why* pp. 170–175 by Bart D. Ehrman.
[64]For a discussion of this point, see *Misquoting Jesus: The Story Behind Who Changed the Bible and Why* p. 90 by Bart D. Ehrman.
[65]For a brief discussion of anti-Jewish adjustments to *Matthew* 27:24–25, see *Misquoting Jesus: The Story behind Who Changed the Bible and Why* pp. 183–194 by Bart D. Ehrman. The book also surveys numerous difficulties associated with identifying the original texts of *New Testament* scriptures.

only explicit delineation of the *trinity* (the division of God into the *Father*, the *Son*, and the *Holy Ghost*) that appears in the *New Testament* comes from the Latin *Vulgate Bible*[66] and does not appear in earlier, better Greek texts.[67] Aware of the problem, Christian scholars in the sixteenth century manufactured a Greek source text to match the Latin text in the *Vulgate Bible*: The church preferred to forge a new Greek source that explicitly supported official church beliefs rather than assemble the most authentic Greek source possible and accurately translate it into Latin. Bearing scars from this period of particularly shoddy and manipulative scholarship, the *King James Bible* comes from a sixteenth century Greek *New Testament* assembled inaccurately from some of the poorest Greek sources available at that time.[68] However, modern recognition of numerous problems in the text has not diminished the status of the poetic *King James Bible*: Modern English-speaking Christians often believe that its text represents the unaltered word of God.

During the second century A.D., some Christians announced new prophecies, some wrote new scriptures, and some led their followers in strange new varieties of worship. Christian leaders became increasingly concerned about the great variety of cults that continued to emerge, each claiming to represent the original teachings of Jesus. In Gnostic cults, spiritual masters spoke of a female divinity named Sophia, sometimes associated with the Holy Spirit; they rejected the world and the god of the Jews as evil; and they taught Christian *gnosis*, or knowledge, in stages that led to worshippers actually becoming Christ.[69] In *Montanist* cults (cults based on the beliefs of the second century Phrygian priest named Montanus), spiritual leaders urged worshippers to find God through asceticism, martyrdom, and ecstatic experiences.[70]

---

[66]The Latin *Vulgate Bible* was translated from Greek by Saint Jerome in the fourth century A.D.
[67]To see textual manipulation associated with church policy about the trinity compare *I John* 5:7–8 in the *King James Bible* with *I John* 5:7–8 in the *Jerusalem Bible*.
[68]See *Misquoting Jesus: The Story Behind Who Changed the Bible and Why* pp. 78–83 by Bart D. Ehrman.
[69]See *The Gnostic Gospels* pp. 134–135 by Elaine Pagels. Also, see the translation of *Pistis Sophia* by G. R. S. Mead.
[70]See *The Earliest Christian Heretics: Readings from their Opponents* pp. 127–135 edited by Arland J. Hultgren and Steven A. Haggmark.

Perhaps most horrifying of all to modern sensibilities, a cult called the *Phibionites* worshipped God with sexual orgies, performing an obscene Eucharist ceremony that treated semen and menstrual blood as the body and blood of Jesus Christ.[71]

For Christians in the second century A.D., the tumultuous events in Judea during the previous century were important only as local color for the story of Jesus. Unaware of Judean politics and the long history of cults that had offered salvation over many centuries, Christian writers portrayed the prospect of heaven as an unprecedented possibility that magically appeared by the grace of a god who had cleansed himself from involvement with Jews. More concerned about advantageously promoting their beliefs than about accurately preserving history, they ignored what happened before Augustus and projected second century realities into forged first century scriptures. For example, *Titus*, a pastoral epistle in the *New Testament*, pretended authorship by Paul while projecting church issues and administrative structures from the second century A.D. into the first century A.D.[72] Ambitiously recreating history, many Christian leaders aggressively pruned, shaped, and transplanted Christian traditions onto conveniently manufactured roots.

By the late second century, most Christians identified the four canonical gospels (*Matthew*, *Mark*, *Luke*, and *John*) as the most important of all gospels. However, many Christians still preferred different gospels. Christians began speaking of Christianity as a "religion," a broad umbrella that embraced acceptable cults and excluded unacceptable cults.[73] Paradoxically, the invention of Christian religion simultaneously invented the "religions" of Judaism and paganism. Christians identified all pagan cults as instances of unacceptable paganism, all non-Christian Jewish cults became Judaism, and unacceptable Christian cults became heresies.

---

[71]See *Lost Christianities: The Battles for Scripture and the Faiths We Never Knew* pp. 198–201 by Bart D. Ehrman.
[72]See *The New Testament: A Historical Introduction to the Early Christian Writings*, Third Edition, pp. 388–391, by Bart D. Ehrman.
[73]The first broad identification of religion as a collection of disparate cults occurred during the early third century A.D. in the writings of Tertullian, a Carthaginian Montanist known as the father of Latin Christianity and the founder of Western theology. See "Judaism—Back to Basics" by Professor Steve Mason in *Biblical Archaeology Review*, Vol. 35, No. 6.

Figure 25-3. A Hellenistic Interpretation of Noah and His Ark Appears on This Coin's Reverse, One of the Earliest Christian Numismatic Images. Phrygia, Apamea, Gordian III. AE 39, ca. 238–244 A.D.

The Hellenization of Christian Iconography

The *New Testament* provides ample evidence that early Christianity assimilated elements of Pythagorean mysticism, Platonic philosophy, Zoroastrian beliefs, and Mithraic cosmology. In addition, the earliest Christian iconography reveals connections with pagan mythology. In literature and art, early Christians Hellenized Semitic metaphors, often portraying scenes from *Old Testament* stories with iconography from Greek myths. For example, the coin in Figure 25-3 shows a picture of Noah and his wife, not in an ark of the dimensions described in *Genesis*, but in a "casket" like the one that carried Deucalion and Pyrrha in Greek flood myths. The appearance of Hellenistic Christian images[74] on early third-century coins indicates a broad acceptance of Christian religious beliefs in many Roman cities long before the reign of Constantine.

Hellenized iconography also reveals close connections between Christians and Eastern cults. For example, excavations beneath Saint Peter's basilica in the Vatican uncovered a chapel floor mosaic with

---

[74] The numismatic images of Noah's Ark match images on early Christian sarcophagi (as in Figure 25-5, for example) in the Vatican collection portraying the ark as a casket like the one that carried Deucalion and Pyrrha.

Chapter 25 | The Birth of a Thousand Cults 667

Figure 25-4. Hellenistic Christian Images of Jesus and Sophia on a Christian Sarcophagus from the Third Century A.D. Vatican Collection of Early Christian Art.

an early image of Jesus: Portrayed as Sol Invictus, Jesus wears a radiate solar crown and drives a four-horse chariot.[75] Sharing iconography, non-Jewish Christianity and Hellenistic Mithraism cooperated, competed, and grew during the second century A.D.[76] Both cults attracted worshippers among the soldiers in Rome's legions who facilitated dispersal of the cults throughout the Roman Empire as well as potentiating each cult's influence on the other.[77]

The earliest Christian images of Jesus Christ portrayed him as a beardless young man (that is, not a bearded Jew) who resembled the cultic god, Attis. For example, an image of Jesus as the "Good Shepherd"[78] appears on the sarcophagus in Figure 25-4. Seated in the left panel of sarcophagus, the deceased man reads Christian scripture. Two

---

[75]The mosaic dates no later than 240 A.D. See "Tracing the Spread of Early Christianity through Coins" by Stanley A. Hudson in *Bible Review*, Fall 1985, pp. 34–44.
[76]See *The Cults of the Roman Empire* pp. 203–207 by Robert Turcan.
[77]For example, the house of Paquo Procolo (retired with citizenship from service in Rome's legions) in Pompeii (a town buried by an eruption of Mt. Vesuvius in 79 A.D.) contained the world's oldest known SATOR Square, a controversial symbol found in legionary contexts from Dura Europus to Hadrian's Wall and associated variously by scholars with Christianity, Judaism, Egyptian cults, and Roman legionary worship of Sol Invictus. In his video series *The Secrets of Christianity* Simcha Jacobovici showed that the house and bakery of Paquo Procolo also contained other Christian symbols, including a fish symbol and a cross.
[78]Worshippers of Attis also referred to him as the "Good Shepherd."

Figure 25-5. Third Century Christian Sarcophagus with Hellenistic Images of Adam and Eve, the Ten Commandments, Nativity, Noah, Jonah, and Moses Striking a Rock. Vatican Collection of Early Christian Art.

other men support and guide the deceased man toward spiritual truth. Also supported by a friend, the wife of the deceased man sits in the right panel of the sarcophagus. On either side of Jesus, the Tree of Life and the Tree of Knowledge stand in the background. Jesus carries a lamb and silently watches as the woman next to him speaks. An unfamiliar figure to modern Christians, the speaking woman represents Sophia (Wisdom). In Gnostic Christianity, Sophia personified the wisdom of the soul that guided all spiritual seekers to eternal life through the discovery of Jesus Christ within them.

Carved in the third century A.D., the sarcophagus in Figure 25-5 provides a Hellenistic overview of important biblical figures. In the top left panel, the sculptor carved nude images of Adam and Eve like semi-divine figures from Greece's mythological Golden Age—no comparable nude portrayals of Adam and Eve exist in ancient Jewish art. To the right of Adam and Eve, Moses receives the Ten Commandments, the tablets surrounded by a Zoroastrian-style nimbus (halo).

Chapter 25 | The Birth of a Thousand Cults   669

Figure 25-6. Religious Amulets from the Third Century A.D. Left: Pagan Amulet Portraying the Crucifixion of Orpheus/Bacchus, Berlin Museum. Right: Gnostic Christian Amulet Portraying Abrasax.

To the right of Moses, three magi dressed like Zoroastrian astrologers bring gifts to Mary and Jesus, who resemble Egyptian portrayals of Isis and Harpokrates. Angels portrayed as Greek Eroti (cupids) frame an empty panel prepared to carry the name of the deceased. On the right half of the sarcophagus (the lower half of Figure 25-5), a raven brings Noah evidence of land as he floats in a casket like Deucalion. Next, a Ketos-style sea-monster consumes, and then disgorges Jonah. On the far right, the sculptor portrays a classical figural criticism of Judaism: Moses reveals the insufficiency of Jewish faith by striking a rock to get water rather than trusting God to make water flow from it.[79]

Some pagan iconography looked Christian and some Christian iconography looked pagan. From the second century A.D., well before the time that Christians broadly adopted the crucifix in their standard iconography, the amulet[80] on the left in Figure 25-6 portrays the god Orpheus/Bacchus crucified like Jesus: This crucifix was a pagan image.

---
[79] See *Numbers* 20:11–13.
[80] A photo of this artifact originally appeared on the cover of *The Jesus Mysteries* by Timothy Freke and Peter Gandy.

Figure 25-7. Alexandrian Coins from the Second Century A.D. with Symbols Reflecting Christian Influence.

From the same period, the amulet on the right portrayed a rooster-headed, snake-legged, scorpion-footed symbol of the Gnostic deity Abrasax: This pagan-looking symbol represented the good god that Gnostic Christians worshipped in opposition to the evil god (Yahweh) worshipped by Jews.

In its first few centuries, Christianity incorporated features from other cults, and other cults adopted Jesus Christ as just another new god in their Hellenistic pantheon. In Alexandria, some Christians believed in Serapis and Isis, and some worshippers of Serapis and Isis believed in Jesus Christ. Figure 25-7 shows second-century Egyptian coins with odd combinations of Christian and pagan symbols. On the top coin, a bust of Serapis accompanies a lamb and a star, pagan

Figure 25-8. Roman Coin Honoring the Isis Festival. Rome, AE 18, ca. Mid-4th Century A.D.

astrological iconography that recalls Paul's comparison of Zeus (hence, Serapis) with God,[81] the common portrayal of Jesus as the Lamb of God,[82] and the appearance of the Star of Bethlehem at the nativity. On the lower coin, Isis holds a lamb, symbolically equivalent to Mary holding the infant Jesus. While overtly pagan, the images on these coins show that some Egyptian officials in the second century A.D. attempted to use numismatic iconography acceptable to both Christian and pagan segments of Egyptian society.

As another example of how the infusion of pagan material enriched Christianity, the Roman coin in Figure 25-8 honored the annual festival of Isis called *Carrus Navalis*. In this festival, worshippers dressed in costumes of Egyptian gods and welcomed Isis' arrival by sea. Then, celebrating with music and dance, they paraded idols of Isis and other Egyptian gods through the streets of Rome. Minted in a period when Christianity was becoming the dominant religion of Rome, the coin

---

[81] In *Acts* 17:28, Paul refers to God quoting from a prayer to Zeus in the *Phaenomena* by Aratus.

[82] As an unconscious memory of the pagan practice of criobolium, baptism in the blood of a lamb or goat (similar to taurobolium, see Chapter 21), Christians still refer to finding salvation through Jesus as being "washed in the blood of the lamb."

bears a reverse that portrays Isis as the mother of Horus/Harpokrates, the ancient Egyptian symbol that gave rise to modern images of the Madonna and child. Jews had no iconographgy or celebration comparable to Carrus Navalis. Echoes of the pagan holiday still survive in Christian celebrations of *Carnival* and *Mardi Gras*.

Magic and Witchcraft in Early Christianity

Most modern Christian histories assert the superiority of Christianity over paganism largely because Christians condemned superstition, magic, and witchcraft.[83] However, Romans also condemned superstition, magic, and witchcraft: They had pioneered the use of accusations of superstition and witchcraft to justify persecutions of Dionysian cults in 186 B.C., Sabazian and Jewish cults in 139 B.C., and Syrian cults on Sicily in 132 B.C. Non-Christian Romans thought of Jesus as nothing more than a magician or sorcerer.[84] Furthermore, some Roman civic authorities persecuted Christian communities precisely because Christian religious beliefs had a reputation for encouraging immorality, superstition, magic, and witchcraft.[85]

Regardless of official Christian proscriptions against divination and witchcraft, the boundaries between Christianity, astrology, and magic have not always been clear. Romans found ample evidence for Christian beliefs in magic and witchcraft in descriptions of the miracles performed by Jesus as documented in Christian gospels. In addition, the announcement of the birth of Jesus by the Star of Bethlehem connected Christianity inseparably with astrology.

---

[83]In Book VIII of *The City of God*, Saint Augustine of Hippo (354–430 A.D.) distinguished between miracles and magic and used the distinction to claim of superiority of Christianity over paganism. At first used to battle paganism, Saint Augustine's writings eventually justified the denunciation of witches and witchcraft.
[84]See *Against Celsus* I 28 and 68, II 32 and 48f, by Origen.
[85]For a description of Roman persecutions of the Christians of Lyons in 177 A.D. for practicing black magic, see *The Enemy Within: 2,000 Years of Witch-Hunting in the Western World* pp. 7–13 by John Demos. Romans persecuted Christian clergy from 235–238 A.D. for teaching immorality and superstition, and Romans persecuted Christians from 250–261 for causing a plague (the same reason that Christians used to persecute Jews in the 14th century).

Figure 25-9. Jesus Watches God Create Adam and Eve with a Magic Wand, and Three Zoroastrian Astrologers Bring Gifts to Mary and Jesus. Vatican Collection of Early Christian Art.

An early Christian sarcophagus in the Vatican portrays both astrology and magic. (See Figure 25-9.) Three Zoroastrian magi bring gifts to the Madonna and child. Pointing to a star, one of the magi—an astrologer—explicitly connects astrology with the birth of Jesus. Between the magi and Adam and Eve, two men—God and his son Jesus—illustrate God's use of magic to create Adam and Eve in the Garden of Eden. As his son watches, God uses a magic wand first to create Adam, and then to create Eve from Adam's side. After their creation, Adam and Eve stand next to God and Jesus, nude, obedient, and unashamed. On this sarcophagus, magic and astrology appear as the most important elements of Christian faith.

Early Christian fathers condemned superstition and magic precisely because some early Christians included these practices as part of their Christian worship. Viewed as cutting-edge philosophy and technology during the early centuries of the first millennium, magic entered every religious community: pagan, Jewish, Christian, Zoroastrian, and more. Modern archaeology has long documented magical charms, beads, and inscriptions connected with early Christians. For example, a burial in Denmark, dated approximately 300 A.D., contained a carved glass bead, a magical Christian amulet that is preserved in the National

Museum of Denmark. The bead carries an anchor symbol[86] associated with early Christianity as well as the word "ABLATHANALBA,"[87] a magical word like "ABRACADABRA." This amulet proves that Christian material and influence reached the edges of the known world by 300 A.D. even as it provides evidence for a long relationship between Christians and magic.

Attempting to rein in superstition and combat heresies, early Christian fathers expanded the hierarchies and powers of church authorities, which facilitated unification and enforcement of policies in Christian communities. Creatively extending church authority into personal beliefs and private behavior, Christians developed new tools for discovery of disobedience to rules. New requirements to confess[88] and to submit to temporal church authority turned Christianity into a powerful social force that the most influential Roman civic authorities simply could not match, a social force just waiting to be harnessed by an inspired Roman leader.

A VITAL BLEND OF PAGAN AND SEMITIC IDEAS

At its core, modern Christianity affirms ideas about salvation broadly comparable to ideas espoused by Hellenistic cults. Centuries before the birth of Jesus, pagans worshipped gods whose death and resurrection gave humanity access to a blessed eternal life. Isis, the universal mother goddess, adapted easily to the role of Mary, the mother of Jesus. Mary gave birth to Jesus on December 25, the same great day

---

[86]In March of 2007 while going through archived material from a Danish burial mound dated ca. 300 A.D., Peter Pentz, archaeologist and curator for the National Museum of Denmark in Copenhagen, recognized that the anchor carved on the amulet was an early Christian symbol.

[87]"ABLATHANALBA" can be translated as "You are our father." The artifact is related to teachings of Basilides, an Alexandrian teacher of Gnosticism in the early second century A.D. In his *Homilies on Luke* 1.1, Origen said that Basilides wrote a gospel.

[88]Written around the end of the first century A.D., the *Didache* (14.1 and 4.14) calls for individuals to confess in the congregation. Also, in *De Lapsis* Chapter 39, Saint Cyprian (Bishop of Carthage from 250–258 A.D.) established confession as a method for Christians who chose not to face martyrdom to return to the church: "Let each confess his sin while he is still in this world, while his confession can be received, while satisfaction and the forgiveness granted by the priests is acceptable to God."

that other virgin goddesses bore solar deities[89] like Mithras, Dusares, Baal-Hammon, etc. Like worshippers of Attis, modern Christians celebrate the possibilities of resurrection and eternal life by decorating evergreen trees; like worshippers of Astarte (Eoster), Christians honor procreation and salvation during Easter, a festival that still bears the goddess' name; and like worshippers of Eleusinian mysteries, Christians perform passion plays honoring the death and resurrection of a savior who offered salvation to all mankind. Some early church fathers even castrated themselves[90] like priests of Cybele. Many ideas about salvation from Greek, Semitic, and Eastern traditions converged easily in Christian cults centered on the death and resurrection of Jesus.

From a historical point of view, little evidence survived about Christian development and diversification in the first century A.D. Much more information survived from the second century, particularly about the disagreements among different types of Christian communities. Then, in the third century A.D., guidance from strong leaders through conflict and persecutions produced the beginnings of Christianity's most important expressions of canon and theology. By the beginning of the fourth century, Christianity began to look very similar to the religion we know today.

Throughout the Roman Empire, metaphors from Eastern cults facilitated the discussion of Christian ideas about salvation in already familiar terms. None of the Jewish disciples of Jesus associated him with the return of the sun after the winter solstice; but claims about his resurrection meant that well-developed metaphorical language about resurrection lay within easy reach of new Christians who converted from pagan cults. All of the original followers of Jesus—poor

---

[89]Reported by Dr. Rami Arav (Director of Excavations and Research, Bethsaida Excavations Project) the earliest cross associated with emerging Christianity in a wine-maker's house in Bethsaida dating to the first century A.D. The cross bears a circular symbol in its center strongly suggesting a solar association. Jesus performed two miracles in Bethsaida and three disciples were born there. Later, the city was given to Herod Philip who renamed it Julias after Augustus' daughter.

[90]*Matthew* 19:12 states, "For there are eunuchs who have been so from birth, and there are eunuchs who have been made eunuchs by men, and there are eunuchs who have made themselves eunuchs for the sake of the kingdom of heaven. Let the one who is able to receive this receive it." The most famous early church father to castrate himself was the Egyptian scholar, Origen (185–254 A.D.), who helped create the list of Christian documents that ultimately were included in the *New Testament*.

and oppressed Jews in Galilee and Judea—opposed Rome's Cult of the Emperor and resisted worshipping Caesar as god; however, as Christianity became more Roman, language that Augustus had used to convince Romans of his divinity begged to be reinterpreted and placed in service to Jesus Christ.

Offering salvation from imminent apocalypse, Christian cults connected the powerful Jewish literary traditions of Jerusalem and Alexandria with the best features of the most advanced Eastern cults. Achieving wide popularity, Christianity attracted pagan converts who imported their favorite beliefs and blended Semitic ideas with Hellenistic science, mysteries, and respect for miracles. The veneration of Mary and maintenance of purity through sexual abstinence[91]—practices related to cults of Isis—entered Christianity along with pagans long accustomed to worshipping Eastern goddesses. However, Jewish literary traditions and the *Old Testament*[92] prevented Christianity from becoming just another Hellenistic cult featuring a solar deity borne of a virgin.

By 313 A.D., Christianity had acquired enough substance, structure, and political power to form a useful alliance with Constantine the Great, a great Roman general struggling to unite and control the Eastern and Western halves of the Roman Empire. After Constantine defeated all rivals and successfully asserted dominance over a reconstituted Roman Empire, he proclaimed tolerance for all cults,[93] specifically granting Christians full authority to worship unhindered throughout the Roman Empire. Because of Constantine, the cross obtained universal recognition as an important Christian symbol.[94] Christians succeeded in unifying and promoting their religion sufficiently such that, by the end of the fourth century, Christianity became not just a highly favored religion in the Roman Empire but the compulsory religion of

---

[91] During an age when fathers and husbands controlled women, voluntarily choosing a life of sexual abstinence offered women the possibility of more control over their lives.
[92] The last books to enter the *Old Testament* were canonized in the context of parallel developments in Christianity and Pharisaic Judaism during the first three centuries A.D.
[93] Constantine the Great formally legalized Christianity in the *Edict of Milan* issued in 313 A.D.
[94] In the *Companion Bible*, Appendix 162, Dr. E. W. Bullinger suggested that the Cross of Constantine actually derived from a symbol associated with Tammuz, a Babylonian solar deity.

the Roman state. From then on, pagans and Jews suffered at the whims of Christian rulers.

The broad historical path along which Christianity developed is littered with bodies of lost cults; and histories written by winners of political, economic, and social wars have long hidden authentic Christian roots. Successful establishment of central religious authorities governing Christianity ensured the cleansing of historical records that preserved authentic Christian origins along with the destruction of divergent points of view. Poorly documented beginnings then allowed church officials to create the history that they wanted.

Under Constantine the Great, church history became a Roman history that hid Christian beginnings while pretending to speak of them. Only history of the emperor's cult mattered and nothing earlier than the birth of Jesus possessed any relevance whatsoever. Regardless, archaeology, numismatics, and history are slowly recovering pieces of a larger and more complex story that began much earlier than the birth of Jesus. Today, it is no longer possible to deny the secret roots of Christianity.

INDEX

Page numbers in italics indicate illustrations or graphics, n indicates a note, and *m* indicates a map.

Aaron, 637
Abraham, 8
Abrasax, Gnostic deity, 310, 670
Aceso, Goddess of Healing Processes, 98
Achelous
　myth of, 44–46
　visit to Sicily, 52–53
Achelous River, 44–45
Achilles and his mother, Thetis, *131*
Acrisius, King of Argos, 277, 278
Actium, Battle of, 490–493, 496, 518, 541
Adam, meaning earth, 158
Adam and Eve, 119n.6, 158, *660*, *668*, *673*
Adar, Phoenician cult of, 55
Adiabene, 533
Adonis, lover of Atargatis, 172
Adon or Adonai, 170, 172
Adranos, river god, *55*
　Sicilian cult of, 55
Adrastus, King of Argos, 95n.11
Aduatuci, Gallic tribe, 390
Aecus, King of Aegina, 87, 87n.4
Aedui tribe, France, 403–404, *404*
Aegates Islands, Battle of the, 228
Aegean Sea, 155*m*
Aegestes, child of Segesta, 64
　and dogs, *65*
Aegipan, son of Zeus, 24
Aegira, Greece, 490, 491
Aegis (shield), 31
Aelianus, Claudius, 55n.7
Aeneas, Trojan prince, 40, *133*, 255, 316
　progenitor of Roman race, 64, 239
　son of Venus, 64, 316
Aeneid (Virgil), 133, 133n.9
Aeolian Islands, 7
Aeolus, King of Thessaly, 48, 49, *49*, 52
Aetolian League, 241, 241n.8, 242
Afghanistan, 168, 187

Afterlife, belief in, 530
　in Zoroastrian view, 144–145
Agamemnon, 491
　and Briseis, 131
　in Trojan War, 131
Agathocles, Tyrant of Syracuse, 226, 227, 231–232
Agdistis, 194, 195, 196, 247
Agenor, King of Tyre, 84, 85
Age of Taurus, 291–293
Ages, 152
Aglaea (Brilliance), of the three charities, 98
Agnosticism, 222
Agriculture, secrets of, 71
Agrigento, 22, 41
Agrippa, military commander, 474, 476, 492–494
　death of, 502
　Julia and, 515, 519
Agrippina the Elder, daughter of Agrippa, 570, 580, 581
Ahura Mazda, *171*, 191
　creator of universe, 142, 266n.3, 267
　equivalent to Zeus, 270, 272
　god of the Zoroastrians, 265–266
　as good, 144–145, 170, 170n.4
　good God of Light, 268
　as Mithra, 142, 144, 266, 267, 268, 277
　spirits of, 142, 143, 174, 266n.3, 267
　twin of Angra Mainyu, 142, 143, 267
　worship of, 170, 243
Ahuras, good spirits, 142, 145
Aitolia, Greek state, 44
Ajax, Locrian hero, 134, *135*
Akarnania, Greek state, 44, 108
Akeldama, tombs of, 625–626
Akhenaten, Pharaoh of Egypt, 180, 180n.22
Akragas, Sicily (Agrigento), 13*m*, 41, 91

679

Akrai, 233
Alcaeus, 114. *See also* Herakles, Greek god
　as baby Herakles, 112, *113*
　name changed to Herakles, 116
　son of Perseus, 108, 110
Alcmene, mother of Herakles, 107, 109, 110, 111, 112
Alesia, Gaul, 404, 405
Alexander Helios, son of Antony and Cleopatra, 470, 485, 498
Alexander III (the Great) of Macedon, 85, 221, 499, 504
　compared with other leaders, 221, 358, 373, 413, 439, 476
　conquest of Persian Empire, 167, 168–169, 171, 182–187
　crowned Pharaoh in Egypt, 187
　death of, and aftermath, 165, 168, 187–188, 192n.7, 193–196, 218, 219, 265, 281, 453
　deification of, 191, 250
　genealogy of, 361
　as Herakles, *185*
　images of, 168, 183, *192*
　and Jewish culture, 168, 172
　King of Macedon, 183
　merger of Eastern and Western culture under, 146, 167, 168
　military exploits of, 189
　scope of influence, 167–188, 371
　son of Zeus/Amon, 187, *192*
　timeline of his life, 183, *184*
Alexandria, cities named, 167, 167n.1, 197, 373
Alexandria, Egypt, 250, 538
　Antony's triumph in, 485
　cultural center, 499
　and defeat of Antony and Cleopatra, 493, 495–497
　expectation of a messiah in, 516
　fall of, 497–500
　Great Library of, 203, 211, 214, 425n.5
　Hellenistic Jews in, 530
　invaded by Octavian, 496
Alexandrian coins, *670–671*
Alexandrian Greeks, 200–201
Alexandrian War, Egypt, 424–426, 427
Alexandropolis, 182
Algeria, 514
Alpheios, river god, 53–54
Amaltheia, Goddess of Plenty, 45
Amazons, 135, 160n.8
Ambibulus, Marcus, prefect of Judea, 489, 589
Ambiones tribes, 321

Ambiorix, King of the *Eburones*, 400
Ammonites, 527
Amon (or Amon-Ra), 193, 193n.8
Amon of Egypt, 60, 99
Amphinomus and Anapias (divine twins), 66–67
Amphitryon, 110–115
　son of Alcaeus, 108, 110
Amulet, 669–670
Amyntas, King of Galatia, 470, 494, *495*
Anat, war goddess, 61, 62
Anatolia (Turkey), 183, 186*m*
　Alexander the Great in, 168, 183, 185
　coins of, 511
　cults in, 193, 438
　god/goddess cults of, 158–160, 265, *271*, 419
　Hellenization of cults in, 193–197
　Pompey's invasion of, 482
　under Rome, 324, 327, 437n.26, 438, 439, 511
　wars in, 168, 182–183, 185, 366, 437n.26, 439
　worship of Mithra in, 265, 327, 419
Anaximander, Ionian philosopher, 152
Anchises, Trojan, 64, 225, 239, 316, 360
Ancient healers, 98–99
Ancient mystery cults, 59n.2. *See also* Mystery cults
Androkles, Sicilian ruler, 50, 62
Andromeda, constellation, 277
Angels, 22, 205, 205n.22
Angra Mainyu, 142–145, 147, 267
　source of all evil, 170n.4, 268
Anguipedal (snake-footed) deity, 309, *310*
Animal-headed gods, 203
Animals
　sacred, 63, 64
　sacrifice of, 174, 254, 280n.19, 295
Ankh (cross), 201
Annunciation, 97, 108, 108n.1, *279*, 593, 593n.52
Anthesteria, ancient festival, 102, 103
Anthesterion, 102, 102n.15
Antigone, execution of, 110
Antioch, 544, 652
Antioch, Incident at, 654
Antiochos, ruler of Commagene, 469
Antiochus, King, 262–263
Antiochus II, and Berenike, 210
Antiochus IV, Seleukid Emperor, 255, 255n.15, 256, *257*
Antiochus XIII, of Syria, deposed, 380
Antipater, father of King Herod the Great, 425n.6

Antonia Major, daughter of Antony and
  Octavia, 468n.27, 498
Antonia Minor, daughter of Antony and
  Octavia, 470, 498, 581, 582
Antonius, Lucius, Antony's brother,
  464–465, 466
Antonius, Marcus, father of Antony, 366
Antony, Marc
  alliance with Cleopatra, 453–477,
    469–475, 477, 480, 508, 538–539
  and Battle of Philippi, 462
  children of, 459, 468, 468n.27, 470,
    475, 498, 513–514, 520
  and control of Greece, 462–463
  cousin of Caesar, 407–408, 416, 440,
    479
  death of, 422, 446, 498, 499, 506, 512
  and death of Caesar, 443, 444, 447
  declared independence from the West,
    485
  defeated by Octavian, 493–494, 497–
    500, 541
  defection of troops, 496
  differences with Octavian and Lepidus,
    467
  as Dionysos, 453–477, 464, 468, 471,
    477, 484, 485
  and disastrous invasion of Parthia, 455,
    470, 473–476, 482
  division of Asia Minor, 470
  establishment over the East, 463–464
  in exile with Lepidus, 445
  and failure to conquer Parthia, 480,
    481, 482
  his military forces defect to Octavian,
    493–494, 496
  his will revealed, 488
  images of, 447, 471
  invasion of Armenia, 480, 482,
    484–486
  and liaison with Cleopatra, 486,
    488–489, 492, 538–539
  power of, 440
  preparations for war, 487–489, 488
  rivalry and civil war with Octavian, 454,
    455, 475, 479–500
  in the Second Triumvirate, 446, 455,
    459–462, 491
  sovereign of Greece, Macedonia, and
    Roman Asia, 485
  support for Hellenism, 223n.2
  tour of Eastern cities with Cleopatra,
    489–491
  treatment of his soldiers, 487
  triumph in Alexandria, 486
  wives of, 455, 460, 464, 467, 468n.27,
    498
Antyllus, Marcus Antonius, son of Antony
  and Fulvia, 468n.27, 498
  death ordered by Octavian, 498
Anubis, Egyptian god, 577
Anubis, son of Osiris, 199
Anytos (Titan), raised Despoena, 95, 97
Aphrodisias, goddess of, 345, 346, 454,
  511
Aphrodite, Eastern goddess, 10, 60, 84,
  196, 197, 211. *See also* Cybele; Eastern Aphrodites; Venus
  cults of, 11, 64, 345
  Goddess of Love, 10, 11, 21, 60, 84
  images of, 21, 63, 64, 140, 457
  ruler of love, 21
Aphrodite, Temple of, 63, 133, 134, 345
Aphrodite Erice. *See* Venus Erice
Aphrodite of Eryx. *See* Venus Erice
Aphrodite Panel of the Ludovisi Throne
  (replica), 9–10
Apis, 498
Apis Bull, 506
Aplustre, 463
Apollo, god, 90, 413
  Augustus as, 518, 519
  as Baal, 574
  birth of, 154
  children of, 28
  and death of Orion, 51
  images of, 92, 114, 129, 130, 280, 281,
    510, 574
  Kreousa and, 9
  Mithridatic War and, 338
  Olympic Games and, 128
  rites of, 97
  son of Zeus, 21
  twin of Artemis, 21
Apollo, Temple of, 504
Apollo, Tripod of, 121
Apollodorus, 163, 163n.13
Apollo Maleatus (Apollo as healer), 98
Apollonius of Tyana, a Pythagorean,
  645–646
  as a possible messiah, 647–648
Apollo of Actium, 510
Appian Way, 373
Apples of the Hesperides, 118
Aquae Sextiae, on Rhone River, 321
Aquarius, constellation, 285
Aquitania, Roman province, 407
Arabian coins, 140
Arabs, 8
  and Jews, relationship between, 88

Aratus of Soli, 377
Arcadia, Peloponnese Peninsula, 94, 96
Arcadian Mysteries, 94, 95
Arcadians, Peloponnese Peninsula, 95, 96
Archaeologists, 140
    designating periods of technological development, 164
    and fossil remains, 137
Archelaos, ruler of Cappadocia, 470
Archelaus, General, 328, 338, 341
Archery, 114
Archias, founder of Syracuse, 30
Archimedes, scientist, 191, 229, 230, 230n.12
Areion (horse), 94, 95, 95n.11
Ares, 11, 55, 84, 259. *See also* Mars
    child of Zeus and Hephaistos, 21, 25
    father of Romulus and Remus, 225
    God of War, 11, 55, 84
Ares, temple of, 11
Arethusa
    myth of Alpheios and, 53–54
    Syracusan water nymph, 70
Arges (Brightener), *19*, 28
Argo, ship, 117n.5
Argolis, *99*
Argonauts, 34, 117n.5, 119
Argos, Greece, 32n.11
Ariadne, daughter of King Minos
    abandoned by Theseus, 41, 75, 102
    wife of Dionysos, 102
Aries, constellation, 284, 516, 558, 561, 563, 565
Ariobarzanes, King of Cappadocia, 325, 327, 334
Aristarchus of Samos, 191, 267, 282, 283
    sun-centered model of universe, 282, 283–*284*
Aristion of Athens, 328
Aristobulus II of Judea, 535, 392
    King of the Jews, 381, 381n.50
    denied kingship of Judea, 536n.13
Aristonicus of Pergamene Kingdom, 307n.5
Aristotle, philosopher, 182, 220–221
Armenia, 324, 377, 473, 484, 533
Arminius, German king, 522
Arsakes I, King of Parthian Empire, 396, 397
Arsinoe IV, sister of Cleopatra, 424, 456–462, 466n.24
    as priestess of Artemis, 433
Artabazes, King of Armenia, 395, 485
Artaxerxes I, Persian king, 176

Artemis, cult of, 11, 160, *161*
Artemis, Eastern goddess, 154, 270, 454, 495
    child of Zeus, *21*, 154
    Goddess of the Hunt, 11, 47, 51, 53, 60, 91, 92, 95, 124, 140
    ruler of prophecy, music, and healing, 21
Artemis, Temple of, 32n.11, 162, 456, 491
Artemis of Ephesos
    Arsinoe IV as priestess, 433
    statue of, 160, *161*, 446, *447*
    temple of, 456
Artifacts, as religious relics, 139
Arverni tribe, France, 402–403
Aryana Vaejah, Kazakhstan, 142
Asclepion, temple complex, 99–100, 647
Asclepius, god of healing, 100, *101*, 117n.5, 127
    child of Apollo, 98
    from Epidauros, 98
    founded healing cult, Eumolpas, 98
    images of, 97, *99*
    killed by Zeus, 28
    mysteries of, 98
Asculum, central Italy, 325
Asherah, goddess, 170, 172, 260
Asia Minor, 12
Asian iconography, 190
Asia Province, 313, 324–325, 348, 427
    created, 307
    Roman control of, 342
    wars in, 366
Assyria, 168
Assyrians, 203, 207
Astarte, fertility goddess, 63, 170, 172, 260, 454
Astarte (Eoster), worshippers of, 675
Asterion, King of Crete, 87
Astrologer (magus), 504
Astrologers, 120, 511
Astrological iconography, 671
Astrological signs
    and crucifixion of Jesus, 631, 649
    and Jesus' birth, 516, 556–566, 630, 649
    and Jonah and the whale, 630
    between Sign of Jonah and Star of Bethlehem, 631–636
    between Sign of Jonah and the crucifixion, 630–631
Astrological symbols, *172*, 511
Astrological terms, 560

Astrological week, seven-day, 269, 269n.9
Astrology, 207, 223, 225
  and birth of Jesus, 672, 673
  and Christianity, 672
  classical, 287, *288*
  descriptions, concepts, and terms of, 558–561
  Hellenistic, 562
  and interpretations of *Matthew* and *Luke*, 559–561, 630
  and Jesus' date of birth, 557–559
  and magic, 673
  popularization of, 606
  and Star of Bethlehem, 520, 559, 630
  under Tiberius, 572–575
Astronomical observations, 206–207
Astronomical software, 559
Astronomy, 204, 211, 287
  ancient, 289
  Hellenization of Eastern and Western, 206–207
  modern, 287
Aswan, Egypt, 309
Atargatis, 190, *334*, 336, 506, 597
  cult of, 260–263, 329, 655
  earth goddess and mistress of beasts, 172
  goddess of Damascus, *484*
  Great Flood and, 193
  as Hera, 186
  images of, *173*, *334*, 346
  prophet of (Eunus), 261–263
  and slave rebellions, 313, 319
  as Syrian Aphrodite, 172–173, *173*, 190, 254, 259, 316, 320, 334
  transformations of, 190, 196
Atargatis, Temple of, 173
Athamas, raised Dionysos, 74
Atheism, 606
Atheistic philosophy, 221, 606
Athena, 240, *241*, 328, *329*
  child of Zeus and Metis, 21
  cult of, 11
  Cybele equal to, 281
  and Dionysos, 97
  and dolphins, *44*
  Enkeladus crushed by (temple carving), 26n.5, *27*, 68
  Goddess of Crafts and Wisdom, 11, 22n.4, 25–26, 26n.5, *27*, 47, 51, 84, 116
  helping Herakles, 118
  and Hephaistos, 29–30
  images of, 21, 31, *51*, *62*, *192*, 193, *241*, *329*
  leaping from Zeus' brain, 26
  and Medusa, *31*
  as a meteor, 140
  olive tree given to Athens, 29
  and owl, *340*
  raped by Hephaistos, 150n.1
  revenges of, 30–33, 113
Athena, Temple of, 32
Athenian Empire, 136n.20
Athenion, astrologer, 319
Athens, Greece, 9, 11, 17, 338, 490–491
  defeated by Sparta, 66
  rivalry with Sicily, 4
  siege of, by Sulla, 339, 339n.12
  weakening of, 30
  wealth of, 29
Athletic games, 128–132, 378–379. *See also* Olympic Games
Athletics, as acts of religious devotion, 128
Athronges, shepherd, 547
Atia, mother of Octavian, 504
Atlas, Titan, 21, 119, 128, 286, *286*
Atoms, 223
Atrebates, Gallic tribe, 390, 397
Atta Clausas, Sabine, 245
Attalids, 240, 240n.5
Attalus I, King of Pergamon, 240, 240n.5, 245
Attalus III, King of Pergamon, 307, 307n.5
Attendants (in astrology), 563
Attis, 195, *196*, *271*, 272, 277, 368
  cults of, 196, 196n.16, 197, 246, 246n.10
  Cybele's consort, 245, 247, 598, 598n.74
  worshippers of, 675
Attrition, Rome's strategy of, 230
Augean Stables, 117, *118*
  divinity of, 575
  images of, 573
  as solar deity, 575
Augeas, King of Elis, 117
Augurs, 344
Augustus Caesar, Emperor, 501, 501n.1
  adoption of Lucius and Gaius as heirs, 519, 520
  adoption of Tiberius, 521–522
  comet prophesizes his death, 522
  concern about succession, 514–515
  and Cult of the Emperor, 516–517, 518, 523

cults under, 512, 518
death of, 522, 603
as divine ruler, 502, 503–512, 516, *578*
Eastern cults under, 502
established the Julio-Claudian dynasty, 570, 570n.3
and goddess cults, 507
images of, *509*, *511*, 577, 578
impact of tragedies involving friends and family on, 519–521
imperial power transferred to Tiberius, 568
inaugurating a new spiritual age, 518–519
Jesus born during reign of, 523–524, 527
Jews and, 570, 610
last years in the reign of, 522, 528
legacy of, 516–522
marriage to Scribonia, 515
ordered First Roman Census, 555–556
proclaimed as a god, 522
reign and power of, 513, 528
religious beliefs of, 516
religious symbols used by, 508–511
responsored the Secular Games, 502, 518, 523
as solar deity, 575
as the son of God, 516, 517, 519, 524
Aulus Allienus, proconsul of Sicily, 429
Aurantis, 543, 544*m*, 550
Autochthonous (earth born), 150
Autolycus, son of Hermes, 114
Autumnal equinox, 283, 286, 292
Avericum, Gaul, 403
Baal, gods called, 170–172, 174, 484, 511
husband of Atargatis, 172
images of, *172*–*173*, *175*, *177*, 178
of Issus, *171*
as male, 574
of the Near East, 60
sky god, 11, 573
of Tarsos, *146*, 171, *172*, *176*, 277, 292
as Zeus, 188
Baalats, goddesses, 170–172
Baal-Hammon, Carthaginian god, 217, 257, 60, 61, 193n.8
Babylon, 147, 168
cultural center, 499
early cultures of, 203
Hellenization of cults in, 174, 203–207
Jews taken to, 176–178, 532
in the Persian Empire, 176–178
Babylonian metaphysics, 205
Babylonian Talmud, 204n.21

Bacchus, 270, 367, 368. *See also* Dionysos
Bacchus, Cult of, 251–252, 254, 255, 259, 370, 511
The Bacchae (Euripides), 93, 396
Bactria, 185
Baetyls, 140, 258, 512
Balaam, seer, 534, 539
Balak, King of Moab, 534, 553
Balsam oil, 483
Bambyce (Hierapolis), Syria, *173*, 193, 193n.13, 196
Baptism, 270, 270n.11, 296, 594, 655
as initiations, 595
Barabbas, 615, 616, 617
"Barbarian" cults, 76
Barbarians, invasions of Italian peninsula, 313
Bar Kokhba Revolt, 643, 662
Bar Mitzvah, 601n.83
Barrenness, 100
Bastet (a cat), 197
Batanea, 543, 544*m*, 550
Bees, symbols, *161*
Beirut, 473
Belgica, Roman province, 397, 407
Bellona, 335, 336
Bel (Lord)-Marduk, 204
Berenike, 209–210
Berenike II, Queen of Egypt, 210, 211, *212*
Berenike IV, Egyptian ruler, 383
Berenikes, sister and wife of Ptolemy, 212–213
Berenike's Hair, Cult of, 211, 213
Berlin, Summer Olympics of 1936 in, 132
Berosus, priest of Babylon, 204, 205, 206, 214, 265, 290–291
Bes, Egyptian god, 145–*146*
Bethlehem, Judea, 555
Bible, 8, 35, 180
as evidence of Christianity, 158
Greek translations of, 112
Hellenistic influence on, 208–209
nativity stories in, 568
Vulgate translation of, 163n.12
Biblical prophecies, fulfilled by Jesus, 592
Biblical stories, connected to Greek mythology, 112, 125
Bipennis (double-headed axe), 511
Birds, symbolization of, 181
Birthing position, ancient, 201
Bithynia, Roman protectorate, 324, 325, 327, 427
wars in, 366
Black Death, 4

Index 685

"Black Madonna" statues, of Virgin Mary, 162
Boccus, King of Mauretania, 333
Body and soul, 89
Boethusians, 549
Boreas, Greek god, 190
Born again, 91
Brahmins, 647
Briearcus, *19*
Brighid, Celtic goddess, 22n.4
Brimos, 68, 76
Briseis, concubine, 130, 131
Britain
　Caesar's invasion of, 397–398
　tribes in, 396
Brontes, cyclopes, *19*, 28
Bronze Age, 154–156, 157, 163, 164
Bronze Race, description of, 154–155
Brothel tokens, 584, 585
Brundisium, 466, 467
Brutus, Lucius Junius, 438–439
　and Battle of Philippi, 462
　and Cassius, and control over Rome, 461
　death of, 462
Brutus, Marcus Junius, 395n.7, 416, 416n.23
　blocking Octavian from power, 444, 445, 446
　in conspiracy against Caesar, 441, 442, 442n.32
Buca, L. Aemilius, moneyer, 444
Buddha, 189
Buddhism, 189
Bull
　Mithras' sacrifice of, 273, *274–275*, 276–277, 295
　symbol of, 181
Byblos, Phoenicia, 199
Byzantine Christians, 140
Byzantion (Istanbul), 485
Caca, Goddess of Excrement, 31–32, *34*
Cacus, son of Medusa, 31–32, 34
Cadiz, Spain, 371
Cadmus, 110
　and Harmonia, 85, 86, *86*
　relationship with Zeus, 24, 35, 84, 85
　son of King Agenor, 85
Caduceus, symbol of Hermes, 100, 510
Caepionis, Servilia, mistress of Caesar, 385, 441n.31
Caesar, Julius, 343n.19, 353–386
　absolute power of, 440
　acquisition of Spanish and Egyptian wealth, 381–383
　African campaigns of, *355*, 428–430, 429
　apotheosis of, 351, 421–449
　Asia Province and, 361–362, 366
　assassination of, *355*, 422, 439–446, 449
　birth and childhood of, *355*, 360–361
　at Bithynian court, 362, 363
　capture of Spain and Massalia, *355*
　Cataline Conspiracy and, 379, 380
　and civil war in Greece, 413–416
　and civil war with Pompey, 21, 409, 418, 421
　and Cleopatra, 417, 422, 423, 444
　coins of, *429–430*
　compared to Alexander the Great, 421
　consequences of his wars, 418–420
　consulships of, *355*, 387, 388
　and Crassus, 353, 354, 388
　crossing the Rubicon, *355*, 409, 421
　cults surrounding, 421, 422, 440, 447
　curator of Appian Way, 355
　as curule aedile, 378–379, 381
　death of his daughter, 398–399
　defeated by Vercingetorix, 402–403
　dictator of Rome, 349, 349n.24, 412, 431–438, 440, 441
　family name of, 360
　fight against Pontic Army, *355*
　and First Triumvirate, 353, 360–364, 388, 392–396
　foreign governorships of, 385, 388, 393
　funeral of, 442–444
　and Gallic Wars, *355*, 387, 388–392, 393, 396–409
　genealogy of, 316–317, 360–361, 360n.13, 361, 429–430
　as a god, 132, 420, 421–449, 438, 676
　high priest of Capitoline Jupiter, 361
　images of, *351*, *355*, *441*
　increasing opposition to, in Rome, 408–409
　judicial officer (praetor), *355*, 379
　and Julian calendar, 213
　kidnapped by pirates, 363–364
　legacy of, 420, 444–446
　marriages of, *355*, 373
　military successes of, *355*, 366–367, 384, 430, *435–439*, 455
　Optimate enemies of, 385, 423–427, 435
　and the Parthians, 439, 441
　and Pompey, 21, 353, 354, 388, 394–395, 399, 408–418, 421

686   Index

and Pompey's alliance with enemies, 400–402, 420
pontifex in Rome, 367
Pontifex Maximus, *355*, 379
and Populares causes, 370–386
praetor, *355*, 379
proconsul of Further Spain, *355*, 381
rivalry with Sulla, *355*
Roman consul, 384
in Roman politics, 378–379, 384–386
in Spain, 371, 440
timeline of his life, *355*
treatment of soldiers, 428, 433–434
triumphs of, 432–434, 439–440, 448
Caesar, Lucius Julius, 361
Caesarea, Judean city, excavations, 550, 611, 612
Caesareum, temple of, 458
Caesarion (Ptolemy XV), 458
   coins related to, *457*
   death ordered by Octavian, 498
   declared co-regent of Egypt, 458, 459
   as King of Kings, 485
   son of Caesar and Cleopatra, 432, 444, 456, 485, 498, 499
Caesarea, 638
Calabrian Apennines, 5
Caledonian Boar hunt, 66
Calendars, 435–436, 435n.25
   astrological, 269
   Egyptian, 206–207, 213
   lunar, 533
   Roman, 417n.26, 422, 440, 520, 520n.31
   solar, 566
   solar, by Essenes, 533n.8
   solar, in Dead Sea Scrolls, 533, 533n.8
   Zoroastrian, 268
Caligula, Emperor, 651
Callimachus, 211
Calpurnia, wife of Caesar, 442
Calydon, 123
Cambyses II, Persian ruler, 169
Cancer, constellation, 285
Canine ancestry, 64
Canis Minor, 274
Cannibalism, symbolic, 97–98
Canonical gospels, 548. *See also* Jesus; Nativity stories
   accounts of the crucifixion in, 619–621
   content of, 592, 594
   contradictory details in, 610
   differences between, 600, 605
   fabrication of scriptures in, 662–665
   Hellenistic Christians in, 639
   historical Jesus in, 598
   and prejudice against Jews, 618
   and Sign of Jonah, 630
   and superiority of Jesus, 596
   sympathetic portrayals of Pilate in, 619
   treatment of Christians and Jews in, 643
   trial of Jesus and, 618
   writing of, 658
Canopic Decree, 212–213, 213n.32, 282n.23
Canopic Gate, 497
Capitoline Hill, 392, 431, 438
Capitoline Jupiter, Temple of, 239, 361, 361n.15, 505
   games honoring, 379
Capitoline Triad, 379n.45
Cappadocia, Roman protectorate, 324, 325, 327, 336, 427, 470, 647
Capricorn, constellation, 285, 511, 514
   as *Gate of Souls*, 454n.5
Carbo, Gnaeus Papirius, 314
Caria, city-state, 136n.21
Carrhae, Parthian battles near, 395
Carrus Navalis, festival, 577, 671, 672
Carthage, 6, 11, 12
   African (Egyptian) influences in, 59–60
   cultural influences in, 12
   destruction of, 312
   Phoenician cults and mythology in, 40–41, 59n.2
   Phoenician ruler of, 133
   Phoenicians in, 40, 59
   and Punic Wars, 227–230, 242, 244, 256–257
   and Pyrrhic War, 227
   slaves from, 256–257
Carthaginian colonies, 12, 59, 63, 76
Carthaginian gods, 59–60, *61*
Carthaginians, 22, 61, 6359
Cassander, ruler of Macedon, 188
Cassiopeia, constellation, 277, 292
Cassius, 446
   and Battle of Philippi, 462
   and Brutus, 460
   death of, 462
   plotted Caesar's death, 460n.14
Castor and Polydeukes (Dioscuri), divine twins, 66, 66n.9, 67, 86, 114
   myths of, 66–67
Castration, 163, 173, 195, 197, 247, 347, 675, 675n.90
Catalina, Lucius Sergius, 379n.46
Cataline, scandal of, 379

Index   687

Cataline Conspiracy, 379, 380
Catastrophic messianism, belief system, 549
Cathedra Petri, 297
Catholic Church, 297, 309
Catholic nuns, 103
Cato, Marcus Portius, Optimate leader, 430
Cattle of Geryon, *118*
Catulus, Quintus, 505
Catuvellauni, British tribe, 398
Celestial equator, 285, 286, 287
Celeus, King of Eleusis, 69
Celibacy, 647
Celtica (Lugdunensis), 397
Celtic cults, trinity in, 398
Celtic moon god, 398
Celtic race, 119
Celtic solar worship, 660–661
Celtic tribes, Gallic Wars and, 389–390, 397–398
Celtine, daughter of Bretannus, 119
Celts, sacking of Rome, 226
Censors, 305
Census. *See* Roman Census of Judea, First
Ceos, *19*
Cepheus, constellation, 277, 292
Cepheus, King of Tegea, 122
Cernunnos, Celtic God of Animals, 22n.4
Cetus, constellation, 277
Chaeronea, Battle of, 183, 340
Chaldaeans, 203, 207
Chaldei, expulsion from Rome, 259
Chalkidian black-figured hydria with Zeus and Typhon, *23*
Chalkidian colonists, in Sicily, 50
Chalkidian Peninsula, Macedonia, 26, 96
Chalkidians, from Euboia, 13*m*
Chalkis, city-state, 470, 471, *484*
Chaos, *19*
Chariot, God's, *177*, 178
Chariot racing, 114, 129
Chariots, 144
Charnel burial, 536
Charybdis, daughter of Poseidon, 29, 34
Cheiron, centaur, 114
Cherubim, of the *Bible*, 22, 180, 484
Chevron (V-shaped symbol), 633, 634
Chimera, female monster, 24
Chi-Rho symbol, *202*–203, 539, 539n.23
Chiron, 48
Chrestus, 654
Christ, earliest mention of, 612
Christian Church, first, 657

Christian cults, 639, 663, 675
 after the crucifixion, 618
 early, 82, 329
 in Judea, 643
Christian divine hierarchy, 22
Christian doctrine, and worship, 659, 661
Christian family values, 599
Christian gnosis (knowledge), 664
Christian iconography, 113n.4, 217, 640n.85, *666*, 669
Christianity
 aspects of Zoroastrianism in, 142, 147
 becoming a religion, 219, 641–677, *650*
 conversions to, 631
 diverse beliefs and traditions in, 639, 641–677
 early components of, 217–218
 early controversies of, 652
 emergence of, 235, 562, 568, 580
 evidence of validity of, 158
 evolution of, 165, 219, 225, 233, 639, 640, 675, 676, 677
 first leaders of, 649–652, 654
 full legal status of, 645
 Hellenistic philosophies and, 218, 296–298
 ideas from Cult of Mithras in, 283, 296–298
 influence from mystery cults in, 84
 influence from paganism in, 22, 149–164, 645, 662, 671, 672, 672n.83
 intolerance of non-Christian beliefs and, 219
 magic and witchcraft in early, 672–674
 Roman Empire and, 344, 644–645, 662, 665, 676
 as a social force, 674
 spiritual origins of, 524, 677
 symbols and images of, 202, 202n.20, 517, *636*, *666*, 667
 timeline of events related to, 649–661, *650*
Christian Jews, 652. *See* Jewish Christians
Christian religion
 and baptism, 655
 confession established, 674n.87
 evolution of, 639
 and possibilities of resurrection, 675
 salvation and, 674
 and simultaneous creation of Judaism and Paganism, 639n.84
 simultaneous creation of Judaism and Paganism and, 639n.84

688 Index

Christians, 662n.60
  as against all Jews, 532
  distinction from Jews, 643
  early beliefs of, 590
  Eastern cults and, 666
  increased numbers of, 643
  need for leadership of, 649–652
  Nero's persecution of, 652, 655
  new prophecies from, 664
  non-Jewish, 631
  and pagan viewpoints, 662
  and Rome, 662, 665
Christian saints, in Sicily, 4
Chrysaor, the battle giant, 32, *34*
Chthonic (underworld) cult, 52, 53
Chthonic deities, 280n.19
Chthonic nymph, *52*
Chthonic rites, 97
Chthonic worship, 81
Church government, 644
Church of Santa Maria, Cosmedin, Rome, 103
Cicero, Marcus Tullius, 380, 446, 446n.42, 460, 505
Cilicia, 333–334, 647
Cilician Gates, capture of, 183
Cilician pirates, 266, 281, 298, 324, 364, 372–373, 392
Cilix, son of King Agenor
  founded Cilicia, 85
Cimbri, Germanic tribe, 314–315
Cinna, Lucius Cornelius, 356, 356n.2
Circe, sorceress, 33, *34*
Circumcision, 256, 259, 569, 652, 653
Cisalpine Gaul, 371, 372, 385, 388, 390, 398, 400, 407, 409
Cista mystica (ritual basket), 468, *468*, 510
Cithaerian lion, 114
Cithara (harp), 574
City-states, 11, 12, 38
  ethnic conflicts among, 12
Civic Crown Award, 362, 363n.19
Claudius, Emperor, 521
  expelled Jews from Rome, 654
Clementia and a gallic trophy, 416, *417*
Cleon, and slave rebellion, 262
Cleopatra Selene, daughter of Antony and Cleopatra, 470, 498
  declared Queen of Cyrenaica (Libya) and parts of Crete, 485
  images of, 514, *515*
  wife of Juba II, 512–514
Cleopatra VII, Egyptian ruler, 382n.53, 383, 417, 423. *See also* Antony, Marc; Caesar, Julius
  Antony and, 469–475, 480, 482, 484
  arrival in Tarsos, 466
  Arsinoe as threat to her power, 456–462, 466n.24
  birth of Caesarion to, 432, 444, 456
  Caesar and, 417, 423
  children with Antony, 459, 468, 468n.27, 470, 474
  children with Caesar, 456, 458, 477
  as co-ruler with Caesarion, 458–459, 477
  as co-ruler with husband/brother Ptolemy XIII, 417, 423–424, *424*, 427
  death of, 498, 499, 506, 512
  divinity of, 483–484, *484*
  focus on security of Egypt, 456, 475–476
  images of, *426*, 426n.9, *434*, *457*, *471*, *472*, *484*, *495*
  as incarnation of Atargatis, 484
  with Iphigenia, *491*
  as Isis, 422, 423, *426*, 453, 454, *457*, 471, 477, *484*, *490*, 514
  marriage to Ptolemy XIV (brother), 425
  possession of Cyprus, 470
  as Queen of Kings, 485
  and resurrection of Ptolemaic Empire, 471, 481, 483
  visit to Cyprus, *457*
  visit to Rome, 431–432
Clodius, Publius, 401
Clophas, brother of Joseph, 601–602
Clymene, wife of Prometheus, 157
Clytemnestra and Castor (twins), 66
Cocalus, King of Camicus, 41–42
Coele-Syria, Pompey in, 381
Coins
  ancient Sicel gods on, *55*
  common Greek themes on, 76
  common numismatic themes on, 76–77
  countermarked, 472–473
  Egyptian, 211–*212*
  Greek, 231
  Jewish, 168
  meaning of numismatic symbols, 140
  minted by Pompey the Great, 358
  minted under John Hyrcanus II, 381, *382*
  qualitative differences in, 231–232
  Roman, 231
  with sexual themes, 584
  showing Zoroastrian influence, *146*
College of Augurs, 344
College of Pontifices, 344, 379, 507
Colline Gate, Battle of, 356

Coma Berenices, 209, 209n.28, 211-212
Comaetho, Taphian princess, 110, 112
Comet, of Caesar, 575
Comitia Centuriata, 304, 305, 323
Comitia Tributa, 305, 323
Commagene, kingdom of, 469
Commentary on the Phaenomena of Eudoxus and Aratus (Hipparchus), 377, 377n.42
Communal meals, 90
Confession, 674n.87
Conon of Samos, astronomer, 211
Constantine I, Emperor (Constantine the Great), 666
  control of Christianity, 645
  public support of Christianity, 162
  uniting the Roman Empire, 676-677
Constantinople, sacred relic in, 139
Constellations, 191, 284-287
  animal, 293
  Aquarius, 285
  Aries, 284
  Cancer, 285
  Canis Minor, 274
  Capricorn, 285
  Cassiopeia, 277
  Cepheus, 277
  Gemini, 285
  Leo, 209, 285
  Libra, 285
  Mithras, 277
  Perseus, 277
  Pisces, 285
  Sagittarius, 285
  Scorpio, 285
  Taurus, 274, 284
  Virgo, 285
  zodiacal, 285
Constellations along the Zodiac and Ecliptic, 293
Copernicus, Nicolaus, astronomer, 191, 299, 299n.40
Coponius, prefect of Judea, 588-590, 589, 610
Corduba, Spain, Battle at, 436-437
Corinth, 6, 652
  Dorians from, 13*m*
Cornelia
  wife of Caesar, 361, 371
  wife of Pompey, 423
Cornucopia (Horn of Plenty), 45
Coroebus of Elis, 132n.6
Cos, Greek city-state, *130*, 494
Cosmic month, 144
Cosmology, 19

Cottus, *19*
Council of Ephesos, 346
Crassus, Marcus Licinius, 353-357, *355*, 379, 388
  beheaded, 395, 396, 400
  campaign against the Parthians, 394
  capture and death of, *355*, 395-396, 400
  consulships of, *355*, 393
  in First Triumvirate, 384, 392-396
  foreign governorships of, 393
  governor of Syria, *355*
  jealousy of Pompey, 356, 390
  leader of Optimates, 342, 342n.18, 356
  pursuit of wealth, 354, *355*, 356-357, 384
  putting down a slave rebellion, 368-369
  timeline of his life, *355*
  war against Spartacus, *355*
Crassus, Publius, death of, 400
Creation, accounts of, in *Genesis*, 174n.6
Creation mythology, 17-35
  Athena's revenge in, 30-33
  First Cyclopes, 27-28
  and forces for change, 42-43
  marriage of Hera to Zeus, 24-25
  monstrous happenings in, 29-30
  and roots of Western culture, 30
  Sicilian *Genesis*, 35
  transformation of Skylla, 33-34
  war with the giants, 25-27
Creator, identified by Plato, 286n.25
Creon, King of Thebes, 110, 116
Crescent and star, 514, 514n.24
Cretan bull, *118*
Cretans, 87
Crete, kingdom of, 14, 31, 41, 44. See also Mycenaean civilization
  Dorians from, 13*m*
  mystery cults in, 83
  Zeus raised on, 20
Creticus, Iullus Antonius, son of Antony and Fulvia, 468n.27, 498
Criobolium, baptism, 507, 507n.9, 671n.82
Crius, *19*
Cronos, God of Time, 9, *19*, 152, 170, 270
  castration of Uranus, 18
  children of, 20
  married sister Rhea, 19
  Zeus' defeat of, 22
  Zeus' father, 26
Cross, 201, 201n.18, 202, 590, 675n.89, 676

Index

as a Christian symbol, 676
symbol of righteousness, 540n.24
Croton, Italy, 89, 90, 91
Crowns, of rulers, 195n.15, 272
Crucifix, 669
Crucifixions, 228, 263, 364, 369, 657. *See also* Jesus, crucifixion of
Cruciform, 235
Crusades, 4
Crux ansate, 202
Cultic practices, Jewish and pagan, 173–174
Cult of the Emperor, 502, 518
Cults, 11, 57, 160–162, 194, 198. *See also* Mystery cults; names of people, gods, and goddesses
  after Jesus' death, 664
  ancient Mediterranean, 1–77
  ancient Sicilian, 57–77
  Augustus and, 503–505
  from colonists, 12
  Eastern, 8, 12
  and first Sicilian immigrants, 37
  Greek, 4
  Mediterranean, 1–77
  Phoenician, 59–63
  of the Roman Empire, 506–515
  survival of, 53, 80
  with undesirable religious beliefs, 218
Cultures, 152, 152n.4
Cumaean Sibyl, 238, 239
Cupid, images of, *457*
Cup of Helios, 119
Cura, earth goddess, 156, 158
Curia Julia, 441
Cursus honorum, 357, 357n.6
Curule aediles (city managers), 305
Cyan (color), 49
Cybele, *196*, 197, 266, 271, 320, 360, 597. *See also* Aphrodite; Venus
  baetyl of, 239
  Eastern mother-goddess, 140, 196
  games honoring, 379, 392
  Great Mother of Pessinus, 316, 320
  High Priest of, 320–321
  images of, 321, *322*, *510*
  invited to Rome, 195, 238–248
  Mother goddess, 334
  presence in Rome and, 245–248
  priesthood of, 507–508, 507n.9, 675
  priests of, 392
Cybele, Cult of, 134, 140, 160–162, 170, 194, 197, 198, 238, 251, 258, 263, 302, 304, 329, 345
  priests of, 347, 347n.22

Sulla's naturalization of, 347
worship ceremonies of, 247–248
Cybele, Temple of, 233, 246, 507
Cyclades Islands, 254
Cyclopes, 18, 19, 19, 20, 27–28, 30, 33
  generations of, 28
  killed by Apollo, 28
  second generation of, 29
The Cyclops (Greek satyr play), 74
Cynicism, 218, 221
Cyprus (Europe), 11
Cyprus, island of, 456
Cyrenaica, Libya, *101*, 493, 496
Cyrene, nymph, *99*, *101*
Cyrus the Great, 176, 177, 178, 178n.14
  unifying policies of, 168–169
Daevas, evil spirits, 143, 144, 145
Daidalos, Greek hero/inventor, 41–42
  mythological roots related to, 41n.3
Damascus, Syria, 484
Danae, mother of Perseus, 108, 112, 280
  and Zeus, 108, 277
Dances, ecstatic, 63
Daniel, book of, 36n.14
Darius I, Persian emperor, 169, 183–184, 187
Darius III, of Persia, 185
Dark Ages, 207
David, House of, 308, 609
David, King of Judea, 308, 535, 561–562. *See also* House of David
Dead Sea Scrolls, 533, 537, 549
Death
  fear of, and mystery cults, 82
  survival after, 223
  in Zoroastrian view, 144
Decan, 566, 566n.68
Decan of Ketos (decan of death), 630–631
Decapolis, 543, 544*m*, 544n.31, 638
  coins from, *597–598*
Decius Mundus
  and scandal involving Paulina, 576
Deification, 215
  death of Caesar and, 446–449
  in Hellenistic Age, 191
Deinara
  Aitolian princess, 45
  daughter of King Oeneas, 122, 123
  married Herakles, 122, 123
Deities
  minor, *205*
  representations of, 140, 181
Deity with three faces, 179, *179*
Delos, island of, 154, 202
  goddess worshippers in, 255

Index   691

oldest synagogue on, 532n.6
slave trade in, 254–255, 372
temple looted on, 338
Delphi, Greece, 97
artifacts at, 83
oracles at, 12
Delphyne, dragon-woman, 24
Demeter, 20, 52, 56, 59, 60, 76, 83, 90
Demeter and dolphins, *69*
Demeter and Persephone, Cult of, 10n.4, 53, 89
Demeter Erinys, 94, 95
Demeter or Persephone, and Triptolemus, *72*
Demetrius, son of Philip V, 241n.6
Democritus, philosopher, 205
Demonology, 204
Despoena, daughter of Demeter, 70, 94, 95, 97
Destiny, 196
Deucalion, 158, 193, 194
Deucalion, Greece, 156–157
Deucalion, son of Titan, 155, 156
Diadochi, 187, 188, 192n.7, 193
The Dialogue of the Savior, 647
Diana, 270
Diaspora (dispersed Jewish community), 528, 528n.2, 529–530, 642, 661
Dictys, 279
Didache, Christian manual, 296n.33
Dido, Queen (formerly Elissa of Tyre), 133
Dio, Cassius, 498
Diocletian, Emperor, persecutions of Christians under, 644n.9
Diodorus Siculus, 6n.1, 163, 163n.14
Diogenes, 221
Diomedes, King of Thrace, 118
Dion, of Syracuse, 192
Dionysian cults, 57, 58, 72–75, 250–254, 510, 511, 672
Dionysian Mysteries, 90, 215
Dionysos, 93, 194, 199, 209, 270, 271, 367. *See also* Bacchus
in battle against the Amazons, 135, 135n.15
birth of, from Zeus, 73
children of, 102
and erotic love, 101–103
God of Wine, Ecstasy, and Fertility, 21, *21*, 56, 59, 68, 72–75
and Herakles, 103
miracles of, 75
murdered by Titans, 97, 98
and Sicily, 72–75
symbol of spiritual salvation, *102*

tyrant of Syracuse, 66
worship of, 97
Dionysos, cult of, 57–58, 68, 217, 263, 370, 655
Dionysos and his stepfather, Silenos, *74*
Dionysos and Katanean brothers, *67*, *68*
Dioscuri, 212, 212n.30–31
Disciples of Jesus. *See* Jesus, disciples of
Divination, 223, 225
Divine and mortal beings, distinction between, 214
Divine conception, 523
Divine ecstasy, 75
Divine fish, 172
Divine power, 101–102
Divine symbols, 574
Divine twins, 66–67
Divine will, 120, 239
Divinity
claims during the Roman Republic, 480
early concepts of, 28
Hellenistic perspective on, 191–193
DNA, 149, 151
Dogs, 98
bred for hunting, 55n.7
sacred, 55
Dolphins, 75
Domitian, Emperor, persecutions of Jews and Christians, 659
Donations of Alexandria, 485
Dorian exiles, 13*m*
Dorian Greeks, 8–9, 10, 11, 30, 48
from Crete and Rhodes, 44
myths and culture of, 9
origins of, 13, 13*m*, 14
Dorians, 95–97
origins of, 17
Doric *peplos*, 8, 11
Dorus, Kreousa's son, 9
King of Winds, 48
progenitor of Dorian Greeks, 48
Doves, sacred, 172–173, 173n.5
Draco, constellation, 108n.2
Dreams, curing disease through, 100
Drugs, healing, 98
Drusus, son of Tiberius, 570, 580
death of, 571, 580
Dualism, 170n.4
Ducetius, Sicel leader, 39
Ducetius' rebellion, 55
Dumuzi, god, 172
Durres, Albanian city (Dyrrachium), 415n.22
Dusares, solar deity, 512, 537
Dyrrachium, 415

Eagles, *177*, 178, 181, *181*, 181n.26, 182, 183n.29, 413, *602*
Earth
  axis of, 283, 290
  equator of, 285
  hemispheres of, 283
  ideas on the origin of, 147
  orbit of, 90
  plane of the ecliptic of, 282n.21, 283
  revolution of, 283, 290
  rotation of, 283, 290
Earth (Juno), 272
Earth-centered universe, 269, *284–287*, *285*
  model of, 282, *284–287*, *285*, 298
Easter, 279–280, 598, 675
Eastern Aphrodites, 196, *196*, 197
Eastern cults, 8, 12, 655, 675, 676
  Christians and, 666
  deterioration of, 499
  Hellenization of, 189–215
  and roots of Christianity, 524
Eastern culture
  under Alexander, 168
  respect for Western cultures, 188
Eastern goddess cults, 162
Eastern goddesses, 194
Eastern ideas, and transformation of Western thought, 225
Eastern mysticism, 198
Eastern traditions, 142–147
  in Greek mythology, 147
  merging with Western ideas, 189
  spread to the West, 146–147
Ebionites, 646. *See also* Jewish Christians
Echidna/Lernian hydra, 24, 117, *118*
Ecliptic, of earth's orbit, 282n.21, *285*, 286, 287
Ecstatic practices, 247
  dance ceremonies, 173
Edict of Milan, 162
Egypt, 76, 168, 185, 439
  Alexander and, 168
  and Alexandrian War, 424–426
  annexation of, 513
  Antony and Cleopatra and, 453–477
  civil war in, 423–424
  cults of, 12, 174, 180, 197–203, 426, 570–572
  divinity of rulers from Caesar, 458–459
  Greek culture in, 6, 214
  influences in Sicily, 40
  mystery cults in, 250
  under Persian Empire, 180
  Rome's defeat of, 167

Egyptian deities
  household worship of, 508
Egyptian Jews, 308
  God of, 180n.19
  in Persian Empire, 180–182
Egyptian mythology, 198–200
Egyptians
  beliefs of, 24, 96
  early astronomy of, 206–207
  view of the Pharaohs, 191
Eileithyia, Goddess of Childbirth, 25, 112
Ein Kerem, Judean village, 593
Einstein, Albert, 18–19, 18n.2
Electrum, 160
Electryon, King of Tiryns, 108
  nine sons killed by pirates, 109
Elephantine Island, Jewish temple on, 180, *180*, 309, 309n.15, 310
Eleusinian Mysteries, 10, 71, 103, 104, 119, 128, 193n.11, 194, 198, 213, 250, 495, 516, 597, 675
  Dorian variation of, 94–95
  first priest of, 98
  in Greece, 345
  initiation ceremony, 97–98
Eleusis, Cult of, 573
Eleusis, near Athens, 10, 10n.4, 71, 103, *104*, 193n.11
  artifacts in, 83
  initiations at, 516
  temple at, 71
Elijah, 594
Elima, Elymian town, 40
Elimo, Trojan prince, 64
Elis, city-state, 132, 138
Elissa, Princess of Tyre, 59, 227n.9
Elizabeth, mother of John the Baptist, 593
Elymians
  colonization in Sicily, 12–13*m*, 37, 40, 42–43, 63, 233
  cults of, 40, 63–65, 76
  origins of, 12, 40, 233
Elymian Temple of Venus, 346
Elysian Fields, 58, 71, 85
Emesa, Syria, 140
Empedocles, Pythagorean philosopher, 91–92, 192
Emperor, Cult of, 516–517, 523, 568, 573, 606
  birth of, 496n.25
  in Judea, 586
  as a loyalty cult, 509
  opposition to, 676
  promoting, 508, *509*
  rise of, 505

Emperors
  divinity determined by the Senate, 516, 523
End of Days, 128n.1, 145, 276, 590, 592, 603, 615
  prophecy of, 499, 516, 534, 536n.14, 567, 642
End of Time. *See* End of Days
Enkeladus, hundred-armed, 26, *27, 34,* 35
Enkoimitiria, 100
Enna, Sicily, 10, 13*m*, 14, 43
  myths and cults in, 56, 67–72
  Persephone abducted by Hades in, 71
Entella, Elymian city, 13, 64
Ephesian coins, 446, *447*
Ephesians, 160, 161
Ephesos, 463, 464
  Antony's headquarters at, 487, 489–490
  near Troy, 147, 433
  temple at, 160
Epicureanism, 218, 222–223
Epicurus, 222–223
Epidauros, 99, 100, 338
Epimetheus, brother of Prometheus, 157
Epinomis (Plato), 220
Epione, Goddess of Easing Pain, 98
Epirote League, 227
Epistles, letters by Paul, 655, 655n.44
Equinoxes
  autumnal, 283, 286, 292
  implications for the Cult of Mithras, 287–298
  precession of, 267, 285, *288*
  shifting in zodiacal constellations and, 288, *288,* 290
  vernal, 268, 283, 286, 292
Eratosthenes of Cyrene, 191, 211, 282n.23
Erginus, King of Minyan Orchomenus, war against Thebes, 115, 116
Erichthonius, King of Athens, 9, 30, 150n.1
Eris, Goddess of Discord and Strife, child of Zeus and Hera, 25
Eros, God of Erotic Love, *21,* 69, 102
  images of, *457*
  pondering a dove, *64*
Eroticism, connection with Christian mysticism, 103
Erotic love, Dionysos and, 101–103
Erymanthian boar, 117, *118*
Eryx, Elymian king, 32, 40, 64–65, 133
  boxed with Herakles, 65
  death by Perseus, 65
Eryx, Elymian town, 40, 63, 64–65, 133
Eryx, Sicily, 13*m*, 14, 346

Eshmoun, God of Health and Healing, 60, 61
  images of, 61
Essenes, 533
Esther, Queen, 177
Eternal life, 201, 202, 598, 674, 675
Eternal youth, 65
Ethics, and logic, 224
Ethnarch of Judea (Herod), 467
Etruria, 379, 380
Etruscans, 226, 239, 239n.2
Euboeans, 13–14
Euboea, Greek island, 13, 50
  Ionians from, 13*m*
  Kataneans from, 66–67
Eucharist ceremony, 296, 296n.33, 604, 605, 615
  compared to murder of Dionysos, 98
  obscene, 665
Eumenia, Phrygian city, changed to Fulvia, 464
Eumolpids, 193, 193n.11, 198
Eumolpus, first priest of Eleusis, 98–101, 119, 125, 193n.11
Eunuchs, 163, 163n.10, 240, 675n.90
Eunus, Sicilian slave, 262
  crowned as King Antiochus, 262, 263
Euripides, 74
Europa
  abducted by Zeus, 85
  ancestors and descendents of, 88
  married King Asterion of Crete, 87
Euryale, a daughter of King Minos, 31, 50
Euryale, Gorgon, 31
Eurymedusa, nymph, *52,* 53
Eurynome, nymph, 25
Eurystheus, King of Thasos, 119
  son of Sthenelus, 112
  and twelve labors of Herakles, 116, 117
Eurytus, King of Oechalia, 114, 120, 121, 124
Eusebius, Father of Church History, 163, 163n.15
Eve
  meaning "life," 158
  source of original sin, 157n.7
"Eve Hypothesis," 164
Evil, 170
  Eastern idea of, 220
  good versus, 143–147
Evil eye, 634, 634n.74
Evil people, 224
Evil spirits, 143
Evolution
  biology, and theory of, 151

comparing ancient and modern ideas of, 150–152
fundamentalist religion and, 151
Greeks' idea of, 150–151
of history and ideas, 149–164
ideas about, 149–164
in mythological genealogies, 97
mythology about, 152–156
Pythagoras' ideas on, 152
scientific evidence of, 151
Excavations, at Paphos, Cyprus, 140
Exodus, book of, 180
Exodus (from Egypt), 534
Eye for an eye, 174, 175
Ezekiel, book of, 178
Ezra, book of, 176
Family values, in religious tradition, 84
Far East, religious beliefs from, 516
Farnese Atlas, 286, *286*, 290, 565
Fasis River, in Mithridatic War, 378
Fates, 24, 35, 206
Father, son, and Holy Ghost, 664
Faustulus, Sextus Pompeius, raised Romulus and Remus, 357–358, *359*
Feeding of five thousand, 604
Fertility, representations of, 74
Festival of Anthesteria, 103
"Field of Blood," 135, 135n.14
Fimbria, in Asia, 342
Fire
  creation of, 157, 224
  Vulcan as, 272
First Jewish War, 642, 643, 656, 657, 661
First Roman Census, 555–556, 567
First Triumvirate, 354, 383–386, 395
  end of, 420
  events leading to, 354–384
  origins of the members of, 354–364
  power of, 384n.54
  renewal of, 392–396
  timelines comparing members, *355*
  weakening of, 393–395
Fish, divine, 172, 173n.5
Flaccus, consul, 338
Flagellation, 270
Flavian dynasty, 582, 657
Flood of Deucalion, 156
Florence, Renaissance in, 4
Flowers, as symbols, *161*
"Forbidden fruit," 119
Fortuna, good luck, 347
Fossils, 135–139
  Miocene, 135
  Pleistocene, 138
Fujin, Shinto god, 190

Fulvia, 466, 520
  children of, 498
  death of, 467
  as Goddess of Victory, 464
  marriages of, 460, 460n.16
  war against Octavian, 464–465, *465*
  wife of Antony, 464, 468n.27
Funerary token, 631, *632*
Furious Demeter and her son, Arcion, 94, 95
Further Spain, 316, 371, 381
Gabatha, 618
Gabinius, Aulus, 373
Gabriel's Revelation, 549
Gadara, coins of, 597
Gadarenes, land of, 371, 436, 437n.26, 597, *598*
Gaea, goddess of the earth, 18, *19*, 20, 22, 25, *34*, 35, 85, 150n.1
  children of, 19
  and death of Orion, 51
  impregnated by Hephaistos, 30
  mother of Tartarus, 22
  mother of Typhon, 22–23
  wife of Zeus, 26
Gaius Cassius Longinus, 395, 395n.7
  and Parthian invasion, 395, 396
Galatea, sea nymph, 29, 33
Galatia, Roman protectorate, 24, 470
Galilean Jews, 586
Galileans, 527, 528, 533
  and Samaritans, 532
Galilee, Judea, 528, 543, 544*m*, 548, 638
  displeasure with rule of, 587
  early Christianity in, 652
  First Jewish War in, 656, 657
  opening Church to non-Jews, 652–655
  ruled by Herod Archelaus, 587
Galileo, 224n.4
Galli (priests), 245, 247
Gallia, and Artemis of Ephesos, *415*
Gallic tribes, 390
Gallic Wars, 388–392
  Britain and, 398–399
  Caesar and, 388–392, 396–409
  Gauls and, 399
  Germanic tribes and, 389–390
  map of tribes and cities in Gaul, 391*m*
  rebellion in the North, 399
Galli of Pessinus, 194
Games, by Octavian, honoring Venus and Caesar, 444
Ganymede, Trojan cupbearer, 65, 74, 362
  and Zeus, 65
Garden of Eden, 119n.6, *660*

Index   695

Garden of the Hesperides, 119, 119n.6
Gaul, 388, 391*m*, 438. *See also* Gallic Wars
    conquest and reorganizaton of,
        407–408
    peace in, 406–407
    Rome and, 391–393
    sacking of Rome by, 312, 313
Gaulanitis (Golan), 544*m*, 550
Gazi, Crete's opium goddess, 84n.1
Geb, 198
Gegenus, 49
Gela, Sicily, 13*m*, 14
Gelas, river god, 44, 45
Gemini, constellation, 66n.9, 191, 285
Gemini twins, *67*, 86, 117n.5, 191, 212,
    212n.30, 242, 294
Gender changing, 121
Genealogies
    in the *Bible*, 88
    Christians' use of, 88
    clues about migrations and relationships
        in, 88
    of Herakles, 131
    mythological, hints of evolution in, 97
General theory of relativity, 18–19
Genesis, book of, 158, 174n.6
Geometric diagrams, *93*
Geometry, 92–93, 287
The Geography (Strabo), 30n.9
Germania, 397
Germanic tribes, 314, 397
    Gallic Wars and, 389–390
Germanicus
    adopted by Tiberius, 522, 570
    death of, 570, 576, 580, 582
    grandson of Antony and Octavia, 570
    named imperial successor before Drusus,
        522, 570
    son of Nero Claudius Drusus, 522
Germans, 312
    Aryan ancestor of, 132
    invasions of Italian peninsula, 313,
        320–321
Germany, Roman legions in, 580
Geryon, 24, 32
    myth of the red cattle of, 32
Gethsemane, garden of, 605, 615
Giants, war with, 25–27, 26–27
    defeat of, 27
Girdle of Hippolyte, *118*
Glaucus, son of Poseidon, 33, 34
Gnaeus Pompeius Magnus. *See* Pompey
    the Great
Gnostic beliefs, 593
Gnostic Christianity, 668

Gnostic Christians, 646, 646n.12
Gnostic cults, 664
Gnosticism, 649
Gnostic Jews, 309n.309
Gnostics, 202, 202n.19, 597
God, in three parts, 225
Goddess cults, 158, 172, 506
    of Anatolia, 345
Goddess worshippers, 255
Godfearers, 643, 643n.4, 644
God of Jews, 182
God of Moses, 177, *177*, 178
Gods. *See also* Olympian Gods
    many claims of divinity, 479–480
    minor, belief in, 204
    and mortals, 85
    multiple, belief in, 169
    and mythologies, interconnecting, 57
    non-existence of, 218
    origins of, 11
    questioning the existence of, 215
    Roman leaders as, 476–477
Gold eagle, 542, *543*
Golden Age, 152–154, 163
Golden apples, 119
Golden Fleece, search for, 34, 117n.5
Golden Race, 154
Good versus evil, 143–147
Gorgons, 31
    description of, 31, 32
    killed by Herakles, 119
Gortyna, Crete, 87, 88
Gortys, 87
Gospels. *See also* Canonical gospels; Synop-
    tic gospels
    conflicting stories of Jesus in, 591–606
    contradictions between, 599–600
    fabrication of scriptures in, 662–665
    on the nativity, 529
The Gospel of the Egyptians, 647
Graccus, Gaius, 305–306
Graiai, monster, 24
Grapes, religious symbol, 146
Gratus, Valerius, prefect of Judea, *589*, 590
Great Bear, constellation, 292n.27
Great Flood, 44
Great Flood of Deucalion, 193
Great Flood of Noah, 163
Great Gymnasium of Alexandria, 485
Great Illyrian Revolt, 522n.34
Great Mother, names of, 158
Great Mother of Mount Ida, 160
Great Mother of Syria, 260
Great Sanhedrin, 651, 586, 614
Great Year, Chaldaean, 291

Greece
  cities of, 6
  culture of (*see* Greek culture)
  mystery cults in, 83
  Persian invasions of, 169
  Roman control over, 462
Greek city-states, 12, 15, 44–45
  under the Persian Empire, 176
  Greek civilization, spread of religious ideas from East to West, 146
Greek coins, 46
Greek colonization, 11, 14, 76
Greek cults, 4, 76
  merging with Rome, 233
  from Rome, 4
Greek culture
  absorption of, 6
  flowering of, 219
Greek exiles, 66
Greek goddess cult, 160, *161*
Greek gods, 15, 17n.1
  compared to Carthaginian gods, 60
  images of, 59
  from Olympus, 11
Greek graves, notes in, 75–76
Greek Heroic Age, 45
Greek iconography, 57–77
Greek islands, 17
Greek mystery cults, 57, 297–298
  Ionian arrivals and, 57
Greek mythology, 17–35. *See also* Mythology(s)
  abduction of Persephone, 10
  associated with Sicily, 35
  compared to native Sicilian mythology, 56
  conflicting stories in, 9
  connection to biblical stories, 111–112
  creation of the universe, 18–19
  divine power in, 28, 191
  "earthiness" of heroes in, 150
  evolution of, 17–35
  influence of, 76
  merger of beliefs with Zoroastrianism, 266
  mother goddess in, 158
  movement to the East, 189
  relative to Herakles' life, 124–125
  and rise of Greek Sicily, 8–11
  Romans' transmission of, 28
  Sicani mythology and, 41–42
  in Sicily, 17–35
  Sicily's influence on, 15, 48–50
  stories of abductions, 86
  twelve Olympian Gods of, 20–21, 20n.3
  view of humanity's role in the world, 164

Greek myths, 15, 66
  associated with Sicily, 35
  beliefs in, 191
  divinity in, 191
  metaphorical power of, 25
  premise of, 35
  similarity with biblical stories, 125
Greek philosophy, 204–205
Greek plays, mystery stories in, 82
Greek polis (free city), 586–587, 588
Greek religious beliefs, 135
Greek rituals, 12
Greeks, 12. *See also* Hellenistic entries; Mycenaean Greeks
  in Asia, 169
  cultural differences with Rome, 231
  exiled, 66
  ideas about evolution, 151–152
  influence on all Mediterranean cults, cultures, and trade, 76
  versus Persian points of view, 147
  and river gods, 44–46
Greek salvation iconography, 57–58
Greek Siceliots, 43–44
Greek temples, 22
Greek women, 8
Griffins, 484
Guarducci, Margherita, 8n.3
Gyane, daughter of King Liparus, 49
Gyges, 19
Gymnosophists (naked philosophers), 647
Hadad, ruler of the heavens, 170, 172, 186
Hades, God of the Underworld, 7, 10, 10n.4, *21*, 46, 59, 83, 119, 270, 572
  myths of, 20, 28, 68, 69
  and Persephone, 70, 71, 86
Hadrian, *190*
Halley's Comet, 211, 212, 519, 523
Halos (nimbus), 496n.25, 631
Hannibal, Carthaginian general, 229, 231, 241, 241n.7, 242, 246, 259, 263, 316, 358, 360, 410
Hanno, brother of Hannibal, 244
Hara Mountain, 143
Hariti, Buddist deity, 190, 190n.1
Harmonia, daughter of Ares and Aphrodite, 84, 85
Harpokrates, son of Isis, 113, 200, 201–202, 311, *312*. *See also* Horus/Harpokrates
Hasdrubal, brother of Hannibal, 244
Hasmonean Jews, 308–309, 310, 311, 529
  destroyed the Samaritan temple, 531
  and Jerusalem Temple Cult, 531–532, 531n.4
Hasmonean rule, Jewish disapproval of, 529

Hathor (a cow), 197
Healing, 91, 98, 604, 649
  performed by Jesus, 596
Healing cult at Epidauros, 98, 99
Healing cults, 98, 100–*101*
Healing drugs, 98, 99
Heaven, 665
  concept of, 147
  in Zoroastrian view, 145
Hebe, Goddess of Youth, 21, 65, 124
  cupbearer of Zeus, 65
Hebrew Bible, 174, 174n.6, 178
  in Aramaic, 208n.25
  codification of, 176
  Masoretic text of, 208, 209
  Ptolemaic version of, 208
  translation into Latin, 208
Hecate, magical moon goddess, 70, 273, 276
Hecatonchires, 18, 19, *19*, 20
Helen of Troy, 66, 67, 86
Heliacal (solar) rising, 206–207
Heliogabalus, sun god, 140
Helios, God of the Sun, 21, 70, 271, 275
Hell, 147, 272
Hellenism, 191, 499, 640
Hellenistic Age, 147, 167–188, 224, 529–539
  complex relations of empires during, 209
  scientific achievements of, 191
Hellenistic Christians, 639
Hellenistic Cult of Mithras, 265–299
  association with Tarsos, 291
  astrological key to, 292, 293
  description of, 266
  duties of worshippers, 276
  emergence of, 266
  and Hellenistic deities, 270
  influenced by Zoroastrianism, 265
  major features of, 298–299
  mixture of beliefs in, 266
  and Olympian deities, 269, 270
  origins of, 272–275
  parallels with Perseus, 277–281
  similarities to Christianity, 296–298
  and Stoic philosophy, 291
Hellenistic cults, 201, 217–218, 345, 348, 375, 502, 573, 674
  Christian beliefs in, 590
  and expectations of religion, 329
  and Jewish cults, 652
  opportunistic, 209–213
  resistance to, 652
  in Roman Republic, 238, 302, 303
Hellenistic deity, *377*
Hellenistic Egypt, 214

Hellenistic entrepreneurs, cults of, 258
Hellenistic Greeks, 33
Hellenistic Jewish Christians, 663
Hellenistic Jews, 311, 646
Hellenistic metaphysics, 225
Hellenistic Mithraism, 373–376, 374n.36, 375n.40, 667
Hellenistic mysticism, 251–253
Hellenistic philosophers, 205
Hellenistic philosophies
  after the death of Jesus, 225
  agnostic, 221
  atheistic, 221
  Cynicism, 221
  Epicureanism, 222–223
  four movements of, 218
  humanistic, 222–223
  Plato and, 220–221
  Skepticism, 222
  Stoicism, 223–224
  theistic, 223–224
Hellenization, 165
  of Atargatis, 194
  of Babylonian cults, 203–207
  of cultic practices, 194
  and cultural homogenization, 188
  defined, 167, 189
  of Eastern cults, 189–215, 213–215, 233
  of Egyptian cults, 197–203
  of goddess cults, 346
  Golden Age of, 165–233
  influence on the *Bible*, 208–209
  Jews' acceptance of, 585
  of Syrian and Anatolian cults, 193–197
  and understanding of spirituality, 167
Hellespont, 183
Helmet of Invisibility (of Hades), 28
Helots, 66, 66n.10
Helvetii, Celtic tribes, 389, 390
Hendin, David, 176
Hephaistos, child of Zeus and Hera, 21, *21*, 26, 32, 34, 270
  and Athena, 29–30, 150n.1
  God of Metalworking, 25, 26, 28, 29, 118
  workshop of, 29
Hera, Goddess of Childbirth and Marriage, 20, 112, 124, 130, 132, 270
  and birth of Dionysos, 72–75
  and Herakles, 122, 124
  wife of Zeus, *21*, 24–25, 73, 97, 111
Heraclitus of Ephesos, 223, 223n.3
Hera/Cybele, 189
Heraean Games, 132, 132n.8
Herakles, Greek god, 34, 59, 61, 371, 372, 413

ancestry of, 108–112, 361
and Athena, 47, 107
birth and infancy of, 111, 112–113
children of, 114, 122, 123, 125
conceived by Alcmene, 107, 111, 112
cult following of, 124, 125
death of, 107, 108, 123, 124
and defeat of Enkeladus, 35
and Dionysos, 103
Doric hero, 156
in the East, 189
fight with Leukaspis, 43–44
founder of Olympic Games, 118, 123, 129
as a god, 125
as grand unifier of Greek mythology, 124–125
Hera and, 107, 116, 124
and horse, wheat, and palm tree, *61*
iconography over time, 190
illness of, 121
Ketos killed by, 136–*137*
killing his three sons and wife, 116
killing of the eagle, 157
and King Eryx, 32, 65
Linus killed by, 114, 115
marriage to Deinara, 45, 122
marriage to Princess Megara, 116
as a mature hero, 122–124
myths about, 44–46, 111–112
place in Greek mythology, 43n.5, 107–125
and red cattle of Geryon, 64–65
semi-divine, 112, 114, *115*
son of Zeus, 112
strength of, 107, 114, *114*, *115*, 191
symbol of spiritual salvation, *102*, 107–125
and Theban army, 115
transcends mortality, 124
twelve labors of, 297
in war against the giants, 122
in war against Troy, 122–124
weaknesses of, 114, 120–121
as a young man, 114–115
Herakles, Temple of, 371
Herding societies, 94
Heresies, 665
Hermaphrodite, 194, 194n.14
Hermaphroditic deities, 197
Hermes, God of Messengers, 24, 70, 85, 90, 100, 120, 121, *196*, 197
child of Zeus and Maia, *21*
Hermes and Persephone, 86
Herod, King of Judea, 425n.5, 427. *See*
also Judea, kingdom of
alliance with Octavian, 496, 497, 541
ancestors of, 308
as an Idumean king, 536
and Antony, and the Parthians, 538–539
appointed by Caligula, 651
assumed kingship of Judea, 470, 539
brutality of, 541–542
and Caesar, 538
as christos, 540
and Cleopatra, 483
cult of, 549–550
death, and aftermath of, 523–524, 528, 543, 545, 547–550, 549, 552, 556, 567
early life of, 537–539
executions of Jewish leaders, 562
family of, 537, 545, 652
flight from Syria, 467
and Jewish cults, 532
and the Jews, 527–531, 534, 541
as King of the Jews, 467–468, 524, 539
last years of, 551
leadership of, 528
and massacre of innocents, 504, 504n.6, 523–524, 552, 562, 601
murders of, 528, 541, 549
murders of his family, 542, 567
plan to murder Jesus, 278, 529, 552
as a possible messiah, 567
and Roman control, 517, 528, 585
rule of his kingdom, 470, 541–543
and slaughter of pious Jews, 549
sons of, 545
as tetrarch of Galilee, 538–539
and wife Mariamne, 538, 539, 541, 542
Herod Agrippa, client-king of Judea, 651–652
Herod Antipas, 552, 600
espousal of liberal Hellenism, 587, 594
and execution of John the Baptist, 649
as tetrarch of Galilee, 545–546, *547*, 550, 552, 587, 588, 616
Herod Archelaus, 543, 545, *546*, 547, 550, 552, 567, 587
Herodian dynasty, legitimacy of, 529
Herodian fortress, Masada, 657
Herodias, wife of Herod Philip, and of Herod Antipas, 594, 595
Herodotus, 136, 136n.17, 168
Herod Philip, 545, *548*, 548, 550, 675n.89
Heroes, 136
Heroic Age, 41n.3, 84, 117n.5, 135n.15, 156, 163, 164

Hesiod, 152, 152n.3, 164
Hesione, daughter of Laomedon, 137
Hestia, virgin Goddess of the Hearth, 20, 21
Hierocles, Sossianus, 648
Hilaria, celebration, 598
Himera, fountain nymph, *46*, 47
Himera, town of, 13, 46–47
Himera (Imera), Battle of, 22
Hindu gods, 144
Hinduism, compared to Zoroastrianism, 143–144
Hindus, perception of the universe, 144
Hipparchus of Rhodes, 267, 282, 283, 284–287, 293, 298
  and precession of the equinoxes, 290, 293, 294n.30, 377
Hipparis, river god, 47, *48*
Hippocamp, 50, *51*, 131
Hippodamas, 52
Hippodameia (Briseis), 131, 132
Hippolyte, Amazon Queen, 118
History
  comparing ancient and modern chronologies, 163–164
  evolution over time, 150
Hitler, Adolf, 132n.8
Holon, 178
Holy Roman Empire. *See also* Roman Empire, 4
Holy See, 297
Holy sites, 76
Holy Spirit, 552, 593, 593n.52, 604, 605, 664
Holy Trinity, 163
Homer, 29, 29n.8, 131, 136, 360
Honeybees, 161
Honi the Circle-Maker, Jewish cult leader, 535, 536
Horse and palm tree, *60*
Horus, son of Isis, 191, 199, 201, 457, 572
Horus/Harpokrates, 113, 311, *312*, 453, 579, *669*, 672
House of David, 627
House of Israel, 638
House of Thebes, 111, 111n.3
Human existence
  comparing perspectives on, 153
Humanity
  creation of, 156–158
  myths about, 156–158
Humans and gods, 85, 141–142
Hundred-handed, *19*
Hybrid deities, 189

Hyccara, Sicani town, 41, 42
Hydra, multi-headed, 24
Hygeia, Goddess of Health and Bathing, 98
Hyksos, Egyptian rulers, 180n.20
Hyperion, *19*
Hypocrites (actors), 548
Hyrcanus I, King of Judea, 308, 531n.4
Hyrcanus II, King of the Jews, 381, 535, 536
Iapetus, 19
Iaso, Goddess of Recuperation from Illness, 98
Ice Age, 154
Ichthyosaur skulls, in Caria, 136, *137*
Iconography
  Asian, 190
  astrological, 671
  Christian, 97, 113n.4, 217, 666–672, 669
  Greek, 76
  Hellenized, 201, 666–672
  Mithraic, 297
  mythic, 62–63, 368n.26
  and mythology and worship, 62–63
  numismatic, 671
  pagan, 76, 659–660, 660, 669
  Phoenician, 62
  religious, 218
  salvation-related, 57–58, 203
  Semitic, 62
Idaean Mother of Pessinus. *See* Cybele
Ides of March, 442, 461, 506
"Idols of Jamnia," 310
Idumea, 543, 544*m*, 545, 550
Idumeans, 308, 527, 528, 531, 537
Ikaros, son of Daidalos, 41, 42
Iliad (Homer), 131, 140
Illyria, 242, 398, 486
  defeat of, 513
Illyrian War, 481
Illyricum, governorships in, 385, 388, 407
Ilos, founded Troy, 65
Image of Poseidon in the form of an ithyphallic ass, *96*
Immorality, 84
Immortality, 65, 66, 70, 91
Imperial cult, 573. *See* Emperor, Cult of
Imperial Rome, 63
Incident at Antioch, 654
Incubation, 100, 100n.14
India, 143–144, 169, 169n.3, 647
  religious beliefs from, 516
Indus Valley, 169, 185
Infertility, 100

Initiation ceremonies, 270n.11
  Greek rituals, 8, 60n.3
  in mystery cults, 58, 82, 83, 84
  offering salvation, 72
  secret, 75
Initiation stories, 511
Ino, Semele's sister, 74
Intellectual climate, in Roman Empire, 606
Invocation of Zeus, pagan prayer, 377
Iolaus, 117
Iole, daughter of Eurytus, 120, 124
Ion, Kreousa's son, 9
Ionian Greeks, 17–18, 30, 66
  in Sicily, 8–9, 10, 13, 14
Ionic *chiton*, 8, 9
Iphicles, son of Amphitryon, 112, 117
Iphigenia, daughter of Agamemnon, 491
  Cleopatra and, *491*, 491–492
Iphitus, son of Eurytus, 120
  killed by Herakles, 120
Iran, 646
Iron Age, 156, 157, 164, 292
Iron Race, 156, 158, 194
Isaiah, and prophecy of virgin birth, 554
Isamula, *623*
Iseum (Temple of Isis), 577, 578
Ishtar, goddess, 172
Isis, goddess
  as Aphrodite, 201
  Cleopatra as, 453, 454, 502
  Cult of, 201–202, 311, *312*, 346, 392, 502, 508, 676
  in Rome, 392
  war against, 392
  images of, *200*, 201, 423, *424*
  importance in Roman politics, 311–312
  many names for, 255, 454n.2
  modified cults of, 214
  as the mother of Horus/Harpokrates, 672
  priests of, 345
  scandal involving Decius Mundus and, 576–579
  symbols of, 201
  worship of, 113, 197, 201, 202
Isis, temples of, 201–202, 484
Isis of Delos, 255
Isis Pelagia, 201
Isis Pharia, 201
Islam, 140
Isles of the Blessed, 156
Israel, kingdom of, 168, 178, 180
Israelites, exodus from Egypt, 534
Issus, Battle of, 185–187
Isthmia, games at, 128
Italian Greeks, 227

Italian peninsula, barbaric invasions of, 312, 313
Italy, Renaissance in, 4
Ithyphallic ass, 87, *96*
Iturea, 543, 544, 544*m*
Iullus Antonius, son of Antony and Fulvia, 520
Iulus, son of Aeneas, 360
Ivy leaves, 102
Jacob (as Hyksos King), ruler of Egypt, 180
Jacob's well, 637
James, brother of Jesus (James the Just), 601, 627, 628, 649, 652, 657
  leadership of, 653
  stoning of, 646, 655
Jannaeus, Alexander, King of Judea, *635*
Janus, Temple of, formal closing of, 512–513
Janus, two-faced god, 242, *244*
Jason and the Argonauts, 117
Jerome, Christian writer, 163, 163n.12, 164
Jerusalem, 173, 637
  after the crucifixion, 618
  civil war with Shechem, 588
  destroyed by Nebuchadnezzar, 176
  First Jewish War in, 656–657
  Jews and Christians in, 642
  under Roman control, 571
  Sanhedrin priests in, 586
  under seige, 657
  walls of, 176
Jerusalem Jews, in Babylon, 177, 178
Jerusalem Temple, 537, 542, 549
  destruction of, 642, 661
  Herod and, 539
Jerusalem Temple Cult, 506, 570, 614, 641, 652
  advocates of, 528, 529, 652
  controlled by Coponius, 588
  diaspora and, 530, 531
  and early Christians, 651
  Hellenistic influences and, 595
  Herod Agrippa and, 652
  Herod and, 308, 309n.9, 537, 539
  legitimacy of, 587
  looking for spiritual guidance outside, 587
  non-Jews in, 643
  perceived corruption and sacrilege in, 506, 527, 536, 570, 587, 595, 642
  prefects and, 606
  Roman influence and, 532, 587n.28, 641
"Jeselsohn Stone," 549n.40

Jesus, 94, 272, 297, 303. *See also* Canonical gospels; End of Days; Messiah; Nativity stories
  accounts of the nativity, 529
  after the crucifixion of, 642, 643n.6, 646, 661
  apostles of (*see also* disciples of), 642
  arrest and trial of, 614–618
  astrological signs at his birth, 516, 556–566, 672
  astrological signs at his crucifixion, 631, 649
  baptism of, 595–596, 603
  belief in catastrophic messianism, 624–625
  in Bethlehem and Egypt, 600
  birth of, 476, 520, 529
  before the birth of, 217, 476, 659
  childhood of, 547–550, 591, 591n.35, 601n.84
  compared to other gods, 591
  compared to other saviors, 596–598, 622
  compared to the Good Shepherd, 597–598
  conflicting gospel stories of, 591–606
  contradictory statements by, 599–600
  crucifixion of, 272, 498, 562, 571, 580, 582, 599, 605, 616–621, 638
  cults of, 639
  date of birth controversy, 523, 524, 529, 557–559, 565, 649
  date of the crucifixion of, 530–531, 555, 649
  disciples of, 551, 596, 597, 600, 603, 638, 642, 648, 675–676, 675n.89
  divine conception of, 523
  divine heritage of, 88
  as a divine savior, 480n.1, 615, 622, 659
  entombment and resurrection of, 621–624, 631
  ethical statements by, 599–600
  fabrication of stories of, 662–665
  as a false messiah, 646
  family of, 601, 627
  family tomb of, 626–628, *629*, 635, 636
  genealogy of, descent from David through Joseph, father of Jesus, 54, 592
  as God, 659
  as the "Good Shepherd," 667
  historical perspective on, 598, 624, 638–640
  images of, *660*, *667*
  in India, 622–623
  Jewish conspiracy against, 618, 624
  John the Baptist and, 593–596, 603
  as "King of the Jews," 616
  as the "lamb of God," 604, 671
  last days of, 592, 607
  the Last Supper, 605
  life and ministry of, 585–591, 603–606, 610
  as the messiah, 585–591, 592, 603–606, 610, 646
  miracles performed by, 511, 596–597, 603–606, 624, 629, 648, 672, 675
  and modern doctrines, 600
  parables of, 597, 604
  and prophecies fulfilled, 592
  resurrection of, 621–622, 631, 675
  and ritual washing of feet, 605
  saving power of, 103–104
  as a solar deity, 631, 658
  as the son of God, 449n.46, 616, 617, 623, 673
  son of Joseph and Mary, 375n.40, 635
  stories about, 348
  teachings of, 91, 571, 587, 593, 647, 662
  timing of his birth, 529
  tomb of, 626–628, 636, *636*
  transfiguration, 603
  "virgin birth" of, 296, 554
  writings of, 90
  as a young man, 600–603
Jesus family tomb, Telpiot, 626–628, 629, 634, 635, 636
Jesus movements, 652, 654, 658, 661
Jesus of Nazareth, 571
Jewish burial customs, 536, 657n.70
Jewish Christians, 652, 653, 657, 659
  Jews and, 656
Jewish cults, 661, 672
  antagonistic, 308–309
  categories of, 528
  coexistence with Christian cults, 82, 672
  diversity of, 174n.6
  ethnic and religious tensions between, 588–590
  Hellenization of, 208–209
  numbers of, 174n.7
  under the Persians, 173–174, 180
  in the Roman world, 529–539
  under Tiberius, 571–572
  use of the *Torah*, 174
Jewish culture, spread of, 168
Jewish kingdoms, 180
Jewish kingship, 381, 528
Jewish laws, 174, 653
  justice in, 175
  purity laws, 174

Jewish magic, 204n.21
Jewish monastic movements, 303
Jewish rebellions, 661
　during childhood of Jesus, 547–551
　in Judea, 656–657, 661
Jewish royalty, 180
Jewish scriptures, 310, 311
Jewish texts, sacred, 533–534
　narrow interpretatons of, 533–534
Jewish War, 627
Jews, 8. *See also* Judea, kingdom of
　and animal sacrifice, 280n.19
　distinction from Christians, 643
　expulsion from Rome, 259
　Hellenistic, 568
　and idols, 611
　and Jewish Christians, 656
　messianic, 568
　Pergamene, 259n.17
　pogroms against, 642, 642n.3
　resistance to Roman control of Judea, 588
　rejection of Jesus, 624
　Roman killings of, 662n.60
　in Rome, 422, 444, 530
　and search for the messiah, 534–537, 609
　and Seleukids, 256
　in Spain, 438
John, gospel of, 549, 594, 597
　and arrest and trial of Jesus, 615, 617
　and crucifixion of Jesus, 620
　Jesus as the "lamb of God," 604
　Last Supper of Jesus mentioned, 605
　miracles of Jesus in, 605–606, 624
John, son of Zebedee, 649
John the Baptist, 303, 375n.40, 587, 651
　death of, 596
　as Elijah, 594n.54
　execution of, 595, 595n.60, 596, 649
　following of, 646–647
　as a possible messiah, 645, 646–647
　relationship with Jesus, 593–596, 603
　supporting role of, 591
Jonah, sign of. *See* Sign of Jonah
Jonah and the whale (Ketos), 629, 630–631, 634
Jonah symbol, 633
Joseph, father of Jesus, 551–556, 601
　age of, 601, 601n.87
　as an old man, 553n.51
　genealogy of, 554
Joseph of Arimathea, family tomb of, 626, 631–632, 634

Joshua, 178, 637
Juba I, Caesar's defeat of, 514
Juba II, King of Numidia, 433, *515*, 520
　client-king of Mauretania, 433
　husband of Cleopatra Selene, 512–514
　in North Africa, 412, 426
　as Scholar King, 514
Judah, kingdom of, 168, 178, 180
　Hellenistic influences in, 534
　Roman administration of, 610
Judaioi, 531, 532. *See also* Judeans
Judaism, 177, 373, 644
　in Alexandria, 506
　conversion to, 569–570
　Gnostic variety of, 309
　and Greek mystery cults, 104
　non-Christian Jewish cults as, 665
　as a religion, 665
　restrictions in, 104
Judaizers, or Godfearers, 569, 570
Judas, gospel of, 591n.36
Judas Iscariot, apostle
　betrayer of Jesus, 626, 642
　death of, 625–626
Judas of Gamala
　Galilean rebel, 550, 551, 587
　son of Hezekiah, 547, 548
Judea, kingdom of, 381, 470, 483, 550. *See also* Herod, King of Judea
　acts of violence and terrorism in, 588
　alliance with Rome, 308–311
　conquered by Babylon, 176
　conservative Jews in, 527
　death of Herod and Roman control of, 538–539
　deposition of Herod Archelaus, 606
　diaspora in, 528
　divided among three sons of Herod, 545
　dominated by Roman Empire, 233, 308–311, 528
　early Christianity in, 652
　Egyptian cults in, 572
　end of Jewish kingship in, 381, 528
　First Census of, 588
　and First Jewish War, 656
　Hasmonean theocracy in, 527
　Hellenistic administrations in, 585, 588
　Hellenistic and Jewish populations in, 588
　under Herod the Great, 527–531, 566–568
　Jewish cults in, 528, 533–534, 572
　Jews, Christians and pagans in, 662

Jews and non-Jews in, 527, 528, 570, 643, 652–655
multiple ethnicities and cults in, 527, 657
Pompey's seige of, 381
under Pontius Pilate, 581, 609–613, 609–640, 611–613
prefects of, 588–590, *589*, 606, 609–611, 610–611
regions of, 543, 544*m*
reorganization of, 544–545
rising power of Rome and, 528
Roman control of, 233, 537–551, 564, 585, 607, 641
transition from Herodian to Roman rule, 570
violence and terrorism in, 588
Judean Jews, 533
compared to other Jews, 530–531
revolution against Rome, 618
Judeans, 531
Judeo-Christian metaphysics, 225
Jugurtha, African ruler, 313, 314, 317, 318, 332, 333, 348
Jugurthine War, 314, 317, 332, 348
Julia, daughter of Augustus, and Livia, 515
deserted by Tiberius, 520
exiled for life, 520, 521
wife of Agrippa, 519
wife of Tiberius, 519
Julia, daughter of Caesar, 363, 385, 399
wed to Pompey, 385, 394
Julia, daughter of Octavian, 469
Julia, wife of Gaius Marius, 316, 320, 370, 371
Julian family, 316–317, 360–361
Julius Caesar. *See* Caesar, Julius
Juno, 270, 272, 273
as Savior of Women, 345
Juno Sospita, 345
in goatskin headdress, *347*
Jupiter (planet)
and the moon, 558–559
occultation by the moon, 564–565
position of, and birth of Jesus, 558
Jupiter, God of the Sky, 231, 266, 270, 274, 276, 297, 386, 502, 504
and Aries, 560–561
Jupiter Capitolinus, 392
Jupiter Sebazius. *See* Sebazius
Jupiter Terminus, 413
Ka'ba, Mecca, 140
Kamarina, nymph, 47, *48*
Kamarina, Sicily, 13*m*

Kantharos, 74
Kassandra, prophetess
raped by Ajax, 134
Katane, Sicily, 13, 13*m*, 66–67, 311
Katanean brothers, Amphinomus and Anapias, 66–67, 463, *464*
Kazakhstan, 169
Kerberos, monster, 24, *118*
Keryneian doe, 117, *118*
Ketos, monster, 108, 629, 630
images of, *669*
killed by Herakles, *137*, 565
Phorcys' sister, 31, *34*, 35, 136, *137*
portrayal as a dragon, 108n.2
Ketuviim, 533
Khabu, 512
Khnum, Egyptian god, 180n.19
Kidnapped women, Arcadian, 94
Kingdom of God, 603. *See also* End of Days
Kingdom of the Dead, 10
King James Bible, 664
King of Kings, Persia, 191
Kitos War, 642
Knowledge, creation of, 157
Kosher animals, sacrifice of, 280n.19
Kosher foods, 533
Kosher lifestyle, 569
Kreousa, 8, 9
Krimissos, river god, 63–64, 65
Kyane, 70
Kynodesme, 129
Kyrbasia, military hat, 394
Labors of Herakles. *See* Herakles
Ladon, serpent, 119, 119n.6
Lake Urmia, 144
Laomedon, King of Troy, 137
Last Judgment, 142
Laurion mines, 339, 339n.13
Lazarus, raising from the dead, 597, 604
Lead votive plaque, *660*
Leda, wife of Tyndareos, 66
seduction of, 47
Lemnos, island of, 25
Leo, constellation, 209, 285, 292
Leontini, Sicily, 13, 13*m*
Lepidus, Marcus Aemilius, 435, 474, 476
and control of North Africa and Spain, 462–463
death of, 519
in exile with Brutus, 445
Roman consul, 428, 443, 445, 455
in Second Triumvirate, 446, 467
Leprosy (Hansen's disease), 596, 596n.68

Lesbos Island, 362
Leto, wife of Zeus, *21*, 154
Leukaspis, Sicani hero, 43–*44*
Lex Gabinia, 373
Lex Talionis, 175
Liberty and Mars, *365*
Libra, constellation, 285
Libya, Africa, 11, 169
Licinius. *See* Lucullus, Lucius Licinius
Life after death, 302, 349
Lilybaeum, Sicilian port, 428
Linus, 114, 115
Lion, head of, 181
Lion attacking a bull, *172*, 176, *177*
Lion fountains, *47*
Lion-headed serpent, 309, 310
Lions, 196, 197
Lion-skin hat, 183
Lipara, Aeolian Islands, 48, 52
Liparus, King, 49
Lituus (auger's wand), 613
Livia Drusilla, 508
  death of, 581
  first empress of Roman Empire, 469, 469n.28
  images of, *509*, 574, 575, *577*
  as Isis, 507
  as Peace (Pax), 510, 574
  third wife of Augustus, 515
  wife and sister of Octavian/Augustus, 469, 481, 495
  wife of Tiberius, 469n.28
Livias, city in Perea, 587
Locris, city-state, 134, 134n.12
Longinus, Gaius Cassius, 318
  in conspiracy against Caesar, 441
  governor of Syria Province, 427
"Lord of the phallus," 193n.8
Lord's Prayer, 377
Lucca, Italy, 392, 396
Lucius Verus, *271*
Lucullus, Lucius Licinius, 348, 366, 372, 378, 380
Ludovisi Throne, 8n.3
Lugdunensis, Roman province, 407
Lugdunum, capital of Gaul (Lyons), 419, 521
Lugh, Celtic sun god, 389–390, 400, 419
  cult of, 419
Luke, gospel of, 549, 555–566, 601, 612
  annunciation in, 593
  astrological terminology in, 562
  author of, 552
  description of the nativity, 551
  Hellenistic religious ideas in, 553
  Jesus' arrest and trial in, 615, 616
  Jesus' crucifixion in, 620

  Jews rejection of Jesus in, 624
  and location of Jesus' birth, 556
  nativity according to, 552, 564
  and Sign of Jonah, 628–630, 635
  writing of, 658
Luna, 270, 315
Lunar eclipse, 542n.26
Luxury, rejection of, 223
Lycia, Kingdom of, 88
Lycians, defeated by Romans, 461
Lydia, state of, 168
Lyre, 114
Lyrnessus, Cilician town, 131
Lysander, the Spartan, 192
Lysanias, ruler of Chalkis, 470, 471–473, *472*
Lysimachus, ruler of Thrace, 188, 192n.7
Mâ, goddess, 194, 336, 345
Maccabee, Judah, 256
Maccabees, 527n.1
  beliefs of, 308–309
  independence from the Seleukids, 256
Macedon (Macedonia), 11, 341
  Alexander and, 182, 227, 240–242, 241–242, 250
  Dorian ancestry of, 95–97
  and Mysteries of Samothrace, 86
  and Punic Wars, 242
Macedonians, 86, 95–97
Madonna and child, images of, 672
Magi
  Babylonian priests, 203, 552, 565, 566
  Hellenized, 511
Magic, 127, 223, 225
  different forms of, 203
  in early Christianity, 672–674
  as part of worship, 673
Magna Mater (the Great Mother), 162
Mago, 244
Magus, King of Cyrene, 210
Maia, wife of Zeus, *21*
Male prostitution, 181–182
Mallos, Cilicia, 147
Mammal bones, 136
Mandeans, cult, 646–647, 646n.13
Mandubii tribe, Alesia, 405
Manetho, 198
Man-headed bulls, 46
Manius Aquillius (the elder), Proconsul of Asia Province, 307, 315
Manius Aquillius (the younger), Roman consul, 307, 319, 327, 336, 396
Marasà, 8n.3
Marathon, Battle of, 169
Marc Antony. *See* Antony, Marc
Marcellus, Gaius Claudius Minor, 408
Marcellus, son of Antony and Octavia, 515

Marcus, Sulla's brother, 339
Marcus Junius Silanus. *See* Silanus, Marcus Junius
Marduk, 178n.15
Mares of Diomedes, *118*
Mariamne, wife of Herod, 538–539, 541, 542, 651
Marius Gaius
 consulships of, 307, 316–319, 320, 323, 337–338
 death of, 337–338, 339
 death of his wife, Julia, 316, 320, 370, 371
 empowerment of Romans under, 329, 332, 335
 march on Rome, 356
 military successes of, 301–329
 political success of, 311, 315–323
 siege of Rome, 359
Mark, gospel of, 103, 549, 599
 account of Jesus' death in, 623
 Jesus' arrest and trial in, 615
 Jesus' crucifixion in, 620
 and tomb of Jesus, 626–627
 writing of, 658
"The Marriage of God," 102
Mars, God of War, 11, 259, *260*, *317*, *365*
Martha, Syrian prophetess, 320, 324, 336
Martyr, meaning of, 651
Mary
 genealogy of, 554, 554n.56
 Great Mother, 346
 Mother of God, 346
 Queen of Heaven, 346
Mary, mother of Jesus, 593, 674
Mary, sister of Jesus, 601
Mary, Virgin, 552, 565. *See also* Virgin Mary, mother of Jesus
 Cult of, 113, 346
 virginity of, 601
Mary Magdalene, 622, 626–628, 626n.55, 647
"Massacre of Innocents," by Herod, 504, 504n.6, 523–524
Massalia (Marseille), 411, 412, 460
Mastectomy, 163
Master of Horse, Antony promoted to, 416
Materialistic theories, 223
Maternus, Julius Firmicus, 558
Mathematics, 92–94
Mathesis (Maternus), 557–558
Matter, creation of, 18
Matthew, gospel of, 549, 556–562, 599–601
 astrological calculations in, 559
 author of, 552

 description of the nativity, 551
 fabricated stories in, 605–606
 Jesus' crucifixion in, 619–620
 and location of Jesus' birth, 556
 massacre of the innocents in, 562
 nativity in, 552–556
 nativity story in, 552–556
 Sign of Jonah and, 628–630, 635
 and trial of Jesus, 619
 and "virgin birth," 554
 writing of, 658
Mauretania, North Africa, 433, 514
Mazaios, Persian *satrap*, 175
Mazaios governor of Transeuphrates and Cilicia, 176
Mazda, the spirit of wisdom, 142, 267
Medea, kingdom of, 168, 473, 482, 485
Medea, king of, 482, 485
Medical procedures, 98
Mediterranean area
 colonization of, 6, 11
 decline of Greek power in, 8
 East and West cultural differences in, 169–170
 as easy access among civilizations, 157
 emergence of Roman culture in, 8, 219
 first century B.C., 243*m*
 number of cults in, 1–77, 13, 158
 Romans compete with Greeks and Phoenicians in, 226
 slave trade in, 258
 spread of mystery cults in, 7–8
 spread of religious ideas in, 6–7, 158
 trade in, 6–7
Medusa, 29, *34*, 45, 52
 Athena and, *31*
 blood from her body, 32–33
 children of, 31
 description of, 31
 killed by Perseus, 32, 65, 108, 277
 parents of, 31
 relationship with Hephaistos, 33
Megara, marriage to Herakles, 116
Megara Hyblaia, Sicily, 6
 Dorians from, 13*m*, 14
Melanippe, daughter of Chiron, 48
Melqart, Carthaginian god, *61*, 602
 bust of, *633*
 portrayal of, 61
 worship of, 61
Mên, *271*, 277
 portrait of, 368
Menahem
 executed by Herod, 605
 possible messiah, 542, 605
Mende, Macedonian town, 96
Messana. *See* Zankle-Messana, Sicily

Messenia, Greece, 50
Messiah, 534
    announcing the coming of, 594
    coming at time of Herod's death, 536
    concept of, 534
    to deliver Jerusalem from evil Rome, 591
    expectation of his coming, 516, 534–537, 543
    prophecy of, 543
    prospective candidates, in the *New Testament*, 645–649
Messianic symbols, *540*
Messina, Sicily, 14, 34
Metallurgy, 29
Metal workers, *19*
Metamorphoses (Ovid), 54
Metapontum, Anatolian Peninsula, 91
Meteorites, 140, 160
    black, in Mecca, 140
    and deities, 140
    sacredness and excavations of, 140
Metis, wife of Zeus, *21*, 26
Midas, King, of Phrygia, 195
Middle East, ethnic groups of, 172–182
Midrash (religious fiction), 552–553
Mikveh (Jewish ritual bath), 594
Milky Way, 113, 292
Milo, Roman gang lord, 401
Miltiades, General in Athens, 169
Minerva, 240, 271
Minos, King of Crete, 41–42, 87
    death of, 42
Minotaur, birth of, 41
Miocene geological epoch
    fossils from, 135
Miracles, 4, 120, 498, 511
    indicating Augustus' divinity, 503–505
    of Jesus, 596
    by possible messiahs, 645–649
    of possible messiahs, 535
Miracle workers, 91, 92
Mithra, solar deity, *271*, 273, 368, 502
    death and resurrection of, 280
    as a redeemer, 268, 269
    and sacrifice of the bull, 267, 273–277, *274*, *275*, 654
    as spirit of the covenant, 142, 144, 265–267, 268
    and the sun, 270, 271, 274
    virgin birth of, 277–280, *278*, 278n.16
Mithradates VI, King of Pontus, 281, 307, 372–378, 396, 413, 427. See also Mithridatic Wars
    and Aristion, 328
    battles in Greece and, 340–342, 342n.17, 354
    challenge to Roman dominance, 323n.23
    defeat of Armenian army, 334
    and interests in Anatolia, 324, 327–329, 336
    and invasion of Bithynia, 363–367
    suicide of, 378, 380, 381n.51
Mithraic art, 274, *275*, *295*
Mithraic iconography, 297
Mithraic shrines, 292–295, *295*
Mithraism, 264
    and Christianity, 298, 375, 631, 654
    initiation into levels of, 269
Mithras, constellation, 277
Mithras, Hellenistic Cult of, 191, 264, 268–281, 297–299, 419
    Roman contact with, 419, 438, 512, 573, 631
Mithridatic Wars, 334, 334n.4, 338–339
    First, 338, 342, 379
    Second, 344, 361–363
    Third, 364–367, 372, 377–379
Mnemosyne, *19*
Moabites, 527
Moloch, Sun God, 55
Monotheism, 22, 142, 170, 170n.4, 173
Monsters, 24, 76
    genealogies of, *34*, 35
    and geographical features, 27–28
    related to Sicily, 28
    versus Zeus, 35
Montanism, 163
Montanist cults, 664
Montanus, castrated priest of Cybele, 162
Moon
    phases of, 102n.15
    revolutions of, 285
Moral pollution, 115
Mordecai, 178n.15
Morocco, 514
Moses
    images of, 259, 297, 309, 532, 572, *668*, *669*
    laws of, 651
    on Mount Sinai, 606, 637
Moshiach (messiah), 381, 534, 539
Mot, God of the Underworld, 62
Mother goddesses, cults of, 217, 240n.4
Motivation, God of the Underworld, 61
Motya, Sicily, 13*m*
Mount Cithaeron, 114
Mount Ebal, 637
Mount Eryx, 235, 261

Mount Etna, 5–6, 24, 26, 28, 32, 55–56
  eruption of, 6n.1, 67
Mount Gerizim, 178, 308, 636, 637
Mount Hara, 144, 268
Mount Ida, 239
Mount of Olives, 656
Mount Olympus, 11, 21, 26, 32, 66, 71,
  138, 272
Mount Vesuvius, eruption of, 658
Mount Zion, 588
Multiple gods, belief in, 169
Munda, Spain, Battle at, 436–437
Museion, (first museum), 197
Music, 114
Mycenae, 108, 109, 110
  decline of the civilization of, 39n.2, 42
Mycenaean Greeks, 38–39
  in early Sicily, 37
  evidence of culture of, 39
Mysteries. *See also* Mystery cults
  for communicating knowledge, 88–89
  interconnections of, 97
  knowledge of, 72
  secrecy of, 75
  seriousness of, 75
  teachers and teachings of, 88–94
Mysteries of Bona Dea, 380
Mysteries of Mende, 96
Mysteries of Samothrace, 84–87
Mystery cults, 250
  and agricultural products, 76
  archaeological evidence of, 83
  comprised of chthonic mysteries, 83
  definition of, 198
  focus of, 81
  highly intellectual, extinction of, 91
  influences on Judeo-Christian scripture,
    103
  initiation into, 58, 82–84, 250, 595
  lost, evidence of, 87–88
  major centers of, 83
  mechanism of, 82–83
  modern traditions from, 103–105
  mythology and, 1
  origins of, 3, 7–8, 7n.2, 81–82
  personal issues and, 81
  in prehistory, 83
  priests of, 81–82, 83
  rituals of, 81–82
  in Roman Empire, 573
  salvation-oriented, 217
  secrets of, 59
  spread of, 7–8, 58–59
Mysticism, 92–93, 225
  eroticism and, 103
Mystics, 91, 91n.8, 92
Mythical horned bird, 145, *146*
Mythic iconography, 368n.26
Mythological creation stories, 19
Mythological genealogies, 97
Mythological heroes, 127
Mythological references, 128
Mythology. *See* Greek mythology
Mythology(s). *See also* Greek mythology
  believability of, 139
  and Christianity, 3
  common themes of, 76–77
  fossils as records of, 138–139
  influence of history on, 37
  living traditions related to, 134–135
  merging of Greek and Sicani, 41–42
  native Sicilian, 37–56
  proving the truth of, 135
  Sicel, 39
  in the Stone Age, 37
Myths. *See also* Greek myths
  premise of, 35
  variations among, 164
Nabataeans
  Arabian cults, 512, 527
  mother of King Herod, 537, 541
  wife of Herod Antipas, 594
Nabatea, next to Judea, 544*m*
Nablus, 178
Nag Hammadi, 647
Nana, daughter of King Sangarios, 195
Nativity. *See also* Jesus
  according to *Matthew* and *Luke*, 572,
    592
  astrological accounts of, in *Matthew* and
    Luke, gospel of, 551, 572
  astrological birth chart in Hellenistic ter-
    minology, 562–563, 563
  astrological context of, 561–562
  and astronomical miracles, 556–557
  and First Roman Census, 555
  historical context of, 555, 561–562
  reconciling contradictions between gos-
    pels, 562–564
  at the time of Herod's death, 551
Nativity scene, 578, *579*
Nativity stories. *See also* Canonical gospels;
    Jesus
  in the canonical gospels, 551–556,
    568
  connecting with history, 555–556
Nature, underlying unity of, 224
Nature deities, 37
Nature worship, 142
Naval warfare, 396

Naxos, Greek island, 6, 7, 13, 14, 56, 72, 74
Naxos, Sicily, 72
Nazareth, Galilee, 548, 552–556, 601, 602
Nazi Aryanism, 132, 132n.8
Neanderthal man, 139
Nebuchadnezzar, King of Babylon, 176, 178
Nehemiah, book of, 176
Nemea, games at, 128
Nemean lion, 24, 117, *118*
Neo-Assyria, 168
Neo-Babylonia, 168
Neophytes, 90
Neo-Platonism, 225, 225n.7
Neo-Pythagorean ideas, 225
Nephthys, 198, 199
Neptune, God of the Sea, 270, 429
Nereids, sea nymphs, 466
Nero, Emperor, 655–657
 and the Jews, 656
 persecution of Christians, 655
Nero Claudius Drusus, brother of Tiberius, 521
Nessus, centaur, 123
Neviim, 533
New Testament, 140, 377
 canonical gospels of, 549
 as canonized collection of Christian documents, 532
 epistles of Paul in, 655
 influence on shaping Western culture, 640
 Jewish cults referred to in, 33
 official accounts of Jesus' life and death in, 97, 639
 other messiahs mentioned in, 596, 645–649
 portrayal of King Herod in, 529
 pretended authorships in, 663–665
 salvation in, 103
 understanding original meaning in, 598–599
Nicomedes II, *363*
Nicomedes III of Bithynia, 325
Nicomedes IV, King of Bithynia, 325, 327, 362, 366, 433
Nike, winged Goddess of Victory, 45, *46*, *64*, *69*, 193, 204, *205*, 231, *232*, 246, 271, 272, *322*, 373, *374*, 385–*386*, *451*, *494*, 496n.25, 505, *506*
Nile flood, 206
Nile River gods, 310
Noah, 158
Noah's Ark, *666*
Non-Christian beliefs, 218

Non-Christian Jewish cults, as Judaism, 665
Non-Jewish Christians, 659, 661
Non-Jews, 652–655
Nonviolence, 90
Noreia, Gaul, 314
Nude images, *181*
Nude pentathletes, 129, *130*
Numbers, book of, 179
Numerical studies, 90
Numidia, African kingdom, 313, 314, 426, 433
Numismatic iconography, 671
Nursing, as symbol of salvation, 113, 113n.4
Nymphs, 46–48, *52*, 53–54, 76, 204
Occult powers, 203, 205
Occult teachings, 120
Oceanus, *19*, 45
Octavia, wife of Antony, 467, 468, 470, 475, 498, 513–514
 claim to divinity, 477
 daughter of Octavian/Augustus, 481, 502, 513
 death of, 502, 519
 divorced by Antony, 480, 490
 grandniece of Caesar, 394, 408
 raised surviving children, 498
Octavia Minor, daughter of Antony and Octavia, 521
Octavian. *See also* Octavian/Caesar
 adopted by Caesar, 476, 499, 501
 advance to Alexandria, end of war, 495–497
 defeat of Antony, 499, 510–513, 541
 divine birth of, 504
 early childhood of, 504–505
 and Egyptian cults, 508
 as a god, 480
 honors showered on, 512–513
 name changed to Augustus, first Emperor of Rome, 494, 500, 501, 541
 nephew of Caesar, 513
 as Octavian Caesar, 496
 resigns consulship, 513
 rivalry and civil war with Antony, 479–500
 as the son of God, 501
 use of propaganda, 480–485, 496
 victory over Antony, 499, 510, 512, 513
 victory over Illyria, 486
Octavian/Caesar, 223n.2, 422, 428, 433, 500. *See also* Augustus Caesar, Emperor
 adopted son of Caesar, 476, 501
 alliance with Sextus Pompey, 469
 and Battle of Philippi, 462

consul, 446
control of North Africa, 475
defeat of Sextus Pompey, 474
divorce from Scribonia, 469
grandnephew of Caesar, 444
inherited divinity of, 455
marriage to Claudia, 460
rivalry and civil war with Antony, 444, 445, 454, 455, 463, 475
rivalry and war with Sextus Pompey, 463, 469
seizes power in Rome, 476
as Son of God, 446–449, *448*, 451, 454, 463
triumvir, 455, 467
victory of, *497*
wives of, 469, 469n.28
Octavius, father of Octavian, 504
Odysseus, 29, 48, 74, 114, 141
Odyssey (Homer), 29, 29n.8, 40, 48, 141
Oechalia, kingdom of, 120, 124
Oedipus, King of Thebes, 110, 124–125
Oeneas, King, 123
Ogyges, first King of Boeotia, 154
Ogygian Deluge, 154, 154n.5, 156
Old Testament, 168, 174, 178n.15, 180, 303, 676
  Egyptian Jews in, 180
  prophecies in, 536, 592
  Torah in, 174
Olympia, Greece, 53, 128, 132, 136, 138, 338
Olympiad, 128, 129, 132
Olympian Goddesses, 11
Olympian Gods, 11, 20–21, 20n.3, 62, 96, 128, 130–131
  chart of, *21*
  identifying, 11
  reign established, 20
  Roman names for, 266n.5
  rulers of the universe, 272
  war with the giants, 25–27
  worship of, 76, 265
Olympic Games, 128, 132
  description of, 129, *130*
  events of, 129
  founded by Herakles, 118, 122, *123*, 129
  history of, 129–130
  mythological basis of, 130–132
  religious nature of, 130
  stadion race, 129
  women forbidden to watch, 130
Omens, 141–142, 395, 429, 430, 439, 442, 459, 506
  divine, 505
Omphale, Queen of Lydia, 120, 121, 489

One god, belief in, 220, 225
On the Characteristics of Animals (Aelianus), 55n.7
Opium, healing drug, 60n.3, 98–99
Optimates, 336–342, 408, 409, 413
  allied with Pompey, 392, 426
  and Caesar, 440
  coins of, *429–430*
  friction with Populares, 303–305, 322–327, 390–391
  and Julian family, 360, 361
  loss of power, 370
  in North Africa, 426
Oracle at Delphi, 12, 30, 91, 98, 116, 120–122, 136, 245
Oracle at the Siwa Oasis, 193
Oracular dreams, 371
Orchomenos, Battle of, 341
Oreios, Euboea, 50
Orestes, son of Agamemnon, 52, 136
Orgies, 84, 252–254
Origen, Father of the Church, 163, 675n.90
Original sin, 88, 157n.7
Orion, *49*, 50–51, 96
Orion, constellation, 51
Orodes II, King of Parthia, 396, *397*, 473
  execution of General Surena, 396n.10
  with moon and stars, 396, *397*
Orontes, river god, 334
Orpheus, 117n.5, 250n.12
  mysteries of, 250
  mystery cults of, 250n.12
  semi-divine hero, 250n.12
"Orphic Life," 90
Orthos, monster, 24
Orthosia, Phoenician city, 484
Ortygia Island, 51, 54
Osiris, 198, 199, 201, 458
Ossilegium, 536
Ossuaries, 536
Ostanes, prophet, 205
Ostia, Roman port, 245, 372
Owens, Jesse, 132
Owls, 340
Pagan cults, 82, 661, 675
Pagan deities, 22, 22n.4, 140, 174
Pagan iconography, 659–660, *660*, 669, 671
Paganism, 100n.14, 139, 162, 640, 644, 652–653, 654, 665, 671
  and Christian viewpoints, 662
  becoming Christians, 652–653, 654
  as a religion, 128, 665
  and Semitic ideas, 674–677
Pagan superstition, 128
Pain, absence of, 222

Pakistan, part of India, 169n.3
Palatine hill, Rome, 31–32, 246
Palatine Temple of Cybele, 246
Palatine Temple of Victory, 246
Palestine
  Jewish kingdoms in, 180
  Jews in, 168
  Philistines in, 168n.2
Palikoi, demon children of Zeus, 55, 56
Palladium, cultic statue, 430
Pallas Athena, 133
Palmyra, Syria, 631
Pan, 46, 204, *205*
Panakaia, Goddess of Medicine, 98
Pandora, wife of Epimetheus, 157, 157n.7
Panhellenic Games, 128, 129
Panias, 544*m*, 550
Panias Gaulanitis (Golan), 543
Pankration, 129
Pannonian rebellion (Great Illyrian Revolt), 522, 522n.34
Panopeus, near Delphi, 156
Panormus, Sicily, 13*m*
Paphos, Cyprus, 140
Parable of the vineyard, 610
Paraclete, 605
Parthenis, 90
Parthia (Iran), 409, 439, 528, 531. *See also* Mithridatic Wars
  Alexander the Great and, 395
  Antony's invasion of, 473–474, 475, 476
  conflict with Medea, 482
  Jews in, 533
  Rome's attack on, 395–396
  and Seleukid Empire, 383
Parthians
  Antony's obsession with, 455
  gains by, 467
  Herod and, 538–539
  invasion of Syria, 466–468
  occupation of Roman territories, 469
  war with, 472
Pasiphae, wife of King Minos, 41
Passion of Christ, 621
Passion plays, 76, 84
Passover, 615, 617
Passover feast, 620, 621
Pater (Father), 297
Patio tomb, 631–632, 635
Patricians, 303
Paul, apostle. *See* Saint Paul, apostle (Saul of Tarsos)
Paulus, L. Aemilius Lepidus, 408
Pausanias, Greek traveler, 156
Pax (Peace), 510
Pax Romana (Roman-enforced peace), 642
Pegasus (winged horse), 32, *34*
Pegasus, constellation, 277, 376
Peloponnese Peninsula, 11, 13*m*, 14, 17, 53, 66, 70, 95, 108, *109*, 242
  herding societies in, 94
Peloponnesian War, 66, 136, 136n.20
  Athens under seige in, 339n.12
Pelops, King, 131
  lost shoulder of, 138–139
  offered as sacrifice, 138
Pelorias, nymph, *49,* 50
Pentathlon, 129
Perea, rebellion in, 543, 544*m*, 549
Pergamene Jews, 259n.17
Pergamene Kingdom, 240, 241, 242, 258, 307
Pergamon, Babylon, 100, *101*, 240n.5, 499
Perimele, seduced by Achelous, 52
Persecutions
  targeting Christians, 652
Persephone, goddess, 47, *60*, 71n.13, 76, 83, 199, 231–232, 468, 468
  abduction by Hades, *21*, 69–72, 94
  child of Zeus and Demeter, 21, 52, 53, 56, 59
  as Eastern Queen of the Dead, 7, 172
  images of, 60
  and Locrian Ajax, 134, *135*
  mystery cults related to, 250n.12
  myths of, 10, 67–72, *69*
  Queen of the Underworld, 59, 75–76
  return to Sicily, 10, 10n.4
Persepolis, Alexander's death in, 187
Perseus, constellation, 277, 292
Perseus, Greek hero, 108, 269, *280*, *281*, *419*
  ancestor of the Persians, 32, 147
  Andromeda saved by, 108
  associated with Baal of Tarsos, 292
  astrological mysteries and, 277
  birth of, 280, 281
  children of, 108
  Eryx killed by, 65
  founder of Tarsos, 292
  Greek hero, 269
  married to Andromeda, 108
  Medusa killed by, 32, 65, 108, 277, 281, *281*, *282*
  miraculous conception of, 277, 278
  as Mithras, 294

myth of, 277–281, 292
  semi-divine hero, 108
Persia, 136n.21, 141, 142, 191
Persian Empire, 167, 168–170, 439
  conquered by Alexander, 168, 182–185
  Jews in, 173, 176–182
  tolerance of different cultures in, 169–170
Persians, 32
  and Greek points of view, 147
  in Syria, 172
Persian Zoroastrians
  worship of Mithra, 145–146, 265–266
Personal deification, 349
Personal freedom, belief in, 169
Personification of Italia, *326*
Personification of Rome, 306, *306*
Perusia (Perugia), Spain, 465, 466
Pessinus (Galatia), 140
Pessinus, temple at, 158–160, 196, 242
Petasus, 197
Petra, Jordan, 512
Phaenomena, pagan prayer in, 377, 377n.42
Phallic symbols, religious use of, 182
Pharaohs, 181, 191
  as gods, 453
  wives of, 181–182, 181n.25
Pharaoh Seti I, Egyptian ruler, *535*
Pharisaic teachings, 309
Pharisees, Jewish cult, 309n.9, 530, 531, 533, 535–536, 597–598
Pharnaces, son of Mithradates VI, 427–428, 433
Pharsalos, Greece, 415, 416
Pheraimon, King of Zankle-Messana, *49*, 50, 62
Phibionites, cult of, 665
Philadelphus, Ptolemy, son of Antony and Cleopatra, 474, 498
  declared King of Syria, Phoenicia, and part of Asia, 485
Philetaerus, 240, *241*
Philip II of Macedon, father of Alexander the Great, 85, 85n.2, 182
Philippi, Battle of, 462
Philip V of Macedon, 241–242, 241n.6
  forms alliance with Carthage, 241–242
Philistines, 168n.2
Phillip II, Roman emperor, 129, *130*
Philo, relative of Herod Antipas, 596
Philosophical movements, 606
Philosophy, 204
  new understandings of, 204

Phoebe, *19*
Phoenicia, 544*m*
  Pompey in, 381
Phoenician city-states, 15
Phoenician colonies, 11–14
Phoenician gods, 62
Phoenicians, 40
  from Carthage, 40
  competition with Romans, 40–41
  cults and mythology of, 59–63
  in early Sicily, 6, 11–14, 37, 40–41
  in Judea, 527
  origins of, 13, 14
  religious beliefs of, 40
  trade of, 31
Phoenix, son of King Agenor, 85
Phorcys, father of Medusa, 31, *34*, 35, 45
Phraates IV, ruler of Parthia, 473
Phrygia, Anatolia, 240n.4, 307
Phrygian (Central Anatolian) mysteries, 194
Phylacteries (boxes of scripture), 534
Physical and Mystical Teachings (Democritus), 205
Physical resurrection, 598
Picenum, Adriatic Coast, 357, 359
Pidyon Ha' Ben ceremony, 179
Pig, 103, *104*
Pilate, Pontius, prefect of Judea, 613, 613, 625
  accused of mass murder, 638
  anti-Jewish policies of, 609, 610
  arrest and trial of Jesus and, 615–619, 641
  arrival in Jerusalem, 581, 603, 607
  assigned to Judea, 571
  controversy surrounding, 641
  crucifixion of Jesus and, 609–640
  deposed, 609
  expulsion from Judea of, 636–638
  historical record of, 610, 624–625
  Jerusalem cult controlled by, 586
  Jesus' arrest and trial and, 614–619
  removal from office, 651
  reputation for cruelty and violence, 641n.1
  ruthless treatment of Jews, 582, 583, 585, 612, 641, 641n.1
Pillars of Herakles, 6, 119
Piracy, 12
Pisa, Italy, 132
Pisces, constellation, 172, 277, 285, 506, 516
Piso, Gnaeus Calpurnius, 576, 580

Pisonis, Calpurnia
  wife of Caesar, 385
Plague, 138
  halted by Pythagorean mystic, 91, *92*
Planets
  motions of, 285, 287
  positions of, 558–561, 562, *563*
Plato, Greek philosopher, 92, 146, 154, 192n.5, 224, 286n.25
  influence on Hellenistic Age, 220–221
Platonic metaphysics, 225
Plebians, 303
Pleiades, star cluster, 51
Pleistocene geological epoch, 136, 136n.19, 138
Pliny the Elder, Roman general, 298
Plotinus, 225
Plutarch, 266
Pluto, god, 270, 272, 273, 276
Pogroms, 642, 642n.3
Polemon, ruler of Pontus, 470
Polycrates, 90n.5
Polydeukes, son of Leda, 66
  myths of, 66–67
Polyphemus, 29, 33, *34*, 35, 74
Polytheism, 22
Pomoerium, boundary of Rome, 508
Pompeii, 667n.77
  Christian graffiti found in, 658
Pompeiopolis, city created by Pompey, 373
Pompeius Aulus, tribune, 321
Pompeius Strabo, Gnaeus, Roman politician, father of Pompey the Great, 357
Pompey, Cnaeus, 426, *436*, 437
Pompey, Sextus, 426, *436*, 437, 446
  alliance with Octavian, 469
  commander of Roman fleet, 460
  control of Sicily and other islands, 467
  death of, 482
  defeated by Octavian, 463, 467, 469, 474, 475, 476
  invasion of Anatolia, 482
  as Son of Neptune, 463, *464*
Pompey, Theater of, *355*, 394, 442
Pompey portrayed as Alexander the Great, *393*
Pompey the Great (Gnaeus Pompeius Magnus), 266, *413*, 504
  alliance with enemies, 400–402
  annexed Syria Province and Judea, *355*
  assassination of, *355*, 418, 420–423
  background of, 354
  and burning of the Senate, *355*
  campaign against Cilician pirates, 266, 372–373, 374, 413
  consul of Rome, *355*
  consulships of, 393
  and Crassus, 388, 392, 393
  death of, and aftermath of, 422–430
  defeat of Populares in Sicily, 360, 361
  defeat of Spartacus, 368–369
  ended Jewish kingship in Judea, 528, 535–536
  and expansion of Roman control, 380–381
  in First Triumvirate, 384, 390, 393
  flight to Egypt, 416–418
  foreign governorships of, 393
  founded Pompeiopolis, *355*
  gave kingship of Judea to Hyrcanus II, 536n.13
  granted proconsular imperium, 365
  images of, 463, *464*
  lust for glory, 357–360
  marriage to Cornelia Metella, *355*, 400
  marriage to Julia Caesar, *355*
  military career of, 357, 358–359
  organizational talents of, 365–366
  portrayed as Alexander the Great, *393*
  rivalry with Caesar, 392–393, 400–403, 408–418
  and Roman politics, 383–384
  in Servile War, *355*
  in Social War, *355*, 357
  sons of, 431, 436, *436*, 437n.36
  in Southern Anatolia, 378
  Sulla's treatment of, 334n.4, 342n.18, 343, 353, 354, 359–360
  in Syria, 381
  and Third Pontic War, *355*
  timeline of his life, *355*
  vanity of, 373–377
  and wars in Spain, *355*
  winning of Third Mithridatic War, 377–378
Pontic army, 341
  in Greece, 338–339, 340
Pontic Empire, 427
Pontifex Maximus, 344, 380, 435
Pontifices, College of, 367
Pontus, kingdom of, 271, 341, 366, 367, 372, 375, 377, 427, 433, 470
  reorganized as a Roman Province, 380
Pope of the Catholic Church, 297, 344
Populares, 303–306, 322–327, 336–341, 359–361, 364, 401
  Caesar and, 390, 391
Poros, King of India, 516
Poseidon, God of the Sea, 20, 21, 29, 34, 270
  children of, 29, 32, 70
  grants Pteralaos invincibility, 109–110

heals Polyphemus, 29
image in the form of an ithyphallic ass, 96
loved by Pelops, 138
and Olympic Games, 128
rape of Demeter, 70, 94, 96
rape of Persephone, 94
revenge acts of, 41, 42
son of Orion, 50
trident of, 28
Posidonius of Apamea, 269n.7
Pozzuoli, Italian city, 258, 512
Praetor, office of, 259, 259n.16, 357, 401
Prefects of Judea, 588–590, *589. See also* Judea, kingdom of
Priam, King of Troy, 119, 360–361
Priests
of Cybele, 392
of the Eleusinian Mysteries, 98
Eumolpids, 98
in mystery cults, 81–82, 83
sacrificial ceremonies, 173
Proconsular imperium, 365, 365n.21
Prometheus, 48
Deucalion created by, 156, 157
myths about, 157
Promised Land, 180
Prophecies, books on, 238
Prophetess, *434*
Prophets, 533
Proskynesis, 193, 193n.9
Prostitutes, 260
Protective deities, 189
Pteralaos, King of the Taphians, 109
Ptolemaic Empire, 471
end of, 499, 516
Ptolemy I, ruler of Egypt, 188, 197–198, *198*, 203, 206–207, 231
Ptolemy II, ruler of Egypt, 203, 209–210, 423, 424
and translation of the *Torah*, 208
Ptolemy III, ruler of Egypt, 203, 209, 210–211
Ptolemy IV, ruler of Egypt, 250
Ptolemy IX, ruler of Egypt, 382
Ptolemy XII, ruler of Egypt, 382, 382n.53, 416, 417, 423, 424
father of Cleopatra VII, 382n.53
and First Triumvirate of Rome, 384
illegitimate son of Ptolemy IX, 382–383
Ptolemy XIII, co-regent of Egypt, 383, 417, 423, 424, 425
Ptolemy XIV, brother/husband of Cleopatra, 425, 431, 431n.18
disappearance of, 458–459
Publius, son of Gaius Marius, *323*, 394

Publius Clodius, gang lord, 380, 391, 392
Publius Crassus, son of Marcus Crassus, 393, 394
death of, 395–396, 400
Publius Quinctilius Varus, military general, 522, 547–548
reorganization of Judea, 544–545
Publius Scipio Nasica, 245
Pulcher, Publius Clodius, 380, 460n.16
Punchmarks, 96
Punic Wars, 219, 227–230, 233, 238
First Punic War, 219, 241
Second Punic War, 219, 238, 241n.7, 242–245, 247, 251, 259, 358
Third Punic War, 256–257
Purification ceremonies, *104*, 110
Purim, 177
Pylus, King of, 121
Pyrrha, first Iron Age woman, 157
and the Great Flood, 193
Pyrrhic War, 219, 226–227
Pyrrho, 222, 264
Pyrrhus, King of Molossia, 227
Pythagoras, 89, 90n.5, 146, 152, 596
influence of, 92
teachings of, 90, 90n.7, 91, 92–94
Pythagorean Mysteries, 88–92
Pythagorean rituals, 90
Pythagorean Theorem, 89
Pythia, games at, 128
Python, monster snake, 97
Quaestors, 305, 357
Queen of Heaven, 162
Queen of the Dead, 172
Quintus Caecilius Metellus Pius Scipio Nasica (QCMPSN), 400, 402, 426, 429
Quirinius, Publius Sulpicius, governor of Syria Province, 520n.32, 550, 553, 555, 557, 610
Qumran, Jewish scriptures found at, 310, 533, 537n.17
Ra, sun god, 181, 182, 198
Rab, Croatia, 139
Races
evolution of, 147
sequential appearance of, 164
Rama I, 190
Ramses II, Pharaoh of Egypt, 180, 180n.21
Rapture, 128, 128n.1
Rasnu (spirit of judgment), 144, 268
"The Rape of the Sabine Women," 226n.8
Reason, declining faith in, 224–225
Red cattle of Geryon, 119
Regional Archaeological Museum, Palermo, Sicily, *47*

Reincarnation, 224
Religion. *See also* Religious beliefs
 ancient religious themes, 123–147
 athletics and, 128–132
 Christianity, Judaism and paganism as, 665
 as a collection of cults, 639, 665n.73
 dichotomies in, 105
 Eastern, 128
 evolution of Western, 127, 128
 and human needs, 127
 origins of, 149–150
 power of, 150
 purpose of, 127
Religious amulets, 669
Religious beliefs
 in afterlife, 530
 deification and, 447
 of earliest inhabitants of Sicily, 35, 43
 in early Roman Empire, 502
 eternal life, 590
 evolution of, 149–164
 in Gallic societies, 419
 immortality of the soul, 549
 in multiple gods, 169
 personal freedom and, 169
 of physical resurrection, 530, 536, 550, 590
 of reincarnation, 594
 of souls' ascent into heaven, 573
 in the time of Jesus, 590–591
 in transmigration of souls, 530
 Zoroaster's concepts and pagan mythologies, 142, 145–146
Religious fundamentalism, 151
Religious iconography, 58, 62–63, 218
Religious implements, 410, 411
Religious offices, 410
Religious persecution
 in Rome, 252–254
 in Sicily, 319
Religious practices, 162–163
Religious relics
 artifacts as, 139
 associated with King Pelops, 138–139
 fossils as, 135–139, 137
 Pelops' scapula as, 138
Religious rituals, 82–83, 129
Religious symbols, 146
 across centuries, 160–162
 on coins, 509, 509, 510
 in Herod's kingdom, 567
 indicating divinity of emperors, 575
 non-Jewish, 545
 power of, 516
 on Roman coinage, 574

 in the time of Jesus, 590
 used by Augustus, 508–511
 used by Christians, 496n.25
Religious theater
 in mystery cults, 82, 83–84
 and reenactments of mythological events, 83
Religious triad, 346
Renaissance, 4
Reshef, image of, 62
Resurrection, 142, 196, 196n.16, 197, 675. *See also* Jesus, resurrection of
 belief in, 530
 as corpse resuscitation, 625
 physical, 309
 spiritual, 624, 625
Retrograde motion, 285
Revenge, killing for, 115
Rex Sacrorum, priest, 344
Rhadamanthus, 87
Rhea, Goddess of Mountains, Forests, and Commerce, 19, 19–20, 225, 386, 507
Rhodes, island of, 14, 44, 363–364, 496
 Dorians from, 13*m*
Rhodians, defeated by Romans, 461
Ring money of Helvetii, 389
Rites of reconciliation, 96
Ritual immersion, 595
Rituals
 of the Romans, 231
 washing of feet, 594
River gods, 37, 44–47, 52, 53–55, 63–64, 76
Roman Asia Province, 517
Roman calendar, 422, 435–436, 435n.25, 440
Roman Census of Judea, First, 550–551
 Jesus and, 555–556
Roman cults, under Tiberius, 572–575
Roman Empire. *See also* Roman Republic; Rome
 after the crucifixion of Jesus, 643, 645
 approval of Tiberius as emperor in, 580
 cults of, 506–515, 569, 571–579, 606, 644
 divinity of emperors in, 502, 503–512
 emerging, 481
 evolution of, 134, 501–524
 expansion of, 4, 519, 522, 676
 foundations of, 57
 Hellenistic cults in, 523
 intellectual climate in, 606
 Jews and non-Jews in, 642
 new provinces in, 517
 population of Jews in, 569, 570

Index   715

renewal of spiritual life in, 502
Roman origins of, 133
transition to, 501–524
undesirable cults, controlling, 508
Roman Forum, 431
Roman Gaul, 318–319
Roman gods and goddesses, 231
Roman mythology, 64, 225
Roman pagans, 84
Roman priests, 231
Roman Republic. *See also* Caesar, Julius; Roman Empire; Rome
    absolute power of Caesar in, 418, 440
    civil war between Antony and Octavian in, 486–498
    claims of divination in, 477
    competition for power in, 476
    consuls in, 304
    control of the Western World and, 353–386
    creation of, 239
    culture of, 238
    elections and offices of, 304–305
    and emergence of Christianity, 235
    emerging claims of divinity in, 480
    end of, 329, 349, 499, 500, 501
    evolving into Roman Empire, 134
    expansion into Hellenistic lands, 311
    First Triumvirate in, 354, *355*
    influence of Hellenistic cults on, 301–303
    Jewish cults in, 529–539
    military successes of, 353–354
    Mithridatic Wars of, 364–365, 366–367, 377–378
    morality and divinity in, 482
    official religion in, 344
    Optimates and Populares friction in, 370–386, 390
    period of wars of, 364–373
    polarization of East and West, 481
    politics in, 303–311
    Second Triumvirate in, 422
    slow death of, 512–515
    struggle among gods in, 476–477
    struggles for power, 479–480
    threats from other countries, 312–315
    transition to the Roman Empire, 501–524
    upper and lower classes in, 304–307
    war between East and West and, 474–475
Rome, 32. *See also* Roman Empire; Roman Republic
    alliances of, 237, 308
    ambiguous relationship with Hellenism, 217, 219, 231, 233, 506
    Carthaginian invasion of, 241, 241n.7
    Christianity in, 373–377
    connection to Pergamene Kingdom, 240, 241–242
    connection with ancient Troy, 134
    conquest of Syracuse, 230
    as a cosmopolitan city, 449
    and cults, 231–232, 237–264, 373, 379
    dependence on slaves, 354
    division into three parts, 462–463
    Eastern lands controlled by, 439
    economic dependence on war, 235, 237
    expulsion of cults, 258–259
    extent of control, 226
    fire in, 655
    First Triumvirate of, 383–386
    foreign governance policies, 229
    founding of, 64, 133, 225, 357
    Greek colonies and, 226
    Hellenism and, 219–220, 229, 231, 233
    Jews in, 422, 530
    maintaining traditional culture of, 233
    new nature of, 349
    possession of Sicily and, 228–229
    preserving the culture of, 237
    provincial rule by, 231–233
    rise of, 225–230
    rituals in, 231
    sacked by Celts, 226
    Second Triumvirate, 422, 455
    slaves in, 254–257
    territorial expansion of, 226
    as a threat to Greek culture, 231, 233, 241–242
    violence and gang lords in, 400–401
    war-based, 225
    wars against Hellenism, 237–264
    wars of, 219–220, 228–229
Romulus and Remus, 40, 225, 357–358
Rosh Chodesh, 565
Royal anchor symbol, *635*
Royal diadem (indicating queen), 8, 101, 231, *232*
Royal House of Pontus, 281
Sabazian cults, 672
Sabazians
    expulsion of, 258–259, 259n.17, 271n.12
    Spartacus and, 367
Sabazius, Thracian god, 250, 258–259, 367–368, 511
    cult of, 258–259, 277, 298, 367, 368, 570, 655
    holding grapes and thyrsus, 368, *368*
    images of, *271*, *368*

Sabbath, 297
Sabines, 226
Sacagawea, 43
Sacred animals, *64*
Sacred Band of Thebes, 183
Sacred bipennis, *346*
Sacred mountains, 157
Sacred owl, 328, *329*
Sacred prostitution, 63
Sacred symbols, *60*
Sacrifice, 254
  of animals, 174, 295
  to Atargatis, 173
  of children, 63n.6, 63n.7, 173
  of kosher animals, 280n.19
  of living children, 63
Sacrificed bull, 267, 273, *274–275*, 507, 508, 654
Sacrificial tripod and heron, 89
Sadducee priests, 614, 615
Sadducees, 309n.9, 530–533, 535, 536
Sagittarius, constellation, 285
Saint Augustine, Christian philosopher, 225
Saint Bridgit, 22n.4
Saint Christopher ("Dog Face"), skull of, 139
Saint Cornely, 22n.4
Saint George and the dragon, 22n.4, 368, 368n.26, 661n.58
Saint Jerome, 596
Saint Mary. *See* Virgin Mary, mother of Jesus
Saint Paul (Saul of Tarsos), apostle
  death of, 655
  forged writings of, 663
  miracles of, 648
  competing with possible messiah, 648
Saint Peter, apostle, 272, 297, 617, 649, 652
  Christian burial site of, 656
  death and tomb of, 655
Saints, 22, 22n.4, 309
Saint Stephen, Christian martyr, 651
Salamis, island near Athens, 169
Salome, daughter of Herodias, 595
Salome, sister of Jesus, 601, 627
Salvation, 104–105, 134, 674
  agricultural products and, 76
  Christian beliefs about, 640
  in Christian cults, 675
  cults offering, 573
  fears associated with, 82
  in Hellenistic Cult of Mithras, 276
  Herakles as a symbol of, 125
  initiation ceremonies offering, 72
  as marriage to Jesus, 103
  meaning of, in ancient times, 58–59
  mysteries and, 75, 81
  mystery cults and, 81
  in *New Testament* scripture, 103
  origins of, 57–77, 83
  representation of, 68
  spreading to all Mediterranean cultures, 75–77
  symbols of, 60, 60n.3, 113
Salvation-related mysteries, 127–128
Samaria, Judea, 145, 178, 181–182, 532, 543, 544*m*, 545, 550
Samaritan cults, 174
Samaritan Jews, 178–179
  and Jerusalem Jews, 178
  Zeus as god of, 187
Samaritan Pentateuch, 208
Samaritans, 533, 534, 637–638
  and acts of violence in Judea, 588–599
  and criticisms of Judaioi, 531–532
  synagogues outside the Levant, 532
Samaritans of Shechem, 308, 527
Samos, island of, 90n.5, 489
  mammal bones found in, 135–136
Samothrace, island of, 7, 85
  artifacts on, 83
  mystery cults in, 81, 84–87
Samothrace, Mysteries of, 73n.15, 85
Samson and Delilah, 112
Sandan, *190*
Sangarios, King (mythical), 195
Sanhedrin priests, 586
Santa Prisca Mithraeum, 277
Santorini, Greek island, 154
Saosyant, spiritual savior, 516
Saraph, Jewish tradition, 309
Sarcophagus, *667*, *668*, *673*
Saronic Gulf, 169
Sarpedon, son of Zeus, 87
Satan, Christian images of, 48
SATOR Square, cult symbols, 658
Saturn, deity, 266, 270, 272, 277, 297, *385*
Saul of Tarsos, Hellenized Jew. *See* Saint Paul (Saul of Tarsos), apostle
Savior(s)
  expected arrival of, 147
  powers attributed to, 622
  prophesized (Saosyant), 144–145
  title of, 453
Sayings gospel, Gnostic point of view in, 593
Scepter, eagle-tipped (religious symbol), 146
Scepter of Zeus, 183, 183n.29

Index   717

Scientific achievements, 223
  during the Hellenistic Age, 191, 266
Scipio. *See* Quintus Caecilius Metellus Pius Scipio Nasica (QCMPSN)
Scipio Africanus, defeated Hannibal, 245, *246*, 247
Scorched-earth policy, 183
Scorpio, constellation, 285
Scribonia, wife of Augustus, 515
Scribonia, wife of Octavian, 469
Scythia, 324
Sea nymphs, 31, 33, 37, 45
Seas, surrounding Greece and Sicily, 7*m*, 155
Seasons, 71, 283
Second Triumvirate, 422, 446, 449, 455, 459, 477
  and Battle of Philippi, 462
  Brutus versus Cassius and, 461
  Caesarion accepted as ruler of Egypt, 477
  domains after Caesar's death, 449, 459, 479–480
  Herod and, 538–539
  leaders of, 422, 446, 455
  Octavian versus Antony and, 479–500
  resolving differences in, 467
  rivalries and civil war for control of Rome, 459–469
Secular Games, 502, 518, 523
Seers, 121, 121n.8
Segesta, Sicily, 13*m*, *40*, 64
Segesta, Trojan maiden, 63–64
Sejanus, administrator of Rome, 581, 582–585
  anti-Jewish policies of, 571
  appointed by Tiberius, 607
  appoints Pontius Pilate as prefect for Judea, 571, 581
  death of, 580, 582
  seduction of Drusus' wife, 580
  substitutes for Tiberius, 609
Sekhmet (a lioness), 197
Selene (moon), 270
Seleucus II, 210, 211
Seleukid Empire, 193, 210, 240, 254, 255n.15, 256, *257*, 380n.49, 383, 469
  and the Jews, 256
Seleukids, 308, 529
Seleukos, ruler of Mesopotamia, 188
Self-castration, 163
Self-mutilation, 162, 163
Selinos, river god, 52, 92
Selinos, Sicily, 13*m*, 91, 92
  artifacts in, 52, 83
  cults in, 53, 56
  temple at, 26–27, 26n.5, 27
Semele, daughter of Cadmus and Harmonia, 73, 87
Semites, 180n.20
Semitic iconography, 297
Semitic ideas, pagan and, 674–677
Senate, Roman, 304
Sepphoris, city destroyed, 548, 549, 602
  rebuilding of, 587
Septuagint, 208, 209, 533, 535, 554, 662
Serapeum, temple in Alexandria, 458
Seraphim, 22
Serapion, governor of Cyprus, 456
Serapis, Lord of the Underworld, 200–201, *312*
  Cult of, 201, 214, 506, 670
Sermon on the Mount, 605–606
Sertorian War, 364–366
Sertorius, Spanish general, 364–365
Servile Wars, 364, 367–369
Seth, Egyptian god, 198, 199
"Seven against Thebes," 95n.11
"Seven Sisters" (star cluster), 51
Sextilis, month (August), 504, 504n.5
Sexual orgies, 84, 665
Sex without passion, 222n.1
Shechem, in northern Israel, 178, 186, 588, 637
Sheep, 114
Shekel, 602
Shimon Bar Jonah. *See* Saint Peter
Sibylline Books, 238–240, 245, 247, 439
Sicani cults, 76
Sicani mythology, 41–42, 41–43
Sicans, 12, 13, 13*m*, 14, 37, 38, 40, 44
Sicarii, 533, 588, 657
Sicel cults, 76
Sicel gods, 46, *55*–56
Siceliots, 63
Sicel kings, 49–50
Sicels, 12, 13, 13*m*, 14, 37, 39, 40, 42
  origins of, 39
Sicilian cults, ancient, 57–77
Sicilian Greeks, 208, 227, 228
Sicilian mythology (native)
  compared to Greek mythology, 56
  role of gods and nymphs in, 47–48
Sicilian river gods, 46–48
Sicily. *See also* Creation mythology
  African culture influences in, 3, 40, 76
  ancient Greek era of, 17–35, 42–43
  archaeologists in, 38–39
  as birthplace of wheat, 68
  Carthaginian colonies in, 14–15

colonization periods of, 3, 7–8, 12–15, 13*m*, 17
Cult of Atargatis in, 261
diverse traditions and cultures in, 3–15, 37, 57, 59, 68, 76
earliest religious traditions in, 35, 43
Eastern cults in, 76
Elymian gods and, 57
Europeans in, 3, 5
evolution of Greek mythology in, 17–35
Greek colonies in, 4, 5, 13, 30, 38, 40, 41–44, 54
Greek culture in, 43–44
history of, 3–4, 5
indigenous tribes of, 13
Ionian Greeks in, 13, 57, 58
land/landforms of, 3–15, 28, 55
maps of, 7, 13
Mediterranean cults in, 1–77
merging of gods and myths in, 37–38
monsters of, 24
native cults in, 12, 57, 76
Near Eastern influences in, 40
non-Greek influences in, 57–65
Phoenician colonies in, 4, 13*m*, 40–41, 57
religious influences in, 6–8
religious persecution in, 319
rivalry with Athens, 4
role in creation mythology, 25
Roman battles for control of, 4, 17, 40, 43, 228
slave revolt in, 319
slaves and slavery in, 4–12, 40, 134, 175
strategic location of, 5
surrounding seas of, 7
trade with Mycenaean Greeks in, 38–39, 41
tribal cultures of, 13
Siculo-Punic images of Anat and Reshef portrayed as Athena, 62
Sidereal year, 207
Sides Iulium (comet), 518
Sign of Jonah, 628–636
and astrological connection with crucifixion, 630–631
earliest depiction of, 631
and internment of Jesus, 631
from Talpiot, 632–633
Silanus, Marcus Junius, 314–315
Silenos, stepfather of Dionysos, *74*
ruled as King of Satyrs, *74*, 75
Silphium, 98–99
Silver Age, 154, 163, 164
Silver Race, 154

Simon Magus (a Samaritan), 645, 648–649
healing miracles of, 649
Simon of Perea, 547, 549
Simon the Zealot, 646
Simpulum (ladle), 613
Single god, Jewish worship of, 174
Sirens (woman-headed birds), 34
Sistine Chapel, 297
Sistrum (rattle), 311, *312*, 514
Skepticism, 218, 222, 225, 264, 606
Skoptsy of Russia, 163, 163n.11
Sky, God of, 9–10. *See also* Jupiter, God of Sky
Sky gods, 9–10, 573
Skylla, sister of Medusa, 29, 31, *34*, 35, 45, 52, 69, *69*
transformation of, 33–34
Slave-operated farms, 312
Slave rebellions, 262–263, 354, 368–369
in Rome, 313
in Sicily, 319
Slavery, 4–12, 40, 186
early association with Sicily, 40
Slaves, 175, 461
Carthaginian, 256–257
Jewish, 255–256
in Rome, 254–257
in Sicily, 40
Slave trade, 5, 254–255, 255–256, 372
Snakes, 98, 100, 103, *104*, 112, 197, 270n.11, 346, 410, *411*, 468, 510
Sneezes, 141, 142
Sober Stone, 116
Social War, 324–327, 335–336, 343
Socrates, 225
Sol, sun god, 315, 573
Solar deities, 631, 658
under Augustus, 512
birth of, 61, 170–172, 217, 257, 310, 419, 419n.29, 502, 675
Jesus as, 631
Solar symbols, 180
Sol Invictus, 271, 573, 631
Solomon, Temple of, 173, 174, 177
Solstice, 285
Solus, Phoenician town, 13, 62
Sophia, female divinity, 664, 668
Sosigenes of Alexandria, scholar, 435
Soter (savior), 102, 198, 231
Sothic calendar, 206–207
Sothis (dog star), 206, 207
Soul
ascent to heaven after death, 573
beliefs about, 224, 530
creation of, 156
at death, 90

immortality of, 91, 223
Plato's view of, 220
Roman ideas of, 231
in Stoic philosophy, 276
transmigration of, 530
in Zoroastrian view, 144
Space, creation of, 18
Spain, 392, 393, 411, 647. *See also* Further Spain
cults in, 438
Rome and, 393, 431
Sparta, city-state, 136n.20
Sparta, King of, 121
Spartacus, gladiatorial slave, 354, 367, 368–369
Spartans, 11, 14, 66, 86
Spear-bearers, 563
Sphinx, 24
Spica (star), 294n.30
Spintriae, *584*, 585
Spiritual and material worlds, 89
Spiritual beings, 143
Spiritual pollution, 116, 119, 122
Spiritual purification rituals, 270n.11
Sraosa, spirit of hearkening to god, 144, 268
Stadion race, 129
Star from Jacob, 539
Star of Bethlehem, 520, 523, 525, 557, 559, 562, 564, *565*, 566, 671, 672
astrological discussions of, 520, 630, 631
Stars, giant (myth), 19
Stephen. *See* Saint Stephen
Steropes, Cyclopes, *19*, 28
Sthenelus, son of Perseus, 108, 110
Stheno, Gorgon, 31
Stoic ideas, 269, 277
and Cult of Mithras, 283
Stoicism, 219, 223–225, 266, 276
existence of God, 218
Stoic philosophers, 269n.7, 573
scientific ideas of, 282–283
Stoic philosophy, 276
Stoics of Tarsos, 277, 291, 298
Stone Age, 12, 37, 152n.4, 164
Strabo, 30n.9
Strait of Gibraltar, 6
Strait of Messina, 12, 29, 33, 34, 39, 48, 50, 55
Stymphalian birds, *118*
Styx River, 45
Suessiones, Gallic tribe, 390
Suetonius, historian, 443n.34, 503n.3
Suicide, 116
Sulla, Lucius Cornelius, Roman dictator
battles of, 336, 340, 341
and Caesar, 361
consulships of, 333, 334, 348, 356
death of, and aftermath of, 349, 354, 362, 365
dictatorship of, 331–349, 354
in exile, 338–342
marriage of, 336, 337
military strategist, 318, 331–334, 353–354
politics of, 332–334, 370
religious reforms under, 344–345
secured Greek Peninsula for Rome, 341
seizes control of Rome, 337
and the Social War, 335–336
treatment of Pompey the Great, 359–360, 392
Sulla, Pompeia, Caesar's wife, 373, 380
Sumerians, 203, 207
Summer solstice, 283, 286, 287
Sun
monotheistic reverence for, 180
worship of, 90
Sun-centered model of universe, 282, 283–*284*, *298*
Superstitions, 231, 672
Surena, Parthian general, 396, 396n.10
execution of, 396n.10
Survival skills, 150
Symbols, persistence of, through history, 160–162
Synoptic gospels, 595, 604
contradictions among canonical gospels, 619, 621
Jesus' arrest and trial in, 614–618
Syracusans (Dorians), 10n.4, 14
Syracuse, Sicily, 13, 13*m*, 14, *43*, 44, 51, 53, *227*
founding of, 30
and Olympia, 54
and Punic Wars, 242
Syria, 76, 172, 188, 196. *See also* Syrian Province
becomes Roman province, 380
Crassus in, 395, 439, 3393
invaded by Parthians, 466–468
Pompey in, 380
Syrian Aphrodite, 172–173, 233, 260, *262*, 316, 334n.5, 506, 507, 634
images of, *510*
Syrian cults, 672
Syrians, in Judea, 529–530
Syria Province, 380, 427, 467, 520, 544, 547
government of, 612

governorship of, 550, 612
  and removal of Coponius, 588–589
Taa Raa Ban, god, 190
Taheb (Samaritan messiah), 636–637
Tallit (Jewish prayer shawls), 533–534
Talpiot tomb, Israel, 627, 628, 634, 635, 636
Tammuz, god, 172
Tanach, or *Hebrew Bible*, 533
Tanit, Carthaginian goddess, 60, 170, 260, 574
Tantalus, King
  offered Pelops as child sacrifice, 138
  in the underworld, 138n.22
Taphian pirates, 108, 109, 110
  war against, 109, 110, 111
Taphos, 108
Taras. *See* Tarentum, Greek colony
Tarentum, Greek colony, 91, *202*, 203, 227, 254
Tarentum, Treaty of, 469
Tarkondimotos, King of Eastern Cilicia, 374, 374n.37, *375*
Tarquinius Superbus, Etruscan king, 239
Tarsians, 277
Tarsos, Anatolia, 427, 516, 573, 647
  Antony's move to, 466
  capital of Cilicia, 183, 277, 291
  displaying city towers, *175*
  Stoics of, 277, 291
Tartarus, 18, 20
Taurobolium, ritual baptism, 507, 508
Tauromenion, temple to Serapis, 233
Taurus, constellation, 274, 277, 284
Taxes. *See* Roman Census of Judea, First
Tax farming, 306, 307, 555
Tefnut, 198
Tegea, city-state, 136
Tekton (laborer), Jesus as, 601
Telesphoros (God of Convalescence), 98
Temple boys, 181, 181n.27
Temples, 174
  architecture of, 174
  to combination deities, 188
Ten Commandments, 655
Tertullian, 163
Tesserae, 584
Tethys, *19*, 45
Teutones, Germanic tribe, 314, 321
Thailand, 190
Thaleia, nymph, 55
Thanatos, as Angel of Death, *445*
Thasos, island of, 85, 102, 108, 110
Thasos, son of King Agenor, 85
Thebes, Greece, 45, 114, 115
  Electra gate in, 110
  founded by Cadmus, 84

Theia, *19*
Themis, *19*
Themistocles, Athenian leader, 169
Theocles, Ionian leader, 13
Theodosius I, Christian emperor, 129, 162
Thera caldera, eruption of, 154, 164
Therapeutae, teacher, 533
Thermoutis (a snake), 197
Theron, King of Akragas (Agrigento), 22, 42
Theseus, Ionian hero, 75, 116, 156
Thespiae, 114
Thespius, King, 114
Thessaly, 11, 12
Thetis, sea nymph, 25, 131, *131*
Thomas, apostle, 597, 654
Thomas, gospel of, 592–593
Thoosa, sister of monsters, 29, *34*
Thoth, 199
Thrace, 250, 461
Thrasyllus, astrologer, 520
Thucydides, 6n.1
Thunder and lightning, 20, 28
Thyrsos, 74
Tiberias, new city, 587
Tiberius, Emperor, 589, 590, *613*
  actions towards Germanicus, 580
  adopted by Caesar, 521–522
  as an administrator, 580, 607
  appointment of Sejanus, 571, 607
  birth chart of, 572
  as co-ruler of the Roman Empire, *520*, *521*
  and Cult of Isis, 578
  death of, 580, 582, 583, 638, 649
  divisions of his reign, 571
  Egyptian cults and Jewish cults under, 571–572
  fading interest in governing, 571, 581
  first hereditary emperor of Rome, 568, 570
  images of, *574, 575, 579, 584, 597*
  immoral behavior by, 582–585
  increasing paranoia of, 581, 582–583
  interest in astrology, 572–575
  and the Jews, 570, 610, 641
  lifts ban on Jewish cults, 582
  marriage to Julia, 519, 521
  marriage to Vipsania, 522
  married Livia Drusilla, 469
  move to Capri, 581–582, 585
  and murder of Germanicus, 570, 576, 580–582, 607, 609
  as office of Pontifex Maximus, 574
  plot to overthrow, 582
  and problems in Judea, 572
  proclaimed as emperor, 579

Index   721

reign and influence of, 579–585, 603
religious and political climate in Rome under, 571–579
reputation of, 582–585
self-imposed exile in Rhodes, 520
son of Livia, 519
support for Cult of the Emperor, 606
tolerance of cults under, 571
Tiberius Gracchus, 305–306
Tigranes II, King of Armenia, *334*, 373, 374, 377, *377*, 378
Tigranocerta, Armenian capital, 378
Tigurine Celts, 319
Time
    creation of, 18
    God of, 9–10
Timelines
    based on scientific evidence, *153*
    of biblical history, *153*
    of mythology, *153*
    of the universe and of human existence, 153
Timotheus, 193, 194, 196, 199, 201, 204
Tiresias, Theban seer, 111, 120, 121, 121n.8
Tiryns, city-state, 108, 109
Titan (Atlas), 286, *286*
Titans, 18, 19, *19*, 20, 45, 76
Titus, Emperor, 250, 656–657, 665
Torah, 178, 179, 208, 208n.24, 533, 553, 593
Trachonitis, 543, 544*m*, 550
Trading centers, early, 14
Transalpine Gaul, 379, 385, 388, 407
    Cimbri invasion of, 314
Transcendent filial piety, 67, *68*
Transformation, 94
    personal fears and, 83
    representations of, 74, 124
    teachings about, 205
    of water into wine, 75n.16
Trapezus, *271*
Tree of Life, 119, *668*
Treviri, tribe, 400, 401
    coins of, 400, *401*
Tribal cults, 76
Tribal groups, prehistoric, 88
Tribunate of the Plebs, 305, 322–323, 336, 337, 343, 370, 373, 378, 407
Tribute Penny, 574, *576*
Trident (Poseidon's), 28
Trigonometric tables, 287
Trinacria, ancient name of Sicily, 5
Trinacrus, Sicilian son of Neptune, 429
Trinity
    in Celtic cults, 398
    concept and worship of, 60, 142, 147
    division of, 664
    in Zoroastrianism, 144
Trinovantes, British tribe, 398, *399*
Tripolis, Phoenician city, 484
Triptolemus, 70, 71, 103, *104*
Triskeles, 400, *401*
    ancient symbol of Sicily, 400, *401*, 429
Troas. See Troy (ancient)
Trojan royalty, *133*
Trojan War, 29, 41n.3, 88, 119, 122–124, 134–140, 491
    beginning of, 12n.6
    myths about, 132–134
    start of, 86
Tropic of Cancer, 286, 287
Tropic of Capricorn, 286, 287
Troy, 40, 64, 65, 239
    fall of, 134
Tryphon, King, 319
Tullianum, prison, 432–433
Tunic, 132
Turkey, 11. *See also* Anatolia (Turkey)
    mystery cults in, 83
Turullius, Decimus, 494, *494*
Twelve labors of Herakles, 116–119, *118*
Twelve signs of the zodiac, 120
Twin caps. *See* Gemini twins
2 Maccabees, 308, 309, 310
Tyche, 507, *597*
    with Atargatis, *484*
    Goddess of Prosperity, 346, 347
Tyndareans, exiles from Peloponnese, 66–67
Tyndareos, first Spartan king
    competition with Zeus for Leda, 66
    myths of, 66–67
Tyndaris, Sicily, 13, 14, 66–67
Typaion Cliff, 130
Typhon (monster), *23*, *343*, 179, 179n.18, 309n.15
    attack on Mount Olympus, 23
    children/grandchildren of, 24
    description of, 23
    myth of, 96
    Zeus' defeat of, 22–24, 26, 35, 84, 85
Tyre, ancient Canaanite city, 11, 40–41, 59, 186–187, 466
Tyrrhenian Sea, 5, 7
Underworld, 18
    judges of, 87
Underworld deities, 68
Unguentarium (container of scented oil), 632
Universe
    changing concept of, 191
    competing models of, 267, 281–287
    cosmological teachings about, 192n.4

creation of, 181, *181*, 267
in Greek mythology, 18–19
in Zoroastrian tradition, 142–143
different views of, 147, 170
Earth-centered model of, 267, 269, 284–287
genealogy of (mythical), *19*
generated by Ra, 181, *181*
seven creations of, 142–143
sun-centered model of, 267, *284*
timeline of, 153
Uranus, God of the Sky, 9–10, 18, *19*, 26, 34, 85, 277, 386
castrated by Cronos, 18
imprisoned his children in Tartarus, 18
Urbs, in Rome, 251, 311
Uxellodunum (near Puy D'Issolu), 406
Uzbekistan, 169
Vajrapani, deity, 189
Valentine's Day, 103
Varuna, the spirit of the spoken word, 142, 267
Varus. *See* Publius Quinctilius Varus, military general
Vatican, 297
Vegetarian food, 90
Veii, city-state, 226
Veils, 87
Velitra, city of Octavian's birth, 504
Vengeance, 174, 175
Veni, vidi, vici, 428, 433
Venus, 225, 271, 305, 316, *317*, 360, *394*. *See also* Aphrodite; Cybele
children of, 64, 239
as Eastern Aphrodite, *445*
ecstatic worship of, 63
images of, *351*, *394*, *445*, *457*
Venus de Milo, Paris, 347
Venus Erice (Syrian Aphrodite), 63, 235, 260, 261, *262*
Venus Erice, Temple of, 64, 134, 233, 261
Venus Genetrix, 431
Venus Genetrix, Temple of, 434
Venus Victrix, 316, 440, *441*, *510*
Vercingetorix, Gallic leader, 402–407, *408*, 432
Vespasian, Emperor, 657
Vesta, Goddess of the Hearth, 344, 345
Vestal Virgins, 133, 344, 356, 430
and Antony's will revealed, 488, 488n.15
Victory. *See* Nike, winged Goddess of Victory
Victory, Palatine Temple of, 246
Victory crowning Roma, *385*, 385–386

Virgil, 64, 133n.9
Virgin birth, 209n.27
Virgin goddesses, 47
Virgin Mary, mother of Jesus, 272, 622, 647
images of, 162, *660*, *669*
mother of James and Salome, 627
and sexual abstinence, 676
virginity of, 601
Virgin(s), 103
in *Hebrew Bible*, 209
Virgo, constellation, 285, 294
Virtue, and will, 224
Vitellius, Aulus, future emperor, 583
Vitellius, governor of Syria Province, 638
Vitellius, Lucius, governor of Syria, 582–583
Volcano eruptions, 5, 6n.1
Vote, right to, 305
Vulcan, 270
Vulgate Bible, 664, 664n.66
Walking on water, 596, 604
Warfare, 114
Wars of Antiochus IV, 255–256
Washing hands, as a Jewish activity, 619
Water into wine, changing, 511, 511n.12, 596, 604
Western culture, 132, 169
Olympic Games' contribution to, 132
pre-Hellenistic, 221
respect for Eastern cultures, 188
Zoroastrian influences in, 146–147
Western religion
relating ancient cults and themes to, 77
sources, themes, and characteristics of, 76–77
Wheat, religious symbol, 68, 146, 231–232, 613
Winged Cherub, 180, *181*
Winged deity and sacred meteorite, 140, 141
Winged Goddess of Victory. *See* Nike, winged Goddess of Victory
Winged serpent chariot, *104*
Winged solar disk, 143, 146, *147*, 180
Winged wheel, *177*, 178
Winter solstice, 61, 61n.4, 283, 286, 287
Wise men (magi), 552, 557, 560–561
Witchcraft, in early Christianity, 672
Women
equality of, 600
Women's ritual games, 130
Worship. *See also* Initiation ceremonies
ecstatic version of, 162–163
recurring themes across centuries, 163

Wreath of ivy, 101
Wrestling, 114
Xenophon, mercenary, 141, 141n.29, 142
Xerxes, King of Persia, 169, 339n.12
Xoanon, representation of Aphrodite, 140
Xouthos, husband of Kreousa, 9
Yahweh, god of the Jews, 258, 309,
    309n.13, 368
  evil god, 670
Zama, Battle of, 247
Zanclus, son of Gegenus, 49, 50
  King of Zankle-Messana, Sicily, 50
Zankle (sickle), 50
Zankle-Messana, Sicily, 13, 13*m*, 14, 39,
    48, 62, 66–67, 227–230
  name changed to Messana, 50
Zarmaros, Brahmin Hindu priest, 516
Zealots, 533, 551, 551n.46, 588, 588n.30
  and First Jewish War, 657
Zela, Anatolia, Pharnaces defeat at,
    427–428
Zeno, 223–224
Zephyrium, 211
Zeus, deity, 174
Zeus, ruler of gods and the universe, 11,
    19–22, *21*, 24, 32, 59, 94, 270, 280,
    362
  defeat of Typhon, 84, 85
  with eagle, *88, 257, 363*
  impregnates Alcmene, 107, 108
  relatives of, 21
  stories about, 11, *21*, 32, 59, 84, 85, 87,
    88, 107, 108, 280, 362, *363*

Zeus/Ahura Mazda, 189
Zeus/Amon, 493, 494, *192*, 193, 193n.8,
    218
Zeus as an eagle ravishing europa in a plane
    tree, 87, *88*
Zeus Melichios, Cult of, 52, 53, 68
Zeus Ouranios, (Jupiter), God of the Sky,
    502, 573
Zodiac, 285, 286, 288, *288*
Zodiacal constellations, 285, *289*
Zoroaster, prophet, 142, 143, 144, 146
Zoroastrian eschatology, 145
Zoroastrian ethics, 143
Zoroastrianism, 168, 170, 170n.4, 203,
    204, 220
  afterlife in, 144–145
  aspects in Christianity, 147
  and astrology, 572–573
  beliefs about Mithra, 265, 267–268
  compared to Hinduism, 143–144
  death, and the soul in, 144
  early worship of, 147, 266
  in Eastern Mediterranean lands, 145,
    146
  influences on the West, 146–147
  merger of beliefs with Greek mythol-
    ogy, 266
  spirituality of, 269–270
Zoroastrians, 179
  influence on non-Zoroastrian cults, 170
  prediction of a Saosyant coming, 516
Zoroastrian traditions, 142–147
  and creation of the universe, 142

About the Author

One of the founders of the Writing Program at the Massachusetts Institute of Technology (MIT), the author won the highest literary prize at MIT. Funded by a career as a Program Manager for early internet companies (for example, Bolt, Beranek, and Newman, Inc.), he privately pursued interests in numismatics, history, and archaeology, eventually retiring from hi-tech and dedicating his efforts toward researching the complex story about the origins of Christianity.

As a numismatist—a coin collector—who had traveled the world pursuing interests in history, the author was invited to join the Society Historia Numorum (SHN). A Boston collectors' organization with a particularly distinguished membership, the SHN served as a mechanism for engaging in numismatic research with other collectors—historians, archaeologists, and writers—exploring the connections between artifacts and history, and publishing his research in numismatic literature.

www.ingramcontent.com/pod-product-compliance
Lightning Source LLC
Chambersburg PA
CBHW071229300426
44116CB00008B/967